GOD'S PATTERN FOR THE CHRISTIAN LIFE

God's Pattern for the Christian Life

Rediscovering the Essential Foundation

THREE VOLUMES IN ONE

The foundation of repentance from dead works and of faith toward God, of the doctrine of baptisms, of laying on of hands, of resurrection of the dead, and of eternal judgment

Hebrews 6:1–2

KEITH SOUTHWORTH

THANKFUL BOOKS

First published 2008

Published by Thankful Books
c/o P.O. Box 2118, Seaford BN25 9AR.

ISBN: 978 1 905084 16 6

Book design and production for the publisher by
Bookprint Creative Services, <www.bookprint.co.uk>
Printed in Great Britain.

Dedicated to my grandchildren

Anna Francesca Southworth
Rebecca Emily Thompson
Rachael Elizabeth Thompson
Lydia Grace Thompson
Joel Ethan Thompson

SUMMARY OF CONTENTS

ACKNOWLEDGEMENTS

I wish to express my gratitude to publishers and copyright holders for giving me permission to use extracts from their books, and also to those who helped me to produce this book. My daughter and son-in-law, Karen and Robert Thompson, provided a computer, a printer and office equipment. They and Christian friends have prayed diligently for me. Peter Holloway, a Systems Consultant, has given vital assistance. Not least my wife Jill has been a true helpmeet at all times. Above all thanks be to God for salvation, the revelation of the scriptures, and life, health and strength to proclaim the truth contained in Hebrews 6:1–2.

PREFACE

God's Pattern for the Christian Life sets forth the conviction that there is a revelation of God's order stated in Hebrews 6:1–2. It is reasoned from the scriptures that this order is of prime importance. It is God's design for the beginning and development of the Christian life. Heb. 6:1–2 declare the following truths.

1. A foundation must be laid for the building of the Christian life.
2. This foundation is precisely defined.
3. This foundation must be laid before the superstructure is built. There is a strict chronological order for the spiritual growth of every Christian: first the foundation, then growth into Christian maturity.
4. This foundation is essential for the support of the superstructure from day one, and as long as the building lasts. The laying of the foundation is essential for the believer throughout his earthly pilgrimage.
5. This foundation must be complete. Otherwise the total building will be affected adversely.

The book is an in-depth exposition of Hebrews 6:1–2. It is a reasoned and thorough study of the meaning and profound significance of these verses.

An overview of the contents of the three volumes

VOLUME ONE

The book begins with a striking example of neglect of God's order in the time of David King of Israel. It is a lesson for New Testament Christians. A basic overall interpretation of Heb. 6:1–2 is stated, followed by examination of conflicting approaches to the verses and differing views concerning the original text. The six elements of the foundation are addressed.

ix

Repentance

The repentance necessary for salvation is defined and distinguished from inadequate repentance. The motivation to repent is examined.

Faith

Faith is addressed in relation to the gospel. It is described as an act of man, and then it is affirmed that it is the result of a special operation of God which is defined as God's calling. The relationship of faith and regeneration is elucidated, and this leads into a consideration of doctrines of infant salvation. It is affirmed that a work of the exceeding greatness of God's power is required to produce saving faith. The relationship between repentance and faith is defined. The amount of knowledge required to receive salvation is considered from the scriptures. Justification by faith is treated and objections to the doctrine are answered. Faith and assurance are dealt with in relation to the initial act of faith, the actual experience of salvation, the subsequent sealing of the Spirit, the tests of the scriptures and the command to make one's calling and election sure. Concluding the studies on repentance and faith, they are set forth as two parts of the essential foundation of Heb. 6:1–2.

VOLUME TWO

The baptism of believers by immersion in water

Its timing and relationship with initial saving faith is stated. It is contended that immersion is the scriptural mode. Objections about the meaning of baptizo, opposing arguments based on the New Testament records of baptisms, or on the symbolism of baptism, or on the meaning of Rom. 6:1–11 and Col. 2:12 are given full consideration. The issue of a baptismal formula is addressed. Attempts to justify infant baptism are dealt with. Infant baptism based on the doctrine of the covenant of grace is examined in-depth. It is concluded that the doctrine is without scriptural basis, and is contrary to the teaching of the scriptures. Seven attempts to validate infant baptism from the New Testament are explained and refuted. The consideration of other arguments leads into infant baptism and church history. The reasons for its rise and prevalence today are put forward. The various alleged benefits of infant baptism are stated, and the related issues of its relationship with holy communion and confirmation are addressed. The different grounds and different subjects qualifying for infant baptism according to paedobaptists are surveyed. The relation of baptism to church membership is defined. Various approaches to the step of baptism are examined. The grounds for rebaptism are stated. Finally reasons are given why baptism is foundational.

The baptism in the Spirit

It is defined with particular attention to Peter's words in Acts 2. It is contended that it is error to affirm that it occurs at conversion. There is extensive treatment of writers holding that stance. The related matters of the laying on of hands, speaking in tongues and the mention of the baptism in the Spirit in the epistles are expounded. The way to receive the baptism in the Spirit is outlined. Spiritual gifts are defined. Finally the baptism in the Spirit is looked at as a part of the foundation for the Christian life.

VOLUME THREE

The resurrection of the dead

The scriptural teaching on death, the intermediate state, the time of the resurrection of the dead and the nature of the resurrection body of believers is stated. A case for one resurrection of all the dead is put forward.

Eternal judgment

Its timing, duration, and its nature as a day of wrath and the revelation of the righteous judgment of God are set out. The prominence of the judgment of deeds at this final judgment is explained. The truth of rewards for believers is elucidated. Attention is drawn to the solemn warnings in the scriptures concerning the final judgment. Eternal conscious punishment is affirmed to be the destiny of unbelievers and fallen angels. The doctrines of the resurrection of the dead and eternal judgment are declared to be part of the essential foundation.

In the last chapter the six elements of the foundation are considered together. Final conclusions are stated.

God's Pattern for the
Christian Life

VOLUME ONE

Repentance
and
Faith

CONTENTS OF VOLUME ONE

A SALUTARY LESSON

They [the Old Testament records of God's dealings with His people] were written for our admonition upon whom the ends of the ages have come (1 Corinthians 10:11).

About 1000 B.C. a man called David became King over all Israel. He captured Jerusalem and made it the nation's capital. Shortly afterwards, at the beginning of his thirty-three year reign, he desired to remove the ark of God from Kiriath-jearim to Jerusalem, a journey of about seven miles. The ark had been made at God's command, and to precise specifications given by God to Moses. With regard to its composition it was a rectangular box made of acacia wood covered with gold inside and outside and measuring approximately 4 × 2½ × 2½ feet. Concerning its significance it was the place where God met with and spoke to His people Israel through the High Priest. The ark therefore was at the heart of God's special relationship with His chosen nation. Sadly, this exceedingly glorious provision for God's presence with His people had been sorely neglected. Apparently the previous king Saul left it in Kiriath-jearim. It had been deposited there finally when the Philistines, enemies of Israel, returned it after they had captured it. This occurred during the time when Samuel was Israel's leader before Saul's reign. The men of the town took the ark into the house of a man called Abinadab and consecrated his son Eleazar to keep it. David purposed to restore the ark to its proper place in the life of the nation. He did this because he loved God and he loved his people. He wanted to fulfil God's intention for the ark and he desired the fulness of God's blessing to be experienced by Israel. So there is no doubt that David's decision and motives were in perfect harmony with God's will. But his plan ended in disaster and death.

The scriptures record the details. They placed the ark on a new cart and took it from the house of Abinadab on the hill. The sons of Abinadab, Uzzah and Ahio, led the cart. When they reached the threshing floor of Nacon Uzzah "put out his hand to hold the ark, for the oxen stumbled. Then the anger of the Lord was aroused against Uzzah, and He struck him because he put his hand to the ark; and he died there before God" (1 Chronicles 13:9–10).

At first David was angry, then he was afraid, and finally he gave up his plan to take the ark to Jerusalem. Instead he took it aside to the house of Obed-edom. His high purpose had resulted in failure and a man's death. And these things had happened before the eyes of all Israel, for David had organised their presence at what was to have been an historic event of great joy and significance for the nation.

No doubt David recalled that he had consulted with the "captains of thousands and hundreds and with every leader" (1 Chronicles 13:1). He had put his plan to them and they were unanimous in their support "for the thing was right in the eyes of all the people" (1 Chronicles 13:4). No one had dissented. He would also reflect that he had made all efforts to organise properly and appropriately the movement of the ark. He had arranged for a new cart to transport the ark, for Uzzah and Ahio to drive the cart, and for the presence of the people and the worship and praise of God during the ark's movement. "Then David and all Israel played *music* before God with all *their* might, with singing, on harps, on stringed instruments, on tambourines, on cymbals, and with trumpets" (1 Chronicles 13:8).

Many who saw this happening and had watched David's rise would have been deeply shocked. The blessing of God was manifestly upon him. This had caused all the tribes to make him their king. David was a mighty man of God. He was a man of victory and success ever since he slew Goliath. From the days when the women of Israel sang "Saul has slain his thousands and David his ten thousands" David had become greater and greater. This failure was totally unexpected. So what went so terribly wrong? David and all his leaders had failed in just one respect. They failed to take into account what God had stated in the scriptures which He had given to them at that time. In the book of Numbers God had given clear commands about the way the ark was to be moved. He commanded that a particular group within Israel, and only that group, should move the ark. The sons of Kohath, one of the three families of the tribe of Levi, had to carry the ark using poles made of acacia wood and covered with gold just like the ark. These poles had to be inserted through four rings on the ark, two rings on each side at the corners (Exodus 25:12–14). The poles were to be kept always in the rings (Exodus 25:15), because God stated that when they transported the ark they must not touch it. If they did they would die (Numbers 4:15). David and his leaders for whatever reason did not do what God had said. They did it their way, a new cart and two men to drive it instead of the Levites carrying it on poles. The priests and Levites did not object even though they were present (1 Chronicles 13:2–6). Consequently Uzzah died. It made no difference that the decision to move the ark was absolutely right, that David's motives were pure, that everyone unanimously agreed with the plan, that David organised the operation properly and that he was so wonderfully blessed by God. Nor did it matter that Uzzah had been given some responsibility with Ahio for the movement of the cart, and was probably trying to prevent any damage to the ark. When scripture is not listened to and obeyed God is still true to His word. He said that the consequence of touching the ark would be death, and so it was.

At this point it is necessary to pause and consider why God determined the death of anyone who touched the ark. At first sight His treatment of Uzzah appears harsh even barbaric. Why didn't God take into account the particular circumstances when Uzzah touched the ark? At that time God had chosen Israel from among the nations. He purposed to dwell with them, and had given them detailed and precise commandments concerning worship and the way to come into His presence. These commands were in force until the coming of the Messiah. The ark and the commandments concerning it were part of God's requirements for Israel to live in a special relationship with Him and to receive cleansing from sin. These rules concerning the ark ceased when Christ died on the cross. The reason why God killed Uzzah was because God was teaching man by these rules the truth about his state before God. Man is born fallen and sinful. If he were to go into God's holy presence without a blood sacrifice for sin he would die. The ark signified God's presence, therefore it must not be touched. To allow it to be touched without punishment would have misled man into thinking he is fit to stand before God without first having received God's cleansing. If the penalty for touching it had been less than death then the truth about the consequences of sin would not have been signified. The awful fact is, that if we die without having received God's forgiveness and cleansing through Christ's blood sacrifice for our sins, we shall come into God's presence at the judgment and be punished with the second death, hell. When these truths are seen to be represented in the commands concerning the ark, we understand why God killed Uzzah.

Let us now return to the record of this event and what happened subsequently. After three months David admitted his failure to obey scripture. He assembled all Israel again. He addressed the Levites "sanctify yourselves . . . that you may bring up the ark of the Lord God of Israel to the place I have prepared for it. For because you did not do it the first time the Lord our God broke out against us, because we did not consult Him about the proper order" (1 Chronicles 15:12–13). Then "the children of the Levites bore the ark of God on their shoulders, by its poles, as Moses had commanded according to the word of the Lord" (1 Chronicles 15:15). This time the ark was carried to Jerusalem without mishap. There was gladness and David "blessed the people in the name of the Lord of hosts. Then he distributed among all the people, among the whole multitude of Israel, both the women and the men, to everyone a loaf of bread, a piece of meat, and a cake of raisins. So all the people departed, everyone to his house" (2 Samuel 6:18–19). Now all was well.

There is a salutary lesson in this record. There exists a real danger for us that just like David and all his leaders we will fail to be careful to listen to and carry out what God has told us in the scriptures. Paul tells us in 1 Corinthians 10:11 that these accounts in the Old Testament Scriptures were caused to be recorded by the Holy Spirit with the express purpose of being a warning to us who live after the coming of Jesus Christ. If we think we do not need these Old Testament stories I remind you what Paul said, "Now all these things happened to them as examples, and they were written for our admonition, upon whom the ends of the ages have come. Therefore let him who thinks he stands take heed lest he fall" (1 Corinthians 10:11–12).

The warning for us contained in this example of David is particularly striking. When we ponder the details was it not remarkable that a man like David and all his leaders so neglected their scriptures? This is all the more surprising when we see that they seem to have done everything else right. They had consulted with everyone, they acted in unity, their objective was right, David's motives were pure, their organisation was thorough and they sought to give glory to God by arranging to worship and praise Him during the transportation of the ark. Let us take note that we can have outstanding leaders, full consultation, unity, right aims, pure motives, excellent organisation and true spiritual worship, yes, all these things and even so, still fail to act in accord with the scriptures. And of course if we do not consult Him about the "proper order" there are consequences dependent on the particular scriptures we neglect to obey.

Against this background let us proceed to consider certain fundamental facts about God's order for Christians declared in the New Testament.

Preliminary Considerations

CHAPTER ONE

THE ESSENTIAL FOUNDATION

The New Testament states God's order for the Christian life. There are two stages of development expressed in simple building terms. The first stage must be completed and then the second activity can begin. First the foundation must be laid. Then the rest of the building can progress. These truths are stated by the writer to the Hebrew Christians in the opening verses of chapter six of his letter. He says "Let us go on to perfection not laying again the foundation of repentance from dead works and of faith toward God, of the doctrine of baptisms, of laying on of hands, of resurrection of the dead, and of eternal judgment." Two distinct actions – laying the foundation and going on to perfection are identified as God's requirements.

These verses contain revelation of the highest importance. They define the Lord's pattern for the commencement and growth of the Christian life. A proper foundation is absolutely essential for a building. When a spectacular edifice is completed the foundation is usually hidden, but it remains vital to the continued existence of all the impressive structure standing upon it. It is indispensable. Just so in the Christian life. A sound and complete foundation is both the starting point and the enduring support for building the Christian life.

The believers to whom the letter to the Hebrews was written had already put in place the foundation. They needed to build upon it, and go on to perfection. In order to prepare the way and to clear the ground for a detailed study of the foundation, let us look first of all at what it means to go on to perfection. The answer is found in the preceding words of the letter in chapter five verses ten to fourteen. The author was speaking of Christ as their High Priest. He started to say that Christ's High Priesthood is "according to the order of Melchizedec" who was a priest of God Most High during the time of Abram as recorded in the book of Genesis chapter fourteen. Before he could continue he found it necessary to halt and to speak plainly to them. He told them that they were difficult to teach because they had become sluggish in receiving the truth. They ought to be able to teach others their faith, that is, simply be able to communicate the message to others. Since they had been Christians for some considerable length of time there was no valid reason for their inadequacy. But their deficiency was such that they needed someone to teach them the first principles of the oracles of God. They required instruction in the ABCs of the word of God, and their spiritual condition was babyhood, for they needed milk, not solid food. They were unable to receive solid food because they lacked the ability to understand the scriptures as they should and to distinguish correct and incorrect interpretations of them. This ability was something they should have developed by feeding on the word of God, and thereby become mature Christians, able to understand and teach the scriptures. Therefore when he exhorted them to go on to perfection he was calling them to achieve this maturity, to progress to a state of being adults instead of babies. They must advance from the basic initial doctrines of Christ to a greater understanding of the truth and a capacity to receive teaching which is solid food. They must build on the foundation of the elementary teachings concerning Christ, which they learned when they received the gospel message.

So in this particular instance the Christians receiving the letter had not built on the foundation they had laid as they should have done. Having now clarified the meaning of going on to perfection and explained the context of verses one and two of Hebrews 6 we can proceed to look at the details of the foundation the Lord requires. Three elements comprise the foundation.

1. Repentance from dead works
2. Faith toward God
3. Doctrine – of baptisms and of laying on of hands, and of the resurrection of the dead and eternal judgment

This third element contains four components:

- water baptism
- baptism in the Holy Spirit with the laying on of hands
- the resurrection of the dead
- eternal judgment

We may note at this point that all these six items form three pairs:

- repentance and faith
- baptism in water and baptism in the Holy Spirit
- resurrection of the dead and eternal judgment.

To provide a comprehensive view of the foundation I shall define concisely these six units which make up the foundation.

Repentance from dead works

Dead works are sins. They are called dead works because they are committed by those "dead in trespasses and sins" (Ephesians 2:1). That is the state of man born into this fallen world until he finds the salvation and true life which only Christ can give. Sins are also termed dead works since they result in death (Romans 6:16 and 21).

Repentance from sins involves the whole of man – his mind, his emotions and his will. To repent means to undergo a radical change of attitude towards oneself and one's conduct before God. There is a realisation of extremely serious personal guilt, a sense of present condemnation and a fear and dread that sins will bring judgment in the future. This condemnation and judgment is seen as entirely deserved and just. Distinct from this apprehension about the consequences of sins the truly penitant feels deeply and keenly grief and shame for sinning against God. He loathes himself for being sinful, and comes to hate sin itself. He desires not to continue in sin. He renounces his former thoughts of himself, of sin and of God and turns to the Lord and His revelation in submission. With a new understanding of the truth about himself, sin and God he views life, death and eternity in a fundamentally different way. No-one can become a Christian unless he repents from dead works. There can be no right relationship with God without repentance. The Christian life cannot begin without repentance.

Faith toward God

The faith designated here is that initial faith in God which together with repentance is required to become a Christian. Like repentance faith involves the mind, the feelings and the will. Faith is the action of a truly repentant person coming to God to receive salvation from the guilt, power and eternal consequences of sin. It is an understanding that God gave His Son to die for sins, that Christ was buried and that God raised Him from the dead. There is a realisation that Jesus Christ can therefore forgive, change a state of condemnation before God to a state of reconciliation, and deliver from future eternal condemnation. The sinner exercising faith knows there is no other way of salvation. The heart is moved towards God perceiving His great mercy. The repentant sinner sees himself as utterly unworthy of such mercy. He considers himself deserving God's wrath; but he is convinced of God's promises of pardon in Christ as stated in the scriptures. He turns to

Christ and puts his trust entirely in Him. He receives Christ as his Saviour, and gives himself to Him as his Lord. He experiences a joy of forgiveness, peace with God and a new power to overcome sin. Repentance from dead works together with faith toward God are absolutely essential to start the Christian life and to be in a right relationship with God. When repentance and faith are exercised what the Bible calls conversion takes place. The sinner's life is fundamentally changed.

Baptisms and Laying on of Hands

Two baptisms are encompassed here for those who have repented and believed in God's salvation in Christ – baptism by total immersion of the body in water in the Name of the Father, the Son and the Holy Spirit, and baptism in the Holy Spirit normally accompanied with the laying on of hands. The latter is distinct from baptism in water. The baptism in the Spirit is an experience of receiving personally the pouring out of the Holy Spirit and being filled with Him.

Resurrection of the Dead and Eternal Judgment

The scriptures declare that there will be a bodily resurrection of every dead human being at the "last day". At that time everyone will be judged individually. Jesus Christ will determine the eternal destiny of each person to either heaven or hell. Only Christians will go to heaven. All Christians will go to heaven but they will have to give account of their service to Christ and will receive rewards or "suffer loss." The rewards or loss will be of eternal duration.

These then are the elements comprising the foundation of the Christian life. There are no exceptions to this divine order. Every Christian must lay precisely this foundation. These are issues of the greatest significance and relevance to all Christians. They concern the essential doctrines which must be believed and acted upon at the beginning of the Christian life. If they are believed and obeyed a foundation is present and the building can develop, and grow to the design of the Architect. But if a sound and complete foundation is not laid it is sheer folly to attempt to build, and the consequences can be serious indeed.

CHAPTER TWO

NEW TESTAMENT EVIDENCE OF THE FOUNDATION

Strong assertions have been made, and at this point you may be questioning the interpretations of the elements of the foundation stated above. If my interpretations are right then the New Testament, especially the book of the Acts of the Apostles, will provide clear evidence that the first Christians began their Christian life with precisely these matters. Let us examine the scriptures to see if this is in fact the case. We shall look at all six elements of the foundation.

We start with repentance. We will find that repentance was an absolutely essential part of the gospel message which Jesus commanded to be preached to every creature. He defined the purpose of His coming as a call to sinners to repent (Mark 2:17). He chose twelve men to "be with Him and that He might send them out to preach" (Mark 3:14). The content of their preaching is recorded in Mark 6:12, "So they went out and preached that *people* should repent." Jesus Himself proclaimed the absolute need for all to repent in terms that none could misunderstand: "There were present at that season some who told Him about the Galileans whose blood Pilate had mingled with their sacrifices. And Jesus answered and said to them, 'Do you suppose that these Galileans were worse sinners than all *other* Galileans, because they suffered such things? I tell you, no; but unless you repent you will all likewise perish. Or those eighteen on whom the tower in Siloam fell and killed them, do you think that they were worse sinners than all *other* men who dwelt in Jerusalem? I tell you, no; but unless you repent you will all likewise perish'" (Luke 13:1–5). The concluding verses of Luke's gospel record that the risen Christ said to His disciples that "repentance and remission of sins should be preached in His name to all nations, beginning at Jerusalem" (Luke 24:47).

The Acts of the Apostles tells us about the spread of the gospel commencing at Jerusalem, and the accounts show clearly that the message they proclaimed was repentance. On the day of Pentecost Peter preached that the Jesus whom they, the Jews, had crucified God had made both Lord and Christ. They said, "What shall we do?" "Then Peter said to them 'Repent and let every one of you be baptized in the name of Jesus Christ for the remission of sins' " (Acts 2:38). Shortly afterwards Peter healed the lame man near the temple in Jerusalem. The people saw this miracle and gathered together attracted in wonder and amazement. Peter preached Jesus to this gathering. He told them that they had killed the Prince of life in ignorance, and said, "Repent therefore and be converted, that your sins may be blotted out" (Acts 3:19). Soon the apostles were imprisoned. The success of their preaching and their miraculous healing filled the Jewish religious leaders in Jerusalem with indignation. An angel of the Lord brought them out of prison and they resumed their gospel witness. When they were asked about their refusal to stop teaching in the name of Jesus, Peter and the other apostles answered "We ought to obey God rather than men. The God of our fathers raised up Jesus whom you murdered by hanging on a tree. Him God has exalted to His right hand *to be* Prince and Saviour, to give repentance to Israel and forgiveness of sins" (Acts 5:29–31).

The gospel was taken to the Gentiles for the first time by Peter when the Spirit of God directed him to go to the house of Cornelius in Caesarea. Cornelius, a Gentile, together with his relatives and friends listened to Peter's message, and while he was still speaking "the Holy Spirit fell upon all those who heard the word" (Acts 10:44). Later Peter was challenged at Jerusalem by some Jewish Christians who believed that Peter should not have eaten with these Gentiles. They believed that this would have resulted in eating foods which were condemned as unclean in the laws given to Moses for the nation of Israel (Leviticus 11). Peter explained to them in detail the events leading to eating with the Gentiles. He concluded saying " 'the Holy Spirit fell upon them . . . If therefore God gave them the same gift as *He gave* us when we believed on the Lord Jesus Christ, who was I that I could withstand God?' When they heard these things they became silent; and they glorified God, saying, 'Then God has also granted to the Gentiles repentance to life' " (Acts 11:1–18).

Paul was explicit to the Athenians. He declared God "now commands all men everywhere to repent" (Acts 17:30).

The apostle reminded the elders of the church at Ephesus of the way he had lived among them. When he met them at Miletus he said "You know . . . how I kept back nothing that was helpful, but proclaimed it to you, and taught you publicly and from house to house, testifying to Jews, and also to Greeks, repentance toward God and faith toward our Lord Jesus Christ" (Acts 20:18–21).

Later Paul became a prisoner of the Romans following an uproar in Jerusalem stirred up by his enemies. After several events he was permitted to speak before king Agrippa. Paul told the king of his past life and his conversion to Christ and calling. He went on "Therefore, king Agrippa, I was not disobedient to the heavenly vision, but declared first to those in Damascus and in Jerusalem, and throughout all the region of Judea, and *then* to the Gentiles, that they should repent, turn to God, and do works befitting repentance" (Acts 26:19–20). This statement proves that Paul always preached repentance.

These scriptures bear clear witness to the centrality of repentance in the gospel proclamation. The Christian life began with repentance.

It is equally clear that faith in Christ was essential to become a Christian. In the early chapters of the Acts of the Apostles we see a constant proclamation of Jesus Christ calling men and women to faith in Him as Saviour (Acts 2, 3, 4, 5, 7 and 8). In chapter nine there is the account of Saul's conversion to faith in Christ. Chapter ten tells of Peter preaching Jesus, saying, "To Him all the prophets witness that, through His name, whosoever believes in Him will receive remission of sins" (Acts 10:43). In the next chapter we read, "Now those who were scattered after the persecution that arose over Stephen traveled as far as Phoenicia, Cyprus, and Antioch, preaching the word to no one but the Jews only. But some of them were men from Cyprus and Cyrene, who, when they had come to Antioch, spoke to the Hellenists, preaching the Lord Jesus. And the hand of the Lord was with them, and a great number believed and turned to the Lord" (Acts 11:19–21). Paul's message at Antioch in Pisidia on his first missionary journey was, "Therefore let it be known to you, brethren, that through this Man, (Jesus Christ) is preached to you the forgiveness of sins; and by Him everyone who believes is justified from all things from which you could not be justified by the law of Moses" (Acts 13:38–39). Towards the end of that first journey "they returned to Lystra, Iconium, and Antioch . . . and . . . they commended them to the Lord in whom they had believed" (Acts 14:21–23). Paul and Silas were imprisoned in Philippi during their second missionary journey, and the keeper of the prison following an earthquake said to them "Sirs, what must I do to be saved?" They said, "Believe on the Lord Jesus Christ, and you will be saved" (Acts 16:30–31).

In Berea "many of them believed" (Acts 17:12). At Corinth "Crispus, the ruler of the synagogue, believed on the Lord with all his household. And many of the Corinthians, hearing, believed and were baptized" (Acts 18:8). On the third missionary journey Paul addressed the elders of the church at Ephesus. He reminded them that he had testified "to

Jews, and also to the Greeks, repentance toward God and faith toward our Lord Jesus Christ" (Acts 20:21).

These records of the spread of the gospel are conclusive proof that faith in the Lord Jesus was at the heart of the gospel and required of everyone who would become a Christian. Though we have treated repentance and faith separately for the sake of clarity, in reality both were preached together at the same time as Paul stated in Acts 20:21. Further consideration of the relationship between them will follow in due course.

We must now turn to baptism in water. The scriptures demonstrate that those who repented and believed in Christ were baptized in water as a next step after conversion. Jesus commanded the eleven apostles to "Go therefore and make disciples of all the nations, baptizing them in the name of the Father and of the Son and of the Holy Spirit" (Matthew 28:19). Again the book of Acts reveals this as the standard practice. We have already noted Peter's exhortation on the day of Pentecost, "Repent, and let every one of you be baptized in the name of Jesus Christ for the remission of sins" (Acts 2:38). The gospel spread to Samaria through a man called Philip. "When they believed Philip as he preached the things concerning the kingdom of God and the name of Jesus Christ, both men and women were baptized" (Acts 8:12). Shortly afterwards Philip witnessed to a man from Ethiopia, a eunuch of great authority under Candace the queen of the Ethiopians. Philip preached Jesus to him. The record then says, "Now as they went down the road, they came to some water. And the eunuch said, 'See *here is* water. What hinders me from being baptized?' Then Philip said, 'If you believe with all your heart, you may.' And he answered and said, 'I believe that Jesus Christ is the Son of God.' So he commanded the chariot to stand still. And both Philip and the eunuch went down into the water, and he baptized him" (Acts 8:36–38).

The Lord sent a disciple named Ananias to Saul a few days after his Damascus road conversion so that Saul might receive his sight and be filled with the Holy Spirit. When he came to Saul and laid hands upon him "immediately there fell from his eyes *something* like scales, and he received his sight at once; and he arose and was baptized" (Acts 9:18).

We have looked at Peter preaching to Cornelius and his household in Caesarea. Immediately following the falling of the Holy Spirit upon those who heard the word Peter said " 'Can anyone forbid water, that these should not be baptized who have received the Holy Spirit just as we *have*?' And he commanded them to be baptized in the name of the Lord" (Acts 10:47–48).

When Lydia a seller of purple is converted in Philippi we read that she was baptized (Acts 16:14–15). In the same town the keeper of the prison and his household heard the word and believed. The scriptures then inform us – "immediately he and all his family were baptized" (Acts 16:31–34).

In Corinth the same pattern is manifest: "And many of the Corinthians, hearing, believed and were baptized" (Acts 18:8).

It is striking that in all these accounts baptism followed conversion without any time delay. The accounts in Acts are compressed summaries of events and some instruction would have taken place, but when full allowance is made for these factors we cannot escape from the conclusion that baptism speedily followed repentance and faith. The first Christians demanded a physical response of those who obeyed the gospel call. It was not an altar call, a coming forward out of a gathering of people, or signing of decision cards or any such invention of man, it was baptism in water.

The manner in which Ananias dealt with Saul three days after his encounter with the Lord Jesus Christ is a striking example of this practice. Saul recounts exactly what happened in Acts 22:12–16: "Then a certain Ananias . . . said . . . 'And now why are you waiting? Arise and be baptized, and wash away your sins, calling on the name of the Lord.'" Remember at that time Saul had not eaten for three days! (Acts 9:9–19). Similarly Peter immediately "commanded" those on whom the Spirit fell in the house of Cornelius to be baptized in the name of the Lord (Acts 10:48). These men wasted no time in laying this part of the foundation.

We come to the next element in the foundation, baptism in the Holy Spirit. We shall have to proceed more slowly to be able to demonstrate that this experience was received at the commencement of the Christian life in New Testament times. Believers are divided on the meaning of this doctrine, and a fuller treatment of various issues will be addressed later. For the time being I will seek to show the pattern in the book of Acts. In Acts 2:2–4 is recorded the first baptism of Jesus' disciples in the Holy Spirit: "Suddenly there came a sound from heaven, as of a rushing mighty wind, and it filled the whole house where they were sitting. Then there appeared to them divided tongues, as of fire, and *one* sat upon each of them. And they were all filled with the Holy Spirit and began to speak with other tongues, as the Spirit gave them utterance." This was a fulfilment of what the risen Christ had promised them just before His ascension into heaven. He had said "You will be baptized in the Holy Spirit not many days from now" (my translation of Acts 1:5). There were crowds gathered in Jerusalem at that time for the feast of Pentecost, Jews "from every nation under heaven" (Acts 2:5). They heard the disciples speaking in their own languages, and they were amazed and perplexed. Peter explained to them what had happened. He said that the disciples were speaking under inspiration. They were prophesying. This would be intelligible to Jews familiar with the Old Testament. They would recall Moses in Numbers 11:25, "Then the Lord came down in the cloud, and spoke to him, and took of the Spirit that *was* upon him, and placed *the same* upon the seventy elders; and it happened, when the Spirit rested upon them, that they prophesied." They would think of their first king Saul. He prophesied among the prophets, and "It became a proverb: '*Is* Saul also among the prophets?'" (1 Samuel 10:11–12). Peter went on to explain that they were prophesying because the Spirit had been poured out upon them in fulfilment of words spoken by the prophet Joel in the scriptures. He quoted Joel to them saying, "And it shall come to pass in the last days, says God, that I will pour out of My Spirit on all flesh; your sons and your daughters shall prophesy, your young men shall see visions, your old men shall dream dreams. And on My menservants and on My maidservants I will pour out My Spirit in those days; and they shall prophesy" (Acts 2:17–18). He then proclaimed Jesus as Lord and Christ. He called on them to repent, to be baptized and said that if they did they would "receive the gift of the Holy Spirit." It is most important to pay careful attention to precisely what Peter meant by those words. Peter said, "you shall receive the gift of the Holy Spirit" and then gave the reason for his assertion, namely, "For the promise is to you and to your children, and to all who are afar off, as many as the Lord our God will call" (Acts 2:38–39). What promise was he referring to? The context permits only one answer. The promise was God's promise to pour out His Spirit on all flesh as declared by Joel and quoted by Peter to them (Acts 2:17–18,33). The experience of the fulfilment of that promise was also defined by Jesus as a baptism in the Spirit, as we have seen (Acts 1:4–5). So we find the disciples' experience of the Spirit on that occasion defined in all of the following ways – baptism in the Spirit (Acts 1:5), being filled with the Spirit (Acts 2:4), the promise of the Holy Spirit (Acts 2:33) and the pouring out of My Spirit (Acts 2:17). Therefore Peter was saying that the baptism in the Holy Spirit was available to them if they would respond to his gospel message. He also stated that this baptism in the Spirit was promised to their children, that is their descendants, and to the Gentiles, "all who are afar off" (Acts 2:39). By these terms he did not mean all their children and all the Gentiles, rather he limited it to those children of the Jews and those Gentiles whom "the Lord our God will call." These are those who will come to God by obeying the gospel call. This promise of God is for the duration of the "last days" (Acts 2:17). The last days began on that Day of Pentecost and will continue until Jesus Christ returns. Therefore, the baptism in the Spirit is available to all converts to Christ until His coming again. The book of Acts gives us the history of converts receiving this promise of the Father, the baptism in the Spirit.

In Acts 8 the spread of the gospel into Samaria is recorded. Verse 12 reads "But when they believed Philip as he preached the things concerning the kingdom of God and the name of Jesus Christ, both men and women were baptized." The good news of these conversions reached the apostles in Jerusalem. They immediately sent Peter and John to these new believers (Acts 8:14). When they arrived they discovered that none of them had received the baptism in the Holy Spirit, and they took immediate rectifying action. This was not a matter for any delay. Notice carefully what the Holy Spirit has caused to be written for our learning. "They sent Peter and John to them, who, when they had come down, prayed for them that they might receive the Holy Spirit. For as yet He had fallen upon none of them. They had only been baptized in the name of the Lord Jesus. Then they laid hands on them, and they received the Holy Spirit" (Acts 8:14–17). Their baptism in the Spirit was a distinct event and experience following their receiving Christ. They experienced the fulfilment of Joel's prophecy, just as Peter had said in Acts 2:39.

When Saul was converted on the Damascus road Ananias was sent by the Lord three days later to lay hands on him that he might be filled with the Holy Spirit. Again the filling with the Spirit was a distinct event from conversion, but with only a short time delay. He was baptized in the Spirit, another fulfilment of Acts 2:39.

The Holy Spirit fell upon those who heard Peter preaching in Cornelius' home. Peter related the occurrence and said, "Then I remembered the word of the Lord, how He said, 'John indeed baptized in water, but you will be baptized in the Holy Spirit.' Therefore if God gave them the same gift as *He gave* to us also after believing in the Lord Jesus Christ, who was I that I could stand in God's way?" (my translation of Acts 11:16; v.17 NASB). Here we see the Gentiles baptized in the Spirit. This took place immediately following their hearing about Jesus Christ, and believing (Acts 15:7–8).

At Ephesus Paul found some disciples of the Lord who had been baptized into John the Baptist's baptism. He tells them of the need to believe in Christ as John had said. They responded and were baptized in the name of the Lord Jesus. The narrative continues "And when Paul had laid hands on them, the Holy Spirit came upon them, and they spoke with tongues and prophesied" (Acts 19:1–6). They were baptized in the Spirit in accordance with Acts 2:39.

There are several references confirming that this was an initial Christian experience in the rest of the New Testament. To the saints at Corinth Paul wrote "He who . . . has anointed us *is* God, who also has sealed us and given us the Spirit in our hearts as a guarantee" (2 Corinthians 1:21–22). He recalls it again in his question to the Galatian believers, "Did you receive the Spirit by the works of the law, or by the hearing of faith?" (Galatians 3:2). Paul said to the Christians at Ephesus concerning Christ, "in whom also, having believed, you were sealed with the Holy Spirit of promise" (Ephesians 1:13). These all refer to a single event in the past, the baptism in the Spirit.

Concerning the laying on of hands B.F. Westcott makes the following illuminating comments. Speaking of the three pairs:

- repentance and faith,
- baptisms and laying on of hands, and
- resurrection of the dead and eternal judgment,

he says in his notes on Heb. 6:1–2 "The three pairs are not however strictly coordinate: μετ ... και π ..., βαπτ .... ἐπιθ. τε χ., αναστ. ν. και κρ. αι. The centre pair are regarded as forming one great subject of teaching in two parts."[1] He then directs the reader to his note on the use of τε in Heb. 9:1, where he states "The conjunction τε is rarely used by itself in the epistles: c i:3 note; vi.5; xii.2; Rom. ii.19; xvi.26; 1Cor.iv.21; Eph.iii.19. It marks something which is not regarded as distinct from and coordinate with that with which it is connected, but which serves to complete the fulness of one main idea."[2] Thus the laying on of hands completes the full meaning of baptisms. The records in the New Testament are wholly in accord with Westcott's comments. The laying on of hands frequently accompanied the baptism in the Spirit (Acts 8:17, 9:17, & 19:6).

Resurrection from the dead and eternal judgment are so closely linked that it is appropriate to look at them together. Is there evidence in the New Testament that instruction in these doctrines was given to converts as a foundation for their Christian living? When we examine the scriptures we find that the gospel was inseparable from these truths. Jesus defined the gospel He commanded them to preach, and His message of eternal life was in the context of a general resurrection of all the dead of mankind and eternal judgment. Let us look at what Jesus said. On one occasion Jesus was challenged by the Jews in

Jerusalem because He had healed on the Sabbath and had said that God was His Father, thereby making Himself equal with God. He answered them, and within His reply were these words; "Most assuredly, I say to you, he who hears My word and believes in Him who sent me has everlasting life, and shall not come into judgment, but has passed from death into life. Most assuredly, I say to you, the hour is coming, and now is, when the dead will hear the voice of the Son of God; and those who hear will live" (John 5:24–25). The dead to whom Jesus is referring here are the spiritually dead in trespasses and sins. Jesus used this word with this meaning on two other recorded occasions, "Let the dead bury their own dead, but you go and preach the kingdom of God" (Luke 9:60); and at the conclusion of His parable of the man who had two sons, concerning the prodigal son's return, the father says, "It was right that we should make merry and be glad, for your brother was dead and is alive again, and was lost and is found" (Luke 15:32). In the epistles we find the use of the term with precisely the same meaning. Paul said to the saints in Ephesus that God "even when we were dead in trespasses, made us alive together with Christ" (Ephesians 2:5). Paul defined his spiritual state and theirs before they became Christians as a state of death. He said the same thing in his letter to the Colossian Christians, "And you, being dead in your trespasses and the uncircumcision of your flesh, he has made alive together with Him, having forgiven you all trespasses" (Colossians 2:13). So Jesus is saying here in John 5:24–25 that all those who have believed, and so passed from a state of spiritual death into life, possess everlasting life and will not "come into judgment." Jesus made abundantly clear what He meant by the words "come into judgment." In the next verses He said that in the future there will be a resurrection of all the dead and everyone will be judged by Him. The eternal destiny of each will be determined by Jesus. It will be either life or condemnation. His actual words were "The Father . . . has granted the Son to have life in Himself, and has given Him authority to execute judgment also, because He is the Son of Man. Do not marvel at this; for the hour is coming in which all who are in the graves will hear His voice and come forth – those who have done good, to the resurrection of life, and those who have done evil, to the resurrection of condemnation" (John 5:26–29). He said to Martha, "I am the resurrection and the life. He who believes in Me, though he may die, he shall live" (John 11:25). Combining what Jesus taught in these verses we see that at the final judgment the believer will not come into "condemnation" but into "life." From the other words of Jesus it is certain that the resurrection of life will be a resurrection to eternal life.

Jesus proclaimed that the resurrection of John 5:29 will be on the "last day." He said, "This is the will of the Father who sent Me, that of all He has given Me I should lose nothing, but should raise it up at the last day. And this is the will of Him who sent Me, that everyone who sees the Son and believes in Him may have everlasting life; and I will raise him up at the last day . . . No one can come to Me unless the Father who sent Me draws him and I will raise him up at the last day . . . Whoever eats My flesh and drinks My blood has eternal life, and I will raise him up at the last day" (John 6:39, 40, 44 and 54). Notice the repetition of the words "at the last day." Jesus used the phrase again towards the end of His ministry on earth. He said "He who rejects Me, and does not receive My words, has that which judges him – the word that I have spoken will judge him in the last day" (John 12:48). This verse leads us to look at the fact that Jesus declared that the final judgment will take place on this last day.

Jesus affirmed a single final judgment in the following verses. "Many will say to Me in that day, 'Lord, Lord, have we not prophesied in Your name?'. . . And then I will declare to them, 'I never knew you; depart from Me, you who practice lawlessness!'" (Matthew 7:22–23). Jesus warned, "I say to you that for every idle word men may speak, they will give account of it in the day of judgment" (Matthew 12:36). He sent out the twelve apostles and He said, "Whoever will not receive you nor hear your words, when you depart from that house or city, shake off the dust from your feet. Assuredly, I say to you, it will be more tolerable for the land of Sodom and Gomorrah in the day of judgment than for that city!" (Matthew 10:14–15). He spoke of those cities who did not repent even though most of His mighty works had been done in them. He said, "Woe to you Chorazin! Woe to you Bethsaida! For if the mighty works which were done in you had been done in Tyre and Sidon, they would have repented long ago in sackcloth and ashes. But I say to you, it will be more tolerable for Tyre and Sidon in the day of judgment than for you. And you, Capernaum, who are exalted to heaven, will be brought down to Hades; for if the mighty works which were done in you had been done in Sodom, it would have remained until this day. But I say to you that it shall be more tolerable for the land of Sodom in the day of judgment than for you" (Matthew 11:21–24). Speaking to the Pharisees he told them "The men of Nineveh will rise up in the judgment with this generation and condemn it, because they repented at the preaching of Jonah; and indeed a greater than Jonah *is* here. The queen of the South will rise up in the judgment with this generation and condemn it, for she came from the ends of the earth to hear the wisdom of Solomon; and a greater than Solomon *is* here" (Matthew 12:41–42). In these verses Jesus is prophesying events at a final judgment of all mankind. He is stating that all mankind of all time will be judged at that one event. There will be different degrees of guilt and punishment. The conduct of some will condemn the misconduct of others, even though they lived during different time periods of history.

In Matthew 25:31–46 Jesus warns us of what will happen at the last day, the day of judgment. All will be judged, and Jesus Christ will separate everyone into one of two groups. One group, the righteous will have eternal life, the other will go away into eternal punishment. Jesus said "When the Son of man comes in His glory, and all the holy angels with Him, then He will sit on the throne of His glory. All the nations will be gathered before Him, and He will separate them one from another, as a shepherd divides *his* sheep from the goats. And He will set the sheep on His right hand, but the goats on the left. Then the King will say to those on His right hand, 'Come you blessed of My Father, inherit the kingdom prepared for you from the foundation of the world': . . . Then He will also say to those on the left hand, 'Depart from Me, you cursed, into the everlasting fire prepared for the devil and his angels': . . . And these will go away into everlasting punishment, but the righteous into eternal life" (Matthew 25:31–34, 41 and 46). Here is eternal judgment. It could not be stated more strongly.

On several occasions the Lord Jesus Christ was equally explicit about the eternal state of those condemned in the day of judgment. He stated the reality of hell in stark words. He explained to His disciples the meaning of one of His parables, "So it will be at the end of the age. The angels will come forth, separate the wicked from among the just, and cast them into the furnace of fire. There will be wailing and gnashing of teeth" (Matthew 13:49–50). On the same occasion He gave them the meaning of the parable of the tares of the field. He said, "The field is the world, the good seeds are the sons of the kingdom, but the tares are the sons of the wicked *one*. The enemy who sowed them is the devil, the harvest is the end of the age, and the reapers are the angels. Therefore as the tares are gathered and burned in the fire, so it will be at the end of this age. The Son of Man will send out His angels, and they will gather out of His kingdom all things that offend, and those who practice lawlessness, and will cast them into the furnace of fire. There will be wailing and gnashing of teeth. Then the righteous will shine forth as the sun in the kingdom of their Father" (Matthew 13:38–43). When He compared the future of the Gentiles who would receive Him as their Saviour with the future of those Jews who would not receive Him as the Messiah, He defined their eternal states in the following words, "And I say to you that many will come from east and west, and sit down with Abraham, Isaac, and Jacob in the kingdom of heaven. But the sons of the kingdom will be cast out into outer darkness. There will be weeping and gnashing of teeth" (Matthew 8:11–12).

Jesus spoke plainly of the imperative need to avoid eternal punishment. He said, "If your right eye causes you to sin, pluck it out and cast *it from* you; for it is more profitable for you that one of your members perish, than for your whole body to be cast into hell. And if your right hand causes you to sin, cut it off and cast *it* from you; for it is more profitable for you that none of your members perish, than for your whole body to be cast into hell" (Matthew 5:29–30). He repeated this warning later in His ministry, "If your hand or foot causes you to sin, cut it off and cast *it* from you. It is better for you to enter into life lame or maimed, rather than having two hands or two feet, to be cast into the everlasting fire. And if your eye causes you to sin, pluck it out and cast *it* from you. It is better for you to enter into life with one eye, rather than having two eyes, to be cast into hell fire" (Matthew 18:8–9).

He instructed His own disciples when being persecuted, "Do not fear those who kill the body but cannot kill the soul. But rather fear Him who is able to destroy both soul and body in hell" (Matthew 10:28). This was a grave warning for Jesus went on to say, "Whoever confesses Me before men, him I will also confess before My Father who is in heaven. But whoever denies Me before men, him I will also deny before My Father who is in heaven" (Matthew 10:32–33).

With the knowledge of these clear teachings directly from the lips of Christ, the apostles were in no doubt about the gospel message He commanded them to preach. At the core of the message of eternal life were two future events – the resurrection of all the dead of mankind and a final judgment at the end of this age, the last day.

The New Testament confirms that this was in fact the gospel they declared. Peter tells the Gentiles that Jesus "Commanded us to preach to the people, and to testify that it is He who was ordained by God *to be* Judge of the living and the dead" (Acts 10:42). This was Peter's initial witness to Cornelius and those with him. When Paul preached the gospel at Athens he declared that God "has appointed a day on which He will judge the world in righteousness by the Man whom He has ordained. He has given assurance of this to all by raising Him from the dead" (Acts 17:31). At Caesarea Paul spoke to the governor Felix, and "as he reasoned about righteousness, self-control, and the judgment to come, Felix was afraid and answered, 'Go away for now; when I have convenient time I will call for you'" (Acts 24:25). Paul wrote to the saints at Rome concerning the "day when God will judge the secrets of men by Jesus Christ, according to my gospel" (Romans 2:16). Paul also says in the same passage that there will be a day of judgment resulting in either eternal life or the wrath of God; "the day of wrath and revelation of the righteous judgment of God, who *'will render to each one according to his deeds'* eternal life to those who by patient continuance in doing good seek for glory, honor, and immortality; but to those who are self-seeking and do not obey the truth, but obey unrighteousness – indignation and wrath, tribulation and anguish on every soul of man who does evil" (Romans 2:5–9). Let there be no misunderstanding of Paul's words, "according to my gospel." These words do not mean that the apostle formulated the content of the message. The content of the gospel he received, embraced and was called by God to give his life to proclaiming, was fully determined by God before he received it. As he stated at the beginning of his letter to the Romans, he was "called to *be* an apostle, separated to the gospel of God which He promised before through his prophets in the Holy Scriptures, concerning His Son Jesus Christ." Therefore to modify the gospel in the slightest was unthinkable to Paul. When some others preached a different gospel he said, "If we, or an angel from heaven, preach any other gospel to you than what we have preached to you, let him be accursed" (Galatians 1:8).

This survey demonstrates that these doctrines concerning the resurrection of the dead and eternal judgment were fundamental and at the heart of the gospel.

We have now completed our examination of the New Testament records concerning repentance from dead works, faith toward God, baptism in water, baptism in the Spirit, and the doctrines of the resurrection of the dead and eternal judgment. I submit that the New Testament scriptures show that these matters were in fact the first concerns of those who became Christians. They began with precisely these things. First they repented and believed in Christ. The next steps were baptism in water and in the Holy Spirit. Sometimes water baptism preceded Spirit baptism. Sometimes they were baptized in the Spirit before baptism in water. Either way these baptisms soon followed conversion. The gospel the converts had obeyed was a message of eternal life. It was in the framework of a last day when there will be a general resurrection of dead mankind and a final judgment with eternal effect. Therefore the interpretation of the foundation elements in Hebrews 6:1–2 is substantiated by the practice of Christians in the book of Acts and the teachings of the New Testament.

References

1. B. F. Wescott, *Epistle to the Hebrews*, Macmillan & Co 1892, page 143.
2. *Ibid.*, page 244.

CHAPTER THREE

OTHER INTERPRETATIONS OF THE FOUNDATION

We must now address other interpretations of Hebrews 6:1–2 to answer objections which may arise to my explanation of the meaning of the passage, and to reveal more fully the truths contained in these verses – "Therefore leaving the discussion of the elementary *principles* of Christ, let us go on to perfection, not laying again the foundation of repentance from dead works and of faith toward God, of the doctrine of baptisms, of laying on of hands, of resurrection of the dead, and of eternal judgment."

Some commentators totally dismiss the approach I have taken and argue that all the elements of the foundation spoken of in this exhortation were items of Old Testament faith and practice. They interpret the elementary principles of Christ as the teachings about Christ in the Old Testament, the types and prophecies concerning Him and His work. They contend that the writer was bidding them to leave those rudimentary matters, and to go on to perfection which they say refers to the full glory of Christ and the New Testament He inaugurated. They affirm the truth that the Old Testament is preparatory to Christianity, and that the New Testament is the fulfilment of the Old Testament types and prophecies. These writers contend that in this sense the Old Testament is the foundation of Christianity. That is an accepted truth, but they take a further step and say that when the writer of the letter used the word foundation in these verses he is to be understood as giving it that meaning. So they interpret "not laying again the foundation" as meaning not returning to the Old Testament requirements and teachings. They conclude that all the elements of the foundation pertained to the Old Testament economy.

They define each element of the foundation as something belonging only to the Old Testament period. They say that repentance from dead works is to be understood as what was required under the old covenant. It was different from the New Testament repentance toward God. Kenneth S. Wuest, in his Word Studies Volume Two, cites John the

Baptist as an example of the preaching of repentance from dead works under the old covenant before Christ brought in the new. Similarly faith toward God is taken to be not the same as faith in the Lord Jesus Christ. A.W. Pink in his commentary on Hebrews speaks of it as a national faith toward God. They render the word translated "baptisms" in Hebrews 6:2 as washings, and relate it to the Old Testament washings as in Exodus 30:18–19, Leviticus 16:4, and Numbers 19:19. Laying on of hands is said to mean the practice found in Leviticus 1:4, "Then he shall put his hand on the head of the burnt offering, and it will be accepted on his behalf to make atonement for him," and in Leviticus 16:21, "Aaron shall lay both his hands on the head of the live goat, confess over it all the iniquities of the children of Israel, and all their transgressions, concerning all their sins, putting them on the head of the goat, and shall send *it* away into the wilderness by the hand of a suitable man." They assert that the doctrines of the resurrection of the dead and eternal judgment are those stated in the Old Testament. They argue that the fuller revelation in the New Testament on all these matters superseded these Old Testament beliefs. Thus they make the foundation to be wholly made up of Old Testament beliefs and practices. They declare that the writer was saying that all these must be abandoned and the new covenant embraced. They must go on to perfection, the new covenant. To return to these Judaistic things they say would be laying again a foundation, namely the foundation of the Old Testament. They point out that the message of the epistle was the immeasurable superiority of Christianity over Judaism, and they argue that their exposition does justice to this central theme and purpose of the letter to the Hebrews whereas other interpretations fail to do so.

It is true that the theme of Hebrews is exactly as they state. But they fail to take account of the fact that at this point the writer had to digress from his central theme, the superiority of Christ as High Priest. He had to deal with the problem of the readers' spiritual condition, their dullness of hearing. Consequently he leaves his argument concerning Christ as High Priest "according to the order of Melchizedek" (Hebrews 5:10), and he does not return to it until chapter seven verse one when he has fully dealt with the serious state of dullness of hearing into which the readers have lapsed. Hebrews 5:11 to 6:20 concerns not the difference between Judaism and Christianity but the condition of the readers described in chapter five verses eleven to fourteen. Those verses read, "you have become dull of hearing. For though by this time you ought to be teachers, you need *someone* to teach you again the first principles of the oracles of God; and you have come to need milk and not solid food. For everyone who partakes *only* of milk *is* unskilled in the word of righteousness, for he is a babe. But solid food belongs to those who are of full age, *that is*, those who by reason of use have their senses exercised to discern both good and evil." The exhortation which follows immediately: "Therefore leaving the discussion of the elementary *principles* of Christ, let us go on to perfection, not laying again the foundation of repentance from dead works and of faith toward God, of the doctrine of baptisms, of laying on of hands, of resurrection of the dead, and of eternal judgment" is the action they need to take in view of their spiritual state. They need to become those of "full age". This is what the call to "perfection" refers to. The Greek words used in both "full age" and "perfection" are the same, one in adjectival form and the other a noun. The meaning in each is completeness in the sense of being fully grown, mature. The NIV translates "full age" as mature and "perfection" as maturity. That version of these verses reads "solid food is for the mature . . . Let us . . . go on to maturity". This shows the connection very clearly. These Christians had degenerated to a condition of dullness. They had become sluggish in their listening to the truth of God. This was not the case with them originally. They were being persecuted, and the writer records that they had forgotten the exhortation which God gave to them as sons, "My son, do not despise the chastening of the Lord, nor be discouraged when you are rebuked by Him" (Hebrews 12:5). This is an example of their dullness. They had failed to see the hostility of their fellow men against them as their heavenly Father's chastening for their good, because they had forgotten the scripture they once knew, namely Proverbs 3:11–12. They had not departed from the faith, but they were in real danger of doing so. They had succumbed to the pressure of persecution to the extent that they had allowed themselves to be wrongly affected by it in that they had become dull of hearing. For this reason the writer said to them earlier in the letter "Therefore we must give the more earnest heed to the things we have heard, lest we drift away" (Hebrews 2:1). The exhortation to go on to perfection is a reiteration of that counsel. They needed to be stirred to a greater diligence in listening to God's truth and obeying it. The writer graciously says "let us" joining himself with them just as he did in chapter two verse one. He wants to encourage them, because this dullness is an extremely serious matter. This is why the writer departs from his central message.

The exhortation to go on to perfection was not a call to embrace the new covenant and not to return to Judaism as asserted by A.W. Pink and Kenneth S. Wuest. They had become true Christians and were partakers of the new covenant. This is clear from the fact that the writer addresses the readers throughout the letter as "brethren". The exhortation was a plea to attain to spiritual maturity. It concerned their personal condition of dullness. Maturity would remedy their dullness of hearing, and the writer would be able to teach them his central theme, the immeasurable superiority of Christianity to Judaism. These two authors are misinterpreting the writer to the Hebrews at this point, and consequently they define the elements of the foundation incorrectly.

Therefore "not laying again the foundation" pertains to spiritual growth. It is in the context of going on to maturity from a condition of spiritual babyhood. The writer is instructing them not to repeat the first steps they have taken in Christian belief and practice as babes in Christ. They must press on to maturity so that they can receive, understand and embrace the more difficult truths concerning Jesus Christ. There is a striking parallel in 1 Peter 1:13 where Peter exhorts Christians whom he addresses as "new-born babes" to "gird up the loins" of their minds. Just as one would gather up a long garment under a belt to walk without hindrance, in like fashion they must remove every hindrance to being attentive to God's word in order to progress from babyhood to maturity. In 1 John 2:12–14 there is the same truth. Three stages of spiritual development are stated. Christians are placed in three categories of spiritual growth, namely, little children, young men, and fathers. 1 John 2:12–14 reads "I write to you, little children, Because your sins are forgiven you for His name's sake. I write to you fathers, Because you have known Him *who is* from the beginning. I write to you, young men, Because you have overcome the wicked one. I write to you, little children, Because you have known the Father. I have written to you, fathers, Because you have known Him *who is* from the beginning. I have written to you, young men, Because you are strong, and the word of God abides in you, And you have overcome the wicked one." Little children are characterised as those who have known the Father. Like young children know their parents and depend on them, in the same way those young in the faith centre on their experience of the gift of forgiveness and their new relationship with God as Father. Fathers have come to a much greater knowledge of God in Christ, Him Who is from the beginning. They have come to know Christ to a degree way beyond their knowledge of Him when they were little children, and even when they grew to be young men in the faith. The young men have matured from childhood. They are strong, the word of God abides in them and they have overcome the wicked one. This is the Christian maturity which the writer to the Hebrews is exhorting them to attain.

According to K.S. Wuest and A.W. Pink "not laying again a foundation" is equivalent to not returning to Judaism. When we pause and consider this we shall see that the writer to the Hebrews would never speak of turning back to the old covenant in such terms. He says that falling away from Christ and returning to Judaism would be tantamount to crucifying again for themselves the Son of God and putting Him to open shame. It is therefore unthinkable that he should speak of such a fearful sin with such awful consequences as "laying again the foundation." Laying a foundation is a positive action pointing forward to further development and progress. Returning to Judaism would be a negative action resulting in eternal ruin. It would be impossible to renew them again to repentance – "For *it is* impossible for those who were enlightened, and have tasted the heavenly gift, and have become partakers of the Holy Spirit, and have tasted the good word of God and the powers of the age to come, if they fall away, to renew them again to repentance, since they crucify again for themselves the Son of God, and put *Him* to an open shame" (Heb. 6:4–6). The epistle is a warning against returning to Judaism under the pressure of persecution. The writer warns of the consequences of backsliding in such a way that we can only conclude that he would never speak of returning to Judaism as "laying the foundation." He says "For if the word spoken through angels proved steadfast, and every transgression and disobedience received a just reward, how shall we escape if we neglect so great a salvation, which at first began to be spoken by the Lord, and was confirmed to us by those who heard *Him*" (Hebrews 2:2–3), and, "For if we sin wilfully after we have received the knowledge of the truth, there no longer remains a sacrifice for sins, but a certain fearful expectation of judgment, and fiery indignation which will devour the adversaries. Anyone who has rejected Moses' law dies without mercy on the testimony of two or three witnesses. Of how much worse punishment, do you suppose, will he be thought worthy who has trampled the Son of God underfoot, counted the blood of the covenant by which he was sanctified a common thing, and insulted the Spirit of grace? For we know Him who said, 'Vengeance is Mine, I will repay,' says the Lord. And again, 'The LORD will judge His people.' It is a fearful thing to fall into the hands of the living God" (Hebrews 10:26–31). Hebrews 10:39 is explicit, drawing back results in perdition. I submit therefore that A.W. Pink's and K.S. Wuest's interpretation of "laying again a foundation of . . . eternal judgment" as equivalent to returning to Judaism is incorrect and not a possible alternative interpretation to the one I have defined.

F.F. Bruce

In his *Epistle To The Hebrews*, revised[1], F.F. Bruce interprets the foundation elements as follows. He says concerning Hebrews 6:1–2, "We are thus given some insight into what was regarded as a suitable foundation of Christian teaching in a non-Pauline church, and one which had a Jewish basis. When we consider the 'rudiments' one by one, it is remarkable how little in the list is distinctive of Christianity, for practically every item could have its place in a fairly orthodox Jewish community. Each of them, indeed, acquires a new significance in a Christian context; but the impression we get is that existing Jewish beliefs and practices were used as a foundation on which to build Christian truth."[2]

He defines the dead works to be repented of as ". . . probably not the works of the law, not even the sacrificial ceremonies prescribed by the cultic law . . ."[3] He continues, "They are works which issue in death because they are evil . . ."[4] He writes, "Repentance from such things was insisted upon in the Old Testament, and in all the strains of Jewish thought and life which were derived from the Old Testament."[5] Faith in God he perceives to be ". . . the way of faith in Christ, but this way had been prepared for them in advance by the Old Testament insistence on faith in God . . ."[6]

He translates the Greek word *baptismos*, in the plural here, as ablutions. He believes it refers to ceremonial washings, quoting Numbers 19 and Ezekiel 36:25 in support. He says the Old Testament instructions about ablutions ". . . provided a further foundation on which the Christian truth could be erected."[7] He also sees a possible reference to a ritual bath for the removal of impurity before baptism mentioned in the writings of Hippolytus.

Laying on of hands, he says, "most probably" applies to ". . . an early Christian practice, associated especially with the impartation of the Holy Spirit."[8] He affirms that it was a practice ". . . inherited from the Old Testament, where it is used especially in commissioning someone for public office, or as part of the sacrificial ritual."[9]

The doctrines of resurrection of the dead and of eternal judgment he declares to be doctrines clearly stated in the Old Testament but given a ". . . fresh and fuller significance because of the coming of Christ into the world."[10]

He asserts the writer does not "go on insisting on these things" (the six foundation elements) because ". . . the 'Hebrews' were exposed to a subtle danger which could not be experienced by converts from paganism. If a convert from paganism gave up Christianity and reverted to paganism, there was a clean break between the faith he renounced and the paganism to which he returned. But it was possible for the recipients of this letter, yielding gradually to pressures from various quarters, to give up more and more those features of faith and practice which were distinctive of Christianity, and yet to feel that they had not abandoned the basic principles of repentance and faith, the realities denoted by religious ablutions and the laying on of hands, the expectation of resurrection and the judgment of the age to come."[11]

Compared with the interpretation of the foundation I have set out in the previous chapter there are the following significant differences.

1. The definitions of the six elements are essentially the same except for the doctrine of baptisms which is interpreted to mean ablutions instead of Christian baptism.
2. The suggestion that the six foundation elements are peculiar to Jewish Christians rather than all Christians.
3. The assertion that these Hebrews were exhorted not to lay the foundation again because they were in danger of shedding the distinctively Christian features of the six elements and reverting to the Old Testament doctrines which had prepared the way for their New Testament faith.

Let us look firstly at the contention that the doctrine of baptisms should be translated "teaching about ablutions", and interpreted as referring to Old Testament ceremonial purifications

To support this exposition he writes guardedly ". . . it may be significant that our author does not use *baptisma*, the Greek noun regularly employed in the New Testament to denote Christian baptism (and the baptism of John), but *baptismos*, which in its two other indubitable New Testament occurrences refers to Jewish ceremonial washings."[12] Those two occurrences are in Mark 7:4 and Hebrews 9:10. Christian baptism is certainly the meaning in Colossians 2:12 and he concedes concerning the original Greek text of that verse that "there is weighty textual evidence" for baptismos as against baptisma.[13] So here is a verse in the New Testament where baptismos was possibly used to speak of Christian baptism. Therefore the argument from the use of baptismos rather than baptisma is inconclusive.

Various translations of the scriptures demonstrate the uncertainty whether to translate baptismos (plural form) as washings or baptisms.

Revised Standard Version	"with instruction about ablutions"
New Revised Standard Version	"instruction about baptisms"
New American Standard Bible	"of instruction about washings"
Good News Bible	"the teaching about baptisms" with footnote on the word baptisms which reads "baptisms; *or* purification ceremonies"
New International Version	"instruction about baptisms"

| New King James Version | "the doctrine of baptisms" |
| New Century Version | "the teaching about baptisms" with a footnote on the word baptisms as follows: "The word here may refer to Christian baptism, or it may refer to the Jewish ceremonial washings" |

According to Simon J. Kistemaker *baptismos* "signifies the 'act alone', whereas *baptisma* is the 'act with the result'."[14] This may explain why the writer chose to use this word rather than *baptisma*. He is referring back to the first steps after conversion to Christ, the actual events of Christian baptism and receiving the Spirit. Converts focused on the "act alone" rather than the "act with the result" as they received these two baptisms.

F.F. Bruce has a further argument for translating the word ablutions. He writes ". . . the plural speaks against a straightforward interpretation in terms of Christian baptism in Hebrews. 6:2."[15] But the plural form of baptismos makes perfect sense if the writer wished to denote Christian baptism and the baptism in the Holy Spirit.

F.F. Bruce says that the six matters "fall naturally into three pairs: *(a)* 'repentance from dead works' goes closely with *(b)* 'faith in God'; *(c)* 'instruction about ablutions' (RSV) goes with *(d)* 'laying on of hands'; while there is patent association between *(e)* 'resurrection of the dead' and *(f)* 'eternal judgement.'."[16] He is absolutely right about the fact of three pairs and interpretation must take account of this manifest pairing. The baptism in the Spirit was normally accompanied with the laying on of hands (Acts 8:17, 9:17, 19:6); and Christian baptism was closely linked in time with the baptism in the Spirit as we have seen from the survey in the previous chapter. Sometimes it preceded the baptism in the Spirit, sometimes it followed that event.

What about F.F. Bruce's assertion that the ablutions of the Old Testament ". . . provided a . . . foundation on which the Christian truths could be erected"?[17] He proceeds to point to the existence of baptist groups in noncomformist Judaism which flourished at the beginning of the Christian era and who practised Old Testament ceremonial ablutions but ". . . did not regard such ablution as a means of removing iniquity from the heart."[18] He says that the epistle may have been sent to believing Jews in Rome; and ". . . the Jewish community in Rome, in particular, probably preserved some characteristic features of this non-comformist Judaism – features which were carried over into Roman Christianity, if the Hippolytean *Apostolic Tradition* may be trusted.

According to Hippolytus, for example, baptism, as the central act of Christian initiation, took place on Easter Day, but on the preceding Thursday the candidate was required to have a ritual bath for the removal of impurity."[19] He concludes ". . . the reference to 'teaching about ablutions' may have had a more direct significance than meets the eye of the twentieth-century reader."[20]

Philip Edgcumbe Hughes writes concerning F.F. Bruce's conjectures, ". . . it is difficult to see how any solidity can be granted to an explanation of this kind which involves a supposition built on a supposition, namely, that the Jewish-Christian community in Rome included a non-conformist baptist group and that some elements of their ablutionary ritual were adopted by the Roman church . . ."[21]

If we were to accept F.F. Bruce's arguments for ablutions we are left with a striking and incredible imbalance. The first pair of repentance and faith and the last pair of resurrection of the dead and eternal judgment are doctrines of magnitude. He would place between them teachings concerning washings which are now obsolete! This is totally unsatisfactory.

Moreover he pairs "laying on of hands" with ablutions. But he defines laying on of hands as ". . . an early Christian practice, associated especially with the impartation of the Holy Spirit, and that is most probably its significance here."[22] He clarifies this statement in a footnote by referring to Acts 6:6, 8:17, 9:12,17 and 19:6. By these words he is in fact linking the laying on of hands with the baptism in the Spirit, but failing to see that baptismos in the plural is speaking of the baptism in the Spirit and Christian baptism.

In conclusion F.F. Bruce's interpretation of baptism as ablutions rather than Christian baptism and the baptism in the Spirit should be rejected for the reasons stated above.

Let us now turn to his assertion that the six foundational elements are peculiar to Jewish Christians rather than all Christians.

The facts overthrow his argument. Repentance and remission of sins was to be preached to all nations at the command of the risen Christ (Luke 24:47). Paul told the learned Athenians "God . . . now commands all men everywhere to repent" (Acts 17:30). He reminded the elders of the church at Ephesus that he testified "to Jews, and also to Greeks, repentance toward God" (Acts 20:21). Concerning faith Paul wrote to the Romans "Is He the God of the Jews only? Is He not also the God of the Gentiles? Yes, of the Gentiles also, since there is one God who will justify the circumcised by faith and the uncircumcised through faith" (Romans. 3:29–30). There was no distinction between Jews and Gentiles to receive salvation. Everyone must repent and believe. The gospel message was not different for the Jew because he had the revelation of God given to the Jews and contained in their Old Testament scriptures.

Similarly Christian baptism was for Jew and Gentile believers alike. Jesus is crystal clear, "Go therefore and make disciples of all the nations, baptizing them in the name of the Father and of the Son and of the Holy Spirit" (Mat. 28:19).

We have noted that the baptism in the Holy Spirit (Acts 1:5) was stated to be a fulfilment of Joel's prophecy promising the Spirit in Acts 2:17–18. Peter says that that promise of the baptism in the Spirit is to Jew and Gentile; it "is to as many as the Lord our God shall call" (Acts 2:39). So again there is no distinction between Jews and Gentiles in the matter of the required baptisms for the foundation.

The New Testament doctrines of the resurrection of the dead and eternal judgment were partially revealed in the Old Testament. But Gentile converts to Christ just as much as Jewish converts to Christ had to refocus their lives in the light of these truths. Paul tells of this fundamental change of values and manner of life in 1 Thessalonians 1:9–10. He wrote to them in these words, "you turned to God from idols to serve the living and true God, and to wait for His son from heaven, whom He raised from the dead, even Jesus who delivers us from the wrath to come."

There is no sound basis for the assertion that the foundation stated in these verses was peculiar to "a non-Pauline church, and one which had a Jewish basis."

Finally let us examine F.F. Bruce's argument that the Hebrews were exhorted not to lay the foundation again because of the danger of shedding the distinctively Christian features of the six elements and reverting to the Old Testament doctrines which had prepared the way for their New Testament faith.

The temptation confronting the Hebrew Christians was not merely to shed a percentage of their belief. It was to go back on their profession of faith in Christ (Heb. 10:32). They were being tempted to cease from confessing Him and bearing abuse because of following Him (Heb. 13:13). They were under pressure to return to Judaism, which was nothing less than hostile to Jesus Christ. The danger therefore was not of shedding some of their faith, it was the danger of renouncing the faith.

Having said that, the question arises why did the writer exhort the readers not to lay again a "foundation of repentance from dead

works and of faith toward God, of the doctrine of baptisms, of laying on of hands, of resurrection of the dead, and of eternal judgment?"
Why did he state these things?
There are several reasons which we do well to ponder.

1. He is clarifying precisely what he means by saying in the previous verse "leaving the discussion of the elementary principles of Christ." The six doctrines of verse 1b and 2 define the first steps in the Christian life. Moreover they are doctrines which centre on Jesus Christ. They concern Him. Repentance and faith are the actions of someone coming to Christ for salvation. Christian baptism properly understood is an act of identification with Christ. Paul wrote to the church at Colossae, "Buried with Him in baptism" (Col. 2:12). The baptism in the Holy Spirit was, and is the action of Jesus Christ. He is the One Who baptizes in the Holy Spirit. All four gospels proclaim so (Mat.3:11, Mark 1:8, Luke 3:16 and John 1:33). The resurrection of the dead and eternal judgment are doctrines which centre on Jesus Christ. Jesus made the following declarations of the magnitude of His power and authority, "The Father . . . has committed all judgment to the Son . . . the hour is coming when all who are in the graves will hear His voice and come forth – those who have done good, to the resurrection of life, and those who have done evil, to the resurrection of condemnation" (John 5:22–29).

   Interpretations of the six elements must therefore be doctrines of Christ, His Person and Work, and pertaining to the beginning of the Christian life. Therefore the following explanations of "baptisms" are clearly wrong.

   a) the baptism of John the Baptist as one of the baptisms.
   That baptism was nothing to do with becoming a Christian. It was a baptism of repentance for the remission of sins, and limited to the ministry of John the Baptist. It cannot be considered as a doctrine of Christ.
   b) the baptism of suffering in Mark 10:38–39 "Are you able to drink the cup that I drink, and be baptized with the baptism that I am baptized with?"
   Jesus prayed concerning this cup in Gethsemane saying, "O My Father, if it is possible, let this cup pass from Me: nevertheless, not as I will, but as You *will*" (Mat. 26:39). Jesus told His disciples about this baptism in response to their request to sit on His right and left hand. It was not one of the elementary doctrines of Christ.

    c) baptisms not stated in scripture.

       Such teachings are the baptism of blood – martyrdom, taught by Thomas Aquinas as one of the baptisms spoken of in this verse; and the baptism of penitential tears or desire, where, as in the example of the believing thief at Christ's crucifixion, water baptism was not possible. This was the teaching of Augustine.

2. The writer is stating precisely what they need to leave. It is striking that the six elements, as we have seen from the New Testament, pertain to the commencement of the Christian walk, spiritual babyhood. They must press on to maturity.
3. The writer is stating in what sense they are to leave these elementary doctrines. They are a foundation for the rest of their life; indispensable but not to be laid again. They are in place with a view to the building of a Christian life, just as a foundation is laid to make possible a building.
4. The writer has been moved by the Holy Spirit to define these unchanging principles of Christian spiritual growth for all Christians until the return of the Lord Jesus Christ. He is stating matters of profound significance for all believers.

References

1. F.F. Bruce *The Epistle to the Hebrews*, Revised, Eerdmans 1990.
2. *Ibid.*, page 139.
3. *Ibid.*, page 139.
4. *Ibid.*, page 140.
5. *Ibid.*, page 140.
6. *Ibid.*, page 141.
7. *Ibid.*, page 141.
8. *Ibid.*, page 142.
9. *Ibid.*, pages 142–143.
10. *Ibid.*, page 143.
11. *Ibid.*, page 143.
12. *Ibid.*, page 141.
13. *Ibid.*, page 141 footnote.
14. Simon J. Kistemaker *Hebrews*, Evangelical Press, 1984, page 155.
15. F.F. Bruce *The Epistle to the Hebrews*, Revised, Eerdmans 1990, page 141 footnote.
16. *Ibid.*, pages 138–139.
17. *Ibid.*, page 141.
18. *Ibid.*, page 142.
19. *Ibid.*, page 142.

20. *Ibid.*, page 142.
21. Philip Edgcumbe Hughes *A Commentary on the Epistle to the Hebrews*, Eerdmans, 1990, page 200.
22. F.F. Bruce *The Epistle to the Hebrews*, Revised, Eerdmans,1990, page 142.

CHAPTER FOUR

ANCIENT MANUSCRIPTS

The various translations of the scriptures have been made not from the original writings of the many parts of the Bible but from copies of copies of copies of those "autographs". The number of these copies available is enormous, in excess of five thousand manuscripts. Where they differ some editions of versions of the Bible, for example the NIV, give footnotes stating other readings in places where the translators are uncertain as to what the original text was. We encounter this problem of differing ancient copies right here in verse two of Hebrews chapter six. The different readings have a significant bearing on the meaning of the text. It is therefore necessary to examine them thoroughly. Some manuscripts of verse two have the Greek word διδαχῆς (genitive) translated "of the doctrine." Other copies have διδαχήν (accusative) translated "instruction" in the NIV.

- διδαχῆς (genitive) gives the following translation,
  Heb 6:1–2 "not laying again the foundation of repentance from dead works and of faith toward God, of the doctrine of baptisms, of laying on of hands, of resurrection of the dead, and of eternal judgment."
- διδαχήν (accusative) has this meaning,
  not laying again a foundation of repentance from dead works and of faith toward God, a foundation consisting in instruction about baptisms and of laying on of hands, of resurrection of the dead and eternal judgment.

The two readings affect the meaning of the verses as follows. If we take the former, the genitive, as representing the true copy of the original writing then there are six elements in the foundation on which the Christian life is built.

1. Repentance
2. Faith

3. The doctrine of baptism in water.
4. The doctrine of the baptism in the Holy Spirit with the laying on of hands.
5. The doctrine of resurrection.
6. The doctrine of eternal judgment.

If we choose the latter, the accusative, then the foundation is essentially two elements,

1. Repentance
2. Faith

R.V.G. Tasker writes in support of the accusative reading, "If διδαχήν is read . . . as it probably should be . . . repentance from dead works and faith in God are equated with the teaching that underlies and gives meaning to baptism and the laying-on-of-hands. . . . This renouncing of a past way of life, whether it be a Jewish or a pagan way, and this turning to God in faith to receive new power from him were symbolized, in early Christian practice, in the initiation ceremonies of 'baptism and the laying on of hands'; and the outstanding characteristics of the new life that a Christian sought to live were the new sense of purpose and the increased sense of seriousness which were imparted to it by the certainty that, because Christ had been raised from the dead, there would be 'a resurrection of the dead' followed by a 'judgment' which would have eternal consequences."[1]

Paul Ellingworth also chooses the accusative. He writes, "It could follow that the items mentioned in v. 2, while included in elementary teaching which the author wishes to leave behind, are not considered 'fundamental' in the same sense as repentance and faith; this would partly reflect the general pattern of the apostolic preaching (Dodd 1936), which included reference to repentance and faith (e.g. Acts 2:38; 3:19; 10:43; 13:36f.), and also, perhaps less strongly, to judgment (especially Acts 10:42), but not to baptism, the laying on of hands, or, at least explicitly, to the resurrection of the dead (but cf. Acts 17;31f.)."[2]

G. Zuntz argues for the accusative reading. He said, "I submit that the genitive is inadmissible. It is stylistically bad, in the midst of so many other genitives which are on a different level both logically and syntactically; besides it makes it impossible to construe the sentence. . . . The meaning then of this over – condensed sentence is that the writer will not dwell upon the doctrines of the Resurrection and the Judgement which constitute the foundation of the Christian life in faith and repentance. They are the subject of the teaching which is given in preparation of the baptism and the laying on of hands; that is, they are propaedeutic; cf. v. 12–vi.1."[3]

As we shall see other scholars totally disagree. If the genitive is accepted there is no problem whatsoever in combining the words of the sentence and interpreting its meaning.

All six elements of the foundation remain present in the verse whether the word in the original text was in the genitive or the accusative. But the accusative essentially reduces six foundation elements to two, namely repentance and faith, with the other four items merely enlarging on the content of repentance and faith. The doctrines of baptism in water, baptism in the Holy Spirit with the laying on of hands, the resurrection of the dead and eternal judgment are subsumed within the elements of faith and repentance. Consequently their importance as essential parts of the foundation of the Christian life is not fully recognised. Only repentance and faith are seen as absolutely essential elements of the foundation. In contrast the genitive reading gives all six elements of the foundation their due weight.

We must pay attention to every word of scripture. The precise meaning is vitally important. The original writings were "God breathed" (2 Tim. 3:16), and the Lord Jesus Christ said that we live by "every word" that proceeds from the mouth of God (Mat. 4:4). Paul gives us a striking example of how carefully and seriously we need to treat each word of the scriptures in Galatians 3:16. He bases his reasoning concerning God's salvation in Christ on the fact that one word, namely seed in Genesis 22:18, is in the singular not the plural. Therefore we must be clear about the precise meaning of the phrase "not laying again the foundation." Without a sound foundation our Christian lives cannot be built as they should be built. Building upon an inadequate or incomplete foundation will mean that only limited development is possible because the foundation will stand little weight. Failure will result if too much is placed on too little. Incomplete foundations can also prevent certain parts of a building from being erected. Therefore we must be certain to lay the foundation God has designed in His wisdom and love for His children. We cannot be vague or unsure of the definition of the foundation. It is absolutely essential that we know what God is instructing us by this word. This is not an academic matter to be relegated to an appendix or mere footnote. It concerns the growth and potential of every Christian!

The actual difference between the two readings is only one letter – διδαχῆς or διδαχήν. The question is, was a letter ς in the original changed wrongly to a letter ν, or was a letter ν in the original modified to a letter ς? I will submit my case for διδαχῆς. In summary I have two reasons. There is at least as good an argument for διδαχῆς as for διδαχήν from the manuscript evidence. Secondly the New Testament considered as a whole teaches the foundation was made up of six elements not two.

At this point let us address the manuscript evidence for διδαχῆς (genitive).

1. This reading is much more widely attested: διδαχήν is only found in the Chester Beatty papyrus P^{46}, the Codex Vaticanus, the Old Latin of Codex Claromontanus (the Greek has the genitive) and the Peshitta Syriac version of the New Testament. Bruce M. Metzger, on behalf of and in cooperation with the Editorial Committee of the United Bible Societies' Greek New Testament, writes "Although the reading διδαχήν, which is in apposition with θεμέλιον of ver.1, is early ($\mathcal{P}$46 B it^d), a majority of the Committee regarded it as a stylistic improvement introduced in order to avoid so many genitives. The reading διδαχῆς is strongly supported by good representatives of all the major types of text . . ."[4]

2. B.F. Westcott argued that ". . . on the whole it seems simpler to take the genitive." He also gave an answer to a recent argument against διδαχῆς put forward by R. McL. Wilson, who states that διδαχήν should be preferred partly because ". . . there is an inversion of order in the Greek, which makes the genitive appear decidedly clumsy."[5] The inversion he refers to is that baptisms is in front of διδαχῆς in the Greek text. It reads thus, Heb 6:1–2 GNT Διὸ ἀφέντες τὸν τῆς ἀρχῆς τοῦ Χριστοῦ λόγον, ἐπὶ τὴν τελειότητα φερώμεθα, μὴ πάλιν θεμέλιον καταβαλλόμενοι μετανοίας ἀπὸ νεκρῶν ἔργων, καὶ πίστεως ἐπὶ Θεόν, **βαπτισμῶν διδαχῆς**, ἐπιθέσεώς τε χειρῶν, ἀναστάσεώς τε νεκρῶν, καὶ κρίματος αἰωνίου. Westcott wrote, " The unusual order is probably to be explained by the emphasis gained for the characteristic contents of the teaching by placing **βαπτισμῶν** first. If **διδαχῆς** were placed first, this would appear to be co-ordinate with μετανοίας (repentance) and πίστεως (faith) rather than the elements which it includes." He adds, "The simple gen. in place of Περι with gen. is remarkable. . . . It seems to express more completely the contents, the substance, of the teaching than the preposition which would give merely the subject."[6]

3. As stated a majority of the United Bible Societies Committee rejected διδαχήν as "a stylistic improvement introduced in order to avoid so many genitives." Certainly there are a great number of genitives: Διὸ ἀφέντες τὸν **τῆς ἀρχῆς τοῦ Χριστοῦ** λόγον, ἐπὶ τὴν τελειότητα φερώμεθα, μὴ πάλιν θεμέλιον καταβαλλόμενοι **μετανοίας** ἀπὸ **νεκρῶν ἔργων**, καὶ

πίστεως ἐπὶ Θεόν, βαπτισμῶν διδαχῆς, ἐπιθέσεώς τε χειρῶν, ἀναστάσεώς τε νεκρῶν, καὶ κρίματος αἰωνίου. All the words in the genitive case are shown in bold type. Philip Edgcumbe Hughes counters this suggestion by contending that ". . . with the long string of genitives on either side it is more likely that διδαχήν was altered to διδαχῆς than the other way around."[7] Paul Ellingworth, however, argues with equal force that διδαχήν may have come into the text instead of διδαχῆς by the copyist wrongly following the final letter ν in some of the surrounding words.[8] There are clearly a number of such words. They are shown in bold in the Greek text of Heb. 6:1–2 Διὸ ἀφέντες τὸν τῆς ἀρχῆς τοῦ Χριστοῦ λόγον, ἐπὶ τὴν τελειότητα φερώμεθα, μὴ πάλιν θεμέλιον καταβαλλόμενοι μετανοίας ἀπὸ νεκρῶν ἔργων, καὶ πίστεως ἐπὶ Θεόν, βαπτισμῶν διδαχῆς, ἐπιθέσεώς τε χειρῶν, ἀναστάσεώς τε νεκρῶν, καὶ κρίματος αἰωνίου.

4. Before the discovery in 1930 of P^{46} written about 200 A.D. the attestation of διδαχήν was generally considered to be too weak to rival the genitive. F.W. Beare wrote concerning the reading διδαχήν, "The addition of P^{46} to the ranks of its supporters turns the probability into a virtual certainty."[9] Sober consideration does not justify his conclusion. P^{46} is not always a reliable witness. Zuntz asks "What then is the quality of P^{46} considered as an individual manuscript?" He answers "In spite of its neat appearance (it was written by a professional scribe and corrected – but very imperfectly – by an expert), P^{46} is by no means a good manuscript. The scribe committed very many blunders. . . . My impression is that he was liable to fits of exhaustion: from the fifth chapter of Hebrews onwards blunders seemed to me much more frequent than before it, . . ." He then proceeds to quote some examples from what he terms "a few bad pages in Hebrews." Of particular relevance to our consideration of the text of Hebrews 6:2 is the following sentence: "In vi.1 he wrote θεμελιοτητα for τελειότητα under the spell of θεμέλιον following; in vi.9 ἐλάβομεν for λαλοῦμεν; in viii. 11 ἕτερος for ἕκαστος." He also details errors in verses 6, and 11 of the sixth chapter of Hebrews.[10] Concerning the scribe who wrote P^{46} he says, "Of his innumerable faults, only a fraction (less than one in ten) have been corrected and even that fraction – as often happens in manuscripts – grows smaller and smaller towards the end of the book. Whole pages have been left without any correction, however greatly they were in need of it."[11]

What then of the Peshitta Syriac version which also supports the accusative reading? This was the official bible of the Syriac Church. Brian Edwards assesses it as follows, "It was completed at the very latest by the end of the third century A.D. and one copy available bears the date A.D. 464; this is the oldest copy of the whole Bible, in any language, for which the date is certainly known. Unfortunately the *Peshitta* is often more of a paraphrase than a translation and it does not really help our search for an accurate text."[12]

In the light of the above there is insufficient reason to argue that διδαχήν should be chosen rather than διδαχῆς.

In the following chapters I shall reason that New Testament doctrine and practice is in harmony with this choice. We shall look at the six elements, and demonstrate that each of them provides the necessary and essential foundation for the development of the Christian into maturity.

References

1. R.V.G. Tasker *Gospel in the Epistle to the Hebrews*, 2nd ed., The Tyndale Press 1956, pages 21–22.
2. Paul Ellingworth *The Epistle to the Hebrews*, Eerdmans and Paternoster 1993, pages 313–314.
3. The British Academy Schweich Lecture on Biblical Archaeology 1946, *The Text of the Epistles: A Disquisition upon the Corpus Paulinum* by G. Zuntz. OUP, 1953 pages 93–94.
4. Bruce M. Metzger *A Textual Commentary On The Greek New Testament*, 2nd ed., United Bible Societies, 2001; page 596.
5. R. McL. Wilson *The New Century Bible Commentary on Hebrews*, Eerdmans, 1987, page 106.
6. B.F. Westcott *The Epistle to the Hebrews*, Macmillan & Co. 1892, page 145.
7. Philip Edgcumbe Hughes *A commentary on the Epistle to the Hebrews*, Eerdmans, reprinted 1990, page 196 footnote.
8. Paul Ellingworth *The Epistle to the Hebrews*, Eerdmans and Paternoster 1993, page 314.
9. F.W. Beare *Journal of Biblical Literature* "The Text of the Epistle to the Hebrews in P^{46}". Vol. 63, No. 4 (Dec 1944) page 394.
10. The British Academy Schweich Lecture on Biblical Archaeology 1946, *The Text of the Epistles: A Disquisition upon the Corpus Paulinum* by G. Zuntz. OUP 1953 page 18.
11. *Ibid.*, page 252
12. Brian Edwards *Nothing But The Truth*, Evangelical Press, 1978, page 158.

Repentance

CHAPTER FIVE

REPENTANCE FROM DEAD WORKS

The words used in the scriptures which are translated into our word repentance mean to think again and change one's mind and have regret for the previous wrong view. These are the basic meanings of the Greek words used in the New Testament, but we must look at the verses teaching repentance to see the full meaning of this doctrine.

In Luke chapter fifteen Jesus spoke three parables to the Pharisees and scribes when they were complaining about Him receiving sinners. All three proclaim that heaven rejoices when sinners repent. The third parable delineates the Pharisees and scribes who, just like the elder brother, do not rejoice when a sinner repents and is restored. The younger brother, commonly known as the prodigal son, is a picture of repentance. The elements of true repentance are found in this parable. Here we have a full and clear statement of what Christ means by repentance.

The downward path of the prodigal is stated in stark and vivid words. We read that he had wasted all his possessions with prodigal living. He had become a pauper, and had attempted to relieve his misery by "joining himself to a citizen" of the foreign country to which he had travelled. This action failed to meet his need. No one gave him anything, and he was perishing with hunger. At this point he repented. "He came to himself." For the first time in his life he saw himself as he really was. Formerly he was only concerned to maximise his own pleasure and enjoy himself to the fullest possible extent. When he became poor he sought a solution to his hunger. But now he turns his eyes on himself. He sees the truth about himself, and he does not turn away from it. He acknowledges it fully, and makes no excuses for himself. He knows that he has committed sins, "Father, I have sinned against heaven and before you." Moreover he knows that he has fallen far short of what he ought to have been, "I am no longer worthy to be called your son. Make me like one of your hired servants." He has what the modern psychologists call low self-esteem. In fact he loathes himself for what he is. He acknowledges his guilt. He is full of sorrow and shame for what he has done and for what he is. He resolves to confess his sins and utter unworthiness, and to leave the far country of sin and live at home as a servant of his father.

Here in this parable are the elements of true repentance from dead works.

1. A realisation of personal guilt before God for sins committed.
2. A realisation of personal guilt before God for not being what one ought to be.
3. Shame for the sins done.
4. Self-loathing for one's sinful nature.
5. Sorrow for sins and sinfulness.
6. A hatred of sin.
7. A desire to cease from sin. True repentance is a change of mind including all of these seven elements. It leads to a change of conduct, namely,
8. Works befitting repentance.

A realisation of personal guilt before God for sins committed

The prodigal son was without any real concern about his guilt before God while he was spending his inheritance and enjoying himself. His conscience may have troubled him at times, maybe even persistently, but it resulted in no personal admission of guilt. He would not accept the truth about his conduct. When he became in need he still did not face his guilt. Rather he directed his efforts to solve the problem caused by his sins. He did not repent until he came to himself, faced up to the truth and acknowledged his guilt. He said "I will arise and go to my father, and will say to him, 'Father, I have sinned against heaven and before you.'" Notice that he made no excuses. He could have blamed his wrong companions. He could have condemned his father for giving him his inheritance too soon, before he was able to act wisely. He could have been angry that no one helped him. He could have blamed society in general for not giving him assistance. True repentance never shifts the blame. It sees the guilt as all one's own. The sinner feels the guilt of sins. He feels stained by sins. The feeling of guilt is awful and constantly in the eyes of the sinner. In the words of David "My sin *is* always before me" (Psalm 51:3). The sinner takes sides against himself with God. He does not argue that God's requirements are too strict. He knows that they are right and that he is wrong. He realises and accepts without reserve that he deserves God's punishment for his sins.

Sins may take many different forms from the prodigal. The sins committed may include idolatry or participating in religion and religious practices not according to God's will. But whatever the sins repentance always means that there is a realisation of guilt before God for having committed those sins.

A realisation of personal guilt for not being what one ought to be

In the same way the prodigal did not face up to the sort of person he was while living for pleasure, nor when he tried to remedy his poverty. He repented only when he came to himself and acknowledged his sinfulness as a person. He planned to say to his father "I am no longer worthy to be called your son. Make me like one of your hired servants." Again he could have blamed the environment in which he had lived. They influenced him wrongly. Or he could have said that he was born that way. He could have argued that he could not help the way he had been made. Therefore his parents were to blame. But the true penitent does not entertain such considerations. He feels and knows the pollution of his own nature. He knows that not only has he done wrong, he is wrong in his essential nature. He is sinful at the very core of his being. When King David repented of his sins of adultery and murder he confessed his sinfulness to God in the words, "Behold I was brought forth in iniquity, and in sin my mother conceived me" (Psalm 51:5). David is not excusing himself here. It is the very opposite. He is fully admitting to God in brokenness and contrition that he is sinful by nature. He pleads for mercy acknowledging that God would be just if he were to punish him for both his transgressions and his sinfulness.

Shame for sins committed

The words the prodigal planned to say to his father reveal shame for what he has done. He feels he is unworthy of his father's name. True repentance is genuinely ashamed of the wrong things done. We have an example of this in 458 B.C. when Ezra went to God's chosen people, the Jews, after they had returned from exile. When God gave them the land of Canaan He commanded them not to marry the nations who inhabited the land. They were to conquer them and utterly destroy them. They were not to make any covenant with them nor show mercy to them (Deut. 7:1–3). Ezra discovered that the people of Israel and the priests and the Levites had taken some of their daughters as wives for themselves and their sons, so that the holy seed was mixed with the peoples of those lands. Indeed, the hand of the leaders and rulers had been foremost in the trespass. Ezra said, "O my God, I am too ashamed and humiliated to lift up my face to You, my God; for our iniquities have risen higher than *our* heads, and our guilt has grown up to the heavens" (Ezra 9:6). Similarly God revealed to the prophet Ezekiel His requirement that the nation be ashamed of their iniquities. He instructed the prophet to "describe the temple to the house of Israel, that they may be ashamed of their iniquities" (Ezek. 43:10).

Self-loathing for one's sinful nature

The prodigal realised he was no longer worthy to be called the son of his father. He loathed himself. In Ezek. 36:25–27 God said to His people that He would cleanse them, give them a new heart and put His Spirit within them. "Then," said God, "you will remember your evil ways and your deeds that *were* not good; and you will loathe yourselves in your own sight, for your iniquities and abominations" (Ezek. 36:31).

Sorrow for sins and sinfulness

The prodigal came to a place of sorrow not just because of his desperate plight, but because of his sinful failure. He was sorry for what he had done and what he was. David wrote of his sorrow for sin in Psalm 38: "For Your arrows pierce me deeply, And Your hand presses me down. *There is* no soundness in my flesh Because of Your anger, Nor *any* health in my bones Because of my sin. For my iniquities have gone over my head; Like a heavy burden they are too heavy for me. My wounds are foul *and* festering Because of my foolishness. I am troubled, I am bowed down greatly; I go mourning all day long. For my loins are full of inflammation, And *there is* no soundness in my flesh. I am feeble and severely broken; I groan because of the turmoil of my heart. . . . I will declare my iniquity; I will be in anguish over my sin." When God called his people to turn from sin He "called for weeping and for mourning, For baldness and for girding of sackcloth" (Isa. 22:12). Shaving off one's hair was an act of contrition as was the wearing of sackcloth. Similarly in Joel 2:12 God said, "Turn to Me with all your heart, With fasting, with weeping, and with mourning."

The prophet Zechariah in the sixth century B.C. predicts repentance following the crucifixion of the Christ. The stress on mourning runs throughout the passage: "And I will pour on the house of David and on the inhabitants of Jerusalem the Spirit of grace and supplication; then they will look on Me whom they pierced. Yes, they will mourn for Him as one mourns for *his* only *son,* and grieve for Him as one grieves for a firstborn. In that day there shall be a great mourning in Jerusalem, like the mourning at Hadad Rimmon in the plain of Megiddo. And the land shall mourn, every family by itself: the family of the house of

David by itself, and their wives by themselves; the family of the house of Nathan by itself, and their wives by themselves; the family of the house of Levi by itself, and their wives by themselves; the family of Shimei by itself, and their wives by themselves; all the families that remain, every family by itself, and their wives by themselves" (Zech. 12:10–14).

Jesus once told a parable in which a tax collector went to pray in the temple. Jesus said of him, "And the tax collector, standing afar off, would not so much as raise *his* eyes to heaven, but beat his breast, saying 'God, be merciful to me a sinner!'" (Luke 18:13). Jesus commended this man's attitude before God. He was sincerely and deeply sorrowful for his sins and sinfulness.

Hatred of sin

The prodigal once thought of his life of sin as the way to happiness. How real is the deceitfulness of sin! Sin was so attractive. Now he has come to see sin in its ugliness. Sin is now seen as filthiness and detested. The scriptures speak of sin as filthiness. Paul wrote to the Corinthian Christians saying, "Therefore, having these promises, beloved, let us cleanse ourselves from all filthiness of the flesh and spirit, perfecting holiness in the fear of God" (2 Cor. 7:1). Covetousness is called the pursuit of "filthy" lucre (Tit. 1:11). Sexual sins are condemned as uncleanness (Rom. 1:24, 6:19, and 1 Thess. 4:7). Sin results in filthy language (Col. 3:8). Even the "good" works of self righteousness are seen to be "filthy rags" (Isaiah 64:6). Indeed all sin is perceived in a new way as "filthiness" (James 1:21). It is therefore hated as contemptible, corrupt, depraved, despicable, foul, impure, indecent, nasty, offensive, sordid and vile.

A desire to cease from sin

The prodigal decided that he wanted leave the far country of sin and be a servant of his father. He wanted this as an abiding state. Repentance is a desire to cease from sin and sins and to serve God. The penitent comes to hate sin and sins and to want to love God and His commands. There is a change of heart, a new disposition. This is what God commanded through His prophet Ezekiel in chapter 14 verse 6: "Therefore say to the house of Israel, 'Thus says the Lord GOD: Repent, turn away from your idols, and turn your faces away from all your abominations.'" Isaiah made the same appeal to his hearers: "Let the wicked forsake his way, and the unrighteous man his thoughts; let him return to the Lord" (Isa. 55:7). This turning must be from the heart. In the days of Jeremiah God said, "And yet for all this her treacherous sister Judah has not turned to Me with her whole heart, but in pretense" (Jer. 3:10). True turning from sin to God is a settled state of heart, a permanent attitude.

Works befitting repentance

Repentance is fundamentally a change of mind, involving the emotions and an inward resolve of the will. It is not a change in a person's actual actions, but it always results in a change of conduct as the result of the change of mind. Genuine repentance will bring about a radical shift of behaviour from sinfulness to obedience to God. Turning from sin results in "works befitting repentance" (Acts 26:20).

The initial act of repentance accompanied with faith in Christ leading to salvation arises from:

1. a realisation of personal guilt before God for sins committed.
2. a realisation of personal guilt before God for not being what one ought to be.
3. shame for the sins done.
4. self-loathing for one's sinful nature.
5. sorrow for sins and sinfulness.
6. a hatred of sin.
7. a desire to cease from sin.

The feelings and emotions associated with these seven elements vary from individual to individual. In some they are intense; in others not so strongly felt. Moreover consciousness of the presence of each of these elements is different in each individual. But despite this marked diversity there will always be changed behaviour. Dependant on the past life the particular works befitting repentance will also vary.

One example of such works is confession of sin and sins. This is what the prodigal did: "And the son said to him, 'Father, I have sinned against heaven and in your sight, and am no longer worthy to be called your son'" (Luke 15:21).

Nehemiah confessed to God, "You *are* just in all that has befallen us; For You have dealt faithfully But we have done wickedly" (Neh. 9:33). The true penitent makes no excuses, and rather than pleading mitigating circumstances, he also confesses those things which render his sins even more culpable.

Following Paul's ministry at Ephesus it is reported, "And many who had believed came confessing and telling their deeds. Also, many of those who had practiced magic brought their books together and burned *them* in the sight of all. And they counted up the value of them, and *it* totaled fifty thousand *pieces* of silver" (Acts 19:18–19). Here, in addition to confession, we have the burning of occult books as the fruit of repentance.

Another example of works befitting repentance is restitution for sins committed. Zacchaeus, a chief tax collector, repented when Jesus met with him. He "stood and said to the Lord, 'Look, Lord, I give half of my goods to the poor; and if I have taken anything from anyone by false accusation, I restore fourfold' " (Luke 19:8).

When John the Baptist preached repentance to prepare the way for the Messiah he demanded works befitting repentance. "So the people asked him, saying, 'What shall we do then?' He answered and said to them, 'He who has two tunics, let him give to him who has none; and he who has food, let him do likewise.' Then tax collectors also came to be baptized, and said to him, 'Teacher, what shall we do?' And he said to them, 'Collect no more than what is appointed for you.' Likewise the soldiers asked him, saying, 'And what shall we do?' So he said to them, 'Do not intimidate anyone or accuse falsely, and be content with your wages' " (Luke 3:10–14).

In the second letter to the Corinthians Paul writes of the sorrow of repentance and the works which followed: "For godly sorrow produces repentance *leading* to salvation, not to be regretted; but the sorrow of the world produces death. For observe this very thing, that you sorrowed in a godly manner: What diligence it produced in you, *what* clearing *of yourselves, what* indignation, *what* fear, *what* vehement desire, *what* zeal, *what* vindication! In all *things* you proved yourselves to be clear in this matter" (2 Cor. 7:10–11). The intensity of their sorrow was expressed in:

1. diligence, literally haste to put matters right,
2. clearing of themselves by their actions,
3. indignation against the sin committed, that is their anger against themselves for what they had done,
4. fear as to whether they had done everything they needed to do to put things right,
5. vehement desire,
6. zeal, and
7. vindication, that is, with a passion for justice to be done.

What a vast difference often exists between early church practice as stated by Paul in Acts 26:19–20, "Therefore, King Agrippa, I was not disobedient to the heavenly vision, but declared first to those in Damascus and in Jerusalem, and throughout all the region of Judea, and *then* to the Gentiles, that they should repent, turn to God, and do works befitting repentance," and the conduct of evangelists and those following up converts to Christ in these days! True repentance will always result in a change of behaviour from sinfulness to righteousness. There is a renouncing of sin, and a settled determination to obey God which translates into a new way of living. Paul wrote to the Christians at Thessalonica and recalled their repentance from dead works. He said, "you turned to God from idols to serve the living and true God" (1 Thess. 1:9).

The apostle Paul proclaimed a difference in God's dealing with mankind after the coming of Christ to earth and His death, resurrection and ascension into heaven. He preached to the men of Athens, "we ought not to think that the Divine Nature is like gold or silver or stone, something shaped by art and man's devising. Truly, these times of ignorance God overlooked, but now commands all men everywhere to repent, because He has appointed a day on which He will judge the world in righteousness by the Man whom He has ordained. He has given assurance of this to all by raising Him from the dead" (Acts 17:29–31). God now commands all men everywhere to repent. The true Christian life begins with repentance and faith.

CHAPTER SIX

INADEQUATE REPENTANCE

The scriptures give us examples of repentance which are not acceptable to God for becoming a Christian. We must consider these and related biblical truths as a warning, and in order to clarify the meaning of true repentance.

In 2 Corinthians chapter seven verses nine to eleven Paul distinguishes between godly sorrow for sin and the sorrow of the world. This worldly sorrow consists in the pain of the consequences of the sin, the dread of punishment, the shame of being discovered, and remorse. There is sorrow for the sin, but only because of the resulting pain. So long as the sin does not result in any painful consequences there is no sorrow for what has been committed. Sin itself is not sorrowed over as done against God. What is sorrowed over is having to bear the consequences of it. The sin is regretted only because it has brought pain to oneself. The sorrow of self pity may be intense because of the painful consequences of sinning. There is a fervent desire to undo, if it were possible, the sin or sins that have brought the painful consequences. But this is not godly sorrow which leads to becoming a true Christian. There is no overall desire to be rid of sin and sinfulness, and no longing to live a life of righteousness.

Acts 24:25 records that Felix the governor of Judea at the time of Paul was "afraid" when Paul spoke to him concerning righteousness, self-control and the judgment to come. Such fear is not the repentance required by God. Even though Felix said, "Go away for now; when I have a convenient time I will call for you," he was only frightened by the truth not truly repentant. This is not the repentance that is necessary to become a Christian. In these days it is so rare to see any fear of God that when it does occur, even to the limited extent as in Felix, it is often mistaken for being ready to become a Christian. Such fear has no desire to leave sin, it is only fearful of the final judgment and finds an immediate solution in putting off any decision. In reality Felix's decision was a refusal to repent at that time, and a sinful

53

presumption that God would give him further opportunity in the future, if and when Felix so wished! The Bible tells us that such an attitude is sin: "Come now, you who say, 'Today or tomorrow we will go to such and such a city, spend a year there, buy and sell, and make a profit'; whereas you do not know what *will happen* tomorrow. For what *is* your life? It is even a vapor that appears for a little time and then vanishes away. Instead you *ought* to say, 'If the Lord wills, we shall live and do this or that.' But now you boast in your arrogance. All such boasting is evil" (James 4:13–16).

In the time of Moses Pharaoh refused to allow God's people to leave Egypt. God caused plagues to come upon the Egyptians, and after the eighth plague recorded in Exodus 10:16–17, "Pharaoh called for Moses and Aaron in haste, and said, 'I have sinned against the LORD your God and against you. Now therefore, please forgive my sin only this once, and entreat the LORD your God, that He may take away from me this death only.'" At first sight this may appear to be repentance. Subsequent events revealed it to be merely acknowledgment of sin under the immediate stress of adverse circumstances rightly seen to be the judgment of God. Once Moses had prayed to God and He had removed the locusts Pharaoh was again unwilling to let God's people go. Such temporary change of mind is worthless however wonderful it may appear at the time. True repentance is a settled hatred of sin and a settled resolve to turn from it. It is a fundamental change of mind, heart and will, renouncing the previous way of life for an entirely new way of life. It is not an action done only because of pressure, and withdrawn once the strain is relieved.

Repentance is more than humbling oneself because of fear of punishment. King Ahab of Israel c. 874 – 852 B.C. committed gross sin. Elijah the prophet delivered God's word to him, "Behold, I will bring calamity on you. I will take away your posterity, and will cut off from Ahab every male in Israel, both bond and free. I will make your house like the house of Jeroboam the son of Nebat, and like the house of Baasha the son of Ahijah, because of the provocation with which you have provoked *Me* to anger, and made Israel sin" (1 Kings 21:21–22). The king humbled himself: "So it was, when Ahab heard those words, that he tore his clothes and put sackcloth on his body, and fasted and lay in sackcloth, and went about mourning" (1 Kings 21:27). But Ahab did not turn from his idolatry.

Herod the tetrarch behaved in similar fashion when he encountered the person and preaching of John the Baptist. In Mark 6:20 we read, ". . . Herod feared John, knowing that he *was* a just and holy man, and he protected him. And when he heard him, he did many things, and heard him gladly." This fear and partial response in doing "many things" did not stop him from subsequently beheading John. Many are affected by God's word and they are restrained in their disobedience of God by fear, and even do certain things to satisfy their tormented conscience, but there is no fundamental breaking with the life of choosing their own way and rejecting God's way. Repentance is a turning to God. It involves stopping, and realising that one is going the wrong way, and then a decisive turn and going on the right road. The whole life is fundamentally changed. It is not a partial reform and forsaking some selected sins, or even a certain reverence for God and fear of Him without that total change of direction.

Today Christians are far too ready to treat actions of the sort Ahab and Herod did as evidence of true repentance. They fail to see that pricked consciences and awakened fears of judgment to come when the gospel is preached can result in responses which do not result in becoming a Christian. For example such persons will readily obey an invitation to walk to the front of a meeting to "receive Christ" and say a prayer, or go to Church, or do good works, or turn from certain sins etc. but they do not surrender themselves to God. They are only concerned to pacify a disturbed conscience, and to relieve the fear of punishment. These are pressing and urgent concerns to them, and they are highly motivated to do anything they think can achieve these purposes. They are unwilling to truly turn to God, but they are most willing to do "many things" (Mar. 6:20).

The scriptures contain the terrible account of the repentance of Judas after he betrayed Jesus: "Then Judas, His betrayer, seeing that He had been condemned, was remorseful and brought back the thirty pieces of silver to the chief priests and elders, saying, 'I have sinned by betraying innocent blood.' And they said, 'What *is that* to us? You see *to it!'* Then he threw down the pieces of silver in the temple and departed, and went and hanged himself" (Mat. 27:3–5). This was the remorse of despair resulting in suicide. It was not repentance acceptable to God and leading to forgiveness. Jesus said that it would have been good for him if he had not been born (Mat. 26:24). It was a state of darkness fearful to contemplate.

Saul is revealed in the scriptures as a man of insincere repentance. When he was king over Israel God commanded him to "go and attack Amalek, and utterly destroy all that they have, and do not spare them. But kill both man and woman, infant and nursing child, ox and sheep, camel and donkey" (1 Sam.15:3). "But Saul and the people spared Agag and the best of the sheep, the oxen, the fatlings, the lambs, and all *that was* good, and were unwilling to utterly destroy them. But everything despised and worthless, that they utterly destroyed" (1 Sam.15:9). Samuel the prophet rebukes the king for his disobedience. Then Saul said to Samuel, "I have sinned, for I have transgressed the commandment of the LORD and your words, because I feared the people and obeyed their voice. Now therefore, please pardon my sin, and return with me, that I may worship the LORD" (1 Sam.15:24–25). This sounds very fine. In reality Saul was blaming the people for his sin. His repentance was not sincere, and God rejected him that day from remaining king over Israel. David was chosen by God to replace Saul, and Saul sought to kill David. After some time while Saul was pursuing David in the wilderness, Saul unknowingly entered a cave where David was hiding, and David had the opportunity to kill Saul. Afterwards when Saul left the cave David informed Saul of what he could have done, and showed him a corner of Saul's robe which he had cut off while he was in the cave unknown to Saul. The scriptures tell us again of fine words by Saul: "So it was, when David had finished speaking these words to Saul, that Saul said, 'Is this your voice, my son David?' And Saul lifted up his voice and wept. Then he said to David: 'You *are* more righteous than I; for you have rewarded me with good, whereas I have rewarded you with evil. And you have shown this day how you have dealt well with me; for when the LORD delivered me into your hand, you did not kill me. For if a man finds his enemy, will he let him get away safely? Therefore may the LORD reward you with good for what you have done to me this day. And now I know indeed that you shall surely be king, and that the kingdom of Israel shall be established in your hand'" (1 Sam. 24:16–20). The next action of David is the reflection of the insincerity of Saul's words. David and his men went up to the stronghold! Saul soon reverted to his purpose to kill David. David was able to penetrate Saul's camp one night, and again he had the opportunity to kill Saul while he was sleeping. David took from Saul's side his spear and jug of water. Then he called to Saul's camp from a hill afar off. Yet again Saul responded with fine words: "Then Saul said, 'I have sinned. Return, my son David. For I will harm you no more, because my life was precious in your eyes this day. Indeed I have played the fool and erred exceedingly'" (1 Sam.26:21). David knew these were worthless words in which he could not trust. Sadly many fine prayers of repentance said in the presence of a man of God, just as Saul spoke before Samuel and David, are equally worthless.

Balaam is a similar example to Saul of repentance that is not genuine. Balaam, because of covetousness, wished to go to curse Israel at the request of an enemy king. Three times the Angel of the Lord stood in the donkey's way as Balaam went on his way: "Then the LORD opened

Balaam's eyes, and he saw the Angel of the LORD standing in the way with His drawn sword in His hand; and he bowed his head and fell flat on his face. And the Angel of the LORD said to him, 'Why have you struck your donkey these three times? Behold, I have come out to stand against you, because *your* way is perverse before Me. The donkey saw Me and turned aside from Me these three times. If she had not turned aside from Me, surely I would also have killed you by now, and let her live.' And Balaam said to the Angel of the LORD, 'I have sinned, for I did not know You stood in the way against me. Now therefore, if it displeases You, I will turn back' " (Num. 22:31–34). His words were right but they were not the desire of his heart. True repentance is from the heart.

Of course it is not always clear whether repentance is genuine or not. There is the case of Achan in the book of Joshua. When Israel conquered Jericho God forbad them taking the "accursed things," the silver and gold and vessels of bronze and iron. Achan disobeyed and God withdrew His help against their enemies, and they were defeated with thirty-six men killed in battle. Achan's sin was discovered. He was asked to confess. "And Achan answered Joshua and said, 'Indeed I have sinned against the LORD God of Israel, and this is what I have done: When I saw among the spoils a beautiful Babylonian garment, two hundred shekels of silver, and a wedge of gold weighing fifty shekels, I coveted them and took them. And there they are, hidden in the earth in the midst of my tent, with the silver under it' " (Josh. 7:20–21). He was then stoned with stones. Was his repentance genuine? We do not know. Often death bed repentance leaves one unsure of its real nature.

CHAPTER SEVEN

THE MOTIVATION TO REPENT

What moves a person to repent?

The scriptures tell us that certain things we might consider to be effective in producing repentance do not result in that change of mind.

We might suppose that if someone returned to life after death and related the fact of eternal judgment, having seen the realities of the state of man after death, then the hearers would surely repent.

Jesus was emphatic that this would not happen. The gospel of Luke records His words: "There was a certain rich man who was clothed in purple and fine linen and fared sumptuously every day. But there was a certain beggar named Lazarus, full of sores, who was laid at his gate, desiring to be fed with the crumbs which fell from the rich man's table. Moreover the dogs came and licked his sores. So it was that the beggar died, and was carried by the angels to Abraham's bosom. The rich man also died and was buried. And being in torments in Hades, he lifted up his eyes and saw Abraham afar off, and Lazarus in his bosom. Then he cried and said, 'Father Abraham, have mercy on me, and send Lazarus that he may dip the tip of his finger in water and cool my tongue; for I am tormented in this flame.' But Abraham said, 'Son, remember that in your lifetime you received your good things, and likewise Lazarus evil things; but now he is comforted and you are tormented. And besides all this, between us and you there is a great gulf fixed, so that those who want to pass from here to you cannot, nor can those from there pass to us.' Then he said, 'I beg you therefore, father, that you would send him to my father's house, for I have five brothers, that he may testify to them, lest they also come to this place of torment.' Abraham said to him, 'They have Moses and the prophets; let them hear them.' And he said, 'No, father Abraham; but if one goes to them from the dead, they will repent.' But he said to him, 'If they do not hear Moses and the prophets, neither will they be persuaded though one rise from the dead'" (Luke 16:19–31).

Miracles do not always bring about repentance

This fact is taught by Christ: "Then He began to rebuke the cities in which most of His mighty works had been done, because they did not repent: Woe to you, Chorazin! Woe to you, Bethsaida! For if the mighty works which were done in you had been done in Tyre and Sidon, they would have repented long ago in sackcloth and ashes" (Matthew 11:20–21). The miracles He did in Chorazin and Bethsaida did not produce repentance, but those same miracles would have done so in Tyre and Sidon at a previous time in history. The record of the Acts of the Apostles demonstrates that miracles greatly assisted the proclamation of the gospel and in leading men and women to repentance and faith. The miracles drew crowds (Acts 2:6, 3:11, 5:16, 8:6–7, 9:33–35, 9:36–42, 14:8–18, 28:9). Miracles also confirmed the word of God (Heb. 2:3–4, Mark 16:20, Acts 2:3, 4:29–31 and 33, 5:12, 6:8, 8:13, 14:3, 15:12, Rom. 15:18–19, 2 Cor. 12:12, and 1 Cor. 2:4–5). These miracles were the means used by the Lord on some occasions to bring people to hear the gospel, and also, in some cases, to produce repentance and faith. We have an example of this in Acts 13:6–12: "Now when they had gone through the island to Paphos, they found a certain sorcerer, a false prophet, a Jew whose name *was* Bar-jesus, who was with the proconsul, Sergius Paulus, an intelligent man. This man called for Barnabas and Saul and sought to hear the word of God. But Elymas the sorcerer (for so his name is translated) withstood them, seeking to turn the proconsul away from the faith. Then Saul, who also *is called* Paul, filled with the Holy Spirit, looked intently at him and said, 'O full of all deceit and all fraud, *you* son of the devil, *you* enemy of all righteousness, will you not cease perverting the straight ways of the Lord? And now, indeed, the hand of the Lord *is* upon you, and you shall be blind, not seeing the sun for a time.' And immediately a dark mist fell on him, and he went around seeking someone to lead him by the hand. Then the proconsul believed, when he saw what had been done, being astonished at the teaching of the Lord." However miracles alone without the working of the Spirit drawing to Christ will not produce conversion. Christ Himself was "a Man attested by God to you by miracles, wonders, and signs which God did through Him" (Acts 2:22). But John records, "although He had done so many signs before them, they did not believe in Him" (John 12:37). Only a small remnant of the nation received their Messiah. As Jesus Himself said, "no one can come to Me unless the Father who sent Me draws him" (John 6:44).

Divine judgments do not always cause repentance

In the Old Testament there is the account of king Manasseh c. 693 – 639 B.C. His genuine repentance as a result of judgment is recorded in 2 Chronicles 33:9–16: "So Manasseh seduced Judah and the inhabitants of Jerusalem to do more evil than the nations whom the LORD had destroyed before the children of Israel. And the LORD spoke to Manasseh and his people, but they would not listen. Therefore the LORD brought upon them the captains of the army of the king of Assyria, who took Manasseh with hooks, bound him with bronze *fetters,* and carried him off to Babylon. Now when he was in affliction, he implored the LORD his God, and humbled himself greatly before the God of his fathers, and prayed to Him; and He received his entreaty, heard his supplication, and brought him back to Jerusalem into his kingdom. Then Manasseh knew that the LORD *was* God. After this he built a wall outside the City of David on the west side of Gihon, in the valley, as far as the entrance of the Fish Gate; and *it* enclosed Ophel, and he raised it to a very great height. Then he put military captains in all the fortified cities of Judah. He took away the foreign gods and the idol from the house of the LORD, and all the altars that he had built in the mount of the house of the LORD and in Jerusalem; and he cast *them* out of the city. He also repaired the altar of the LORD, sacrificed peace offerings and thank offerings on it, and commanded Judah to serve the LORD God of Israel."

However, the book of Revelation tells us that certain plagues come upon mankind by God's decree, but they do not produce repentance: "But the rest of mankind, who were not killed by these plagues, did not repent of the works of their hands, that they should not worship demons, and idols of gold, silver, brass, stone, and wood, which can neither see nor hear nor walk. And they did not repent of their murders or their sorceries or their sexual immorality or their thefts" (Revelation 9:20–21). The scriptures indicate that Manasseh was a rare exception to the reality that calamities do not bring men and women to repentance.

The goodness of God is designed by God to lead men to repentance (Rom. 2:4)

This goodness is God's kindness active for mankind. Paul stated this great truth concerning God's goodness in his words at Lystra. The people thought he was a god because he healed a man who had been lame. He said to them, "Men, why are you doing these things? We also are men with the same nature as you, and preach to you that you should turn from these useless things to the living God, who made the heaven, the earth, the sea, and all things that are in them, who in bygone generations allowed all nations to walk in their own ways. Nevertheless He did not leave Himself without witness, in that He did good, gave us rain from heaven and fruitful seasons, filling our hearts with food and gladness" (Acts 14:15–17). Jesus declared that His Father "makes His sun rise on the evil and the good, and sends rain on the just and on the unjust" (Matthew 5:45). David in one of his psalms expressed the same truth: "The LORD *is* good to all, And His tender mercies *are* over all His works" (Psa. 145:9).

This goodness of God is not confined to the provision of man's physical needs. It extends to His ordination of rulers and governments to restrain evil for the preservation and good of humanity: "Let every soul be subject to the governing authorities. For there is no authority except from God, and the authorities that exist are appointed by God" (Rom.13:1). Sometimes rulers are corrupt and oppressive, and they do not carry out God's ordained task stated in Rom.13:4: "he (the ruling power) is God's minister, an avenger to *execute* wrath on him who practices evil." When they fulfil God's purpose they are "God's minister to you for good." They save man from violence and anarchy. This is God's goodness to mankind.

God's riches of goodness is also expressed in His forbearance and longsuffering with man's sinfulness and sinful behaviour day by day. His goodness is manifest in His restraint in punishing men for their sins. He holds back from executing His wrath, and He delays the day of final judgment. He is longsuffering in bearing with man's sins. The express purpose of this longsuffering is to provide time for men to repent. He "is longsuffering toward us not willing that any should perish but that all should come to repentance" (2 Peter 3:9). Each day the sinner offends God. Each day the cumulative guilt and offense increases. Each day the offensiveness of the sinner is aggravated by not responding to the goodness of God in repentance. But God continues to exercise forbearance and longsuffering! This is intended to influence men to repent. If they think on these things, and acknowledge them as true in their own lives it will move them to repent. The reality is that men in general do not accept the goodness of God to them, but wilfully choose not to acknowledge it because of their sinful attitude towards God. So the goodness of God, without the working of the Holy Spirit in a person's heart, does not bring about repentance.

Repentance that brings a person into relationship with God always requires a mighty work of the Spirit of God. This truth will be addressed in subsequent chapters. People returning to life after death, calamities, judgments, miracles, and even the riches of God's goodness without His operation on the heart will not produce this change. All we have considered brings out the depth and extent of the change of mind called repentance which is essential to become a Christian.

A final word is necessary. We must distinguish clearly between repentance bringing salvation and the repentance that is required after conversion. The Christian, despite his fundamental change of mind, often falls into sinful ways or sinful attitudes and must repent of those sins. He must repent specifically of those sins. John wrote to Christians saying, "If we say that we have no sin, we deceive ourselves, and the truth is not in us" (1 John 1:8). This repentance for particular sins must be distinguished from repentance with faith to receive salvation. These acts of repentance are fundamentally different from the initial repentance to become a Christian. Repentance at conversion to Christ is necessary to enter the kingdom of God. Repentance for particular sins after conversion concerns the believer's walk before God in the kingdom. There are examples of such repentance in the book of Revelation in 2:5,16, and 22; 3:3,19. This repentance is a matter of putting matters right with God, but now as one of His children, not as one outside the kingdom. The repentance that is part of conversion to Christ can never be repeated. But the repentance for sins after conversion is needed each time they are committed. Hebrews 6:1 speaks only of repentance at conversion.

Faith

CHAPTER EIGHT

FAITH TOWARD GOD

We now consider the second element in the foundation of the Christian life. This is faith toward God, which together with repentance, is essential to become a Christian. FAITH IS BELIEF IN THE GOSPEL

The gospel is the good news of God's salvation for everyone who will believe. The salvation it brings is deliverance from,

- the wrath of God in this life,
- the wrath of God at the Final Judgment Day,
- God's eternal punishment for sinfulness and sins.

The wrath of God in this life

The wrath of God comes upon men and women from birth. The first man disobeyed God and by that action all mankind became alienated from God. All mankind descended from him, and were born with, and continue to be born with, a sinful disposition that hates the true God. They wish to shut Him out of the universe He created, and above all, out of their lives. They want to be away from His presence, and to be free from His rule over them. This is their natural and settled state of mind. Consequently they are, in the words of scripture, "by nature children of wrath" (Eph. 2:3), that is, justly under the wrath of God because of their sinful nature. Babies, in respect of their nature, do not begin life as innocent before God. Their sinful nature is present at birth and manifests itself as the years go by. Sins are the inevitable products of the heart disposition towards God. Bad companions, influences and opportunities provided by circumstances may increase the range and number of sins committed, but environment alone is not the cause of sinful actions. The fundamental explanation of man's sinful behaviour is his sinful nature from birth. The problem of sin is within. In the words of the Son of God, "For from within, out of the heart of men, proceed evil thoughts, adulteries, fornications, murders, thefts, covetousness, wickedness, deceit, lewdness, an evil eye, blasphemy, pride, foolishness. All these evil things come from within and defile a man" (Mark 7:21–23).

In spite of his sinful disposition man does have a sense of right and wrong. He has a conscience. He is capable of doing good actions. Jesus Christ affirmed this capability: "If you then, being evil, know how to give good gifts to your children, how much more will *your* heavenly Father give the Holy Spirit to those who ask Him!" (Luke 11:13). It is striking that at the same time as He says, "you know how to give good gifts to your children," He also defines human nature as "evil." The following record reveals that Jesus was unambiguous and explicit in this assessment of man: "Now as He was going out on the road, one came running, knelt before Him, and asked Him, 'Good Teacher, what shall I do that I may inherit eternal life?' So Jesus said to him, 'Why do you call Me good? No one *is* good but One, *that is*, God. You know the commandments: "Do not commit adultery," "Do not murder," "Do not steal," "Do not bear false witness," "Do not defraud," "Honor your father and your mother." ' And he answered and said to Him, 'Teacher, all these things I have kept from my youth' " (Mark 10:17–20). Notice that this man was able to reply that he had kept the commands mentioned by Jesus. The world would say that he was "good." Jesus stated categorically that the man, and every individual person of all of mankind, were not good. All have a sinful nature from birth. No one is good but God. Because of this sinful nature man is under God's wrath.

The wrath of God in this life also comes upon men and women because of sins. They refuse to face up to the truth about God revealed in creation, and to respond to it as they should. This suppression of the truth is the natural expression of their sinful nature. They are unwilling to acknowledge what God shows clearly to them by the universe He has made, namely His eternal power and Godhead. They do not glorify Him as God, nor give thanks to Him in response to that revelation of Himself. In God's sight they are without excuse for these sins of omission. Moreover because of their hatred of the true God they gladly embrace lies, ideas, philosophies or religions which get rid of the true God by denying His existence or by replacing Him with a god or gods of man's invention. Consequently God, in holy and righteous wrath, gives men up to their debased thoughts and sinful behaviour. This behaviour is defined in the Bible as sexual immorality, lewdness, lust, adultery, fornication, lesbianism, homosexuality, unrighteousness, wickedness, blasphemy, filthy language, covetousness, anger, wrath, maliciousness, envy, theft, extortion, murder, strife, lying, deceit, evil-mindedness, backbiting, violence, drunkenness, pride, boasting, occult practices, idolatry, inventing evil things, disobedience to parents, and the lack of the following qualities – moral values, trust-worthiness, love, forgiveness and mercy (Rom. 1:18–31). This wrath of God in handing men over to sin must not be thought of only in terms of the suffering and pain that are often the direct consequence of sins. For example the homosexual may develop AIDS and suffer most terri-bly. The wrath of God experienced by men in this life is the action of God in giving men up to their sinful conduct regardless of whether or not sinning brings ruin in this life.

His wrath is revealed in giving them up to the expression of their lusts. He lets them indulge as they wish, but He is in no way the author of their sins. He permits them to do what they freely choose to do. In that way He punishes sin with sin. Make no mistake this is not correc-tive. The effect is to make the sinner worse. Sin repeated is a downward path. This action of God is truly fearful and terrible to contemplate once one's eyes have been opened to see it. Fallen man's state is described in John's gospel: "the wrath of God abides on him" (John 3:36).

Men generally do not perceive that God deals with them in this way. They are unaware that God is active towards them in this manner. They are completely blind to it. They are not conscious of God's wrath upon them. For those with eyes to see, God displays His wrath in handing men over to their sins. It is a holy and just punishment for sinful attitudes and behaviour. It is a terrible punishment, but it is measured and mixed with goodness and mercy. It is essential to see this truth of God's wrath in the context of His total dealings with His creatures. Otherwise we will not have a true understanding or appreciation of His wrath. God deals with mankind in goodness and mercy as well as wrath. As we have noted previously He constantly provides for man's needs (Acts 14:17). He restrains sinners through the agency of human government. He is longsuffering with man's rebellion. He is forbearing towards man's continual sinfulness and sinning. He holds back His wrath against the sinner in the face of daily increasing guilt. Above all, God has no pleasure in the guilt and punishment of man. He desires rather that man will repent and believe the gospel so that he will no longer be under God's wrath. In the wonderful words of scripture, "God so loved the world that He gave His only begotten Son, that whoever believes in Him should not perish but have everlasting life" (John 3:16).

When these facts are given due consideration we can better under-stand God's wrath. It is clear that there is nothing irrational or uncon-trolled in God's wrath. We sinful beings are accustomed to thinking of anger in those terms. God exercises His wrath with total self-control, in absolute righteousness and in perfect justice. However this does not mean that He is devoid of emotion in this particular dealing with mankind. The scriptures are clear. Just as he is moved with pity and compassion for those in need, He is also moved to wrath, even at times fury and fierce anger, by the behaviour of sinners.

This wrath of God is no deficiency in the Godhead. To think of it as such borders on blasphemy. The wrath of God is one aspect of the glory of God. It is a perfection of the Divine character. A.W. Pink expresses this truth, "Now the wrath of God is as much a Divine perfection as is His faithfulness, power, or mercy. It *must be so*, for there is no blemish whatever, not the slightest defect in the character of God; yet there *would be* if 'wrath' were absent from Him! Indifference to sin is a moral blemish, and he who hates it not is a moral leper. How could He who is the Sum of all excellency look with equal satisfaction upon virtue and vice, wisdom and folly? How could He who is infinitely holy disregard sin and refuse to manifest His 'severity' (Rom. 9:12) toward it? How could He who delights only in that which is pure and lovely, loathe and hate not that which is impure and vile?"[1]

The wrath of God at the Final Judgment Day

Despite the consequences of many sins men often enjoy the pleasures of sin during this life. But a day of reckoning is certain to come for every man and woman. There will be a Final Judgment Day: "And as it is appointed for men to die once, but after this the judgment" (Heb. 9:27), and "Do not marvel at this; for the hour is coming in which all who are in the graves will hear His voice and come forth – those who have done good, to the resurrection of life, and those who have done evil, to the resurrection of condemnation" (John 5:28–29).

Those who live rejecting God are stacking up each day sins before God. They are amassing a wealth of guilt which will bring upon them wrath in the day of wrath and revelation of the righteous judgment of God: "in the day of wrath and revelation of the righteous judgment of God, who 'will render to each one according to his deeds': . . . to those who are self-seeking and do not obey the truth, but obey unrighteousness – indignation and wrath, tribulation and anguish, on every soul of man who does evil, of the Jew first and also of the Greek" (Rom. 2:5–6, and 8–9).

All will be revealed on that Day: "in the day when God will judge the secrets of men by Jesus Christ, according to my gospel" (Rom. 2:16). All actions, words and thoughts of each individual will be judged: "For God will bring every work into judgment, Including every secret thing, Whether good or evil" (Eccl. 12:14).

All sins will bring not just God's righteous condemnation but also His holy wrath upon the guilty one. That wrath will be unspeakably fearful on the day. The book of the Revelation foretells the terror men will experience when they are judged by the Lord Jesus Christ: "I looked when He opened the sixth seal, and behold, there was a great earthquake; and the sun became black as sackcloth of hair, and the moon became like blood. And the stars of heaven fell to the earth, as a fig tree drops its late figs when it is shaken by a mighty wind. Then the sky receded as a scroll when it is rolled up, and every mountain and island was moved out of its place. And the kings of the earth, the great men, the rich men, the commanders, the mighty men, every slave and every free man, hid themselves in the caves and in the rocks of the mountains, and said to the mountains and rocks, 'Fall on us and hide us from the face of Him who sits on the throne and from the wrath of the Lamb! For the great day of His wrath has come, and who is able to stand?' " (Rev. 6:12–17).

God's eternal punishment for sinfulness and sins

Every soul of man found guilty at that Final Judgment will be sentenced to eternal punishment in Hell. The scriptures tell us that Hell is a place:

1. prepared for the Devil and his angels (Mat. 25:41).
2. of everlasting fire (Mat. 25:41).
3. of suffering tribulation (Rom. 2:9).
4. of suffering distress (Rom. 2:9).
5. of continual and eternal torment (Rev. 20:10).
6. of weeping (Mat. 13:42).
7. of no rest (Rev. 14:11).
8. of the undying worm (Mark 9:48). This probably speaks of the never ending torment of a guilty conscience.
9. of the blackness of darkness (2 Pet. 2:17).
10. of everlasting punishment (Mat. 25:46).
11. of destruction in the sense of ruin (2 Thess. 1:8–9).
12. of the second death (Rev. 21:8). Death in this verse means existing in a wrong way, debased and wretched.
13. of utter hopelessness. It is eternal. There will be no second chance and no annihilation.
14. of the gnashing of teeth (Mat. 13:42). This probably speaks of the anger of those suffering in Hell.

This place, and all the punishment experienced there, will be the unending execution of God's wrath and indignation against sinful angels and sinful mankind.

The gospel is the good news that there is a way to be saved from God's wrath in this life, at the Final Judgment and for all eternity. God sent His Son into the world to die in the place of sinners to make a propitiation for sin. Christ appeased the holy and righteous wrath of God the Father against sinners by taking the punishment of sin upon Himself. Christ died and shed His blood as an atoning sacrifice. He died the just for the unjust, and did all that was necessary to bring men into fellowship with God. "God was in Christ reconciling the world to Himself" (2 Cor. 5:19).

God's justice was upheld by the death of Christ. His holy law was vindicated and established because Christ bore the penalty of breaking the law. That law stated, "Cursed is everyone who does not continue in all things which are written in the book of the law, to do them" (Gal. 3:10). The law also said, "Cursed is everyone who hangs on a tree" (Gal. 3:13). This referred to the person who was executed because of breaking the law and then hung upon a tree. Christ took that curse of death for breaking the law when He died on the cross, that is on a tree, in the place of and for sinners. Mercy therefore can be given to sinners who repent and believe without any waiving of God's law, justice and righteousness.

This salvation from the wrath of God through faith includes forgiveness of sins, washing from the filthiness of sin, the gift of the perfect righteousness of Christ imputed to the believer to stand legally righteous before God, God's action separating the believer from the world to Himself and for His service, adoption into God's family, becoming a partaker of the divine nature, newness of life with power by the Holy Spirit to overcome sin and to be holy, bodily transformation at the return of Christ to this world to become conformed to the Risen Glorified Jesus Christ, and eternal blessedness as joint heirs with Christ of all things.

Reference

1. A.W. Pink *The Attributes of God*, Bible Truth Depot, 1962, pages 75–76. (Later edition by Baker 2006.)

CHAPTER NINE

WHAT IS THE FAITH THAT THE GOSPEL REQUIRES TO OBTAIN SALVATION?

It is a response of obedience from the heart to the truth of the gospel understood by the mind, and affecting the emotions. Speaking of the Christians at Rome Paul wrote of their conversion to Christianity in precisely these terms: "But God be thanked that *though* you were slaves of sin, yet you obeyed from the heart that form of doctrine to which you were delivered" (Rom. 6:17). Knowledge of the message is essential. Equally there must be a submission of the will to God's way of salvation. Moreover there is a felt need of salvation, and a desire for it involving the emotions. The degree of emotion varies from person to person. The expression of such feelings also varies from person to person. But the realisation of the need of salvation, and the step taken to obtain it are always accompanied with emotion. In addition to these elements of knowledge (the mind), submission (the will), felt need and desire (emotions), action is required to gain salvation.

The Bible defines that action of faith in various ways

The relationship between repentance and faith will be considered at a later stage, but as we look at several terms in the Bible defining the action of faith which gains salvation we must remember that such faith must always be accompanied by repentance.

1.   It is calling on the name of the Lord for salvation (Acts 2:21 and Rom. 10:13)
It is asking the Lord Jesus Christ to have mercy and to give salvation.

2.   It is "receiving Christ"
"But as many as received Him, to them He gave the right to become children of God, to those who believe in His name: who were born, not of blood, nor of the will of the flesh, nor of the will of man, but of God" (John 1:12–13). Receiving Christ is believing His words to be true, and

responding to them so that He becomes a personal Saviour and Lord. It is to say to Jesus Christ, "I believe what You say about Yourself and Your coming to earth to die to seek and to save that which is lost. I acknowledge You as Lord, and ask You to be my Saviour from sin and its consequences."

3.   It is "coming to Christ"
"Come to Me, all *you* who labor and are heavy laden, and I will give you rest" (Mat. 11:28). This record of the words of Jesus speaks of the action of turning to Christ out of a real sense of need to be delivered from the burdens of life. Jesus says, "Take My yoke upon you and learn from Me, for I am gentle and lowly in heart, and you will find rest for your souls." Coming to Christ is to give oneself to Christ taking His yolk which is easy and His burden which is light. The fallen life of separation from God is often a life of labour and heavy load. Walking one's own way instead of God's way has many different pathways resulting in toil and weariness of soul. The prophet Isaiah asks, "Why do you spend money for *what is* not bread, And your wages for *what* does not satisfy? Listen carefully to Me, and eat *what is* good, And let your soul delight itself in abundance" (Isa. 55:2). So many people toil for wealth, and spend, and yet are not satisfied. Similarly multitudes of zealous men and women practise an almost innumerable variety of non-Christian religious beliefs with a continual sense of burden and no rest of soul. Equally huge numbers of people practise empty nominal Christian religion and ritual sometimes with great devotion but no rest of soul. Many of the religious requirements they follow are like those of the scribes and Pharisees at the time of Christ's first coming. Jesus said of them, "For they bind heavy burdens, hard to bear, and lay *them* on men's shoulders" (Mat. 23:4). There are very many pathways of toil and burden. To come to Christ is to turn from one's own way and to give oneself to Him asking Him for rest.

4.   It is looking to Christ
"The next day John saw Jesus coming toward him, and said, 'Behold! The Lamb of God who takes away the sin of the world!' " (John 1:29). Faith sees Christ as the complete answer to one's spiritual need. It is not Christ plus something else, but Christ alone for salvation. Faith relies only on Christ. It says "I have nothing to present to gain God's favour; there is nothing I can do to merit His blessing; I only deserve condemnation. But I trust only in Christ and His completed work for my salvation."

5.   It is an act of submission to God's way of salvation

"For they being ignorant of God's righteousness, and seeking to establish their own righteousness, have not submitted to the righteousness of God" (Rom. 10:3). In this verse of scripture Paul states why the Jews, except for a remnant, rejected their Messiah, the Lord Jesus Christ. They sought to become righteous before God by their own good works and religious practice. It was therefore offensive to be told that their own righteousness was totally unacceptable to God. It nullified their personal achievement. It completely destroyed their pride in their own good works. They had to humble themselves, and acknowledge the worthlessness of their own righteousness, and admit that they could not achieve salvation by their own goodness and actions. They were required to renounce all self-merit, admit their utter helplessness, and ask Christ to give them righteousness to stand without condemnation before God. This action of submission for those who take pride in their own righteousness is a huge step to take. This submission is of crucial importance. To get right with God, as the prophet Isaiah declared, it is necessary to cast aside one's own opinions as well as that behaviour which is not right in the sight of God: "Let the wicked forsake his way, And the unrighteous man his thoughts; Let him return to the Lord, And He will have mercy on him; And to our God, For He will abundantly pardon" (Isa. 55:7). It is no small matter for men and women to surrender their own thoughts to God's gospel as His appointed and only way of salvation.

6.   It is described as "eating Christ"

"This is the bread which comes down from heaven, that one may eat of it and not die. I am the living bread which came down from heaven. If anyone eats of this bread, he will live forever; and the bread that I shall give is My flesh, which I shall give for the life of the world" (John 6:50–51). This passage of scripture speaks of the appropriation of Christ. Faith that saves believes in Christ not just as the Bread of Life that one may eat and not die; it believes *and eats*. It believes in a *personal* Saviour. It says "the Son of God who loved *me* and gave Himself for *me*" (Gal. 2:20 italics mine).

7.   It is defined as "fleeing for refuge and laying hold of the hope" promised in the gospel (Heb. 6:18)

The realisation of the danger of God's wrath at the Judgment Day causes one to go to Christ for salvation with a sense of an urgent and great need for deliverance that He alone can give. That deliverance is grasped hold of as most precious and not to be lost.

8.   The scriptures also speak of faith as "embracing" the gospel promises (Heb. 11:13)

This focuses on the manner in which the emotions are profoundly moved when the gospel is obeyed. The promises are so wonderful and trustworthy that they are believed and appropriated with great eagerness and feeling.

This initial act of faith which obtains salvation must not be confused with physical responses to the gospel. It has become the custom of many who preach the gospel to ask hearers to become Christians by raising a hand, coming to the front or some similar action. There is no doubt that many have done such actions, and for them their physical action has been simultaneous with and inseparable from their repentance and faith. They have been truly saved. In reality all that was necessary was their repentance and faith. The repentance and faith demanded by the gospel are spiritual actions between the individual and God: they require no physical actions other than those involved in private prayer. They do not include the physical responses sometimes demanded by evangelists. Such physical response was an additional requirement of the preacher, not of God. Only repentance and faith are required by God. None of the verses in the New Testament speaking of confessing Christ before men can be used legitimately to sanction calling for a physical response to receive salvation. They all speak of the confessing of a salvation which has been previously received; of confessing Christ after receiving Him as Lord and Saviour.

This physical movement gospel gets much response because of certain facts about human behaviour stated in the scriptures. Firstly, when sinners are confronted with the gospel conscience is often disturbed. The immediate reaction is a desire to ease the feeling of guilt by doing good things. Herod Antipas, ruler over Galilee at the time of Jesus, is an example of this characteristic behaviour of fallen human nature. He was rebuked by John the Baptist for his immorality in marrying Herodias his brother's wife. To satisfy Herodias Herod put John in prison. She wanted to kill John, but as Mark 6:20 says, "Herod feared John, knowing that he *was* a just and holy man, and he protected him. And when he heard him, he did many things, and heard him gladly." Notice Herod "did many things" as well as protecting him from Herodias. He attempted to relieve his guilty conscience by doing many good things to offset his sin. He did not repent of his sinful union with Herodias. In just the same way men and women will gladly do good works when confronted with the gospel. They will readily do something other than repent and change their way of life. Therefore the requirement for physical motion gets a willing response, whereas repentance would not. In reality the Herod decisions are worthless. Herod killed John the Baptist despite his doing "many things." When Jesus was sent to Herod by Pilate and Herod questioned Him with many words, it is recorded that Jesus "answered him nothing." Christ did not have a single word for him.

Secondly, the high level of response to the physical movement gospel is explained in the scriptures by sinful human nature's exceedingly strong preference to do works to obtain God's favour rather than to come to God, and humbly receive salvation as an undeserved gift. Sinful man wants to earn salvation, and then glory in personal achievement, and receive the praise of men. God's way of salvation is only for those who are poor in spirit, those who have come to the end of themselves. They realise there is nothing in themselves, nor in what they have done or are trying to do, that they can present to God to obtain salvation. God alone can save them. There is no place for pride, and this is highly offensive to sinful human nature. In contrast salvation by works is much more attractive.

The record of a man called Naaman in the Old Testament is a clear example of this strong preference for works. He was a great man, commander of the army of the king of Syria. One day he made the terrible discovery that he was a leper. Eventually he went to the prophet Elisha to be healed. Elisha gave him a simple and clear message: "And Elisha sent a messenger to him, saying, 'Go and wash in the Jordan seven times, and your flesh shall be restored to you, and *you shall* be clean' " (2 Kings 5:10). He reacted with fury: "But Naaman became furious, and went away and said, 'Indeed, I said to myself, "He will surely come out *to me*, and stand and call on the name of the LORD his God, and wave his hand over the place, and heal the leprosy. *Are* not the Abanah and the Pharpar, the rivers of Damascus, better than all the waters of Israel? Could I not wash in them and be clean?" ' So he turned and went away in a rage. And his servants came near and spoke to him, and said, 'My father, *if* the prophet had told you *to do* something great, would you not have done *it?* How much more then, when he says to you, "Wash, and be clean"?' " (2 Kings 5:11–13). Here we see his willingness to do "something great" instead of washing seven times. He had to humble himself by acknowledging his uncleanness (seven washes), and by obeying exactly what God said through His prophet – washes in Jordan not any other river. Great works were not acceptable. Notice what is most significant. He would have had no objection to doing "something great." Men and women, like Naaman, readily do works. They are willing to respond to an appeal to do some self-glorifying great action, like coming to the front to receive Christ or publicly pledging their commitment. In contrast the obedience of repentance and faith is offensive.

Some evangelists, keen to appear successful, exploit these characteristics of human behaviour seen in Herod and Naaman. Thereby they get visible impressive results in terms of physical response to their appeals/invitations. They subtly change the requirements of the gospel from repentance and faith to a physical response routine that superficially seems to be biblical and helpful. Counselling usually has a key role in the physical response gospel. Sadly such counselling is often done without a faithful presentation of the absolute need for repentance and faith as defined by the word of God. The counselled is directed in such a way that they need to give only verbal assent to the truths put before him/her, and repeat the words of prayers said by the counsellor. Real repentance and true faith from the heart are not essential to advance through this process and finally to be told "You are now a Christian." This is a diluted untrue gospel made easy to get results. Such "converts" don't last of course. The subsequent inevitable falling away is accounted for, not in terms of failure to preach faithfully repentance and faith, but in terms of deficiency in following up the ones who made decisions. The truth is also pleaded that some temporary "converts" follow the preaching of the gospel as stated by Jesus in the parable of the sower: "But he who received the seed on stony places, this is he who hears the word and immediately receives it with joy; yet he has no root in himself, but endures only for a while. For when tribulation or persecution arises because of the word, immediately he stumbles" (Mat. 13:20–21). To plead this explanation for the falling away is invalid when the true gospel is not being proclaimed.

In stating these sad realities about some evangelism I do not wish to depreciate the place of counselling in the furtherance of the gospel. But counselling must ever be true to God's requirements of repentance and faith. The scriptures teach clearly that counselling and helping people, one to one, to obtain salvation are means used by the Holy Spirit for the proclamation and progress of the gospel. There are clear proofs of this in the Acts of the Apostles. The apostle Peter proclaimed on the day of Pentecost that Jesus, Whom they had crucified, God had made both Lord and Christ. The record continues, "Now when they heard *this*, they were cut to the heart, and said to Peter and the rest of the apostles, 'Men *and* brethren, what shall we do?' Then Peter said to them, 'Repent, and let every one of you be baptized in the name of Jesus Christ for the remission of sins; and you shall receive the gift of the Holy Spirit. For the promise is to you and to your children, and to all who are afar off, as many as the Lord our God will call.' And with many other words he testified and exhorted them, saying, 'Be saved from this perverse generation'" (Acts 2:37–40). Peter gave counsel after his message. Indeed he used "many other words." He directed them to do three things: to repent, to be baptized (which we shall see later is the expression of faith) and to "be saved from this perverse generation." The generation of Jews living at that time were perverse in their rejection of Jesus the Son of God, and he exhorted them not to be influenced and destroyed by following their example.

Another account of counselling tells of an evangelist called Philip: "Now an angel of the Lord spoke to Philip, saying, 'Arise and go toward the south along the road which goes down from Jerusalem to Gaza.' This is desert. So he arose and went. And behold, a man of Ethiopia, a eunuch of great authority under Candace the queen of the Ethiopians, who had charge of all her treasury, and had come to Jerusalem to worship, was returning. And sitting in his chariot, he was reading Isaiah the prophet. Then the Spirit said to Philip, 'Go near and overtake this chariot.' So Philip ran to him, and heard him reading the prophet Isaiah, and said, 'Do you understand what you are reading?' And he said, 'How can I, unless someone guides me?' And he asked Philip to come up and sit with him. The place in the Scripture which he read was this: 'He was led as a sheep to the slaughter; And as a lamb before its shearer is silent, So He opened not His mouth. In His humiliation His justice was taken away, And who will declare His generation? For His life is taken from the earth.' So the eunuch answered Philip and said, 'I ask you, of whom does the prophet say this, of himself or of some other man?' Then Philip opened his mouth, and beginning at this Scripture, preached Jesus to him. Now as they went down the road, they came to some water. And the eunuch said, 'See, here is water. What hinders me from being baptized?' Then Philip said, 'If you believe with all your heart, you may.' And he answered and said, 'I believe that Jesus Christ is the Son of God.' So he commanded the chariot to stand still. And both Philip and the eunuch went down into the water, and he baptized him" (Acts 8:26–38).

These accounts fully endorse the offering and giving of help to those who wish to know more about the gospel. On some occasions they endorse also the giving of help to those, like the Ethiopian eunuch, who do not initially request it. But they give no authorisation nor support to the physical motion gospel. The Biblical act of exercising faith to receive salvation must not be confused with man's inventions.

WITHOUT A SPECIAL OPERATION OF GOD UPON MAN NO ONE WOULD EXERCISE THE FAITH NECESSARY TO GAIN SALVATION

Jesus declared, "No one can come to Me unless the Father who sent Me draws him; and I will raise him up at the last day. It is written in the prophets, 'And they shall all be taught by God.' Therefore everyone who has heard and learned from the Father comes to Me" (John 6:44–45). Without this work of God no one is able to come to Christ. It is absolutely essential for the exercise of faith. This special operation of God is a twofold work. It is defined as a drawing to Christ, and as a hearing and learning from the Father. It is an inward work on the heart, and an enlightening work. The hearer is turned from an attitude of hatred and rebellion towards the truth to love for it. Also the Spirit teaches with such power the truths of the gospel to the hearer that faith is the result *in every case*: "everyone who has heard and learned from the Father comes to Me."

We can understand the absolute necessity for this special operation of God when we realise the state of mind mankind has towards God. As previously stated, the Bible declares that man is a fallen creature. His disposition towards God is one of enmity. He hates a holy God. He wishes to do as he pleases, and to have absolutely no interference from God in his life. He desires to live apart from the one true God, to keep Him and His requirements completely out of his life. He abhors God's assessment of him as sinful by nature and deeds. In rebellion he asserts man's essential goodness. Man wants to go his own way, and not to have to give account to God at a Final Judgment Day. He does not want a righteous and just God as his Judge at the end of his life. He is totally against a God who will condemn men and women to eternal punishment in hell unless they repent and believe the gospel. God is offensive to him even in His offer of mercy. He is offended at God's command to repent in order to receive that mercy. He stumbles at God's insistence that man can do nothing to save himself from God's punishment of sin. It is unpalatable that God requires him to humble himself and ask Christ to save him. This God destroys his pride in human goodness, ability and good works. Not only that, he also sees it as intolerable that God declares that all other religions are not ways to God, and that Jesus Christ is the only way to be restored to a right relationship with God. This God and His ways are detestable to him.

These attitudes are not new. Sinful nature has always been the same since the fall of man. It was just the same when Jesus the eternal Son of God came to earth. How did they react to God coming among them in the flesh? The sacred record tells us in the words of Jesus Himself: "The world . . . hates Me" (John 7:7). In that same gospel we read, "And this is the condemnation, that the light has come into the world, and men loved darkness rather than light, because their deeds were evil. For everyone practicing evil hates the light and does not come to the light, lest his deeds should be exposed" (John 3:19–20). Jesus was the light among men, and consequently He was hated.

These truths show the absolute need for a special operation of God if men are going to believe. Men do not want God. They want the absence of God. They hate the light and love the absence of light, the darkness. Their choice is clear-cut and set. Just as the Bible says, "There is none who understands; There is none who seeks after God" (Rom. 3:11). This fixed disposition of enmity towards God means that no one is willing to exercise faith to gain salvation unless drawn by the Father. But this disposition is not the only cause of unwillingness. Man's understanding is darkened. His thoughts are perverted by his disposition. He loves the arguments, or philosophies or religions which get rid of the true God, either by denying His existence, or by denying the possibility of knowing whether He exists, or by replacing Him with another god or gods. He considers such to be wisdom. In contrast the gospel is sheer foolishness to him. He is so set in this way of thinking that the scripture says that he "does not receive the things of the Spirit of God, for they are foolishness to him; nor can he know *them*, because they are spiritually discerned" (1 Cor. 2:14).

Man is not only in darkness and blind to the truth, but blind to the fact that he is blind. He thinks that he can see. He thinks he is wise. He does not think that he is in darkness, and in need of Jesus Christ the Light of the world. Therefore he does not see any sense or relevance in the gospel message. This terrible blindness is not just the result of the sinful God-hating heart within him. It is the work of Satan. Paul wrote of this blinding of the devil in his second letter to the Christians at Corinth: "But even if our gospel is veiled, it is veiled to those who are perishing, whose minds the god of this age has blinded, who do not believe, lest the light of the gospel of the glory of Christ, who is the image of God, should shine on them" (2 Cor. 4:3–4). The devil is always active to prevent a positive response to the gospel message: "When anyone hears the word of the kingdom, and does not understand *it*, then the wicked *one* comes and snatches away what was sown in his heart" (Mat. 13:19). This is one of the ways the devil blinds the minds of men. How else does the devil blind men? The Bible reveals much about his methods. Here are some of them:

1.   He casts doubt on God's word
At the start of mankind his opening words to Eve were, "Has God indeed said, 'You shall not eat of every tree of the garden'?" (Gen. 3:1). This is still the activity of Satan. In various ways he causes people to doubt the revelation God has given in the sixty-six books of the Bible.

2.   He declares that God's word is not true
Eve said to the devil, "We may eat the fruit of the trees of the garden; but of the fruit of the tree which *is* in the midst of the garden, God has said, 'You shall not eat it, nor shall you touch it, lest you die.' " Then the serpent said to the woman, "You will not surely die" (Gen. 3:2–4).

3.   He deceives that sin will bring happiness, and that obedience to God will result in loss
"For God knows that in the day you eat of it your eyes will be opened, and you will be like God, knowing good and evil" (Gen. 3:5). The serpent asserts that they will lose out unless they disobey God. Disobedience will bring huge benefit.

4.   He uses philosophies and religions to provide men with an alternative to the truth about God and His ways

5.   He provides counterfeit Christianity using his own false prophets
Jesus warned that they would appear harmless, but in fact be ravenous wolves in sheep's clothing (Mat. 7:15). The New Testament speaks very clearly of the reality and presence of these false prophets. Paul wrote of them to Timothy: "But know this, that in the last days perilous times will come: For men will be lovers of themselves, lovers of money, boasters, proud, blasphemers, disobedient to parents, unthankful, unholy, unloving, unforgiving, slanderers, without self-control, brutal, despisers of good, traitors, headstrong, haughty, lovers of pleasure rather than lovers of God, having a form of godliness but denying its power. And from such people turn away!" (2 Tim. 3:1–5). The crucial words here are, "having a form of godliness but denying its power." Such claim to be Christian, and there is the "form of godliness." They

have church buildings, ministers, creeds, baptisms and various forms of remembering the Lord's death. But they deny the power of godliness. They subtly modify the scriptures to remove the requirement of the new birth through the word of God and by the Spirit of God. They have their own teaching on the new birth, but it is false and brings about no real godliness of life. They teach about the Holy Spirit, but they have no experience of Him. The Spirit does not indwell them. He is not at work in them enabling them to cease from sins and to be holy. They know nothing of "praying in the Holy Spirit" (Jude 20). All such experience of the power of God in human lives they deny by false teachings, just as Paul went on to tell Timothy: "For the time will come when they will not endure sound doctrine, but according to their own desires, *because* they have itching ears, they will heap up for themselves teachers; and they will turn *their* ears away from the truth, and be turned aside to fables" (2 Tim. 4:3–4). We see this fulfilled in these days across the world. Wherever there are true Christian believers there are also pseudo-Christians and pseudo-Christian ministers and pseudo-Christian churches. Such are the means through which Satan destroys millions of souls.

The Bible affirms this reality of Satan and his evil work upon and in mankind. In Eph. 2:2 the scripture speaks of "the prince of the power of the air, the spirit who now works in the sons of disobedience." This spirit is the devil, a spiritual power at work in mankind. His work is so effective that he causes people to behave disobediently towards God. This working of the devil is something men are usually unaware of. Several scriptures enlighten us of the reality of his evil power at work in daily life in specific terms: James reveals his use of the tongue to cause blasphemy: "And the tongue *is* a fire, a world of iniquity. The tongue is so set among our members that it defiles the whole body, and sets on fire the course of nature; and it is set on fire by hell" (James 3:6). Set on fire by hell means set on fire by satanic activity. Clear manifestations of this are many of the swear words used in Britain. They are expressions of contempt of realities hated by the devil. False doctrines are attributed to satanic activity: "Now the Spirit expressly says that in latter times some will depart from the faith, giving heed to deceiving spirits and doctrines of demons, speaking lies in hypocrisy, having their own con-science seared with a hot iron, forbidding to marry, *and commanding* to abstain from foods which God created to be received with thanksgiving by those who believe and know the truth" (1 Tim. 4:1–3). The devil uses deceiving spirits and demons to propagate false religions to destroy men's souls during these latter times between the first coming and the return of Jesus Christ. These are just two manifestations of the reality of the work of the devil in humanity.

Fallen mankind is very happy to listen to Satan. They are at one with him in their enmity against God. Consequently it is easy for the devil to carry out his blinding activities. The Bible states the relationship of mankind with the devil in stark terms: "the whole world lies *under the sway of* the wicked one" (1 John 5:19). Satan is the god of this age (2 Cor. 4:4), the period until the return of Jesus Christ. The devil has usurped God's place, and fallen man is subject to him. Satan's power and deception are so great, that man thinks he is free to do as he wishes, and not in any bondage to evil spiritual power.

Man is unable to come to Christ because of his own disposition. He hates the Light. He hates the true God. Therefore he is totally unwilling. He is also unable to come because his understanding is darkened, and the truth of the gospel is foolishness to his way of thinking. Not least, he is unable to come because Satan so blinds him that he cannot see the light of the gospel. For these reasons a special work of God is necessary in order that faith be exercised.

CHAPTER ELEVEN

THIS SPECIAL OPERATION OF GOD IS DEFINED IN THE BIBLE AS GOD'S CALLING

True saving faith the result of God's calling

The scriptures reveal that God calls some of mankind to Himself. There are a number of scriptures addressing Christians which state this great truth:

> "God *is* faithful, by whom you were called into the fellowship of His Son, Jesus Christ our Lord" (1 Cor. 1:9).

> "But you *are* a chosen generation, a royal priesthood, a holy nation, His own special people, that you may proclaim the praises of Him who called you out of darkness into His marvelous light" (1 Pet. 2:9).

> "But may the God of all grace, who called us to His eternal glory by Christ Jesus, after you have suffered a while, perfect, establish, strengthen, and settle *you*" (1 Pet. 5:10).

> "Therefore, brethren, be even more diligent to make your call and election sure, for if you do these things you will never stumble" (2 Pet. 1:10).

> "But we are bound to give thanks to God always for you, brethren beloved by the Lord, because God from the beginning chose you for salvation through sanctification by the Spirit and belief in the truth, to which He called you by our gospel, for the obtaining of the glory of our Lord Jesus Christ" (2 Thess. 2:13–14).

> "God who has saved us and called *us* with a holy calling, not according to our works, but according to His own purpose and grace which was given to us in Christ Jesus before time began" (2 Tim. 1:8–9).

81

This action of God calling individuals to Himself reveals the truth of the gospel to the hearer and causes a response of obedience to the message. These two aspects of God's action in calling are stated by Jesus in John 6:44–45, "No one can come to Me unless the Father who sent Me draws him; and I will raise him up at the last day. It is written in the prophets, 'And they shall all be taught by God.' Therefore everyone who has heard and learned from the Father comes to Me." The people listening to Jesus did not believe that He, the eternal Son of God, came from heaven. They said, "Is this not Jesus, the son of Joseph, whose father and mother we know?" Therefore they did not come to Him to receive eternal life. At this point Jesus says that all those who have heard and learned from the Father do come to Him. If they have revelation from God, and are taught by Him, they will receive Him. They will know that He has come down from heaven. This revelation is a hearing and learning from the Father. It is a being taught by God personally, One to one tuition. It is something additional to hearing the message of the gospel; but it is not additional truth to that contained in the gospel. It makes the difference from disobedience to the gospel to willing obedience to it in repentance and faith. It is a drawing to Jesus Christ.

What does God do when He calls someone to Himself?

1.   God opens the eyes to see the truth of the gospel

It is a revelation of the truth by the Spirit not just a hearing of the truth. In Matthew 16:13–17 we have a record which declares this revealing of the truth: "When Jesus came into the region of Caesarea Philippi, He asked His disciples, saying, 'Who do men say that I, the Son of Man, am?' So they said, 'Some *say* John the Baptist, some Elijah, and others Jeremiah or one of the prophets.' He said to them, 'But who do you say that I am?' Simon Peter answered and said, 'You are the Christ, the Son of the living God.' Jesus answered and said to him 'Blessed are you, Simon Bar-jonah, for flesh and blood has not revealed *this* to you, but My Father who is in heaven.' " Notice the last words. No man revealed this to Peter. It was revelation from God the Father. It was the hearing and learning from the Father. Jesus stated this fact of revelation on several occasions during His ministry: "At that time Jesus answered and said, 'I thank You, Father, Lord of heaven and earth, that You have hidden these things from *the* wise and prudent and have revealed them to babes' " (Mat. 11:25). He is speaking concerning the truths of his kingdom, and saying clearly that the Father reveals them to some and hides them from others. We have the same distinction in Mat. 13:10–11, "And the disciples came and said to Him, 'Why do You speak to them in parables?' He answered and said to them, 'Because it has been given to you to know the mysteries of the kingdom of heaven, but to them it has not been given.' " His disciples were given revelation, the rest were not.

This revelation includes a realisation that the message is from God even though written or spoken by men: "For this reason we also thank God without ceasing, because when you received the word of God which you heard from us, you welcomed *it* not *as* the word of men, but as it is in truth, the word of God, which also effectively works in you who believe" (1 Thess. 2:13). By the revelation of truth through the Spirit He dispels that darkness of the mind which dismisses the gospel as foolishness. The truth of God's word is seen in such a manner that the hearer is absolutely convinced that the message is true. The truth revealed to be true compels belief. The hearer is fully persuaded that all other views which are in any way contrary to the message are false. There is a realisation that in this message alone is the truth about God. Peter expressed this conviction as recorded in John 6:66–69: "From that *time* many of His disciples went back and walked with Him no more. Then Jesus said to the twelve, 'Do you also want to go away?' But Simon Peter answered Him, 'Lord, to whom shall we go? You have the words of eternal life. Also we have come to believe and know that You are the Christ, the Son of the living God.' " Peter knew that no one other than Jesus had the words of eternal life.

True faith in God is not the product of imagination. We may imagine certain things concerning God, and successfully persuade oneself that these things are true. True Christian faith is not believing what we concoct in our thoughts. Even less is it believing simply what we wish to be true. It is response to the truth revealed through the word of God by the Spirit of God. It is only possible when God opens the eyes to see the truth of the gospel. The person whose eyes are opened has come into knowledge and understanding of the truth. The message received is seen to be totally reasonable, and in no way contrary to reason. God's revelation is not a sort of hypnosis creating a blind unreasoning faith, a mere attitude or frame of mind with no defined content. Nor is faith an act of intuition. Responding to God's revelation is altogether different from mere intuition. The eyes are opened to truth. The message is addressed to the mind, and it is understood and acted upon intelligently. God does not call men to believe something beyond knowledge and understanding. Faith is not a leap in the dark. It is the response to light. God reveals truth, and faith soberly and intelligently embraces it.

The gospel is God's word. It may be preached by someone filled with the Holy Spirit. Miracles may confirm the message as truly from God.

The hearer may have seen the truth and power of the gospel in the transformed lives of Christians. He may have heard also their witness about the things God has done for them. But unless God opens the eyes of the hearer to the truth he will see but not see, will hear but will not hear and will not understand. Jesus said, "Therefore I speak to them in parables, because seeing they do not see, and hearing they do not hear, nor do they understand. And in them the prophecy of Isaiah is fulfilled, which says: 'Hearing you will hear and shall not understand, And seeing you will see and not perceive' " (Mat. 13:13–14). Jesus also said, "And the Father Himself, who sent Me, has testified of Me. You have neither heard His voice at any time . . ." (John 5:37). Those Jews read the Old Testament scriptures which were the very oracles of God. They heard John the Baptist proclaim Jesus as the Son of God. They saw the miracles Jesus did which bore witness that God the Father had sent Him into the world. He spoke the words of God to them (John 3:34 and 17:8). But despite all these things they never heard the voice of God!

Those called by God have their ears unstopped and their eyes opened by the Spirit. The Spirit's work is not to speak some additional message; it is to make them really see the truth that is being presented to them. So, when He calls, they hear God's voice, and they learn the truth. They have ears to hear (Mat. 11:15 and 13:9).

2.   He brings to an end the blinding by the god of this age which prevents one from seeing the light of the gospel

This action of God is described in scripture when Paul wrote to the Christians at Corinth: "But even if our gospel is veiled, it is veiled to those who are perishing, whose minds the god of this age has blinded, who do not believe, lest the light of the gospel of the glory of Christ, who is the image of God, should shine on them. For we do not preach ourselves, but Christ Jesus the Lord, and ourselves your bondservants for Jesus' sake. For it is the God who commanded light to shine out of darkness, who has shone in our hearts to *give* the light of the knowledge of the glory of God in the face of Jesus Christ" (2 Cor. 4:3–6). Paul is stating in these verses that Christians are people delivered by God from blindness caused by Satan. They now see the light. They know that they have come to the knowledge of the truth.

3.   He opens the heart to obey the gospel

The truth of the gospel is not modified or added to when God calls. The difference is that there is a new capacity to receive the truth. In the course of Paul's evangelism we have an example of this aspect of God's call: "Now a certain woman named Lydia heard *us*. She was a seller of purple from the city of Thyatira, who worshiped God. The Lord opened her heart to heed the things spoken by Paul" (Acts 16:14). The significant words are, "the Lord opened her heart." Heart in the scriptures includes the mind and governs all the actions of a man. When God calls He not only reveals the truth of the gospel, He so works in the heart that the hearer totally surrenders to the truth. The hearer rejects thoughts and beliefs now seen to be wrong. There is a willing wholehearted obedience to the demands of the truth. People hearing the gospel may be convinced that the message is true, that it applies to himself or herself, that they ought to obey it and have no real excuse for not doing so. They may be greatly disturbed and emotionally moved. But they do not repent and believe. When God calls they do. His call makes the difference because it opens the heart to obey the gospel.

4.   God brings about the new birth when He calls

In John's gospel there is the record of a conversation between Jesus and a religious teacher and leader of the Jews: "This man came to Jesus by night and said to Him, 'Rabbi, we know that You are a teacher come from God; for no one can do these signs that You do unless God is with him.' Jesus answered and said to him, 'Most assuredly, I say to you, unless one is born again, he cannot see the kingdom of God.' Nicodemus said to Him, 'How can a man be born when he is old? Can he enter a second time into his mother's womb and be born?' Jesus answered, 'Most assuredly, I say to you, unless one is born of water and the Spirit, he cannot enter the kingdom of God. That which is born of the flesh is flesh, and that which is born of the Spirit is spirit. Do not marvel that I said to you, "You must be born again." The wind blows where it wishes, and you hear the sound of it, but cannot tell where it comes from and where it goes. So is everyone who is born of the Spirit'" (John 3:2–8). This new birth is essential in order to "see the kingdom of God," and "to enter the kingdom of God." To be a Christian you must be born again. The new birth is "of water and the Spirit." The meaning of water is defined in the following scriptures as the word of God. In Eph. 5:26 we read of "the washing of water by the word." The gospel washes clean of the stain of sin like water washes clean that to which it is applied. Jesus spoke to His disciples of this washing of the word of God: "You are already clean because of the word which I have spoken to you" (John 15:3). Therefore we see that the new birth is by the word of God and the work of the Spirit of God. This is confirmed as Jesus continues his conversation with Nicodemus and answers his question concerning the new birth, "How can these things be?" Jesus replies, "And as Moses lifted up the serpent in the wilderness, even so must the Son of Man be lifted up, that whoever believes in Him should not perish but have eternal life" (John 3:14–15). Jesus refers to an event recorded in Num. 21:4–9: "Then they journeyed from Mount Hor by the Way of the Red Sea, to go around the land of Edom; and the soul of the people became very discouraged on the way. And the people spoke against God and against Moses: 'Why have you brought us up out of Egypt to die in the wilderness? For *there is* no food and no water, and our soul loathes this worthless bread.' So the LORD sent fiery serpents among the people, and they bit the people; and many of the people of Israel died. Therefore the people came to Moses, and said, 'We have sinned, for we have spoken against the LORD and against you; pray to the LORD that He take away the serpents from us.' So Moses prayed for the people. Then the LORD said to Moses, 'Make a fiery *serpent*, and set it on a pole; and it shall be that everyone who is bitten, when he looks at it, shall live.' So Moses made a bronze serpent, and put it on a pole; and so it was, if a serpent had bitten anyone, when he looked at the bronze serpent, he lived." Jesus is saying that just as people did not perish physically but lived when they looked at the elevated bronze serpent believing in God's promise through Moses, so people will not perish eternally but receive eternal life when they look at Christ lifted up on the cross believing in His work there for sinners. Eternal life can be obtained through faith in Christ. In these words He is giving Nicodemus the message of the word of God through which he can be born again. Later accounts of Nicodemus in John's gospel show that the new birth did take place in his life at some point after his conversation with Jesus.

This instrumentality of the word of God in giving eternal life is stated again in John 6:63: "It is the Spirit who gives life; the flesh profits nothing. The words that I speak to you are spirit, and *they* are life." Jesus is saying that the words which He speaks are the product of the life-giving Spirit, and consequently they bring life when received with faith. The new birth is through the word and the Spirit, just as Jesus had told Nicodemus. The New Testament states this instrumentality of the word of God elsewhere in the following passages both of which are addressed to Christians:

"Of His own will He brought us forth by the word of truth, that we might be a kind of firstfruits of His creatures" (James 1:18).

"having been born again, not of corruptible seed but incorruptible, through the word of God which lives and abides forever" (1 Pet. 1:23).

This new birth is entirely a work of God: "But as many as received Him, to them He gave the right to become children of God, to those who believe in His name: who were born, not of blood, nor of the will of the flesh, nor of the will of man, but of God" (John 1:12–13). This verse explicitly declares that God alone brings about the new birth. Physical descent from someone born again will not pass it on. It is not "of blood." Nor can it be produced as the result of human decision, "not of the will of the flesh." Man can only produce offspring who belong to humankind. Flesh gives birth to flesh, (John 3:6). Only God, through His word and by the Holy Spirit, can accomplish the new birth, and bring about children of God. No man can cause it to happen in any other person. It is not "of the will of man." The false doctrine of the new birth by means of baptism, held by Roman Catholicism, Anglo-Catholics and Lutherans, places the power to bring about the new birth in the hands of men. The priest believes that the new birth is produced by performing the sacrament of baptism. God reserves that power strictly to Himself. He does it through the instrumentality of the Spirit and the word. He uses men and women to proclaim that word, and consequently they also become His instruments to bring about the new birth when He chooses. Examples of this are found in 1 Cor. 4:15, "For though you might have ten thousand instructors in Christ, yet *you do* not *have* many fathers; for in Christ Jesus I have begotten you through the gospel," and Philemon 10, "Onesimus whom I have begotten while in my chains." But these human instruments have absolutely no power in themselves to produce the new birth.

This new birth changes man's disposition from loving darkness and hating Jesus Christ the Light of the world. When born again the light is loved instead of the darkness. There is a change of heart. The prophet Ezekiel declared God's word, "I will give you a new heart and put a new spirit within you; I will take the heart of stone out of your flesh and give you a heart of flesh" (Ezek.36:26). This is what happens in the new birth. The tremendous change is seen in John 3:19–21. The behaviour before the new birth is defined in verses 19 and 20. The changed conduct is seen in verse 21.

Verses 19–20: "And this is the condemnation, that the light has come into the world, and men loved darkness rather than light, because their deeds were evil. For everyone practicing evil hates the light and does not come to the light, lest his deeds should be exposed."

Verse 21: "But he who does the truth comes to the light, that his deeds may be clearly seen, that they have been done in God."

CHAPTER TWELVE

FAITH AND THE NEW BIRTH (1)

The relationship of faith and the new birth requires further consideration. It is defined in the following sentences.

The new birth occurs as a result of:

1. God's direct immediate operation on the heart,
2. His indirect working by the word and the Spirit and,
3. man's response of repentance and faith. That response is the result
   of God's direct and indirect work.

In harmony with the above we see the change of heart wrought in the
new birth attributed to obeying the gospel in the following words of
Peter: "Since you have purified your souls in obeying the truth through
the Spirit in sincere love of the brethren, love one another fervently
with a pure heart, having been born again, not of corruptible seed but
incorruptible, through the word of God which lives and abides forever,
because 'All flesh is as grass, And all the glory of man as the flower
of the grass. The grass withers, And its flower falls away, But the word
of the LORD endures forever.' Now this is the word which by the gospel
was preached to you" (1 Pet. 1:22–25). Again in the Acts of the Apostles
we read that God "made no distinction between us and them, purifying their hearts by faith" (Acts 15:9). Peter is pointing out that God
made no difference between Jewish believers and Gentiles who
received Christ. When the Gentiles believed their hearts were purified.
Notice it was when they exercised faith.

But if the new birth is not of the will of the flesh, nor of the will of
man, how can it include man's repentance and coming to Christ for
salvation? These are voluntary actions. The scriptures reveal that
repentance and faith are given by God as a result of His direct and indirect work. Concerning that faith which saved Christians Paul says that
it was "not of yourselves" it was "the gift of God" (Eph. 2:8). In the
same way, repentance is the gift of God: "The God of our fathers raised

up Jesus whom you murdered by hanging on a tree. Him God has exalted to His right hand *to be* Prince and Savior, to give repentance to Israel and forgiveness of sins" (Acts 5:30–31), and, "When they heard these things they became silent; and they glorified God, saying, 'Then God has also granted to the Gentiles repentance to life'" (Acts 11:18). Because repentance and saving faith are wholly the result of God's operation, the new birth is truly of God. Hence Paul speaks of Christians as "His workmanship created in Christ Jesus" (Eph. 2:10).

Every person in whom God works the new birth is so affected that without a single exception they come to Christ: "It is written in the prophets, 'And they shall all be taught by God.' Therefore everyone who has heard and learned from the Father comes to Me" (John 6:45). Their new birth is not dependent on their cooperation with God. The special operation of God brings about their repentance and coming to Christ in every case. But they are not forced to come. They decide freely from the heart. Left to themselves, without the special operation of God, not a single one would ever come. The only reason anyone comes is because of God's decision to save them as Jesus stated in John 6:44 and 65 "No one can come to Me unless the Father who sent Me draws him; and I will raise him up at the last day," and, "Therefore I have said to you that no one can come to Me unless it has been granted to him by My Father." Therefore in the light of these New Testament scriptures it is inadequate and incorrect to define the new birth only as God's immediate operation upon the heart of man.

John Murray contends that ". . . regeneration is used in two distinct senses in the New Testament: (1) in the restricted sense of recreative action on the part of God in which there is no intrusion in contribution of agency on our part; (2) in a more inclusive sense, that is to say, a sense broad enough to include the saving response and activity of our consciousness, a saving activity which is always through the Word of the truth of the gospel."[1] He defines the restricted sense of the term as ". . . a change wrought by the Spirit in order that the person may savingly respond to the summons, or demand of the call, embodied in the gospel call."[2] Having defined regeneration in this restricted sense he goes on to say, "But it may be objected that if regeneration precedes faith, then the person is saved before he believes and we have the anomaly of the person saved by regeneration while he is still an unbeliever. The answer to this objection is simply that there is no such state or condition of regeneration without faith always coincident; the priority of regeneration is logical and causal, not chronological. If we were to posit a case of regeneration without faith then we should have to say that the person merely regenerate is not saved. But there is no such case. . . . Regeneration is the act of God and God alone, but it is directed to the renewal which produces faith as the specific instrument of salvation and justification."[3] He also affirms, "The priority of regeneration and the fact that it must not be separated from faith must be borne in mind even in the case of regenerate infants. . . where regeneration takes place in the case of an infant there is the immediate transition from the kingdom of darkness to the kingdom of God, and even though intelligent faith cannot be in exercise, nevertheless there is that which we may and must call the germ of faith."[4]

In contrast to these statements the Bible presents the new birth as the entrance into new life not merely the potential to enter, not simply the capability to believe. Every New Testament statement referring to it, either as a state: "whoever is born of God" (1 John 5:18), or as something that has happened in the past: "having been born again" (1 Pet. 1:23), speaks of the new birth as bringing about salvation; never as an intermediate state between being lost and saved. John Murray is right in asserting that the regenerating work of God in the heart cannot be separated from faith. He is wrong in failing to see that the reason it cannot be separated is because faith is the gift of God, and is included in the work of the new birth wrought by God. His restricted meaning of regeneration is not taught in the Bible.

Dr. Martyn Lloyd-Jones also contended for a restricted meaning of regeneration. He wrote, "So as we consider what we mean by regeneration, the one important thing, it seems to me, is that we must differentiate it from conversion. . . . But regeneration is not conversion and for this reason: conversion is something that we do whereas regeneration . . . is something that is done to us by God. . . . Conversion is something that follows upon regeneration. The change takes place in the outward life and living of men and women because this great change has first of all taken place within them.

You can look at it like this: there is all the difference between planting the seed and the result of planting that seed. Now regeneration means the planting of the seed of life and obviously that must be differentiated from what results or eventuates from that. There is a difference between generation and birth. Generation takes place a long time before the birth takes place. Generation is one act. It leads subsequently, after certain processes have been going on, to the actual process of birth. So it is good to hold the two things separately in our minds, and remember that when we are talking about regeneration we are talking about generation, not the actual bringing forth, the birth.

Now the effectual call comes in the actual birth, and that is what gives a proof of the fact that men and women are alive. The call is effectual:

they believe. Yes, but that means that the process of generation, the implanting of the seed of life, must have already taken place."[5]

Certain conclusions must follow if we were to accept Dr. Martyn Lloyd-Jones's definition of regeneration.

1.   Regeneration and faith are distinctly separated to the degree that a long time may elapse between the two

The New Testament never speaks of such a separation. Every born-again person is a believer: every believer is born again. Moreover it never speaks of two stages of regeneration – implanting the seed of life and subsequently actual birth.

2.   We can therefore have regenerate persons who have never exercised the faith through which salvation is received

Dr. Martyn Lloyd-Jones states that infants who "cannot receive truth" can be regenerated and go to heaven.[6]

He says "There are a number of texts that suggest that our regeneration takes place through and by means of the word." He goes on to quote two such texts, namely James 1:18 and 1 Pet. 1:23, and to say ". . . I drew a distinction between the act of regeneration and the coming to birth and said that there may be a long interval between the two. Now I suggest to you that both these texts I have quoted are concerned about the bringing to birth. . . . The word is used, not in the act of generating, but in the bringing out into life of that which has already been implanted within."[7]

In reply to these arguments, the New Testament never speaks of the new birth as merely the act of generating as distinct and apart from bringing to birth.

He goes on to argue as a matter "of great importance"[8] that Old Testament saints were regenerate, and to assert ". . . it is clear that it is not the word that actually performs the act of regeneration."[9] He says that "those saints did not receive the promise in full"[10] and he quotes Heb. 11:39–40, "And all these, having obtained a good testimony through faith, did not receive the promise, God having provided something better for us, that they should not be made perfect apart from us."

Though the Old Testament saints did not receive the promise in full, in the light of the following scriptures it is clear that they did receive and believe the word. Therefore could not the word as well as the Holy Spirit have been the means of their regeneration?

"just as Abraham 'believed God, and it was accounted to him for righteousness' " (Gal. 3:6).

"the Scripture, foreseeing that God would justify the Gentiles by faith, preached the gospel to Abraham beforehand, *saying,* 'In you all the nations shall be blessed'" (Gal. 3:8). Notice the words "preached the gospel to Abraham."

Jesus declared "Your father Abraham rejoiced to see My day, and he saw *it* and was glad" (John 8:56).

"These all died in faith, not having received the promises, but having seen them afar off were assured of them, embraced *them* and confessed that they were strangers and pilgrims on the earth" (Heb. 11:13). The Old Testament saints saw the promises afar off, were assured of them and embraced them.

He further argues also as a matter "of great importance"[11] that his definition of regeneration makes possible the salvation of infants. He says, "Now we all believe, do we not, that there are infants and children who have gone and who will go to heaven and spend their eternity in the presence of God. . . . Now, if you want to insist upon the fact that regeneration always follows upon hearing the word and believing it and accepting it – how can an infant be saved? The infant cannot receive truth, it does not have the ability; it does not have understanding, it has not awakened to these things. So is there no hope for any infant? We do not believe that, we obviously reject such a suggestion. And the answer is, of course, that a child is regenerated in exactly the same way as anybody else, because it is the action of this almighty being, of God Himself through the Holy Spirit. He can implant the seed of spiritual life in an unconscious infant with the same ease as He can do it in an adult person. Therefore you see why it is important for us to consider whether regeneration is something that happens indirectly through the word or whether it is indeed the direct operation of God upon us."[12]

In the light of Martyn Lloyd-Jones's statements this matter of infant salvation has great bearing on the correct definition of the new birth. This is a particularly difficult subject to address because for those whose infants have died their pain is often acute. It is therefore a subject where it is not always easy to prevent desires for comfort affecting the way we read and interpret the scriptures. Also the helplessness of infants rightly moves us to treat them with tenderness, and to look upon them as ones to be cared for with love. Our natural feelings towards these little ones, let alone the intense love of parents and often other members of a family, can affect the way we hear God's word. Let us therefore look carefully and prayerfully to see what the Bible teaches.

Romans chapter five reveals that God made the first man Adam the representative of all mankind who would descend from him. Accordingly when he disobeyed God his guilt came upon every individual human being born after his disobedience: "Therefore, . . . through one man's offense *judgment* came to all men, resulting in condemnation, . . . by one man's disobedience many were made sinners" (Rom. 5:18–19). This means that all infants are guilty before God. It means that it is contrary to the truth to speak of infants as innocent. They sinned in their representative Adam. Infants die, and it is because Adam's sin is imputed to them, that is, is reckoned by God as belonging to them. Therefore to go to heaven they need salvation. They must be regenerated. This leads us to a careful examination of the scriptures concerning infants in the next chapter.

References

1. John Murray *Collected Writings of John Murray, 2:Systematic Theology*, Banner of Truth 1977, page 197.
2. *Ibid.*, page 172.
3. *Ibid.*, page 262.
4. *Ibid.*, page 199.
5. Dr. Martyn Lloyd-Jones *God The Holy Spirit*, Copyright © 1997 Elizabeth Catherwood and Ann Desmond. Reproduced by permission of Hodder and Stoughton Limited, page 77.
6. *Ibid.*, pages 92–93.
7. *Ibid.*, page 91.
8. *Ibid.*, pages 91–92.
9. *Ibid.*, page 92.
10. *Ibid.*, page 92.
11. *Ibid.*, pages 91–92.
12. *Ibid.*, pages 92–93.

CHAPTER THIRTEEN

FAITH AND THE NEW BIRTH (2):
THE NEW BIRTH AND INFANT SALVATION

Do any scriptures state that children dying in infancy will go to heaven?

Let us examine those verses which some say do give assurance that such infants will have eternal life.

1. *"But now he is dead; why should I fast? Can I bring him back again? I shall go to him, but he shall not return to me" (2 Sam. 12:23)*
These are the words of King David after the death of his son born to him through Bathsheba. The words, "I shall go to him," are taken to mean that he would be reunited with his son in heaven. The true meaning may simply be that David is expressing the fact that he too will go to the realm of the dead. The words of David probably echo Jacob's when he thought that his son Joseph had been killed by a wild beast: "Then Jacob tore his clothes, put sackcloth on his waist, and mourned for his son many days. And all his sons and all his daughters arose to comfort him; but he refused to be comforted, and he said, 'For I shall go down into the grave to my son in mourning.' Thus his father wept for him" (Gen. 37:34–35). Gen. 37:35 reveals the Old Testament belief in Sheol, the place where all the dead are gathered indiscriminately, both saints and sinners. It is most likely that David's words voice this belief and nothing more.

2. *"Then little children were brought to Him that He might put His hands on them and pray, but the disciples rebuked them. But Jesus said, 'Let the little children come to Me, and do not forbid them; for of such is the kingdom of heaven'" (Mat. 19:13–14)*
Mark 10:13–16 and Luke 18:15–17 also record this event. When we compare the three accounts it is clear that Jesus is not saying that children belong to the kingdom. He is rather saying that His kingdom is composed only of those who receive it as a little child. Mark 10:15

and Luke 18:17 add the following verse: "Assuredly, I say to you, whoever does not receive the kingdom of God as a little child will by no means enter it." Entrants to the kingdom must be like children in their humble position of helplessness and dependence. They must come to the realisation that there is nothing they can present to God for their salvation – no self righteousness, no good works, absolutely nothing! They cannot save themselves. They must turn to Christ and put their trust only in Him and His saving work for sinners. In humility they must depend on Christ alone for salvation. The kingdom of heaven is composed of such childlike believers.

If "such" in Mat. 19:13–14 is taken to mean infants then we must conclude:

a) that all infants are in the kingdom in that early stage of their lives. This is regardless of who are their parents, and regardless of where they are born.
b) that such infants who die will go to heaven regardless of parentage and nationality.
c) that the majority of the world's population do not continue to be in the kingdom when they progress from infancy.
d) that countless millions of souls are lost after being saved in infancy.
e) that those who are converted to Christ are in fact saved for the second time, having been saved once in infancy, then fallen away and then saved again! The new birth can only occur once in a lifetime.

It is clear that we arrive at a position impossible to square with the New Testament if we interpret Mat. 19:14 "of such is the kingdom of heaven" to mean that the kingdom of heaven is composed of infants.

3.   *"Then He came to Capernaum. And when He was in the house He asked them, 'What was it you disputed among yourselves on the road?' But they kept silent, for on the road they had disputed among themselves who* **would be the** *greatest. And He sat down, called the twelve, and said to them, 'If anyone desires to be first, he shall be last of all and servant of all.' Then He took a little child and set him in the midst of them. And when He had taken him in His arms, He said to them, 'Whoever receives one of these little children in My name receives Me; and whoever receives Me, receives not Me but Him who sent Me'"* (Mark 9:33–37)

Matthew also gives his account of this incident: "At that time the disciples came to Jesus, saying, 'Who then is greatest in the kingdom of heaven?' Then Jesus called a little child to Him, set him in the midst of them, and said, 'Assuredly, I say to you, unless you are converted and become as little children, you will by no means enter the kingdom of heaven. Therefore whoever humbles himself as this little child is the greatest in the kingdom of heaven. Whoever receives one little child like this in My name receives Me. But whoever causes one of these little ones who believe in Me to sin, it would be better for him if a millstone were hung around his neck, and he were drowned in the depth of the sea' " (Mat. 18:1–6).

Jesus uses a little child to teach his disciples concerning who is the greatest in His kingdom. Firstly He says that there is no entrance into the kingdom at all unless one is willing to humble oneself and acknowledge one's total dependence on God just as a child is dependent on adults. It is pride which is expressed in wanting to be the greatest. To enter the kingdom of God pride in oneself, one's good works or good life and in one's own thoughts must be renounced. It is only those who realise their wretched sinfulness and repent of their own thoughts and submit to God's truth and in genuine humility say "God be merciful to me a sinner" who get into the kingdom. They cast themselves entirely upon God's mercy for acceptance. They are absolutely dependent on God. There is no room for pride: "Where *is* boasting then? It is excluded. By what law? Of works? No, but by the law of faith" (Rom. 3:27).

Jesus then goes on to say that every member of the kingdom partakes of greatness. This is taught in verse 5: "Whoever receives one little child like this in My name receives Me." The "little child like this" is the believer who has become childlike in dependence when entering the kingdom. When a believer is received Christ is also received because of the union between Christ and His followers: Jesus said, "He who receives you receives Me, and he who receives Me receives Him who sent Me" (Mat. 10:40). So real is this union that when Saul persecuted Christians the Lord Jesus Christ said to him, "Saul Saul why are you persecuting Me?" (Acts 9:4). Christ is so united with his disciples that persecution of them is in reality persecution of Him. This great truth of the union of Christ with believers is found again in the words of Christ concerning His return and final judgment: "When the Son of Man comes in His glory, and all the holy angels with Him, then He will sit on the throne of His glory. All the nations will be gathered before Him, and He will separate them one from another, as a shepherd divides *his* sheep from the goats. And He will set the sheep on His right hand, but the goats on the left. Then the King will say to those on His right hand, 'Come, you blessed of My Father, inherit the kingdom prepared for you from the foundation of the world: for I was hungry and you gave Me food; I was thirsty and you gave Me drink; I was a stranger and you took Me in; I *was* naked and you clothed Me; I was sick and you visited Me; I was in prison and you came to Me.' Then the righteous will answer Him, saying, 'Lord, when did we see You hungry and feed *You*, or thirsty and give *You* drink? When did we see You a stranger and take *You* in, or naked and clothe *You?* Or when did we see You sick, or in prison, and come to You?' And the King will answer and say to them, 'Assuredly, I say to you, inasmuch as you did *it* to one of the least of these My brethren, you did *it* to Me'" (Mat. 25:31–40). What they did to His brethren, that is to His followers, they did to Christ.

In the same way when a believer is received Christ is thereby received. In that sense the believer is great in the kingdom because of the union with Christ. The disciples were thinking of some disciples being greater than other disciples. Jesus is telling them that every believer is great. He goes on to apply that truth in verse 6: "But whoever causes one of these little ones who believe in Me to sin, it would be better for him if a millstone were hung around his neck, and he were drowned in the depth of the sea." Actions against believers are actions against Christ. Therefore Jesus warns against despising any believer: "Take heed that you do not despise one of these little ones, for I say to you that in heaven their angels always see the face of My Father who is in heaven" (Mat. 18:10). These little ones refers back to verse 6, not literal children, but believers who are dependent on God just as little ones are dependent on adults.

4.   *"For the promise is to you and to your children, and to all who are afar off, as many as the Lord our God will call" (Acts 2:39)*
The promise referred to by Peter in this message on the day of Pentecost is the prophecy of Joel he had quoted earlier in the message ending with the words recorded in Acts 2:21, "And it shall come to pass *That* whoever calls on the name of the LORD Shall be saved." This provides no ground whatsoever for infant salvation. The promise is for the children of the Jews who will hear the call of God. The promise is explicitly to "as many as the Lord our God will call." It has nothing to do with infants who cannot hear and understand the call of God. It gives no basis for assertions of salvation for children or infants simply because they have Christian parents.

5.   *"But to the rest I, not the Lord, say: If any brother has a wife who does not believe, and she is willing to live with him, let him not divorce her. And a woman who has a husband who does not believe,*

if he is willing to live with her, let her not divorce him. For the unbelieving husband is sanctified by the wife, and the unbelieving wife is sanctified by the husband; otherwise your children would be unclean, but now they are holy. But if the unbeliever departs, let him depart; a brother or a sister is not under bondage in such cases. *But God has called us to peace. For how do you know, O wife, whether you will save* your *husband? Or how do you know, O husband, whether you will save* your *wife?" (1 Cor. 7:12–16)*

Paul is addressing the problem encountered by converts to Christianity who were married to an unbeliever. The crucial words for our consideration are "your children . . . are holy." Some interpret these words to mean that the children of a believing parent will go to heaven if they die, and proceed to argue that it must mean also that the children of believing parents will go to heaven. Some believe that the child and the unbelieving spouse are brought into the community of the church through the sanctification of the unbelieving partner by the believing spouse. The verse however does not teach that the child is brought into the community of the church. The church is only composed of those born again. Clearly from verse sixteen the unbelieving partner is unsaved, yet in some real sense "sanctified," that is, set apart by God. In what sense is the unbelieving spouse sanctified? Charles Hodge wrote, ". . . the meaning is, not that they are rendered inwardly holy, nor that they are brought under a sanctifying influence, but that they were sanctified by their intimate union with a believer, just as the temple sanctified the gold connected with it; or the altar the gift laid upon it, Matt. 23,17.19. The sacrifice in itself was merely a part of the body of a lamb, laid upon the altar, though its internal nature remained the same, it became something sacred. Thus, the pagan husband, in virtue of his union with a Christian wife, although he remained a pagan, was sanctified; . . ."[1] The sanctification of the unbelieving spouse, therefore, means that the marriage bed is "undefiled" (Heb. 13:4). Consequently the children are not unclean, but the opposite, holy. This sanctification results in the child being accounted holy, set apart by God. In what sense is the child holy? T. E. Watson argues that since ". . . the holiness of the children is not inferred from the faith of the believing parent, but from the sanctification of the unbelieving party . . . it follows that the holiness of the children cannot be superior, either as to nature or degree, to that sanctification of the unbelieving partner from which it is derived."[2] Therefore the holiness of the child is not regeneration. It is that it is not unclean, not the offspring of a defiling union. It would seem that Paul wrote these words because some of the believers at Corinth may have thought that their marriage to an unbeliever defiling, and therefore they were obliged to divorce their partner. T. E. Watson says, "they would be acquainted with Nehemiah 13:23–27 and Ezra 10:17 from which they might deduce that a 'mixed' marriage was unclean in God's eyes, so that a Christian ought to divorce or leave his or her unbelieving partner."[3] Let us look at the passages in Ezra and Nehemiah and related Old Testament verses. "When these things were done, the leaders came to me, saying, 'The people of Israel and the priests and the Levites have not separated themselves from the peoples of the lands, with respect to the abominations of the Canaanites, the Hittites, the Perizzites, the Jebusites, the Ammonites, the Moabites, the Egyptians, and the Amorites. For they have taken some of their daughters *as wives* for themselves and their sons, so that the holy seed is mixed with the peoples of *those* lands. Indeed, the hand of the leaders and rulers has been foremost in this trespass.' So when I heard this thing, I tore my garment and my robe, and plucked out some of the hair of my head and beard, and sat down astonished" (Ezra 9:1–3). This intermarriage was contrary to God's clear commands recorded in Deut. 7:1–4, "When the LORD your God brings you into the land which you go to possess, and has cast out many nations before you, the Hittites and the Girgashites and the Amorites and the Canaanites and the Perizzites and the Hivites and the Jebusites, seven nations greater and mightier than you, and when the LORD your God delivers them over to you, you shall conquer them *and* utterly destroy them. You shall make no covenant with them nor show mercy to them. Nor shall you make marriages with them. You shall not give your daughter to their son, nor take their daughter for your son. For they will turn your sons away from following Me, to serve other gods; so the anger of the LORD will be aroused against you and destroy you suddenly." Ezra fasted and prayed. The people made a covenant to divorce the foreign women. They investigated to find out who had married foreign women. Those who were guilty sent their wives and children away. Within a short time of a few years Nehemiah encounters this same disobedience: "In those days I also saw Jews *who* had married women of Ashdod, Ammon, *and* Moab. And half of their children spoke the language of Ashdod, and could not speak the language of Judah, but spoke according to the language of one or the other people. So I contended with them and cursed them, struck some of them and pulled out their hair, and made them swear by God, *saying,* 'You shall not give your daughters as wives to their sons, nor take their daughters for your sons or yourselves. Did not Solomon king of Israel sin by these things? Yet among many nations there was no king like him, who was beloved of his God; and God made him king over all Israel. Nevertheless pagan women caused even him to sin. Should we then hear of your doing all this great evil, transgressing against our God by marrying pagan women?' " (Neh. 13:23–27). These verses with their exceedingly strong condemnation of mixed marriages would explain why some believers needed to be instructed not to divorce an unbelieving spouse whom they had married before conversion. In addition to these scriptures, the Corinthians were aware also that believers must not marry unbelievers. Marriage, whenever it is undertaken, must be to another believer; as Paul commanded "only in the Lord" (1 Cor. 7:39). Therefore in the light of these considerations 1 Cor. 7:14 gives no ground to assert that infants who die will go to heaven.

There remains one other scripture which gives revelation on this matter.

6.   "For he will be great in the sight of the Lord, and shall drink neither wine nor strong drink. He will also be filled with the Holy Spirit, even from his mother's womb" (Luke 1:15)
Since John the Baptist was filled with the Spirit in his mother's womb there is absolute certainty that he was regenerate since only the regenerate can be filled with the Spirit. It is certain that had he died as an infant he would have gone to heaven. However, he did not die as an infant.

Conclusion

There is not a single verse of scripture which teaches that infants who die will go to heaven. Moreover there is no recorded instance in the whole Bible where an infant who died is declared to have gone to heaven.

References

1. Charles Hodge *The First Epistle to the Corinthians*, 6th ed Banner of Truth Trust, 1959, page 116.
2. T. E. Watson *Should Infants Be Baptized?* Baker 1978, page 39.
3. *Ibid.*, page 40.

CHAPTER FOURTEEN

FAITH AND THE NEW BIRTH (3): THE NEW BIRTH AND INFANT SALVATION CONTINUED

Some contend for infant salvation using arguments other than specific texts of scripture. Many like to think that, just as in Old Testament times the children were included in the Old Covenant of God with Israel, so in the New Covenant following the death and resurrection of Christ the children of believers are included in that New Covenant. The New Covenant gives eternal life. Therefore if they die as infants they will go to heaven. The truth is that such children are guilty in Adam. They are fallen as regards their nature and need to be saved just as any other child born into this world. Christian parents do not give to their children an automatic entitlement to the New Covenant. Like the rest of mankind they are lost until they are born again. The new birth is not "of blood." John declares, "But as many as received Him, to them He gave the right to become children of God, to those who believe in His name: who were born, not of blood, nor of the will of the flesh, nor of the will of man, but of God" (John 1:12–13). The new birth is not of physical descent. Only when offspring receive Christ will they partake of the New Covenant. Only then will they go to heaven when they die.

Similarly there are those who affirm that infants of Christian parents are included in the church of Jesus Christ because of the faith of their parents. Accordingly they affirm that should they die they will go to heaven. The new birth is essential to belong to the Church of Jesus Christ, and the new birth has nothing whatever to do with natural descent. Christian parents do not give birth to offspring who are Christians at birth. Such offspring will not enter the Church of Jesus Christ until they are born again. History demonstrates that many children of believing parents grow up and die as unbelievers. They were never born again. They were never included in the Church of Jesus Christ.

But what about the infants of Christian parents if those infants die in infancy? Will God treat them as a special group and regenerate them before death?

101

Wayne Grudem

In his *Systematic Theology* Wayne Grudem contends from Luke 1:15 and Psalm 22:10 that "Salvation usually occurs when someone hears and understands the gospel and then places trust in Christ. But in unusual cases like John the Baptist, God brought salvation before this understanding. And this leads us to conclude that it certainly is possible that God would also do this where He knows the infant will die before hearing the gospel.

How many infants does God save in this way? Scripture does not tell us, so we simply cannot know. Where scripture is silent, it is unwise for us to make definitive pronouncements. However, we should recognise that it is God's frequent pattern throughout scripture to save the children of those who believe in him (see Gen 7:1; cf. Heb. 11:7; Josh. 2:18; Ps. 103:17; John 4:53; Acts 2:39; 11:14(?); 16:31; 18:8; 1 Cor. 1:16;7:14; Titus 1:6). These passages do not show that God automatically saves the children of all believers . . . but they do indicate that God's ordinary pattern, the 'normal' or expected way in which he acts, is to bring the children of believers to himself. With regard to believers' children who die very young, we have no reason to think that it would be otherwise."[1]

In reply the following points should be considered.

1. He starts from the argument that the regeneration of infants is possible based on Luke 1:15 and Psalm 22:10. He puts forward Psalm 22:10, "From My mother's womb You *have been* My God" as a similar example to Luke 1:15. He takes the words to be words uttered by David and referring to him, but it is more likely that they speak of the Messiah, Jesus Christ. They link with another glorious Messianic prophecy: "Listen, O coastlands, to Me, And take heed, you peoples from afar! The LORD has called Me from the womb; From the matrix of My mother He has made mention of My name" (Isa. 49:1). These are words spoken by Christ. If Psalm 22:10 refers to Jesus Christ then it is not an example of God's dealings with fallen humanity in infancy.

   Luke 1:15 speaks of John the Baptist, of whom Jesus said, "But what did you go out to see? A prophet? Yes, I say to you, and more than a prophet. For this is *he* of whom it is written: 'Behold, I send My messenger before Your face, Who will prepare Your way before You.' Assuredly, I say to you, among those born of women there has not risen one greater than John the Baptist" (Mat. 11:9–11). John was the Forerunner of the Messiah. He was unique in that he was filled with the Spirit "even from his mother's womb." This was an exceptional enduement for his exceedingly great task. It enabled him to begin his work *even when he and Jesus were both in the womb:* "Now Mary arose in those days and went into the hill country with haste, to a city of Judah, and entered the house of Zacharias and greeted Elizabeth. And it happened, when Elizabeth heard the greeting of Mary, that the babe leaped in her womb; and Elizabeth was filled with the Holy Spirit. Then she spoke out with a loud voice and said, 'Blessed *are* you among women, and blessed *is* the fruit of your womb! But why *is* this *granted* to me, that the mother of my Lord should come to me? For indeed, as soon as the voice of your greeting sounded in my ears, the babe leaped in my womb for joy. Blessed *is* she who believed, for there will be a fulfilment of those things which were told her from the Lord'" (Luke 1:39–45). John bore witness to the Messiah by leaping for joy inside his mother's womb when in the presence of Mary who was pregnant with Jesus Christ. This is the explanation of John being regenerate and filled with the Spirit in his mother's womb.

This regeneration and filling with the Holy Spirit was probably unique in the total history of mankind, and probably never to occur again in any individual in the future. John's regeneration and filling of the Spirit had nothing to do with providing salvation for someone who was going to die in infancy. John was destined to grow up and fulfil his unique and momentous ministry. Therefore to base hope of infant salvation from Luke 1:15 is at best tenuous.

2. If we accept that God's ordinary pattern is to save the children of believers this does not mean that we can say this pattern operates with regard to believers' children who die very young. As we have seen there is no proof from Luke 1:15 and Psalm 22:10 that God regenerated or will regenerate any infant other than John the Baptist. It is simply surmise to assume that He works in that way. It is surmise built upon surmise to go on to say He will regenerate believer's children who die very young. This is not stated anywhere in the scriptures.

3. Wayne Grudem supports his speculations by reference to 2 Sam. 12:23. He argues, "This can only imply that he would be with his son in the presence of the Lord forever."[2] We have seen above that this verse probably means only that he would join his son in Sheol; the place where all the dead were gathered indiscriminately, both saints and sinners.

4. With regard to the infants who die having unbelieving parents he says the scripture is silent as to their future state. He says, "We simply must leave that matter in the hands of God and trust him to be both just and merciful."[3] But it is indisputable that God saves some of the offspring of unbelievers who grow up and repent

and believe the gospel. He does not suggest from that pattern of His dealings that it is reasonable therefore to conclude that He will save some of unbelievers' children who die very young. Is he not inconsistent? If the pattern of God's dealings applies in the case of believers' children why not in the case of unbelievers' children?

For these reasons I submit that Wayne Grudem is deriving conclusions of hope beyond what his quoted texts will support.

Some take a different and definite stance. They contend that all infants who die in infancy will be saved. They assert that God has elected to save all such infants regardless of parentage or race.

C.H. Spurgeon

The famous preacher C.H. Spurgeon said in a sermon on Luke 18:17, "We know that *infants* enter the kingdom, for we are convinced that all of our race who die in infancy are included in the election of grace, and partake in the redemption wrought out by our Lord Jesus. Whatever some may think, we believe that the whole spirit and tone of the word of God, as well the nature of God himself, lead us to believe that all who leave this world as babes are saved. . . . My solemn persuasion is that the child of a Mahometan, or a Papist, or a Buddhist, or a cannibal, dying in infancy, is as surely saved as the child of a Christian."[4] God has not stated that "all of our race who die in infancy are included in the election of grace" and "are saved." Why this total silence if C.H. Spurgeon's belief is true? Why has God not revealed this to be so?

But let us consider the grounds for his belief. He bases his belief on "the whole spirit and tone of the word of God, as well as the nature of God himself." Let us weigh the following scriptures to see if he really has valid ground for his conviction.

1. In many places in the Bible we find God's instructions to kill babes and children (Deut. 3:1–6 cf. Deut. 2:34; Deut. 7:1–2; Deut. 20:16–18; Josh. 6:17–21)
The record is absolutely explicit in 1 Sam. 15:1–3, "Samuel also said to Saul, 'The LORD sent me to anoint you king over His people, over Israel. Now therefore, heed the voice of the words of the LORD. Thus says the LORD of hosts: "I will punish Amalek *for* what he did to Israel, how he ambushed him on the way when he came up from Egypt. Now go and attack Amalek, and utterly destroy all that they have, and do not spare them. But kill both man and woman, infant and nursing child, ox and sheep, camel and donkey." ' " These commands pertain to God's covenant with the nation of Israel containing commands concerning

warfare. That covenant is now obsolete. But these verses are a true record of God's dealings with mankind at that time and a revealing of Him Who is eternally the same.

2.   God's judgments on nations including Israel brought destruction on infants as well as adults

The destruction of the firstborn in Egypt at the time of the Exodus must have involved some babes and infants. In the same way the judgments of the Flood and Sodom and Gomorrah fell upon infants as well as adults.

Hosea the prophet proclaimed the doom of the kingdom of Israel: "Samaria is held guilty, For she has rebelled against her God. They shall fall by the sword, Their infants shall be dashed in pieces, And their women with child ripped open" (Hos. 13:16). Assyria would destroy them as the rod of God's anger (Isa. 10:5). In this terrible fall of the Northern Kingdom God declares concerning Himself, "So I will be to them like a lion; Like a leopard by the road I will lurk; I will meet them like a bear deprived *of her cubs*; I will tear open their rib cage, And there I will devour them like a lion. The wild beast shall tear them" (Hos. 13:7–8). Their conquest in 721 B.C. with all its suffering and devastation was the manifestation of God acting in judgment. In that judgment He did not spare infants.

When judgment fell upon the Southern Kingdom of Judah in 587 B.C. the horrors of suffering and death came upon the children as Jeremiah prophesied: "Therefore I am full of the fury of the LORD. I am weary of holding *it* in. 'I will pour it out on the children outside, And on the assembly of young men together; For even the husband shall be taken with the wife, The aged with *him who is* full of days' " (Jer. 6:11 cf. Jer. 9:21 and Lam. 2:11–12). Concerning these events the scripture says, "The LORD has fulfilled His fury, He has poured out His fierce anger. He kindled a fire in Zion, And it has devoured its foundations" (Lam. 4:11). That fierce anger of God fell upon infants and adults alike when it fell upon Judah.

In the prophecies of Isaiah we read of the day of God's fierce anger against Babylon (Isa. 13:13) and in verse sixteen, "Their children also will be dashed to pieces before their eyes." God said, "Behold, I will stir up the Medes against them, Who will not regard silver; And *as for* gold, they will not delight in it. Also *their* bows will dash the young men to pieces, And they will have no pity on the fruit of the womb; Their eye will not spare children. And Babylon, the glory of kingdoms, The beauty of the Chaldeans' pride, Will be as when God overthrew Sodom and Gomorrah" (Isa. 13:17–19).

3.   *We read of God's judgment on King David*

"Then Nathan departed to his house. And the LORD struck the child that Uriah's wife bore to David, and it became ill. David therefore pleaded with God for the child, and David fasted and went in and lay all night on the ground. So the elders of his house arose *and went* to him, to raise him up from the ground. But he would not, nor did he eat food with them. Then on the seventh day it came to pass that the child died. And the servants of David were afraid to tell him that the child was dead. For they said, 'Indeed, while the child was alive, we spoke to him, and he would not heed our voice. How can we tell him that the child is dead? He may do some harm!' " (2 Sam. 12:15–18). Notice God struck the child. The child was not guilty of David's sins of adultery and murder. David had repented: "So David said to Nathan, 'I have sinned against the LORD.' And Nathan said to David, 'The LORD also has put away your sin; you shall not die. However, because by this deed you have given great occasion to the enemies of the LORD to blaspheme, the child also *who is* born to you shall surely die' " (2 Sam. 12:13–14). David pleaded, fasted and wept for the child, but God took him.

4.   *At the birth of Jesus Herod the king of Judea sought to kill Him.*
He put to death all the male children who were in Bethlehem and in
all its districts from two years old and under

"An angel of the Lord appeared to Joseph in a dream, saying, 'Arise, take the young Child and His mother, flee to Egypt, and stay there until I bring you word; for Herod will seek the young Child to destroy Him'" (Mat. 2:13). Joseph heeded the message and stayed in Egypt until Herod died. The other infants and children were massacred. William Hendriksen estimates that the total number of them was not more than fifteen to twenty.[5] Whatever the number was, the fact is that God did not warn their parents/guardians. He did not act to preserve them.

5.   *In the terrible destruction of Jerusalem in A.D. 70 infants as well*
as adults experienced great tribulation

In AD 66 the Jews revolted against Roman rule. The Romans under Titus took the city in AD 70. The destruction of Jerusalem was the final stage of the victory of Rome over the Jewish uprising. Jesus foretold this event and said that it would be God's judgment for all the righteous blood shed by the hands of the wicked since the time of Abel. All that guilt would be laid on the generation living at that time: "Therefore, indeed, I send you prophets, wise men, and scribes: *some* of them you will kill and crucify, and *some* of them you will scourge in your synagogues and persecute from city to city, that on you may come all the righteous blood shed on the earth, from the blood of righteous Abel to the blood of Zechariah, son of Berechiah, whom you murdered between the temple and the altar. Assuredly, I say to you, all these things will come upon this generation. O Jerusalem, Jerusalem, the one who kills the prophets and stones those who are sent to her! How often I wanted to gather your children together, as a hen gathers her chicks under *her* wings, but you were not willing! See! Your house is left to you desolate" (Mat. 23:34–38). Because all that guilt would be laid on that generation the most fearful punishment would come. Jesus said, "But woe to those who are pregnant and to those who are nursing babies in those days!" (Mat. 24:19), and, "For then there will be great tribulation, such as has not been since the beginning of the world until this time, no, nor ever shall be" (Mat. 24:21).

I submit that the scriptures do not support C.H. Spurgeon's contention that his belief is justified by "the whole spirit and tone of the word of God, as well as the nature of God himself."

J. Oliver Buswell

Like C.H. Spurgeon, J. Oliver Buswell writes in his *A Systematic Theology of the Christian Religion*, ". . . I do most assuredly believe that those who die in infancy are saved through the atonement of Christ, and are regenerated by the power of the Holy Spirit."[6] He wrote, ". . . I *postulate* (and I frankly state that it is but a postulate, yet in harmony with, and not at all contrary to the Scriptures) that the Holy Spirit of God prior to the moment of death, does so enlarge the intelligence of one who dies in infancy . . . that they are capable of accepting Jesus Christ."[7] He believed that this supernaturally enlarged intelligence to be "the means by which faith is imparted and regeneration accomplished by the Holy Spirit."[8] He believed his postulate harmonized two lines of scriptural truth, namely God's care for children, and that there is no salvation apart from faith in our Lord Jesus Christ. Like John Murray he realized that regeneration and faith cannot be separated. He goes much further than John Murray who states that where regeneration occurs in the case of an infant "there is that which we may and must call the germ of faith." J. Oliver Buswell and John Murray both see very clearly that regeneration and faith cannot be separated in the application of salvation. They assert that some infants are regenerated. Accordingly they devise ways in which regenerate infants are given faith. Scripture does not state that some infants are regenerated, nor does it speak of faith in infants. They have moved from what God has revealed into beliefs arising from their own reasoning and speculation.

Some reason that since God elects out of mankind whom He will to salvation, it is reasonable to conclude that some infants who die in infancy are included in the elect and therefore will go to heaven. This may be, but it would be equally reasonable to believe that God preserves the lives of all His elect until He calls them into His kingdom. The scripture tells us plainly that God determines our lifespan: "Come now, you who say, 'Today or tomorrow we will go to such and such a city, spend a year there, buy and sell, and make a profit'; whereas you do not know what *will happen* tomorrow. For what *is* your life? It is even a vapor that appears for a little time and then vanishes away. Instead you *ought* to say, 'If the Lord wills, we shall live and do this or that.' But now you boast in your arrogance. All such boasting is evil" (James 4:13–16). Such preservation seems more in accord with Paul's words in Rom. 8:28–30, "And we know that all things work together for good to those who love God, to those who are the called according to *His* purpose. For whom He foreknew, He also predestined *to be* conformed to the image of His Son, that He might be the firstborn among many brethren. Moreover whom He predestined, these He also called; whom He called, these He also justified; and whom He justified, these He also glorified." Those whom He foreknew, the elect, He also called. This appears to be a statement with universal application. All the elect are called. If this is so, then it implies that without exception they are preserved through infancy to the time of their individual repentance and faith. This link between election and calling is also stated in Paul's letter to believers at Thessalonica: "But we are bound to give thanks to God always for you, brethren beloved by the Lord, because God from the beginning chose you for salvation through sanctification by the Spirit and belief in the truth, to which He called you by our gospel, for the obtaining of the glory of our Lord Jesus Christ" (2 Thess. 2:13–14).

In conclusion what is revealed in the scriptures?

1. The scriptures tell us that infants are guilty of Adam's sin, are by nature children of wrath and must be born again to enter heaven.
2. John the Baptist was regenerated and filled with the Spirit even in the womb for a unique ministry.
3. There is no recorded case in the whole Bible of any infant born again and dying in infancy.
4. They don't tell us anywhere that God's will is to regenerate infants or any particular group of infants during infancy.
5. To choose to believe that all or some infants who die will go to

heaven goes beyond what is revealed in the Bible. Some creeds add to the scriptures pronouncements beyond God's revelation. The Westminster Confession reads "Elect infants , dying in infancy, are regenerated, and saved by Christ through the Spirit, who worketh when, and where, and how he pleaseth . . ."[9] The Presbyterian Church North U.S.A revised this Confession in 1903. The above article was modified concerning those dying in infancy, stating belief in the inclusion of all dying in infancy in the election of grace and belief in their regeneration and salvation by Christ through the Spirit.

The doctrine of the new birth and infant salvation

We have examined the arguments for infant salvation in depth because it is clear that the way we define regeneration can be linked to, and affected by belief in infant salvation. We must derive our doctrine from what scripture teaches, not from a desire to provide salvation for infants who die. There is an understandable wish and pressure from others to affirm hope for infants who die, but this must not cause us to add to what the scriptures reveal. The new birth is through the Spirit and the word of God responded to in repentance and faith. This is taught in James 1:18, 1 Peter 1:23 and John 3:5, and must not be modified to provide regeneration for those dying in infancy. The scriptures do not give sufficient ground for such modification.

There are extremely serious consequences of a restricted doctrine of regeneration

1.   A restricted view of regeneration, not including man's repentance and faith, makes possible the false gospel of baptismal regeneration
The belief that the new birth is produced by baptism is not possible if it comprises of

a) God's direct immediate operation on the heart
b) His indirect working by the word and the Spirit, and
c) man's response of repentance and faith as a result of God's direct and indirect work.

It is possible if regeneration is only God's immediate operation on the heart. One only needs to add to that restricted definition of the new birth the error that it is produced by baptism and the final product is the lie of baptismal regeneration. This terrible error has deluded, and is deluding millions of souls that they are born again when they are not. It provides a way to manufacture false Christians on demand, when God alone decides who will be born again "The wind blows *where it wishes*, and you hear the sound of it, but cannot tell where it comes from and where it goes. So is everyone who is born of the Spirit" (John 3:8).

2. A restricted view of regeneration can lead to serious errors concerning the need to preach the gospel to every creature

James P. Boyce draws the following conclusion from a separation of regeneration from conversion. He says that there is antecedence of regeneration in relation to conversion and "in some cases an appreciable interval" between regeneration and conversion; and speaking of this time interval, "There is no reason why it should not be true of some heathen. The missionaries of the cross have been sought by men, who knew nothing of Christianity, but whose hearts, unsatisfied with the religion of their fathers, were restlessly seeking for what their soul was crying out"[10] The logic cannot be faulted. If regeneration is limited to a direct immediate work of God then yes, He works wherever He wills so why not on the heathen? And if there is sometimes an appreciable time between regeneration and conversion why not upon the heathen before they hear and believe the gospel? Logic however takes us even further than James P. Boyce – why rule out the possibility of God regenerating heathen who will never hear the gospel ? Moreover if God so regenerates, would such heathen go to heaven? And if the answer is yes, then God can save without the preaching of the gospel and missionaries are not needed always for the fulfilment of God's saving purposes!

References

1. Taken from *Systematic Theology* by Wayne A. Grudem. Copyright © 1994 by Wayne Grudem. Used by permission of IVP and Zondervan, page 500.
2. *Ibid.*, page 501.
3. *Ibid.*, page 501.
4. C.H. Spurgeon *The Metropolitan Tabernacle Pulpit* 1878, Volume 24, Pilgrim Publications, Pasadena, Texas, pages 583/584.
5. William Hendriksen *Commentary on Matthew*, Banner of Truth 1974, page 181.
6. J. Oliver Buswell *A Systematic Theology of the Christian Religion* 1979, volume 2, page 161.
7. *Ibid.*, page 162.
8. *Ibid.*, page 162.
9. *See* chapter X section 3.
10. James P. Joyce *Abstract of Systematic Theology* 1887, Ernest C. Reisinger, Fred A. Malone Christian Gospel Foundation, page 381.

FAITH AND THE NEW BIRTH (4): THIS SPECIAL OPERATION OF GOD TO PRODUCE THE FAITH THAT SAVES IS A WORK OF THE EXCEEDING GREATNESS OF GOD'S POWER

In Paul's letter to the Christians at Ephesus he prays "that the God of our Lord Jesus Christ, the Father of glory, may give to you the spirit of wisdom and revelation in the knowledge of Him, the eyes of your understanding being enlightened; that you may know . . . what *is* the exceeding greatness of His power toward us who believe, according to the working of His mighty power which He worked in Christ when He raised Him from the dead and seated *Him* at His right hand in the heavenly *places*, . . . And you *He made alive*, who were dead in trespasses and sins in which you once walked according to the course of this world, according to the prince of the power of the air, the spirit who now works in the sons of disobedience, among whom also we all once conducted ourselves in the lusts of our flesh, fulfilling the desires of the flesh and of the mind, and were by nature children of wrath, just as the others" (Eph. 1:17, 18a, 19, 20:2:1–3). He wanted them to be enlightened by God so that they would come to know "the exceeding greatness of God's power" which had caused them to be born again, "made alive". Notice it is not simply God's power, not even the greatness of that power, but the exceeding greatness of that power that they needed to know. It is evident therefore that Christians are either in a state of knowledge and understanding on this matter or not. The Greek word used here indicates a knowledge that is thorough, accurate and full. It is truth stated in God's word and revealed by the Holy Spirit. The Christians to whom Paul wrote were true believers, and were sealed with the Holy Spirit (Eph. 1:13), but they lacked this knowledge and understanding. They needed an "opening" of the scriptures on this matter (Luke 24:32). Paul prays that they will be illumined to see that the very same power, which raised Jesus from the dead and exalted Him far above all, had brought about in them the new birth. Only that exceeding greatness of power had transformed their lives from being dominated by the prince of the power of the air, the influence of this God rejecting world, and the lusts of the flesh and of the mind. They had been the slaves of sin and devoid of righteousness (Rom. 6:20). God's action changed them by setting them free from the power of sin and Satan. Previous to their conversion they were by nature children justly incurring the wrath of God from birth. Now they have been given exceedingly great and precious promises through which they may be partakers of the divine nature (2 Peter 1:4). They are new creatures. They are His workmanship, created in Christ Jesus for good works, which God prepared beforehand that they should walk in them (Eph. 2:10). Now they live in fellowship with God. They are able to present themselves and all their powers and faculties to God for His service and holiness of life. When God created the heavens and the earth there was the exercise of the "greatness of His might" (Isa. 40:26). When God causes men and women to be born again He exercises the "*exceeding* greatness of His power."

By this exceeding greatness of power the Father "draws" men to Christ. The word draw expresses a very powerful action. It is used elsewhere in the scriptures to speak of drawing in a fish net (John 21:6,11), of dragging prisoners (Acts 16:19; 21:30) and of dragging people into the courts (James 2:6).

There is no violation of man's free will by God's call. Before that drawing of the Father man acted freely in rejecting the truth. He exercised his choice in accord with his fallen human nature. When born again he acts freely according to his new disposition. He chooses from his heart to receive and act upon that which the Father has taught him. He is not forced to come to Christ.

This new birth is a mysterious operation as well as a work of power: "The wind blows where it wishes, and you hear the sound of it, but cannot tell where it comes from and where it goes. So is everyone who is born of the Spirit" (John 3:8). This working of God is inscrutable, but the results are visible – repentance and faith and changed behaviour. He works the new birth in whomever He chooses, whenever He chooses.

Objection: Why does God command that the gospel be preached to all if He only calls some to Himself?

The gospel is the expression of God's love for fallen humanity. It declares that salvation is available to all who will repent and believe. It is a real and sincere offer of forgiveness and eternal life to all who hear. God desires that every hearer of the gospel will repent and believe and obtain salvation. Ezekiel 33:11 expresses God's heart towards sinful man, "Say to them: '*As* I live,' says the Lord GOD, 'I have no pleasure in the death of the wicked, but that the wicked turn from his way and live. Turn, turn from your evil ways! For why should you die, O house of Israel?'" Jesus revealed exactly the same feeling, "O Jerusalem, Jerusalem, the one who kills the prophets and stones those who are sent to her! How often I wanted to gather your children together, as a hen gathers her chicks under *her* wings, but you were not willing!" (Mat. 23:37).

God commands obedience to the gospel from every hearer, "Truly, these times of ignorance God overlooked, but now commands all men everywhere to repent, because He has appointed a day on which He will judge the world in righteousness by the Man whom He has ordained. He has given assurance of this to all by raising Him from the dead" (Acts 17:30–31). Man's inability to obey the gospel is because of sin. His sinful nature means that he is unwilling to repent and believe: "And this is the condemnation, that the light has come into the world, and men loved darkness rather than light, because their deeds were evil. For everyone practicing evil hates the light and does not come to the light, lest his deeds should be exposed" (John 3:19–20). That was the state of humanity when Jesus came to earth. It is just the same today. Man's understanding is darkened so that the gospel is foolishness to him; but this is because of sin. It is because of the sinful hardness of his heart: "being darkened in their understanding, excluded from the life of God, because of the ignorance that is in them, because of the hardness of their heart" (Eph. 4:18 NASB). His sinfulness also gives the devil the opportunity to have power over his life. His desires, both of the flesh and of the mind, through the fall have become perverted into lusts. It is therefore easy for Satan to deceive by suggesting that satisfying those lusts will bring happiness. Equally the devil has no problem in persuading men to believe arguments, philosophies and religions instead of God's truth, because man's sinful heart loves darkness. Therefore the reasons for man's unwillingness to receive the gospel are all ultimately caused by his personal sinfulness.

When Moses addressed the nation of Israel shortly before his death and Israel's entry into the promised land he set before them life and blessing if they would walk in His ways and keep His commands. He said on that occasion, "For this commandment which I command you today *is* not *too* mysterious for you, nor *is* it far off. It *is* not in heaven, that you should say, 'Who will ascend into heaven for us and bring it to us, that we may hear it and do it?' Nor *is* it beyond the sea, that you should say, 'Who will go over the sea for us and bring it to us, that we may hear it and do it?' But the word *is* very near you, in your mouth and in your heart, that you may do it" (Deut. 30:11–14). Moses was saying that God's commands were not too difficult for them to understand and obey. Paul applies these words to the gospel message affirming the very same truth (Rom. 10:6–9). The gospel is not too difficult to understand and to obey. Just as Israel had no valid excuse for disobedience the gospel hearer likewise has no excuse for not obeying the message.

God's sincerity and love in the offer of salvation, and His right to command what man ought to do, is not diminished one whit by man's sin. That He calls some, and not all, is a profound mystery. That mystery is stated in John 3:8: "The wind blows where it wishes, and you hear the sound of it, but cannot tell where it comes from and where it goes. So is everyone who is born of the Spirit." There is an unsearchableness in God's dealings with man, "The wind blows where it wishes." But two facts are crystal clear: only man's sin prevents him receiving the salvation offered in the gospel, and if God were to call no one He would not be unjust. Justice requires only man's punishment for guilt in Adam and personal sins and sinfulness. Man has no right whatsoever to mercy and the offer of salvation.

CHAPTER SIXTEEN

THE RELATIONSHIP BETWEEN REPENTANCE AND FAITH

To receive salvation both repentance and faith are essential. The question is often asked, which comes first? The truth is that both are the result of the calling of God. Everyone who hears and learns from the Father (John 6:45) is moved to both repent and to believe. Therefore when the soul is drawn to Christ both repentance and faith unite to receive salvation. The call of God never produces repentance without also bringing about faith. Equally the call of God never causes faith that is not accompanied with repentance.

However it is striking that the New Testament, when mentioning repentance and faith together, always places repentance first. There is a sense in which repentance must precede the act of faith which receives salvation. To ask for salvation from the guilt, power and penal consequences of sin presupposes repentance. Robert L. Dabney states this truth succinctly, "Repentance feels the disease, faith embraces the remedy."[1] When the prodigal returned to his father in the parable told by Jesus in Luke 15 he first repented: "But when he came to himself, he said, 'How many of my father's hired servants have bread enough and to spare, and I perish with hunger! I will arise and go to my father, and will say to him, "Father, I have sinned against heaven and before you, and I am no longer worthy to be called your son. Make me like one of your hired servants" ' " (Luke 15:17–19). After coming to that change of mind he took the step of faith and went to his father.

In actual experience there may be some time lapse between coming to a place of repentance and the exercise of faith to receive salvation. A person may be broken and contrite over having turned to one's own way, but for a time may not come to faith in Christ for salvation. There will be a belief in God in this state of repentance. Indeed there must be a belief in God's existence and Godhead for any exercise of repentance. It is repentance towards God. But such belief is not the same as the exercise of faith which brings salvation. That belief in God may well include some understanding of His goodness (Acts 14:17, Psalm 145:9

and Mat. 5:45), forbearance and longsuffering. Indeed these very things may lead to repentance. But they contain no revelation of how a sinner may be forgiven and be in a right relationship with God.

C.H. Spurgeon tells of his state prior to conversion. He wrote, "For five years, as a child, there was nothing before my eyes but my guilt, and though I do not hesitate to say that those who observed my life would not have seen any extraordinary sin, yet as I looked upon myself, there was not a day in which I did not commit such gross, such outrageous sins against God, that often and often have I wished I had never been born . . . It was my sad lot, at that time, to feel the greatness of my sin, without a discovery of the greatness of God's mercy[2] . . . It was not so much that I feared hell, as that I feared sin; and all the while, I had upon my mind a deep concern for the honour of God's name, and the integrity of His moral government. I felt that it would not satisfy my conscience if I could be forgiven unjustly."[3] These words speak of repentance not merely conviction of sin. He acknowledges and loathes his sins and sinfulness. He sought to overcome that sinfulness, and said "I tried and failed."[4] He did not know how to get his sins forgiven. He records "While under concern of soul, I resolved that I would attend all the places of worship in the town where I lived, in order that I might find out the way of salvation. . . . I went time after time, and I can honestly say that I do not know that I ever went without prayer to God, and I am sure there was not a more attentive hearer than myself in all the place, for I panted and longed to understand how I might be saved."[5] Eventually he went to a little Primitive Methodist Chapel and the preacher took as his text "Look unto Me, and be ye saved, all the ends of the earth." He wrote, "I saw at once the way of salvation . . . My spirit saw its chains broken to pieces, I felt that I was an emancipated soul, an heir of heaven, a forgiven one, accepted in Christ Jesus, plucked out of the miry clay and out of the horrible pit, with my feet set upon a rock, and my goings established. I thought I could dance all the way home."[6]

I have narrated this account at length to demonstrate that there can be a period of time between repentance toward God and coming to faith in Jesus Christ. Why the delay? Spurgeon himself says, "Oh, that somebody had told me this before, 'Trust Christ, and you shall be saved.' Yet it was, no doubt, all wisely ordered, . . ."[7] God's dealings show that not only can there be delay, but also the need for repentant souls to be directed to Christ and His cross. The gospel is repentance toward God and faith in Jesus Christ.

Of course in the experience of some they are moved to repentance not just because of coming to a realisation and acknowledgement of

God's existence, goodness, forbearance and longsuffering; they also hear of the love of God in giving His Son to die for sinners. This also melts their heart. Indeed it may be that this action moves them above all else to repent. In such cases the message of the cross is used by the Spirit to bring about both repentance and faith.

Faith in Christ for salvation must always be accompanied with repentance. Christ is the Saviour not only from the guilt of sin but also the power of sin. He gives the power to overcome sin and sinfulness, to live in obedience to God and to be holy. He brings in a New Covenant for all who receive Him. The blessings of the New Covenant are stated in Heb 8:10–12: "For this *is* the covenant that I will make with the house of Israel after those days, says the LORD: I will put My laws in their mind and write them on their hearts; and I will be their God, and they shall be My people. None of them shall teach his neighbor, and none his brother, saying, 'Know the LORD,' for all shall know Me, from the least of them to the greatest of them. For I will be merciful to their unrighteousness, and their sins and their lawless deeds I will remember no more." God does not abolish His Ten Commandments for Christians. He puts them in their minds and on their hearts. He gives the believer understanding of His commands and a desire to keep them. He has intimate fellowship with Christians. They all know Him. He is merciful to them; He forgives their sins and does not remember their transgressions. It is impossible for anyone to want the salvation Christ gives if they are not repentant. If they wish to continue walking their own way, then they are opposed to God writing His laws upon their hearts, and they have no desire whatsoever for fellowship with a holy God. They might want a Saviour from the penal consequences of their sin, but they have no wish to change their behaviour. Christ never gives salvation to such. Many of them profess to be believers in Christ. On that day He will say, "I never knew you; depart from Me, you who practice lawlessness" (Mat. 7:23).

Some argue that faith precedes repentance. They contend that a convicted sinner cannot repent until given hope that God will be merciful. The truly repentant sinner does not condition his willingness to repent on the assurance of mercy. The truly penitent is sorrowful for sins regardless of whether or not there is forgiveness and mercy. Indeed he feels utterly unworthy of the least crumb from God's table. He does not see his penitence as meriting any favour, or making any reparation for past sins. It is perfectly true, as stated above, that the love of God demonstrated on the cross of Christ may move one to repentance. But that is not to say that saving faith precedes repentance. An awakening to the reality of God's love for the world leading to repentance, is not the same as receiving salvation through faith. Such faith sees the love, and is moved to repentance. Saving faith not only sees the love and repents, it also acts to take the salvation offered by that love.

R.T. Kendall contends for faith coming before repentance. He argues, "The Puritans, after Calvin, often defined repentance as turning from every known sin. Now if you define repentance as turning from every known sin, and also insist that repentance must go before faith, then it means one must prepare oneself for salvation; a person must have a change in their life, someone must have a complete break from sin before they have even reached the place where they can even qualify for faith."[8] The New Testament never presents repentance as a qualification for faith. The message of the gospel is not repent first and then believe. It is always repent and believe. Repentance is to be preached together with the forgiveness of sins; "Then He said to them, 'Thus it is written, and thus it was necessary for the Christ to suffer and to rise from the dead the third day, and that repentance and remission of sins should be preached in His name to all nations, beginning at Jerusalem'" (Luke 24:46–47). This is exactly what the apostles did preach. Peter on the day of Pentecost proclaimed repentance and forgiveness of sins: "Now when they heard *this*, they were cut to the heart, and said to Peter and the rest of the apostles, 'Men *and* brethren, what shall we do?' Then Peter said to them, 'Repent, and let every one of you be baptized in the name of Jesus Christ for the remission of sins; and you shall receive the gift of the Holy Spirit'" (Acts 2:37–38). A little later Peter preaches again in Jerusalem. He says, "Repent therefore and be converted, that your sins may be blotted out, so that times of refreshing may come from the presence of the Lord" (Acts 3:19). Peter and the apostles are brought before the high priest and the council at Jerusalem because of their preaching. The scripture records their response: "But Peter and the *other* apostles answered and said: 'We ought to obey God rather than men. The God of our fathers raised up Jesus whom you murdered by hanging on a tree Him God has exalted to His right hand *to be* Prince and Savior, to give repentance to Israel and forgiveness of sins'" (Acts 5:29–30). When Peter took the gospel to the Gentiles He preached Jesus Christ and faith in Him saying, "To Him all the prophets witness that, through His name, whoever believes in Him will receive remission of sins" (Acts 10:43). There is no mention of repentance in his message, but when Peter reported the events following his preaching the Christians in Jerusalem said, "Then God has also granted to the Gentiles repentance unto life" (Acts 11:18). They knew that there is no salvation without repentance. In many of the accounts of preaching in the Acts of the Apostles only faith is mentioned (Acts 13:38, 16:31) or only repentance (Acts 17:30). The accounts are concise summaries. Every detail is not mentioned. But Paul gives an insight into his preaching in his words to the elders of the church at Ephesus. He said, "I kept back nothing that was helpful, but proclaimed it to you, and taught you publicly and from house to house, testifying to Jews, and also to Greeks, repentance toward God and faith toward our Lord Jesus Christ" (Acts 20:20–21). The gospel was a message of repentance and faith proclaimed together.

Repentance in this gospel proclamation must be defined correctly. Faith for salvation must be accompanied with repentance, but it is imperative that a true definition of repentance is kept in mind at this point. It is to think again and change one's mind about oneself and one's conduct before God. Specifically it means:

1. Coming to a realisation of personal guilt before God for sins committed.
2. A realisation of personal guilt before God for not being what one ought to be.
3. Shame for sins.
4. Self-loathing for one's sinful nature.
5. Sorrow for sins and sinfulness.
6. A hatred of sin.
7. A desire to cease from sin.

Repentance must be distinguished from the works befitting repentance which follow it when Christ's salvation from sin is received

The repentant sinner cannot in his or her own strength mortify sins and be holy. It is by the Spirit of God mortification is achieved. An unconverted person may reform in some respects, but when Christ is received then comes the power to overcome sin and to be righteous. Preaching repentance therefore is calling upon men and women to see themselves and their behaviour as God sees them, and to be genuinely sorry, deeply ashamed and really wanting from the heart deliverance from sin's guilt, power and consequences. Preaching repentance and faith in Christ also calls upon men and women to turn to Jesus Christ for mercy, forgiveness and deliverance from sin. When Christ is received then works befitting repentance will result immediately (Acts 26:20). An example of such works is recorded at Ephesus: "And many who had believed came confessing and telling their deeds. Also, many of those who had practiced magic brought their books together and burned *them* in the sight of all. And they counted up the value of them, and *it* totaled fifty thousand *pieces* of silver" (Acts 19:18–19). The preaching of repentance in the gospel therefore does not demand works befitting repentance before faith is exercised for salvation. It presents the requirements of repentance and faith together. Works befitting repentance follow conversion.

References

1. Taken from *Lectures in Systematic Theology* by the Zondervan Corporation. Copyright © 1972 by Zondervan Publishing House. Used by permission of Zondervan, page 658.
2. C. H. Spurgeon *Autobiography: 1, The Early Years*, Banner of Truth, Reprinted 1976, pages 58–59.
3. *Ibid.*, pages 79–80.
4. *Ibid.*, page 81.
5. *Ibid.*, pages 86–87.
6. *Ibid.*, pages 88–89.
7. *Ibid.*, page 88.
8. R.T. Kendall *Are You Stone Deaf To The Spirit or . . . Rediscovering GOD?*, Christian Focus Publications, 1994, page 61.

CHAPTER SEVENTEEN

HOW MUCH KNOWLEDGE IS REQUIRED TO BECOME A CHRISTIAN?

In the light of all that has been stated one may ask how much does one need to know to become a Christian. Many true believers will confess that they knew very little when they entered the kingdom. The scriptures are clear that there must be sufficient knowledge imparted by the Spirit to bring about repentance and faith. Knowledge of the scriptures and doctrine may be very limited. But there will be enough knowledge and understanding of the gospel truths to repent and believe. Becoming a Christian is not merely an emotional experience. It is obeying a message. The obedience required is repentance and faith.

In Paul's letter to the Romans it is striking how often the apostle speaks of this obedience to the gospel.

"Through whom we have received grace and apostleship to bring about *the* obedience of faith among all the Gentiles for His name's sake" (Rom. 1:5 NASB).

"but to those who are self-seeking and do not obey the truth, but obey unrighteousness – indignation and wrath" (Rom. 2:8).

"But God be thanked that *though* you were slaves of sin, yet you obeyed from the heart that form of doctrine to which you were delivered" (Rom. 6:17).

"But they have not all obeyed the gospel. For Isaiah says, 'Lord, who has believed our report?' " (Rom. 10:16).

"For I will not dare to speak of any of those things which Christ has not accomplished through me, in word and deed, to make the Gentiles obedient – in mighty signs and wonders, by the power of the Spirit of God, so that from Jerusalem and round about to Illyricum I have fully preached the gospel of Christ" (Rom. 15:18–19).

121

"Now to Him who is able to establish you according to my gospel and the preaching of Jesus Christ, according to the revelation of the mystery which has been kept secret for long ages past, but now is manifested, and by the Scriptures of the prophets, according to the commandment of the eternal God, has been made known to all the nations, *leading* to obedience of faith; to the only wise God, through Jesus Christ, be the glory forever. Amen" (Rom. 16:25–27 NASB).

This fact that the gospel demands the obedience of repentance and faith runs through the New Testament.

"Then the word of God spread, and the number of the disciples multiplied greatly in Jerusalem, and a great many of the priests were obedient to the faith" (Acts 6:7). The term faith here stands for the gospel.

"when the Lord Jesus is revealed from heaven with His mighty angels, in flaming fire taking vengeance on those who do not know God, and on those who do not obey the gospel of our Lord Jesus Christ" (2 Thess. 1:7–8).

"Peter, an apostle of Jesus Christ, To the pilgrims of the Dispersion in Pontus, Galatia, Cappadocia, Asia, and Bithynia, elect according to the foreknowledge of God the Father, in sanctification of the Spirit, for obedience and sprinkling of the blood of Jesus Christ: Grace to you and peace be multiplied. . . . Since you have purified your souls in obeying the truth through the Spirit in sincere love of the brethren, love one another fervently with a pure heart, having been born again, not of corruptible seed but incorruptible, through the word of God which lives and abides forever" (1 Pet. 1:1–2, 22–23).

Obedience means that there is true understanding of the gospel's demands. Saving faith hears the message and has sufficient knowledge and understanding to obey it by repenting and believing.

The apostle Peter, shortly before his death wrote his second epistle. He addressed it "to those who have obtained like precious faith with us by the righteousness of our God and Saviour Jesus Christ" (2 Pet. 1:1). He is writing to Christians, probably those to whom he wrote in his first letter, namely, "the pilgrims of the Dispersion in Pontus, Galatia, Cappadocia, Asia, and Bithynia, elect according to the foreknowledge of God the Father, in sanctification of the Spirit, for obedience and sprinkling of the blood of Jesus Christ." Peter is speaking of saving faith.

It is significant that he asserts that their faith in every case is of equal standing to his own and the other apostles, cf. vs.16–18. It is like faith, of the same value, equally precious. In some young converts their knowledge of the Bible and its doctrines would be very very small. But their faith had brought about their salvation, just as Peter and the other apostles had been saved by grace through faith. Saving faith may only know enough of the truth to enable repentance toward God and faith in Christ to obtain salvation, but it is not to be despised because the knowledge of truth is small. That knowledge of the gospel taught by the Spirit leads to faith which is as precious as the faith of an apostle. It is a knowledge imparted by God Himself (John 6:45).

CHAPTER EIGHTEEN

JUSTIFICATION BY FAITH

No treatment of faith would be adequate without dealing with justification. When we look at the New Testament's definition of the gospel we find that justification through the righteousness of God and received by faith is the gospel. Paul declared, "I am not ashamed of the gospel of Christ, for it is the power of God to salvation for everyone who believes, for the Jew first and also for the Greek. For in it the righteousness of God is revealed from faith to faith; as it is written, 'The just shall live by faith'" (Rom. 1:16–17). *The Westminster Shorter Catechism*, Ques.33 defines justification as "an act of God's free grace, wherein He pardons all our sins, and accepts us as righteous in His sight, only for the righteousness of Christ imputed to us, and received by faith alone." God justifies the ungodly through faith. The sinner who believes is accounted legally righteous before God, because God imputes the righteousness of Christ to the believer. He reckons it to their account. He treats the believer as if that righteousness were actually his righteousness. He gives the gift of the righteousness of Christ to the believer. That person no longer stands before God in the filthiness of the stains of sins committed throughout life, nor in the filthy rags of his own righteousness by means of good works, religious practice, prayers etc. Instead the sinner who believes stands before God clothed in the righteousness of Christ. Justification is God's legal declaration as Judge that there is no condemnation, since the sinner now has the righteousness which is from God by faith.

It is important to stress that the believer is justified by the imputed righteousness of Christ. Faith is simply the instrument which receives that righteousness. Faith is the organ by which the believer appropriates the righteousness of Christ as the ground of justification. Faith is not the ground of justification.

Justification is only possible because of the work of Christ. The Son of God became man, placed Himself under the law, obeyed it perfectly and bore its penalty for sins. Thus God's law was upheld and established. The sinner's sins were transferred to Christ, and He died for those sins in the place of the sinner. The believing sinner is now forgiven. His sins are now atoned for. God does not impute sin to the believer. Justice has been done. Sin was punished fully, and God made known His justice in not sparing His own Son. Thus He revealed Himself to be both "just and the justifier of the one who has faith in Jesus" (Rom. 3:26). It is true of course that men crucified the Lord Jesus Christ. They acted freely and sinfully, but they only did what God planned in eternity past to be done (Acts 2:23 and 4:27–28). God delivered His Son to death, to the shedding of His blood by the hands of sinful men.

God's holy wrath against sin was appeased by Christ's death as a sacrifice for sins. He was propitiated. Consequently the sinner is no longer under the wrath of God. That anger is now turned away. The righteousness of Christ, Who fulfilled all the requirements of God's law, is transferred to the sinner who believes. Justification is more than forgiveness. It is wholly inadequate to define justification as merely 'just as if I'd never sinned'. That is a sad and gross depreciation of God's saving work in Christ. Justification is the gift of the perfect righteousness of Another, Jesus Christ, to the believer. The believer is accepted by God, and stands before God complete in Christ. God is reconciled. The believer has peace with God. The believer is also assured of salvation from the wrath of God at the final judgment. In the words of Paul, "Much more then, having now been justified by His blood, we shall be saved from wrath through Him. For if when we were enemies we were reconciled to God through the death of His Son, much more, having been reconciled, we shall be saved by His life" (Rom. 5:9–10). God has done this glorious work of justification and reconciliation through Christ. He raised His Son from the dead for the justification of believers (Rom. 4:25). By this action the Father proclaimed His complete satisfaction with the sacrifice of Christ.

Justification is instantaneous the moment the sinner believes in Christ. He then receives "the righteousness which is from God" (Phil. 3:9). That righteousness is the same righteousness received by every other Christian. It is identical. It is a complete, perfect righteousness. It is the righteousness of Christ given to the account of each believer. It can never be added to: it cannot be improved. It is perfect. The believer stands before God righteous, because the righteousness of Christ is constantly accounted to the believer by God from the moment of saving faith. He is justified once and for all time by God's legal declaration. From that moment onwards the believer is "in Christ." Nothing can destroy that new standing before God. Sins committed after conversion do not affect that legal standing before God. When sin is committed the standing is unaffected, because it is based on the imputed righteousness of Christ, not on the conduct of the believer. That is not to say that it does not matter if a believer sins. Even less is it to say that a believer is free to sin. When the believer is justified through faith there is a new relationship with God as well as a new legal standing before Him. Believers are adopted into God's family, and God is their Father. They are now His children. When a believer sins that new family relationship is not lost. But fellowship with God the Father is affected. He is displeased with the sin. He requires that it be confessed, and He promises to be faithful and just to forgive and to cleanse from all unrighteousness when it is confessed (1 John 1:9). Moreover, sinning by the believer can have very serious consequences. Such sins will not only destroy the experience of blessedness of walking daily with God, and rob the believer of the joy of intimacy with the Father, they will bring further results. The scriptures tell us of those consequences of sinning. We shall state them in the next chapter.

CHAPTER NINETEEN

THE CONSEQUENCES OF SIN FOR THE BELIEVER JUSTIFIED BY FAITH

The consequences of sinning for the believer are serious.

Reaping what we sow

Paul wrote to the Galatian believers, "Do not be deceived, God is not mocked; for whatever a man sows, that he will also reap. For he who sows to his flesh will of the flesh reap corruption, but he who sows to the Spirit will of the Spirit reap everlasting life" (Gal. 6:7–8). The Christian has a choice in this life. He can "put off, concerning your former conduct, the old man which grows corrupt according to the deceitful lusts and be renewed in the spirit of your mind and . . . put on the new man which was created according to God, in true righteousness and holiness" (Eph. 4:22–24). There are two ways of living. The "old man" is living according to the fallen nature, the flesh; and the "new man" is living according to the Spirit and in His power. Each way of life will yield corresponding harvests. The harvest of the flesh is evident: "adultery, fornication, uncleanness, lewdness, idolatry, sorcery, hatred, contentions, jealousies, outbursts of wrath, selfish ambitions, dissensions, heresies, envy, murders, drunkenness, revelries, and the like" (Gal. 5:19–21). In contrast, "the fruit of the Spirit is love, joy, peace, longsuffering, kindness, goodness, faithfulness, gentleness, self-control" (Gal. 5:22–23). Every believer is producing daily a harvest. If they sow to the flesh they reap corruption. They produce rottenness. If they walk in the Spirit they partake of life. There is no deviation from these fixed rules. God is not mocked. What God has stated will always come to pass. Man likes to think he can sow to the flesh, and, in his case, not reap the consequences. He has a great capacity to deceive himself in this way.

What we sow we reap. There are striking examples in the history of God's dealings with mankind of this inexorable rule. Lot did not value the purity of his daughters (Gen. 19:8). The time came when they did not value his purity (Gen. 19:33–35). Jacob deceived his father in the matter of the firstborn (Gen. 27:23). Later Jacob was deceived in the matter of the firstborn (Gen. 29:21–26). King David committed adultery and then murder (2 Sam. 11:2–17). The same sins were committed by his sons Amnon (sexual sin) and Absalom (murder) (2 Sam. 13). Nathan the prophet pronounced to David, "Why have you despised the commandment of the LORD, to do evil in His sight? You have killed Uriah the Hittite with the sword; you have taken his wife *to be* your wife, and have killed him with the sword of the people of Ammon. Now therefore, the sword shall never depart from your house, because you have despised Me, and have taken the wife of Uriah the Hittite to be your wife. Thus says the LORD: 'Behold, I will raise up adversity against you from your own house; and I will take your wives before your eyes and give *them* to your neighbor, and he shall lie with your wives in the sight of this sun'" (2 Sam. 12:9–11). The sword indeed never departed. Absalom rebelled against his father and lay with his wives (2 Sam. 16:22). His son Adonijah rebelled against him at the very end of David's life (1Kings 1:5). It must be noted as a matter of the greatest significance that David repented and acknowledged his sin (2 Sam. 12:13 and Psalm 51). Even so, Nathan said to David, "the Lord has put away your sin; you shall not die However, because by this deed you have given great occasion to the enemies of the LORD to blaspheme, the child also *who is* born to you shall surely die" (2 Sam. 12:13–14). The child did die, and what David had sown, sexual sin and murder, came down upon his head in his own family. David suffered terrible long term consequences of his sinning, even though the Lord put away his sin.

Wicked Haman built gallows for godly Mordecai. God overruled so that Haman hung dead on them! (Esther 5:14–7:10).

These are Old Testament examples of God's dealings, but the New Testament tells us that "they were written for our admonition, upon whom the ends of the ages have come" (1 Cor. 10:11). God still deals with mankind in the same way. Paul spells it out to believers, "But he who does wrong will be repaid for what he has done, and there is no partiality" (Col. 3:25). That repayment is very often in this life, and, if not, at the final judgment. There is no partiality with God: all will repaid, to believers as well as to unbelievers.

God's Fatherly chastisement of believers, His children

This is a further consequence of sinning. Thus we see Christians at Corinth judged by the Lord for eating and drinking at the Lord's Supper in an unworthy manner (1 Cor. 11:20–34). They did not discern the Lord's body and consequently many were weak physically, many were sick and many had died. The ones who had died were stated to be sleeping. Sleeping is used in the New Testament to depict the death of believers in anticipation of the resurrection (see Mat. 27:52, Luke 8:52, John 11:11–14, Acts 7:60, 13:36, 1 Cor. 15:6, 18 and 51, 1 Thess. 4:13–18, 2 Pet. 3:4). This judgment of God therefore did not take away their salvation. This is beyond dispute because the passage goes on to say that these judgments were Divine chastisements (Heb. 12:7–11) on the church at Corinth so that believers "may not be condemned with the world" (1 Cor. 11:32). The sins committed, even though they did not bring eternal punishment, resulted in very real suffering in this life and, in some cases, premature death. This fact that the sins of Christians sometimes lead to death is found elsewhere in the New Testament (Acts 5:1–10, James 5:20, and 1 John 5:16). The truth that sickness is sometimes the result of sin is clearly taught by James in his epistle (chapter 5:15–16). All these New Testament verses teach that Christians can and do experience very real consequences for sin.

The chastisements of God administered to His children to rebuke and correct them are not confined to physical afflictions. They take many forms. God may bring a blight on work and efforts (Hag. 1:6–11). The people of God at that time were failing to seek first the kingdom of God and His righteousness. Sometimes they are calamities (Gen. 14:12). The loss of possessions and captivity was a warning to Lot about living in Sodom for which he had a carnal love. It was designed to correct him from that wrong affection. God's chastisement is always perfectly suited to the particular believer and God's particular purpose. Therefore it is highly varied in its content and specific intentions. But Divine chastening deals with believers sins, and is always painful (Heb. 12:11). Only afterward, if it is received aright and the lesson learned, is the benefit gained – "the peaceable fruit of righteousness."

There is clear teaching in God's word that many chastisements come upon believers because of sins which could be avoided. Indeed sometimes further chastisement is needed and administered by the Father because the believer does not respond aright to the rod of correction.

The loss of usefulness in God's service

This is also a serious result of sinning. Paul says that he constantly disciplines his body. Literally he says that he strikes it under the eyes so as to make blue wounds (1 Cor. 9:27). He thus describes all the privations and suffering he inflicts upon his body in order to fulfil His service of preaching the gospel. This discipline was essential, otherwise he would be rejected from God's service. The Old Testament records that Saul was rejected by God from being king over Israel because of his sinful disobedience (1 Sam. 13:1–14; 15:1–26, 35).

These men held high office in God's service. All believers, however, can be unfruitful and barren in the knowledge of our Lord Jesus Christ (2 Pet. 1:8). Some of the sins causing many Christians to become unfruitful in God's service are stated by Jesus in His parable of the sower – the "cares of this world, the deceitfulness of riches, and the desires for other things entering in choke the word, and it becomes unfruitful" (Mark 4:19).

The book of Revelation tells us that Christ constantly looks at each local church (Rev. 2–3). He judges each, assessing their works, doctrine and love, and He delivers his verdict on them. Just like Laodicea, a particular church may become "lukewarm" (Rev. 3:16). If so, Christ says that unless that church is zealous and repents He will vomit it out of His mouth. A local church may become useless in God's service, and be rejected. The decline of usefulness to God of individual churches, of denominations and church groups is often because those churches, denominations and church groups do not hear what Christ says by the Spirit (Rev. 3:22). Decline of usefulness to God is not always apparent. The church at Sardis had a reputation of being alive when in truth it was dead (Rev. 3:1).

Sin results in unfruitfulness in God's service, in individual Christians whatever their calling, in individual churches and in denominations and church groups.

The loss of blessing

Sinning can forfeit blessings which otherwise would have been experienced. God's love for His children is the love which moved Him to give His Son to die at Calvary. The Father promises to pour out His blessings in this life upon His children provided that they are obedient to Him. Sadly Israel did not obey and missed God's blessings on their lives. Psalm 81:11–16 records the sorry tale: "But My people would not heed My voice, And Israel would *have* none of Me. So I gave them over to their own stubborn heart, To walk in their own counsels. Oh, that My people would listen to Me, That Israel would walk in My ways! I would soon subdue their enemies, And turn My hand against their adversaries. The haters of the LORD would pretend submission to Him, But their fate would endure forever. He would have fed them also with the finest of wheat; And with honey from the rock I would have satisfied you." Many believers walk according to their own thoughts instead of the way God would direct them. They are afflicted with "enemies" they would not have if they were obedient. They suffer loss of the knowledge of God and

His word so that their souls do not prosper as they might have done. They miss out in their satisfaction in God and the things of God.

Someone may object that these verses are from the Old Testament, and that the Old Covenant is no longer in operation for New Testament believers. God still blesses His children when they are obedient, and they still lose His best by disobedience. The following verses state this so clearly: "Finally, all *of you be* of one mind, having compassion for one another; love as brothers, *be* tenderhearted, *be* courteous; not returning evil for evil or reviling for reviling, but on the contrary blessing, knowing that you were called to this, that you may inherit a blessing. For 'He who would love life And see good days, Let him refrain his tongue from evil, And his lips from speaking deceit. Let him turn away from evil and do good; Let him seek peace and pursue it. For the eyes of the LORD *are* on the righteous, And His ears *are open* to their prayers; But the face of the LORD *is* against those who do evil.' " (1 Pet. 3:8–12).

"For bodily exercise profits a little, but godliness is profitable for all things, having promise of the life that now is and of that which is to come" (1 Tim. 4:8). Notice godliness brings benefits in this life. These benefits are not to be limited to spiritual matters: "Godliness is profitable for all things." The believer can enjoy His blessing on the totality of daily life and all that concerns him. This is beautifully expressed in the prayer of John for Gaius, "Beloved, I pray that you may prosper in all things and be in health, just as your soul prospers" (3 John 1:2). John prays that to the degree that Gaius's soul is prospering, that is to the degree that he is walking aright with and before God, that God will match that prosperity in his spiritual walk with prosperity in all temporal matters of his life and in his personal health. Believers miss out in these things if they not obedient.

It may be objected that frequently it is the wicked who prosper, and the righteous often "had trial of mockings and scourgings, yes, and of chains and imprisonment. They were stoned, they were sawn in two, were tempted, were slain with the sword. They wandered about in sheepskins and goatskins, being destitute, afflicted, tormented – of whom the world was not worthy. They wandered in deserts and mountains, *in* dens and caves of the earth" (Heb. 11:36–38). These facts are manifestly true. But the following truths reveal that there is no real disharmony with the assertion that obedience brings blessings.

1. The prosperity of the wicked makes it impossible for them to receive eternal life

"Then Jesus looked around and said to His disciples, 'How hard it is for those who have riches to enter the kingdom of God!' And the disciples were astonished at His words. But Jesus answered again and said to them, 'Children, how hard it is for those who trust in riches to enter the kingdom of God! It is easier for a camel to go through the eye of a needle than for a rich man to enter the kingdom of God.' And they were greatly astonished, saying among themselves, 'Who then can be saved?' But Jesus looked at them and said, 'With men *it is* impossible, but not with God; for with God all things are possible'" (Mark 10:23–27). Jesus states that riches will always prevent a person from becoming a Christian unless God intervenes. Riches therefore are not an unmixed blessing. Without the grace of God they will destroy the soul eternally in hell!

2. *The Christian who suffers loss in this life receives back in this life more than he loses*

Jesus Himself taught this: "Then Peter began to say to Him, 'See, we have left all and followed You.' So Jesus answered and said, 'Assuredly, I say to you, there is no one who has left house or brothers or sisters or father or mother or wife or children or lands, for My sake and the gospel's, who shall not receive a hundredfold now in this time – houses and brothers and sisters and mothers and children and lands, with persecutions – and in the age to come, eternal life'" (Mark 10:28–30). In Luke's gospel "a hundredfold" is stated to be "many times more." Believers belong to the family of God. In Christ they have spiritual fathers (1 Cor. 4:15), spiritual mothers (Rom. 16:13), spiritual brothers (Heb. 13:22), spiritual sisters (Rom. 16:1), and spiritual children through the gospel (Philemon 10). Separation from natural family relatives in the service of Christ is more than compensated for by new bonds of pure love and fellowship of the Spirit with others in the family of God. This is so real and precious. It is an experience known only to the children of God. It breaks through barriers of culture, race, financial differences and social status, and throws open many houses of believers to those who forsake their home for the service of Christ. The bonds with other believers are so strong in God that believers often share with other believers the produce of their "lands." Thus some believers receive income from the occupations and possessions of others. This income is so wonderful in the way God moves His people to give that it compensates many times over for the income lost in leaving home and occupation for His sake and the gospel. Paul rejoiced greatly when the Church at Philippi gave to him. His joy was not simply on account of meeting his need and caring for him; but because it was the fruit of their faith, and it abounded to their account before God, "a sweet-smelling aroma, an acceptable sacrifice, well pleasing to

God" (Phil. 4:17–18). He was thrilled to see this expression of the grace of God in their lives.

Someone will object that the servants of Christ sometimes suffer hunger and poverty in the service of their Master. Yes they do. Paul wrote of hunger and thirst (2 Cor. 11:27) as his experience in fulfilling God's will. He also wrote, "I know how to be abased, and I know how to abound. Everywhere and in all things I have learned both to be full and to be hungry, both to abound and to suffer need. I can do all things through Christ who strengthens me" (Phil. 4:12–13). Even in poverty there was an experience of Christ giving supernatural strength. Such experience is exceedingly precious.

But does not Jesus say that in addition to these compensations for loss of home, relatives and income there will be persecutions? Yes He does. But persecutions are in reality a blessing in this life because they result in a fuller knowledge of Christ through the fellowship of Christ's sufferings. For Paul nothing could compare in value to knowing Christ, "Yet indeed I also count all things loss for the excellence of the knowledge of Christ Jesus my Lord, for whom I have suffered the loss of all things, and count them as rubbish, that I may gain Christ and be found in Him, not having my own righteousness, which *is* from the law, but that which *is* through faith in Christ, the righteousness which is from God by faith that I may know Him and the power of His resurrection, and the fellowship of His sufferings, being conformed to His death" (Phil. 3:8–10). Through persecutions Paul came to know Christ in the fellowship of His sufferings. That was a precious blessing to him. It is to all true Christians.

Persecutions are also a blessing in this life because they result in a greater experience of God. Paul wrote, "Blessed *be* the God and Father of our Lord Jesus Christ, the Father of mercies and God of all comfort who comforts us in all our tribulation, that we may be able to comfort those who are in any trouble, with the comfort with which we ourselves are comforted by God. For as the sufferings of Christ abound in us, so our consolation also abounds through Christ" (2 Cor. 1:3–5). Paul said that God had ministered to him during persecution in so wonderful a way that he had come to know Him experimentally as the Father of mercies, as the One who saw, pitied and acted in response to his condition. He had also come to know Him experimentally as the God of all comfort. This knowledge of God had come only because of, and in proportion to, his sufferings in the service of God. Paul was blessed not only in his increase of the knowledge of God, but also because this experience enabled him to minister comfort to other Christians, and so enable them to endure their sufferings (2 Cor. 1:4–6). Persecution enlarged his ministry to other believers.

Paul gave another reason to reckon persecutions a blessing. In his second letter to the Corinthian church he said, "And He said to me, 'My grace is sufficient for you, for My strength is made perfect in weakness.' Therefore most gladly I will rather boast in my infirmities, that the power of Christ may rest upon me. Therefore I take pleasure in infirmities, in reproaches, in needs, in persecutions, in distresses, for Christ's sake. For when I am weak, then I am strong" (2 Cor. 12:9–10). The apostle took pleasure in persecutions because in that situation of weakness he experienced the power of Christ.

There is yet another specific reason given in scripture for accounting persecutions a blessing: "And not only this, but we also exult in our tribulations, knowing that tribulation brings about perseverance; and perseverance, proven character; and proven character, hope" (Rom. 5:3–4 NASB). The testing of faith in persecutions results in stead-fastness which produces proven character. That, in turn leads to a strengthening of hope in the Christian. He is more confident of the glorious future which God has determined for His children. For these reasons Paul says believers are glad when they suffer persecutions. They know that they will produce these blessings.

The Acts of the Apostles records that the apostles were persecuted for preaching Christ, and they were beaten. Their reaction was to con-sider it a blessing. They rejoiced that they were counted worthy to suffer shame for His name (Acts 5:41). Paul tells the Christians at Philippi that they have been granted a gracious privilege to suffer for Christ (Phil. 1:29). Similarly Peter writes to persecuted Christians, "If you are reproached for the name of Christ, blessed *are you*, for the Spirit of glory and of God rests upon you. On their part He is blasphemed, but on your part He is glorified" (1 Pet. 4:14). Peter says that Christians are blessed in persecution because the Spirit of glory and of God rests upon them. We have an example of this when Paul and Barnabas were persecuted for preaching at Antioch in Phrygia. They were expelled from that region. Were the disciples at Antioch downcast and demor-alised by the expulsion? Far from it, "they were filled with joy and with the Holy Spirit" (Acts 13:52).

Persecutions therefore are a great blessing to Christians in this life. They also result in great blessing in the life to come. Jesus taught, "Blessed are those who are persecuted for righteousness' sake, For theirs is the kingdom of heaven. Blessed are you when they revile and persecute you, and say all kinds of evil against you falsely for My sake. Rejoice and be exceedingly glad, for great *is* your reward in heaven, for so they persecuted the prophets who were before you" (Mat. 5:10–12). This leads us to the next consideration.

Loss of rewards at the final judgment

Sinning will result in loss of rewards at the final judgment. Treatment of this truth anticipates future chapters. Therefore it will suffice to say at this point that all believers will have to give account of their use of their time and talents at that final judgment seat of Christ. If they have failed to serve as they should there will be a loss of reward, but not of salvation (1 Cor. 3:15).

So we see that sinful conduct after a believer is justified has very serious consequences:

1. Reaping the harvest of sinful behaviour.
2. God's chastisement.
3. Loss of usefulness to God.
4. Loss of blessing.
5. Loss of rewards.

I have dealt with this matter at length because generally the grave consequences of waywardness are not known. It is thought simply that God is willing to forgive. This ignorance is evident in the absence of a fear of God. The New Testament speaks of this fear as an essential part of Christian living. It characterised the first Christians:

> "Then fear came upon every soul, and many wonders and signs were done through the apostles" (Acts 2:43); and, "Then the churches throughout all Judea, Galilee, and Samaria had peace and were edified. And walking in the fear of the Lord and in the comfort of the Holy Spirit, they were multiplied" (Acts 9:31).

This fear of God was enjoined upon them:

> "Therefore, having these promises, beloved, let us cleanse ourselves from all filthiness of the flesh and spirit, perfecting holiness in the fear of God" (2 Cor. 7:1).

> "Therefore, my beloved, as you have always obeyed, not as in my presence only, but now much more in my absence, work out your own salvation with fear and trembling" (Phil. 2:12).

> "Therefore, since we are receiving a kingdom which cannot be shaken, let us have grace, by which we may serve God acceptably

with reverence and godly fear. For our God *is* a consuming fire" (Heb. 12:28–29).

"And if you call on the Father, who without partiality judges according to each one's work, conduct yourselves throughout the time of your stay *here* in fear" (1 Pet. 1:17).

"submitting to one another in the fear of God. Wives, submit to your own husbands, as to the Lord . . . . Children, obey your parents in the Lord, for this is right . . . . Bondservants, be obedient to those who are your masters according to the flesh, with fear and trembling, in sincerity of heart, as to Christ not with eyeservice, as men-pleasers, but as bondservants of Christ, doing the will of God from the heart, with goodwill doing service, as to the Lord, and not to men, knowing that whatever good anyone does, he will receive the same from the Lord, whether *he is* a slave or free" (Eph. 5:21–22, 6:1 and 6:5–8).

CHAPTER TWENTY

OBJECTIONS TO THE DOCTRINE OF JUSTIFICATION BY FAITH

Several objections are raised in opposition to justification by faith.

Such a legal transaction excludes grace

The meeting of all the law's demands by the obedience and death of Christ was the grace of God in action to bring salvation.

Justification by faith is really a legal fiction

It is true that the believer is an ungodly sinner, but it is also true that in God's sight believers are clothed in the righteousness of Christ. Given that imputed righteousness they are truly righteous before God.

Such teaching leads to sin because it requires no works of righteousness of one's own to be right with God

This is not true for many reasons.

a) True saving faith that appropriates the righteousness of Christ for justification is always accompanied with repentance, which is a turning from sin.
b) Those who receive justification are profoundly grateful to God. They love Him because He first loved them. They are moved by love to obey Him.
c) God fulfils His New Covenant and puts His laws in their mind and writes them on their hearts.
d) They are set free from sin, and His divine power has given them all things that pertain to life and godliness.

Consequently true faith is always demonstrated by works. If there are no works following profession of salvation through faith then in reality there is no true faith, just as James asserts: "Thus also faith by itself, if it does not have works, is dead" (James 2:17). James goes on to point out that Abraham proved that he had true faith by his work of offering

Isaac his son on the altar. Thus James argues, "You see then that a man is justified by works, and not by faith only" (James 2:24). James is addressing a different matter to Paul. He is attacking empty profession of faith. He is not saying in contradiction of Paul that justification is by works. In the previous verse James quoted Genesis 15:6 "Abraham believed God and it was accounted to him for righteousness." These words recorded his justification by faith long before he offered Isaac (Gen. 22:9). James is saying that true faith, distinct from mere profession, is seen in works. Works always flow from true faith. So in that sense justification is by faith and works. The justified man shows his true faith by works. His use of the word faith is different to Paul's. James means simply profession of faith. Paul means true saving faith when he speaks of justification by faith. Therefore both are in total harmony. They both state in different ways that a man or woman is only justified by true faith.

- Paul – Justification by true faith.
- James – Justification by profession of faith plus works which prove it to be true faith. No justification by profession of faith alone without accompanying works, because such faith is not true faith. It is empty and worthless (James 2:19).

This brings us to a further objection:

The final judgment is according to works

It is absolutely true that this will be a judgment of works (Mat. 12:36–37; 16:27; 25:31–46; John 5:29; Rom. 2:5–10; 14:10–12; 2 Cor. 5:10; Rev. 20:11–15). The key to understanding these verses aright, and seeing that they are in perfect harmony with the scriptures which teach justification by faith, is the fact that true faith always results in works. Christ, the Judge of all, on that day, will see true believers revealed by their works. Their works will be the evidence of faith. They will enter heaven not on the merit of their works, but on the merit of Christ's righteousness given to them through faith.

The Roman Catholic gospel of justification

Roman Catholicism teaches that justification is by means of an infused righteousness, not an imputed righteousness. This infused righteousness is a state of grace by which a person becomes actually just before God. It is to be made righteous. It is a righteousness put within a person changing them internally. On that basis God declares the person justified. This personal state of grace, a state of righteousness, is attained through sacraments and obedience to the ten commandments and the precepts of Roman Catholicism. The process starts with the sacrament of baptism. This is said to bring about the new birth, the forgiveness of sins and membership of the Body of Christ. From then on this state of grace is maintained by means of sacraments, and obedience to the ten commandments and the precepts of Roman Catholicism. The sacraments in addition to baptism are:

- Confirmation – through which baptismal grace is increased and deepened.
- The Mass – by which Christ is offered for the living or the dead to make satisfaction for sins and to obtain other graces and blessings.
- Penance – by it sins committed after baptism are forgiven through confession and absolution of the priest bringing reconciliation with God and the Church.
- Anointing of the Sick – for the seriously ill. Through this sacrament grace is given and forgiveness of sins when the person is unable to receive penance.
- Matrimony – through which grace is received to live in the married state.
- Holy Orders – by which grace is given to serve as bishops, priests and deacons.

The precepts of Roman Catholicism concern attendance at Mass, confession of sins, reception of Holy Communion, fasting and abstinence and contribution to the material needs of the Church.

The grace of justification therefore can be increased by good works according to this gospel. Equally it can be lost if mortal sin is committed. A distinction is made between sins. Some are venial; some are mortal. The former weaken the grace and love of God in the soul. The latter destroy the grace of God in the soul. Therefore if a mortal sin is committed the state of justification is lost, and the right to heaven is lost. The state of grace can be regained through the sacrament of penance or the sacrament of anointing the sick.

According to Roman Catholicism the eternal punishment of sin is remitted through the sacrament of penance. But there is also a temporal punishment for sin. That punishment may be here on earth or after death in purgatory. Sin can be atoned for and the temporal punishment removed in a variety of ways – prayers, fasting, acts of mercy, suffering, service to others, the denial of one's own needs, indulgences etc. Indulgences are partial or plenary giving partial or full remission of the temporal punishment of sin. They can be applied to souls in purgatory.

The sacraments are essential for the state of grace. There are conditions which have to be fulfilled however, in order for a sacrament to be valid and efficacious. One of these is that the minister must have the intention at least of doing what the Church does. As Cardinal Bellarmine, the personal theologian of the Pope at the time of the Reformation, said, "No one can be certain with the certainty of faith that he has a true sacrament, since the sacrament is not formed without the intention of the minister, and no one can see the intention of another."[1] Potentially this destroys the justification of a Roman Catholic. The priest may fail to minister the necessary grace of God in the sacrament; and this failure will not be apparent.

This alternative way of justification requires a church, sacraments, a special priesthood and works in addition to Christ. The true gospel proclaims that only faith in Christ is needed to be justified. The Holy Spirit moved Paul to write concerning those who distorted the gospel in this way, "But even if we, or an angel from heaven, preach any other gospel to you than what we have preached to you, let him be accursed. As we have said before, so now I say again, if anyone preaches any other gospel to you than what you have received, let him be accursed" (Gal. 1:8). These words are a most solemn condemnation. Make no mistake they apply to the teaching of Roman Catholicism as stated above.

This other gospel of justification presents a Christ whose work for man's salvation is inadequate. A special priesthood and sacraments and man's good works are also essential in Roman Catholicism to remit sins and to be justified. The whole system tears down the work of Christ to reconcile God and man. It overthrows His glorious all sufficient work of redemption. Professing to be Christianity, it is in fact an enemy of Christ. It is counterfeit Christianity inspired by Satan to destroy eternally the souls of men and women.

Reference

1. Tom, 1, p.488, prag. 1721, quoted by H.M. Carson, *Dawn or twilight*, IVP Revised edition 1976.

CHAPTER TWENTY ONE

FAITH AND ASSURANCE OF SALVATION (1)

We must now address the relationship between faith and assurance of salvation.

Assurance the essence of the initial act of faith which receives salvation

This is so because:

1. The one coming to Christ with saving faith comes with a total conviction that the gospel message is absolutely true
Saving faith is belief with all one's heart in Christ's words and His work for man's salvation. There is no doubt about Christ's power to save. The initial act of saving faith is an act of full assurance that the gospel is truth. There are two reasons for this total conviction that the gospel is absolutely true. Firstly, the one coming for salvation, drawn by the Father, has come to a state of willingness to do God's will. The drawing of the Father brings about a desire to do the will of God. Jesus said that when that willingness exists then that person knows assuredly that Christ's teaching is from God. Jesus said, "If anyone wants to do His will, he shall know concerning the doctrine, whether it is from God or *whether* I speak on My own *authority*" (John 7:17).

Secondly, anyone coming to Christ for salvation has heard and learned of the Father (John 6:45). Consequently they are fully persuaded that what they have heard and learned is true. That persuasion is more than the influence of truth on the mind and conscience. Such influence can be very strong, and can produce considerable results. When Paul spoke to Felix, governor of Judea A.D. 52–60, the great man was afraid: "Now as he reasoned about righteousness, self-control, and the judgment to come, Felix was afraid and answered, 'Go away for now; when I have a convenient time I will call for you'" (Acts 24:25). When saving faith is exercised there is a personal teaching by

141

God in addition to the impact of the truth of the gospel. The one drawn of the Father hears the gospel, and in contrast to others also hears and learns from God. This teaching of the Father does not add to the content of the message, but He causes it to be really heard, understood and heeded voluntarily. This hearing and learning of the Father causes full assurance in the initial act of saving faith that the gospel is true.

2.   *The gospel message promises a complete salvation to those who obey it. It declares justification once and for all for the believer*

Through the imputed righteousness of Christ there is no condemnation before God as Judge, and no separation ever from His love. By the one offering of Christ for sin He has perfected believers forever (Heb. 10:14). They are "in Christ". They are permanently in a right relationship with God. They have been set apart to God, and for God, through the offering of the body of Christ once for all (Heb. 10:10). They receive the gift of eternal life, and the gifts and callings of God are irrevocable (Rom. 11:29). He does not give eternal life to anyone and then take it away. He does not call anyone into the kingdom and later cast them out. As Jesus said, "All that the Father gives Me will come to Me, and the one who comes to Me I will by no means cast out. For I have come down from heaven, not to do My own will, but the will of Him who sent Me. This is the will of the Father who sent Me, that of all He has given Me I should lose nothing, but should raise it up at the last day. And this is the will of Him who sent Me, that everyone who sees the Son and believes in Him may have everlasting life; and I will raise him up at the last day" (John 6:37–40). Those who are called by the Father into the kingdom are ones given by the Father to Christ. The Father's will is that Jesus should lose not a single one of them. Jesus will not fail to carry out His Father's command. He said, "My sheep hear My voice, and I know them, and they follow Me. And I give them eternal life, and they shall never perish; neither shall anyone snatch them out of My hand. My Father, who has given *them* to Me, is greater than all; and no one is able to snatch *them* out of My Father's hand" (John 10:27–29). These are the absolute promises Jesus gives in the glorious gospel message. He has done, and will do everything necessary to secure the believer's salvation. This gospel therefore is a message which gives full assurance of salvation to the believer. These great truths cannot be believed without producing full assurance of a right relationship with God for time and eternity. The writer to the Hebrews speaks of this "full assurance of faith" (Heb. 10:22).

Assurance from the experience of conversion which results from repentance and faith

1.   When a person is converted there is an experience of knowing God and the blessings flowing from His love
The convert experiences the fulfilment of the New Covenant brought in through Christ. The New Covenant is stated in Heb. 8:11–12, "None of them shall teach his neighbor, and none his brother, saying, 'Know the LORD,' for all shall know Me, from the least of them to the greatest of them. For I will be merciful to their unrighteousness, and their sins and their lawless deeds I will remember no more." The impact of this new fellowship with God varies from person to person. But there is always a conscious experience of salvation. This is affirmed by Peter when he wrote his first letter. He said to the new converts to Christ, "desire the pure milk of the word that you may grow thereby if indeed you have tasted that the Lord is gracious" (1 Pet. 2:3). Tasting is a vivid sensation. At the time of their new birth they experienced the mercy and goodness of God in such a way that it was memorable in every case. So he reminds them of that first experience of God. There was a wonderful consciousness of forgiveness and coming into a right relationship with God, and of the experience of His blessing. At that time they came to know God, and became conscious of being related to God as children in His family. There was for the first time an awareness of the Heavenly Father's love. Their spirits witnessed to them that they were His children.

2.   Conversion brings about a union with God
It is a union with the Father, and with the Son and with the Holy Spirit as stated in the following verses:

> "Paul, Silvanus, and Timothy, 'To the church of the Thessalonians in God the Father and the Lord Jesus Christ: Grace to you and peace from God our Father and the Lord Jesus Christ'" (1 Thess. 1:1). Christians are " in God the Father."

> They are also "in Christ" (Phil. 1:1).

> And they are "in the Spirit" (Rom. 8:9).

This union means that each Person of the Trinity indwells the believer. Eph. 2:22 tells us that God the Father indwells, Christ indwells (Col. 1:27 and Rom. 8:10) and the Holy Spirit also indwells (Rom. 8:9). There is conscious fellowship with the Father, the Son and the Holy Spirit (1 John 1:3 and 2 Cor. 13:14). This fellowship with the Father and the Son was promised to disciples by Jesus. He said, "If anyone loves Me, he will keep My word; and My Father will love him, and We will come to him and make Our home with him" (John 14:23). He also promised that the Holy Spirit would be Another Comforter strengthening, aiding, and encouraging just as Jesus ministered in these ways to His disciples while He was on earth. The union with Christ is profound and powerful: "But he who is joined to the Lord is one spirit *with Him*" (1 Cor. 6:17). He likens the union between a believer and Christ to the union of marriage, "The two become one flesh." John speaks of it as a vine and the branches. He reveals the power of Christ given to believers by that union. It enables them to bear "much fruit" (John 15:1–8).

It is a sheer impossibility for anyone to begin to partake of these amazing blessings which always come when the gospel is obeyed, and not to be conscious of a wonderful closeness to God hitherto unknown. From such experience comes an assurance of salvation and being His.

3.   Conversion causes a changed relationship with unbelievers

When a person receives salvation there is an experience of a great change of one's relationship to non-Christians. God separates those He calls from the rest of mankind. They are no longer of the world, mankind living separated from God and in enmity against Him. They become conscious of being fundamentally different to unbelievers. They perceive a real difference in the way they relate to non-Christians. There is a fundamental disharmony. The unbeliever is determined to exclude God from his life. The believer has come to know that closeness to God is the most precious experience on earth. The unbeliever walks through life motivated by fallen human nature, driven by desires of the mind and of the flesh perverted through sin. The believer is now set free from the power of sin and moved by the Holy Spirit to live in obedience to God. The unbeliever is ruled over by the prince of the power of the air, who powerfully works in him so that he fulfils his desire. The believer at the moment of saving faith is delivered from the power of darkness and transferred into the kingdom of the Son of God's love. So the believer and non-believer belong to two different and opposing kingdoms. This is what Jesus meant when He said, "Do not think that I came to bring peace on earth. I did not come to bring peace but a sword. For I have come to 'set a man against his father, a daughter against her mother, and a daughter-in-law against her mother-in-law'; and 'a man's enemies will be those of his *own* household.' He who loves father or mother more than Me is not worthy of

Me. And he who loves son or daughter more than Me is not worthy of Me" (Mat. 10:34–37). Jesus stated that the unbeliever hates the believer, because God chooses him out of the world. He told His disciples, "If you were of the world, the world would love its own. Yet because you are not of the world, but I chose you out of the world, therefore the world hates you" (John 15:19). The new convert therefore frequently experiences the same treatment from relatives and friends about which Peter wrote. He said, "Therefore, since Christ suffered for us in the flesh, arm yourselves also with the same mind, for he who has suffered in the flesh has ceased from sin, that he no longer should live the rest of *his* time in the flesh for the lusts of men, but for the will of God. For we *have spent* enough of our past lifetime in doing the will of the Gentiles – when we walked in lewdness, lusts, drunkenness, revelries, drinking parties, and abominable idolatries. In regard to these, they think it strange that you do not run with *them* in the same flood of dissipation, speaking evil of *you*. They will give an account to Him who is ready to judge the living and the dead" (1 Pet. 4:1–5). The true Christian experiences pressure from the world to do as they do rather than to be holy as God is holy. The true Christian identifies with these truths. This incompatibility with non-Christian relatives and friends does not always result in persecution or total breakdown of those relationships, but there is a definite discord. The believer stands back and looks at his experience of a changed relationship with unbelievers, and knows that the explanation of that change is entering God's kingdom. In this way he is assured that he is truly saved.

FAITH AND ASSURANCE OF SALVATION (2): THE SEALING OF THE SPIRIT

In addition to the assurance stated above the convert can have a further experience which also gives assurance of salvation both present and future.

Assurance by the sealing of the Spirit

The sealing of the Spirit is a conscious experience of being baptized in the Spirit after conversion. It is distinct from the new birth. It should follow conversion without delay. This experience of the baptism in the Spirit will be treated in depth in later sections. At this stage the relationship with assurance is our focus. A seal is a mark of authentication. A seal of wax on a letter or document certifies its author and contents. In the same way the sealing of the Spirit certifies that a believer truly is the Lord's. It gives assurance to the believer that he is among those who are His. The seal also speaks of security. Thus the sealing of the believer declares his security. New Testament verses which refer to the baptism in the Spirit as the sealing of believers are:

> "In Him you also *trusted*, after you heard the word of truth, the gospel of your salvation; in whom also, having believed, you were sealed with the Holy Spirit of promise, who is the guarantee of our inheritance until the redemption of the purchased possession, to the praise of His glory" (Eph. 1:13–14).

> "And do not grieve the Holy Spirit of God, by whom you were sealed for the day of redemption" (Eph. 4:30).

> "Now He who establishes us with you in Christ and has anointed us *is* God, who also has sealed us and given us the Spirit in our hearts as a guarantee" (2 Cor. 1:21–22).

In these verses Paul is writing to Christians. He says that they were sealed with the Holy Spirit of promise. This took place after they had believed. The Greek participle translated "having believed" (Eph. 1:13) is an aorist indicating a single completed action. It can express antecedent action. The AV captures the meaning: "in whom also after that ye believed, ye were sealed with the Holy Spirit of promise." The sealing followed faith in the gospel. It is most likely that some, if not all of the twelve he ministered to recorded in Acts 19:1–6, received this epistle. They had believed and been baptized following their faith in Christ (Acts 19:1–5). Acts 19:6 narrates their subsequent sealing with the Holy Spirit of promise: "And when Paul had laid hands on them, the Holy Spirit came upon them, and they spoke with tongues and prophesied." Notice how the Spirit is designated in Eph. 1:13, "the Holy Spirit of promise", recalling the promise of the Father through Joel (Acts 2:17–18). As stated previously, the baptism in the Spirit is the promise of the Father (Acts 1:5 and 2:16–18), and is for every believer (Acts 2:39). It is a conscious and glorious experience of the presence and power of the Holy Spirit. The words of scripture speaking of it reveal the greatness of the baptism in the Spirit:

- The anointing (1 John 2:20).
- The Spirit coming upon (Acts 19:6)
- The Spirit falling upon (Acts 8:16 and 10:44)
- The pouring out of the Spirit abundantly (Tit. 3:5–6)
- A being made to drink of the Spirit (1 Cor. 12:13).
- A being filled with the Spirit (Acts 2:4).
- A pouring out of the Spirit inspiring prophecy (Acts 2:17–18).

All these terms denote a definite event that blesses the believer with an unforgettable experience of the presence and power of the Spirit. That experience gives the believer a profound sense of God's acceptance and strong assurance of salvation.

This sealing is defined as the "guarantee" of the Christian's inheritance. The inheritance is the glorious future state of the Christian in heaven. Then the believer will have a new spiritual body conformed to Christ's, and there will be a new heavens and a new earth wherein will dwell righteousness. The Greek word translated "guarantee" is ἀρραβών which means a deposit which in itself is a guarantee of full payment later. The guarantee is the first instalment of that future bliss. It is called the "firstfruits of the Spirit" (Rom. 8:23). The present experience is the same in kind as will be experienced in the age to come, just as the firstfruits are the same as the final harvest. It is a foretaste and a sure pledge of the blessing in the future. It is the absolute guarantee that there will be a wonderful fulfilment of the hope of the Christian. The Christian will be kept for the day of redemption, the final consummation.

This same truth is taught in Rom. 5:3–5, "And not only *that*, but we also glory in tribulations, knowing that tribulation produces perseverance; and perseverance, character; and character, hope. Now hope does not disappoint, because the love of God has been poured out in our hearts by the Holy Spirit who was given to us." Paul refers to the experience of the sealing of the Spirit, "the Holy Spirit who was given to us." He asserts that the hope of the Christian is developed and strengthened through tribulation. There is a process. Tribulation produces perseverance, which in turn produces character, and which in turn produces hope. Then he gives a reason why that hope will not lead to disappointment. It is because the love of God has been poured in their hearts by the Holy Spirit Who was given to them. It is because of the sealing of the Spirit. The tenses of the verbs are significant. The verb "was given" is an aorist participle indicating a single decisive act. It refers to the specific time in the past when each believer received the promise of the Father, the gift of the Spirit. The verb "has been poured out" is in the perfect tense denoting a continuing state after a past action. It was a single event of sealing, and an abiding foretaste and guarantee of the future inheritance. Therefore their hope will not disappoint. The experience is defined as a pouring into the heart of the love of God. The love of God for His children is experienced powerfully and vividly. Other verses of Paul speaking of this experience of sealing illuminate his meaning. In the same letter he said, "For you did not receive the spirit of bondage again to fear, but you received the Spirit of adoption by whom we cry out, 'Abba, Father.' The Spirit Himself bears witness with our spirit that we are children of God" (Rom. 8:15–16). This receiving of the Spirit is the single event of sealing. The convert before this sealing has a witness in his own spirit that he is a son of God. Through the sealing of the Spirit there is added another witness, the Spirit Himself. The Spirit witnesses with the believer's spirit that he is a child of God. The experience of God's love at the sealing of the Spirit creates in the child of God the love and confidence to cry out "Abba Father." Therefore the Spirit is called here "the Spirit of adoption." It is not by receiving the Spirit of adoption that the Christian is adopted and becomes a son of God. He has already been adopted by the Father at conversion. As Paul says to the Galatians, "And because you are sons, God has sent forth the Spirit of His Son into your hearts, crying out, 'Abba, Father!'" (Gal. 4:6). The verb cry out expresses extremely strong feeling. It is fervent, earnest, importunate, intense expression. The sense of God's love is so great it causes the believer to cry out in this intense way 'Abba Father.' These words speak of love and intimacy, of a consciousness of relationship and of absolute confidence of acceptance. These verses reveal the impact and abiding result of experiencing the love of God when receiving the promise of the Father, the sealing of the Spirit.

The Holy Spirit witnesses with the believer's spirit that he is a child of God. It is an immediate witness of God by the Spirit. He does not speak in an audible voice, but there is an experience of His presence as a glorious reality. It gives absolute certainty to the believer that he is His. It is distinct from assurance gained by testing one's life before the scriptures, and distinct from assurance from the words and promises of scripture.

As stated previously, at the time of conversion the believer is conscious of being in a new relationship with God. Conversion is a wonderful experience of coming to know God. The believer is His child and is adopted into His family. Having become His child the believer's own spirit witnesses to the fact. Afterwards by the sealing of the Spirit God gives an additional witness, the witness of the Spirit. The Spirit witnesses along with the believer's spirit that he is a child of God. It is not the Spirit witnessing to the believer's spirit, but with the believer's spirit. It gives wonderful and strong assurance. It is a stronger assurance than the full assurance of faith in the gospel. It is stronger than the assurance of the believer's own spirit gained from the experience of conversion. It is stronger because the love of God is felt in a greater degree. This twofold witness is a divine pattern seen throughout God's dealings with mankind.

> "Whoever is deserving of death shall be put to death on the testimony of two or three witnesses; he shall not be put to death on the testimony of one witness" (Deut. 17:6).

> "Moreover if your brother sins against you, go and tell him his fault between you and him alone. If he hears you, you have gained your brother. But if he will not hear, take with you one or two more, that 'by the mouth of two or three witnesses every word may be established.' And if he refuses to hear them, tell *it* to the church. But if he refuses even to hear the church, let him be to you like a heathen and a tax collector" (Mat. 18:15–17).

> "This *will be* the third *time* I am coming to you. 'By the mouth of two or three witnesses every word shall be established' " (2 Cor. 13:1).

"Do not receive an accusation against an elder except from two or three witnesses" (1 Tim. 5:19).

"Anyone who has rejected Moses' law dies without mercy on the testimony of two or three witnesses" (Heb. 10:28).

Even Jesus had three witnesses – John the Baptist, the works He did and the Father.

"But I have a greater witness than John's; for the works which the Father has given Me to finish – the very works that I do – bear witness of Me, that the Father has sent Me. And the Father Himself, who sent Me, has testified of Me" (John 5:36–37).

There is another aspect of this truth of the sealing of the Spirit. It is that the sealing authenticates converts as true believers. In the early years of the church we see that the sealing of the Spirit was decisive in the development of the church. It proved to Jewish Christians, despite their exceedingly strong prejudice, that Gentiles must be accepted into the church. The record of the significance of the sealing of the Spirit is given in detail in Acts 10. Peter was led by God in a dramatic manner to go to a Gentile named Cornelius and his household of Gentiles who had come to believe in the God of Israel, and who had embraced the revelation of God given in the Old Testament scriptures. Cornelius and his household loved and feared God. He gave alms generously to the people, and prayed to God always. He knew God just as the Old Testament Jewish believers did. He was accepted by God just as they were (Acts 10:35). He had been cleansed from sin (Acts 10:15–16) just as they were (Psa. 32:1–2). However, not being a proselyte to the Jewish faith, in the sense of submitting to circumcision and baptism, the Jews regarded him and his household as ritually unclean Gentiles. Irina Levinskaya states that Cornelius was an idolater. She asserts that he participated in the official cult of offerings to the pagan gods because of his official position as a centurion in the Cohors Italica.[1] Such participation is an assumption. It is not stated by Luke, and is inconsistent with the facts of his devotion to God, his fear of God and God's sending an angel to him (Acts 10:2–3). The problem for the Jews of going to his home to eat with him was purely his lack of circumcision (Acts 11:3). Otherwise he had "a good reputation among all the nation of the Jews" (Acts 10:22). The barrier is stated by Peter: "You know how unlawful it is for a Jewish man to keep company with or go to one of another nation. But God has shown me that I should not call any man common or unclean" (Acts 10:28).

Because of this long standing tradition and practice the Jewish Christians, and even the leading apostle Peter, could not grasp that the gospel had to be preached to uncircumcised Gentiles. They were so locked into their tradition of being God's chosen people that the crystal clear words of Jesus commanding the preaching of the gospel to all nations fell on blocked ears. It appears that for many years, possibly seven, the apostles and first Christians failed to obey Christ's command to preach the gospel to every creature. They did not go to the Gentiles. Even Peter needed a special visitation from God to remove his prejudice. He was given a vision and an audible voice from heaven. The vision and voice were given no less than three times. Peter's ears needed a lot of unblocking! His fellow Jewish Christians had the same ear blockage. During the years after the Pentecost of Acts 2 there is only one recorded instance of the gospel being taken to a Gentile, the Ethiopian eunuch. On that occasion very special and extraordinary directions were given by God to Philip. He received remarkable instruction first from an angel of the Lord speaking to him, and then from the Holy Spirit also speaking to him: "Now an angel of the Lord spoke to Philip, saying, 'Arise and go toward the south along the road which goes down from Jerusalem to Gaza.' This is desert. So he arose and went. And behold, a man of Ethiopia, a eunuch of great authority under Candace the queen of the Ethiopians, who had charge of all her treasury, and had come to Jerusalem to worship, was returning. And sitting in his chariot, he was reading Isaiah the prophet. Then the Spirit said to Philip, 'Go near and overtake this chariot' ... Then Philip opened his mouth, and beginning at this Scripture, preached Jesus to him" (Acts 8:26–29, 35).

So we read that when the gift of the Holy Spirit was poured out on Cornelius and his household as Peter preached to them, "those of the circumcision who believed were astonished, as many as came with Peter, because the gift of the Holy Spirit had been poured out on the Gentiles also" (Acts 10:45). They were staggered that Gentiles received the same gift as the Jewish believers (Acts 11:17), the Holy Spirit of promise (Acts 2:17–18). Peter's actions immediately following the outpouring are of the greatest significance: "Then Peter answered, 'Can anyone forbid water, that these should not be baptized who have received the Holy Spirit just as we *have*?' And he commanded them to be baptized in the name of the Lord" (Acts 10:47–48). That outpouring of the Spirit proved conclusively, even to the six Jewish believers (Acts 11:12), who were of the circumcision, that these Gentiles were truly the Lord's people, and must not be denied baptism. God had sealed them with the Holy Spirit. Thereby God acknowledged them as His, "So

God, who knows the heart, acknowledged them by giving them the Holy Spirit, just as *He did* to us" (Acts 15:8).

They did not request Peter to wait and see if the subsequent lives of these Gentiles verified their discipleship. The sealing of the Spirit was considered to be absolute proof that they were in the kingdom. Nothing more was needed. The natural reaction of the Jewish Christians was to forbid water baptism to such Gentiles who were uncircumcised. Now in view of the sealing of the Spirit it was unthinkable to refuse water baptism. The facts indicate that, without that sealing, they would have opposed the baptizing of Cornelius and his household, even if those Gentiles had affirmed their belief in Jesus as Saviour after Peter's message.

Afterwards we read, "Now the apostles and brethren who were in Judea heard that the Gentiles had also received the word of God. And when Peter came up to Jerusalem, those of the circumcision contended with him, saying, 'You went in to uncircumcised men and ate with them!'" (Acts 11:1–3). Peter explained his actions in detail (Acts 11:5–16). He concluded by stating that God had sealed Cornelius and his household saying, "Therefore if God gave to them the same gift as *He gave* to us also after believing in the Lord Jesus Christ, who was I that I could stand in God's way?" (Acts 11:17 NASB). Their response was unanimous, positive and unequivocal: "When they heard these things they became silent; and they glorified God, saying, 'Then God has also granted to the Gentiles repentance to life'" (Acts 11:18). They acknowledged that God had authenticated these Gentiles as His by sealing them with the Holy Spirit. Therefore they could not withstand God. From that point onwards in history there was no longer any question of the inclusion of Gentiles in the Church of Jesus Christ. God's sealing of Cornelius and his household settled the matter once and for all. This was an event of the greatest significance in the early years of the church.

Later we read of some Jewish Christians insisting on Gentiles being circumcised in order to be saved. The issue was not the inclusion of the Gentiles in the church of Jesus Christ. That was not in dispute. What was now in dispute were the conditions for entry. Were they repentance and faith, or repentance and faith plus circumcision? "Now the apostles and elders came together to consider this matter. And when there had been much dispute, Peter rose up and said to them: 'Men and brethren, you know that a good while ago God chose among us, that by my mouth the Gentiles should hear the word of the gospel and believe. So God, who knows the heart, acknowledged them by giving them the Holy Spirit, just as *He did* to us, and made no distinction between us and them, purifying their hearts by faith. Now therefore, why do you test God by putting a yoke on the neck of the disciples which neither our fathers nor we were able to bear?'" (Acts 15:6–10). Peter refers back to his going to Cornelius and his household. Significantly he argues that God "acknowledged them." God testified that they were truly His children. He did this without them being circumcised. He showed His acceptance of them by sealing them with the Holy Spirit of promise. Peter contended that if God so accepted these uncircumcised Gentiles then their insistence on circumcision was tantamount to trying God to see whether He would change His will, and whether He would inflict punishment upon them for requiring Gentiles to be circumcised in order to be saved. Peter's argument prevailed and the Council of Jerusalem declared to the Gentile Christians that they did not need to be circumcised. God's sealing of Cornelius and his household was decisive again in settling a matter of the greatest magnitude in the development of the church. These events demonstrate that the sealing of the Spirit certified to other believers beyond any question that that person was the Lord's.

There is another significant fact contained in the sealing of Cornelius and his household. Cornelius and those believing Gentiles were totally accepted as the Lord's by Peter and the six Jewish believers with him and later by other Jewish believers (Acts 11:18 and 15). That unreserved acceptance was most meaningful to the Gentiles. They had been used to partial acknowledgment. This new acceptance no doubt gave them assurance that they were indeed "fellow citizens with the saints and members of the household of God" (Eph. 2:19). In this way it assured them of their salvation. So we see in these events that the sealing of the Spirit proved to other sealed believers that the one sealed was truly the Lord's, and that the resulting acceptance of other believers brought further assurance to the sealed believer.

The baptism in the Spirit has been considered above from the limited perspective of assurance of present and future salvation. Consequently we have looked only at the New Testament verses which refer to the experience as a sealing. This sealing of the Spirit is an unforgettable event in which the believer is conscious of a powerful experience of the Holy Spirit. We shall see in later chapters that the scriptures define the baptism in the Spirit as a dramatic and vivid experience. The sealing of the Spirit gives a great assurance of present and future salvation to the believer.

References

1. Irina Levinskaya *The Book of Acts in its First Century Setting, Vol. 5,* Eerdmans and Paternoster 1996, page 121.

CHAPTER TWENTY THREE

FAITH AND ASSURANCE OF SALVATION (3): ASSURANCE BY EXAMINATION AND ADDITION

There are two further ways through which the believer can be assured of salvation.

Assurance by self-examination using the tests of the scriptures

There was an occasion when some sought to undermine Paul's apostolic authority to speak to the church at Corinth. Paul commanded the Corinthians to examine themselves as to whether they were in the faith (2 Cor. 13:5). He was sure of the outcome. He knew that their self-examination would testify that Christ was in them. Therefore they must admit that Christ spoke through Paul since they had been converted through his ministry. Their coming to faith proved conclusively that Christ spoke in Paul. Therefore let them cease to question his authority. Implicit in this incident is the fact that the true Christian can check his or her spiritual state by self-examination using the tests of the scriptures, and be assured thereby of being in the faith. This assurance from the scriptures of being in the faith is addressed in John's first epistle. It was written to Christians under attack by false teachers and false professors. He stated several tests to determine and confirm true profession:

1. *Walking in the light*
"If we say that we have fellowship with Him, and walk in darkness, we lie and do not practice the truth. But if we walk in the light as He is in the light, we have fellowship with one another, and the blood of Jesus Christ His Son cleanses us from all sin" (1 John 1:6–7). Walking in the light of God's word results in fellowship with other Christians and the confession of sins and cleansing from sin.

2. *Obedience to God's Commandments*
"Now by this we know that we know Him, if we keep His commandments. He who says, 'I know Him,' and does not keep

His commandments, is a liar, and the truth is not in him. But whoever keeps His word, truly the love of God is perfected in him. By this we know that we are in Him " (1 John 2:3–5).

3.   *Walking as He walked*
"He who says he abides in Him ought himself also to walk just as He walked" (1 John 2:6).

4.   *Loving those who are true believers*
"He who says he is in the light, and hates his brother, is in darkness until now. He who loves his brother abides in the light, and there is no cause for stumbling in him" (1 John 2:9–10).

"We know that we have passed from death to life, because we love the brethren. He who does not love *his* brother abides in death" (1 John 3:14).

5.   *Practising righteousness*
"Little children, let no one deceive you. He who practices righteousness is righteous, just as He is righteous. He who sins is of the devil, for the devil has sinned from the beginning. For this purpose the Son of God was manifested, that He might destroy the works of the devil. Whoever has been born of God does not sin, for His seed remains in him; and he cannot sin, because he has been born of God. In this the children of God and the children of the devil are manifest: Whoever does not practice righteousness is not of God, nor *is* he who does not love his brother " (1 John 3:7–10). Christians live righteous, but not perfect lives (1 John 1:7–10). Unbelievers and false professors do not live righteously. They turn to their own way.

6.   *Loving in deed and truth*
"But whoever has this world's goods, and sees his brother in need, and shuts up his heart from him, how does the love of God abide in him? My little children, let us not love in word or in tongue, but in deed and in truth. And by this we know that we are of the truth, and shall assure our hearts before Him. For if our heart condemns us, God is greater than our heart, and knows all things. Beloved, if our heart does not condemn us, we have confidence toward God" (1 John 3:17–21).

7.   *By the gift of the Spirit, the baptism in the Spirit*
"And by this we know that He abides in us, by the Spirit whom He has given us " (1 John 3:24).

8.   Confession that Jesus is the Son of God

"Whoever confesses that Jesus is the Son of God, God abides in him, and he in God" (1 John 4:15).

9.   Believing that Jesus is the Christ

"Whoever believes that Jesus is the Christ is born of God, and everyone who loves Him who begot also loves him who is begotten of Him" (1 John 5:1).

John gave these tests because their assurance was under attack from false teachers and false professors. These teachers and professors were seeking to lead them astray (1 John 3:26). It is important to realise that these tests were not given because it is normal for converts to lack assurance. The normal healthy Christian state is one of full assurance. Christians under attack from false teachers and false professors can, and often do, have their assurance undermined. When this occurs they need to apply the tests of John's first epistle to regain that full assurance.

Let us now look at another important means of being sure of salvation.

Assurance by diligent addition

The apostle Peter wrote a letter to Christians shortly before his death. He said, "But also for this very reason, giving all diligence, add to your faith virtue, to virtue knowledge, to knowledge self-control, to self-control perseverance, to perseverance godliness, to godliness brotherly kindness, and to brotherly kindness love. For if these things are yours and abound, *you will be* neither barren nor unfruitful in the knowledge of our Lord Jesus Christ. For he who lacks these things is shortsighted, even to blindness, and has forgotten that he was cleansed from his old sins. Therefore, brethren, be even more diligent to make your call and election sure, for if you do these things you will never stumble; for so an entrance will be supplied to you abundantly into the everlasting kingdom of our Lord and Savior Jesus Christ" (2 Pet. 1:5–11). Peter is saying that believers can be sure that God has called them and elected them into His kingdom by adding certain things to their lives. The verb "add" is drawn from Athenian drama. The word originally referred to the training and staging of the chorus paid for by a rich patron. Hence it came to mean to supply lavishly. All those who have come to true saving faith (2 Pet. 1:1) can be sure that they are called and chosen by God. Their assurance of salvation can be made firm by their diligent efforts. They are able to add to their faith "virtue, to virtue knowledge, to knowledge self-control, to self-control perseverance, to perseverance godliness, to godliness brotherly kindness, and to brotherly kindness love" (2 Pet. 1:5–7).

- Virtue is excellence in the sense of living in a manner befitting their profession of being Christians.
- Knowledge is understanding God's truth and also His will.
- Self-control means the ability to stop self from behaving contrary to God's will and to conform behaviour to God's word.
- Perseverance is literally "remaining under." It means continuing steadfast in spite of difficulties, discouragements, dangers and even the threat of death.
- Godliness is reverence for God and love for Him.
- Kindness must be exercised to other believers, and it must be genuine, "not in word or in tongue, but in deed and in truth" (1 John 3:18).
- Love. The Greek means that sort of love which seeks the good of the one to whom it is directed, and is prepared to act sacrificially for that person. It is not restricted to believers, but is to be exercised to all, even enemies.

Believers have no excuse for not adding these qualities to their faith because they have been given "all things that *pertain* to life and godliness" and exceedingly great and precious promises that through them they may be partakers of the divine nature (2 Pet. 1:3–4). Peter goes on to say that if they do have these additions abounding in their lives they will be fruitful. Also "they will never stumble." They will not backslide, and fall away from the faith. They will enter the everlasting kingdom of Jesus Christ. They can be assured that final salvation will surely be theirs. It is important to stress that Peter is merely commanding standard Christian duty when he requires them to be diligent to add these qualities to their lives. He is only saying in different words what Paul commanded: "Therefore, my beloved, as you have always obeyed, not as in my presence only, but now much more in my absence, work out your own salvation with fear and trembling; for it is God who works in you both to will and to do for *His* good pleasure" (Phil. 2:12–13). Any believer fulfilling this basic Christian duty will thus enjoy assurance. It will come naturally to the diligent disciple as a by-product of their spiritual progress. In addition to assurance because of

1. conviction that the gospel is true,
2. confidence in Christ as Saviour,
3. the actual experience of conversion and its results,

4. the sealing of the Spirit,
5. applying the tests of 1 John.

The believer who obeys Peter's command also enjoys an assurance resulting from the diligent addition of these qualities. As he exerts himself in gaining or continuing in these things the Lord is pleased. His face shines upon him. The effect of that state of blessedness is to give assurance that he is called and elect.

In contrast, if anyone fails to add these things to their faith their spiritual state is unhealthy. Such a one is living with his eyes closed to God's requirements. In that sense he is spiritually blind. He is also short-sighted. Life is lived as if there were no final reckoning. The final judgment and giving account for one's stewardship before Christ (Rom. 14:10–12) are not in his thoughts. Moreover he has lapsed into a state of having forgotten that once he was cleansed from sins. The greatest event in his past and the most significant day in his future therefore have no effect on the way he lives. This is the condition of the backslider. For such there is no assurance of their calling and election. The joy and peace that accompanies the righteous walk of the believer (Rom. 14:17), departs as he lapses from the way of righteousness. Assurance as stated in 1–5 above fades. This is not to say that backsliders do not often still assert that they are the Lord's. Usually they still have hopes of heaven. But the scriptures are explicit. In their lapsed state they will go to hell just as surely as unbelievers. The New Testament promises eternal salvation only to those who persevere in the faith. Heaven is conditional on continuance. The word of God is crystal clear:

> "Moreover, brethren, I declare to you the gospel which I preached to you, which also you received and in which you stand, by which also you are saved, if you hold fast that word which I preached to you" (1 Cor. 15:1–2).

> "And you, who once were alienated and enemies in your mind by wicked works, yet now He has reconciled in the body of His flesh through death, to present you holy, and blameless, and above reproach in His sight – if indeed you continue in the faith, grounded and steadfast, and are not moved away from the hope of the gospel which you heard, which was preached to every creature under heaven, of which I, Paul, became a minister" (Col. 1:21–23).

> ". . . you stand by faith. Do not be haughty, but fear. For if God did not spare the natural branches, He may not spare you either.

Therefore consider the goodness and severity of God: on those who fell, severity; but toward you, goodness, if you continue in *His* goodness. Otherwise you also will be cut off" (Rom. 11:20–22).

All these verses contain an "if." Final salvation is conditional on perseverance. Some may ask "How can this be reconciled with other verses in the New Testament such as, 'My sheep hear My voice, and I know them, and they follow Me. And I give them eternal life, and they shall never perish; neither shall anyone snatch them out of My hand. My Father, who has given *them* to Me, is greater than all; and no one is able to snatch *them* out of My Father's hand' (John 10:27–29), and, 'All that the Father gives Me will come to Me, and the one who comes to Me I will by no means cast out. For I have come down from heaven, not to do My own will, but the will of Him who sent Me. This is the will of the Father who sent Me, that of all He has given Me I should lose nothing, but should raise it up at the last day. And this is the will of Him who sent Me, that everyone who sees the Son and believes in Him may have everlasting life; and I will raise him up at the last day' (John 6:37–40)'?" God will preserve His elect, but He does it through means. He employs commands, promises, exhortations and warnings. A.W. Pink has written excellent words on this matter: "The older writers were wont to illustrate the consistency between God's purpose and our performance of duty by an appeal to Acts 27. The ship which carried the apostle and other prisoners encountered a fearful gale and it continued so long and with such severity that the inspired narrative declares *'all hope that we should be saved was then taken away'* (v.20). A Divine messenger then assured the apostle, *'Fear not Paul, thou must be brought before Caesar; and lo God hath given thee all* (the lives of) *them that sail with thee,'* and so sure was the apostle that this promise would be fulfilled, he said unto the ship's company *'Be of good cheer, for there shall be no loss of life among you, but of the ship, for I believe that it shall be even as it was told me'* (vv. 21–25). Yet next day, when the sailors feared that they would be smashed upon the rocks and started to flee out of the ship, Paul said to the centurion *'except these abide in the ship, ye cannot be saved'* (v.31)!

Now there is a nice problem which we would submit to the more extreme Calvinists: how can the positive promise *'there shall be no loss of life'* (v. 22) and the contingent *'except these abide in the ship ye cannot be saved'* (v.31) stand together? How are you going to reconcile them according to your principles? But in reality there is no difficulty: God made no absolute promise that He would preserve those in the ship regardless of their use of appropriate means. They were not irrational creatures He would safeguard, but moral agents who must discharge their own responsibility, and neither be inert nor act presumptuously."[1]

Not only is heaven conditional on perseverance, counterfeit faith is revealed by falling away. Jesus taught this in His parable of the sower: "But he who received the seed on stony places, this is he who hears the word and immediately receives it with joy; yet he has no root in himself, but endures only for a while. For when tribulation or persecution arises because of the word, immediately he stumbles" (Mat. 13:20–21). Just as the hearer responds immediately to the gospel, he responds immediately to tribulation or persecution arising from his profession. He did not expect such to follow. Immediately this happens he ceases to profess faith. Initially the blessings of the message were the great attraction. There was never a heart to do the will of God. There was no true conversion. In this sense it is incorrect to refer to this passage of scripture as speaking of temporary faith. It denotes temporary profession, not temporary true faith. It is not true conversion; it is pseudo conversion. It is counterfeit faith that appears genuine for a time.

Conclusions

Assurance of salvation both now and for the future is the normal state of the Christian. God gives assurance by:

1. opening the eyes to the truth of the gospel.
2. by the promises of the gospel.
3. by the actual experience of conversion.
4. by the sealing of the Spirit.
5. by self-examination in the light of the scriptures.
6. by addition to one's faith.

The believer who uses these means of grace enjoys assurance, and triumphs over the world, the flesh and the devil.

Reference

1. A.W. Pink *Eternal Security*, Guardian Press 1974, page 87. Later edition by Baker 1996.

CHAPTER TWENTY FOUR

REPENTANCE AND FAITH PART OF THE ESSENTIAL FOUNDATION

Repentance and faith are essential for building a Christian life. It cannot begin without them. Only by them can there be entrance into the kingdom of God. Repentance and faith are also foundational in the Christian life in another sense. The change of mind, which is repentance, and the new belief in Christ, are essential for daily life after conversion. Repentance and faith must be understood as initial actions through which salvation is received at a point in time; and also as settled new states of heart and mind towards God and Christ which are basic for Christian living in the following ways.

Repentance

1. The new views of sin, sins, God and His commands contained in repentance are indispensable to walk daily before God in the way He requires

At conversion the believer turned from his sinful ways and sinful thoughts to serve the living God. From that time that commitment must be constant. Indeed God's will for every believer is the full implementation and outworking of the repentance exercised at conversion. Learning and understanding God's will is necessary for that new dedication to be worked out as God desires. The new convert often has very little knowledge of the scriptures, and sometimes has been taught a misinterpretation of them. The New Testament gives abundant and detailed instructions concerning daily behaviour in this world. Those commands must be learned, and understood with "all wisdom and spiritual understanding" to walk "worthy of the Lord, fully pleasing Him, being fruitful in every good work" (Col. 1:9–10). But this growth of knowledge of God's will and godly conduct will only come about where the heart constantly desires to cease from sin and obey God. These new desires born in repentance are an essential foundation for life throughout the Christian's earthly pilgrimage.

2. The new shame for sins committed before conversion is essential throughout the Christian life

When a person repents there is shame for sins committed. This is an element in the change of mind about sin and sins. To live the Christian life as God commands sins must continue to be seen after conversion as something to be ashamed of. This does not mean that the believer must constantly remember past sins, nor devote effort to recall them. It does mean that the Christian must never cease to feel shame for past sins whenever such conduct comes to mind. This shame springs from seeing sins in their true light, and that perception of sins is always essential for the Christian walk. It moves the Christian to turn from sin to holiness. Paul made this clear when he wrote to the Christians at Rome, "For when you were slaves of sin, you were free in regard to righteousness. What fruit did you have then in the things of which you are now ashamed? For the end of those things *is* death" (Rom. 6:20–21). He defined their state before conversion as "slaves of sin." This was true of every single one of them, even the most respectable. There was no righteousness whatsoever in their lives. They never sought to obey and please the one true God. It was no concern to them to do what was right in His eyes. Some of them had sought to be righteous according to their own concept of righteousness. But it was their idea of right-eousness, not God's true standard. In God's sight it was "filthy rags," literally a garment of menstruation (Isa. 64:6). So he reminds them of the result of their behaviour. What was it? It was spiritual death, separation from God. He states the fact that they are now ashamed of their past conduct. He does not say that they ought to be ashamed. He says that they are ashamed. This is a mark of a true Christian. He is ashamed of the sinful things done before conversion. The wretched-ness of sinning is seen in its true colours, regardless of whether the sins are condemned by the world or sanctioned by the world. Self-righteousness also is seen for what it is – filthy rags, to be ashamed of as much as the filth of overt sins. Shame for past sins is fundamental for Christian living. Where it is not present sin will not be seen aright and not renounced. God and His word will not be obeyed.

3. The new view of self in true repentance is essential to walk acceptably before God

Repentance re-assesses self in God's sight. It is an attitude of humility expressed in the actions and prayer of the repentant tax collector: "And the tax collector, standing afar off, would not so much as raise *his* eyes to heaven, but beat his breast, saying, 'God, be merciful to me a sinner!' " (Luke 18:13). Like the tax collector the repentant sinner is poor and contrite, (Isa. 66:2). He knows that he cannot plead anything in himself to merit mercy; is conscious that he has no deeds to present to God to gain His favour, and that he can do nothing at all to earn mercy. Poverty stricken he can only plead for mercy. Such humility is essential to enter the kingdom. As Jesus said, "Blessed are the poor in spirit for theirs is the kingdom of God" (Mat. 5:3). That humility is also essential for the life after conversion. God's requirement is to "walk humbly" with Him each day (Mic. 6:8). It is absolutely and gloriously true that the repentant sinner is forgiven and accepted as righteous in Christ. But the believer must never forget throughout life that he is a sinner unworthy of the least crumb of mercy, and fully deserving of eternal punishment. He must continue to see himself according to truth. Salvation is entirely by grace, God's unmerited favour. God justifies the ungodly (Rom. 4:5). The divine design of the way of salvation is to exclude any pride and boasting of man. The New Testament is explicit: "Where *is* boasting then? It is excluded. By what law? Of works? No, but by the law of faith" (Rom. 3:27), and, "For by grace you have been saved through faith, and that not of yourselves; *it is* the gift of God, not of works, lest anyone should boast" (Eph. 2:8–9). Consequently Paul said, "But God forbid that I should boast except in the cross of our Lord Jesus Christ, by whom the world has been crucified to me, and I to the world" (Gal. 6:14). Only in the new estimation of self which comes by repentance will there be this humility, a genuine appreciation of the grace of God in salvation, and deep gratitude to God for His grace and mercy.

Paul exemplifies this Christian humility. He was deeply conscious that he was saved and an apostle only because the "grace of our Lord was exceedingly abundant" towards him (1 Tim. 1:14). He stated repeatedly his low estimation of himself because of past sins, "For I am the least of the apostles, who am not worthy to be called an apostle, because I persecuted the church of God" (1 Cor. 15:9 written in A.D. 55). Because of his enduring shame for past sins he considered himself not worthy to be called an apostle. In fact he went even further because of his continued repentant state of mind. He counted himself below the least of all other believers: "To me, who am less than the least of all the saints, this grace was given, that I should preach among the Gentiles the unsearchable riches of Christ" (Eph. 3:8 written sometime in A.D. 59–61). But this statement is not his lowest estimate of himself. He even said that he was the chief of sinners: "This *is* a faithful saying and worthy of all acceptance, that Christ Jesus came into the world to save sinners, of whom I am chief" (1 Tim. 1:15 written sometime in A.D. 61–63). Notice he said "of whom I am chief" not of whom I was chief. The word "chief" means foremost, of the first rank. Paul wrote these words because of his sins before conversion. He was not being excessively humble. He had committed many exceedingly evil deeds. He believed that they really did make him a sinner of the first rank. He related his past life to King Agrippa: "Indeed, I myself thought I must do many things contrary to the name of Jesus of Nazareth. This I also did in Jerusalem, and many of the saints I shut up in prison, having received authority from the chief priests; and when they were put to death, I cast my vote against *them*. And I punished them often in every synagogue and compelled *them* to blaspheme; and being exceedingly enraged against them, I persecuted *them* even to foreign cities" (Acts 26:9–11). Throughout his life he never forgot the past sins he committed. He never ceased to be repentant of them. Consequently he was humble even as an apostle. He knew that it was only "by the grace of God" that he was what he was (1 Cor. 15:10). When his apostleship was attacked he could assert, "in nothing was I behind the most eminent apostles, though I am nothing. Truly the signs of an apostle were accomplished among you with all perseverance, in signs and wonders and mighty deeds" (2 Cor. 12:11–12). Alongside his claim to equality with the greatest apostles are the words "though I am nothing." There is no contradiction between his claim to equality and his discounting of himself. Paul knew that he "became a minister according to the gift of the grace of God given to me by the effective working of His power" (Eph. 3:7). He knew that his apostleship was a gift of God, unmerited by him; and that his ministry was the "effective working of God's power." It was all the grace of God. He was nothing.

It is striking that Paul's estimation of himself descended lower and lower as the years went by. With reference to his statements above, notice the dates of the letters 1 Cor. A.D. 55, Eph. sometime within A.D. 59–61, 1 Tim. 1 sometime within A.D. 61–63. As his knowledge of God and God's truth grew he saw the guilt of his sins more fully and clearly than when he first repented. His change of mind about self became even greater. He still saw himself as a sinner, but a worse sinner than he had realised and acknowledged previously. As the Christian grows in knowledge and grace there is an increased comprehension of the guilt and gravity of sin. Consequently there is more humility, a greater appreciation of the grace of God and deeper gratitude for salvation. The believer does not mature out of the repentant state at conversion. The opposite is true. Spiritual growth develops and strengthens the initial repentance. Repentance is not only essential for the Christian throughout life, it grows as the Christian develops.

Faith

Faith, like repentance, continues and must continue after the initial act of faith for salvation. The Christian is not a person who believed once in the past to be saved. A Christian is a person who constantly possesses faith. As Peter said, Christians are those who have "obtained" faith. They have received it as a gift from God. They are called believers. Non-Christians are named unbelievers (2 Cor. 6:15). Faith is essential for the daily walk of the Christian: "The just shall live by faith."

1.   It is through faith in Christ that the believer continually has access to God, the Father

Through faith in Christ the Christian gains access to God, the Father (Eph. 2:18). Christ is the Way to the Father and there is no access except by Him (John 14:6). "For Christ also suffered once for sins, the just for the unjust, that He might bring us to God" (1 Pet. 3:18). The express purpose of His suffering was to bring men to God, to bring them into fellowship and communion with Him. He died that they might know Him as a loving heavenly Father. Through faith in Christ the Christian has boldness and confidence to come into His Presence. Paul affirmed to fellow Christians, "Christ Jesus our Lord, in whom we have boldness and access" (to God the Father Eph. 2:18) "with confidence through faith in Him" (Eph. 3:12). The Christian can come before a holy God with boldness because he believes that Christ has died for his sins in his place, and Christ's righteousness is imputed to him. He knows that he stands justified in God's sight and accepted in the Beloved, Jesus Christ the Son of God. He believes also that he is coming to the Father Who loves him so much that He gave His only begotten Son to save him. He comes with that confidence. In the words of the writer to the Hebrews the Christian can "draw near.. in full assurance of faith" (Heb. 10:22). At God's throne of grace the believer continually obtains mercy and finds grace to help in times of need (Heb. 4:19). Access to the Father and the blessings of that access are through the continual exercise of faith. "The just shall live by faith."

2.   Faith governs the life of the Christian

Paul stated the place of faith in the Christian's life in these words, "the *life* which I now live in the flesh I live by faith in the Son of God, who loved me and gave Himself for me" (Gal. 2:20). Paul lived in the light of Christ's love and death for him. He knew that that sacrificial love had brought him salvation. He was moved to love Christ in return. His love was expressed in obedience to Christ's commands. True love for God is expressed always in this way. As Jesus stated, "He who has My commandments and keeps them, it is he who loves Me" (John 14:21). We therefore have a wonderful sequence – faith appropriates the love of God in Christ – faith loves in return – obedience to Christ's commands flows from that love. Thus the scripture says faith works by love (Gal. 5:6). In this way faith in Christ produces good works. Those works spring from it. The daily good works of the Christian are dependent on sustained faith. Faith in the reality of Christ's love and sacrifice is the dynamic motivator. It governed the way Paul lived so much so that he said "it is no longer I who live, but Christ lives in me" (Gal. 2:20). He was so diligent to obey Christ's words that Christ truly directed his behaviour to the extent that he could say Christ was living in his body. Christ was using his body to speak words, and to do actions. This was the effect of faith. It is important we notice that Paul says "the life which I now live in the flesh." His words emphasise that the life of faith in Christ is a life lived in this world, and in the various conditions that occur in this world. In every condition the life of faith can be lived, and is to be lived by the Christian. Paul lived it as a free man or as a prisoner, when he had abundance and when he was in want (Phil. 4:11–13), as an apostle working signs and wonders or as a tent maker earning his keep (Acts 18:3). The Christian life cannot be lived without faith. Without it there will not be love for Christ. Without that love there will not be obedience to His commands.

3.   Faith enables the Christian to overcome the world
"For whatever is born of God overcomes the world. And this is the victory that has overcome the world – our faith. Who is he who over-comes the world, but he who believes that Jesus is the Son of God?" (1 John 5:4–5). At conversion the Christian overcame the world by faith. There was deliverance from "this present evil age" (Gal. 1:4). God delivered from the power of darkness into the kingdom of the Son of His love (Col. 1:13). But the Christian convert remains in this world though no longer of it. So the Christian lives in an alien world. It is rebellious against God, and under the influence of Satan (Eph. 2:1). The Christian is surrounded by bad examples, pressures to conform to the world, sometimes persecution or loss because of refusal to conform, and temptations to yield to the benefits and pleasures the world offers by turning from the way of godliness. It is a world where the power of Satan is present, and the Christian is subject to his attacks (Eph. 6:16 and 1 Pet. 5:8). It is the exercising of faith that enables him to overcome all these opposing influences. His faith in Christ as we have seen moves him to love Christ, and that love desires to please Him in all things. This

desire is so real and strong that it conquers all opposition. It is even willing to sacrifice life itself if necessary to please Christ. It is a desire that comes from faith in Christ. Faith brings victory.

4.   *There can be no continuance of the Christian's acceptance by God, and no assurance of final salvation unless faith is maintained*
We have already seen that perseverance in faith is essential (1 Cor. 15:1–2, Col. 1:23 and Rom. 11:20–22). These last verses spell out the Christians position in the kingdom: "Well *said*. Because of unbelief they were broken off, and you stand by faith. Do not be haughty, but fear. For if God did not spare the natural branches, He may not spare you either. Therefore consider the goodness and severity of God: on those who fell, severity; but toward you, goodness, if you continue in *His* goodness. Otherwise you also will be cut off." The Christians (in this case Gentiles in the church at Rome) stand "by faith." If they lapse from faith they will not continue in His goodness. They will be "cut off" just as the unbelieving Jews were. The writer to the Hebrews asserts the same need for perseverance in faith. He quotes from Habakkuk the Old Testament prophet, "Now the just shall live by faith; But if *anyone* draws back, My soul has no pleasure in him" (Heb. 10:38). He warns of drawing back to perdition (Heb. 10:39). It is true that Christians are kept by the power of God for final salvation at Christ's return. But it is "through faith" that God preserves His people (1 Pet. 1:5). Continued faith is essential to arrive in heaven.

As with repentance faith can develop and be strengthened by the Christian growing in knowledge and grace. The Christians at Thessalonica gave cause for thanksgiving to God because their faith grew exceedingly (2 Thess. 1:3). Greater understanding of God's word especially of Christ's Person and Work produces an even stronger faith in Him. In turn this reinforces love for Christ, which results in an increased zeal to obey His commands. This growth of faith is built upon the foundation of initial saving faith.

True repentance and true saving faith are essentially abiding changes of heart and mind. The believer is called to continue in the new stance before God, and grow in knowledge and grace. However that new position is subject to attack. False teaching can cause the Christian to believe in error instead of the truth. Also temptation from the world, the flesh and the devil can lead astray from the forsaking of sin implicit in repentance. The following are examples of lapses from the state of repentance and faith exercised at conversion and onwards. They demonstrate that the settled states of faith and repentance are indispensable for the Christian life.

The Galatian Christians soon after their conversion turned to a false gospel. It was Christ plus circumcision and keeping Old Testament laws as the means of salvation instead of faith in Christ alone for justification (Gal. 1:6). They were bewitched from continuing in the truth (Gal. 3:1). Paul called them back to the truth they had believed when they became Christians. At that time they believed in Christ in order to be justified, knowing that by the works of the law no flesh shall be justified (Gal. 2:16). He saw their moving away to a perversion of the gospel as extremely serious. He said, "I am afraid for you, lest I have labored for you in vain" (Gal. 4:11). He warned, "Indeed I, Paul, say to you that if you become circumcised, Christ will profit you nothing" (Gal. 5:2). He was passionately concerned about their falling away from true faith in Christ. He wrote, "I could wish that those who trouble you would even cut themselves off!" (Gal. 5:12). His anxiety for them was so real that he declared, "My little children, for whom I labor in birth again until Christ is formed in you" (Gal. 4:19). These verses all reveal the extreme seriousness of their lapse from faith. The Christian life is built on the foundation of faith. If that collapses the life is not possible.

Similarly because of temptation the believer may lapse from the fundamental renunciation of sin intrinsic in repentance. Demas forsook Paul "having loved this present world" (2 Tim. 4:10). He was once a valued fellow labourer with Paul. He is mentioned along with Mark and Luke, who were writers of scripture and missionary workers of prominence, (Philemon 24). Later when Paul suffered imprisonment Demas abandoned him because his heart turned to the love of the things offered by the world rather than the service of Christ. That state of heart was incompatible with repentance and living as a Christian should.

These cases of lapsing from the settled states of repentance and faith reveal clearly the key place they have in the Christian walk. It cannot continue without them. They are essential parts of the foundation on which the Christian life is built.

God's Pattern for the
Christian Life

VOLUME TWO

Baptism in Water
and
Baptism in the
Holy Spirit

CONTENTS OF VOLUME TWO

Baptism in Water

THE BAPTISM OF BELIEVERS BY IMMERSION IN WATER: ITS TIMING AND RELATIONSHIP WITH FAITH

Let us proceed to the next element of the essential foundation for a Christian life. At this point I am concerned to avoid any misunderstanding. Only repentance and faith are essential for salvation. Water baptism is not. It is, however, an essential part of the total foundation on which the Christian life must be built. We shall present this doctrine, and then explain how it is foundational.

The Bible teaches that when a man repents and believes the gospel he must be baptized immediately by total immersion

The following scriptures in the Acts of the Apostles show the practice of the first Christians.

1. On the Day of Pentecost

"Then Peter said to them, 'Repent, and let every one of you be baptized in the name of Jesus Christ for the remission of sins; and you shall receive the gift of the Holy Spirit. For the promise is to you and to your children, and to all who are afar off, as many as the Lord our God will call.' And with many other words he testified and exhorted them, saying, 'Be saved from this perverse generation.' Then those who gladly received his word were baptized; and that day about three thousand souls were added *to them*" (Acts 2:38–41). This was the conclusion of Peter's message on the day of Pentecost. He calls his hearers to repent and be baptized. It is unthinkable that he means repent now and after some time be baptized. The following words: "Then those who gladly received his word were baptized; and that day about three thousand souls were added to *them*" indicate an immediate response.

2. The Samaritans

"Then Philip went down to the city of Samaria and preached Christ to them. And the multitudes with one accord heeded the things spoken by Philip, hearing and seeing the miracles which he did. For unclean spirits, crying with a loud voice, came out of many who were possessed; and many who were paralyzed and lame were healed. And there was great joy in that city. But there was a certain man called Simon, who previously practiced sorcery in the city and astonished the people of Samaria, claiming that he was someone great, to whom they all gave heed, from the least to the greatest, saying, 'This man is the great power of God.' And they heeded him because he had astonished them with his sorceries for a long time. But when they believed Philip as he preached the things concerning the kingdom of God and the name of Jesus Christ, both men and women were baptized. Then Simon himself also believed; and when he was baptized he continued with Philip, and was amazed, seeing the miracles and signs which were done" (Acts 8:5–13). Again the account tells us that baptism followed faith. There was no probationary period for these converts. There is not the slightest indication from the behaviour of the apostles when they came that such examination should have taken place. The conduct of the apostles, Peter and John, shows conclusively that they fully accepted the Samaritan converts as the Lord's. The record continues, "Now when the apostles who were at Jerusalem heard that Samaria had received the word of God, they sent Peter and John to them, who, when they had come down, prayed for them that they might receive the Holy Spirit. For as yet He had fallen upon none of them. They had only been baptized in the name of the Lord Jesus. Then they laid hands on them, and they received the Holy Spirit" (Acts 8:14–17). The apostles would not have prayed for them to receive the Holy Spirit if they had not believed they were truly converted. They knew that the Holy Spirit is given only to those who repent and believe, to those called by God into His kingdom (Acts 2:38–39). As Jesus said, the Spirit cannot be received by non-believers (John 14:17). When they prayed the Spirit was received by these baptized converts.

But what about Simon? Does not his subsequent conduct reveal that it is better to wait for a period before baptizing converts? Let us look at his behaviour after his baptism: "And when Simon saw that through the laying on of the apostles' hands the Holy Spirit was given, he offered them money, saying, 'Give me this power also, that anyone on whom I lay hands may receive the Holy Spirit.' But Peter said to him, 'Your money perish with you, because you thought that the gift of God could be purchased with money! You have neither part nor portion in this matter, for your heart is not right in the sight of God. Repent therefore of this your wickedness, and pray God if perhaps the thought of your heart may be forgiven you. For I see that you are poisoned by bitterness and bound by iniquity.' Then Simon answered and said,

'Pray to the Lord for me, that none of the things which you have spoken may come upon me' " (Acts 8:18–24). The narrative demonstrates that the practice of baptizing upon the profession of faith in Christ did result in baptizing someone who by the indications of the text may not have been a true believer. But it is not certain that Simon was unregenerate. His sin may have been a gross sin of a true Christian leading to death (1 John 5:16) unless he repented. He was bitter with envy of Philip, and "bound by iniquity." It is clear, however, that there is not the slightest hint of any condemnation of Philip for baptizing without delay the Samaritan converts including Simon.

3.   The Ethiopian eunuch
"Then Philip opened his mouth, and beginning at this Scripture, preached Jesus to him. Now as they went down the road, they came to some water. And the eunuch said, 'See, here is water. What hinders me from being baptized?' So he commanded the chariot to stand still. And both Philip and the eunuch went down into the water, and he baptized him" (Acts 8:35–36,38). Again the record demonstrates that baptism followed faith without delay. Indeed the account shows that the Ethiopian eunuch himself requested to be baptized at the very first opportunity. It must have been on the same day. Is it not reasonable to conclude that Philip had told him to be baptized, and that in the fire of love that accompanies conversion, the moment he saw water he wanted to be obedient to God's will? The eunuch asked, "What hinders me from being baptized?" Philip baptized him at once.

4.   Saul
"And Ananias went his way and entered the house; and laying his hands on him he said, 'Brother Saul, the Lord Jesus, who appeared to you on the road as you came, has sent me that you may receive your sight and be filled with the Holy Spirit.' Immediately there fell from his eyes *something* like scales, and he received his sight at once; and he arose and was baptized" (Acts 9:17–18). This is the record of Ananias, a devout disciple in Damascus, ministering to Saul three or four days after Saul was converted. Saul was truly born again, a true believer before Ananias entered the house. This is apparent from Ananias's opening words He says, "Brother Saul." He addresses him as a believer, a brother in Christ. He went on to say, "And now why are you waiting? Arise and be baptized, and wash away your sins, calling on the name of the Lord" (Acts 22:16). The scriptures tell us that Saul responded immediately and was baptized (Acts 9:18). Please take note of Ananias's question "Why are you waiting?" Ananias seems to be

surprised that Saul was not already baptized. He commanded him to delay no longer.

5.   Cornelius and his relatives and close friends

"While Peter was still speaking these words, the Holy Spirit fell upon all those who heard the word. And those of the circumcision who believed were astonished, as many as came with Peter, because the gift of the Holy Spirit had been poured out on the Gentiles also. For they heard them speak with tongues and magnify God. Then Peter answered, 'Can anyone forbid water, that these should not be baptized who have received the Holy Spirit just as we *have*?' And he commanded them to be baptized in the name of the Lord" (Acts 10:44–48). These events follow Peter's preaching of Christ to Cornelius and those gathered in his household. Peter knew that the Lord had called them into His kingdom because the Holy Spirit was poured out upon them. It is significant that immediately he asserted that no one could have valid grounds to say that they should not be baptized at once. He commanded Cornelius and his fellow believers to be baptized. Observe that he did not simply put before them baptism as God's will. He commanded them to do it. When their faith in Christ was manifest the next immediate step was baptism in water. Peter's words and actions reveal his doctrine of water baptism. He believed that it must follow faith without delay.

6.   The Philippian jailor and his household

"Then he called for a light, ran in, and fell down trembling before Paul and Silas. And he brought them out and said, 'Sirs, what must I do to be saved?' So they said, 'Believe on the Lord Jesus Christ, and you will be saved, you and your household.' Then they spoke the word of the Lord to him and to all who were in his house. And he took them the same hour of the night and washed *their* stripes. And immediately he and all his family were baptized. Now when he had brought them into his house, he set food before them; and he rejoiced, having believed in God with all his household" (Acts 16:29–34). Here is the story of the conversion of the Philippian jailor and those in his household. The members of the household may have been family members or servants or both. It is stated that they all heard the gospel and all believed. Their baptisms were immediate (verse 33).

7.   Disciples at Ephesus

"And it happened, while Apollos was at Corinth, that Paul, having passed through the upper regions, came to Ephesus. And finding some disciples he said to them, 'Did you receive the Holy Spirit when you believed?' So they said to him, 'We have not so much as heard whether there is a Holy Spirit.' And he said to them, 'Into what then were you baptized?' So they said, 'Into John's baptism'. Then Paul said, 'John indeed baptized with a baptism of repentance, saying to the people that they should believe on Him who would come after him, that is, on Christ Jesus.' When they heard *this*, they were baptized in the name of the Lord Jesus" (Acts 19:1–5). These disciples had been baptized into John the Baptist's baptism. Their spiritual state was one of obedience to God but lacking in knowledge of Christ. Their understanding was limited to what they had been taught as ones responding to the ministry of John the Baptist. They were obedient to his ministry, but appear not to know anything of Christ beyond what John had taught. Paul directs them to faith in Christ (verse 4). Verse 5 records their immediate response of faith in Christ, expressed straightaway in baptism.

There are two other passages in the Acts of the Apostles telling of water baptisms. They do not state the time period between faith and baptism. They do not give any indication that baptism did not follow faith without delay.

"Now a certain woman named Lydia heard *us*. She was a seller of purple from the city of Thyatira, who worshiped God. The Lord opened her heart to heed the things spoken by Paul. And when she and her household were baptized, she begged *us*, saying, 'If you have judged me to be faithful to the Lord, come to my house and stay.' So she persuaded us" (Acts 16:14–15). This is a concise account of the baptism of Lydia and her household. Though the faith of her household is not mentioned, it is in harmony with the totality of the records in Acts and all the teaching of the New Testament to assume that they also heard the gospel and believed. Baptism followed. "And many of the Corinthians, hearing, believed and were baptized" (Acts 18:8). This is the summary account of conversions at Corinth when Paul proclaimed Jesus as the Christ.

Turning to the rest of the New Testament it is significant that in every instance where water baptism is mentioned the writer always takes for granted that all of the Christians to whom he writes have been baptized (Rom. 6:1–4; 1 Cor. 1:13; Gal. 3:27; Col. 2:12 and 1 Pet. 3:21). This is in harmony with baptism at the commencement of their Christian faith.

The practice of delaying baptism until after a period of instruction in the faith or after a probationary period is completely foreign to the New Testament. To be in accord with its teaching all converts must be baptized when converted. This applies to children just as much as adults. When they repent and believe they should be baptized. It is not scriptural to fix a lower age limit for baptism. It is an indisputable fact that God does give repentance and faith to some children. To deny this is to refuse to face the facts of the history of God's dealings. If a young child can understand enough to repent and believe he can understand enough to be baptized. It is true that children can be persuaded wrongly into taking actions. It is also a fact that they will do things to please their parents. And like adults they will be willing to carry out religious acts to ease a guilty conscience when not truly repentant. But some do truly repent and believe. They are truly born again. To deny baptism to them is contrary to God's revealed will and a hindrance to their spiritual development. It is to deprive them of the blessing of baptism, and to prevent them from laying a part of the foundation on which their Christian life is to be built.

Water baptism linked to faith

Baptism is the expression of faith in Christ by a physical action. This explains why it followed faith without delay in New Testament practice. This close connection between faith and baptism also explains certain New Testament scriptures below which at first sight appear to say that baptism in water is the means of salvation:

Peter wrote, "There is also an antitype which now saves us – baptism (not the removal of the filth of the flesh, but the answer of a good conscience toward God), through the resurrection of Jesus Christ" (1 Pet. 3:21).

Paul told of Ananias saying to him just after his conversion, "And now why are you waiting? Arise and be baptized, and wash away your sins, calling on the name of the Lord" (Acts 22:16).

Paul said to the Christians in Galatia, "For as many of you as were baptized into Christ have put on Christ " (Gal. 3:27).

These words speaking of baptism saving and washing away sins, and putting on Christ are explained by the fact that true baptism is inseparable from faith, because it is the expression of faith in Christ. Perhaps this is seen most strikingly in Peter's words on the day of Pentecost. Having declared Jesus to be Lord and Christ he directs his hearers to repent and be baptized: "Then Peter said to them, 'Repent, and let every one of you be baptized in the name of Jesus Christ for the remission of sins; and you shall receive the gift of the Holy Spirit' " (Acts 2:38). He does not tell them to repent and believe. He instructs them to repent and express belief in Christ by baptism. He declares that if they do repent and are baptized they will receive the remission of sins. That remission of sins is not by means of repentance and baptism without faith. It is by repentance and baptism as the expression of faith. Baptism is simply faith expressed in a divinely designed symbolic action. The convert is immersed in water thereby signifying death and burial with Christ. He then emerges out of the water signifying rising with Christ: "Therefore we were buried with Him through baptism into death, that just as Christ was raised from the dead by the glory of the Father, even so we also should walk in newness of life" (Rom. 6:4), and, "Buried with Him in baptism, in which you also were raised with *Him* through faith in the working of God, who raised Him from the dead" (Col. 2:12). The convert by the action of being baptized is expressing his faith:

- In Christ's death, burial and resurrection.
- In his personal union with Christ in His death, burial and resurrection: "baptized into Christ Jesus" (Rom. 6). This union with Christ has wonderful meaning.

1.   It is a representative union
Romans 5:12–21 sets forth this union of Christ with believers. Adam the first man sinned. Sin entered the world and death through sin. Death spread to all men because all sinned in their representative Adam. Through his offence judgment came to all men resulting in condemnation. God judged Adam and all his descendants in their representative Adam. His sin was imputed to them. Christ in the same way is the representative of all who believe in Him: "Therefore, as through one man's offense *judgment* came to all men, resulting in condemnation, even so through one Man's righteous act *the free gift came* to all men, resulting in justification of life. For as by one man's disobedience many were made sinners, so also by one Man's obedience many will be made righteous" (Rom. 5:18–19). Christ died and rose from the dead as the Representative of His people. He bore the full punishment for their sins in their place as their Substitute. What He did is reckoned by God as though they had done it. Therefore in Christ the believer has paid the penalty of sin which is death. By His sacrifice believers are justified. Thus the same principle of representative union applies with respect to Adam and all mankind, and to Christ and all believers. This is God's way of salvation.

2.   It is also a vital union
Baptism signifies the believer's death, burial and resurrection with Christ. At conversion the believer is united with Christ in the "likeness"

of His death and resurrection. The believer's death and resurrection are in the "likeness" of Christ's, not identical. Christ's death was physical, the believer's is spiritual. The convert, in his representative Christ, died to sin, was crucified, buried and rose from the dead and is alive to God. Paul wrote, "we judge thus: that if One" (that is Christ) "died for all, then all" (that is all believers) "died; and He died for all, that those who live should live no longer for themselves, but for Him who died for them and rose again" (2 Cor. 5:14–15). At conversion the believer was set free from the reigning power of sin in his life and enabled to walk in newness of life. In Christ the former unconverted person was crucified, so that the convert might no longer be the slave of sin but present himself to God as alive from the dead to serve Him. Baptism signifies this death to the old life and rising with Christ to walk in newness of life. The Christian is in a new position. He is no longer the slave of sin. He is alive to God in Christ Jesus, and able to live to God. Baptism is a symbol of this great change.

3.   *This union with Christ is the source of all spiritual blessings for the Christian*

Paul gave praise to God when he wrote to the Christians at Ephesus: "Blessed *be* the God and Father of our Lord Jesus Christ, who has blessed us with every spiritual blessing in the heavenly *places* in Christ" (Eph. 1:3). He goes on to mention some of them – election, adoption, acceptance, redemption, forgiveness of sins, an inheritance, and the Holy Spirit as the guarantee of that inheritance (Eph. 1:4–14). All these blessings are "in Christ". Union with Christ is the meaning of water baptism: "baptized into Christ Jesus" (Rom. 6:3).

CHAPTER TWO

WHY IS BAPTISM NECESSARY?

We have seen that the convert in the act of being baptized is affirming his new position in Christ. By repentance and faith he has already come into that position. His baptism does not bring it into being. So we may ask why is baptism necessary? God commands it. So even if it seems unnecessary we must submit to His will, and faith recognises that God's command is given to His children in perfect wisdom and love. I suggest that the scriptures reveal some reasons for the symbolic act.

Baptism focuses the mind on the essential truths of the gospel

If we compare the meaning of baptism with Paul's definition of the gospel we see the correspondence between the two. "Moreover, brethren, I declare to you the gospel which I preached to you, which also you received and in which you stand, by which also you are saved, if you hold fast that word which I preached to you – unless you believed in vain. For I delivered to you first of all that which I also received: that Christ died for our sins according to the Scriptures, and that He was buried, and that He rose again the third day according to the Scriptures" (1 Cor. 15:1–4). Baptism speaks explicitly of Christ's death, burial and resurrection (Rom. 6:3–4 and Col. 2:12) and the washing away of sins (Acts 2:38 and 22:16).

Baptism focuses the mind on the new relationship with Christ

The believer enacts his union with Christ in the act of immersion. He is buried with Christ in baptism and raised with Christ (Col. 2:12). Paul reminded the Christians at Rome, "We were buried with Him through baptism into death, that just as Christ was raised from the dead by the glory of the Father, even so we also should walk in newness of life" (Rom. 6:4). At this point it will be helpful to consider the two ordinances commanded by the Lord requiring symbolic actions, namely

13

baptism in water and the breaking of bread. The symbols of the Lord's death in the Lord's Supper, bread and wine, point to the facts of His broken body and the shedding of his blood. They provide a focus point for believers to remember their Saviour's death and the blessings resulting from it. Thus believers are enabled to look by faith at the cross and appropriate again the love of Christ. Faith can and does contemplate the sacrifice of Christ and His love without any action using symbols, but these symbols do assist faith. In this way the Lord's Supper is a wonderful and powerful means of grace to believers. Similarly in the act of water baptism, the death, burial and resurrection of Christ, and the union of the believer with Christ is represented vividly. Faith already exists, but it is helped by the symbolism of the act. It is directed to focus on the truths contained in the symbolic act. Thus the faith of a convert is assisted.

Baptism is an affirmation of the new spiritual state that has been entered into through faith and repentance

Baptism is God's appointed way for the convert to express his new faith in Christ. As seen from the record in the Acts of the Apostles it is God's immediate requirement of those who have come to believe the gospel. It manifests Divine wisdom. The symbolism of the action speaks so powerfully of Christ, union with Christ and the blessings of salvation. The action is so simple. The convert only requires water and one other believer to baptize him. Faith in Christ is wonderfully helped by taking this decisive step. By the dramatic action of baptism the convert affirms his new faith in Christ, and the blessings received from Him. He says, "Christ is now my Lord and Saviour. My sins are washed away. I am 'in Christ'." The convert thus declares the tremendous change that took place at conversion. The new believer is strengthened in God.

Baptism signifies a convert's decision to live for God through Jesus Christ

It is a renunciation of the life of sin lived before repentance and faith, and a commitment to serve the living God.

The symbolic action of baptism is of profound significance

Baptism is more than a wonderful symbolic action. It is more than a sign to focus and strengthen faith. God has invested it with profound significance. Baptism is God's affirmation of the new spiritual state of the believer before God. In that sense God seals to the believer all that is signified by baptism. As noted above we have seen that God has ordained two symbolic actions for believers, baptism and the Lord's Supper. The symbolic actions in the latter are of great significance. This is clearly revealed in the following words concerning the Lord's Table. When believers eat the bread and drink the cup they "proclaim the Lord's death till He comes. Therefore whoever eats this bread or drinks *this* cup of the Lord in an unworthy manner will be guilty of the body and blood of the Lord. But let a man examine himself, and so let him eat of the bread and drink of the cup. For he who eats and drinks in an unworthy manner eats and drinks judgment to himself, not discerning the Lord's body. For this reason many *are* weak and sick among you, and many sleep. For if we would judge ourselves, we would not be judged. But when we are judged, we are chastened by the Lord, that we may not be condemned with the world" (1 Cor. 11:26–32). These verses reveal the great significance of the symbolic actions. God says they "proclaim the Lord's death." The consequences of not carrying out the symbolic actions at the Lord's Supper in the right manner are extremely grave. The bread remained bread, and the wine remained wine, but the Corinthians were guilty of the body and blood which the bread and cup symbolized when they took them unworthily. Their failure to respect the symbols was so serious in the sight of God that it resulted in premature death for some! The symbolic actions at the Lord's Table are of profound meaning. To fail to recognise that meaning in the way some Christians at Corinth did at the time of Paul's letter continues to bring God's chastisement in the form of weakness, sickness and death to believers. It is evident therefore that God takes these symbolic actions most seriously. Believers partaking of the bread and wine in an unworthy manner are reckoned by God Himself to be guilty of what is symbolized, the Lord's body.

In the same way the symbolic action of baptism is of profound significance. When a true believer is baptized, God reckons that all that is signified by baptism concerning the believer is in fact true. Baptism is God's declaration that the convert is "in Christ." The believer by being baptized embraces that Divine declaration. It is a momentous and unique event in the life of the believer. The convert affirms his new state by the act of baptism, and God sees and acknowledges that affirmation. In the words of Peter baptism is "the answer of a good conscience toward God" (1 Pet. 3:21). The believer knows that through Christ he is forgiven and accounted righteous. He is now justified by faith. There is no longer any condemnation of God upon him. He has a good conscience before God. He declares this spiritual standing by being baptized. Baptism is a decisive and unforgettable action in which he can declare before God his faith in Christ and new position in Christ in the knowledge that God also declares his new standing by what is signified in baptism. Indeed it is God who has commanded him to affirm his faith and his new state by being baptized. The new standing existed from the moment of conversion. In baptism both God and the convert affirm it. This strengthens his faith, and seals to him the reality of his union with Christ. This understanding of baptism further explains those verses quoted above – 1 Pet. 3:21, Acts 22:16 and Gal. 3:27, which speak of baptism saving, washing away sins and putting on Christ.

Conclusion

These are some of the reasons why God has commanded water baptism. We shall see later that He has ordained it to be part of the foundation of the Christian life.

CHAPTER THREE

THE MODE OF BAPTISM

As stated immersion is the mode of baptism, and the only mode sanctioned by the scriptures.

The meaning of the Greek word *baptizo* is "to dip, immerse."

Liddell & Scott's *Greek – English Lexicon* gives the following meaning: *baptizo* – I. to dip repeatedly, dip under: to bathe. II. to baptize. Hence *baptisma* that which is dipped, *baptismos* a dipping in water: baptism.

Thayer's *Greek English Lexicon of the New Testament* says, *baptizo* is

1. to dip repeatedly, to immerse, submerge.
2. to cleanse by dipping or submerging, to wash, to make clean with water; to wash one's self, bathe.
3. metaphor, to overwhelm.
    baptisma – immersion, submersion.
    baptismos – a washing, purification effected by means of water.

It is clear from these authorities that the primary meaning is dip or immerse, and the secondary meaning is wash.

Turning to the New Testament, was the meaning the primary meaning when used of Christian baptism or the secondary meaning? The crucial question is, What precisely did Jesus mean by the verb baptize in His command to baptize converts recorded in Mat. 28:19? Was it a charge to immerse in water, or to pour water on converts or to sprinkle water on them? Let us look at the evidence in the scripture records of baptizing. The meaning of the word baptize is clearly immersion when the disciples were baptized in the Spirit recorded in Acts 2:2–4. We read, "suddenly there came a sound from heaven, as of a rushing mighty wind, and it filled the whole house where they were sitting." Consequently the disciples were immersed in the sound of the Holy Spirit. They were totally submerged as it filled "the whole house where they were sitting." The sound was an emblem of the presence of the Spirit. They were therefore immersed in the Spirit. This experience was defined by Jesus as a baptism. He predicted to the apostles, "you will be baptized in the Holy Spirit not many days from now" (Acts 1:5; my trans.). This baptism was not a sprinkling, or even just a pouring of the Spirit upon them. It was a pouring out of the Spirit (Acts 2:17) to such a degree that it brought about a total filling of the entire house and a consequent complete immersion of the disciples in the Spirit. William J. Larkin Jr. says, "In the Old Testament such a loud sound often accompanied a theophany (Ex 19:16,19; 20:18; compare Heb 12:19). A violent, rushing wind symbolizes the Holy Spirit (Ezek 37:9–14; compare Lk 16:16). The sound fills the whole house. What has arrived is an all-encompassing divine presence."[1]

From this occurrence of baptism we may learn about the mode of John's baptism, because Jesus predicted this baptism in the Spirit in words which related it to John's baptism, "for John truly baptized in water, but you will be baptized in the Holy Spirit not many days from now" (Acts 1:5; my trans). Jesus spoke of this future event as similar to the past event of John's baptism in that it too would be a baptism. Therefore the meaning of the verb baptize in the first part of the verse must be the same in the second part of the verse. He stated that in distinction to that past event the baptism would be in the Holy Spirit instead of in water. On the day of Pentecost, when they were baptized in the Holy Spirit, they were immersed. It follows, therefore, that those baptized in water by John were also immersed.

Let us suppose for a moment that John the Baptist did not immerse when he baptized. Suppose that he sprinkled the candidates with water. The apostles to whom Jesus said "for John truly baptized in water, but you will be baptized in the Holy Spirit not many days from now" would have been fully aware of John's practice. They would remember the sight of John baptizing. Accordingly when they heard the words of Jesus, at that time before the Day of Pentecost, they would have expected to be sprinkled with the Spirit. The prediction would have mislead them, because they were not merely sprinkled with the Spirit. They were immersed in an outpouring of the Spirit that flooded and filled the whole of the house where they were. The prediction of Jesus would not have been truly fulfilled. To suggest that John the Baptist did not immerse therefore is a serious error. It denies the veracity of the Lord Jesus Christ in His ministry as the Prophet (Acts 3:22–23). Similarly, if John had simply poured water on those he baptized, the apostles would have only expected that the Spirit would be poured upon them. They would not have looked for a pouring that would be so copious as to immerse them. Again they would have found the prediction of Jesus misleading. After the event they would have said that Jesus led them to expect much less than their actual experience. Far from misleading the apostles surely Jesus refers to John's baptism to make as plain as possible what would happen on the Day of Pentecost. He told them to think of the actual action taken by John when he baptized, and to expect an identical event to happen to them, but in the Spirit instead of in water. When they were immersed in the Spirit the prophecy of Christ was fulfilled to the letter. So we conclude that John the Baptist must have immersed when he baptized.

From the fact that John the Baptist immersed those he baptized we may make a further deduction. The disciples of Jesus baptized for a period alongside the ministry of John the Baptist. We may deduce that they also practised immersion. Otherwise we must give different meanings to the verb baptize in the following verses, "After these things Jesus and His disciples came into the land of Judea, and there He remained with them and baptized. Now John also was baptizing in Aenon near Salim, because there was much water there. And they came and were baptized. For John had not yet been thrown into prison.... Therefore, when the Lord knew that the Pharisees had heard that Jesus made and baptized more disciples than John (though Jesus Himself did not baptize, but His disciples), He left Judea and departed again to Galilee" (John 3:22–24 and 4:1–3). So we see that baptize meant totally immerse

- in John's baptisms,
- the baptisms carried out by the disciples of Jesus at the time of John's ministry
- and the baptism in the Spirit predicted by Jesus.

This leads to a further conclusion. In the light of these facts it is evident that the command to "go therefore and make disciples of all the nations, baptizing them in the name of the Father and of the Son and of the Holy Spirit" would be understood by the apostles as a command to "immerse" in the name of the Father and of the Son and of the Holy Spirit. It is surely impossible that the verb baptize could have meant something different from its meaning in these other baptisms.

Only immersion is an adequate symbol of union with Christ in His death, burial and resurrection

This is in accord with Paul's declaration to Christians in his letter to Colosse, "buried with Him in baptism, in which you also were raised with *Him* through faith in the working of God, who raised Him from the dead" (Col. 2:12). Burial stresses the reality of death, precedes and gives meaning to resurrection. As we have seen Rom. 6:3–4 speaks of baptism and its meaning: "do you not know that as many of us as were baptized into Christ Jesus were baptized into His death? Therefore we were buried with Him through baptism into death, that just as Christ was raised from the dead by the glory of the Father, even so we also should walk in newness of life." The mode of baptism is inseparable from its meaning. To change the mode of baptism from immersion changes the meaning of God's ordinance. Sprinkling or pouring can portray the washing away of sins, but cannot symbolize union with Christ in His death burial and resurrection. We have seen that in the ordinance of the Lord's Supper God requires that believers understand and give reverence to what is signified. Therefore to modify the mode of baptism from immersion is a grave desecration of God's ordinance. It ceases to signify union with Christ. It fails to symbolize what God intends it to mean.

Immersion is the correct interpretation of *baptizo* when used in the scriptures concerning Christian baptism because of the testimony of church history

The following quotations state that immersion was the practice of the first Christians and continued as common practice for over a thousand years throughout Christendom. It is inconceivable that this would have occurred unless *baptizo* had been taken by the apostles and subsequent Christians to mean its primary meaning, namely immerse.

John Calvin (1509–1564) ". . . it is evident that the term *baptise* means to immerse, and that this was the form used by the primitive church."[2]

A.W. Argyle states St Thomas Aquinas (1224–1274) said, "Christ's burial is more clearly represented by immersion; wherefore this manner is more frequently in use and more commendable."[3]

It is true that soon after the apostolic period affusion (the pouring of water on the head) was practised. This is revealed in the Didache. Scholars find it difficult to date this writing. A range of dates from before 50 A.D. to the third century or later have been proposed. It is clear, however, that the Didache preferred immersion where possible, and that immersion was the normal mode in the first four centuries. Affusion was practised sometimes in cases of sickness or where immersion was inconvenient. A.W. Argyle writes, "After the fourth century immersion had begun to be replaced in some churches by a copious affusion on the head, the person being baptized standing in the water. . . . As Aquinas testifies, even after the spread of affusion, immersion continued to be widely practised and advocated. . . . The mere sprinkling of the head . . . first became the generally recognized custom in the western church after the thirteenth century, but even then the eastern church retained, and still retains, complete immersion of infants."[4] Concerning that eastern Greek Orthodox Church, Erroll Hulse says, "To them baptism literally means to dip or submerge. Their own language preserves the correctness of the word even if tradition has supplanted the Biblical requirement that only believers qualify for immersion."[5]

References

1. William J. Larkin Jr. *Commentary on Acts* IVP 1995, page 49.
2. John Calvin *Institutes* Book IV Chapter 15 section 19.
3. A.W. Argyle *Christian Baptism*, Edited by A. Gilmore, London: Lutterworth 1959, page 219.
4. *Ibid.*, pages 219–220.
5. Errol Hulse *The Testimony of Baptism*, Carey Publications 1982, Page 27.

OBJECTIONS TO THE DOCTRINE OF BAPTISM BY IMMERSION (1)

It will be necessary to refute a number of arguments in this and succeeding chapters.

The first one is the contention that *baptizo* can be used to denote an action which neither indicates nor implies immersion

1. It is argued that in Luke 11:38 "When the Pharisee saw it, he marveled that He had not first washed before dinner," the word translated washed is baptizo *and refers only to washing of the hands* This reference to hand washing is deduced from comparison with Mark 7:3 "For the Pharisees and all the Jews do not eat unless they wash *their* hands in a special way, holding the tradition of the elders." It is contended that the method of washing the hands was done in two ways, namely by dipping the hands in water or by pouring water over them.

However, Luke 11:38 may refer not to Mark 7:3 but to Mark 7:4 *"When they come* from the marketplace, they do not eat unless they wash. And there are many other things which they have received and hold, *like* the washing of cups, pitchers, copper vessels, and couches." The meaning of Mark 7:4 is uncertain. It may mean that contact with the market place increased defilement and therefore required the total washing of immersion. Some manuscripts of this verse contain the word *baptizo* for wash, others read the word *rhantizo*, which means to sprinkle. It is not certain which is correct. If *baptizo* is the reading then the washing after going to the market place could be immersion. This would harmonise with the reference to the washing (*baptismos*) of cups, pitchers, copper vessels, and couches in the remainder of the verse. John Murray, who argues against the contention that immersion is the mode of baptism required by scripture, concedes that *baptizo*, if it is the correct reading in this verse, could mean immersion, and baptismos could refer to the total immersion of cups, pitchers, copper vessels and even couches. He quotes from rabbinic tradition to support the immersion of couches.[1]

In the light of these possible interpretations of Mark 7:4 it is also possible and reasonable to relate Luke 11:38 "When the Pharisee saw *it*, he marveled that He had not first washed (*baptizo*) before dinner" to such a practice of total immersion, rather than the hand washing of Mark 7:3. It is not conclusive that *baptizo* in Luke 11:38 refers to the washing of hands. Immersion as the meaning cannot be dismissed.

2.   *Hebrews 9:10 is also used to argue that* baptizo *and its cognates can mean washing by other means than immersion*

The verse reads, "*concerned* only with foods and drinks, various washings, and fleshly ordinances imposed until the time of reformation." The Greek word translated washings in this verse is literally baptisms – βαπτισμοῖς. It is argued that these washings include the OT rituals in the verses following this scripture, namely, "For if the blood of bulls and goats and the ashes of a heifer, sprinkling the unclean, sanctifies for the purifying of the flesh, how much more shall the blood of Christ, who through the eternal Spirit offered Himself without spot to God, cleanse your conscience from dead works to serve the living God?" (Heb. 9:13–14), and, "For when Moses had spoken every precept to all the people according to the law, he took the blood of calves and goats, with water, scarlet wool, and hyssop, and sprinkled both the book itself and all the people, saying, 'This *is* the blood of the covenant which God has commanded you.' Then likewise he sprinkled with blood both the tabernacle and all the vessels of the ministry. And according to the law almost all things are purified with blood, and without shedding of blood there is no remission" (Heb. 9:19–22). These verses declare purification through sprinkling the unclean. It is contended that, "various washings" (baptisms) in verse 10 refers to these actions of sprinkling, and therefore baptism is used to denote actions other than immersion.

To answer these arguments we must first address the translation of this verse. The correct translation of the verse is disputed by scholars, and their disagreement is evident if the reader compares various versions of the Bible. I suggest that the translation given by F.F. Bruce best captures the meaning, "Those gifts and sacrifices, in addition to matters of food and drink and various ablutions, are material ordinances imposed until the time of reformation."[2] The old covenant, in addition to the arrangements for the gifts and sacrifices of the tabernacle worship, imposed rules for the daily life of the Israelites. These rules concerned foods and drinks and associated washings. But these regulations together with the gifts and sacrifices were literally only "ordinances of flesh." They only provided ceremonial outward cleanness. They could not make the worshipper perfect in regard to the conscience.

If the translation above is correct then the "various washings" do not refer to, nor include the purifications through the blood of sacrifices. The washings of verse 10 are only those linked with the commands about foods and drinks for daily life, not about the gifts and sacrifices of the tabernacle worship, and not about any washings associated with those gifts and sacrifices. Commenting on this verse 10 Paul Ellingworth says, "It is, however, true that for the moment, the author's attention has turned from the Day of Atonement, and indeed from any kind of sacrifice, to the wider range of cultic regulations; the main OT background is now Lv.11 rather than Lv.16. Lv.11, concerned mainly with food, also contains several references to purification with water, especially v.40 λούσεται ὕδατι (cf. Heb. 10:22b). Since the author has noted fatal deficiencies even in the day of Atonement liturgy, the entire OT cultus, by an implied *a fortiori* argument, is considered as similarly ineffective."[3] Donald Guthrie states that the foods and drinks and various washings, ". . . were concerned with peripheral matters, although they were considered to be important. They are not to be identified with the gifts and sacrifices of the earlier verse, but they are accompaniments of them."[4]

So what exactly do "foods and drinks, various washings" refer to in the old covenant regulations? Lev. 11, 17:15–16 and Deut. 14:3–21 explain the meaning of foods and drinks and various washings. These scriptures give clear and comprehensive definitions of clean and unclean foods. To eat of unclean foods rendered an Israelite unclean, defiled and unholy. Similarly in Lev. 11 there are stipulations concerning drinks and washings:

a) The following verses of Lev. 11 state what may and may not be drunk in certain circumstances, and the requirement to immerse particular items in specified cases.

"These also *shall be* unclean to you among the creeping things that creep on the earth: the mole, the mouse, and the large lizard after its kind; the gecko, the monitor lizard, the sand reptile, the sand lizard, and the chameleon. These *are* unclean to you among all that creep. Whoever touches them when they are dead shall be unclean until evening. Anything on which *any* of them falls, when they are dead shall be unclean, whether *it is* any item of wood or clothing or skin or sack, whatever item *it is*, in which *any* work is done, it must be put in water. And it shall be unclean until evening; then it shall be clean. Any earthen vessel into which *any* of them falls you shall break; and whatever *is* in it shall be unclean: in such a vessel, any edible food upon which water falls becomes unclean, and any drink that may be drunk from it becomes unclean. And everything on which *a part* of *any such* carcass falls shall be unclean; *whether it is* an oven or cooking stove, it shall be broken down; *for* they *are* unclean, and shall be unclean to you. Nevertheless a spring or a cistern, *in which there is* plenty of water, shall be clean, but whatever touches any such carcass becomes unclean" (Lev. 11:29–36).

b) The following verses required the washing of clothes.

"By these" (that is the previously specified unclean foods) "you shall become unclean; whoever touches the carcass of any of them shall be unclean until evening; whoever carries part of the carcass of any of them shall wash his clothes and be unclean until evening" (Lev. 11:24–25).

"And if any animal which you may eat dies, he who touches its carcass shall be unclean until evening. He who eats of its carcass shall wash his clothes and be unclean until evening. He also who carries its carcass shall wash his clothes and be unclean until evening" (Lev. 11:39–40).

"And every person who eats what died *naturally* or what was torn *by beasts, whether he is* a native of your own country or a stranger, he shall both wash his clothes and bathe in water, and be unclean until evening. Then he shall be clean. But if he does not wash *them* or bathe his body, then he shall bear his guilt" (Lev. 17:15–16).

The various washings of Heb. 9:10 refer to these immersions and washings here in Lev. 11 and 17. They are all washings by dipping or immersion, not by pouring or sprinkling. As Lev. 11 and 17 reveal, the various washings are bound up with the food and drink regulations. Consequently they are mentioned together. A correct interpretation of various washings in Heb 9:10 therefore

• does not relate them to the gifts and sacrifices of the tabernacle worship.
• relates them to Lev. 11 and 17:15–16.
• distinguishes them from the purifications in Heb. 9:13–14 and 19–22.

• does not substantiate the contention that "various washings" (pl of baptismos) means anything other than washings by dippings/immersions.

3.   Mat. 3:11, "He will baptize you in the Holy Spirit and fire" (my translation) is also appealed to to prove that baptizo does not always mean immerse

Firstly it has been argued that the fulfilment of this as regards the baptism in the Holy Spirit was truly an event of immersion (Acts 2). Secondly the baptism of fire was an immersion in judgment. John was speaking of the nation of Israel when he said these words. Let us look at the surrounding verses. We shall see that fire means judgment. Those of the nation who received the Messiah would be blessed with a baptism in the Holy Spirit, those who rejected Him would suffer terrible judgment: "and do not think to say to yourselves, 'We have Abraham as *our* father.' For I say to you that God is able to raise up children to Abraham from these stones. And even now the ax is laid to the root of the trees. Therefore every tree which does not bear good fruit is cut down and thrown into the fire. I indeed baptize you in water unto repentance, but He who is coming after me is mightier than I, whose sandals I am not worthy to carry. He will baptize you in the Holy Spirit and fire. His winnowing fan *is* in His hand, and He will thoroughly clean out His threshing floor, and gather His wheat into the barn; but He will burn up the chaff with unquenchable fire" (Mat. 3:9–12: my translation of v. 11). In this verse we have *baptizo* used metaphorically. It was an immersion in judgment, just as Jesus prophesied before His death, "Therefore, indeed, I send you prophets, wise men, and scribes: *some* of them you will kill and crucify, and *some* of them you will scourge in your synagogues and persecute from city to city, that on you may come all the righteous blood shed on the earth, from the blood of righteous Abel to the blood of Zechariah, son of Berechiah, whom you murdered between the temple and the altar. Assuredly, I say to you, all these things will come upon this generation" (Mat. 23:34–36). The judgment of God took away the kingdom of God from the Jews and gave it to a new nation of believers in Christ who were predominantly Gentiles (Mat. 21:43). It culminated in the destruction of Jerusalem in A.D. 70. This was a baptism of the fire of Divine judgment. It was an overwhelming punishment on the nation.

We have further metaphorical use of *baptizo* in Luke 12:50, "But I have a baptism to be baptized with, and how distressed I am till it is accomplished!" These are the words of Jesus as He anticipates the overwhelming suffering of His sacrificial death. He knew from the Old Testament scriptures the anguish which lay before Him. He knew that

He would be disfigured to a degree that He would no longer resemble a man (Isa. 52:14). He was fully aware of the prophecy in Psalm 22 of His words during future sufferings: "I am poured out like water, And all My bones are out of joint; My heart is like wax; It has melted within Me. My strength is dried up like a potsherd, And My tongue clings to My jaws; You have brought Me to the dust of death. For dogs have surrounded Me; The congregation of the wicked has enclosed Me. They pierced My hands and My feet; I can count all My bones. They look *and* stare at Me. They divide My garments among them, And for My clothing they cast lots" (Psa. 22:14–18). He knew from these and other prophecies that He was going to have an overwhelming experience of anguish and pain. He was going to be submerged in agony. Suffering was not merely poured upon Him. He was overwhelmed by it.

Mark 10:38–39 also speaks of baptism as an overwhelming experience of suffering: "But Jesus said to them, 'You do not know what you ask. Are you able to drink the cup that I drink, and be baptized with the baptism that I am baptized with?' They said to Him, 'We are able.' So Jesus said to them, 'You will indeed drink the cup that I drink, and with the baptism I am baptized with you will be baptized' " (Mark 10:38–39). For James that baptism would be martyrdom (Acts 12:20); for John banishment to the Isle of Patmos. They were indeed immersed in suffering.

4.   *1 Cor. 10:1–2 are verses also used to argue that* baptizo *does not always mean immerse*

They read, "Moreover, brethren, I do not want you to be unaware that all our fathers were under the cloud, all passed through the sea, all were baptized into Moses in the cloud and in the sea." These verses recall the exodus of the children of Israel from Egypt under the leadership of Moses. Their experience of being under the cloud (Exod. 13:21–22), and going through the sea with the waters on both sides of them standing as walls (Exod. 14:22), is called a baptism. They went through the sea. In that sense they were in the sea. Figuratively speaking they were immersed in the sea. Equally the Israelites were in the cloud in that they walked in its light, (Exod. 14:20). They were immersed in it in that sense. This interpretation surely makes more sense than to suggest that "baptized" in the cloud and in the sea is a figure of pouring or sprinkling.

5.   *Quotations from the Septuagint version of the Old Testament are also argued from to say that* baptizo *does not always signify immersion*

This translation of the Old Testament into Greek was carried out in the third century B.C. *Baptizo* only occurs twice, in 2 Kings 5:14 and Isaiah

21:4. Concerning the latter John Murray says that its use is figurative and, "It would appear that nothing very determinative regarding the precise import of βαπτίζω can be derived in this instance."[5] He says of 2 Kings 5:14, "Without doubt he bathed himself in Jordan; but there is no evidence derived from the terms used either in Hebrew or Greek, or from the details of the narrative, to prove that Naaman immersed himself."[6] His leprosy surely required the total washing of his body. The Hebrew verb means to dip, and so this total washing was by dipping seven times in the river. The Hebrew is not pouring or sprinkling. It is dipping.

Conclusion

All the verses used to contend that baptizo can be used to denote an action which neither indicates nor implies immersion are inconclusive. In every case the evidence is consistent with immersion. A.H. Strong's words concerning baptize remain true, "every passage where the word occurs in the New Testament either requires or allows the meaning 'immerse'."[7]

References

1. John Murray *Christian Baptism*, Presbyterian and Reformed Publishing Company 1972, page 19 footnote.
2. F.F. Bruce *The Epistle to the Hebrews* Revised, Eerdmans 1990, page 206.
3. Paul Ellingworth *The Epistle to the Hebrews*, Eerdmans and Paternoster 1993, page 442.
4. Donald Guthrie *Hebrews*, IVP and Eerdmans Reprinted 1993, page 184.
5. John Murray *Christian Baptism*, Presbyterian and Reformed Publishing Company 1972, page 10.
6. *Ibid.*, page 13.
7. A.H. Strong *Systematic Theology*, Pickering and Inglis Nineteenth printing 1956, page 934.

CHAPTER FIVE

OBJECTIONS TO THE DOCTRINE OF BAPTISM BY IMMERSION (2)

Arguments against interpreting the New Testament records of baptisms as accounts of immersions

John's baptism

"Then all the land of Judea, and those from Jerusalem, went out to him and were all baptized by him in the Jordan River, confessing their sins" (Mark 1:5).

"It came to pass in those days *that* Jesus came from Nazareth of Galilee, and was baptized by John in the Jordan" (Mark 1:9).

"And immediately, coming up out of the water, He saw the heavens parting and the Spirit descending upon Him like a dove" (Mark 1:10 mgn.).

"Now John also was baptizing in Aenon near Salim, because there was much water there. And they came and were baptized" (John 3:23).

John Murray contends that "in the river Jordan"[1] may be nothing more than a designation of location. He states that "into Jordan"[2] ". . . does not necessarily imply immersion. Standing in the water or on the brink of the river would satisfy completely the idea expressed."[3] He says that the choice of the river Jordan and Aenon could have been to avoid disrupting limited water supplies by the presence of large multitudes, and also to meet the needs of those multitudes and possibly animals used by them to travel there. He concludes that the choice of these places "does not prove that they were selected because they afforded the amount of water requisite for immersion."[4] Before these arguments John Murray concedes, "At the outset it should be understood that John may have baptized by the mode of immersion; there does not appear to be evidence by which immersion could be disproved.

29

Furthermore, if John baptized by the mode of immersion there is in this very consideration a good reason for choosing Jordan and Ainon as the sites of administration – there was abundant water in both places. And the expressions used with reference to Jordan, namely, 'in the river Jordan' and 'into the Jordan' could readily be taken as reflecting, to some extent at least, on the actual mode."[5] Please note the admission "there does not appear to be evidence by which immersion could be disproved."

Louis Berkhof questions whether John the Baptist was capable of the enormous task of immersing the multitudes that came to him, or whether he simply poured water on them as some of the early inscriptions would seem to indicate. Wayne Grudem answers, "Certainly over a period of several days he would have been capable of immersing many hundreds of people, but it is also possible that his disciples (Matt. 9:14; et al.) assisted him with some of the baptisms."[6] Affusion was practised in the early ages of the Church, as we have seen from the Didache, but to suggest on the basis of such early inscriptions that John baptized by pouring is pure speculation.

Turning again to Mark 1:10 Wayne Grudem points out that "The Greek text specifies that he came 'out of ' (ek) the water, not that he came away from it (this would be expressed by Gk. apo). The fact that John and Jesus went into the river and came up out of it strongly suggests immersion, since sprinkling or pouring of water could much more readily have been done standing beside the river, particularly because multitudes of people were coming for baptism."[7] Jay E. Adams argues against immersion from the parallel account in Mat. 3:16. He says, "In Mark's account ek is used, but in Matthew, apo While ek can mean 'away from' as well as 'out of,' apo can not mean 'out of,' but only 'away from.' Thus from the parallel accounts, it is certain that Mark used ek in the sense of apo in this instance. Thus Matthew and Mark meant to say 'he went away from' the water."[8] In fact it is by no means certain that Mark used ek in the sense of apo. The following Bible Translations all translate ek as 'out of' not 'away from' – NIV, New Revised Standard Version, New American Standard Bible, Good News Bible, and New Century Version. This list of some translations demonstrates that many biblical scholars do not agree with Jay E. Adams. The two accounts of Matthew and Mark are complementary. Robert H. Gundry writes, "Matthew's ἀπό does not negate the thought of emergence contained in Mark's ἐκ, but it indicates more clearly Jesus' complete departure from the waters of the Jordan. The differences suggest, then, that Matthew did not want anybody to think Jesus stayed in the river to confess his sins. He had none. He was fulfilling all righteousness. That Matthew rarely retains εὐθύς (Mark has it often) lends further support to this understanding."[9]

J. Oliver Buswell argues against immersion as John's mode. He says, "In a country in which people wore sandals, the most natural action would be to step down into the edge of the water for purposes of baptism, and then to step back out of the water after the baptism had been performed."[10] He goes on to say, "The current of the Jordan River is sometimes very swift. Friends of ours, attempting to be immersed in the Jordan at the place where John was baptizing, have reported that they were in danger of being swept away by the current. In all probability the person being baptized, with John, simply stepped down into the edge of the water; John dipped the water of baptism in his hand, or in a gourd; the baptism was by sprinkling or pouring; and then of course the person baptized came up from, or out of, the water."[11] He also states that the words translated "much water" in John 3:23 "literally say 'many waters'. In this geographical area, there are many springs, but there is no natural body of water large enough for immersion. John and his disciples could baptize a great many people at the different springs, but immersion was out of the question."[12]

John A. Broadus gives a great deal of information about the river Jordan. In his long description of the river he says that the traditional place of Christ's baptism is nearly opposite Jericho, but the place cannot be determined. "At the traditional place the river is, in spring (when most travellers visit it), both too deep and too swift for fording. Yet just before Easter several thousand Greek and Oriental pilgrims (in the Middle Ages there were sometimes 100,000) go to this place – men, women and children – and immerse themselves . . ."[13] These facts prove that immersion was not out of the question at the Jordan. Moreover the springs at Aenon would provide abundant water for immersion.

Acts 2:41 "Then those who gladly received his word were baptized; and that day about three thousand souls were added to them"

Louis Berkof asks, "Did the apostles find enough water in Jerusalem, and did they have the necessary facilities, to baptize three thousand in a single day by immersion?"[14] The Pool of Siloam was one source of water fed by the Gihon spring, a copious and perennial stream. Baker's *Encyclopedia of the Bible* states, "It is known that later" (i.e. after the time of king Hezekiah 715–686 B.C.) "2 aqueducts, 13 and 41 miles in length, brought water into Jerusalem. They merged at the Roman reservoirs near Bethlehem. On reaching the city, the water was carried to the temple area by means of underground pipes (cf. Ez. 47:1; Jl 3:18). In NT times, the Jewish historian Josephus stated, Pontius Pilate appropriated some 'Corban' money from the temple treasury for work on an aqueduct. . . . The Romans brought the science of aqueduct engineering to a fine art."[15] John Gill suggests that, as well as pools in Jerusalem, there were private baths and facilities in the temple available for their use.[16] D. Bridge and D. Phypers say, "Sceptical scholars long denied the historical accuracy of the Day of Pentecost narrative (Acts 2) on the grounds that sufficient water would not have been available to the apostles to baptize three thousand people in the forecourts of the Temple. However, recent discovery of at least twenty ritual baths in the houses near the Temple's southern staircase, and further discovery that the Old City had (and still has) a huge number of underground cisterns to collect and store rainwater, often with easy access by carved staircases, have answered that objection."[17] The other disciples with the apostles provided enough help to baptize the large numbers. The text of Acts 2:41 does not necessitate that all the 3,000 converts added to the church were baptized that same day.

Acts 8:36, 38–39 "Now as they went down the road, they came to some water. And the eunuch said, 'See, here is water. What hinders me from being baptized?' So he commanded the chariot to stand still. And both Philip and the eunuch went down into the water, and he baptized him. Now when they came up out of the water, the Spirit of the Lord caught Philip away, so that the eunuch saw him no more; and he went on his way rejoicing."
Jay E. Adams changes the translation to read, both Philip and the eunuch "went down to the water" instead of into the water: and, when they came up "away from the water."[18] Again his translation is contrary to Bible translators of the N.I.V., New Revised Standard Version, New American Standard Bible, Good News Bible, and New Century Version. He has no solid ground for his alternative translation.

J. Oliver Buswell writes "The region along that road is desert country (Acts 8:26) and there is no natural body of water available for immersion. . . . The presumption is that it was a shallow pool beside the road such as is often seen in desert country after a shower."[19] He also affirms that the eunuch thought of baptism because he had just read Isa. 52:15 "So shall he sprinkle many nations." He continues, "He probably was familiar with Ezekiel 36:25 'Then shall I sprinkle clean water on you and ye shall be clean from all your filthiness and from all your idols will I cleanse you. A new heart also will I give you and a new spirit will I put within you and will take away the stony heart out of your flesh and I will give you an heart of flesh. And I will put my spirit within you and cause you to walk in My statutes and ye shall keep My judgments and do them.' (Ezekiel 36:25–27). And the Ethiopian knew the Old Testament idea of ceremonial cleansing by the sprinkling of water. It is thus quite easy to see what caused the Ethiopian to ask for baptism. Here again the going down into the water was not in any sense a part of the baptizing for both of them went down into the water. Neither did the coming up out of the water constitute any part of the baptizing, for they both came up out of the water. The baptizing was an act quite distinct from going down and coming up. Wearing sandals, as was the custom in those days, they doubtless stepped down into the water (it may have been a few inches deep) and Philip baptized the eunuch, doubtless by dipping and pouring or sprinkling, as suggested by numerous Old Testament references. There is then, not one instance in the New Testament in which baptism itself is said to involve the going down into the water, or a coming up out of the water."[20]

Concerning the alleged shortage of water for immersion Simon J. Kistemaker says ". . . closer to Gaza, a brook called Wadi el-Hashi flows north of the city into the Mediterranean Sea. Another possibility is that pools in that area provided a suitable place for baptism."[21]

It is agreed that the records in the New Testament are silent concerning the administration of baptism. Only the actions immediately before and immediately after are recorded on some occasions. But those actions do accord more naturally with immersion than with either pouring or sprinkling. Neither pouring nor sprinkling require both of them going down into the water and coming up out of it. Immersion does. Sprinkling, and even pouring, would only need Philip to go into the water. Moreover these phrases "went down into the water" and "came up out of the water" are most inappropriate if the water was only a few inches deep.

The reasons for the silence about the precise actions involved in the actual immersion of the person baptized are:

- the crystal clear meaning of the word baptize was immerse,
- the fact that just how the person is immersed does not matter. From the evidence in the early centuries of the church it seems that immersion was sometimes accomplished by the administrant standing with the candidate who knelt in the water and bowing him forward. The crucial point of the ordinance is that immersion signifies burial. How the immersion is achieved is of no consequence. To specify a precise method of immersion would detract from the meaning of the symbolic action.

The sprinkling of the blood of Jesus (1 Pet. 1:2), prophesied in Isaiah 52:15, is distinct from baptism. It is the application of the blood of Christ to believing sinners thereby bearing and putting away their sins. That is what Isaiah prophesied, not the baptisms of people of the nations.

Buswell contends that sprinkling is the mode of baptism indicated by the Old Testament. There was no ordinance in the Old Testament comparable to New Testament baptism. Circumcision was not the equivalent as we shall see later. His argument, however, is proved to be wrong by the Jewish practice of baptism by total immersion of Gentile proselytes when they were converted to Judaism. That baptism signified both dedication and cleansing. This shows that the Jews did not deduce from the Old Testament that they should sprinkle their converts. It is uncertain just when proselyte baptism began. Most scholars believe it preceded Christian baptism. But if it began later, unbelieving Jews would surely not have modelled their baptism of Gentile converts to Judaism on Christian practice. With the Old Testament in their hands they decided to immerse when they baptized. It did not suggest sprinkling to them.

Acts 9:18 "Immediately there fell from his eyes something like scales, and he received his sight at once; and he arose and was baptized."

Louis Berkhof questions "Does Acts 9:18 indicate in any way that Paul left the place where Ananias found him, to be immersed in some pool or river?"[22] The account is condensed. It certainly does not rule out going to some pool or river. John Gill argues that ". . . it is highly probable there was a bath in the house, in which it might be performed; since it was the house of a Jew, with whom it was usual to have baths to wash their whole bodies . . ."[23]

Jay E. Adams writes, "In every account, that of Luke, and those of Paul, one finds either Ananias saying, 'Stand up and be baptized' or the statement, 'he stood up and was baptized.' This reads literally 'standing up, he was baptized' (see Acts 22:12–16 and Acts 9:17–18). How can Saul have been immersed if he was baptized on the spot as he stood up?"[24] These accounts in Acts record in concise manner a sequence of events. Saul having fasted totally from food and water for three days is either seated or lying down when Ananias comes to him. This is stated explicitly in Acts 22:16. It is also recorded that he was weak when Ananias went to him (Acts 9:19). To be baptized he must rise from that state of being seated or lying down, and then proceed to be baptized. Just as we might say "Get up and go to work." The two actions are sequential. He first arose and subsequently was baptized.

Acts 10:47–48 " 'Can anyone forbid water, that these should not be baptized who have received the Holy Spirit just as we **have***?' And he commanded them to be baptized in the name of the Lord. Then they asked him to stay a few days."*

Louis Berkhof asks "Does not the account of the baptism of Cornelius create the impression that water was to be brought and that those present were baptized right in the house?"[25] This objection to immersion as the mode is based on suppositions:

1. that they were baptized in the house. The text gives absolutely no indication where they were baptized.
2. that water had to be brought to the house.

From these suppositions it is deduced that baptism was not by immersion. They are suppositions without any basis. The argument amounts to no more than "I imagine that it was not possible to immerse because of certain factors which I imagine, therefore it was not possible."

Acts 16:33 "And he took them the same hour of the night and washed **their** *stripes. And immediately he and all his family were baptized."*

J. Oliver Buswell alleges that this baptism was not by immersion because, "It must be realized that dwelling houses of those days were not even equipped with bathtubs. Even a wealthy person must go to a public bath for bathing . . . there would probably be a well in the courtyard, and water for washing the apostles' wounds and for baptizing the jailor and his household, could be secured with the greatest facility."[26] (In this quotation please note that he uses the word baptizing to mean pour water upon or sprinkle with water). Robert L. Reymond asserts, ". . . Paul would have hardly taken the jailor's household to a river after midnight . . ."[27] Louis Berkhof suggests that the jailor would not have dared to take Paul and Silas outside the city, when he was commanded to keep them safely.[28] It is stated that the jailor did take them to his home after midnight (Acts 16:34), so why not to any suitable place for immersion if it was necessary?

Conclusion

The New Testament accounts of baptisms are consistent with immersion.

References

1. John Murray *Christian Baptism*, Presbyterian and Reformed Publishing Company, 1972, page 28.
2. *Ibid.*

3. *Ibid.*
4. *Ibid.*
5. *Ibid.*, page 27.
6. Taken from *Systematic Theology* by Wayne A. Grudem. Copyright © 1994 by Wayne Grudem. Used by permission of IVP and Zondervan, page 967 footnote.
7. *Ibid.*, pages 967–968.
8. Jay E. Adams *The Meaning and Mode of Baptism*, Presbyterian and Reformed Publishing Company 1975, page 42.
9. Robert H. Gundry *Matthew*, Eerdmans Second Edition, 1994, page 51.
10. J. Oliver Buswell *A Systematic Theology of the Christian Religion* Vol. 2 1979, page 246.
11. *Ibid.*, page 247.
12. *Ibid.*, page 247.
13. John A. Broadus *Commentary on Matthew*, Kregel Publications 1990, page 43.
14. Louis Berkhof *Systematic Theology*, Banner of Truth 1959, page 630.
15. Walter A. Elwell (ed) *Baker Encyclopedia of the Bible* Vol. 1 A-C Baker Books 1997, page 143.
16. John Gill *Body of Divinity* Vol. 2, Baker Book House 1978, page 645.
17. Donald Bridge and David Phypers *The Water that Divides*, Christian Focus, Tain, Scotland 2008 ISBN 978-184550-308-6, pages 23–24 (1998 edition).
18. Jay E. Adams *The Meaning and Mode of Baptism*, Presbyterian and Reformed Publishing Company 1975, page 42.
19. J. Oliver Buswell *A Systematic Theology of the Christian Religion* Vol. 2 1979, page 247.
20. *Ibid.*, page 248.
21. Simon J. Kistemaker *New Testament Commentary Acts*, Baker 1995, page 319.
22. Louis Berkhof *Systematic Theology*, Banner of Truth 1959, page 630.
23. John Gill *Body of Divinity* Vol. 2, Baker Book House 1978, page 645.
24. Jay E. Adams *The Meaning and Mode of Baptism*, Presbyterian and Reformed Publishing Company 1975, page 49.
25. Louis Berkhof *Systematic Theology*, Banner of Truth 1959, page 630.
26. J. Oliver Buswell *A Systematic Theology of the Christian Religion* Vol. 2 1979, page 249.
27. Dr. Robert L. Reymond *A New Systematic Theology of the Christian Faith.* Copyright © 1998, Thomas Nelson, Inc., page 933. Used by permission of Thomas Nelson, Inc.
28. Louis Berkhof *Systematic Theology*, Banner of Truth 1959, page 630.

CHAPTER SIX

OBJECTIONS TO THE DOCTRINE OF BAPTISM BY IMMERSION (3)

Arguments against immersion as the mode based on interpretation of the symbolism of baptism

1. Louis Berkhof contends that washing is the meaning of baptism
He writes, "... Scripture makes it abundantly clear that baptism symbolizes spiritual cleansing or purification, Acts 2:38; 22:16; Rom. 6:4f; 1 Cor. 6:11; Tit. 3:5; Heb. 10:22; 1 Pet. 3:21; Rev. 1:5. This is exactly the point on which the Bible places all emphasis, while it never represents the going down and coming up as something essential."[1]

It is agreed that baptism symbolizes the washing away of sins, and that this is taught in Acts 2:38 and 22:16. But it also symbolizes union with Christ. This aspect of the symbolism is given equal, if not more, prominence in the New Testament. The washing away of sins flows from that union. It is only one of the spiritual blessings which all come from being "in Christ." To make the symbolism of baptism to speak essentially of only one blessing rather than all the blessedness of being "in Christ" is to minimize the meaning of baptism. It takes no account of the change of life and new commitment expressed by the believer in baptism. The believer affirms union with Christ in the likeness of His death and the likeness of His resurrection (Rom. 6:3–11).

Louis Berkhof's quoted verses other than Acts 2:38 and 22:16 do not support his contention that washing is symbolised by baptism. 1 Cor. 6:11, Tit. 3:5, Heb. 10:22 and Rev. 1:5 (quoted below) all refer to the new birth, not water baptism. The washing they speak of is "the washing of water by the word" (Eph. 5:26). It is the cleansing by the word of God of which Jesus spoke to His disciples: "You are already clean because of the word which I have spoken to you" (John 15:3).

1 Cor. 6:11 "And such were some of you. But you were washed, but you were sanctified, but you were justified in the name of the Lord Jesus and by the Spirit of our God."

Tit. 3:5 "not by works of righteousness which we have done, but according to His mercy He saved us, through the washing of regeneration and renewing of the Holy Spirit."

Heb. 10:22 "let us draw near with a true heart in full assurance of faith, having our hearts sprinkled from an evil conscience and our bodies washed with pure water." (Notice that it is "pure water". This surely refers to the word of God not the water of baptism).

Rev. 1:5 "and from Jesus Christ, the faithful witness, the firstborn from the dead, and the ruler over the kings of the earth. To Him who loved us and washed us from our sins in His own blood."

Turning to the other verses quoted, 1 Pet. 3:21 does not focus on washing but on salvation, and the response to God from a good conscience, having experienced justification through faith; and Rom. 6:4f teaches that the essential symbolism of baptism is precisely what Louis Berkhof desires to deny. It is union with Christ in His death, burial and resurrection. If baptism only symbolizes washing from sins then pouring or sprinkling would indeed be an adequate symbol. But only immersion can symbolize death, burial and resurrection.

2. Jay E. Adams states that water baptism does not symbolize death, burial and resurrection. It symbolizes Holy Spirit baptism

He asserts that the Holy Spirit baptisms recorded in Acts 2 and 10 set the norm for all Christian baptism. He contends that these baptisms were outpourings of the Spirit not immersions in the out-poured Spirit. On this basis he argues that water baptism must be done by pouring or sprinkling since it symbolizes this descent of the Spirit into the Christian's life.[2] Reasons for affirming that the Holy Spirit baptisms in Acts 2 and 10 were immersions in the Spirit have been given above. Consequently even if water baptism were intended to symbolize Holy Spirit baptism immersion would be the correct mode.

The argument that burial with Christ in Rom. 6 cannot be appealed to as providing an index to the mode of baptism

John Murray agrees that the leading thought in the passage is union with Christ. He says, "It is very easy to point to the expression 'buried with him' in verse 4 and insist that only immersion provides an analogy to burial. But such a procedure fails to take account of all that Paul says here. It should be noted that Paul not only says 'buried together' (συνετάφημεν) but also 'planted together' (σύμφυτοι) and 'crucified together' (συνεσταυρώθη). These latter expressions indicate the union with Christ which is symbolised and sealed by baptism just as surely as does 'buried together'. But it is only too apparent that they do not bear any analogy to immersion. . . . When all of Paul's expressions are taken into account we see that burial with Christ can be appealed to as providing an index to the mode of baptism no more than can crucifixion with him. And since the latter does not indicate the *mode* of baptism there is no validity to the argument that burial does. The fact is that there are many aspects to our union with Christ. It is arbitrary to select one aspect and find in the language used to set forth the essence of the mode of baptism." He continues, "In Rom. 6:3 Paul says 'As many of us as were baptized into Christ Jesus were baptized into His death', and in Galatians 3:27 'For as many of you as were baptized into Christ did put on Christ.' It would be just as legitimate to insist that there is a reference to the mode of baptism in Galatians 3:27 as in Romans 6:3. But in Galatians 3:27 the figure used by the apostle to set forth the import of baptism into Christ has no resemblance to immersion. It is the figure of putting on a garment. The plain inference is that Paul is not alluding to the mode of baptism at all. And neither may we suppose that he is in Rom. 6:2–6."[3]

It is agreed that "planted together", "crucified with Him" and putting on Christ say nothing about the mode of baptism. But John Murray fails to take account of one decisive fact. Paul does link baptism with burial "we were buried with Him through baptism". It is therefore not arbitrary to select this one aspect and find in it the essence of the mode of baptism. It is the aspect of union with Christ selected by the apostle when speaking of baptism again in Col. 2:12 "buried with Him in baptism, in which you also were raised with *Him* through faith in the working of God, who raised Him from the dead." That burial should be the aspect providing an index to the mode of baptism demonstrates Divine wisdom. Burial speaks of the reality of death and resurrection (Acts 24:15). Burial with Christ, perfectly symbolized by immersion, declares death with Christ and resurrection with Him. It is a comprehensive symbol of union with Christ.

References

1. Louis Berkhof *Systematic Theology*, Banner of Truth 1959, page 628–629.
2. Jay E. Adams *The Meaning and Mode of Baptism*, Presbyterian and Reformed Publishing Company 1975, Chapter IV.
3. John Murray *Christian Baptism*, Presbyterian and Reformed Publishing Co. 1972, pages 30–31.

CHAPTER SEVEN

OBJECTIONS TO THE DOCTRINE OF BAPTISM BY IMMERSION (4)

Arguments that deny that Rom. 6:1–11 and Col. 2:12 refer to water baptism

Louis Berkhof misinterprets Rom. 6:4f and Col. 2:12 as not speaking directly of baptism with water. He says ". . . they do not speak directly of any baptism with water at all, but of the spiritual baptism thereby represented. They represent regeneration under the figure of a dying and a rising again."[1]

To deny direct reference to water baptism in these passages is to deny that "baptized into Christ Jesus" (Rom. 6:3), and "buried with Him in baptism" (Col. 2:12) refer to water baptism. In Romans 6 Paul is arguing against those who said "Let us sin that grace may abound." The thrust of Paul's argument is that his readers knew that in the act of baptism they were baptized into His death. The old way of life, when they were unconverted, had passed away: "knowing this, that our old man was crucified with *Him*, that the body of sin might be done away with, that we should no longer be slaves of sin" (Rom. 6:6). That is what water baptism signified. So Paul argues in the light of that knowledge of having died to sin, symbolized in the act of baptism, "How shall we who died to sin live any longer in it?" (Rom. 6:2). He is not reminding them directly of their regeneration. He is reminding them of their water baptism and its meaning. His argument is most powerful. He refers to a definite event in each of their lives and to its meaning.

Dr. Martyn Lloyd-Jones also concludes that baptism by water is not in the mind of the Apostle at all in Rom. 6. It is the baptism that incorporates believers into Christ and joins them to Him. It is the baptism stated in 1 Cor. 12:13: "For by one Spirit we were all baptized into one body – whether Jews or Greeks, whether slaves or free – and have all been made to drink into one Spirit."[2]

At this point we must look in depth at the correct translation of 1 Cor. 12:13 with reference to "by one Spirit" and "into one body"

A study of various translations of the New Testament will reveal that the words "For by one Spirit" can be translated "For in the one Spirit." The New Revised Standard Version reads "For in the one Spirit we were all baptized into one body." The New International Version has a footnote stating it can be translated baptized "with or in" one Spirit. Grammatically both translations are correct, because the Greek word ἐν has both meanings. Which of the two is intended by the writer can only be decided by the immediate context, and the context of the whole teaching of the New Testament.

The true meaning of this verse, however, requires a further decision about another Greek word which also has different possible translations. The word is εἰς which is translated "into" in the phrase "into one body" in 1 Cor. 12:13. It can be translated "into" or "for" or "with a view to." An example of the translation "for" is found in the same letter in 1 Cor. 16:1: "the collection for the saints." The verse reads,

"Now concerning the collection **for the saints,** as I have given orders to the churches of Galatia, so you must do also."

Περὶ δὲ τῆς λογείας τῆς **εἰς τοὺς ἁγίους** ὥσπερ διέταξα ταῖς ἐκκλησίαις τῆς Γαλατίας, οὕτως καὶ ὑμεῖς ποιήσατε (1 Cor. 16:1 GNT).

Εἰς is translated "for" numerous times in the New Testament. Its root meaning is "direction towards." Consequently it characteristically expresses movement into. But it can also express purpose, with a view to, and so can be translated "for." So let us look at εἰς used with βαπτίζω in the New Testament. It can indicate the element in which the immersion is made e.g. Mark 1:9 "in (εἰς) the Jordan." When we look at the rest of the uses of εἰς with βαπτίζω in the New Testament we see this root meaning of "direction towards" coming through. As above (1 Cor. 1:16) key words are in bold type.

Baptism directed towards expressing repentance

"I indeed baptize you in water **unto repentance,** but He who is coming after me is mightier than I, whose sandals I am not worthy to carry. He will baptize you in the Holy Spirit and fire" (Mat. 3:11 my translation).

ἐγὼ μὲν ὑμᾶς βαπτίζω ἐν ὕδατι **εἰς μετάνοιαν,** ὁ δὲ ὀπίσω μου ἐρχόμενος ἰσχυρότερός μού ἐστιν, οὗ οὐκ εἰμὶ ἱκανὸς τὰ ὑποδήματα βαστάσαι· αὐτὸς ὑμᾶς βαπτίσει ἐν πνεύματι ἁγίῳ καὶ πυρί (Mat. 3:11 GNT).

Baptism directed towards the remission of sins

"Then Peter said to them, 'Repent, and let every one of you be baptized in the name of Jesus Christ **for the remission of sins;** and you shall receive the gift of the Holy Spirit' " (Acts 2:38).

Πέτρος δὲ πρὸς αὐτούς, Μετανοήσατε, [φησίν,] καὶ βαπτισθήτω ἕκαστος ὑμῶν ἐπὶ τῷ ὀνόματι Ἰησοῦ Χριστοῦ **εἰς ἄφεσιν τῶν ἁμαρτιῶν** ὑμῶν καὶ λήμψεσθε τὴν δωρεὰν τοῦ ἁγίου πνεύματος (Acts 2:38 GNT).

"John came baptizing in the wilderness and preaching a baptism of repentance **for the remission of sins"** (Mark 1:4).

ἐγένετο Ἰωάννης [ὁ] βαπτίζων ἐν τῇ ἐρήμῳ καὶ κηρύσσων βάπτισμα **μετανοίας εἰς ἄφεσιν ἁμαρτιῶν** (Mark 1:4 GNT.).

"And he went into all the region around the Jordan, preaching a baptism of repentance **for the remission of sins"** (Luke 3:3).

καὶ ἦλθεν εἰς πᾶσαν [τὴν] περίχωρον τοῦ Ἰορδάνου κηρύσσων βάπτισμα μετανοίας **εἰς ἄφεσιν ἁμαρτιῶν** (Luke 3:3 GNT).

Baptism directed towards the Lord Jesus

"For as yet He had fallen upon none of them. They had only been baptized **in the name of the Lord Jesus"** (Acts 8:16).

οὐδέπω γὰρ ἦν ἐπ' οὐδενὶ αὐτῶν ἐπιπεπτωκός, μόνον δὲ βεβαπτισμένοι ὑπῆρχον **εἰς τὸ ὄνομα τοῦ κυρίου Ἰησοῦ** (Acts 8:16 GNT).

"When they heard *this,* they were baptized **in the name of the Lord Jesus"** (Acts 19:5).

ἀκούσαντες δὲ ἐβαπτίσθησαν **εἰς τὸ ὄνομα τοῦ κυρίου Ἰησοῦ** (Acts 19:5 GNT).

"Or do you not know that as many of us as were baptized **into Christ Jesus** were baptized **into His death?"** (Rom. 6:3).

ἢ ἀγνοεῖτε ὅτι, ὅσοι ἐβαπτίσθημεν **εἰς Χριστὸν Ἰησοῦν, εἰς τὸν θάνατον αὐτοῦ** ἐβαπτίσθημεν (Rom. 6:3 GNT).

"Therefore we were buried with Him through baptism **into death,** that just as Christ was raised from the dead by the glory of the Father, even so we also should walk in newness of life" (Rom. 6:4).

συνετάφημεν οὖν αὐτῷ διὰ τοῦ βαπτίσματος **εἰς τὸν θάνατον,** ἵνα ὥσπερ ἠγέρθη Χριστὸς ἐκ νεκρῶν διὰ τῆς δόξης τοῦ πατρός, οὕτως καὶ ἡμεῖς ἐν καινότητι ζωῆς περιπατήσωμεν (Rom. 6:4 GNT).

"For as many of you as were baptized **into Christ** have put on Christ" (Gal. 3:27).

ὅσοι γὰρ **εἰς Χριστὸν** ἐβαπτίσθητε, Χριστὸν ἐνεδύσασθε (Gal. 3:27 GNT).

Baptism directed to John's baptism

"And he said unto them, 'Unto **what then** were ye baptized?' And they said, '**Unto John's baptism**'" (Acts 19:3 AV).

εἶπέν τε, **Εἰς τί οὖν** ἐβαπτίσθητε; οἱ δὲ εἶπαν, **Εἰς τὸ Ἰωάννου βάπτισμα** (Acts 19:3 GNT)

Baptism directed towards Paul

"Is Christ divided? Was Paul crucified for you? Or were you baptized **in the name of Paul?**" (1 Cor. 1:13).

μεμέρισται ὁ Χριστός; μὴ Παῦλος ἐσταυρώθη ὑπὲρ ὑμῶν, ἢ **εἰς τὸ ὄνομα Παύλου** ἐβαπτίσθητε (1 Cor. 1:13 GNT).

"lest anyone should say that I had baptized **in my own name**" (1 Cor. 1:15).

ἵνα μή τις εἴπῃ ὅτι **εἰς τὸ ἐμὸν ὄνομα** ἐβαπτίσθητε (1 Cor. 1:15 GNT).

Baptism directed towards Moses

"all were baptized **into Moses** in the cloud and in the sea" (1 Cor. 10:2).

καὶ πάντες **εἰς τὸν Μωϋσῆν** ἐβαπτίσθησαν ἐν τῇ νεφέλῃ καὶ ἐν τῇ θαλάσσῃ (1 Cor. 10:2 GNT).

Baptizing directed towards the name of the Father, the Son and the Holy Spirit
"Go therefore and make disciples of all the nations, baptizing them **in the name** of the Father and of the Son and of the Holy Spirit" (Mat.28:19).

Robert. H. Gundry states ". . . 'in the name of' means 'with fundamental reference to' . . ."[3]

πορευθέντες οὖν μαθητεύσατε πάντα τὰ ἔθνη, βαπτίζοντες αὐτοὺς **εἰς τὸ ὄνομα** τοῦ πατρὸς καὶ τοῦ υἱοῦ καὶ τοῦ ἁγίου πνεύματος (Mat. 28:19 GNT).

James D.G. Dunn argues against εἰς meaning "for" in 1 Cor. 12:13, and asserts ". . . we can always assume that in Paul it has the basic sense of 'motion towards or into' some goal."[4]

R. Schnackenburg however, writes, "We ought to set βαπτίζειν εἰς in parallelism with πιστεύειν εἰς; the latter suggests the direction of faith, but it does not express any mystical movement to Christ . . . The expression ἁμαρτάνειν εἰς Χριστὸν [to sin against Christ] (1 Cor. 8:12) should also be compared."[5] Concerning Gal. 3:27 and Rom. 6:3 he says, "Christ is not a 'sphere' into which we are plunged, but the personal Christ with all that happened to him; our baptism 'to Christ' has the goal of uniting us with Christ and with everything that happened to him."[6]

So I assert that 1 Cor. 12:13 can and should be translated "For in one Spirit we were all baptized for one body." This means that the verse is not speaking of entering the body of Christ. It is speaking of the baptism in the Spirit. This translation harmonises with the last part of the verse, "and we were all made to drink of one Spirit" (NRSV). When they were baptized in the Spirit they were immersed in Him and so they were truly made to drink of the Spirit. They were filled with the Spirit.

This translation and interpretation also is in perfect harmony with the immediate context. Paul is saying to the Christians at Corinth that they had all received the baptism in the Spirit. They were the body of Christ, and each one a part of it. This experience had brought different gifts of the Spirit. They needed to keep before them the fact that the gifts were for the benefit of the body, the church. They had the manifestations of the Spirit for the common good (1 Cor. 12:7). They all needed each other's gift to function in the body and for the body.

The translation and interpretation of "in one Spirit" is also in harmony with all the other verses speaking of baptising in the Spirit. Those verses all state that Jesus Christ is the One Who baptizes in the Holy Spirit:

"I indeed baptize you in water unto repentance, but He who is coming after me is mightier than I, whose sandals I am not worthy to carry. He will baptize you in the Holy Spirit and fire" (Mat 3:11; my translation: an alternative possible translation to "with water" and "with the Holy Spirit" as stated in the NRSV).

"I indeed baptized you in water, but He will baptize you in the Holy Spirit" (Mark 1:8; my translation: an alternative possible translation to "with water" and "with the Holy Spirit" as stated in the NASB, and the NRSV).

"John answered, saying to all, 'I indeed baptize you in water; but One mightier than I is coming, whose sandal strap I am not worthy to loose. He will baptize you in the Holy Spirit and fire' " (Luke 3:16

my translation; "in the Holy Spirit" an alternative possible translation to "with the Holy Spirit" as stated in the NRSV).

"I did not recognize Him, but He who sent me to baptize in water
said to me, 'He upon whom you see the Spirit descending and
remaining upon Him, this is the One who baptizes in the Holy
Spirit'" (John 1:33 NASB).

"for John truly baptized in water, but you will be baptized in the
Holy Spirit not many days from now" (Acts 1:5; my translation).

The NIV states in the marginal notes on all the verses above that "in
water" is a possible translation.

The book of Acts records Jesus fulfilling His ministry as the Baptizer
in the Spirit. On the Day of Pentecost Jesus Himself baptized the
disciples in the Holy Spirit, as Peter declared, "This Jesus God has
raised up, of which we are all witnesses. Therefore being exalted to the
right hand of God, and having received from the Father the promise of
the Holy Spirit, He poured out this which you now see and hear" (Acts
2:32–33). Peter tells of the falling of the Holy Spirit on Cornelius and
those in his household. He said, "And as I began to speak, the Holy
Spirit fell upon them, as upon us at the beginning. Then I remembered
the word of the Lord, how He said, 'John indeed baptized in water,
but you will be baptized in the Holy Spirit'" (Acts 11:15–16; v.16 my
translation: "in water" see mgn. NIV). Jesus baptized Cornelius and his
household in the Holy Spirit just as He baptized the disciples on the
Day of Pentecost.

This great ministry of the Lord Jesus Christ as the Baptizer in the
Spirit is proclaimed by Matthew, Mark, Luke and John as seen in
the scriptures above.

Nowhere in the Old or New Testament is the Holy Spirit ever spoken of as One Who baptizes. This fact rules out the translation "by one Spirit."

Wayne Grudem says, "... there is a grammatical argument that
supports the translation 'in one Spirit we were all baptized into one
body' in 1 Cor. 12:13: if Paul had wanted to say that we were baptized
by the Holy Spirit, he would have used a different expression. To be baptized 'by' someone in the New Testament is always expressed by the
preposition hypo followed by a genitive noun." He cites Mat. 3:6; Mark
1:5; Luke 3:7; Mat. 3:13; Mark 1:9 and Luke 7:30 all speaking of baptism
by John the Baptist, and Mat. 3:14 relating John's statement that he

needed to be baptized by Jesus. He concludes, "Therefore, if Paul had wanted to say that the Corinthians had all been baptized *by* the Holy Spirit he would have used *hypo* plus the genitive, not *en* plus the dative."[7]

"For in one Spirit we were all baptized for one body" commends itself as a correct translation when we compare 1 Cor. 12:13 with other baptisms mentioned in the New Testament.

In each baptism we have:
The baptized.
The baptizer.
The element in which one is baptized.
What the baptism is with reference to.

The baptism of 1 Cor. 10:2
The baptized – Israel.
The Baptizer – God.
The elements in which one is baptized – the cloud and the sea.
What the baptism is with reference to – Moses.

John's Baptism
The baptized – the repentant.
The baptizer – John the Baptist.
The element in which one is baptized – water.
What the baptism is with reference to – remission of sins.

Christian Baptism
The baptized – the one obedient to the gospel.
The baptizer – a Christian.
The element in which one is baptized – water.
What the baptism is with reference to – union with Christ, the remission of sins.

Baptism in the Spirit 1 Cor. 12:13
The baptized – the believer.
The Baptizer – The Lord Jesus Christ.
The Element in which one is baptized – the Holy Spirit.
What the baptism is with reference to – the body of Christ, the church.

If we translate "by one Spirit" and "into one body" in 1 Cor. 12:13, we have the following consequences,
The one baptized – the believer.

The Baptizer – The Holy Spirit
The element in which one is baptized – *BLANK*
What the baptism is with reference to – entrance into the body of
Christ.

- There is a significant gap. In what does the Holy Spirit baptize the
  Christian?
- This baptism cannot be the same baptism mentioned in Mat. 3:11,
  Mark 1:8, Luke 3:16, John 1:33, Acts 1:5 and 11:16 because in all
  these verses Jesus is the One baptizing.
- We would have only one verse in the whole of the New Testament
  where this baptism by the Holy Spirit is mentioned!

These consequences demonstrate that "By one Spirit we were all
baptized into one body " cannot be the correct translation of the Greek
text. Dr. Martyn Lloyd-Jones is therefore linking Rom. 6:3 with a
mistranslation of 1 Cor. 12:13. The baptism in Rom. 6:3f is not baptism
by the Spirit into one body.

The correct translation and interpretation of 1 Cor. 12:13 is of the
greatest importance. 1 Cor. 12:13, incorrectly translated and misinterpreted, is used repeatedly as a crucial argument to assert wrong teachings about water baptism and the baptism in the Spirit. I submit that
the correct translation and interpretation of 1 Cor. 12:13 shows that it
speaks of baptism in the Spirit *for*, not into, the body.

References

1. Louis Berkhof *Systematic Theology*, Banner of Truth 1959, page 628.
2. D.M. Lloyd-Jones *An Exposition of Chapter 6 Romans*, Banner of Truth
   1975, page 35.
3. Robert H. Gundry *Matthew*, Second Edition Eerdmans 1994, page
   596.
4. James D.G. Dunn *Baptism in the Holy Spirit*, SCM Press 1977, page
   128.
5. R. Schnackenburg *Baptism in the Thought of Paul*, E.T. Oxford:
   Blackwell 1964, page 23.
6. *Ibid.*, page 25.
7. Taken from *Systematic Theology* by Wayne A. Grudem. Copyright ©
   1994 by Wayne Grudem. Used by permission of IVP and Zondervan,
   page 768 footnote.

CHAPTER EIGHT

THE ALLEGED BAPTISMAL FORMULA

Many believe that Mat. 28:19 states the actual words to be used in the act of baptizing a convert. Mat. 28:19 reads, "Go therefore and make disciples of all the nations, baptizing them in the name of the Father and of the Son and of the Holy Spirit." These words "in the name of the Father, and of the Son and of the Holy Spirit" are pronounced at most baptisms.

In the second decade of the last century some Pentecostal Christians looking at the Acts of the Apostles decided that the correct words to be used at baptism are not found in Mat. 28:19. Rather they are stated in the Acts of the Apostles, "in the name of Jesus Christ" (Acts 2:38), or "in the name of the Lord Jesus" (Acts 8:16 and 19:5). They taught that only baptism "in the name of Jesus" was true baptism. Very soon they denied the Trinity. They affirmed that Jesus is the name of the Father, the Son and the Holy Spirit in Mat. 28:19. Using this misinterpretation of Mat. 28:19 and the fact that God is One, they declared that Jesus is the Father, the Son and the Holy Spirit. They asserted that there is no salvation unless one is baptized using the right words. In 1993 these Oneness heretics numbered over 5 million worldwide, their members having doubled in the period from 1970. Within their ranks there are splits concerning the right baptismal formula, each group insisting that their particular words are the only ones effective to wash away sin. The variants are "in the name of Jesus," "into Jesus' name," "in the name of the Lord Jesus" and "into the name of the Lord Jesus Christ."

Careful examination of Mat. 28:19 and the above texts in the Acts of the Apostles reveal that these verses do not give actual words to be pronounced at baptisms. That is not their purpose. We shall look at each verse to ascertain exactly what is being said : "baptizing them in (εἰς) the name of the Father and of the Son and of the Holy Spirit" (Mat. 28:19). The Greek word shown in brackets and translated 'in' means "with reference to." Jesus is defining Christian baptism. Those who baptize must do it with reference to the name of the Father and of the Son and of the Holy Spirit. John's baptism was "for (εἰς) repentance" (Mat. 3:11). It was "with reference to" repentance. Jesus is not giving actual words to be pronounced at baptism. There is no evidence of the use of these Trinitarian words in the New Testament records of baptisms, nor in any of its statements concerning baptism in the Acts of the Apostles and the Epistles.

"Then Peter said to them, "Repent, and let every one of you be baptized in (ἐπὶ) the name of Jesus Christ for (εἰς) the remission of sins; and you shall receive the gift of the Holy Spirit" (Acts 2:38). "In" is the Greek word ἐπὶ and it means "on the authority of." It is used with that meaning in Acts 4:17–18, 5:28 and 40 which verses refer to speaking or teaching in the name of Jesus. The word translated for, εἰς, means "with reference to," "with a view to." Again there is nothing liturgical in this verse.

The same is true of Acts 8:16, "For as yet He had fallen upon none of them. They had only been baptized in (εἰς) the name of the Lord Jesus", and Acts 19:5, "When they heard *this*, they were baptized in (εἰς) the name of the Lord Jesus."

The same meaning of εἰς is found in the following verses:

"Or do you not know that as many of us as were baptized into (εἰς) Christ Jesus were baptized into (εἰς) His death?" (Rom. 6:3).

"Is Christ divided? Was Paul crucified for you? Or were you baptized in (εἰς) the name of Paul?" (1 Cor. 1:13).

". . . all were baptized into (εἰς) Moses in the cloud and in the sea" (1 Cor. 10:2).

"For in one Spirit we were all baptized for (εἰς) one body – whether Jews or Greeks, whether slaves or free – and have all been made to drink of one Spirit" (1 Cor. 12:13; my translation).

Acts 10:48 uses another Greek word in relation to baptism. The word is ἐν translated in as shown, "And he commanded them to be baptized in (ἐν) the name of the Lord." The phrase "in the name of the Lord" could be translated as going with "commanded." This is perfectly possible grammatically. If we do so it means "with the authority of Jesus Christ."

The verses below all contain ἐν and in each of them it can be translated "with the authority of."

"Then Peter said, 'Silver and gold I do not have, but what I do have I give you: In (ἐν) the name of Jesus Christ of Nazareth, rise up and walk'" (Acts 3:6).

"But Barnabas took him and brought *him* to the apostles. And he declared to them how he had seen the Lord on the road, and that He had spoken to him, and how he had preached boldly at Damascus in (ἐν) the name of Jesus" (Acts 9:27).

"And this she did for many days. But Paul, greatly annoyed, turned and said to the spirit, 'I command you in (ἐν) the name of Jesus Christ to come out of her.' And he came out that very hour" (Acts 16:18).

"In (ἐν) the name of our Lord Jesus Christ, when you are gathered together, along with my spirit, with the power of our Lord Jesus Christ, deliver such a one to Satan for the destruction of the flesh, that his spirit may be saved in the day of the Lord Jesus" (1 Cor. 5:4–5).

"But we command you, brethren, in (ἐν) the name of our Lord Jesus Christ, that you withdraw from every brother who walks disorderly and not according to the tradition which he received from us" (2 Thess. 3:6).

"My brethren, take the prophets, who spoke in (ἐν) the name of the Lord, as an example of suffering and patience" (James 5:10).

"Is anyone among you sick? Let him call for the elders of the church, and let them pray over him, anointing him with oil in (ἐν) the name of the Lord" (James 5:14).

In all these texts doing something in the name of the Lord is doing something at His direction and with His authority.

Conclusions

1. The close examination of Mat. 28:19 and the baptismal verses in Acts 2:38, 8:16, 10:48 and 19:5 show that they contain no words to be pronounced at baptism.
2. The mention of the Trinity in Matthew relates to the activity of those baptizing converts. They baptize with reference to the Father, the Son and the Holy Spirit.
3. The verses in Acts 2:38, 8:16 and 19:5 refer to the convert's act of being baptized. The convert submits to being baptized at the direction of Jesus Christ and with reference to Him.

CHAPTER NINE

ATTEMPTS TO JUSTIFY INFANT BAPTISM: THE INVENTION OF THE COVENANT OF GRACE (1)

We shall look at arguments from the Old Testament and the New Testament to justify infant baptism. First of all we shall address the invention of the covenant of grace. It is argued that

- There is one covenant of grace during Old Testament times and the New Testament era.
- During these two great periods therefore there is a continuity of people in covenant relationship with God. There is the church of the Old Covenant (Acts 7:38) and the church of the New Covenant. There is one people of God before and after Christ.
- The Old Covenant included infants born of covenant members, so the New Covenant, which is greater in blessing, must surely also include them.
- The sign of the Old Covenant was circumcision. Male babies of Old Covenant members were circumcised eight days after birth. Under the New Covenant baptism in water has replaced circumcision as the sign of the covenant. Therefore infants of Christian parents are to be baptized as covenant children.

It is misleading to speak of one covenant of grace. The Bible never does. It is certainly true that God predetermined salvation through Christ before the creation of the universe. He announced that salvation immediately after man's fall: "And I will put enmity Between you and the woman, And between your seed and her Seed; He shall bruise your head, And you shall bruise His heel" (Gen. 3:15). These words predict the Messiah, the Seed of the woman. Over the succeeding thousands of years God wrought salvation by means of a number of covenants, not by one covenant of grace differently administered. They were God's chosen way to bring salvation. We shall look at each covenant and thereby see the gradual outworking of God's great purpose.

51

The Covenant with Noah

God made a covenant with Noah and all who came out of the Ark. From Adam until this covenant we have at least 1,650 years. God declared that he would never again cause a universal destruction of life as He had done during the Flood (Gen. 8:21–9:17). This exercise of forbearance and longsuffering with mankind in its sinfulness, instead of giving to man his just deserts of destruction, has allowed life to continue and multiply on earth after Noah. God will continue to be faithful to His word as long as the earth remains (Gen. 8:22). When Christ returns the earth will be burned with fire (2 Pet. 3:10). From the time of Noah until then this covenant of non-destruction of life has made possible, and will continue to make possible, the fulfilment of God's purpose to gather out of mankind a multitude no man can number to salvation and eternal glory. This covenant permitting sinful man to live and multiply was absolutely essential for the outworking of God's plan of salvation. Succeeding covenants are progressive stages towards God's saving action in Christ.

The Covenant with Abraham

Around 300 years later God promised Abraham that He would:

a)   make him a great nation (Gen. 12:2).
b)   bless him (Gen. 12:2)
c)   make his name great (Gen. 12:2).
d)   bless those who blessed him, and curse those who cursed him (Gen. 12:3).
e)   give that nation a land of their own (Gen. 15:18).
f)   make him a father of many nations (Gen. 17:5–6).
g)   be their God (Gen. 17:8).
h)   give victory over enemies (Gen. 22:17).
i)   bless all the nations through one of his descendants (Gen. 22:18). This was a prediction of Jesus Christ, descended according to the flesh from Abraham.

The Covenant with Israel at Mount Sinai

When the nation came into being it was in slavery for four hundred years, then delivered by God and led to the promised land, just as God predicted (Gen. 15:13–16). When they left Egypt God made a covenant with the nation at Mount Sinai. This was 430 years after the covenant with Abraham. Just as that covenant did not annul the previous one with Noah, so this covenant at Mount Sinai did not annul the covenant with

Abraham. God gave them the Ten Commandments, and regulations for life and worship. He promised them blessings if they obeyed Him (Exod. 19:5–6 and 23:25–33). He warned of punishment for transgression (Exod. 22:22–24). This covenant was a development of the Abrahamic covenant. It was a covenant with the nation that had come into existence and had been delivered from Egypt as a fulfilment of that Abrahamic covenant. Now as a nation God made a covenant which gave them a revelation of His will for the ordering of their lives under His rule until the Messiah came. It was a great advance on previous revelation from God. Besides the sublime revelation of the Ten Commandments the many civil and social laws were a manifestation of God's attributes. The requirements for the worship of God were not only the means of maintaining their special relationship with God, but also pointed forward as types of the salvation through the Christ Who would come.

The Covenant with Israel in the land of Moab

At the end of the wilderness wanderings of Israel for forty years, and just before entering the promised land, the Lord made a further covenant with the nation (Deut. 29:1). This did not annul the previous covenants. It was a renewal of the covenant at Mt. Sinai. It contained promises of great blessing if they were obedient to God (Deut. 28:1–14). It also warned of terrible judgments including the loss of the land if they were disobedient (Deut. 28:15–68).

The Covenant with David

Several hundreds of years later God made a covenant with King David. He said that the Messiah would be a descendant of the family of David according to the flesh. Thus his house and his kingdom would be established forever (2 Sam. 7:16 and Luke 1:31–33). This covenant gave further revelation concerning the Messiah. He would be a King and of the line of David.

The New Covenant

When Christ came he brought in the New Covenant prophesied by Jeremiah. "Behold, the days are coming, says the LORD, when I will make a new covenant with the house of Israel and with the house of Judah – not according to the covenant that I made with their fathers in the day *that* I took them by the hand to lead them out of the land of Egypt, My covenant which they broke, though I was a husband to them, says the LORD. But this *is* the covenant that I will make with the house of Israel after those days, says the LORD: I will put My law in their minds, and write it on their hearts; and I will be their God, and they shall be My people. No more shall every man teach his neighbor, and every man his brother, saying, 'Know the LORD,' for they all shall know Me, from the least of them to the greatest of them, says the LORD. For I will forgive their iniquity, and their sin I will remember no more" (Jer. 31:31–34).

The Bible does not speak anywhere of one covenant of grace. It does tell us clearly that in eternity past God planned and purposed eternal life for some of fallen mankind. The following verses reveal this wonderful truth:

"Paul, a bondservant of God and an apostle of Jesus Christ, according to the faith of God's elect and the acknowledgment of the truth which accords with godliness, in hope of eternal life which God, who cannot lie, promised before time began, but has in due time manifested His word through preaching, which was committed to me according to the commandment of God our Savior" (Tit. 1:1–3).

"Blessed *be* the God and Father of our Lord Jesus Christ, who has blessed us with every spiritual blessing in the heavenly *places* in Christ, just as He chose us in Him before the foundation of the world, that we should be holy and without blame before Him in love, having predestined us to adoption as sons by Jesus Christ to Himself, according to the good pleasure of His will" (Eph. 1:3–5).

Concerning the gospel Paul wrote, "But we speak the wisdom of God in a mystery, the hidden *wisdom* which God ordained before the ages for our glory" (1 Cor. 2:7), and "who has saved us and called *us* with a holy calling, not according to our works, but according to His own purpose and grace which was given to us in Christ Jesus before time began" (2 Tim. 1:9).

This purpose of God fashioned and determined in eternity past is a glorious fact. But it is not correct to call it a covenant of grace. The scriptures never do so. Some theologians in the sixteenth century invented the doctrine. They, and those who have followed them, have chosen without scriptural sanction to call the plan of the One God in Three Persons for the salvation of fallen man a covenant.

CHAPTER TEN

ATTEMPTS TO JUSTIFY INFANT BAPTISM: THE INVENTION OF THE COVENANT OF GRACE (2)

The variety of definitions of the so-called "covenant of grace" reveals that the doctrine is of man and not of God. Louis Berkhof writes about the variety of representations respecting the parties in the covenant of grace. He says, "Some consider them to be the triune God and man, either without qualification, or qualified in some way, as 'the sinner,' 'the elect,' or 'man in Christ'; others, God the Father, as representing the Trinity, and Christ as representing the elect; and still others, since the days of Coccejus, distinguish two covenants, namely, the covenant of redemption (*pactum salutis*) between the Father and the Son, and, as based on this, the covenant of grace between the triune God and the elect, or the elect sinner."[1] These different views arose because men have sought to define God's plan as a covenant without biblical warrant. Louis Berkhof declares himself as one of those who distinguishes two covenants, the covenant of redemption between the Father and the Son, and as based on this the covenant of grace between the triune God and sinful men. He goes on to say, ". . . we should bear in mind what Shedd says: . . . 'The covenant of grace and redemption are two modes or phases of the one evangelical covenant of mercy.'[2] "[3] He gives what he believes to be scriptural data for the covenant of redemption as follows. His arguments are the following, italicised, sentences.

1. *"Now we find that in the economy of redemption there is, in a sense, a division of labour: the Father is the originator, the Son the executor, and the Holy Spirit the applier. This can only be the result of a voluntary agreement among the persons of the Trinity, so that their internal relations assume the form of a covenant life."[4]*
The Bible never calls that agreement of the Persons of the Trinity a covenant. It is too simplistic to define the relations between the Persons of the Trinity as "the form of a covenant life." One God in Three Persons is a profound mystery beyond explanation in terms of a covenant life.

2.   *The eternal plan of God for salvation is indicated to be "of the nature of a covenant. Christ speaks of promises made to Him before His advent, and repeatedly refers to a commission which He had received from the Father, John 5:30,43; 6:38–40;17:4–12. And in Rom. 5:12–21 and 1 Cor. 15:22 He is clearly regarded as a representative head, that is, as the head of a covenant."*[5]

3.   *"Wherever we have the essential elements of a covenant, namely contracting parties, a promise or promises, and a condition, there we have a covenant. In Ps. 2:7–9 the parties are mentioned and a promise is indicated. . . . Again in Ps. 40:7–9 . . . the Messiah expresses His readiness to do the Father's will in becoming a sacrifice for sin. . . . The statement in Luke 22:29 is particularly significant: 'I appoint unto you a kingdom, even as My Father appointed unto me.' The verb used here is* **diatithemi**, *the word from which* **diatheke** *is derived, which means to appoint by will, testament or covenant."*[6]

Nowhere in the Bible is there any text declaring a covenant between Christ and God the Father. Promises, a commission and acting in a representative capacity do not prove the existence of a covenant. These things are simply the putting into action the plan and purpose of the Triune God which had been predetermined before the creation of man. The arrangement between the Father and the Son included an arrangement with the Holy Spirit. Christ could not have carried out His mission apart from the work of the Spirit. Without Him the incarnation (Luke 1:35), His Ministry on earth (Luke 4:18) and His final offering of Himself would not have been possible (Heb. 9:14). Concerning the contracting parties Louis Berkhof makes no mention in 2 and 3 of the Holy Spirit. The verses he quotes refer only to the relationship between the Father and Christ. So we only have two of the three parties involved. They could not have contracted together without contracting with the Holy Spirit. But he fails to demonstrate and prove a covenant concerning all three parties. To ignore the reality of the work of the Spirit and omit Him from a so-called covenant between the Father and the Son reveals that the so-called covenant of redemption is an invention of man not the truth of scripture.

Salvation was purposed and accomplished by One God in Three Persons. The oneness in the Godhead must not be denied. It is stated in the following verses:

"Hear, O Israel: The LORD our God, the LORD *is* one!" (Deut. 6:4).
At creation we see this oneness: "Then God said, 'Let Us make man in Our image, according to Our likeness; let them have dominion

over the fish of the sea, over the birds of the air, and over the cattle, over all the earth and over every creeping thing that creeps on the earth' " (Gen. 1:26).

"Then the LORD God said, 'Behold, the man has become like one of Us, to know good and evil. And now, lest he put out his hand and take also of the tree of life, and eat, and live forever' " (Gen. 3:22).

"Come, let Us go down and there confuse their language, that they may not understand one another's speech" (Gen. 11:7).

And at the time of Isaiah, "Also I heard the voice of the Lord, saying: 'Whom shall I send, And who will go for Us?' Then I said, 'Here *am* I! Send me' " (Isa. 6:8).

With regard to Luke 22:29 the verb can mean 'assign, confer' as well as 'make a covenant'. Since the disciples will also receive a kingdom just as Christ has, assign is the meaning.

4.   "There are two Old Testament passages which connect up the idea of the covenant immediately with the Messiah, namely,Ps. 89:3 . . . and Isa. 42:6,.."[7]
Ps. 89:3–4 states the covenant made by God with David that the Messiah would be born of his line according to the flesh. It reads, "I have made a covenant with My chosen, I have sworn to My servant David: 'Your seed I will establish forever, And build up your throne to all generations.' " It says absolutely nothing about another covenant between the Father and the Son.
Isa. 42:6 reads, "I, the LORD, have called You in righteousness, And will hold Your hand; I will keep You and give You as a covenant to the people, As a light to the Gentiles." This verse predicts that Jesus Christ would bring people of all nations into a new covenant relationship with God. It does not speak of a covenant between the Father and the Son.

5.   "Moreover, there are passages in which the Messiah speaks of God as His God, thus using covenant language, namely, Ps. 22:1, 2, and Ps. 40:8."[8]
This language expresses Christ's position as the Servant of the Father. It does not reflect a covenant between the Father and the Son. It is the manifestation of the subordination of the Son to the Father as predetermined by all three Persons in the Godhead.

6.   "The counsel of redemption is the eternal prototype of the
historical covenant of grace. This accounts for the fact that many
combine the two into a single covenant. The former is eternal, that is,
from eternity, and the latter, temporal in that it is realised in time.
The former is a compact between the Father and the Son as the Surety
and Head of the elect, while the latter is a compact between the
triune God and the elect sinner in the Surety."[9]

Louis Berkhof thus argues from an alleged covenant of redemption
to establish the existence of a covenant of grace. The scriptures never
speak of a covenant of redemption nor of a covenant of grace.

While there are great truths contained in covenant theology a careful
study of the covenants in scripture does not support the concept of one
covenant of grace. It will be argued that the facts revealed concerning
the nature of covenants are contrary to the doctrine of one covenant of
grace.

References

1. Louis Berkhof *Systematic Theology*, Banner of Truth 1959, page 265.
2. William G.T. Shedd *Dogmatic Theology* Volume 2 Part B page 360.
   Reprinted 1979 Klock & Klock.
3. Louis Berkhof *Systematic Theology*, Banner of Truth 1959, page 265.
4. *Ibid.*, page 266.
5. *Ibid.*, page 266.
6. *Ibid.*, page 266.
7. *Ibid.*, page 266.
8. *Ibid.*, pages 266–267.
9. *Ibid.*, page 270.

CHAPTER ELEVEN

ATTEMPTS TO JUSTIFY INFANT BAPTISM: THE INVENTION OF THE COVENANT OF GRACE (3)

At this point some will still object that, though there is no statement of the covenant of grace in scripture, it is a truth contained in the scriptures, just as the term Trinity is not found in the Bible but expresses the true doctrine concerning God in the Bible. I shall argue that the concept of the covenant of grace is contrary to the scriptures. Firstly it is necessary to remove possible misunderstandings. Whilst opposing the use of the term "one covenant of grace" it is agreed that there is:

One plan and purpose of God

It was announced in Gen 3:15, predetermined by the triune God before the creation of the universe and put into action through the various covenants stated above. The different arrangements for different periods of history are all stages in the outworking of one plan of salvation achieved through the death of Jesus Christ.

One way of salvation for man after the fall

It is always by grace through faith. The benefits of Christ's death were applied to believers before Calvary just they are applied to believers after Calvary. During the period after the fall God gave revelation resulting in some exercising faith. God called some individuals into fellowship with Himself. We read of this in Heb. 11:4–7: "By faith Abel offered to God a more excellent sacrifice than Cain, through which he obtained witness that he was righteous, God testifying of his gifts; and through it he being dead still speaks. By faith Enoch was taken away so that he did not see death, 'and was not found, because God had taken him'; for before he was taken he had this testimony, that he pleased God. But without faith *it is* impossible to please *Him*, for he who comes to God must believe that He is, and *that* He is a rewarder of those who diligently seek Him. By faith Noah, being divinely warned of things not yet seen, moved with godly fear, prepared an ark for the saving of his household, by which he condemned the world and became heir of the righteousness which is according to faith." It is striking that these men were righteous before God through faith. From Gen. 4:26 "Then *men* began to call on the name of the LORD" we know that men besides Abel, Enoch and Noah were saved before the Flood. After the Flood we also read of the God of Shem (Gen. 9:26). He was in fellowship with God.

The New Testament is crystal clear that Abraham and David were justified by faith: "What then shall we say that Abraham our father has found according to the flesh? For if Abraham was justified by works, he has *something* to boast about, but not before God. For what does the Scripture say? 'Abraham believed God, and it was accounted to him for righteousness.' Now to him who works, the wages are not counted as grace but as debt. But to him who does not work but believes on Him who justifies the ungodly, his faith is accounted for righteousness, just as David also describes the blessedness of the man to whom God imputes righteousness apart from works: 'Blessed *are those* whose lawless deeds are forgiven, And whose sins are covered; Blessed *is the* man to whom the LORD shall not impute sin'" (Rom. 4:1–8). So throughout Old Testament times we find one way of salvation.

One people of God

The people of God are all those down through the ages who have had true faith in God. Both believers before the cross of Christ and those after the cross will be perfected together (Heb. 11:40). In Romans 11 Paul affirms the unity of believers from Abraham onwards. He says that the people of God are like an olive tree whose root and fatness were the patriarchs and Israel before Christ came. The Jews who did not believe in the Messiah were branches broken off the tree. The Gentiles who believe have been grafted into the tree, and with the believing Jews they became partakers of the root and fatness of the olive tree. So we have one people of God composed of Jewish believers before and after Christ together with Gentile believers.

Covenant theology is right in asserting these truths. But it goes too far in declaring the existence of one covenant of grace in operation from the fall of man onwards. There are certain characteristics of all covenants of God with men throughout the Bible. Covenants are always announced before implementation. When they are announced their contents are always explicit. This so-called covenant of grace is never stated in scripture. Its content is never declared. Unlike all the other covenants God made with man this one is never announced. From Genesis to Revelation it cannot be found. And yet we are told this covenant is in operation from the Fall to the Final Return of the Lord Jesus Christ!

Covenants of God with men are always fixed arrangements for a defined period during which there is absolutely no deviation from, or modification to those arrangements. Therefore living under a covenant one can expect it to be constantly in force and continually applied during the stated time period. A covenant gives absolute assurance that there will be no change in the arrangement. Once declared its contents are fixed for the defined period of time. If another covenant is made at a later date to run concurrently with the previous one the content and application of the previous one is unaffected. To speak of the covenant of grace as administered differently in the various periods of the history of mankind is to reveal a serious failure to understand the basic meaning of the word covenant as used in the scriptures. If the covenant of grace existed it could not be administered differently. A covenant is a fixed unchangeable arrangement.

Let us look at some statements by writers who believe in the covenant of grace in the light of these biblical characteristics of covenants between God and men. Wayne Grudem argues, "Although the essential elements of the covenant of grace remain the same throughout the history of God's people, the specific provisions of the covenant vary from time to time."[1] He defines those essential elements as follows:

"The *parties* to this covenant of grace are God and the people whom he will redeem." . . .

"The *condition* (or requirement) of participation in the covenant is *faith* in the work of Christ the redeemer (Rom. 1:17; 5:1; et al.)," and, ". . . Old Testament believers were saved by looking forward to the work of the Messiah who was to come and putting faith in Him." . . .

". . . the condition of *continuing* in that covenant is said to be obedience to God's commands." . . .

"The *promise* of blessings in the covenant was a promise of eternal life with God." . . .

"The *sign* of this covenant (the outward, physical symbol of inclusion in the covenant) varies between the Old Testament and the New Testament. In the Old Testament the outward sign of beginning the covenant relationship was circumcision. The sign of continuing the covenant relationship was continuing to observe all the festivals and ceremonial laws that God gave the people at various times. In the new covenant, the sign of beginning a covenant relationship is baptism, while the sign of continuing in that relationship is participation in the Lord's Supper."[2] He goes on to say concerning the various forms of the covenant, "At the time of Adam and Eve, there was only the bare hint of the possibility of a relationship with God found in the promise about the seed of the woman in Gen. 3:15 and in God's gracious provision of clothing for Adam and Eve (Gen. 3:21). The covenant that God made with Noah after the flood (Gen. 9:8–17) was not a covenant that promised all the blessings of eternal life or spiritual fellowship with God, but simply one in which God promised all mankind and the animal creation that the earth would no longer be destroyed by a flood. In this sense the covenant with Noah, although it certainly does depend on God's grace or unmerited favor, appears to be quite different in the parties involved (God and mankind, not just the redeemed), the condition named (no faith or obedience is required of man), and the blessing that is promised (that the earth will not be destroyed again by flood, certainly a different promise from that of eternal life). The sign of the covenant (the rainbow) is also different in that it requires no active or voluntary participation on man's part. . . . But beginning with the covenant with Abraham (Gen. 15:1–21; 17:1–27), the essential elements of the covenant of grace are all there."[3]

Please note that he lists the sign of circumcision as one of the essential elements. Yet this sign was not introduced by God until the Covenant with Abraham. As stated this was at least 2,000 years after Adam. So for a period of at least approximately one third of the whole of the history of man, while this so-called covenant of grace was in being, an essential element of it was missing! This essential element was added to the content of the covenant of grace "beginning with the covenant with Abraham." The content of a covenant never changes in this fashion.

It is striking how covenant theology passes over the period from Adam to Abram. It asserts that the covenant of grace was in existence during this time. The truth is that for this considerable period of history their philosophy of the existence of a covenant of grace does not fit the facts of scripture.

Pierre-Charles Marcel says concerning this covenant of grace, "It is first disclosed in Gen. iii:15. From the very beginning grace is implicitly offered to all, to Adam and to his posterity, to Noah and to his posterity, according to rules and conditions of which we are largely ignorant. Up to the time of Abraham Holy Scripture tells us nothing of a formal establishment of the covenant of grace in the sense which it assumed from that time on."[4] A covenant always has a clearly declared content. Gen. 3:15 does not contain such. Thus this covenant of grace, unlike all other covenants of God with man in the whole of scripture, is stated to be in existence but undisclosed in its content from Adam to Abraham!

Louis Berkhof writes, "Up to the time of Abraham there was no formal establishment of the covenant of grace. While Gen. 3:15 already contains the elements of this covenant, it does not record a formal transaction by which the covenant was established. It does not even speak explicitly of a covenant. . . . In the transaction with Abraham the particularistic Old Testament administration of the covenant had its beginning, and it becomes perfectly evident that man is a party in the covenant and must respond to the promises of God by faith."[5] Louis Berkhof not only admits that there was no announcement of the covenant or its contents before Abraham, he is saying also that the covenant was not administered for the two thousand years or more before Abraham. This is at least half of the period from the fall of man to the coming of the Messiah. Covenants have a clearly defined starting time and duration. From start to end they are administered precisely according to their defined content. It is sheer nonsense to speak of an existing covenant not being administered for two minutes let alone two thousand years.

Robert L. Reymond says in similar fashion, "In sum, the two emphases of the first eleven chapters of Genesis are the pervasive fact and power of human sinfulness and God's holy recoil against sin in every form. And while we see evidences of the divine operations of salvific grace in accordance with the covenant of grace, it is equally true that we see it only minimally displayed.

But with the call of Abraham, the covenant of grace underwent a remarkable advance, definitive for all time to come. . . . The fact that the Bible sweeps across the thousands of years between the creation of man and Abraham in only eleven chapters, with the call of Abraham coming in Genesis 12, suggests that the information given in the first eleven chapters of the Bible was intended as preparatory 'background' to the revelation of the Abrahamic covenant."[6]

We read the words, "But with the call of Abraham, the covenant of grace underwent a remarkable advance . . ." A covenant cannot advance. Its contents are fixed. The stark fact is that his whole argument of one covenant of grace is contrary to scripture. Instead of one covenant of grace we have during the stages of mankind's history the following periods of covenants between God and man:

1. From Adam till Noah:
   no covenant between God and man.
2. From Noah to Abraham:
   the operation of God's covenant with Noah and his descendants.
3. From Abraham to Moses at Mt. Sinai:
   the operation of God's covenant with Noah and his descendants
   the operation of God's covenant with Abraham

4. From Mt Sinai to Moses in Moab:
   the operation of God's covenant with Noah and his descendants
   the operation of God's covenant with Abraham
   the operation of God's covenant at Mt.Sinai
5. From Moses in Moab until king David
   the operation of God's covenant with Noah and his descendants
   the operation of God's covenant with Abraham
   the operation of God's covenant at Mt.Sinai renewed at Moab
6. From David until the ascension of Jesus Christ
   the operation of God's covenant with Noah and his descendants
   the operation of God's covenant with Abraham
   the operation of God's covenant at Mt. Sinai renewed at Moab
   the operation of God's covenant with David
7. From the ascension of Christ to His Second Coming
   the operation of God's covenant with Noah and his descendants
   the operation of God's covenant with Abraham – through Christ
   all nations are being blessed with salvation (Gen. 12:3, Gen. 22:18
   and Gal. 3:13–16).
   the operation of God's covenant with David – Christ is reigning
   since His ascension, as declared in Acts 2:29–33: "Men *and*
   brethren, let *me* speak freely to you of the patriarch David, that he
   is both dead and buried, and his tomb is with us to this day.
   Therefore, being a prophet, and knowing that God had sworn with
   an oath to him that of the fruit of his body, according to the flesh,
   He would raise up the Christ to sit on his throne, he, foreseeing
   this, spoke concerning the resurrection of the Christ, that His soul
   was not left in Hades, nor did His flesh see corruption. This Jesus
   God has raised up, of which we are all witnesses. Therefore being
   exalted to the right hand of God, and having received from the
   Father the promise of the Holy Spirit, He poured out this which
   you now see and hear." Christ will continue his reign throughout
   this period (1 Cor. 15:25–26).
   the operation of the New Covenant replacing and fulfilling the
   covenant at Mt. Sinai renewed at Moab. The New Covenant has
   replaced the Covenant at Mount Sinai (Heb. 8:13 and Gal. 3:19).

Some will argue that the covenant with Abraham is still operational
during the period of the New Covenant in a wider sense than salvation
for all nations through Christ. They see Israel's return to the land as
proof of their contention. That return is not the result of the Abrahamic
and Mosaic covenants being in operation. Under those covenants the
possession of the land depended on obedience to all God's statutes and

ordinances. If not they would be vomited out of it (Lev. 18:24–30; 20:22–26; Deut. 4:25–27,40; and Deut. 8:17–19). The return to the land is not explained in terms of national repentance and obedience to God required under the Mosaic covenant. These actions did not happen. Its explanation is purely in a sovereign act of God.

References

1. Taken from *Systematic Theology* by Wayne A. Grudem. Copyright © 1994 by Wayne Grudem. Used by permission of IVP and Zondervan, page 520.
2. *Ibid.*, pages 519–520.
3. *Ibid.*, page 520.
4. Pierre-Charles Marcel *The Biblical Doctrine of Infant Baptism*, James Clarke and Co. reprinted 2002, page 66.
5. Louis Berkhof *Systematic Theology*, Banner of Truth 1959, page 295.
6. Dr. Robert L. Reymond *A New Systematic Theology of the Christian Faith*, Copyright © 1998 Thomas Nelson Inc., pages 512–513. Used by permission of Thomas Nelson, Inc.

CHAPTER TWELVE

ATTEMPTS TO JUSTIFY INFANT BAPTISM: THE INVENTION OF THE COVENANT OF GRACE (4)

The assertion of one covenant of grace does not acknowledge sufficiently the great differences between the various periods listed in the previous chapter and between the various covenants.

In the period from Adam to Noah there was no covenant at all with man. God evidently gave sufficient revelation of truth for men like Abel to exercise faith, but He made no covenant with them.

The covenant with Noah was one of the most decisive events in the history of man. The whole of history from the Fall of Adam onwards to the Return of Christ is divided into two distinct periods of colossal difference by the covenant with Noah. Before that covenant man was subjected to destruction in this life on account of his sinfulness. After the covenant that destruction, though still deserved and fully justified as a punishment, was no longer administered (Gen. 8:21).

The covenant with Abraham created a nation in a special relationship with Himself, distinct from all other nations, and from whom would be born the Messiah Who would bless all nations. The covenant decreed that the nation initially would be in slavery for four hundred years, and then be delivered by God and led by Him to a land given to them by God.

The nature of this special relationship of the nation with God is clarified by the covenant at Mt. Sinai, which was renewed at Moab. This Mosaic covenant relationship with God was an exceedingly great and unique blessing. Moses addressed Israel with these words, "For ask now concerning the days that are past, which were before you, since the day that God created man on the earth, and *ask* from one end of heaven to the other, whether *any* great *thing* like this has happened, or *anything* like it has been heard. Did *any* people *ever* hear the voice of God speaking out of the midst of the fire, as you have heard, and live? Or did God *ever* try to go *and* take for Himself a nation from the midst of *another* nation, by trials, by signs, by wonders, by war, by a mighty hand and an outstretched arm, and by great terrors, according to all that the LORD your God did for you in Egypt before your eyes? To you it was shown, that you might know that the LORD Himself *is* God; *there is* none other besides Him" (Deut. 4:32–35).

The covenants with Abraham and at Sinai and Moab brought the nation into a relationship with God, and a certain knowledge of God. He made known His acts to them in the Exodus and subsequent interventions on their behalf (Psa. 103:7). He was their Ruler (Deut. 33:5). They were all His subjects. He revealed His will for them in the moral, civil and ceremonial laws which He gave to them. He provided a way of cleansing from sin. He administered blessings for obedience or curses for disobedience upon them. These covenants declared great temporal blessings if they obeyed all God's laws. But they pronounced terrible temporal punishments for disobedience.

The New Covenant is so profoundly different to the Mosaic covenant that the Holy Spirit defines it precisely in contrast to the covenant at Mt. Sinai. The very first thing God says about this New Covenant is that it will be "not according to the covenant that I made with their fathers in the day when I took them by the hand to lead them out of the land of Egypt; because they did not continue in My covenant, and I disregarded them, says the LORD" (Heb. 8:9). The giving of the various laws was a wondrous and precious revelation of God and His will. But the Mosaic covenant gave no grace to obey the laws. In the New Covenant there is a glorious internal work, "I will put My laws in their mind and write them on their hearts" (Heb. 8:10). The nation at Sinai said to Moses, " 'You go near and hear all that the LORD our God may say, and tell us all that the LORD our God says to you, and we will hear and do *it*.' Then the LORD heard the voice of your words when you spoke to me, and the LORD said to me: 'I have heard the voice of the words of this people which they have spoken to you. They are right *in* all that they have spoken. Oh, that they had such a heart in them that they would fear Me and always keep all My commandments, that it might be well with them and with their children forever!' " (Deut. 5:27–29). They did not have such a heart. The New Covenant is immeasurably superior to the Mosaic covenant because it gives a new heart to every single person who is in the New Covenant.

Paul writes of the glory of the New Covenant compared with the covenant at Sinai, "Not that we are sufficient of ourselves to think of anything as *being* from ourselves, but our sufficiency *is* from God, who also made us sufficient as ministers of the new covenant, not of the letter but of the Spirit; for the letter kills, but the Spirit gives life. But if the ministry of death, written *and* engraved on stones, was glorious, so that the children of Israel could not look steadily at the face of Moses because of the glory of his countenance, which *glory* was passing away, how will the ministry of the Spirit not be more glorious? For if the ministry of condemnation *had* glory, the ministry of righteousness exceeds much more in glory. For even what was made glorious had no glory in this respect, because of the glory that excels" (2 Cor. 3:5–10).

Paul makes the following contrasts between the Mosaic and the New Covenants

1. The covenant at Sinai was the ministration of the letter of the law written on tablets of stone. The New Covenant is the ministration of the Spirit writing the laws of God upon the heart

2. The former is external, the latter is internal

3. The letter kills. The Spirit gives life
    The law kills because it arouses the sinful passions of fallen human nature. When man in his fallen state is faced with the requirements of God's law sinfulness within him is aroused by the law and works with great power within him. He is incited by the law, because of sin within, to do the very things the law forbids. That sinfulness produces sinful actions and sinful thoughts resulting in spiritual death. Paul gives his own experience of this. He says, "What shall we say then? *Is* the law sin? Certainly not! On the contrary, I would not have known sin except through the law. For I would not have known covetousness unless the law had said, 'You shall not covet.' But sin, taking opportunity by the commandment, produced in me all *manner of evil* desire. For apart from the law sin *was* dead. I was alive once without the law, but when the commandment came, sin revived and I died. And the commandment, which *was* to *bring* life, I found to *bring* death. For sin, taking occasion by the commandment, deceived me, and by it killed *me*. Therefore the law *is* holy, and the commandment holy and just and good. Has then what is good become death to me? Certainly not! But sin, that it might appear sin, was producing death in me through what is good, so that sin through the commandment might become exceedingly sinful. For we know that the law is spiritual, but I am carnal, sold under sin" (Rom. 7:7–14). Paul is saying that sin within him used the law, which is holy just and good, as an opportunity to produce sins and so bring death. Sin is so powerful and able to deceive that it can even use God's holy law, which, if kept, would result in life, to produce death. Thus the New Testament tells us that when the law came it caused sin to abound (Rom. 5:20). Sin's use of the law of God explains why Paul declares that "the strength of sin *is* the law" (1 Cor. 15:56). So in this way the giving of

the law, because it incites the sinful passions within man, results in death. The letter kills. In contrast the Spirit gives life. He fulfils the prophecy given by Ezekiel, "I will give you a new heart and put a new spirit within you; I will take the heart of stone out of your flesh and give you a heart of flesh. I will put My Spirit within you and cause you to walk in My statutes, and you will keep My judgments and do *them*" (Ezek. 36:26–27).

4. The giving of the law was glorious (2 Cor. 3:7). The ministry of the Spirit is more glorious
The latter is so much more glorious that in comparison the former may be said to be no longer glorious.

5. The letter is a ministry of condemnation, the Spirit is a ministry of right-eousness and exceeds much more in glory
Sin uses the law as the opportunity to arouse sinfulness. This brings condemnation before God. The breaking of the law is transgression and brings God's wrath (Rom. 4:15). The Spirit brings about justification, imputed righteousness, and also righteousness of conduct in the Spirit (Rom. 8:1–4).

The New Covenant also is gloriously superior to the Mosaic covenant because it brings one into intimate fellowship with God
"For this *is* the covenant that I will make with the house of Israel after those days, says the LORD: I will put My laws in their mind and write them on their hearts; and I will be their God, and they shall be My people. None of them shall teach his neighbor, and none his brother, saying, 'Know the LORD,' for all shall know Me, from the least of them to the greatest of them" (Heb. 8:10–11).

God said to Abraham that He would be God to him and to his descendants (Gen. 17:7–8). When the Israelites were in Egypt God said, "I will take you as My people, and I will be your God. Then you shall know that I *am* the LORD your God who brings you out from under the burdens of the Egyptians" (Exod. 6:7); and later under the Mosaic covenant with them when formed into a nation, "I will set My taber-nacle among you, and My soul shall not abhor you. I will walk among you and be your God, and you shall be My people" (Lev. 26:11–12). As stated above this relationship with God was a family/national bond. God gave revelation of Himself and His will. He displayed the power of His might. It was not individual fellowship with God. The national relationship with God was not one of personal union and communion. It did not depend on obedience for its existence, and it was not terminated by the nation's disobedience.

Obedience would bring blessings, and disobedience curses. But their disobedience did not break His covenant relationship with them. In spite of their sinfulness as a nation God was still their God and still acted as their God. Ezekiel gives us the record of God acting for the nation in spite of constant sinfulness. He delivers God's word to Israel, "On that day I raised My hand in an oath to them, to bring them out of the land of Egypt into a land that I had searched out for them, 'flowing with milk and honey,' the glory of all lands. Then I said to them, 'Each of you, throw away the abominations which are before his eyes, and do not defile yourselves with the idols of Egypt. I *am* the LORD your God.' But they rebelled against Me and would not obey Me. They did not all cast away the abominations which were before their eyes, nor did they forsake the idols of Egypt. Then I said, 'I will pour out My fury on them and fulfill My anger against them in the midst of the land of Egypt.' But I acted for My name's sake, that it should not be profaned before the Gentiles among whom they *were*, in whose sight I had made Myself known to them, to bring them out of the land of Egypt" (Ezek. 20:6–9). In spite of rebellion God brought His people out of Egypt. Afterwards in the wilderness Ezekiel continues, "So I also raised My hand in an oath to them in the wilderness, that I would not bring them into the land which I had given *them*, 'flowing with milk and honey,' the glory of all lands, because they despised My judgments and did not walk in My statutes, but profaned My Sabbaths; for their heart went after their idols. Nevertheless My eye spared them from destruction. I did not make an end of them in the wilderness" (Ezek. 20:15–17). These verses explain why God said, "My soul shall not abhor you." God chose to be in a special relationship with them, to be their God, in spite of their sinfulness. They were manifestly not in fellowship with Him. At times in their history they saw His mighty works, but He was only their God in an external manner. They did not know Him, in the sense that they had no love for Him. Both Isaiah and Jeremiah testify to this; "Hear, O heavens, and give ear, O earth! For the LORD has spoken: 'I have nourished and brought up children, And they have rebelled against Me; The ox knows its owner And the donkey its master's crib; *But* Israel does not know, My people do not consider'" (Isa. 1:2–3); and, " 'And *like* their bow they have bent their tongues *for* lies. They are not valiant for the truth on the earth. For they proceed from evil to evil, And they do not know Me,' says the LORD" (Jer. 9:3).

There were those within the nation who did know God. We read of the midwives before the Exodus, "Then the king of Egypt spoke to the Hebrew midwives, of whom the name of one *was* Shiphrah and the name of the other Puah; and he said, 'When you do the duties of a midwife for the Hebrew women, and see *them* on the birthstools, if it *is* a son, then you shall kill him; but if it *is* a daughter, then she shall live.' But the midwives feared God, and did not do as the king of Egypt commanded them, but saved the male children alive" (Exod. 1:15–17). Such godly persons were ever present in the nation. But they were a tiny minority. The nation considered as a nation did not know God. In contrast everyone in the New Covenant knows the Lord. Notice how it is emphasised: "None of them shall teach his neighbor, and none his brother, saying, 'Know the LORD,' for all shall know Me, from the least of them to the greatest of them" (Heb. 8:11). This knowledge is true fellowship with God. This knowledge is always accompanied with real love for God. It goes beyond obedience to daily rules, and the keeping of all the ceremonial laws.

The New Covenant is superior to the Mosaic covenant because of the remission of sins.
"For I will be merciful to their unrighteousness, and their sins and their lawless deeds I will remember no more" (Heb. 8:12). The Mosaic covenant only provided an outward external ceremonial cleansing. It purified the flesh (Heb. 9:13). It satisfied God's requirements under that national covenant, but it could not make the worshipper perfect in regard to the conscience (Heb. 9:9). The blood of bulls and goats could not take away sins. The worshippers were never made perfect, and this was demonstrated by fact that there had to be a continual offering of sacrifices year by year. Those sacrifices reminded them of their sins every year. Moreover the way into the Holiest of All was limited to the High Priest just once a year. There was no access for any except him. Under the New Covenant all believers have continual access to the Father (Eph. 2:18).

In the New Covenant, in contrast to the priests standing ministering and offering repeatedly the same sacrifices which can never take away sins, Christ has sat down at the right hand of God having perfected for ever those in the covenant.
They are justified by the blood of His once for all sacrifice for sin. Their hearts are sprinkled from an evil conscience. They have boldness to enter the Holiest by the blood of Jesus, by a new and living way which He consecrated for all those in the New Covenant.

The Mosaic covenant "imposed" its ceremonial laws until the coming of the New Covenant.
It was a heavy burden. Peter referred to it at the council of Jerusalem as a "yoke which neither our fathers nor we were able to bear" (Acts

15:10). In like manner Paul says the Mosaic covenant enslaved. It brought bondage (Gal. 4:24). The New Covenant brings freedom (Gal. 5:1). Paul says that the law was like a jailor keeping man in prison. There was no escape until faith in Christ came: "But before faith came, we were kept under guard by the law, kept for the faith which would afterward be revealed" (Gal. 3:23).

The New Covenant includes mankind from every nation, tribe, people and language.
The covenants with Abraham and Moses were confined to one nation. God said to Israel, "You only have I known of all the families of the earth" (Amos 3:2). The Psalmist said of God, "He declares His word to Jacob, His statutes and His judgments to Israel. He has not dealt thus with any nation; And *as for His* judgments, they have not known them. Praise the LORD!" (Psa. 147:19–20). A few Gentiles occasionally shared in the blessings of those covenants, and benefited from the ministry of prophets of Israel as they came in contact with the people of Israel. Before Christ came, only one prophet Jonah, on one occasion, was sent to preach to Gentiles. Significantly he was sent from Joppa, a foreshadowing of Peter the apostle going from the same place to take the gospel to Gentiles for the first time (Jonah 1:3 and Acts 10:5). It was only after the death of Christ that Gentiles who obeyed the gospel ceased from being aliens from the commonwealth of Israel and strangers from the covenants of promise, having no hope and without God in the world, and became fellow citizens with the saints and members of the household of God (Eph. 2:12–19). This change in God's covenantal dealings was breathtakingly great and wonderful. The inclusion of the Gentiles was prophesied clearly to Abraham, and later through other prophets. It was a tremendous sea change when it happened.

All these verses show the tremendous difference between the Mosaic covenant and the New Covenant. John expresses the contrast succinctly, "For the law was given through Moses, *but* grace and truth came through Jesus Christ" (John 1:17). To assert that these covenants are different administrations of the one covenant of grace effectively undermines the tremendous differences and contrasts between them, and fails to give proper weight to their differing functions in God's way of salvation. This leads us to the next consideration.

The covenants before Christ were given to prepare the way for Christ and the New Covenant

Only after they had run for their appointed time was He sent by the Father when "the fulness of the time had come" (Gal. 4:4). After the fall of man God could have sent His Son to redeem mankind without any delay. But "'My thoughts *are* not your thoughts, Nor *are* your ways My ways,' says the LORD. 'For *as* the heavens are higher than the earth, So are My ways higher than your ways, And My thoughts than your thoughts'" (Isa. 55:8–9). So we have thousands of years of God's dealings with mankind, and His sovereign control over the events of history before the death of Christ. As we read in the prophet Daniel, "All the inhabitants of the earth *are* reputed as nothing; He does according to His will in the army of heaven And *among* the inhabitants of the earth. No one can restrain His hand Or say to Him, 'What have You done?'" (Dan. 4:35). Nothing prevents His purpose coming to pass. He works mysteriously in events and in the actions of men left to do their own freewill to bring about what He has decreed. He even uses the sinful actions of men to bring about His purposes. But He is never the author of sin. We see God working in this way in the life of Joseph. His brothers acted in jealousy and sold him into slavery, and he was taken to Egypt. Later Joseph said, "So now *it was* not you *who* sent me here, but God; and He has made me a father to Pharaoh, and lord of all his house, and a ruler throughout all the land of Egypt" (Gen. 45:8). In that position he was able to save his family from starvation.

Therefore the delay in sending Christ to die was not because God was hindered in any way. Man's sinful actions did not cause any delay. As in the case of Joseph God used the sinful actions of man to fulfil His purpose. The scriptures tell us in a prayer addressed to God the Father, "For truly against Your holy Servant Jesus, whom You anointed, both Herod and Pontius Pilate, with the Gentiles and the people of Israel, were gathered together to do whatever Your hand and Your purpose determined before to be done" (Acts 4:27–28).

God chose to send His Son only after the events of history had run their course according to His decrees. Because His judgments are unsearchable and His ways past finding out (Rom. 11:33), we cannot say why so long a period of history transpired before the coming of Christ. But we do have a revelation of God's working in the various covenants. We see that they prepared for the coming of Christ. Noah's covenant saved man from that time onwards from universal destruction. This was essential to achieve God's ultimate purpose of redeeming from mankind a multitude no man can number. The covenant with Abraham was necessary to fulfil God's chosen purpose that the Christ should be a son of Abraham according to the flesh, and that the nation of the Jews should be created to whom, and from whom, would come the Messiah. The creation of this nation followed the development of nations, and the confusion of speech which God brought about at Babel (Gen. 11). The covenant at Sinai, renewed at Moab, centred on the giving of law. Gal. 3:19 says it was "added" to the Abrahamic covenant. The law came in a secondary place, not of prime importance. It served three purposes, all of which prepared for the coming of Christ:

a)   To increase transgressions in the way we have explained above
"Moreover the law entered that the offense might abound. But where sin abounded, grace abounded much more" (Rom. 5:20). The divine purpose was to reveal that "where sin abounded grace abounded much more" (Rom. 5:20). The increase of the trespass as a result of the law demonstrated that grace superabounded. It caused the exceeding greatness of God's grace to be made manifest.

b)   To give the knowledge of sin
It did that in the following ways. It defined sin as transgression of the law. It makes us aware of what sin is, and that when we break the law we are sinning. Secondly, it brings a knowledge of the terrible power of sin within. Paul relates how he came to this experimental knowledge of sin. He said, "What shall we say then? *Is* the law sin? Certainly not! On the contrary, I would not have known sin except through the law. For I would not have known covetousness unless the law had said, 'You shall not covet.' But sin, taking opportunity by the command-ment, produced in me all *manner of evil* desire. For apart from the law sin *was* dead" (Rom. 7:7–8). The apostle says that when he really tried to obey the command not to covet he found that sin within him incited him to covet. He found himself utterly unable to overcome that power within him. He came to know sin in a way he had not known before. As a Pharisee he knew that it was a sin to covet, but he was unaware of the power of sin within him. Sin in that sense was "dead." Now he knew the awful reality of that power. He found himself to be in its grip. Only Christ could deliver him. This leads us to the final purpose of the giving of the law.

c)   To lead us to Christ
"Therefore the law was our tutor *to bring us* to Christ, that we might be justified by faith" (Gal. 3:24). The word tutor literally means boy leader. It refers to a slave of Roman times who looked after and conducted a freeborn youth to and from school. Just as the tutor led the boy to school, so the law is intended to lead to Christ. The law does this by giving the knowledge of sin so that we turn to the Saviour from sin.

The Mosaic covenant also prepared for the coming of Christ in that essential elements of it spoke of the good things to come in the New

Covenant. The Mosaic covenant included the ordinances of divine service and the earthly sanctuary, the tabernacle, with all the ceremonial law. These were a copy and shadow of Christ and the blessings of the New Covenant (Heb. 8:5 and 10:1). A copy is a type pointing forward to the antitype. A shadow gives a representation of that from which it is projected. It also points to the substance of which it is but a shadow. That substance is the Person and work of Christ.

The tabernacle and its worship were symbolic. They were a parable (παραβολὴ Heb. 9:9) speaking of Christ and the New Covenant. In connection with what has been said above concerning the nation's knowledge of God it is important to point out that parables were used by Christ to conceal truth from those to whom it was not revealed: "And the disciples came and said to Him, 'Why do You speak to them in parables?' He answered and said to them, 'Because it has been given to you to know the mysteries of the kingdom of heaven, but to them it has not been given. For whoever has, to him more will be given, and he will have abundance; but whoever does not have, even what he has will be taken away from him. Therefore I speak to them in parables, because seeing they do not see, and hearing they do not hear, nor do they understand'" (Mat. 13:10–13). Mark is explicit in his account of Jesus' answer to the question "Why do you speak in parables?" "He said to them, 'To you it has been given to know the mystery of the kingdom of God; but to those who are outside, all things come in parables, so that "Seeing they may see and not perceive, And hearing they may hear and not understand; Lest they should turn, And *their* sins be forgiven them"'" (Mark 4:11–12). Contrary to popular thinking parables were not used to reveal the truth, but to conceal it from those to whom it was not given to know the mysteries of the kingdom of God. Just as Jesus constantly used parables, God spoke in parable through the tabernacle and its worship to the nation before Christ came. It was a glorious revelation of truth to those to whom God gave understanding of its meaning. It was a concealing of truth from the rest.

Characteristic of God's dealings with mankind before the coming of Christ is God's use of people and events as well as covenants to be types and shadows of the good things to come in the gospel. In this way, as well as by predictions through His prophets, the Old Testament scriptures speak of Christ. When the Risen Christ met the disciples on the road to Emmaus it is recorded, "And beginning at Moses and all the Prophets, He expounded to them in all the Scriptures the things concerning Himself" (Luke 24:27). Jesus said during His ministry to the Jews who were seeking to kill Him, "You search the Scriptures, for in them you think you have eternal life; and these are they which testify of Me" (John 5:39). Thus God used the covenants to prepare for Christ's coming to speak of Him through their predictions, types and shadows. When He came history had become pregnant with all these promises and predictions, and the covenants had run for the appointed times in the perfect wisdom of God.

The covenant of grace concept blurs this preparatory nature of covenants before Christ. It is willing to admit a progressive increase of revelation in the covenants, but by imagining one covenant of grace operating throughout history it overthrows the fact that the covenants before Christ were designed to bring about the coming of Christ in the manner determined by the Triune God before creation, and to prepare the way for the New Covenant. The various covenants are presented rather as different forms of simply one covenant of grace.

CHAPTER THIRTEEN

ATTEMPTS TO JUSTIFY INFANT BAPTISM: THE INVENTION OF THE COVENANT OF GRACE (5)

The significance of our consideration of the covenants in relation to the teaching of Pierre-Charles Marcel

The stages in the history of God's dealings with mankind do not support the contention of paedobaptists of infants being included in their alleged covenant of grace. Paedobaptist covenant theologians, who, like Pierre-Charles Marcel, assert the existence of this covenant of grace from the fall of Adam, have a very great problem. For at least half of the whole of the history of man before Christ came, their alleged covenant of grace was in operation without any indication whatsoever of including infants. It is only with the advent of the covenant with Abraham that infants are included in one of the so-called various forms of the covenant of grace.

Some would point to Noah and the inclusion of his family in the Ark to argue for the inclusion of family members in the covenant dealings of God before Abraham: "But I will establish My covenant with you; and you shall go into the ark – you, your sons, your wife, and your sons' wives with you" (Gen. 6:18). The covenant was stated in Gen 8:21 to 9:17. God instructed Noah to take all his family into the Ark because their survival was essential for the carrying out of the Divine command after the flood, "So God blessed Noah and his sons, and said to them: 'Be fruitful and multiply, and fill the earth' " (Gen. 9:1). The command was repeated, "And as for you, be fruitful and multiply; Bring forth abundantly in the earth And multiply in it" (Gen. 9:7). Noah's family were commanded to go into the Ark for the same reason as the living creatures were, to repopulate the earth. There are no other indications of family salvation recorded in scripture during the period from Adam to Abram.

The teaching of one covenant of grace gives a false impression of God's dealings with mankind. It minimizes the very real differences of the covenants given at different times to lead up to, and bring about

God's fixed plan and purpose of salvation through Christ. The whole history of God's dealings with man before and after Christ tends to be made level. For some paedobaptists there is really only one covenant in operation throughout history. Pierre-Charles Marcel effectively eliminates the differences between the Covenant with Abraham and the New Covenant by simply referring to circumcision as "the sacrament of the covenant of grace,"[1] and then also referring to baptism as a "sacrament of the covenant of grace."[2] This one covenant of grace operating from the Fall of Adam onwards thus overrides the different covenants and their different conditions. Instead of circumcision being seen as a requirement of the Covenant with Abraham, and baptism as a requirement of the New Covenant, both covenants, and their great differences, disappear from view. Circumcision and baptism are linked as different sacraments of the one covenant of grace. By alleging this one covenant of grace differently administered before and after Christ he can assert that *"Baptism has taken the place of circumcision as the sacrament of admission into the covenant."*[3]

He states that God imposed the covenant on the descendants of Abraham. He then argues "Since *in this way* the condition of participation in the covenant depends on God alone, faith is no longer the requisite condition of membership. The covenant of grace was not established with man in his capacity as believer, because faith is itself *the fruit* of the covenant. Faith not being a condition *of* the covenant, but a condition *in* the covenant, the covenant precedes faith."[4] He states that under the New Covenant the same applies as under the Abrahamic covenant, because there is one covenant of grace. He contends that this one covenant of grace therefore now includes the children of believers because of the character of the covenant, "It was never simply concluded with one or other person taken individually – always *his posterity* is included in it: it is a covenant *'from generation to generation.'* "[5] By imposing one covenant of grace across all history from Abraham onwards he is able to take the content of the Abrahamic covenant and apply it to the period of the New Covenant. Thus he can argue that infants of believers are in the covenant of grace and should receive its sign, baptism, regardless of their inability to believe. He states, "Since the children of believers are 'set apart,' separate from the profane world, 'holy' – to use the biblical expression – from the moment of their birth; since God includes them in the covenant and they belong to Christ's body the Church; in short, since they participate in all the promises and all the spiritual realities signified and sealed in baptism, we say that they are fit to receive it; *there is no other reason for administering baptism to them.*"[6] Notice his final words in italics. The only basis for infant baptism is the alleged inclusion in the covenant of grace. Pierre-Charles Marcel says, "With the rejection of the covenant of grace every possible foundation of infant baptism disappears."[7] What an admission! Since there is no covenant of grace there is no ground for the practice of infant baptism!

In order to deal with Marcel's arguments thoroughly let us consider male circumcision under the Abrahamic covenant. It is important to note that it had a different meaning for Abraham than for the others to whom God stated it must be administered. For him it was the seal of the righteousness imputed to him by faith (Rom. 4:11). It was also a sign of all the promises God had made to him in the covenant. Some of these promises were specifically for Abraham and applied to no one else, e.g. "I will make your name great." (Gen. 12:2). For all other males it was the sign of belonging to a family which would become a nation. It was a sign that that family/nation was in a special relationship with God as stated in God's covenant with Abraham. Abraham's male off-spring, and any male born in the household, both children of a concu-bine or of a slave, had to be circumcised. As regards boys of slaves, both those born of slaves who belonged to the household at the time of the birth of the boy, and those boys who had been born before their parents passed into control of the Hebrew master, had to be circumcised. If such were not circumcised then they were "cut off from his people," and regarded by God as having broken God's covenant (Gen. 17:7).

The only qualification for circumcision was being a male descen-dant of Abraham, or belonging to the household of Abraham, or the household of one of his descendants. Circumcision placed males in the covenant. Female descendants of Abraham were in the covenant without the requirement of circumcision. The qualification for entry into the New Covenant is repentance and faith, the new birth by the word of God and the Holy Spirit: "But as many as received Him, to them He gave the right to become children of God, to those who believe in His name: who were born, not of blood, nor of the will of the flesh, nor of the will of man, but of God" (John 1:12–13). No one can get into the New Covenant on the basis of having a believing parent. John 1:12–13 rules this out in the most emphatic and unambiguous manner. Having a parent in the Abrahamic covenant automatically placed a child in that covenant. Marcel denies this difference in the entry qualifications to the two covenants. He makes entry to both covenants dependent only on being the offspring of a member of the covenant with Abraham or of a member of the New Covenant. He states that it is imperative that the baptism of an infant does not take place unless there is assurance that at least one of the parents is a believer because the infant is only in the covenant if a parent or parents is/are in the covenant. He also insists that there must be assurance that Christian religious instruction will be given to the child.

Circumcision placed one in a special relationship with God as one of His people to whom the Abrahamic covenant applied. It meant belonging to a family/nation whom God dealt with in a special way and to whom promises were made. As God's plan progressed it incorporated one in a nation experiencing His mighty acts and receiving the revelation of His will at Mt. Sinai and Moab for the worship of God, and the ordering of national and daily life. In addition to further promises of blessing there were warnings of curses for disobedience. That special relationship with God signified by circumcision did not mean personal fellowship with God. It signified God's special relationship with a family/nation. Marcel correctly states "Circumcision did not make a Jew of the man who received it; as such, it gave him neither the knowledge nor the grace necessary for him to be one of the true children of Israel. . . . It assured to him the privileges of the theocracy."[8]

Some within, or dwelling with, the family/nation did come into fellowship with God. They were the true Israel within the nation of Israel (Rom. 9:6). That true Israel, together with those who knew God before the time of Abraham, were the people of God, the Church of God in the time before Christ. The nation of Israel was not the Church. A minority within it were. Marcel asserts wrongly that the whole nation of Israel was the Church, and that the Christian Church, since it also comes under the covenant of grace, is the same Church. To support his argument he quotes Acts 7:38 saying, "In the New Testament the people of Israel are called 'the church' (Acts 7:38)."[9] This scripture refers to the ἐκκλησία "the assembly" or "congregation" of Israel. The word is often translated church in the New Testament, but it is not correct to translate it church in Acts 7:38. The word can mean a company of Christians, or the whole body of Christians scattered throughout the earth, or simply a gathering as in Acts 19:32 and 41, or the assembly or gathering of the Israelites. It is incorrect to translate it church in this verse. The correct translation in Acts 7:38 is assembly or congregation. By mistranslating this verse Marcel wrongly equates the Church with the whole nation of Israel in Old Testament times, and by applying the false concept of one covenant of grace across all history he affirms that the Christian Church of the New Covenant is the continuation of the nation of Israel. On this spurious basis he argues for the continuation of inclusion of the offspring of believers as members of the Christian Church, and the baptism of them as infants.

Marcel goes on to define the church of the New Covenant as being composed of both regenerate and unregenerate just as Israel under the Abrahamic covenant was composed of the nation of Israel and the true Israel within it. This flies in the face of the New Testament. Everyone in the New Covenant has experienced the new birth. By its very nature no one can be in it and be unregenerate. In contrast, the Abrahamic covenant included the unregenerate. The unregenerate are outside the New Covenant. But not according to Marcel. He says that the children of believers are born in the covenant and members of the Christian Church even before they repent and believe and when they are unregenerate. This betrays a fundamental blindness to the content of the New Covenant. It also demonstrates that he selects from the covenants before Christ what suits his concept of the covenant of grace, and overthrows the content of the New Covenant to accommodate the infant baptism of the unregenerate.

All in the New Covenant are born again, and they are members of the Church, the true people of God. It is acknowledged that there are false professors and false prophets and teachers among the true Church of God. But none who are unregenerate are in the New Covenant: "The Lord knows those who are His" (2 Tim. 2:19). The unregenerate are not counted by Him as in His Church.

Pierre-Charles Marcel fails to take account of the typical and preparatory nature of the covenant with Abraham. The nation that came into being was "a kingdom of priests and a holy nation" (Exod. 19:6). The nation and priests are described by the New Testament as but a copy and shadow of the heavenly things of the New Covenant. The nation was holy in that it was separated to God for His special dealing. It was not holy in the sense of being regenerate and truly in fellowship with God. God's order of working is revealed by Paul, "However, the spiritual is not first, but the natural, and afterward the spiritual" (1 Cor. 15:46). So the nation and kingdom of Israel prefigured the nation and kingdom of the Church of the New Covenant. The apostle Peter describes that Church in words recalling Exod. 19:6, "But you *are* a chosen generation, a royal priesthood, a holy nation, His own special people, that you may proclaim the praises of Him who called you out of darkness into His marvelous light; who once *were* not a people but *are* now the people of God, who had not obtained mercy but now have obtained mercy" (1 Pet. 2:9–10). These verses are the fulfilment of the type declared in Exod. 19:6. The nation of Israel experienced natural blessings typical of spiritual blessings under the New Covenant. One of the most outstanding examples of this is the deliverance from Egypt, pointing to salvation from the bondage of sin. Under the Abrahamic covenant supplemented with the Mosaic covenant we have an earthly political kingdom and nation. Under the New Covenant we have a kingdom and nation not of this world (John 18:36). It is the Israel of God (Gal. 6:16), made up of believers from all nations individually born again, and individually called out of darkness into His marvellous light. First the natural and then the spiritual. Natural birth sufficed for the natural nation. Spiritual new birth (1 Pet. 1:22–23) is necessary for the spiritual nation.

If we adopt Marcel's concept of the covenant of grace we have three categories of people:

- the unsaved outside the covenant
- the saved in the covenant, and
- children of believers who are unsaved but in the covenant.

He says of children who have at least one believing parent, "These children do not inherit salvation and eternal life. Salvation is not hereditary! They inherit only the promises. It behoves them thereafter to receive the *content* of the promise by faith and repentance, and thus by regeneration and conversion, and to live a life consecrated to the Lord. Then, and then only, will they be heirs of *the things promised*. The heritage is only communicated to the heir who receives the promise *with faith*."[10] He says of these children of believers "Since they have been born into the covenant, children and young people and also adults, although overtaken by the evil of life and tormented by religious questions, are not and should never be considered as proselytes. *For them the content of our message is not the same as that which we address to proselytes.* Since they are within the covenant, the promises which concern them, the demands of God, the possibility of their responding to them, and also their responsibility, are quite different."[11] These words reveal that Marcel is advocating another gospel, with all the fearful consequences of such an action: "But even if we, or an angel from heaven, preach any other gospel to you than what we have preached to you, let him be accursed. As we have said before, so now I say again, if anyone preaches any other gospel to you than what you have received, let him be accursed" (Gal. 1:8–9). These are solemn words. Let us look at what he claims to be "quite different." He asserts that the child has the promise of God to be his God, because He promises the believing parent to be the God of his/her posterity. This is true under the Abrahamic covenant, but not under the New Covenant. The promises of salvation in the gospel are exactly the same to everyone. It makes absolutely no difference to the promises whether or not one's parent or parents are Christian or non-Christian. The demands of God also are exactly the same whether or not a person has a believing parent. Repentance and faith are essential, and nothing else. For someone with a believing parent or parents Marcel says that faith is necessary to remain in the covenant, not to enter it. He says correctly that they are "under obligation to repent and believe."[12] But he defines repenting and believing as responding to God's promise "I shall be your God, and you shall be My people."[13] To refuse to respond is to break the existing covenant God already has with them.

Marcel says that children born in the covenant "have the *possibility* of freely, voluntarily, and consciously choosing between good and evil, blessing and cursing, life and death (Dt. 30:11–20, and all similar texts), the possibility and the liberty of confirming the covenant offered by God and of loving and serving their Redeemer;"[14] and, "Viewed from the angle of man's corruption and his inability to do good, this possibility is in itself something altogether extraordinary which ought justly to excite our wonderment. This possibility and this liberty are already the work of the special grace of God."[15] He continues, "God, according to the promise, restores liberty of choice to the children of the covenant, with the result that, confronted with the alternative of life or death, they are able voluntarily and freely to embrace the one or the other."[16] God does this "by internal regeneration and by making the proclamation of the Gospel efficacious for them."[17] The New Testament, as stated previously, does teach the drawing of the Father (John 6:44). But such drawing always results in coming to Christ. It never gives merely a liberty to choose to repent and believe or to refuse to do so. But Marcel states that despite this possibility and liberty of confirming the covenant some remain unregenerate. His "work of the special grace of God" is his own invention. It fits his scheme, but it is contrary to scripture.

He says of their responsibility, "The fact of being born in the covenant with all the promises and benefits it conveys, lays an increased responsibility upon them."[18] The truth is that they are not in the covenant. To tell them so is a lie. It is a dangerous lie, because it could blur the reality of their position. They are as lost and bound for hell as all others who have not repented and believed in Christ. Lying to them that they are in the covenant is a false gospel. The New Testament declares that there are only two categories of people:

- the saved in the New Covenant
- the unsaved not in the New Covenant
- it is also clear that there is only one gospel.

Conclusions

There is no case for infant baptism in the teachings of Pierre-Charles Marcel. His deviation from the truth of the gospel is extremely serious. It is common to consider these matters as simply differences among Christians which Christians should tolerate. Gal. 1:8–9 states the attitude required by their Lord to such errors.

References

1. Pierre-Charles Marcel *The Biblical Doctrine of Infant Baptism*, James Clarke and Co., Ltd. reprinted 2002, page 94.
2. *Ibid.*, page 152.
3. *Ibid.*, page 155.
4. *Ibid.*, pages 101–102.
5. *Ibid.*, page 107.
6. *Ibid.*, page 192.
7. *Ibid.*, page 199.
8. *Ibid.*, page 178.
9. *Ibid.*, page 95.
10. *Ibid.*, page 108.
11. *Ibid.*, page 135.
12. *Ibid.*, page 131.
13. *Ibid.*, page 102.
14. *Ibid.*, pages 108–109.
15. *Ibid.*, page 109 footnote.
16. *Ibid.*, page 110.
17. *Ibid.*, page 110 footnote.
18. *Ibid.*, pages 131–132.

CHAPTER FOURTEEN

ATTEMPTS TO JUSTIFY INFANT BAPTISM FROM THE NEW TESTAMENT (1)

We shall examine seven attempts to justify the practice of infant baptism based on the New Testament.

The silence of the New Testament

In view of the inclusion of infants in the covenant from the time of Abraham it is argued that if they were now excluded after the death of Christ then an express command to that effect was necessary, and would have been given by the Lord. But no such instruction exists.

This argument treats the first New Testament Christians as if they were unaware of the differences between the Abrahamic covenant and the New Covenant. They knew that they were in the New Covenant. Accordingly we read of Paul's teaching in the Acts of the Apostles, "but they have been informed about you that you teach all the Jews who are among the Gentiles to forsake Moses, saying that they ought not to circumcise *their* children nor to walk according to the customs" (Acts 21:21). Their knowledge of the New Covenant is also revealed in Paul's letter to the Corinthians. He reminds them of the doctrine he had received from the Lord and delivered to them. He had delivered to them the very words of Christ: "This cup is the new covenant in My blood." They knew that circumcision had ceased.

They also knew that the only way of entrance into the New Covenant was by repentance and faith. That New Covenant was as clear as crystal. There was a tremendous change in the position of the children of members of the Abrahamic covenant and the children of parents in the New Covenant. Under the former they entered the national covenant by birth. Now they could only enter the New Covenant by repentance and faith, the new birth. They knew that the only way of becoming His people now was entrance into that New Covenant. They did not need an express command to cease admission of their infants into the New Covenant. Its nature made plain what they should do. They did not think according to the false concept of one covenant of grace overriding the Abrahamic, Mosaic and New Covenants. They knew that their children could enter that New Covenant if, and only if, they would repent and believe.

This leads us to another argument from the silence of the New Testament. It is contended that that there are no cases in the New Testament of the baptism of children/adults born of parents already Christian and brought up by them. There is no doubt that these baptisms occurred, and equally no need for them to be recorded.

There is also silence in the New Testament about infant baptism. There is not a single conclusive case of infant baptism in the New Testament records. Oscar Cullman says this silence is explained by the fact that we have records of a missionary situation where there would be little opportunity for such practice. He says that such opportunities would only occur when a whole house which included infants was converted, and when children were born after the conversion of one or both of the parents.[1] Given the huge numbers of converts, (Acts 2:41, 5:14 etc.) there would be an abundance of opportunities!

Louis Berkhof explains the silence about infant baptism saying, "Converts would not at once have a proper conception of their covenant duties and responsibilities. Sometimes only one of the parents was converted, and it is quite conceivable that the other would oppose the baptism of the children. Frequently there was no reasonable assurance that the parents would educate their children piously and religiously, and yet such assurance was necessary."[2] It is certain that had these imaginary difficulties actually existed the apostles and leaders of the church would have dealt with them. Indeed it is inexplicable that the New Testament contains no teaching about infant baptism if God intended such practice under the New Covenant.

Pierre-Charles Marcel argues that the New Testament makes no reference to women partaking of the Lord's Supper. It is silent just as it is silent about infant baptism. He says that women's admission to the Lord's Table is rightly based on the truths of scripture and so is infant baptism. Here we see the crux of the matter. Silence on a specific matter is not always significant where the teachings of the scriptures reveal God's will and the application of the truth is plain and clear for those willing to submit and obey. The first Christians would behave according to their understanding of the gospel and the covenants. Without express statements or records we can say with confidence, in the light of, and in harmony with all the doctrine of the New Testament, that they would baptize children who repented and believed in Christ, and that they would not baptize any infants.

Paedobaptists sometimes argue that the New Testament passages dealing with baptism relate only to adults and therefore have no bearing on the issue of infant baptism. If the apostles did in fact practise infant baptism is it not truly remarkable that there is no proven case of a single infant being baptized in the New Testament records, no command to baptize infants and there is no teaching about it in the New Testament? Baptism in the New Testament in its insistence on repentance and personal faith rules out infants. Therefore teaching would have been essential both to institute the practice and to define its meaning for infants. Such teaching did arise, but as we shall see it was after the days of the New Testament.

The one covenant of grace argument that baptism has replaced circumcision based on Col. 2:11–12

This is asserted by those who hold to the one covenant of grace error. They give essentially the same meaning to circumcision and baptism, and say that both signs are for the offspring of those in the alleged one covenant from Abraham onwards. Col. 2:11–12 reads, "In him you were also circumcised with the circumcision made without hands, by putting off the body of the sins of the flesh, by the circumcision of Christ, buried with Him in baptism, in which you also were raised with *Him* through faith in the working of God, who raised Him from the dead." This verse does not support their contention that baptism is substituted for circumcision. It teaches that Christians have experienced a "circumcision made without hands." This is in contrast to, and has replaced the circumcision of the Abrahamic covenant. It is clearly not baptism because that is done by hands. It is putting off the body of sins of the flesh by the circumcision of Christ. It is dying to sin (Rom. 6:2–6). This is the new birth, the circumcision of the heart. As Paul wrote of this in his letter to the Romans, "For he is not a Jew who *is one* outwardly, nor *is* circumcision that which *is* outward in the flesh; but *he is* a Jew who *is one* inwardly; and circumcision *is that* of the heart, in the Spirit, not in the letter; whose praise *is* not from men but from God" (Rom. 2:28–29). Circumcision with hands has been replaced by the circumcision of the heart wrought not with hands but by God. Indeed the typical meaning of Old Testament circumcision is to point to this circumcision of the heart under the New Covenant. Again we see the outworking of God's method, first the natural and then the spiritual (1 Cor. 15:46). Baptism has not replaced Old Testament circumcision. Baptism is mentioned in the verse because it signifies that union with Christ through which the circumcision of the heart was effected. The Council of Jerusalem in Acts 15 addressed the crucial question whether converted Gentiles needed to be circumcised. If baptism had replaced circumcision then there would have been an instant answer to the question. We find no trace of that immediate answer in the deliberations that took place. No one said that Gentiles did not need to be circumcised because baptism had replaced circumcision. This fact is decisive.

The passages relating Jesus' reception of children – Mat. 19:13–15, Mark 10:13–16 and Luke 18:15–17

Oscar Cullman says that the Gospel writers transmitted the account "with the evident intention of having it regarded as a standard for the discussion of the Baptism of infants, which was perhaps already acute." He says, "Christ's hand, according to the evangelists laid in blessing on the children, is there the instrument of the Spirit, just like the hand which he laid on the sick. Those infants in the Gospels (βρέφη Luke 18:15) enter through the action of Jesus into fellowship with him. Certainly this is not Baptism; yet this event from the very earliest of times is quite rightly adduced as a legitimation of infant Baptism, in which nothing else is at stake than the reception of children into fellowship with Jesus Christ: 'Forbid them not!' Μὴ κωλύετε."[3] It is not possible for infants to have fellowship. We should rather think of those who brought little ones to Jesus for blessing having in mind such events as Jacob's blessing of Ephraim and Manasseh as recorded in Gen. 48:13–16.

Cullman says, "As early as the first century, whenever someone who had come to faith was brought for Baptism, enquiry was made whether any hindrance existed, that is, whether the candidate had really fulfilled the conditions demanded."[4] He sees evidence of this in the following texts Acts 8:36 (hinders), 11:17 (withstand), Mat. 3:14 (prevent), and the Gospel of the Ebionites, Epiphanias 30:13 (prevented). In all these texts the Greek verbs κωλύω and διακωλύω are used and translated as shown. He argues that they reveal evidence of a rudimentary liturgy, which would be, "What hinders so-and-so from being baptized?" Or the candidate asks, "What hinders me from being baptized?" He then argues from the use of the same Greek verb κωλύω in Mark 10:14 that it must be understood as having this baptismal reference. He says that the account of Jesus' blessing of the children was transmitted in order to "recall to the remembrance of Christians of their time an occurrence by which they might be led to a solution of the question of infant Baptism. If this is so, we wholly understand that this story – without being related to Baptism – was fixed in such a way that a baptismal formula of the first century gleams through it."[5]

An examination of Acts 8:36; 10:47; 11:17, Mat. 3:14 and the Ebionite Gospel does not reveal the alleged liturgy. R.E.O. White says, "If we set out the passages for comparison, and include Mar x 13f, as Cullman does, accepting for the moment his assumption that this passage *is* a baptismal one, we find that the hindrance is advanced by different actors, on different grounds, and is removed by very different types of answer."[6] It is therefore not valid to assert the presence of a baptismal formula in Mark 10:14. There is no real evidence that Matthew, Mark and Luke wrote their accounts or "fixed" them to refer to infant baptism.

The Special Commission on Baptism of the Church of Scotland makes the following assertions from the records of children in the gospels.

1) Referring to Mark 10:14, Mat. 19:14 and Luke 18:16, "The Kingdom of God of which Jesus spoke was already present in Himself, and Jesus' action was one that brought these children into direct relation to Himself and to His Kingdom. . . . What we can quite certainly say is that *our Lord, who stated so clearly that the Kingdom of God belongs to little children, could not have refused to allow them to share in the sacrament of initiation into that Kingdom, which is Baptism.*"[7]

As detailed in a previous chapter these verses do not mean that infants are in the kingdom of God. They teach rather that the kingdom of God is composed of those who receive it like children in their helplessness and dependence.

2) With reference to Mat. 18:3, Mark 10:15, Luke 18:17 and John 3:3, 5, all of which state a condition of entrance into the Kingdom the following is affirmed, "*If the condition of entrance into the Kingdom of God is at the same time being born of water and of the Spirit, and becoming like a little child, it is incredible that our Lord would have us refuse Baptism to those children whom even adult candidates for Baptism need to resemble in order to enter the Kingdom of God. It is 'as little children' that all must be baptized, whatever their actual age.*"[8]

Being born of water and the Spirit is coming to repentance and faith. The water indicates the word of God in its power to cleanse from sin. There is no reference to water baptism in John 3:5. All of these verses state in different ways the need to obey the gospel to enter the kingdom. Infants cannot fulfil this absolute requirement.

3) Quoting Mark 9:37 "Whoever receives one of these little children in My name receives Me; and whoever receives Me, receives not Me but

Him who sent Me" it says that in one of the original uses of these words Jesus may have been speaking of actual children. The document continues, "It has been suggested that in the phrase 'receiving in the name' the words are those used in the Jewish adoption of a foundling child. In the Zadokite communities such reception was probably accompanied by washings. St. Peter uses the same expression, 'in the name of Christ,' in the Pentecost call to Baptism. Be that as it may, we have certainly here an injunction to receive in the name of Christ those whom the world regards as least important, and it is this reversal of the usual order of things that makes infant Baptism the natural custom of the Church. *Our Lord, who bids His disciples receive little children in His name, cannot refuse to receive them Himself in the sacrament of Baptism.*"[9]

Concerning the phrase "receiving in the name" and the probable associated washings done by the Zadokites it must not be forgotten that they also circumcised those they adopted. The phrase applied to circumcision as much as to baptism. The phrase "in the name of" ("ἐπὶ τῷ ὀνόματι") occurs several times in the New Testament – of the coming of false prophets, working miracles, speaking, preaching and teaching. It is only used once of baptism in Acts 2:38. The use of the phrase in this verse in relation to baptism by Peter and its use in relation to the baptismal practice of the Zadokites therefore does not validate interpreting "receives one of these little children in My name" to mean to baptize them. R.E.O. White says concerning Mark 9:37, ". . . if 'receive' in the first clause means 'reception into Christ, into the kingdom, and baptism' then plainly the same meaning should hold for the second clause – which is absurd."[10]

Matthew records more fully the incident in which Jesus uttered the words in Mark 9:37. "These little children" in Mark are defined by Matthew as those who are converted and become as little children, "At that time the disciples came to Jesus, saying, 'Who then is greatest in the kingdom of heaven?' Then Jesus called a little child to Him, set him in the midst of them, and said, 'Assuredly, I say to you, unless you are converted and become as little children, you will by no means enter the kingdom of heaven. Therefore whoever humbles himself as this little child is the greatest in the kingdom of heaven. Whoever receives one little child like this in My name receives Me. But whoever causes one of these little ones who believe in Me to sin, it would be better for him if a millstone were hung around his neck, and he were drowned in the depth of the sea'" (Mat. 18:1–6). Accordingly Jesus is not speaking of little ones but rather of little ones who believe in Him. He is saying all such must be treated as the greatest in the kingdom of heaven. He is so united with them that to receive them in His name is to receive Him. He is speaking of receiving disciples not infants.

References

1. Oscar Cullman *Baptism in the New Testament*, SCM 1950, Page 25.
2. Louis Berkhof *Systematic Theology*, Banner of Truth 1959, page 634.
3. Oscar Cullman *Baptism in the New Testament*, SCM 1950, page 42.
4. *Ibid.*, page 75.
5. *Ibid.*, page 78.
6. R.E.O. White *The Biblical Doctrine of Initiation*, Hodder & Stoughton 1960, page 336.
7. *The Biblical Doctrine of Baptism*, The Saint Andrew Press Edinburgh 1958, page 49.
8. *Ibid.*, page 50.
9. *Ibid.*, page 51.
10. R.E.O. White *The Biblical Doctrine of Initiation*, Hodder & Stoughton 1960, page 331.

CHAPTER FIFTEEN

ATTEMPTS TO JUSTIFY INFANT BAPTISM FROM THE NEW TESTAMENT (2)

"Then Peter said to them, 'Repent, and let every one of you be baptized in the name of Jesus Christ for the remission of sins; and you shall receive the gift of the Holy Spirit. For the promise is to you and to your children, and to all who are afar off, as many as the Lord our God will call' " (Acts 2:38–39)

Those holding the one covenant approach to justify infant baptism grasp eagerly at this verse for support of their view. They fasten on the words "the promise is to you and your children." They argue that this means that children are included in the covenant of grace just as they were in the time of Abraham. They ignore the remainder of the verse which defines the promise as to "as many as the Lord our God will call." This is the call of God which results in repentance and faith, which we looked at in an earlier chapter. Some of Peter's hearers heard that call, and consequently they "received his word and were baptized."

Peter is acutely conscious of just entering a new period of God's dealings with mankind. The prophesied last days have just begun: "And it shall come to pass in the last days, says God, That I will pour out of My Spirit on all flesh; Your sons and your daughters shall prophesy, Your young men shall see visions, Your old men shall dream dreams. And on My menservants and on My maidservants I will pour out My Spirit in those days; And they shall prophesy" (Acts 2:17–18). The promise continued, "And it shall come to pass *that* whoever calls on the name of the LORD shall be saved" (Acts 2:21). The speaking in tongues on that day was the fulfilment of that Old Testament prophecy. Peter stands at the first day of a new era. He looks forward down through the future time of the last days. He sees this glorious promise is for "as many as the Lord our God will call" during the last days. He speaks of future generations of Jews, "your children." Some of them will be called. He also speaks of those "who are afar off," the Gentiles. Some of them also will be called. Therefore "your children" did not refer to infants and children of those listening to Peter on the day of Pentecost. It referred to Jews of coming generations who would be called by God.

When the actual content of the promise "to your children" is considered it is absurd to interpret "your children" as including infants. The promise is salvation for those who call on the name of the Lord (Acts 2:21). Infants cannot do that. The promise is to engage in prophetic action (Acts 2:17–18). Infants cannot do that.

Whole families were baptized (Acts 11:48, 16:15, 33; and 1 Cor. 1:16)

It cannot be assumed that infants or children too young to repent and believe were present in any of the incidents to which the above verses refer. There were certainly servants present on at least one occasion (Acts 10:7). In all the cases, except one, we are informed that faith preceded the baptism of each individual. In the case of the household of Cornelius (Acts 11:48), Peter said that God purified their hearts by faith (Acts 15:9). Everyone in the Philippian household of the prison officer heard the word of God and believed (Acts 16:32 and 34). Concerning the baptism of the household of Stephanas, Paul said, "they have devoted themselves to the ministry of the saints" (1 Cor. 16:15). It can therefore be concluded that the household did not include infants. This leaves the record of Lydia and her household. The account simply says, "she and her household were baptized." It records her prior faith, but not that of the members of her household, nor who they were.

These accounts are in total harmony with the doctrine that repentance and faith must precede baptism and that it is not for infants. They provide not a shred of evidence for baptizing family members regardless of individual faith and solely on the basis of family solidarity.

Pierre-Charles Marcel argues for the spiritual solidarity of the family united under its head. He says that the following families were saved through the faith of one of their members: the family of Zaccheus (Luke 19:9), that of the nobleman (John 4:53), of Cornelius (Acts 10:2), of Lydia (Acts 16:14f.), of the gaoler (Acts 16:30–33), of Crispus (Acts 18:8), and of Onesiphorus (2 Tim. 1:16).[1]

These texts do not support Marcel's argument. Luke 19 records only the conversion of Zaccheus. The record states expressly the reason why salvation came to his house, "because he also is a son of Abraham." His faith resulted in his salvation, and thus in Zaccheus salvation was present in the household. His faith did not save anyone other than himself. With reference to the nobleman of John 4 we are told that "he himself believed, and his whole household" (John 4:53). The faith of the whole household, including the nobleman's servants, is placed alongside the faith of the nobleman. We have seen that the households of Cornelius and the Philippian jailor heard and believed the gospel. Luke tells us that "Crispus, the ruler of the synagogue, believed on the Lord with all his household" (Acts 18:8). Again the faith of his household is alongside the faith of Crispus. Paul's mention of the household of Onesiphorus is explained in terms of the common faith of all in the household. That faith is evident in that Paul sends Christian greetings to them (2 Tim. 4:19). The mention of the household is not an example of a family automatically being blessed because of the head of the household having faith. It is an example of a household united in faith and commitment to the service of Jesus Christ. These texts do not teach Marcel's contention, "In God's eyes parents and their children are *one*. By divine right parents are the authorized representatives of their children; they act for them; they engage in spiritual obligations because of them and for them, and also in their name. Such is the order of God."[2] It is a fact that in every generation there are examples of whole households, composed of a family or a family and servants, with each individual having come to faith in Christ. It is equally a fact that often not all members of a household are believers. There is nothing in the New Testament remotely suggesting that the conversion of a father or mother changes the spiritual standing of children in the family. Indeed far from resulting in solidarity in the family the gospel often divides families. Jesus said, "Do not think that I came to bring peace on earth. I did not come to bring peace but a sword. For I have come to 'set a man against his father, a daughter against her mother, and a daughter-in-law against her mother-in-law'; and 'a man's enemies will be those of his *own* household.' He who loves father or mother more than Me is not worthy of Me. And he who loves son or daughter more than Me is not worthy of Me" (Mat. 10:34–37). Luke records His startling words, "If anyone comes to Me and does not hate his father and mother, wife and children, brothers and sisters, yes, and his own life also, he cannot be My disciple" (Luke 14:26). Jesus is saying that doing His will sometimes mean total disregard of the wishes of loved ones. In the same way it will mean absolute disregard for one's own life. Even that may have to be sacrificed. The disciple's actions therefore sometimes result in strife in families. The unsaved deeply resent the believer's total allegiance to Jesus Christ because it results in complete rejection of their wishes whenever there is a clash between those desires and doing His will. These words of Jesus negate Marcel's spiritual solidarity of the family concept. They also demonstrate the difference between the

Abrahamic covenant and the New Covenant. In the former all the family were included; in the latter families are often torn apart. Jesus Himself said, "Do *you* suppose that I came to give peace on earth? I tell you, not at all, but rather division. For from now on five in one house will be divided: three against two, and two against three. Father will be divided against son and son against father, mother against daughter and daughter against mother, mother-in-law against her daughter-in-law and daughter-in-law against her mother-in-law" (Luke 12:51–53).

Children are called saints in the New Testament

"To the saints and faithful brethren in Christ *who are* in Colosse: Grace to you and peace from God our Father and the Lord Jesus Christ" (Col. 1:2) linked with, "Children, obey your parents in all things, for this is well pleasing to the Lord" (Col. 3:20) is used to argue that children are among the saints, and therefore, if recognised as saints, there is no reason for them not to receive baptism. It is perfectly true that some children repent and believe and become saints. Paul's command is addressed only to such believing children. It is not addressed to all the children of believers at Colosse. This is confirmed by the parallel passage in Paul's letter to the Ephesians. There he exhorts the believers to "be filled with the Spirit, speaking to one another in psalms and hymns and spiritual songs, singing and making melody in your heart to the Lord, giving thanks always for all things to God the Father in the name of our Lord Jesus Christ, submitting to one another in the fear of God" (Eph. 5:18–21). He then defines that submission in specific commands. He tells wives to submit to husbands, and states alongside balancing statements of the duties of husbands. He follows with a command to children to obey, that is to submit, to parents in the Lord. "In the Lord" means that the children are to obey their parents as part of their service to their Lord and Saviour Jesus Christ. He gives two reasons for doing so. Firstly it is right behaviour, and secondly he reminds the children, " 'Honor your father and mother,' which is the first commandment with promise: 'that it may be well with you and you may live long on the earth' " (Eph. 6:2–3). He then commands fathers concerning their conduct. He continues to define the required submission by finally addressing Christian bondservants, "Bondservants, be obedient to those who are your masters according to the flesh, with fear and trembling, in sincerity of heart, as to Christ; not with eyeservice, as men-pleasers, but as bondservants of Christ, doing the will of God from the heart, with goodwill doing service, as to the Lord, and not to men, knowing that whatever good anyone does, he will receive the same from the Lord, whether *he is* a slave or free"

(Eph. 6:5–8). Again he balances these commands with the duties of Christian masters. Therefore it is clear from these parallel passages in Colossians and Ephesians that Paul is addressing children who are believers. These verses give no warrant for the baptism of infants.

"All were baptized into Moses" (1 Cor. 10:2)

It is argued from this that since children were included in this baptism, and since it is presented as a type of Christian baptism, it substantiates the contention that the infants of believers should be baptized. At that time everyone in the nation was in covenant relationship with God. Under the New Covenant the new Israel of God is composed of individuals from all nations who have heard, understood and responded to the gospel in obedience. Just as Israel were in union with Moses symbolized by their baptism so Christians are in union with Christ symbolized by baptism. The point Paul was making is that all partook of the blessings "but with most of them God was not well pleased" (1 Cor. 10:1–5). He was warning Christians that though they had been baptized and had enjoyed God's blessings they could fall into sin just as Israel did. His warning was addressed to believers who had experienced spiritual food and drink. Just as Israel ate the supernatural manna and drank the supernaturally provided water, so Christians have "tasted that the Lord is gracious" (1 Pet. 2:3). Paul was not envisaging any infants among the Christians whom he was addressing. He was speaking to believers who had enjoyed a conscious experience of spiritual food and drink. Also he was not dealing with the subject of baptism at all, but with temptation. All that we can infer about baptism from these verses is:

- all Christians were baptized, just as all Israel was baptized.
- all baptized Christians partake of spiritual food and drink just as Israel ate and drank supernatural provision.
- all Christians need the warnings of these verses.

References

1. Pierre-Charles Marcel *The Biblical Doctrine of Infant Baptism*, James Clarke & Co Ltd. Reprinted 2002, page 117.
2. *Ibid.*, page 117.

CHAPTER SIXTEEN

OTHER ATTEMPTS TO JUSTIFY INFANT BAPTISM, NOT BASED ON THE SCRIPTURES

The argument that infant baptism gives proper weight to the objectivity of God's salvation

It is argued that Baptists place too much emphasis on the subjective response to the gospel by linking baptism to faith. Believer baptism emphasises the faith of the candidate. Infant baptism better points to the action of God in Christ to bring reconciliation. Thus infant baptism bears witness to God's action to make salvation possible for man. It is contended that it is better to focus on God's glorious saving work rather than on individual faith.

New Testament believer baptism was not centred on the faith of the one being baptized. Baptism followed and expressed faith in the Person and Work of Christ. It was subjective and objective. It declared Christ's death burial and resurrection as much as the convert's personal response of faith and union with Christ. Believer baptism by immersion as stated in the New Testament proclaims God's saving work far more clearly than infant baptism. It does so because it points vividly to the death, burial and resurrection of Christ. Moreover it asserts with clarity the truth that salvation is not received apart from personal faith.

Proselyte Baptism

Michael Green argues from the fact that whole families were baptized when coming into Judaism. He says this included "the tiniest children," ... "even sometimes on the day of their birth. Indeed children were admitted to baptism even when only one parent joined Judaism."[1] He asserts, "The only model the earliest Christians had for baptismal practice was proselyte baptism, with which they would have been quite familiar. This being so, would it not have been unthinkable for them to have excluded children from baptism?"[2]

Several facts make it unthinkable that they would have included their children in baptism. Proselyte baptism was not the only model available to them. They had also the example of John's baptism expressly stated by Jesus to be "from heaven" not "from men" (Mat. 21:25). His baptismal practice was in accordance with God's revelation to him. He was not directed by any baptismal practice of men. He was not influenced in the slightest by what others did. He did not baptize infants.

Moreover the argument that Jewish proselyte baptism was a model for Christian baptism does not support the infant baptism of all children of believers, only those born before conversion of the parent(s). As A. Gilmore reasons, "For example, if we are going to argue that children of Christians should be baptized because children of proselytes were baptized, then we must also argue that Christian children born subsequent to their parents' conversion should not be baptized because the proselytes' children born subsequent to their parent's conversion were not baptized."[3] Also there were elements in Jewish proselyte baptism that had no place in Christian baptism. All the males were circumcised. The head of the family offered sacrifices. For all of these reasons it is contended that proselyte baptism was not the model for Christian baptism.

Some say that 1 Cor. 7:14 reflects customs of Jewish proselyte baptism, "For the unbelieving husband is sanctified by the wife, and the unbelieving wife is sanctified by the husband; otherwise your children would be unclean, but now they are holy" Just as children born after the conversion of a proselyte were not baptized because they belonged to the family and so were born into holiness, some say these children of a believer were also born into holiness. Various conclusions are drawn from this interpretation. Some argue that this passage thus excludes baptism of the children of a believer when the son/daughter became a believer. Others argue that on the ground of this collective family holiness there is a basis for infant baptism. Still others assert that, since Jews always circumcised male children born after the mother's conversion to Judaism, and that since baptism replaced circumcision, the earliest Christian parents therefore baptized their infants. In these ways believer's baptism is eliminated and infant baptism justified. These diverse arguments demonstrate that elements of proselyte baptism are fed into 1 Cor. 7:14 to support a paedobaptist stance. In reality Paul makes no reference whatsoever to Jewish proselyte baptism nor to Christian baptism in this verse. In a previous chapter the meaning of holy applied to the children in this verse has been shown to be simply not illegitimate on account of the partner being an unbeliever.

References

1. Michael Green *Baptism, Its Purpose Practice and Power*, Hodder & Stoughton 1987, page 68.
2. *Ibid.*, page 68.
3. A. Gilmore *Christian Baptism*, London Lutterworth 1959, page 74.

CHAPTER SEVENTEEN

ATTEMPTS TO JUSTIFY INFANT BAPTISM FROM CHURCH HISTORY

Before we look at church history it is important to bear in mind some scriptural truths. Firstly the letter to the Galatians teaches us that erroneous practice can become present among Christian believers with truly remarkable speed. The Galatian Christians were persuaded that faith in Christ for justification was insufficient and that they must also be circumcised and keep the law in order to saved. Paul wrote at the beginning of his letter, "I marvel that you are turning away so soon from Him who called you in the grace of Christ, to a different gospel" (Gal. 1:6). He was amazed that they were defecting so soon after their conversion. So evidence of the early practice of infant baptism could simply be evidence of early defection. Secondly, the New Testament is full of warnings about false prophets and that these teachers will have success: "Now the Spirit expressly says that in latter times some will depart from the faith, giving heed to deceiving spirits and doctrines of demons" (1 Tim. 4:1). The latter times are the times between the first and second coming of Jesus Christ. Paul also says, "For the time will come when they will not endure sound doctrine, but according to their own desires, *because* they have itching ears, they will heap up for themselves teachers; and they will turn *their* ears away from the truth, and be turned aside to fables" (2 Tim. 4:3–4). False teachers will abound to meet the demand for them. Therefore the writings of the so-called fathers do not prove the legitimacy of infant baptism when they mention it. They merely testify, dependent on the reliability of the document, to its presence among those professing to be Christians.

Turning to the facts of history there are no writings before Tertullian which mention infant baptism. This takes us to around 200 A.D. Paedobaptists claim earlier mentions, but the sources they quote are inconclusive.

Polycarp c. 70–155/160

Just before his martyr's death he claimed to have served Christ for eighty-six years. It is asserted that this indicates that he was baptized as an infant, and therefore the practice was established in the early days of the church. His statement does not prove that he was baptized as an infant, or give any indication of just when he was baptized. His service for Christ could have commenced prior to his baptism.

Justin Martyr c. 100–165

He wrote of many men and women, who became disciples of Christ "from their childhood" (ἐκ παίδου). These words can apply not only to babes but also to children old enough to repent and believe and understand the meaning of baptism.

Irenaeus

In a writing c. 180 he said concerning Jesus Christ, "For He came to save all through means of Himself – all, I say, who through Him are born again to God – infants, and children, and boys, and youths, and old men. He therefore passed through every age, becoming an infant for infants, thus sanctifying infants; a child for children, thus sanctifying those who are of this age, . . . A youth for youths becoming an example to youths, thus sanctifying them for the Lord. So likewise He was an old man for old men, that He might be a perfect Master for all . . ."[1] The phrase translated "born again to God" is taken to refer to baptism, but it is not certain that it does refer to baptism. Moreover in this passage Irenaeus says that Christ became an old man which is obviously error.

These writings do not establish sure evidence of infant baptism. The argument that this absence of evidence for infant baptism demonstrates that the practice was not present in the first years of the church is strengthened by the fact that allusions to baptism by early writers speak of believer baptism.

The Epistle of Barnabas c. A.D. 120–130

He wrote ". . . we indeed descend into the water full of sins and defilement, but come up, bearing fruit in our heart having the fear [of God] and trust in Jesus in our spirit."[2]

The Shepherd of Hermas c. A.D. 140

In this writing baptism is administered to people who have reached years of understanding.

The Didache

This writing, probably the first half of the second century, contains extremely detailed instructions for baptism. In them the candidate is commanded to fast before baptism and the time period for the fast is specified. Defined teaching preceded the act of baptism.[3] The total absence of any mention of infants amidst all this detail is only satisfactorily explained by the fact that infants were not baptized.

So we come to Tertullian flor. c. A.D. 197–225

His writings contain the earliest conclusive evidence of the rite of infant baptism. And we find that Tertullian attacked the practice of infant baptism. He declared that the benefits of baptism are best reserved for later years. This is certainly evidence of the practice. But it tells against it being an apostolic institution. If it had been it is at least unlikely that Tertullian would have opposed it.

Origen A.D. 185–254

He declared in his commentary on Romans, "the church has a tradition from the apostles to give baptism even to infants."[4] Paul K. Jewett makes the following points. Origen's writings were translated from Greek to Latin by a man called Rufinus. He was concerned to avoid the bad reputation of being the translator of what were viewed as heretical treatises. Consequently he modified the text of what Origen wrote so much that there is substantial doubt that these are Origen's actual words. Even if Origen wrote the words quoted above the veracity of them must be assessed. The claim of apostolic tradition for a particular practice would be a useful argument, but not necessarily according to the truth.[5]

Cyprian

In A.D. 251 or 253 he stated that infants should be baptized at birth not delaying until the eighth day in order to secure the forgiveness of original sin. This reveals that the practice of infant baptism was then established in North Africa, since his writing represents the consensus of sixty-six bishops of that region met together in council to discuss whether or not such baptism should be delayed until the eighth day following the analogy of circumcision in the Old Testament (Gen. 17:2). Does this not indicate the apostolic origin of infant baptism? Paul K. Jewett makes the following telling points: "If infant baptism were indeed practiced from apostolic times, would the question of *when* it should be given require so much deliberation after nearly two hundred years? Nor should one overlook the fact that the bishops not only decided *when* infants should be baptized but also elaborated at length on the reasons *why*. And in setting forth these reasons they made no appeal to an earlier tradition; rather their epistle has the aura of a pioneering endeavor on the part of men who were thinking their way through a subject for the first time."[6]

Augustine 354–430

Concerning the practice of infant baptism he wrote, "And if any one seek for divine authority in this matter, though what is held by the whole Church, and that not as instituted by councils, but as a matter of invariable custom, is rightly held to have been handed down by apostolic authority."[7] Notice it is a matter to be believed. He supplies no proof. He also believed that infant baptism imparted regeneration.

By the fifth century infant baptism had become the general practice of the church. This continued for a thousand years as the universal practice, with occasional opposition. In the eastern church, at the beginning of the ninth century, a group called Paulicians practised believers' baptism and not infant baptism. In the west at the commencement of the twelfth century Peter of Bruys taught believers' baptism and denied infant baptism. It was the Anabaptists who restored the truth of believers' baptism to the church in the sixteenth century. From the fifth century until then darkness prevailed. Infants were regenerated through baptism. Those paedobaptists who are so eager to point to this prevailing practice of infant baptism during those centuries need to stop and recognise that the practice prevailed when the professing church fell into apostasy and perverted the message of Christianity into a false gospel of salvation by means of sacraments and priests.

References

1. Writings of Irenaeus *Against Heresies* Book 2 xxii 4, Ante-Nicene Fathers 1, page 391.
2. The Epistle of Barnabas xi, Ante-Nicene Fathers 1 page 144.
3. The Didache vii.
4. Origen *Commentary On Romans* as cited in W.Wall *The History Of Infant Baptism*, Griffiths 1705, page 51.
5. Paul K. Jewett *Infant Baptism & The Covenant Of Grace*, Eerdmans 1978 page 31.
6. Ibid., page 19.
7. Augustine *On Baptism, Against The Donatists* IV xxiv – 32 Nicene and Post-Nicene Fathers Series 1 Vol. IV page 461.

CHAPTER EIGHTEEN

THE RISE AND PREVALENCE OF INFANT BAPTISM

How did the practice of infant baptism arise if not taught by the apostles? Why has it been so present down through the centuries? Several factors account for its rise and presence.

A. W. Argyle says that a belief arose that the baptism of Christ "conferred upon baptismal waters a sanctifying potency."[1]

Argyle cites Ignatius c. A.D. 110 who asserted that Christ's baptism gave baptismal waters a sanctifying power. A.W. Argyle also states that as the belief in this potency developed the need for repentance and faith declined. Many, even today, still have a superstitious faith of this sort when they have the baby "done". They believe "something" of significance actually happens to the infant.

A.W. Argyle asserts that another factor arising in the early centuries A.D. was "an increasing concentration upon typological exegesis of Scripture in regard to baptism."

He states that this went together with a failing grasp of the New Testament doctrine of baptism. He says, ". . . in view of the conception of Christian salvation as a new exodus, a new deliverance from the worse than Egyptian bondage of sin and a new entrance into a new Canaan effected by the death, burial and resurrection of Christ which are symbolized in Christian baptism, special emphasis is laid upon the baptismal interpretation of the crossing of the Red Sea and of Jordan. In keeping with this typological exegesis milk and honey were administered to the newly baptized as a symbol of spiritual entrance into the promised land 'flowing with milk and honey'."[2] He cites an example of such in Apostolic Tradition 23.2 written by Hippolytus in the third century A.D.

The teaching of Cyprian, Ambrose (c. 339–397) and Augustine that infants were delivered from the guilt of original sin and regenerated by infant baptism

By the fifth century infant baptism had become the general practice of the church. These men, especially Augustine, are often highly esteemed. Consequently some may be surprised that they taught infant baptismal regeneration. It should not surprise us when we remember that the great apostle Peter deviated into extremely serious error concerning circumcision. Paul recounts how he had to rebuke Peter in the presence of the believers who had seen his fall from the truth of the gospel. He wrote, "Now when Peter had come to Antioch, I withstood him to his face, because he was to be blamed; for before certain men came from James, he would eat with the Gentiles; but when they came, he withdrew and separated himself, fearing those who were of the circumcision. And the rest of the Jews also played the hypocrite with him, so that even Barnabas was carried away with their hypocrisy. But when I saw that they were not straightforward about the truth of the gospel, I said to Peter before *them* all, 'If you, being a Jew, live in the manner of Gentiles and not as the Jews, why do you compel Gentiles to live as Jews? We *who are* Jews by nature, and not sinners of the Gentiles, knowing that a man is not justified by the works of the law but by faith in Jesus Christ, even we have believed in Christ Jesus, that we might be justified by faith in Christ and not by the works of the law; for by the works of the law no flesh shall be justified' " (Gal. 2:11–16).

The carnal nature of fallen man prefers ritual religion to the gospel demands for repentance and faith

Consequently a way of making children Christian simply by ritual is most attractive. In later centuries the Roman Catholic and Eastern Orthodox Churches enhanced ritual religion by the development of sacramentalism and doctrines exalting priests by giving them special power to dispense God's blessings. This process reached maturity in the centuries preceding the Reformation.

Historical events

The conversion of the Roman Emperor Constantine early in the fourth century was a watershed in the history of the church. It resulted in Christianity being elevated into the position of being the only legitimate faith in the empire. The Emperor used his power to coerce all to embrace Christianity. The church was no longer composed only of believers. It became composed of all within the state. Membership of the state automatically meant membership of the official religion. The official religion was used politically as a tool to cement society together. Consequently other belief was not tolerated. Being born into the state therefore meant being born into an official religion. There were lasting effects of this change. From then onwards for over a thousand years the secular power was viewed by the church as a means of coercing submission to the one religion and using the sword against dissenters. There was no deviation from this concept of one legitimate state religion.

Infant baptism as initiation into that religion was in perfect harmony with this state church concept. The two went hand in hand, born into the state and born into state religion. Therefore there was no reason to delay initiation into that religion. Moreover infant baptism was a most effective way of enforcing the one state religion. Consequently Emperor Justinian 527–565 made infant baptism compulsory. The Emperor Charlemagne forced those he conquered to be baptized or die. In A.D. 785 he also ordered the Saxons to have their infants baptized in their first year or pay a heavy fine. From Constantine onwards all those who wished to promote or perpetuate the state church concept were utterly committed to infant baptism. The Reformers, Zwingli, Luther, and Calvin, did not break with this concept of state religion which had prevailed for a thousand years. In alliance with secular power they sought to reform state religion. They were committed therefore to the use of infant baptism to maintain unity in the church state. Timothy George writes, "In 1526 Zwingli persuaded the Zurich Council to establish a baptismal register in every parish. This device, together with the decision to expel those citizens who refused to submit their infants for baptism, enabled the magistrates to make infant baptism an instrument for political conformity. This policy went hand in glove with Zwingli's program of reform, which presupposed the identity of the visible church with the populace of the Christian city or state: 'A Christian city is nothing other than a Christian church.' "[3]

At the time of the Reformation the Anabaptists saw from the New Testament that the church is not all persons in a given locality, but a society of believers separated by God from all others in a given locality. They saw that a false Christendom, a false church, depended upon infant baptism. The true church is a fellowship of believers. Take away infant baptism and replace it with believers' baptism and the false state church concept collapses. The state is then composed of Christians and non-Christians. Tragically the Reformers initially killed Anabaptists for their denial of the validity of infant baptism. The Anabaptists threatened to overthrow the state church order to which the Reformers were committed. Dependent on secular power, and wedded to the state church concept, it is not surprising therefore that the Reformers sought to justify infant baptism. But they were also committed to the principle of sola scriptura. Scripture was for them the sole authority over against human opinion and ecclesiastical tradition. So it is understandable that in their attempt to legitimise the practice of state infant baptism by scripture they appealed to the Old Testament period when God was in covenant relationship with a nation. The problem was that there was no support for infant baptism in the New Testament. Consequently they formulated the one covenant of grace error which enabled them to assert the continuance of Old Testament arrangements in New Testament times. Zwingli stated that it is clear to all believers that the New Covenant is the Abrahamic covenant except merely that Christ was only promised in that covenant but in the New Covenant was made manifest.[4]

The one covenant of grace was further developed by later Reformers. Kaspar Olevianus 1536–1587 and Zacharias Ursinus 1534–1583 are prominent in that development. They produced the Heidelberg Catechism of 1563. Philip Schaff says, "It is stated that, next to the Bible, *The Imitation of Christ*, by Thomas à Kempis, and Bunyan's *Pilgrim's Progress*, no book has been more frequently translated, more widely circulated and used."[5] In that catechism question 74 reads, "Are infants to be baptized?" The answer given is "Yes; for since they, as well as their parents, belong to the covenant and people of God, and both redemption from sin and the Holy Ghost, who works faith, are through the blood of Christ promised to them no less than to their parents, they are also by Baptism, as a sign of the covenant, to be ingrafted into the Christian Church, and distinguished from the children of unbelievers, as was done in the Old Testament by Circumcision, in place of which in the New Testament Baptism is appointed."

Some early Christian fathers had linked circumcision and baptism. Cyprian c. A.D. 200/210–258, and Gregory of Nazianzus c. A.D. 325–390 made this connection. But no one before the Reformers put forward the one covenant of grace teaching. It was a new invention. Donald Bridge and David Phypers state, "Whatever the strength of the position it was quite unknown before the Reformation and cannot be found in any form in any of the writings of the early Fathers."[6]

The arguments of the Reformers for infant baptism need to be seen and assessed in the context of their time. Their approach was affected by their alliance with secular power, and commitment to the state church concept. It is important to see that this is revealed in other stances taken by them. They endorsed the use of the sword of the state to punish heretics, and to enforce religious unity. They were utterly opposed to freedom for the individual Christian to worship in the way he believed to be right. Consequently they failed to reform the church in its doctrine of baptism; and they failed to restore a true doctrine of the church as composed only of believers.

Their contention for infant baptism led to the presence of infant baptism in the creeds of the reformed churches formed in the sixteenth century. The Lutheran churches, national churches of Switzerland, France, Holland and Belgium, the Anglican church, and the Presbyterian church all embraced infant baptism in their creeds. These creeds have perpetuated the belief and practice of infant baptism down through the centuries.

The creeds of the sixteenth century Reformation have also been the basis of subsequent creeds which have had great impact on the course of church history. The Westminster Confession of the seventeenth century was drawn up by an assembly of English and Scottish ministers to "undertake the reformation of religion in the kingdoms of England and Ireland in doctrine, worship, discipline, and government, according to the Word of God and the example of the best reformed churches," and to "bring the churches of God in the three kingdoms to the nearest conjunction and uniformity in religion." Following "the example of the best reformed churches" the resultant Westminster Confession continued to assert infant baptism. It has been of great influence on Presbyterian churches. The Congregationalists adopted it with some modifications in their Savoy Declaration of faith 1658. Accordingly they included infant baptism as stated in the Westminster Confession. The Westminster Confession was a comprehensive expression of Calvinistic theology and of the biblical truths declared in that system of doctrine. The work of the assembly at Westminster was a truly great achievement in the course of church history, and of profound and lasting influence. The basic fault marring such a glorious work is stated by Philip Schaff, "The chief fault of the Assembly was that it clung to the idea of a national State Church, with a uniform system of doctrine, worship, and discipline, to which every man, woman, and child in three kingdoms should conform."[7] Consequently it clung also to infant baptism.

It is significant that the Baptist Confession of 1688 is simply the Westminster Confession modified in its statements concerning the church and the sacraments. It is significant because it demonstrates:

• that the doctrines of baptism and of the church are inseparable. A national state church demands infant baptism, a church of believers requires believers' baptism. Therefore they changed the statements concerning both church and sacraments.

- those believing in believers' baptism were at one with those believing the Westminster Confession "in all the fundamental Articles of the Christian religion."
- the Baptists who drew up this confession thereby recognized fully the work of the Reformers in restoring truths of God's word to the church.
- the failure of the Reformers to restore a true doctrine of the church and a true doctrine of water baptism.

That failure had an abiding effect in helping to perpetuate infant baptism to this day. It is seen in its influence on Methodist churches through the Church of England. These churches are a daughter of the Church of England. John Wesley and his followers during his lifetime did not break with the Church of England. John Wesley believed strongly in infant baptism and contended for it. Consequently the Methodist churches formed after his death adopted the belief and practice of infant baptism.

Thus looking at church history we see that the Roman Catholic Church and the Eastern Orthodox Church have always practised infant baptism. Both of these churches cannot be counted as true Christian churches having declared categorically their absolute opposition to the gospel at the time of its recovery in the Reformation. Since then they have never changed their stance of denial of the gospel truth of justification by imputed righteousness received by faith. Major Protestant and Nonconformist denominations have embraced this error of infant baptism. Their deviation has been traced back to the failure of the Reformers to break with the state church concept. Thus infant baptism has been perpetuated in the name of Christ in spite of the voices down the centuries calling for a return to New Testament truth, and in spite of the coming into being of Baptist Churches in the seventeenth century, and the rise of new Church groups practising believers' baptism, such as the Open Brethren in the nineteenth century and the Pentecostal Churches and Restoration Churches of the twentieth century.

Ministers of denominations practising infant baptism often find it too costly to obey their conscience, resign and move to another denomination standing for the truth of believers' baptism

H.M. Carson was Vicar of St. Paul's in Cambridge for seven years. His greatest problem with Anglicanism was infant baptism.[8] He came to see that baptism is only for believers. But he tells of the ordeal of contemplating secession in his book *Farewell To Anglicanism*. He writes of the serious problems he faced as a family man – loss of income, pension, widows' pension, orphans' pension, home and the question of suitable future employment after leaving his position. He was concerned for the welfare of his children. In addition he felt the added trauma of leaving Cambridge and the people with whom he had close bonds in Christian fellowship. One can imagine something of the strain and stress he experienced as he considered secession. It was an ordeal to face it, and then an ordeal when he took the step.[9] Not many are willing to pay the considerable price of following their conscience.

The desires of Christian parents to differentiate their children, and a refusal to acknowledge that until their children repent and believe the gospel they are just as lost as all other children of non-Christian parents

The practise of infant dedication by many churches who believe believers' baptism is sadly infant baptism in disguise and a manifestation of these desires even among baptists. There is no biblical warrant to sanction Christian parents always dedicating their children to the Lord. Hannah's action in dedicating Samuel to the Lord's service (1 Sam. 1–2) in gratitude for being given a child was her personal act. Her action does not teach that it is God's will that every child born of a Christian parent should be dedicated to God. Moreover Hannah's dedication of Samuel was not done in a service but in private prayer before his birth.

There is no basis for dedication in appealing to Luke 2:12–24, which records the presentation of Jesus to the Lord. This was done in accord with the requirements of Exod. 13 concerning redemption of the firstborn. These obligations no longer exist under the New Covenant.

Jesus blessing the children has no element of thanksgiving for the children nor of dedication of them to the Lord. It cannot be used legitimately to justify infant dedication just as it cannot validate infant baptism.

The elements of the dedication service often resemble an infant baptism – the commitments by the parents and church to bring up the child in the nurture and admonition of the Lord, the prayers said for the child and the parents, the naming of the child and the laying of hands upon the child or the taking up of the child into the minister's hands. As regards thanking God for the child, praying for the child and the parents, the acknowledging of commitments of parents and the church there is no need for a dedication service for expression of these actions. Indeed there are very real dangers in the practice of this special rite:

a) The delusion that the child, though not yet a believer, is somehow differentiated from children not dedicated. There are only two groups of people on earth, the saved and the unsaved. This stark reality is blurred by dedication. Failure to accept fully that the child is lost until born again is a disincentive to prayer for the child and conscientious effort to bring up the child in the nurture and admonition of the Lord.

b) The making of vows by parents and church members without heeding the warning of Eccles 5:2,4–5, "Do not be rash with your mouth, And let not your heart utter anything hastily before God. For God is in heaven, and you on earth; Therefore let your words be few. . . . When you make a vow to God, do not delay to pay it; For He has no pleasure in fools. Pay what you have vowed – Better not to vow than to vow and not pay." How many parents have stumbled later when their grown child decided to obey God's call to a course of action involving sacrifice. They gave their child to God to use as He wished. But when the time came to fulfil the vow they were unwilling for that sacrifice. And how many church members make vows to pray for the child and the parents and then fail to do so?

c) Thanking God for the child, praying for him, nurturing him in the Lord are ongoing obligations which cannot be discharged by one dedication service. But many parents rest on the fact that their child has been "done" and their realisation of daily responsibility is seriously undermined.

The Anglican Thanksgiving Service for the Birth of a Child 2000 is prefaced by the statement that the minister may state before the service begins that this service is not the same as baptism. The parents are not required to make any promises, and the service contains the giving of a copy of one of the gospels to the parents, with words stating that it is the good news of God's love and exhorting them to take it as their guide. The service makes provision for the parents to recognize the role of supporting friends. After the giving of the gospel the minister may address the supporting friends asking them to say that they will do all they can with God's help to help and support the parents in bringing up the child. Also the minister may address the wider family and friends asking them also to say that they will do all they can with God's help to help and support the family. By designing the service in this way the church can avoid the charge of indiscriminate baptism of the children of unbelievers. Non-Christians can be steered to this service rather than infant baptism. It gets rid of all the difficulties of any preparation for baptism, and any requirements that certain conditions be met.

In spite of these provisions to distinguish the service from infant baptism it still provides a means of satisfying the carnal desires of non-Christians for ritual religion instead of the reality that the only way to God is through repentance and faith in Jesus Christ. Despite the safeguards, in some cases it will still be regarded as a substitute for baptism. In any event it presents a false message that God can be approached through such a service without having received Jesus Christ as Lord and Saviour. His words are absolute, "I am the way, the truth, and the life. No one comes to the Father except through Me" (John 14:6).

Mark 10:13–16 does not authorise such a practice of thanksgiving. There we have parents/guardians bringing children to Jesus to lay His hands on them and to pray for God's blessing upon them. The children were young enough for Jesus to take them in His arms and some of them were infants according to Luke's account. Their parents were not coming to give thanks to God. They came for blessing. Just what they had in mind we do not know. We can assume some knowledge of the Old Testament and some knowledge of Jesus. In the tradition of the Old Testament teaching we may conclude that they believed that Jesus had special power to bless by the laying on of hands. Some may have come with strong faith; others just thinking that their child might receive something. They believed that His touch was necessary (Mark 10:13). Their request was inspired by the belief that some definite and special blessing could come to the child through that touch.

Some have concluded that Mark 10:13–16 gives ground for a service to pray for God's blessing on infants. The facts do not support this conclusion. Jesus did not command or even suggest to the parents to bring the children to Him for blessing. They took the initiative. While exercising His ministry on earth Jesus was attested by God by miracles, wonders, and signs which God did through Him (Acts 2:22). He was anointed with the Spirit more than any other anointed ones (Heb. 1:9). The faith which prompted their action was inspired by that attestation. It was also the taking of an opportunity only available to them for a limited period of time. Jesus would not remain there. In addition to their prayers to God for blessings on their children here was a unique occasion to obtain a special blessing from God through a special man of God. Jesus' earthly ministry has ended. Now He is the Risen and Ascended Christ. Believers can seek His blessing on their little ones at any time and at all times. His blessing is no longer confined to physical touch during a limited time of opportunity. Christian parents can seek God's blessing on their children every day. They can go to Him boldly with full assurance of faith. Therefore believers should not be encouraged look for blessing through one special service. Their eyes should be directed to the Lord to Whom they can go with full assurance at all times.

The activity of Satan to destroy souls by deluding people that infant baptism makes them Christian

The Bible is clear that the source of false teachings is Satan and demons. Here are some of the verses teaching this:

"Now the Spirit expressly says that in latter times some will depart from the faith, giving heed to deceiving spirits and doctrines of demons" (1 Tim. 4:1).

Note that when Paul speaks of "latter times" he is referring to the period between Christ's first coming and His return to earth.

"And no wonder! For Satan himself transforms himself into an angel of light. Therefore *it is* no great thing if his ministers also transform themselves into ministers of righteousness, whose end will be according to their works" (2 Cor. 11:14–15).

Paul is saying that Satan has his ministers to propagate his teachings, and that they appear to be ministers of righteousness. In reality they are ravenous wolves in sheep's clothing.

The demands of the gospel are plain and clear, repent and believe. The only way into the kingdom is obedience to those demands. Infant baptism in some of its forms is another gospel. It presents an alternative access into the kingdom. It sometimes claims to make infants regenerate. Sometimes it adds other things after infant baptism such as further sacraments or confirmation. But these things often take place with no requirement for repentance and faith as stated in the New Testament. Sometimes the only requirement for the child and subsequent adult who has been baptized as an infant is that he/she continues to give assent to the faith and attend some Church services. If these things are done he/she is considered to be a Christian. No conversion is necessary. The progression to adult Christian living is thus seen as gradual development. This is indeed perfectly possible in the production of pseudo-Christians who have the form of godliness but no experience of its power. But real Christians have come to a place of repentance and faith. Repentance is not gradual development. It reaches a point of crisis and together with faith the change of mind and life that the Bible calls conversion takes place. The person's life history is cut in two. The unconverted life before salvation and the new life found in Christ. There is a radical change.

Distinct from such false prophets propagating these doctrines of infant baptism, some who practise infant baptism insist that it must be followed by repentance and faith to become a Christian. Even then infant baptism detracts from the fact that there is no entrance whatsoever into the Church of Jesus Christ, and no participation whatsoever in eternal salvation until there is repentance and faith. The amount of detraction depends on precisely what is taught about infant baptism, *and* the perception of its effect by the recipient in later years of understanding. Any detraction is very grave. It seriously undermines the truth about one's utterly lost state before God, and consequently undermines the essential and urgent need to repent and believe.

Infant baptism has been, and continues to be, one of the most effective tools used by Satan to destroy the souls of mankind. Infant baptism has produced pseudo-Christians. It has deceived men that they are Christian when they are not, that they are bound for heaven when they are bound for hell. It has populated professing Christian churches with the unregenerate. It has been the means of creating state religion professing to be Christianity, but which is not true Christianity. Thus it has disgraced the name of Christ. The false Christians, false Christian churches and false Christianity produced by infant baptism have been, and are a stumbling block to non-Christians. Consequently the devil delights in infant baptism. He works for its continuance and advance.

References

1. A.W. Argyle *Christian Baptism*, Edited by A. Gilmore, London Lutterworth 1959, page 187
2. *Ibid.*, pages 189–190.
3. Timothy George *The Theology of the Reformers*, Broadman Press and Apollos Reprinted 1992, pages 143–144.
4. *Corpus Reformatorum* Vol. 91 p.635.
5. Philip Schaff *The Creeds of Christendom*. Vol. 1. Reprinted 1996 by Baker Books by arrangement with Harper and Row, Sixth Edition page 536.
6. Donald Bridge David Phypers *The Water That Divides*, Christian Focus, Tain, Scotland 2008 ISBN 978–184550–308–6, page 31 (1998 edition).
7. Philip Schaff *Creeds of Christendom* vol.1 Reprinted 1996 by Baker Books by arrangement with Harper and Row, Sixth Edition, page 730.
8. H.M. Carson *Farewell to Anglicanism*, Henry E. Walter Ltd.1969, page 141.
9. *Ibid.*, page 24.

CHAPTER NINETEEN

THE ALLEGED BENEFITS OF INFANT BAPTISM

We shall look at different benefits from the practice of infant baptism as stated by paedobaptists.

Pierre-Charles Marcel

BENEFITS FOR THE INFANT

1. a declaration that the infant is a member of the body of Christ
He considers children born to Christian parents as already belonging to God from their birth. Baptism does not make them children of God. It declares "that they are received into the Church as being already members of Christ's body."[1] Consequently according to Pierre-Charles Marcel the church is composed of both regenerate and unregenerate persons.

2. a sign, seal and pledge of regeneration
Marcel states that the posterity of believers share in the benefits of God's grace and consequently they are regenerated or will be. Baptism is given to them as "a sign, seal, and pledge of this regeneration."[2] However, elsewhere he qualifies this statement. He states that the promises of God for salvation to the children of believers are given only in a collective sense. They are not given to each individual child. Thus the promise of the covenant does not mean that all the posterity of believers will come to saving faith. He says some will not.[3]

3. the creation of an environment as a means of grace
He affirms that baptism is *"immediately"* for the child "a means of grace."[4] This is because baptism as a seal of the promise of the covenant brings about a strengthening of faith which creates a beneficial environment for the child. Though the infant is ignorant of the meaning of baptism the little child has real benefit because all the participants are conscious that baptism means that the infant is in the

covenant with all its promises. They know that he is "a child of the Kingdom." Thus the parents and the Church view the child differently. This is of crucial importance for the future of the child. They know that he is a child of God loved by Him, and that they are obligated to instruct the child so that he may walk according to the covenant. Thus they are moved to pray for the fulfilment of the promise declared in baptism. In this way the faith of parents and the Church is strengthened by baptism. It sets the standard for the child's religious education. In all these ways baptism creates a beneficial spiritual environment for the child.[5]

4.   an encouragement to faith

Baptism in future days will strengthen the young person's belief. It will confirm God's promises and give assurance of being the "heir designate" of promised blessings. It will make the young one "more inclined to serve the Lord" who received him/her from birth.[6]The child will only be saved when he comes to faith.[7]If in due course they do not repent and believe they break the covenant.[8]

BENEFITS TO THE PARENTS, AND THE CHURCH

Baptism blesses the parents and all who thereby confess their faith. Baptism confirms and seals their faith. It is a blessing to them. Baptism also confirms their obligations. It is a commitment to educate the child in God's works and commands and to set an example of the Christian walk. Marcel regards it a great mistake to consider the infant the only real beneficiary of baptism. It is the sign and seal of God's promise to the parents and the church as well as to the child.[9] Baptism also signifies to the parents and the Church the spiritual rights of the child: right to the fulfilment of the promises; right to fellowship with Christ; right to citizenship in the Church; right to eternal life; right to pardon; right to be instructed in God's works and commands; right to the obedience of his parents to God's commands for his/her education; right to their prayers; and right to the faithful ministry of the Church.[10] Infant baptism "has a collective efficacy."[11] It strengthens parents "anew in the grace of their own baptism." It strengthens them in their sense of obligation to educate their child in the faith.[12] Baptism is an encouragement "to serve God more wholeheartedly" because it declares that God cares for their children.[13] All the believers, including the minister, are blessed. "The whole Church is purified and sanctified by this baptism . . ."[14]

The belief that regeneration is accomplished by infant baptism, held by Roman Catholicism, Lutherans and Anglo-Catholics

Infant baptism gives the new life of sanctifying grace, cleanses from original sin, makes one a child of God, a member of the church of Christ and an heir to the kingdom of heaven. Luther believed that God gives infants faith when they are baptized.

Michael Green

Michael Green writes as an evangelical Anglican. He says it effects "nothing at all" if the infant who was baptized never comes to Christ. He declares, "For baptism is like a cheque which may be said to convey to us a thousand pounds, but which does nothing of the sort if we do not cash it."[15] He then refers to Anglican baptismal liturgies speaking of baptized infants as born again and inheritors of the kingdom of heaven. Of infant baptism he says, "The child is said to repent (through its sponsors); it is said to believe; and consequently it is said to be born again. It is no more literally born again than it literally repents and believes. This is all the language of faith, of covenant, and it must be taken as such."[16] Accordingly he writes, "So baptism is often spoken of in very realist language, as if it effected what it symbolised. But it does not effect our justification, new birth, and a life full of the Spirit *until and unless we cash the cheque*, and claim personally what has been made over to us in the purposes of the generous heavenly Father. So you are not 'saved' if you remain a baptized unbeliever. You are not a Christian."[17] He then adds words indicating that infant baptism has actually done something. He goes on, "But you bear upon your body the mark of how much God the Father cares for you, of what Christ did for you, of what new birth in the Spirit could mean to you – if only you will trust him and obey."[18] In other words when the infant grows to understanding of his baptism he will see it as a statement of God's action to save, of His taking the initiative to redeem, and His promises to save.

John Wesley

He taught that all infants by baptism receive remission of sins, are regenerated, and are made members of Christ and of His Church, heirs of the kingdom of heaven. He also taught that the grace then bestowed would be lost by subsequent sin, in which case it was necessary to be born again a second time. Infant baptism gave regeneration, but this regeneration was lost at the commencement of actual sin around nine years of age. In a sermon entitled "The Marks of the New Birth" he says, "Lean no more on the staff of that broken reed, that you *were* born again in baptism. Who denies that ye were then made children of God, and heirs of the kingdom of heaven? But, notwithstanding this, ye are now children of the devil. Therefore ye must be born again. And let not Satan put it into your heart to cavil at a word, when the thing is clear. Ye have heard what are the marks of the children of God: All ye that have them not on your souls, baptized or unbaptized, must needs receive them, or without doubt ye will perish everlastingly. And if ye have been baptized, your only hope is this, that those who were made the children of God by baptism, but are now the children of the devil, may yet again receive 'power to become the sons of God;' that they may receive again what they have lost, even the 'Spirit of adoption, crying in their hearts. Abba, Father!' "[19] The benefit of infant baptism therefore did not last beyond the first few years of life.

George Whitfield

The evangelist distinguished between being born of water in baptism and being born of the Spirit in conversion. Baptism with water was inadequate. There must also be baptism with the Holy Spirit, conversion.

Belief that baptism is actually a means of strengthening the work of grace in the heart

Some Reformed theologians assume that some infants are already regenerated before baptism and therefore possess the seed of faith. They believe that God through baptism strengthens this seed of faith in the infant.

Belief that infant baptism may be the means of salvation

Charles Hodge says ". . . those parents sin grievously against the souls of their children who neglect to consecrate them to God in the ordinance of baptism. Do let the little ones have their names written in the Lamb's book of life, even if they afterwards choose to erase them. Being thus enrolled may be the means of their salvation."[20] It would seem that Hodge considers infant baptism as the means to salvation because it brings about membership of the visible church. He considers this membership to be of great benefit placing one in a position to be brought to salvation: "It is good to be under the watch and care of the people of God. It is good to have a special claim upon their prayers and upon their efforts to bring us into, or keep us in the paths of salvation."[21]

Conclusions

The sheer diversity of belief is striking. The spectrum of benefit for the infant ranges from salvation to "nothing at all." Moreover there is great difference of belief in the benefits of infant baptism for the parent(s) and for the believers present at the baptism.

References

1. Pierre-Charles Marcel *The Biblical Doctrine of Infant Baptism*, James Clarke & Co., Ltd. Reprinted 2002, page 218.
2. *Ibid.*, page 223.
3. *Ibid.*, page 112.
4. *Ibid.*, page 225.
5. *Ibid.*, pages 224–225.
6. *Ibid.*, page 227.
7. *Ibid.*, page 108.
8. *Ibid.*, page 131.
9. *Ibid.*, pages 219–220.
10. *Ibid.*, page 226.
11. *Ibid.*, page 228.
12. *Ibid.*, page 228.
13. *Ibid.*, page 228.
14. *Ibid.*, pages 228–229.
15. Michael Green *Baptism Its Purpose, Practice And Power*, Hodder & Stoughton 1987, page 90.
16. *Ibid.*, page 93.
17. *Ibid.*, page 90.
18. *Ibid.*, page 90.
19. *The Works of John Wesley* Vol. 5 Baker Books 1991, pages 222–223.
20. Charles Hodge *Systematic Theology* Vol. iii, James Clarke & Co.1960, page 588.
21. *Ibid.*, pages 587–588.

CHAPTER TWENTY

INFANT BAPTISM AND HOLY COMMUNION

Paedobaptists are usually keen to assert that the meaning of baptism for infants is the same as that for adults. This creates a difficulty. Those baptized in the New Testament practised the breaking of bread. When infant baptism arose history is clear that communion was also administered to babes. This has always been the practice in the Eastern Orthodox churches, and continues today. The Western Roman Catholic Church did so until the thirteenth century. Paul K. Jewett says that ". . . in the Roman Catholic Church it appears to have been dropped because of the theory of transubstantiation, the fear being that infants and small children might crumble the host or slaver the blood."[1] If baptism really does have the same meaning for infants and children as for adults then infants and children should receive communion. Almost all paedobaptists of other churches have not permitted this and do not do so today. In some rare cases it is allowed. Paul K. Jewett cites the United Presbyterian Church in the U.S.A. where baptized children who have not made a profession of faith may partake of communion subject to certain conditions being fulfilled[2]. A tiny minority of paedobaptists have advocated this practice.

In 1998 Donald Bridge and David Phypers wrote of a "growing practice of Family Communion in the Church of England" where children are encouraged to be present and to receive a blessing at the communion rail although as yet not partaking of the elements.[3]

There is growing unease among paedobaptists with the traditional stance on this matter. Michael Green says, "Another of the questions that is currently vexing many of the main-line churches which practise infant baptism, is whether or not the baptised children of Christian families should be entitled to receive Holy Communion. . . . Baptism is unambiguously the sacrament of entry into the church, and we must stick with that. Baptists have sometimes pointed (with good reason) to the inconsistency of Anglicans who claim that baptism is the rite of entry into the church and then behave as if confirmation really was!

Their criticism is just. I believe we must grasp the nettle firmly and maintain both that baptism is the rite of entry and that children who have been baptised may take their share in the Holy Communion with their parents."[4] Thus we see paedobaptists increasingly divided as to whether infant baptism gives the benefit, or should give the benefit, of admission to the breaking of bread.

At this point we may pause to note a glaring inconsistency in the reasoning of some of those who contend for infant baptism on the basis of one covenant of grace.[5] The inconsistency is that they argue for children of Christian parentage to be baptized on the basis of infant circumcision under the Abrahamic covenant, but exclude them from Holy Communion even though that same Abrahamic covenant required the Passover to be celebrated by whole households. "Now the LORD spoke to Moses and Aaron in the land of Egypt, saying, 'Speak to all the congregation of Israel, saying: "On the tenth of this month every man shall take for himself a lamb, according to the house of *his* father, a lamb for a household. And if the household is too small for the lamb, let him and his neighbor next to his house take *it* according to the number of the persons; according to each man's need you shall make your count for the lamb." ' " (Exod. 12:1,3–4). Clearly infants would not eat but children would. Their presence is confirmed by God's further instruction: "And it shall be, when your children say to you, 'What do you mean by this service?' that you shall say, 'It *is* the Passover sacrifice of the LORD, who passed over the houses of the children of Israel in Egypt when He struck the Egyptians and delivered our households' " (Exod. 12:26–27). Children of those members of the Abrahamic covenant were included simply because they were part of the household and because they could eat the Passover. Their understanding of the meaning of the feast was not a condition of their participation. But the meaning of the meal was to be explained to them when they asked. Covenant theologians admit the truth that the Lord's Supper of the New Covenant has replaced the Passover of the Abrahamic covenant. On the ground that children of Christian parentage are in the covenant paedobaptists give them infant baptism. If they are in the covenant, then on the very same ground these baptized children should partake of the bread and the wine, just as children of the Abrahamic covenant ate the Passover regardless of whether they understood its meaning. The paedobaptist argues that the New Covenant cannot be less generous than the Abrahamic covenant. Yet the paedobaptist won't allow believer's children to the Lord's Supper even though under the old covenant children ate the Passover! The Anabaptists instantly pointed out the Reformers' inconsistency in this matter.

Conclusion

These glaring and persistent problems of inconsistency arise because of the departure from God's word teaching that water baptism is for believers only.

References

1. Paul K. Jewett *Infant Baptism And The Covenant Of Grace*, Eerdmans 1978, page 195 footnote.
2. Ibid., page 207 footnote.
3. Donald Bridge and David Phypers, *The Water That Divides*, Christian Focus, Tain, Scotland, 2008. ISBN 978–184550–308–6, page 148 (1998 edition).
4. Michael Green, *Baptism, Its Purpose, Practice and Power*, Hodder & Stoughton, 1987, pages 108–109.
5. In this section I draw upon Paul K. Jewett, *Infant Baptism & The Covenant Of Grace*, Eerdmans, 1978, pages 202–206.

CHAPTER TWENTY ONE

INFANT BAPTISM AND CONFIRMATION

There are those who argue that infant baptism without confirmation is an incomplete initiation into the community of the church. Romanism teaches that the Holy Spirit is given in greater measure than at baptism by the sacrament of confirmation. Some Anglicans believe that the Holy Spirit is given for the first time to the one being confirmed. Baptism has not given the Spirit. So confirmation is essential to complete the process of Christian initiation. Other Anglicans deny such a position. They see confirmation essentially as an opportunity to profess personal faith. That was not possible as an infant, but is clearly a part of baptism in the New Testament. So in that sense baptism is completed when confirmation takes place. Also some consider confirmation as entrance into full membership of the Church of England. Infant baptism alone does not do that. Again the benefit of infant baptism needs to be supplemented with confirmation. Whatever view is held of the meaning of confirmation one cannot escape the fact that in some way it completes the initiation process commenced by the rite of infant baptism. Confirmation declares the inadequacy of the benefits of infant baptism. Indeed, for many confirmation has far greater importance than infant baptism. It precedes first communion and admits to full church membership.

Infant baptism plus confirmation is, and has proved to be, the means of producing pseudo-Christians. It is an alternative to true repentance and faith followed by baptism. In practice it is far less demanding. It tells unregenerate wordlings that they are Christian, and can be a huge hindrance to them ever becoming true Christians.

Some would seek to find biblical basis for confirmation in the incidents recorded in the Acts of the Apostles. They point to Acts 8:5–17 and 19:1–6 where the apostles laid hands on baptized believers and the Holy Spirit was given. They also refer to the mention of baptisms and laying on of hands in Hebrews 6:2. These passages, as we shall see in detail later, speak of a baptism in the Spirit. They have nothing to do with young people professing a faith previously expressed for them by godparents.

How did confirmation arise? By the fifth century infant baptism was generally practised. Also the elements of the rite of infant baptism (as for adult baptism) included the imposition of hands for the bestowal of the Holy Spirit. With the rise of clericalism, the presence of a bishop was judged to be essential for this laying on of hands. It was impossible for him to be available for all infant baptisms as they took place, because they were carried out as soon as possible after birth in the belief that such baptism was essential for salvation. Consequently there came about a time delay between the water baptism and the laying on of hands to confer the Holy Spirit. By the fifth century this laying on of hands by a bishop was called confirmation. It was not until the thirteenth century that baptism and confirmation became separated in the Roman Catholic Church by a period of seven to fourteen years. The Eastern Church continued the confirmation of babes. The Reformation gave birth to the Protestant doctrine of confirmation as an act of confirming baptismal vows made for one when an infant. It was their invention arising from three factors: firstly their commitment to infant baptism, which required a subsequent profession of faith, secondly the then current Roman Catholic practice of confirmation, and thirdly the reading back into church history the practice of priestly instruction of children who had been baptized as infants. In this way the invention of infant baptism gave birth to another invention, confirmation.

CHAPTER TWENTY TWO

THE DIFFERENT GROUNDS, SUBJECTS AND PLACES FOR INFANT BAPTISM

Paedobaptists state different grounds to justify their practice

1. To regenerate
The Roman Catholic, Greek Orthodox, Lutheran Churches and some Anglicans affirm actual regeneration through their sacramental infant baptism.

2. Because an infant of Christian parentage is included in the covenant of grace

3. Because an infant of Christian parentage is included in the covenant of grace **and** on the presumption of future regeneration

4. Simply on the ground of presumed future regeneration of infants having a Christian parent or parents
Some presume regeneration in all cases; others only in the case of elect children.

5. On the ground of the faith of the infant being affirmed by sponsors speaking for him/her
This practice is followed in Lutheran and Anglican Churches. It preserves the New Testament essential connection of baptism and faith. But it is incompatible with the whole of the New Testament to assert that anyone can repent and believe for another person. There is no basis in scripture for sponsors, usually called godparents. The Bible demands personal faith for salvation. The pious words of sponsors at infant baptisms are utterly worthless and displeasing to God. They fly in the face of His revealed way of salvation in the New Testament.

6. Simply that God is said to command infant baptism

7. *Because Jesus blessed children*

8. *Because infant baptism expresses the fact that God takes the initiative in saving mankind*
Before man turns to God for salvation, God provides a Saviour.

Conclusion

The diverse grounds alleged to justify infant baptism arise from the fact that in reality it has no basis in scripture.

Paedobaptists also differ concerning which infants should baptized

1. National state church religion as we have seen baptizes all infants born in the state.
2. Some paedobaptists will baptize the children of unbelievers upon the faith of sponsors.
3. Others simply require the parents or a parent to have been baptized.
4. Others say only the children of believing parents or believing guardians should be baptized.
5. Some go further and state that before an infant is baptized there should be assurance of the faith of at least one parent, and also that the parent(s) will see that the child is instructed in the Christian faith.
6. John Baillie goes so far as to say that infant baptism has no significance unless the child is to be brought up in a Christian home and within the Christian community: "If he is not effectively received into such a community, if there is *nobody* who is caring for his Christian upbringing, then the outward ritual – the washing with water – is not Christian baptism at all, and means nothing." (*Baptism and Conversion*, 1964, page 44 used by permission of Oxford University Press). This presents the problem of assessing whether a parent or parents actually do have faith. Yet paedobaptists often attack believers' baptism on the ground that one cannot always discern whether true faith is present in the candidate for baptism!
7. Some adopt a pragmatic approach. Giving infant baptism may be the means of eventually leading the whole family to Christ. Also if the minister refuses the parents can go to another church willing to fulfil their request. Donald Bridge writes, "Twenty years ago, when we first published this book, David firmly advocated restricting infant baptism to families where at least one parent was a practising, worshipping Christian. Nine recent years in two country parishes have taught him otherwise. It is simply not worth giving

the church a bad image in these communities which such a policy would produce. So he explains the obligations listed in the service, as clearly as possible. The parents should, by prayer, example and teaching, encourage growing children to 'learn to be faithful in public worship and private prayer, to live by trust in God, and come to confirmation'. Through a regular midweek 'Scramblers' service for carers with their pre-school children, through family services, through other children's activities, and through encouraging parents to attend *Alpha* courses in basic Christian understanding, David tries to encourage parents to begin to keep the baptismal promises they make on their children's behalf. Some, in varying degrees, respond. Most do not. But David is persuaded that this pastoral approach to the situation is the only practical one in the Church of England today with its long cultural tradition of indiscriminate paedobaptism.

In April 1997, Archbishop George Carey in a well-trailed sermon pleaded for indiscriminate baptism, and gave his reasons. He maintained that the welcome thus extended to his parents in his infancy began a process that eventually led to their conversion and to his! There is no final solution to the problem of 'which infants are eligible' for baptism."[1]

The statement that there is "no final solution to the problem of 'which infants are eligible' for baptism" is striking. Among paedobaptists there is clearly diverse theory and practice in this matter. Such is only to be expected when a practice is followed contrary to God's revealed will that only repentant believers are to be baptized.

Where should infants be baptized?

Some contend that baptism must be conducted in the presence of the local church. Oscar Cullman wrote, "The faith of the congregation though not to be represented as vicarious faith does yet at the moment of the baptismal event belong to the act of baptism. Attention must here be drawn to the Church that *prays* for the person being baptized (Acts viii 15). It prays that God may complete the miracle of baptism in the baptized person, whether adult or infant. *This* faith which has the person baptized as its object is in fact an indispensable element in the baptismal act."[2] Acts 8:15 is nothing to do with baptism in water. The record tells us that this had taken place previously. It concerns the distinct and separate experience of the baptism in the Spirit. The need for a congregation of God's people to be present for baptism is certainly not indispensable according to the New Testament. The Ethiopian eunuch was not baptized in the presence of any other Christian than Philip (Acts 8:38). Paul was baptized by Ananias probably without the presence of any other Christians (Acts 9:18). The baptism of the Philippian jailor and his household (Acts 16:33) was carried out by Paul and Silas only. Yet again the doctrine of infant baptism is accompanied with assertions which have no validity when examined by scripture.

Conclusions

Infant baptism, however defined, is clearly something quite distinct from baptism as stated in the New Testament. There, baptism is an action to express personal faith in Christ as Saviour, and personal commitment to live unto God through Christ. Baptism thus strengthens faith and commitment. It is also God's seal to the convert of the union with Christ signified by baptism. All these things are impossible for an infant.

References

1. Donald Bridge and David Phypers *The Water that Divides*, Christian Focus, Tain, Scotland 2008 ISBN 978–184550–308–6, page 145 (1998 edition).
2. Oscar Cullman *Baptism in the New Testament*, SCM 1950, page 54.

CHAPTER TWENTY THREE

BELIEVERS' BAPTISM BY IMMERSION AND ENTRY INTO THE CHURCH OF JESUS CHRIST

The church of Jesus Christ is composed of all those who have truly repented and believed in Him for salvation. Therefore the moment a person repents and believes, even before baptism, he is in the church of Jesus Christ. The New Testament pattern is that converts were baptized without delay and joined other believers in the local church. Thus baptism coincided with the start of the Christian life and also membership of the Christian church.

An example of this is seen in the conversion of Saul. After his conversion Ananias a disciple in Damascus is sent by the Lord to minister to Saul. The Lord tells Ananias that Saul has been converted. He is now a member of the church which he formerly persecuted. Ananias recognises this fact by addressing Saul as "Brother Saul" (Acts 9:17). "Brother" had a very definite meaning. It acknowledged that Saul was now adopted into the family of God, was born of God and belonged to the church of Jesus Christ. It is significant that at this point in time Saul was not yet baptized. Ananias dealt with that matter immediately. Forthwith Saul joined with the disciples at Damascus (Acts 9:19).

Today true converts to Christ may not hear about believers' baptism by immersion until some considerable time after conversion, and there is a time gap before they are baptized. That time gap may be lengthened by the effect on them of erroneous teaching on baptism. During that time they may seek to belong to a church practising believers' baptism. Some would receive them into membership. Others would require baptism first. It is true conversion, not baptism, which brings entry into the church of Jesus Christ. It is therefore contrary to biblical truth to insist on baptism before allowing membership in a local church. If there is true conversion the applicant is already a member of Christ's church, and must be recognised as such. This does not mean that the duty of obedience to the Divine command to be baptized should not be impressed fully on the applicant, just as all other New Testament commands should be pastorally enjoined as appropriate.

Baptism is about union with Christ. But of course union with Christ means that one is in His body, the church composed of all believers. Water baptism is therefore a signification of membership of Christ's church by association. It is essential to realise that true converts who are not baptized are just as much in that body of Christ as those who are baptized. When they are baptized they are signifying their existing union with Christ. They are not entering the church of Jesus Christ. They are not even signifying their existing membership in it. They are signifying their existing union with Christ. Water baptism is designed by God to speak about union with Christ, not about union with His body.

CHAPTER TWENTY FOUR

THE APPROACH TO BAPTISM AND REBAPTISM

Baptism and the approach of the candidate

From all that has been said it will be clear that the new convert should take the step immediately. It is the expression of repentance and faith in Christ. It should be done to obey the Lord's command.

1. Often believers are moved to be baptized in order to testify to unbelievers of their faith in Christ. Sometimes this becomes the primary focus of the event
Testimony to others of one's faith in Christ is not the essential meaning or purpose of baptism. It is an action of the believer directed towards God. There is no need for the presence of anyone other than the one who baptizes the convert. This is clear from the records in Acts 8:26–38, 9:18 and 19:5. To make baptism essentially a public testimony of faith is foreign to the New Testament. It is a failure to understand the significance of baptism. Baptism was not ordained by the Lord for this purpose. In the same way the breaking of bread is not an action directed towards unbelievers. It is an action done in obedience to the Lord's command focusing faith on the Person and work of Christ.

2. Some direct believers to be baptized to follow Christ's example
Christ submitted to John's baptism. It is therefore a sheer impossibility for believers to follow Christ's example because John's baptism no longer exists. It ceased with John. Christian baptism is distinct from and different from John's baptism. Its meaning and purpose is not the same as John's baptism. That was for the remission of sins to prepare for the coming of the Messiah. Thus we see disciples who knew only John's baptism were baptized again in the name of the Lord Jesus (Acts 19:1–5).

Their baptism by John did not mean they did not need Christian baptism.

3. Many believers approach baptism expecting, or at least hoping for, a conscious experience of blessing during the act of being baptized

Sometimes this occurs. But it should not be the reason for taking the step of baptism. The essential blessing of baptism is to understand its meaning as symbolising union with Christ, His death and resurrection for the believer, and the believer's death and resurrection with Christ. To focus on looking for an encounter with God in baptism is to direct one's eyes elsewhere from what they should be fixed upon – union with Christ in His death and resurrection.

Stephen Gaukroger says that candidates should have an expectation of encountering the Holy Spirit in the baptismal service. He writes, "In many churches the laying on of hands now accompanies baptism. The leaders lay their hands on the person's head and pray, 'May God bless you and fill you with His Holy Spirit as you are baptised', or something like that."[1] This is to confuse two quite distinct baptisms. In the New Testament they are linked in so far as they both occur at the commencement of the Christian life, but they are never fused together as one event. Baptism in the Spirit may follow immediately upon water baptism as in Acts 19:5–6, but Spirit baptism is never presented as a part of water baptism. Moreover water baptism is never stated to be the means of receiving the baptism in the Spirit.

He puts forward guidelines on how to prepare for baptism. He states the things to be done in "the weeks and months before your baptism:

- Open yourself up to the Holy Spirit so that He can convict you of your sins. Repent of the sins he shows you, and so get right with God.
- Think through the basics of the faith. Join a discipleship course. Make sure you are doing the simple things well.
- Be in touch with God through prayer and Bible reading.
- Fast, perhaps for a day each week.
- Keep a spiritual journal.
- Think about your whole life and the task or tasks which God wants you to do.
- Meet regularly with a 'spiritual director'."[2] He defines this director as ". . . someone you can go to for help and encouragement, who can review all the aspects of your life with you."[3]

This approach bears no resemblance to New Testament baptism. It merits the criticism that some who practise believers' baptism have created a new rite with new conditions quite different from the immediate conversion baptism we find throughout the New Testament. There we find no room for a lengthy period of instruction or preparation, and there is not the slightest hint of probation before baptism. To teach such practice appears very spiritual. In reality it is a departure from the Bible.

What about rebaptism?

True baptism is a once for all event not to be repeated. But there are cases where rebaptism is essential. The following baptisms are not valid in the light of New Testament truth.

1.   *All infant baptisms*
Baptism is for believers only.

2.   *Baptism not conducted by immersion*
We have seen the significance given to the emblems in the Lord's Supper. They represent the body and blood of the Lord. Failure to recognise their meaning and to partake of them unworthily can bring judgment. The significance of immersion is also to be taken most seriously. It represents death burial and resurrection. It represents union with Christ. Sprinkling or affusion do not signify what baptism is meant to represent.

There are those who are unable to be immersed on account of bad health. In these cases there is no obligation to obey the command to carry out this ordinance. It is not in accord with scripture to apply sprinkling instead.

3.   *Any baptism that was carried out before conversion*
Not infrequently persons in churches practising believer's baptism are baptized without true repentance and genuine saving faith. This often occurs in the case of children and young people. Some of them are truly born again later in life and then wish to be baptized. Their request should be granted. It is important to say that a rebaptism carried out for any of these three reasons is not truly a rebaptism, it is rather true baptism for the first time.

References
1. Stephen Gaukroger *Being Baptised*, Scripture Union, Reprinted 2006, page 58, ISBN 1 85999 768 6. Used with permission. Also taken from *Being Baptized* by Simon Fox; Stephen Gaukroger, page 54. Copyright © 1993. Used by permission of Zondervan.
2. Stephen Gaukroger *Being Baptised*, Scripture Union, Reprinted 2006,

page 40, ISBN 1 85999 768 6. Used with permission. Also taken from *Being Baptized* by Simon Fox; Stephen Gaukroger, page 40. Copyright © 1993. Used by permission of Zondervan.

3. Stephen Gaukroger *Being Baptised*, Scripture Union, Reprinted 2006, page 39, ISBN 1 85999 768 6. Used with permission. Also taken from *Being Baptized* by Simon Fox; Stephen Gaukroger, page 37. Copyright © 1993. Used by permission of Zondervan.

CHAPTER TWENTY FIVE

THE BAPTISM OF BELIEVERS PART OF THE ESSENTIAL FOUNDATION

Some deny that water baptism is a necessary part of the foundation on which the Christian life is built. Salvationists do not practise water baptism. Their founder William Booth did not observe this ordinance and that of breaking of bread on the grounds that these ordinances divided Christians. Many other Christians who do practise true water baptism do not understand it as an essential part of the foundation for the Christian life. Also many Christians, who believe in water baptism by immersion of believers only, do not wish to insist that it is an essential step for all Christians. They know that such insistence prevents working with many other Christians who do not practise biblical water baptism. Indeed the prevailing climate among Christians is to plead for toleration of the different doctrines of water baptism. Like William Booth many are motivated to seek to avoid division. That motive never justifies the overthrow of God's truth. The sacrifice of truth will prove greater loss than any gain thereby. To trim God's word to achieve His purposes is the arrogance of saying we are wiser than God.

In what ways then is water baptism foundational?

Baptism is a part of the foundation of the Christian life because along with repentance and faith it is designed by God to be part of the whole experience of conversion to Christ

We have seen that true scriptural baptism is inseparable from repentance and faith. Because it is the expression of that repentance and faith, the blessings that come through repentance and faith are ascribed to baptism. It remits sins (Acts 2:38). It washes away sins (Acts 22:16). It saves one's soul (1 Pet. 3:21).

Baptism declares most powerfully and with great clarity what has happened through obeying the gospel

Baptism signifies the new standing into which the Christian has come. A great change has taken place for time and eternity. The convert is

135

now "in Christ". Baptism impresses most vividly the truth declared in the word. By baptism God says to the true convert that he is "in Christ". That is his standing before God. That is the truth about him. The symbolic action declares most powerfully that the believer is united with Christ in His death, burial and resurrection. What happened to Him has also happened to the believer. He has been crucified, buried and raised with Christ. His sins are forgiven. He can reckon himself dead to sin and alive to God. All this is signified and sealed to the convert by baptism. This is of the greatest value to the new Christian. These are the first things he needs to grasp. The convert who is not baptized by immersion at the start of his Christian life lacks this wonderful Divine attestation of what has happened. The Christian who has not been baptized does not have God's appointed sign and seal of his new position "in Christ". It is God's way of signifying what happens when converted to Christ. By it He says personally to the convert that a great change has occurred. It makes the reality of that change even more definite. It gives clarity and certainty about what has happened.

The Christian for the rest of his life on earth has the memory of water baptism which was a vivid portrayal of his identification with Christ

That union with Christ not only dealt with his sins but also determines the way in which the Christian is to live every day after conversion.

The truths declared in baptism are truths he must hold on to throughout his earthly pilgrimage. In Christ the Christian died to sin once for all (Rom. 6:10–11). Therefore he must reckon himself dead to sin and not let sin reign any more in his life (Rom. 6:12). Moreover, just as Christ lives to God, so the Christian must reckon himself alive to God, and walk in newness of life (Rom. 6:11 and 14). He must acknowledge the truth about himself, and live in accordance with that truth. He is no longer the slave of sin (Rom. 6:17). Therefore he must cease from sin. He has become the slave of righteousness (Rom. 6:18). Therefore he must live in obedience to God. In simple words the Christian is to live in accordance with who he is in Christ. And that was declared in baptism. Baptism is a constant reminder to the Christian of these facts which are essential for him to live the way he should.

Paul teaches these same truths in his letter to the Colossians. He reminds them that they were buried with Christ in baptism and raised with Him (Col. 2:12). He goes on to say that since they were raised with Christ they should seek those things which are above, where Christ is, sitting at the right hand of God. They should set their minds on things above, not on things on the earth, for they died, and their life is hidden with Christ in God. Fundamental to their living is to realise that they are "in Christ". This fact is to govern all their conduct, and this fact is affirmed by baptism. It tells the Christian to live in accordance with his new union with Christ.

Baptism is a single act never to be repeated. But the impact of the event is intended to abide throughout the rest of life on earth. To live in accordance with its meaning is to live aright. The Christian who has not been baptized does not have that means of grace declaring the basic facts about his new position "in Christ". Understanding these facts is key to Christian living.

Some will object that Christians can know these facts without being baptized. This is true. In the same way Christians can remember the Lord's death without breaking bread and drinking the cup. But Divine wisdom and love appointed the physical actions of eating bread and drinking from a cup to aid our faith and to be a means of blessing to us. A Christian who does not observe the breaking of bread does not experience the particular blessing that God gives through that means. The early Christians and apostles valued the blessing of the Lord's Supper very highly from the evidence of the New Testament. We find that "they continued steadfastly in the apostles' doctrine and fellowship, in the breaking of bread, and in prayers. Then fear came upon every soul, and many wonders and signs were done through the apostles. Now all who believed were together, and had all things in common, and sold their possessions and goods, and divided them among all, as anyone had need. So continuing daily with one accord in the temple, and breaking bread from house to house, they ate their food with gladness and simplicity of heart, praising God and having favor with all the people. And the Lord added to the church daily those who were being saved" (Acts 2:42–47). The breaking of bread was prominent in their activities. They considered it most important to obey this ordinance of the Lord, and it was a means of grace to them alongside doctrine, fellowship and prayers. They experienced constant miracles and the joy of seeing others coming to Christ. These were blessings indeed, but they continued to break bread. The remembrance of Christ's death through the breaking of bread can be one of the means of God's richest blessing for the Christian. In the same way water baptism is intended to be a means of great blessing at conversion and throughout earthly life. It is a constant reminder that the believer is "in Christ" and must live in dedication to God.

Baptism is also a foundation because it is a defence against errors which would wreck one's Christian life

Water baptism expresses simply but so powerfully what it means to be a Christian. Consequently it is a real preservative against error. This is clearly demonstrated in the following New Testament passages.

Paul had to contend against false doctrine with all his might. In his letter to the Romans he confronts the terrible teaching called antinomianism. This error has never ceased to attack the Church of Jesus Christ, and will continue to do so until Christ returns. Paul declared the glorious truth of God's abounding grace: "Where sin abounded, grace abounded much more, so that as sin reigned in death, even so grace might reign through righteousness to eternal life through Jesus Christ our Lord" (Rom. 5:20–21). From these facts about sin and grace Antinomians reasoned wrongly that men should continue in sin so that grace may also continue to abound. The apostle's answer is most significant. He reminds his readers of their baptism in water. He tells them again what it symbolized. He states that baptism symbolises a believer's union with Christ, which has come about at conversion. He says that they were baptized into Christ Jesus. It expresses the glorious reality of being "in Christ." Christ died to sin once for all, was buried, was raised from the dead and lives to God. When they were baptized they enacted in symbol the fact that they were united with Him in His death, burial, resurrection and living unto God. Of course they did not die physically and so Paul writes, "united together (that is with Christ) in the likeness of His death." Spiritually they were united with his death, because He was their representative. His acts were their acts. Therefore when He died to sin they died to sin in Him. At baptism they carried out an act symbolising this identification with Christ. They acknowledged in that act that what He did as their representative, they did. In Christ they died to sin once for all. Their former unconverted person died to the old life dominated by sin. Consequently they are now free from the dominion of sin. Indeed the express purpose of their once for all death to sin in Christ was that they should no longer be slaves of sin (Rom. 6:6). Because of this union with Christ through conversion and expressed in baptism, they must "reckon themselves dead indeed to sin, but alive to God in Christ Jesus" (Rom. 6:11). They must not let sin reign in their mortal bodies, that they should obey it in its lusts. They must not present their members as instruments of unrighteousness to sin, but present themselves to God as being alive from the dead, and their members as instruments of righteousness to God (Rom. 6:12–13). Baptism is therefore the clearest statement, when correctly understood, of the believers relationship to sin. It means that they have died to it once for all in Christ their representative, and just as Christ rose from the dead and dies no more, they are alive to God in the likeness of Christ's resurrection and they walk in newness of life.

Paul knew that they knew these truths. In the passage he constantly appeals to their knowledge: "What shall we say then? Shall we continue in sin that grace may abound? Certainly not! How shall we who died to sin live any longer in it? Or do you not know that as many of us as were baptized into Christ Jesus were baptized into His death? Therefore we were buried with Him through baptism into death, that just as Christ was raised from the dead by the glory of the Father, even so we also should walk in newness of life. For if we have been united together in the likeness of His death, certainly we also shall be *in the likeness* of *His* resurrection, knowing this, that our old man was crucified with *Him,* that the body of sin might be done away with, that we should no longer be slaves of sin. For he who has died has been freed from sin. Now if we died with Christ, we believe that we shall also live with Him, knowing that Christ, having been raised from the dead, dies no more. Death no longer has dominion over Him" (Rom. 6:1–9).

Note carefully that Paul argues from their act of baptism to answer the subtle suggestion, "Shall we continue in sin that grace may abound?" He might have used other arguments. He could have reminded them of their repentance. He could have argued that when they repented they turned from sin. He could have directed them to consider that returning to sinning would be inconsistent with faith in a Saviour from sin's guilt and power. He could have reminded them of their calling to be holy as God is holy. He might have used so many great New Testament truths to counter this false teaching. But, directed by the Holy Spirit, he reminds them of the meaning of their baptism. He recalls what happened when they were baptized. It is a decisive argument. As they remembered their baptism they would be preserved from the error of sinning that grace may abound. This is proof that baptism is foundational in that it is a defence against error.

There is another clear example in the New Testament where the apostle returns his readers to baptism in water as something absolutely basic and as an antidote to erroneous teaching. In the epistle to the Colossians Paul speaks of false teachers propagating "philosophy and empty deceit, according to the tradition of men, according to the basic principles of the world, and not according to Christ" (Col. 2:8). Those addressed in the letter were in danger of succumbing to these errors. Paul takes them back to their baptism when they were buried with Him (that is Christ), and in which they were also raised with him (Col. 2:12). He says, "Therefore, if you died with Christ from the basic principles of the world, why, as *though* living in the world, do you subject yourselves to regulations – 'Do not touch, do not taste, do not handle,' which all concern things which perish with the using – according to the commandments and doctrines of men?" (Col. 2:20–22). They died to these things with Christ at conversion, and they symbolised that death at baptism. Paul reminds them of that fact. It is the same argument as Romans. Their baptism meant union with the death of Christ, therefore they must remember the truth about themselves. They died to the basic principles of the world. Therefore they must live in the light of that truth. Note again that the apostle argues against serious error from the fact and meaning of water baptism. It was a foundation for life.

There is a third occurrence of water baptism in the New Testament where yet again fundamental truth symbolised by baptism is used by Paul to counter error. The Christians addressed in Paul's letter to the Galatians had come under the evil influence of Judaizers. These Judaizers taught that in addition to faith in Christ it was necessary to be circumcised and to conform in other respects to Jewish law to attain salvation. Midway through his epistle he says, "For you are all sons of God through faith in Christ Jesus. For as many of you as were baptized into Christ have put on Christ. There is neither Jew nor Greek, there is neither slave nor free, there is neither male nor female; for you are all one in Christ Jesus" (Gal. 3:26–28). Baptism symbolised the believer's union with Christ, which had been entered into through faith prior to baptism. It also signified the believer putting on Christ, that is, appropriating the benefits of Christ's saving work. The Son of God came to earth and became truly man, placed Himself under God's law and met all its requirements for believers. As their representative He shed His blood and suffered death in their place for their sins. This was the penalty the law demanded. Consequently the believer receives remission of sins. His debt has been paid in full by Christ. As the believer's representative Christ rendered perfect obedience to God. Therefore the righteousness of Christ is reckoned by God to be the believer's righteousness; it is imputed to him. Before salvation the sinner is clothed in the filthy garments of sin. Afterwards he is forgiven and he puts on the robes of the righteousness of Christ. He stands before God without condemnation and accepted in Christ. The believer now stands in grace, complete in Christ, and blessed with all spiritual blessings, including adoption. He is no longer a slave entangled with a yoke of bondage. He is no longer attempting to be justified by keeping laws. Putting on Christ means gaining these blessings. Baptism was a concrete expression of faith in

Christ. It was so closely related to faith that he speaks of the act of baptism effecting this putting on of Christ. Believers are therefore free from keeping the law as a means of justification. It is striking that Paul refers to their baptism to refute the error they were being subjected to.

These New Testament verses in Rom. 6, Col. 2 and Gal. 3 state fundamental truths concerning the Christian from the meaning of water baptism. That meaning of baptism was the means of refuting extremely serious errors which had the potential of wrecking the spiritual lives of those Christians. Baptism is thus not only a positive and clear statement of a believer's conversion, his standing before God and of his death to sin and walking in newness of life, it is thereby also a strong defence against erroneous teachings coming against the Christian. The Christian who is not baptized does not have this preservative from error. It is true that he has other means of grace to keep him from falling, but in knowledge, wisdom and love God has appointed water baptism as a defence against false teaching. Just as a foundation preserves the superstructure, so baptism preserves the believer.

Because true water baptism is foundational it has been, is, and will be fiercely attacked by Satan and his hosts

This is seen in several ways.

1.   Water baptism is an action observed by principalities, powers, the rulers of the darkness of this age, spiritual hosts of wickedness in the heavenly places (Eph. 6:12)
Water baptism signifies and seals truths about the convert which enrage Satan and his hosts. It symbolises that they have lost a slave, that Christ has gained a follower, and that that follower has laid part of his foundation for the building of his Christian life. This explains why many Christians go through a real spiritual battle before being baptized, why many experience great opposition from those who want them to accept their baptism as an infant as valid before God, and why converts from other religions to Christianity are sometimes persecuted unto death for being baptized.

2.   Rev. 12:1–4 reveals that one of Satan's methods is to attempt to destroy God's work at the very start
Satan is depicted in these verses as a "great fiery red dragon having seven heads and ten horns and seven diadems on his heads . . . [he] stood before the woman [the true Israel of God in the person of Mary] who was ready to give birth, to devour her Child [the infant Jesus] as soon as it was born." Satan used Herod the king to fulfil his purpose.

Herod, in an attempt to kill Jesus, put to death all the male children who were in Bethlehem and in all its districts from two years old and under. Joseph was warned by an angel to flee to Egypt, and Jesus was saved from an early death. These scriptures teach a most important truth: Satan constantly seeks to destroy at birth. As we have seen, water baptism is a most wonderful means of strengthening the Christian immediately after the birth of the Christian life. Thus it is diametrically opposed to Satan's objective to "devour" the Christian as soon as his new life in Christ has begun. Consequently the devil is very happy when gospel proclamation is not followed with the requirement of converts to be baptized, and he does his utmost to overthrow true water baptism by whatever way he can.

3.   Water baptism is inseparable from the gospel of repentance and faith

As we have seen, when men permit water baptism without the personal repentance and faith of the one being baptized, they preach another gospel, or, at best, their declaration of the true gospel of repentance and faith is seriously undermined. Consequently Satan knows that he can effectively attack the proclamation of the gospel by false doctrines of baptism. Thus Satan targets true water baptism because through unscriptural substitutes he can overthrow, or at least hinder the preaching of the true gospel. Sadly the seriousness of error on this issue of water baptism is often not perceived.

Baptism in the Holy Spirit

CHAPTER TWENTY SIX

THE BAPTISM IN THE SPIRIT

"Therefore, leaving the discussion of the elementary *principles* of Christ, let us go on to perfection, not laying again the foundation of repentance from dead works and of faith toward God, of the doctrine of baptisms, of laying on of hands, of resurrection of the dead, and of eternal judgment" (Heb. 6:1–2). We come to the fourth element of the foundation for the Christian life, the baptism in the Spirit. We must begin with a thorough examination of the scriptures so that we arrive at a true definition of this term.

Predicted by John the Baptist

"I indeed baptize you in water unto repentance, but He who is coming after me is mightier than I, whose sandals I am not worthy to carry. He will baptize you in the Holy Spirit and fire" (Mat. 3:11; my trans.).

"I indeed baptized you in water, but He will baptize you in the Holy Spirit." (Mark 1:8; my trans.).

"John answered, saying to all, 'I indeed baptize you in water; but One mightier than I is coming, whose sandal strap I am not worthy to loose. He will baptize you in the Holy Spirit and fire'" (Luke 3:16; my trans.).

"I did not recognize Him, but He who sent me to baptize in water said to me, 'He upon whom you see the Spirit descending and remaining upon Him, this is the One who baptizes in the Holy Spirit'" (John 1:33 NASB).

John the Baptist is recorded in all four gospels predicting that Jesus Christ would come after him and baptize in the Holy Spirit.

Predicted by Jesus Christ

"Behold, I send the Promise of My Father upon you; but tarry in the city of Jerusalem until you are endued with power from on high" (Luke 24:49).

"The former account I made, O Theophilus, of all that Jesus began both to do and teach, until the day in which He was taken up, after He through the Holy Spirit had given commandments to the apostles whom He had chosen, to whom He also presented Himself alive after His suffering by many infallible proofs, being seen by them during forty days and speaking of the things pertaining to the kingdom of God. And being assembled together with *them*, He commanded them not to depart from Jerusalem, but to wait for the Promise of the Father, 'which,' *He said*, 'you have heard from Me; for John truly baptized in water, but you will be baptized in the Holy Spirit not many days from now.' Therefore, when they had come together, they asked Him, saying, 'Lord, will You at this time restore the kingdom to Israel?' And He said to them, 'It is not for you to know times or seasons which the Father has put in His own authority. But you shall receive power when the Holy Spirit has come upon you; and you shall be witnesses to Me in Jerusalem, and in all Judea and Samaria, and to the end of the earth.' Now when He had spoken these things, while they watched, He was taken up, and a cloud received Him out of their sight" (Acts 1:1–9; v.5 my trans.).

These verses tell us that the baptism in the Spirit is also called by Jesus the Promise of the Father. Jesus also says that they will receive power when the Holy Spirit has come upon them. The baptism in the Spirit is a coming upon of the Spirit and a reception of power to be witnesses to Christ. The verses also state that the first fulfilment of that promise took place on the day of Pentecost.

On the day of Pentecost

"When the Day of Pentecost had fully come, they were all with one accord in one place. And suddenly there came a sound from heaven, as of a rushing mighty wind, and it filled the whole house where they were sitting. Then there appeared to them divided tongues, as of fire, and *one* sat upon each of them. And they were all filled with the Holy Spirit and began to speak with other tongues, as the Spirit gave them utterance. And there were dwelling in Jerusalem Jews, devout men, from every nation under heaven. And when this sound occurred, the multitude came together, and were confused, because everyone heard them speak in his own language. Then they were all amazed and marveled, saying to one another, 'Look, are not all these who speak Galileans? And how *is it that* we hear, each in our own language in which we were born? Parthians and Medes and Elamites, those dwelling in Mesopotamia, Judea and Cappadocia, Pontus and Asia, Phrygia and Pamphylia, Egypt and the parts of Libya adjoining Cyrene, visitors from Rome, both Jews and proselytes, Cretans and Arabs – we hear them speaking in our own tongues the wonderful works of God.' So they were all amazed and perplexed, saying to one another, 'Whatever could this mean?' " (Acts 2:1–12).

It seems that the disciples went out of the house where the Spirit came upon them. They mingled with the multitude of Jews from every nation gathered in Jerusalem for the Feast of Pentecost. The speaking in tongues was defined as "utterance." M.R. Vincent says, "A peculiar word, and purposely chosen to denote the *clear, loud* utterance under the miraculous impulse. It is used by later Greek writers of the utterances of oracles or seers. So in the Septuagint, of prophesying. See 1 Chron. 25:1; Deut. 32:2; Zech.x.2; Ezek. 13:19."[1] The sound of their "utterance" attracted the multitude. It would also seem that the disciples were spread, rather than standing in a group close together, so that each could be heard clearly. This is indicated by the fact that hearers who spoke the particular spoken language, knew that "the wonderful works of God" were being proclaimed. All the hearers heard someone speaking their own language/dialect as well as the languages/dialects they did not understand (Acts 2:6,8). The baptism in the Spirit was being filled with the Spirit *and* speaking in tongues.

Peter's explanation of what had happened

"So they were all amazed and perplexed, saying to one another, 'Whatever could this mean?' Others mocking said, 'They are full of new wine.' But Peter, standing up with the eleven, raised his voice and said to them, 'Men of Judea and all who dwell in Jerusalem, let this be known to you, and heed my words. For these are not drunk, as you suppose, since it is *only* the third hour of the day. But this is what was spoken by the prophet Joel: "And it shall come to pass in the last days, says God, That I will pour out of My Spirit on all flesh; Your sons and your daughters shall prophesy, Your young men shall see visions, Your old men shall dream dreams. And on My menservants and on My maidservants I will pour out My Spirit in those days; And they shall prophesy. I will show wonders in heaven above And signs in the earth beneath: Blood and fire and vapor of smoke. The sun shall be turned into darkness, And the moon into blood, Before the coming of the great and awesome day of the LORD. And it shall come to pass *That* whoever calls on the name of the LORD Shall be saved" ' " (Acts 2:12–21).

The declaration of the wonderful works of God through the miraculous tongue speaking was not a proclamation of the gospel. That was to follow through Peter speaking in the common Aramaic language which they all knew. But the tongue speaking arrested the attention of the crowd. It also signalled the start of a new era in God's dealings with His people and mankind. Acts 2:17 and 18 tell us that Joel prophesied that in the last days God would pour out His Spirit upon all flesh. Peter said that on that day of Pentecost this prophecy was fulfilled. The last days had begun. This was the explanation of what had happened.

The promise spoken by the prophet Joel

The baptism in the Spirit, is the fulfilment of Joel's prophecy.

Let us look carefully at the prophecy. *God would pour out His Spirit on all flesh*. The key word here is "all". In contrast to previous times there would no longer be any limitation on account of sex, age or rank. Sons and daughters (both sexes), young men and old men (all ages) and menservants and maidservants (all ranks including those of lowest rank) will partake of this outpouring of the Spirit. Before that time God had poured out His Spirit on a few selected individuals. Usually they were male, old rather than young and high ranking as leaders of God's people, such as prophets, priests, and kings. Here are examples:

> "See, I have called by name Bezalel the son of Uri, the son of Hur, of the tribe of Judah. And I have filled him with the Spirit of God, in wisdom, in understanding, in knowledge, and in all *manner of* workmanship, to design artistic works, to work in gold, in silver, in bronze, in cutting jewels for setting, in carving wood, and to work in all *manner of* workmanship" (Exod. 31:2–3). This man was appointed and endued by God for very special work in the construction of the Tabernacle.

> "And Balaam raised his eyes, and saw Israel encamped according to their tribes; and the Spirit of God came upon him" (Num. 24:2).

> "When the children of Israel cried out to the LORD, the LORD raised up a deliverer for the children of Israel, who delivered them: Othniel the son of Kenaz, Caleb's younger brother. The Spirit of the LORD came upon him, and he judged Israel. He went out to war, and the LORD

delivered Cushan-rishathaim king of Mesopotamia into his hand; and his hand prevailed over Cushan-rishathaim" (Judg. 3:9–10).

"Then all the Midianites and Amalekites, the people of the East, gathered together; and they crossed over and encamped in the Valley of Jezreel. But the Spirit of the LORD came upon Gideon; then he blew the trumpet, and the Abiezrites gathered behind him" (Judg. 6:33–34).

"Then the Spirit of the LORD came upon Jephthah, and he passed through Gilead and Manasseh, and passed through Mizpah of Gilead; and from Mizpah of Gilead he advanced *toward* the people of Ammon" (Judg. 11:29).

Concerning Samson, "And the Spirit of the LORD began to move upon him at Mahaneh Dan between Zorah and Eshtaol" (Judg. 13:25).

"And the Spirit of the LORD came mightily upon him, and he tore the lion apart as one would have torn apart a young goat, though *he had* nothing in his hand. But he did not tell his father or his mother what he had done" (Judg. 14:6).

"Then the Spirit of the LORD came upon him mightily, and he went down to Ashkelon and killed thirty of their men, took their apparel, and gave the changes *of clothing* to those who had explained the riddle. So his anger was aroused, and he went back up to his father's house" (Judg. 14:19).

"When he came to Lehi, the Philistines came shouting against him. Then the Spirit of the LORD came mightily upon him; and the ropes that *were* on his arms became like flax that is burned with fire, and his bonds broke loose from his hands" (Judg. 15:14).

Concerning King Saul, "Then the Spirit of the LORD will come upon you, and you will prophesy with them and be turned into another man" (1 Sam. 10:6).

Concerning King David, "Then Samuel took the horn of oil and anointed him in the midst of his brothers; and the Spirit of the LORD came upon David from that day forward. So Samuel arose and went to Ramah" (1 Sam. 16:13).

"Then the Spirit came upon Amasai, chief of the captains, *and he said:* '*We are* yours, O David; We *are* on your side, O son of Jesse! Peace, peace to you, And peace to your helpers! For your God helps you.' So David received them, and made them captains of the troop" (1 Chron. 12:18).

At the time of King Asa, "Now the Spirit of God came upon Azariah the son of Oded" (2 Chron. 15:1).

In the reign of Jehoshaphat, "Then the Spirit of the LORD came upon Jahaziel the son of Zechariah, the son of Benaiah, the son of Jeiel, the son of Mattaniah, a Levite of the sons of Asaph, in the midst of the assembly" (2 Chron. 20:14).

During the reign of Joash, "Then the Spirit of the LORD came upon Jahaziel the son of Zechariah, the son of Benaiah, the son of Jeiel, the son of Mattaniah, a Levite of the sons of Asaph, in the midst of the assembly" (2 Chron. 20:14).

Ezekiel the prophet, "Then the Spirit of the LORD fell upon me, and said to me, 'Speak! "Thus says the LORD: Thus you have said, O house of Israel; for I know the things that come into your mind" ' " (Ezek. 11:5).

Elizabeth and Zacharias the mother and father of John the Baptist, "And it happened, when Elizabeth heard the greeting of Mary, that the babe leaped in her womb; and Elizabeth was filled with the Holy Spirit" (Luke 1:41).

"Now his father Zacharias was filled with the Holy Spirit, and prophesied" (Luke 1:67).

John the Baptist, "For he will be great in the sight of the Lord, and shall drink neither wine nor strong drink. He will also be filled with the Holy Spirit, even from his mother's womb" (Luke 1:15).

It is therefore clearly incorrect to say that the Spirit was only *upon* God's people in Old Testament times, only *with* God's people during the ministry of Jesus and only *in* God's people after Pentecost. From the time of Bezalel, in the time of Moses, up to the day of Pentecost recorded in Acts 2 there were individuals filled with the Spirit. The difference at Pentecost was that God would give that filling to *every one* of His people.

It is significant that Peter adds to Joel 2:29 the word "My" twice. Joel 2:29 NASB reads, "Even on the male and female servants I will pour out My Spirit in those days." Peter expands it to bring out the meaning, "And on My menservants and on My maidservants I will pour out My Spirit in those days; And they shall prophesy" (Acts 2:18). He is making it clear that the Spirit will be poured out on those who are *His* people.

"All flesh" is defined further by Peter to mean Jews and Gentiles who respond to the gospel and are saved through Jesus Christ (see verses 38–39). Peter declares that the promise proclaimed by Joel is to the Jews to whom he is speaking, to their descendants down through the future centuries and to "all who are afar off," the Gentiles (see Eph. 2:11–13,17). It is to all whom the Lord will call to himself. This change in God's dealings with His people was breathtaking. That God would pour out His Spirit on *every one* of His people instead of just specially selected individuals was exceedingly wonderful and astonishing. Equally, if not more, staggering was the fact that this blessing would be for Gentiles also.

From the day of Pentecost onwards until the return of Jesus Christ God has promised to pour out His Spirit on every Christian. Every believer is promised the baptism in the Spirit: "And it shall come to pass in the last days, says God, That I will pour out of My Spirit on all flesh; Your sons and your daughters shall prophesy, Your young men shall see visions, Your old men shall dream dreams. And on My menservants and on My maidservants I will pour out My Spirit in those days; And they shall prophesy" (Acts 2:17–18). Young men seeing visions and old men dreaming dreams recalls Num. 12:6: "Then He said, 'Hear now My words: If there is a prophet among you, I, the LORD, make Myself known to him in a vision; I speak to him in a dream.' " Seeing visions and dreaming dreams therefore refers to prophesying in this verse. It is significant that Peter adds to Joel's prophecy (Joel 2:29) the words "they shall prophesy" at the end of verse 18. Peter is not modifying the meaning of Joel's sacred oracle. The apostle would not dare to do that. He is rather making absolutely clear the import of the prophet's words, and thereby showing their fulfilment. J.A. Alexander wrote these words: "The last clause, *they shall prophesy*, is added by the Apostle to remove all ambiguity and doubt as to the effusion of the Spirit promised. As if he had said: 'the Spirit which I thus pour out will be one of prophetic inspiration.' This precise specification, in a case where general and comprehensive terms might seem appropriate, arises from the fact that this was the precise form in which the promise was fulfilled at Pentecost."[2]

The Father's promise through Joel was not simply to pour out His Spirit

It is most important to note that the Father's promise through Joel was a promise that He would do that with the specific result "they shall prophesy."

We must also understand that the speaking in tongues on that day was prophesying. O. Palmer Robertson states, "When the twelve apostles began to speak in languages they had never studied, Peter indicated that they were fulfilling Joel's prophecy. Joel had prepared God's people for that moment by stating that in the last days God would pour out his Spirit on all flesh. He prophesied that sons and daughters would *speak in tongues*.

Is that what Joel said?

No, that is not what Joel said.

What did Joel say? He said that sons and daughters would *prophesy*. Yet Pentecost is clearly characterised as the great day of tongues-speaking.

Has Peter perverted Scripture? Has he twisted Joel's prophecy to make it say what he wanted to hear?

No, he has not. But his application of Joel's prophecy to 'tongues' points to a basic understanding about the nature of tongues. Tongues must be regarded as a subset of prophecy. So Joel's prediction about prophecy in the last days gave some preparation for the phenomenon of tongues. From Peter's application of Joel's words on the day of Pentecost, it becomes clear that tongues are a form of prophecy."[3]

The fulfilment of the promise of the Father on this first occasion consisted in:

- the pouring out of the Spirit upon each, "they were all filled with the Holy Spirit," *and*
- each one prophesying, all "began to speak with other tongues".

Joel's prophecy would not have been fulfilled if there had only been an outpouring of the Spirit and no prophesying

To understand fully the meaning of the promise of the Father through Joel we must be clear that this pouring out of the Spirit was an additional and different experience of the Spirit to the disciple's experience of regeneration which they had received before the day of Pentecost. It was an outpouring causing them to prophesy.

The noise like a rushing mighty wind and the appearance of tongues of fire that separated and rested on each of them were heralds respectively of the pouring out of the Spirit and of the prophesying. They marked the beginning of the new dispensation of the last days. Consequently they were never repeated.

Those Jews who knew the Old Testament scriptures would recall other passages as well as Joel's prophecy when they saw and heard the speaking in tongues: "Then the LORD came down in the cloud, and spoke to him, and took of the Spirit that *was* upon him, and placed *the same* upon the seventy elders; and it happened, when the Spirit rested upon them, that they prophesied, although they never did *so* again. But two men had remained in the camp: the name of one *was* Eldad, and the name of the other Medad. And the Spirit rested upon them. Now they *were* among those listed, but who had not gone out to the tabernacle; yet they prophesied in the camp. And a young man ran and told Moses, and said, 'Eldad and Medad are prophesying in the camp.' So Joshua the son of Nun, Moses' assistant, *one* of his choice men, answered and said, 'Moses my lord, forbid them!' Then Moses said to him, 'Are you zealous for my sake? Oh, that all the Lord's people were prophets *and* that the LORD would put His Spirit upon them!' " (Num. 11:25–29). This desire of Moses was fulfilled on the day of Pentecost, and promised for the future, throughout the last days. Some of the Jews would recognize this as the answer to the prayer of Moses, and be filled with awe at God's wondrous dealings.

They would also remember incidents in the life of Saul the first king of Israel. Samuel said to Saul, "After that you shall come to the hill of God where the Philistine garrison *is*. And it will happen, when you have come there to the city, that you will meet a group of prophets coming down from the high place with a stringed instrument, a tambourine, a flute, and a harp before them; and they will be prophesying. Then the Spirit of the LORD will come upon you, and you will prophesy with them and be turned into another man" (1 Sam. 10:5–6).

"When they came there to the hill, there was a group of prophets to meet him; then the Spirit of God came upon him, and he prophesied among them. And it happened, when all who knew him formerly saw that he indeed prophesied among the prophets, that the people said to one another, 'What *is* this *that* has come upon the son of Kish? *Is* Saul also among the prophets?' Then a man from there answered and said, 'But who *is* their father?' Therefore it became a proverb: '*Is* Saul also among the prophets?' And when he had finished prophesying, he went to the high place" (1 Sam. 10:10–13).

"Then Saul sent messengers to take David. And when they saw the group of prophets prophesying, and Samuel standing *as* leader over them, the Spirit of God came upon the messengers of Saul, and they also prophesied. And when Saul was told, he sent other messengers, and they prophesied likewise. Then Saul sent messengers again the third time, and they prophesied also. Then he also went to Ramah, and came to the great well that *is* at Sechu. So he asked, and said, 'Where *are* Samuel and David?' And *someone* said, 'Indeed *they are* at Naioth in Ramah.' So he went there to Naioth in Ramah. Then the Spirit of God was upon him also, and he went on and prophesied until he came to Naioth in Ramah. And he also stripped off his clothes and prophesied before Samuel in like manner, and lay down naked all that day and all that night. Therefore they say, '*Is* Saul also among the prophets?' " (1 Sam. 19:20–24).

These records would come back to the minds of Jews who knew the scriptures. They would also remember wonderful prophetic promises to pour out the Spirit:

The voice of Wisdom, Jesus Christ "Turn at my rebuke; Surely I will pour out my spirit on you; I will make my words known to you" (Prov. 1:23).

The words of Isaiah the prophet, "Until the Spirit is poured upon us from on high, And the wilderness becomes a fruitful field, And the fruitful field is counted as a forest" (Isa. 32:15), and, "For I will pour water on him who is thirsty, And floods on the dry ground; I will pour My Spirit on your descendants, And My blessing on your off-spring" (Isa. 44:3).

They would think of the prophet Ezekiel, " 'And I will not hide My face from them anymore; for I shall have poured out My Spirit on the house of Israel,' says the Lord GOD" (Ezek. 39:29).

Some would recall the pouring out of the anointing oil symbolising the pouring out of the Spirit: "And you shall anoint Aaron and his sons, and consecrate them, that *they* may minister to Me as priests. And you shall speak to the children of Israel, saying: 'This shall be a holy anointing oil to Me throughout your generations. It shall not be poured on man's flesh; nor shall you make *any other* like it, according to its composition. It *is* holy, *and* it shall be holy to you' " (Exod. 30:30–32). This was the command of God Himself.

All these scriptures would illuminate the meaning and impact of

Peter's declaration that Joel's prophecy had been fulfilled before their eyes and in their ears that day.

To complete our interpretation of Peter's quotation from Joel's prophecy let us look at the remaining verses from Joel: "I will show wonders in heaven above And signs in the earth beneath: Blood and fire and vapor of smoke. The sun shall be turned into darkness, And the moon into blood, Before the coming of the great and awesome day of the LORD" (Acts 2:19–20). In the Old Testament great national disasters are sometimes described in such apocalyptic language which uses symbols to disclose the message. Examples are: "For the stars of heaven and their constellations Will not give their light; The sun will be darkened in its going forth, And the moon will not cause its light to shine" (Isa. 13:10). This was a prophecy foretelling the destruction of Babylon. It was not to be interpreted as literal language. Isaiah also prophesies the sudden doom of Idumea using the same apocalyptic language: "All the host of heaven shall be dissolved, And the heavens shall be rolled up like a scroll; All their host shall fall down As the leaf falls from the vine, And as *fruit* falling from a fig tree. 'For My sword shall be bathed in heaven; Indeed it shall come down on Edom, And on the people of My curse, for judgment' " (Isa. 34:4–5). The prophet Ezekiel employs the same language when he predicts the fall of Egypt: " 'When *I* put out your light, I will cover the heavens, and make its stars dark; I will cover the sun with a cloud, And the moon shall not give her light. All the bright lights of the heavens I will make dark over you, And bring darkness upon your land,' Says the Lord GOD" (Ezek. 32:7–8). Thus the words in verse 19–20 of Acts 2 predict in apocalyptic language the destruction of the Jerusalem which was imminent when Peter spoke. It happened in A.D. 70. The words also foretell that the Jews "will fall by the edge of the sword, and be led away captive into all nations. And Jerusalem will be trampled by Gentiles until the times of the Gentiles are fulfilled" (Luke 21:24). The last part of Acts 2:20 refers to the final judgment day at the return of Christ.

"And it shall come to pass *That* whoever calls on the name of the LORD Shall be saved" (Acts 2:21) was fulfilled on the day of Pentecost. The promise extends throughout the last days. Peter, having quoted from Joel, then states that Jesus of Nazareth Whom they wickedly crucified, has been raised from the dead by God. He is exalted to the Father's right hand, and has received from the Father the promise of the Holy Spirit. Jesus has been made both Lord and Christ by God the Father, and has "poured out this which you now see and hear" (Acts 2:33,36). He has filled the disciples with the Spirit and caused them to speak in tongues. He has baptized them in the Holy Spirit. Some realise the terrible sin they have committed: "Now when they heard *this*, they were cut to the heart, and said to Peter and the rest of the apostles, 'Men *and* brethren, what shall we do?' " (Acts 2:37). Peter responds, "Repent, and let every one of you be baptized in the name of Jesus Christ for the remission of sins; and you shall receive the gift of the Holy Spirit. For the promise is to you and to your children, and to all who are afar off, as many as the Lord our God will call" (Acts 2:38–39). Peter refers here to the promise of Joel: "And it shall come to pass in the last days, says God, That I will pour out of My Spirit on all flesh; Your sons and your daughters shall prophesy, Your young men shall see visions, Your old men shall dream dreams. And on My menservants and on My maidservants I will pour out My Spirit in those days; And they shall prophesy" (Acts 2:17–18). Therefore his words "you shall receive the gift of the Holy Spirit" can only have had one meaning for his hearers: they would have the Spirit poured out upon them and they would prophesy. They would not simply expect the Spirit to be poured upon them. That was only part of the promise. Joel also promised that they would prophesy. In the fulfilment of Joel's prophecy before their eyes that prophesying had taken the form of speaking in tongues not learned by the speaker. Consequently they also would expect to speak in tongues they had not learned. Peter's words also state that the promise of the Spirit is for all who are called into the kingdom throughout the last days (Acts 2:39). Every believer has the promise of the baptism in the Spirit.

Commentators and theologians generally give insufficient attention to the meaning of Peter's words to his hearers. They impose on them a meaning divorced from Peter's reference to Joel and divorced from the Jew's knowledge of the Old Testament. They choose rather to misinterpret them according to their own predetermined traditional theology of the Spirit. Consequently they place their own meaning on Peter's utterance.

Conclusion

The baptism in the Spirit is the promise of the Father, the fulfilment of Joel's prophecy (Joel 2:28–29), an experience of being filled with the Spirit with the result that one prophesies. It is given to those who are regenerated by the Spirit. It is an enduement of power for witness to Christ. It is ministered by the exalted Lord Jesus Christ, and is for everyone who obeys the gospel during the last days, which span from the Pentecost of Acts 2 until Christ's return. *This definition is formulated from the words of Jesus Christ and the apostle Peter.*

References

1. M.R. Vincent *Word Studies in the New Testament*, Vol.1 Hendrickson Second Edition 1888, page 449.
2. J.A. Alexander *A commentary on the Acts of the Apostles*, Banner of Truth 1963, page 64.
3. O. Palmer Robertson *The Final Word*, Banner of Truth 1993, pages 42–43.

CHAPTER TWENTY SEVEN

THE BAPTISM IN THE SPIRIT DURING THE LAST DAYS: THE ONGOING FULFILMENT OF JOEL'S PROPHECY

We have shown that the baptism in the Spirit is the fulfilment of the promise of the Father through Joel, and that it is for every believer down through the centuries of the last days until the return of Jesus Christ. Consequently as the gospel spreads out from Jerusalem we find further records of baptisms in the Spirit, further fufilments of the Father's promise. These records flesh out the meaning of Peter's statements in Acts 2:38–39.

Let us look more closely at the fulfilments of the promise. Each one will provide further revelation concerning receiving the promise of the Father.

Acts 8:5–24 The Samaritan converts

"Then Philip went down to the city of Samaria and preached Christ to them. And the multitudes with one accord heeded the things spoken by Philip, hearing and seeing the miracles which he did. For unclean spirits, crying with a loud voice, came out of many who were possessed; and many who were paralyzed and lame were healed. And there was great joy in that city. But there was a certain man called Simon, who previously practiced sorcery in the city and astonished the people of Samaria, claiming that he was someone great, to whom they all gave heed, from the least to the greatest, saying, 'This man is the great power of God.' And they heeded him because he had astonished them with his sorceries for a long time. But when they believed Philip as he preached the things concerning the kingdom of God and the name of Jesus Christ, both men and women were baptized. Then Simon himself also believed; and when he was baptized he continued with Philip, and was amazed, seeing the miracles and signs which were done. Now when the apostles who were at Jerusalem heard that Samaria had received the word of God, they sent Peter and John to them, who, when they had come down, prayed for them that they might receive the Holy Spirit. For as yet He had fallen upon none of them. They had only been baptized in the name

THE PROMISE FULFILLED

"I will pour out My Spirit . . ."	And they shall prophesy."
Acts 2:4 "They were all filled with the Holy Spirit"	**Acts 2:4** "and began to speak with other tongues as the Spirit gave them utterance."
Acts 8:17 "they received the Holy Spirit"	**Acts 8:18** "Simon saw that . . . the Holy Spirit was given"
Acts 9:17 "And Ananias went his way and entered the house; and laying his hands on him he said, 'Brother Saul, the Lord Jesus, who appeared to you on the road as you came, has sent me that you may receive your sight and be filled with the Holy Spirit.'"	**1 Cor. 14:18** "I thank my God I speak with tongues more you all": Paul.
Acts 10:44 "While Peter was still speaking these words, the Holy Spirit fell upon all those who heard the word."	**Acts 10:45–46** "And those of the circumcision who believed were astonished, as many as came with Peter, because the gift of the Holy Spirit had been poured out on the Gentiles also. For they heard them speak with tongues and magnify God."
Acts 19:6 "the Holy Spirit came upon them"	**Acts 19:6** "and they spoke with tongues and prophesied"

of the Lord Jesus. Then they laid hands on them, and they received the Holy Spirit. And when Simon saw that through the laying on of the apostles' hands the Holy Spirit was given, he offered them money, saying, 'Give me this power also, that anyone on whom I lay hands may receive the Holy Spirit.' But Peter said to him, 'Your money perish with you, because you thought that the gift of God could be purchased with money! You have neither part nor portion in this matter, for your heart is not right in the sight of God. Repent therefore of this your wickedness, and pray God if perhaps the thought of your heart may be forgiven you. For I see that you are poisoned by bitterness and bound by iniquity.' Then Simon answered and said, 'Pray to the Lord for me, that none of the things which you have spoken may come upon me.' "

Verse 12 tells us that the Samaritans believed the gospel and were baptized in water. They became Christians. They received salvation.

Verse 14. Peter and John were sent to shepherd the new converts. Philip had the ministry of an evangelist, the enduement and gifts to lead men and women to receive Christ. His work was limited to bringing them to true faith and then baptizing them in water. He did not lead them into the experience of the promise of the Father. After his ministry these Samaritan believers needed pastoral and teaching ministry. All members of the kingdom of God need to be shepherded by those appointed by the Holy Spirit (Acts 20:28).

Verses 15–16. Peter and John discover something on their arrival and take immediate action (v.17).

How did the apostles know that the Spirit had fallen upon none of them?

Answer – Joel's prophecy told them that when He fell upon believers they prophesied. Not one of them had prophesied so therefore none had received the Holy Spirit. If believers received the Spirit at the same time as coming to faith in Christ and without any prophesying then these Samaritans would have been considered by the apostles to have already received the Spirit. The evidence is strong that they were genuine converts. Philip would not have baptized them unless they had repented and believed. Also if they had not been truly saved Peter and John would have dealt with them very differently. They would have ministered to them as those who needed true conversion. The apostles knew that they were saved but also that the Spirit had not yet fallen upon them.

What did Simon see, for which he was willing to pay money, and which he would have used to impress others, vs. 19 and 9–11?

Answer – he saw prophesying. This answer meets all the requirements of the record. No other suggested answers do so. *To any honest reader it is indisputable that there must have been some clear visible sign of the receiving/falling upon of the Holy Spirit in the lives of converts up to that point in time.*

We have Luke's account of the increase of the numbers of believers before the Samaritans were converted.

Acts 2:41 – 3000.
Acts 2:47 – "the Lord added daily those who were being saved."
Acts 4:4 – about 5000 men in total.
Acts 5:14 – "believers were increasingly added to the Lord, multitudes."
Acts 6:7 – "the number of the disciples multiplied greatly in Jerusalem."

From Acts 2:38–39 and 8:15–17 we can deduce that a standard pattern of Christian experience of the Spirit had come into being since the events of Acts 2. Converts experienced a pouring out of the Spirit upon them and they prophesied. *No prophesying meant no experience of the receiving of the Spirit.* If this pattern is denied how did the apostles know that not a single one of them had received the Holy Spirit? If, in some cases, there was a baptism of the Spirit simultaneous with conversion and with no prophesying then the apostles would not have known that the Spirit had not fallen on any of them. He may have done so at their conversion.

We see in this record of a fulfilment of the promise of the Father further revelation concerning the receiving of the promise by converts

1. the promise did not occur in their lives when they exercised true faith in Christ.
2. nor did it happen when they were baptized in water.
3. it required prayer and the laying on of hands to receive the Spirit.
4. the implication is clear. If they had not had ministry concerning the promise of the Father they would have remained without the experience of the promise of the Father. The promise of the Father in this instance was not fulfilled without ministry to the Samaritans and their willingness to receive that ministry.
5. there was a definite time lapse between their regeneration and their baptism in the Spirit.
6. the receiving of the promise was described as a falling upon them of the Spirit and as receiving the Spirit.

Acts 9:1–18 Saul

"Then Saul, still breathing threats and murder against the disciples of the Lord, went to the high priest and asked letters from him to the synagogues of Damascus, so that if he found any who were of the Way, whether men or women, he might bring them bound to Jerusalem. As he journeyed he came near Damascus, and suddenly a light shone around him from heaven. Then he fell to the ground, and heard a voice saying to him, 'Saul, Saul, why are you persecuting Me?' And he said, 'Who are You, Lord?' Then the Lord said, 'I am Jesus, whom you are persecuting. It *is* hard for you to kick against the goads.' So he, trembling and astonished, said, 'Lord, what do You want me to do?' Then the Lord *said* to him, 'Arise and go into the city, and you will be told what you must do.' And the men who journeyed with him stood speechless, hearing a voice but seeing no one. Then Saul arose from the ground, and when his eyes were opened he saw no one. But they led him by the hand and brought *him* into Damascus. And he was three days without sight, and neither ate nor drank. Now there was a certain disciple at Damascus named Ananias; and to him the Lord said in a vision, 'Ananias.' And he said, 'Here I am, Lord.' So the Lord *said* to him, 'Arise and go to the street called Straight, and inquire at the house of Judas for *one* called Saul of Tarsus, for behold, he is praying. And in a vision he has seen a man named Ananias coming in and putting *his* hand on him, so that he might receive his sight.' Then Ananias answered, 'Lord, I have heard from many about this man, how much harm he has done to Your saints in Jerusalem. And here he has authority from the chief priests to bind all who call on Your name.' But the Lord said to him, 'Go, for he is a chosen vessel of Mine to bear My name before Gentiles, kings, and the children of Israel. For I will show him how many things he must suffer for My name's sake.' And Ananias went his way and entered the house; and laying his hands on him he said, 'Brother Saul, the Lord Jesus, who appeared to you on the road as you came, has sent me that you may receive your sight and be filled with the Holy Spirit.' Immediately there fell from his eyes *something* like scales, and he received his sight at once; and he arose and was baptized."

Verses 6, 11 and 17 speak of Saul as truly born again. Ananias would not have addressed Saul as brother unless he had been born again into the family of God.

Verse 17. Three days later after conversion he was filled with the Spirit, verse 9. It is not recorded that he prophesied. 1 Cor. 14:18 proves that Paul certainly did speak in tongues and was thankful to God for being able so to do.

Further revelation concerning the receiving of the promise of the Father

1. Saul did not receive the promise when he believed in Christ.
2. There was a time lapse of three days between coming to faith in Christ and the receiving of the promise (Acts 9:9).
3. The record indicates that he received the promise through the ministry of Ananias who laid hands upon him.
4. Ananias was not an apostle, simply a devout man (Acts 22:12). The laying on of apostolic hands was not required for the fulfilment of the promise.
5. The Lord Himself sent Ananias to minister the promise to Saul (Acts 9:17).
6. Saul was baptized in water after receiving the promise.
7. The receiving of the promise was described as a filling with the Spirit.

Acts 10:1–48 Cornelius and his household

"There was a certain man in Caesarea called Cornelius, a centurion of what was called the Italian Regiment, a devout *man* and one who feared God with all his household, who gave alms generously to the people, and prayed to God always. About the ninth hour of the day he saw clearly in a vision an angel of God coming in and saying to him, 'Cornelius!' And when he observed him, he was afraid, and said, 'What is it, lord?' So he said to him, 'Your prayers and your alms have come up for a memorial before God. Now send men to Joppa, and send for Simon whose surname is Peter. He is lodging with Simon, a tanner, whose house is by the sea. He will tell you what you must do.' And when the angel who spoke to him had departed, Cornelius called two of his household servants and a devout soldier from among those who waited on him continually. So when he had explained all *these* things to them, he sent them to Joppa. The next day, as they went on their journey and drew near the city, Peter went up on the housetop to pray, about the sixth hour. Then he became very hungry and wanted to eat; but while they made ready, he fell into a trance and saw heaven opened and an object like a great sheet bound at the four corners, descending to him and let down to the earth. In it were all kinds of four-footed animals of the earth, wild beasts, creeping things, and birds of the air. And a voice came to him, 'Rise, Peter; kill and eat.' But Peter said, 'Not so, Lord! For I have never eaten anything common or unclean.' And a voice *spoke* to him again the second time, 'What God has cleansed you must not call common.' This was done three times. And the object was taken up into heaven again. Now while Peter wondered within himself what this vision which he had seen meant, behold, the men who had been sent from Cornelius had made inquiry for Simon's house, and stood before the gate. And they called and asked whether Simon, whose surname was Peter, was lodging there. While Peter thought about the vision, the Spirit said to him, 'Behold, three men are seeking you. Arise therefore, go down and go with them, doubting nothing; for I have sent them.' Then Peter went down to the men who had been sent to him from Cornelius, and said, 'Yes, I am he whom you seek. For what reason have you come?' And they said, 'Cornelius *the* centurion, a just man, one who fears God and has a good reputation among all the nation of the Jews, was divinely instructed by a holy angel to summon you to his house, and to hear words from you.' Then he invited them in and lodged *them*. On the next day Peter went away with them, and some brethren from Joppa accompanied him. And the following day they entered Caesarea. Now Cornelius was waiting for them, and had called together his relatives and close friends. As Peter was coming in, Cornelius met him and fell down at his feet and worshiped *him*. But Peter lifted him up, saying, 'Stand up; I myself am also a man.' And as he talked with him, he went in and found many who had come together. Then he said to them, 'You know how unlawful it is for a Jewish man to keep company with or go to one of another nation. But God has shown me that I should not call any man common or unclean. Therefore I came without objection as soon as I was sent for. I ask, then, for what reason have you sent for me?' So Cornelius said, 'Four days ago I was fasting until this hour; and at the ninth hour I prayed in my house, and behold, a man stood before me in bright clothing, and said, "Cornelius, your prayer has been heard, and your alms are remembered in the sight of God. Send therefore to Joppa and call Simon here, whose surname is Peter. He is lodging in the house of Simon, a tanner, by the sea. When he comes, he will speak to you." So I sent to you immediately, and you have done well to come. Now therefore, we are all present before God, to hear all the things commanded you by God.' Then Peter opened *his* mouth and said: 'In truth I perceive that God shows no partiality. But in every nation whoever fears Him and works righteousness is accepted by Him. The word which *God* sent to the children of Israel, preaching peace through Jesus Christ – He is Lord of all – that word you know, which was proclaimed throughout all Judea, and began from Galilee after the baptism which John preached: how God anointed Jesus of Nazareth with the Holy Spirit and with power, who went about doing good and healing all who were oppressed by the devil, for God was with Him. And we are witnesses of all things which He did both in the land of the Jews and in Jerusalem, whom they killed by hanging on a tree. Him God raised up on the third day, and showed Him openly, not to all the people, but to witnesses chosen before by God, *even* to us who ate and drank with Him after He arose from the dead. And He commanded us to preach to the people, and to testify that it is He who was ordained by God *to be* Judge of the living and the dead. To Him all the prophets witness that, through His name, whoever believes in Him will receive remission of sins.' While Peter was still speaking these words, the Holy Spirit fell upon all those who heard the word. And those of the circumcision who believed were astonished, as many as came with Peter, because the gift of the Holy Spirit had been poured out on the Gentiles also. For they heard them speak with tongues and magnify God. Then Peter answered, 'Can anyone forbid water, that these should not be baptized who have received the Holy Spirit just as we *have*?' And he commanded them to be baptized in the name of the Lord. Then they asked him to stay a few days."

It will help us to compare this record with Acts 11:1–18, especially verses 15–17:

"Now the apostles and brethren who were in Judea heard that the Gentiles had also received the word of God. And when Peter came up to Jerusalem, those of the circumcision contended with him, saying, 'You went in to uncircumcised men and ate with them!' But Peter explained *it* to them in order from the beginning, saying: 'I was in the city of Joppa praying; and in a trance I saw a vision, an object descending like a great sheet, let down from heaven by four corners; and it came to me. When I observed it intently and considered, I saw four-footed animals of the earth, wild beasts, creeping things, and birds of the air. And I heard a voice saying to me, "Rise, Peter; kill and eat." But I said, "Not so, Lord! For nothing common or unclean has at any time entered my mouth." But the voice answered me again from heaven, "What God has cleansed you must not call common." Now this was done three times, and all were drawn up again into heaven. At that very moment, three men stood before the house where I was, having been sent to me from Caesarea. Then the Spirit told me to go with them, doubting nothing. Moreover these six brethren accompanied me, and we entered the man's house. And he told us how he had seen an angel standing in his house, who said to him, "Send men to Joppa, and call for Simon whose surname is Peter, who will tell you words by which you and all your household will be saved." And as I began to speak, the Holy Spirit fell upon them, as upon us at the beginning. Then I remembered the word of the Lord, how He said, "John indeed baptized in water, but you will be baptized in the Holy Spirit." If therefore God gave them the same gift as *He gave* us when we believed on the Lord Jesus Christ, who was I that I could withstand God?' When they heard these things they became silent; and they glorified God, saying, 'Then God has also granted to the Gentiles repentance to life' " (my trans. of v.16).

Cornelius and those gathered in his household were not typical Gentiles (verses 1–2, 3–4, 7–8, 22, 30–33, 35, and 37). Cornelius and those gathered with him already had a relationship with the God of Israel as the Old Testament saints did. In addition they had some knowledge of Jesus.

In Acts 11:17 referring back to this event the text reads literally, "If then God gave the same gift to them as he gave to us having believed in the Lord Jesus Christ." The Greek word translated "having believed" is an aorist participle which indicates here a completed action in the past. The NASB translates the verse, "Therefore if God gave to them the same gift as *He gave* to us also after believing in the Lord Jesus Christ, who was I that I could stand in God's way?" Their believing took place before receiving the gift of the Spirit. The latter followed immediately after their coming to faith in Christ.

It is stated that they received precisely the *same* experience of the Holy Spirit as Peter and the other Jews at the beginning. That was not an experience of regeneration, but of the pouring out of the Spirit and prophesying after having come to faith in Christ.

Peter is reminded of the outpouring of the Spirit on the day of Pentecost because on both occasions the promise of the Father was fulfilled by God taking action unilaterally. No one prayed or laid hands on the recipients. Also on both occasions He poured out His Spirit at one moment of time on a group of believers. All the other recorded fulfilments of the promise of the Father up to that time were experienced through the laying on of hands on each individual believer (Acts 8:15–17 and 9:17). The Samaritans and other converts would have received the Holy Spirit individually at different moments of time. Consequently Peter's mind goes all the way back to the Pentecost of Acts 2 and Christ's prediction of it (Acts 1:5).

They also received the *same* experience of the Spirit as the apostles, and elders of the church at Jerusalem (Acts 15:4–12): "And when they had come to Jerusalem, they were received by the church and the apostles and the elders; and they reported all things that God had done with them. But some of the sect of the Pharisees who believed rose up, saying, 'It is necessary to circumcise them, and to command *them* to keep the law of Moses.' Now the apostles and elders came together to consider this matter. And when there had been much dispute, Peter rose up and said to them: 'Men and brethren, you know that a good while ago God chose among us, that by my mouth the Gentiles should hear the word of the gospel and believe. So God, who knows the heart, acknowledged them by giving them the Holy Spirit, just as *He did* to us, and made no distinction between us and them, purifying their hearts by faith. Now therefore, why do you test God by putting a yoke on the neck of the disciples which neither our fathers nor we were able to bear? But we believe that through the grace of the Lord Jesus Christ we shall be saved in the same manner as they.' Then all the multitude kept silent and listened to Barnabas and Paul declaring how many miracles and wonders God had worked through them among the Gentiles."

Notice that the "us" of verse 8 is composed of the apostles *and* elders at Jerusalem (verse 4). At least some of those elders would not have received the first outpouring of the Spirit recorded in Acts 2:4. They must have received the Holy Spirit at some later time(s). If Paul was only referring to the apostles and disciples recorded in Acts 2:1–4 he would have had to say "just as He did to *some* of us." This is further proof that the converts on the day of Pentecost (Acts 2) and converts afterwards who joined the Jerusalem church all received the same experience of the baptism in the Spirit. The Spirit was poured upon them and they prophesied.

What happened to Cornelius and those with him was a further fulfilment of the promise of the Father. The Spirit was poured out upon them and they prophesied. The proof that the Spirit had been poured out upon them was the inspired utterance (Acts 10:46). This tongue speaking was sufficient to fully convince "those of the circumcision" (Acts 10:44–47). They were "astonished" (verse 45), but it was proof to them that the Spirit had been poured out, even on the Gentiles. It was conclusive evidence that God had accepted the Gentiles. He had justified their hearts by faith and poured out His Spirit upon them. No one should prevent them from being baptized in water. The changed attitudes of these prejudiced Jews (Acts 10:23 and 11:12), is explained by the following facts. They knew that normal Christian experience up to that time was to prophesy when receiving the Holy Spirit. Thus speaking in tongues and magnifying God was for them the result of the pouring out of the Spirit. They recognised that Joel's prophecy (Acts 2:17–18) had been fulfilled before their eyes. They knew that that promise is only for believers, therefore these Gentiles must have been granted repentance unto life. Their hearts must have been cleansed by faith.

Further revelation concerning the receiving of the promise of the Father

1. These Gentiles were already in fellowship with God before Peter addressed them.
2. They had put their faith in God, but the revelation they had of Him was limited to that given before the coming of Christ. Now they embraced the message that the Messiah had come and brought salvation. They received the Christ immediately they heard Peter's words, and God poured out His Spirit upon them. Their faith in Christ was followed instantly with the experience of the promise of the Father.
3. In this instance God did not use any person(s) to pray for them or to lay hands on them to receive the promise. By giving them the promise of the Father God purposed to make it absolutely clear that He had granted salvation to the Gentiles, and that He made no distinction between Jews and Gentiles (Acts 11:17–18 and 15:8–9). The extremely strong prejudice of the Jews about Gentiles was overcome by this Divine action. God had poured out His Spirit on them. Therefore He had accepted them. Consequently the Jewish believers must accept them (Acts 10:47–48).
4. They were baptized in water after receiving the promise.
5. They received the same experience of the Spirit as on the day of Pentecost in Acts 2, but this time no one recognised any of the languages being spoken. There was not a gathering of the Jews of the Dispersion as on the previous occasion.
6. They spoke in tongues and magnified God. This was the form the prophesying took on this occasion. "Magnified God" is parallel to "they spoke in tongues." Both verbs describe the same activity. The meaning of "magnified God" is revealed by the statement that on the day of Pentecost the speaking in tongues was declaring the wonderful works of God (Acts 2:11).
7. The receiving of the promise is described as "the Holy Spirit fell."

Acts 19:1–6 Disciples at Ephesus

"And it happened, while Apollos was at Corinth, that Paul, having passed through the upper regions, came to Ephesus. And finding some disciples he said to them, 'Did you receive the Holy Spirit when you believed?' So they said to him, 'We have not so much as heard whether there is a Holy Spirit.' And he said to them, 'Into what then were you baptized?' So they said, 'Into John's baptism.' Then Paul said, 'John indeed baptized with a baptism of repentance, saying to the people that they should believe on Him who would come after him, that is, on Christ Jesus.' When they heard *this*, they were baptized in the name of the Lord Jesus. And when Paul had laid hands on them, the Holy Spirit came upon them, and they spoke with tongues and prophesied' (Acts 19:1–6).

Verse 2: Something caused Paul to ask this question, "Did you receive the Holy Spirit when you believed?" There are two explanations. There is a certain lack of the Presence of the Spirit when believers meet together without having been baptized in the Spirit. There is a real difference between the worship and fellowship of a group of believers filled with the Spirit and the worship and fellowship of a group of believers not baptized in the Spirit. In the latter there is also an absence of the manifestation of the Presence of the Spirit through the operation of spiritual gifts (1 Cor. 12:7). There are no gifts of tongues, the interpretation of tongues and prophecy (1 Cor. 14).

The aorist participle translated "when you believed" can also be translated "since you believed" (AV). Both translations are possible grammatically. Since the receiving of the Spirit should closely follow conversion in the Divine intention the first translation is to be preferred. Whatever translation is chosen this question establishes that it is possible to believe unto salvation and not receive the Spirit. If every believer receives the Spirit at conversion Paul would not have asked the question. *It is clear that Paul believed it possible to be a true believer and not have received the Holy Spirit. His doctrine is revealed here just as much as in the epistles.*

Verse 3. Paul takes it for granted that as disciples they have been baptized. He also expected them to have heard of the Holy Spirit when they were baptized in the name of the Father, the Son and the Holy Spirit.

In verse 5 It becomes apparent that they were disciples whose knowledge was limited to the revelation of God up to the time of John the Baptist's ministry. They had embraced the truth they knew, but they had not come under Christ's ministry nor heard the gospel. Paul tells them of Christ, Whom John had told them to believe in, and with that new knowledge of Jesus they were baptized in His name. There is no question that they were now true believers.

Verse 6: With reference to the question in verse 2, "Did you receive the Holy Spirit when you believed?" we have Paul ministering the Holy Spirit when they did come to faith in Christ. This event was after their water baptism, and even though it followed immediately, it was a separate experience from their coming to faith in Christ. Paul did not conclude that now they had believed in Christ they had therefore received the Spirit. He took the further action of laying his hands upon them for a fulfilment of the promise of the Father. By this time Paul had written his epistles to the Galatians and two letters to the Thessalonians. There was no contradiction between his doctrinal teaching and his practice as a missionary. His actions were in accord with his doctrine, and his doctrine in accord with his actions. His actions reveal his doctrine.

Further revelation concerning the receiving of the promise of the Father

1. the receiving of the promise followed true faith in Christ and water baptism.
2. they received when Paul laid his hands upon them.
3. the pouring out is recorded as "the Holy Spirit came upon them."
4. "they spoke with tongues and prophesied." The latter verb is parallel to "they spoke in tongues" and describes that action.

These accounts in the Acts of the Apostles are the evidence of the ongoing fulfilment of Acts 2:17–18. They are also intended by the Holy Spirit to reveal the manner in which God chooses to fulfil the promise of the Father to converts. They are therefore of the greatest importance in formulating doctrine concerning the promise of the Father, the baptism in the Spirit. These narratives are the record of God's action in pouring out His Spirit. His actions were in accordance with the truth He revealed to those who wrote the New Testament.

When we come to the epistles in the New Testament we find that the recipients of the letters are addressed as those who have been baptized in the Spirit at the start of their Christian life. The following scriptures refer back to the event:

"Now hope does not disappoint, because the love of God has been poured out in our hearts by the Holy Spirit who was given to us" (Rom. 5:5).

"For you did not receive the spirit of bondage again to fear, but you received the Spirit of adoption by whom we cry out, 'Abba, Father.' The Spirit Himself bears witness with our spirit that we are children of God" (Rom. 8:15–16).

"Now we have received, not the spirit of the world, but the Spirit who is from God, that we might know the things that have been freely given to us by God" (1 Cor. 2:12).

"For in one Spirit we were all baptized for one body – whether Jews or Greeks, whether slaves or free – and have all been made to drink of one Spirit" (1 Cor. 12:13, my trans.).

"Now He who establishes us with you in Christ and has anointed us *is* God, who also has sealed us and given us the Spirit in our hearts as a guarantee" (2 Cor. 1:21–22).

"This only I want to learn from you: Did you receive the Spirit by the works of the law, or by the hearing of faith?" (Gal. 3:2).

"In Him you also *trusted*, after you heard the word of truth, the gospel of your salvation; in whom also, having believed, you were sealed with the Holy Spirit of promise" (Eph. 1:13).

"Therefore I remind you to stir up the gift of God which is in you through the laying on of my hands. For God has not given us a Spirit of fear, but of power and of love and of self-control" (2 Tim. 1:6–7, my trans. of v.7).

"But when the kindness and the love of God our Savior toward man appeared, not by works of righteousness which we have done, but according to His mercy He saved us, through the washing of regeneration and renewing of the Holy Spirit, whom He poured out on us abundantly through Jesus Christ our Savior" (Tit. 3:4–6).

"For *it is* impossible for those who were once enlightened, and have tasted the heavenly gift, and have become partakers of the Holy Spirit" (Heb. 6:4).

"But the anointing which you have received from Him abides in you, and you do not need that anyone teach you; but as the same anointing teaches you concerning all things, and is true, and is not a lie, and just as it has taught you, you will abide in Him" (1 John 2:27).

All these verses remind the readers of their baptism in the Spirit. We have seen that in exactly the same way readers were reminded of their baptism in water. Both took place at the beginning of the Christian life. Consequently there is an absence of any instruction in the epistles to be baptized in water or to be baptized in the Spirit.

In the light of these receptions of the promise of the Father and New Testament statements we can define the baptism in the Spirit more fully

It is the promise of the Father, the fulfilment of Joel's prophecy (Joel 2:28–29), an experience of being filled with the Spirit with the result that one prophesies. In all cases where that prophesying occurs and is recorded it takes the form of speaking in tongues. It is given to those who are regenerated by the Spirit. It is ministered by the exalted Lord Jesus Christ, and is for everyone who obeys the gospel in the last days, which span from the Pentecost of Acts 2 until Christ's return. It is an enduement of power from on high in order to function in the body of Christ for the body of Christ, a sealing of the Spirit giving assurance of being a child of God, a foretaste and assurance of the heavenly inheritance that God has prepared for the Christian, and an abiding experience that teaches the believer.

It is described in various terms in the scriptures:

> being filled with the Spirit and speaking in other tongues
> a pouring out of the Spirit resulting in prophesying
> the promise of the Father
> the gift of the Holy Spirit
> the falling upon of the Spirit
> the receiving of the Spirit
> the coming upon of the Holy Spirit
> being made to drink the Spirit
> the anointing of the Spirit
> the sealing of the Spirit.

It is promised to every believer and normally received through the ministry of another believer or believers with the laying on of hands.

Conclusions

- This survey of the New Testament records after Acts 2 demonstrates that the interpretation of Peter's words in Acts 2:16–18 and 38–39 explains fully the experiences of the Spirit recorded in Acts 8:15–17, 9:17, 10:44–46 and 19:6.
- These passages enable us to define the baptism in the Spirit.
- The baptism in the Spirit is distinct from, and follows the new birth. We shall deal with this matter in the next chapter.

CHAPTER TWENTY EIGHT

THE BAPTISM IN THE SPIRIT AND CONVERSION

Many interpreters try to show that the baptism in the Spirit always occurs at conversion. They oppose the truth of the baptism in the Spirit as previously stated.

The chief argument employed is the mistranslation and misinterpretation of 1 Cor. 12:13.

They accept the translation of the verse: "For by one Spirit we were all baptized into one body." *or* "For in the one Spirit we were all baptized into one body" NRSV.

It has been reasoned previously in chapter seven concerning water baptism that the correct translation is, "For in one Spirit we were all baptized for one body." The mistranslation "into one body" links Spirit baptism with entry into the body of Christ, the church, which takes place at conversion. It leaves no place for a subsequent Spirit baptism after regeneration. The correct translation means that the baptism in the Spirit is for the benefit of the body. It does not state that it occurs at conversion. For the Corinthians and New Testament Christians it happened like water baptism following conversion. Sometimes it occurred immediately after conversion (Acts 10:44 and 19:5–6), sometimes with some considerable time lapse (Acts 8:15–17). 1 Cor. 12:13 cannot be used as conclusive proof that the baptism in the Spirit occurs at conversion.

The records in Acts 2, 8, 9, 10 and 19

All of these chapters reveal a two stage experience of regeneration followed by baptism in the Spirit. The usual way of overthrowing this pattern as being of any relevance to Christians today is twofold. Firstly Peter's words in Acts 2:16–18 and 38–39 are misinterpreted. Secondly they are not applied to explain these events. We shall examine the other explanations put forward.

It is pointed out that the disciples, who numbered around 120 (Acts 1:15), lived before and after the giving of the Spirit. This fact is used to account for their two stage experience of regeneration and subsequent baptism in the Spirit. It is acknowledged that they were truly born again before being filled with the Spirit. They had to wait for the giving of the Spirit. But now that the Spirit has been given it is asserted that the baptism in the Spirit occurs at conversion, and therefore the experience of the 120 is not a pattern for today. Jesus said that the Spirit would not be given until He was glorified: "On the last day, that great *day* of the feast, Jesus stood and cried out, saying, 'If anyone thirsts, let him come to Me and drink. He who believes in Me, as the Scripture has said, out of his heart will flow rivers of living water.' But this He spoke concerning the Spirit, whom those believing in Him would receive; for the Holy Spirit was not yet *given*, because Jesus was not yet glorified" (John 7:37–39). Peter links the giving of the Spirit on the day of Pentecost directly to the glorification of Jesus Christ. He said, "This Jesus God has raised up, of which we are all witnesses. Therefore being exalted to the right hand of God, and having received from the Father the promise of the Holy Spirit, He poured out this which you now see and hear" (Acts 2:32–33).

Before the exaltation of Christ the Spirit was not given *as He was on that day of Pentecost*. This argument based on the timing of the giving of the Spirit fails to take account of Peter's definition of that giving of the Spirit in Acts 2:16–18. He says that it was the fulfilment of God's promise to pour out His Spirit on all of His people causing them to prophesy. Before that time God did pour out His Spirit on a *few* selected individuals from among all who were His people. The giving of the Spirit meant that God would now pour out His Spirit on *all* of His people. That was the difference.

Peter defines the baptism in the Spirit as a great and glorious blessing given to those who are already His people, those who are already regenerate. It was not an operation of God to make them His people, to regenerate them. It was distinct from regeneration and additional to regeneration. To receive that blessing believers no longer have to wait as the 120 did. But when it is received it is still distinct from regeneration and subsequent to it.

If the baptism in the Spirit occurs at conversion since Jesus was glorified then the records in Acts 8:15–17, 9:1–17, 19:1–6 should read differently! That doctrine leaves no room for the definite two stage experience of conversion and subsequent experience of the Spirit stated in those accounts. Consequently we shall see that interpreters holding the view that the baptism in the Spirit occurs at conversion find various ways of negating those accounts as evidence of a two stage experience. We shall look at their interpretations below.

R.G. Gromacki, *The Modern Tongues Movement*

Acts 2:1–13; 8:5–25; 10:44–48 and 19:1–7

Referring to the verses above he says, "These four accounts served to introduce the Holy Spirit to four different classes of people. They were unique. They were never intended to become a permanent pattern for an experience to be sought by Christians. This is demonstrated by the facts that no two of these four accounts are completely identical and that the Book of Acts is basically transitional in character."[1] He admits that in Acts 2, 8 and 19 the Spirit was received after salvation,[2] but he asserts, "As Laurin wrote 'We must not make the tragic spiritual mistake of "teaching the experience of the apostles but rather experience the teaching of the apostles."' The experience of the apostles is found in transitional Acts, whereas the teaching of the apostles is clearly set forth in the epistles. . . . There is no lapse of time between conversion and the reception of the Spirit. . . . Since God was introducing a new dispensation, He did things in the early life of the church which were not necessary for the later stages of the Apostolic era or permanent church life. These unusual receptions of the Holy Spirit attended by various phenomena, including speaking in tongues, fall into this category."[3] He writes, "These four unusual receptions of the Holy Spirit, evidenced by speaking in tongues in at least three cases, occurred when the gospel and the Holy Spirit were being introduced to four different classes of people who were in existence after Christ's ascension: Jews, both Christian and unsaved; Samaritans; Gentiles; and the disciples of John the Baptist. When the gospel was given later to members of these four groups, there is no record that the Holy Spirit was received in an unusual way attended by speaking in tongues. Thus these experiences were introductory and temporary in character, not permanent."[4] In this way he is able to assert "When a person *believes* in Christ *for salvation*, at that moment he is baptized in the Holy Spirit."[5]

Answers

1. In spite of his argument that we must base doctrine on the apostolic teaching rather than the experiences of Acts he ignores completely that the apostle Peter says that the promise of the Father, first fulfilled as recorded in Acts 2, is for every believer throughout the last days (Acts 2:16–18 and 38–39). In Acts 2, 8, 10 and 19 we have instances of believers receiving the promise in the last days. That promise was, and is, for "as many as the Lord our God shall call" throughout the last days. In that sense it is absolutely wrong to say

that these events in Acts are unique and not a pattern for all other believers living in the last days. In effect he is contradicting Peter and saying the promise of the Father is not for all believers since the Pentecost of Acts 2. He is saying that the promise of the Father was only for a few special cases at the beginning.

2. Each instance of the promise being fulfilled is different, but an experience of the pouring out of the Spirit, and subsequent prophesying is constant in them all.

3. Because the promise of the Father applies during the totality of the last days we may conclude that converts during New Testament days experienced its fulfilment in their lives. There is nothing in the New Testament which does not harmonise with that stance. Indeed there is no record anywhere in the New Testament of any believer receiving the Spirit without the manifestation of prophesy (we shall see that Paul's question "Do all speak with tongues?" relates to the gift of tongues for use in the church not the tongue speaking which is part of the baptism in the Spirit). Moreover there is no instance in the New Testament where the Spirit is received at the point in time of coming to faith in Christ. It always follows. As we have seen it followed immediately in the case of Cornelius and those with him. It followed water baptism in Acts 19:5–6 very quickly. The promise of the Father is for every convert as soon they have received Christ, but not until they have been born again.

4. He is also incorrect to argue that these happenings were determined by the alleged transitional order recorded in the Book of Acts. The outpourings of the Spirit and speaking in tongues took place simply because the last days began ten days after the ascension of Jesus. The Father has promised to pour out His Spirit on everyone He calls into His kingdom in the last days. The whole of the period of Acts until the return of Christ is called the last days, the final era of God's dealings with mankind before Eternal Judgment. Believers now are living under precisely the same dispensation as the Christians of the time of the Acts of the Apostles. They partake of the same New Covenant and have the same promise of the Father recorded by Joel.

5. If all these events were unique in the way he states them to be then we have no record in the New Testament of a baptism in the Spirit in the case of a "normal" conversion.

Acts 19

He writes, "This phenomenon authenticated the messenger (Paul) and the message to these disciples. It was an objective evidence that the Holy Spirit had indeed been given as Paul had said. Since there are no Old Testament saints living today, this experience cannot be repeated."[6]

Answer

Their experience was the fulfilment of the promise of the Father proclaimed and predicted by Joel. That promise of the Father is to as many as the Lord our God shall call. It was for those twelve once they came to faith in Christ. The twelve were no longer Old Testament saints when Paul baptized them in water. They were New Testament saints.

A.A. Hoekema, *What About Tongue Speaking?*

Acts 8

He writes, "But now the question arises: why were these special gifts of the Spirit bestowed on the Samaritans? One answer, and an important one, would be to say that here in Samaria the power of the gospel was thus conquering the occult power of magical arts. This would be important because of the local situation. But an even more important reason would be this: the Samaritan church was thus placed on full equality with the Jerusalem church, since to the Samaritans also were given the special gifts of the Spirit. Thus the Jewish Christians, who tended to look down on the Samaritans, would be assured that the Samaritans had equal rights in the church with themselves. We could thus call what happened in Samaria a kind of extension of Pentecost, made necessary because the Church was now expanding into what was previously hostile territory. Given the Jewish prejudice against the Samaritans, it can well be imagined that it would take a tremendous demonstration of the power of the Spirit to convince die-hards among the Jewish Christians that it was really proper to bring the gospel to the Samaritans."[7]

Answers

1. Special gifts were not given nor required to conquer the occult power of magic arts. The gospel had already conquered, and miracles had already taken place there before the Spirit fell upon them.
2. The account indicates no prejudice whatsoever in the Jewish Christians against the Samaritan converts. As soon as they hear of their conversion they send Peter and John to shepherd them. It is not valid to assume because Jews had no dealings with Samaritans (John 4:9), that Christian Jews would have the same hostility. There is nothing in the narrative to indicate that they did. Instead everything points to their ready and full acceptance of them as brothers and sisters in Christ.

3. The words "it can well be imagined" are appropriate. There is no indication whatsoever in the record that any Jewish Christians needed convincing that it was proper to bring the gospel to the Samaritans.

Acts 19

He asks "Why, now, did these twelve disciples at Ephesus receive the gift of tongues and the gift of prophecy – two of the special gifts of the Holy Spirit? Because they had not even heard about the outpouring of the Holy Spirit, and therefore had to be convinced beyond the shadow of a doubt that this great redemptive fact had indeed occurred. . . . In other words, here was a kind of extension of Pentecost to Ephesus, necessary because a prominent group of believers there (Bruce calls them the nucleus of the Ephesian church) had an understanding of Christianity which was wholly inadequate . . . glossolalia at Ephesus occurred primarily for the sake of these Ephesian believers, and for the sake of the Ephesian church of which they were to form the nucleus."[8]

Answer

This ignorance of events on the day of Pentecost Acts 2 would apply to other converts just as much as to these Ephesians, and converts would normally become the nucleus of a new local church as the gospel spread to new territory.

J.F. MacArthur Jr., *Charismatic Chaos*

Acts 8

"The reason for the interval between the Samaritans' salvation and their receiving the Holy Spirit is that they were living in a period of transition between the covenants.

The hatred between Jews and Samaritans was well known. If these Samaritans had received the Holy Spirit at the moment of salvation without any supernatural sign or fanfare, the terrible rift between the Jews and Samaritans might have continued in the Christian church. . . . If the Samaritans had started their own Christian group, the age-old rivalries and hatreds could have been perpetuated, with a Jewish church competing against Samaritan and Gentile assemblies. Instead, God withheld the giving of the Spirit to the Samaritans until the Jewish apostles could be with them. Everyone needed to see – in a way that could not be disputed – that God's purpose under the New Covenant transcended the nation of Israel and included even Samaritans in one church.

It was also important that the Samaritans understand the power and authority of the apostles. It was important for the Jews to know that the Samaritans were part of the body of Christ, and it was important for the Samaritans to know that the Jewish apostles were the channels of divine truth.

A point of grammar in Acts 8:16 makes the meaning clear: 'He had not yet fallen upon any of them; they had simply been baptized in the name of the Lord Jesus.' The Greek word for 'not yet' is *oudepō*. The term does not simply signify something that *has not* happened, but something that *should have happened* but has not yet. In other words, the verse is saying that the Samaritans were saved, but for some peculiar reason what *should* have happened – the Holy Spirit's coming – had not yet occurred."[9]

Answers

1. Before the events of Acts 8:15–17 the Jewish and Samaritan Christians accepted fully that God's purpose under the New Covenant transcended the nation of Israel and included the Samaritans in the one church of Jesus Christ. The Samaritans knew that God had received them; and the conversion of the Samaritans was acknowledged without question by the church at Jerusalem. For that reason alone they sent Peter and John to them. They heard of their receiving of the word of God, their obedience to the gospel. Peter and John would not have prayed and laid hands on them to receive the Holy Spirit unless they were absolutely sure they had become true Christians. They knew the words of Christ Who said explicitly that those belonging to the world cannot receive the Spirit (John 14:17). They recognised that these Samaritan converts were no longer of the world, but chosen out of the world. Equally the Samaritan believers accepted, without the slightest hint of any reserve, the ministry of the apostles. The receiving of the Spirit was not necessary to convince the Samaritans that the Jewish apostles were channels of God's truth. Moreover, the Samaritans had already experienced God's salvation through the ministry of a Jew, Philip. They also had seen this Jew working mighty miracles (Acts 8:6–7). The alleged danger of separation and rivalry is contrary to the facts in the narrative. There was immediate and full acceptance of the Samaritan converts by the Jewish Christians and by Peter and John: there was immediate and full acceptance of the apostles by the Samaritan believers.

2. Peter and John prayed and laid hands on them because they knew that the receiving of the Spirit was a promise given to them to be

appropriated as soon as they became Christians. In that sense they should have received the Spirit earlier.

Acts 19:1–6

J.F. MacArthur Jr. says, "Why did Paul lay hands on them? It seems he did it to demonstrate that they were no longer to follow John the Baptist's teaching, but that of the apostles. And why were the Ephesian believers given tongues? The tongues demonstrated that although they had first come into their relationship with God under the Old Covenant, they were now part of the church with everyone else. Like those who had experienced Pentecost, they were now living under the New Covenant."[10]

Answers

It is striking that he makes no mention of the coming of the Spirit upon them. In the light of Acts 8:17 and 9:17 Paul surely laid his hands upon them for them to receive the promise of the Father. The tongues occurred because they received that promise of the Father.

D. Bridge and D. Phypers, *Spiritual Gifts and the Church*

Acts 2, 8, 9, 10 and 19

They write with reference to Acts 2, 8, 10 and 19, "On all four occasions when reception of the Holy Spirit and speaking in tongues are explicitly or implicitly connected, groups of people, not individuals are concerned. Hence it is doubtful exposition to use these incidents today to press personal experiences on individuals following the pattern of any one of them.

All four occasions when speaking with tongues occurred affected the unity of the church. At Pentecost, the unity of Christians within the body of Christ was symbolised and expressed. The church was publicly recognised as a distinct entity in the Jewish nation, preaching its message, practising its ordinances, and receiving new members. In Samaria, Caesarea and Ephesus three communities with particular problems which threatened the continued unity of the church were integrated in an unmistakable way. Each was a special occasion."[11]

Answers

1. The argument from groups: The fact that on several occasions in the book of Acts groups of converts are said to be baptized in water does not mean that the command to be baptized in water should not be pressed upon individuals. Examples of such group baptisms in

water in Acts are 2:41, 8:12, 10:48, 16:15, 16:33, 18:8 and 19:5. In the same way group baptisms in the Spirit do not mean that individuals should not be taught to receive the promise of the Father. Group baptisms in water require precisely the same ministry to each individual as when only one person is baptized. When the apostles laid hands on the Samaritans they laid their hands on each individual in turn. Moreover not all receptions of the Spirit in Acts are groups of people. There is an example of an individual second experience. Paul was filled with the Spirit three days after his conversion when Ananias went to him. D. Bridge and D. Phypers argue that Paul was not converted until he carried out the advice of Ananias, "Get up, be baptized and wash your sins away, calling on his name" (Acts 22:16 NIV). They say that he was converted then, and at the same time was filled with the Spirit. They write, "Paul's experience followed the norm of New Testament teaching. His conversion and his filling with the Spirit were not two separate experiences but one, both aspects of which gave meaning to the other."[12] Paul was converted on the Damascus road. He who previously was breathing threats and murders against the disciples of the Lord (Acts 9:1) said to the Lord Jesus Christ, "Lord, what do you want me to do?" (Acts 9:6). How can such a change be less than conversion? Ananias addressed him as 'brother Saul' before he ministered to him. That term brother was used with great meaning by Christians in those days. To be a brother in Christ meant that you had been born again into the family of God. In the New Testament brethren is one of the commonest ways of addressing fellow believers.

2. The argument that factors concerning unity made these occasions special and not the normal pattern for believers: Concerning speaking in tongues affecting the unity of the church, the only evidence is found in the case of Cornelius and those gathered with him. There is no indication that the Spirit was given on the day of Pentecost to express unity. If tongues were given to mark out the distinct entity of the church in the Jewish nation then it follows that those converted on the day of Pentecost and thus added to the church would also speak in tongues. Nor is there any evidence in Acts 8 of a threat to unity. There is no mention whatsoever of any problems or even potential problems. There is absolutely no threat of division even hinted at in Acts 19.

Acts 19

D. Bridge and D. Phypers assert, "That they received the Holy Spirit as part of their baptismal ceremony (Acts 19:6) is again further evidence of the close connection the early Christians saw between conversion and the reception of the Holy Spirit."[13]

Answer

They received the Holy Spirit at a point in time after faith in Christ. We have a clear record of an experience of the Spirit after the experience of receiving Christ.

Simon J. Kistemaker, *New Testament Commentary: Acts*

Acts 8

He says, "However, God sent the apostles Peter and John to Samaria to signify that through the apostles he officially approved a new level of development in the church: adding the Samaritan believers. God confirmed this new phase by sending the Holy Spirit as a visible sign of his divine presence." He adds, in relation to the conversion of Cornelius and those with him, ". . . God once again approved of a new period in the growth of the church by sending his Spirit (10:44). I conclude, then, that as the apostles fulfilled the mandate to be witnesses in Jerusalem, Samaria, and the Gentile world (1:8), God sanctioned every initial stage with the outpouring of the Holy Spirit."[14]

Answer

God's will was crystal clear. He had commanded that the gospel be preached to every creature. There was not any question about His approval of the adding of Samaritan believers to the church. He had commanded that the gospel be taken to them, led Philip so to do, and through him brought men and women into His kingdom. The Samaritans were not wondering whether God approved of their becoming believers. They had found salvation in Christ. Great miracles and signs were happening before their eyes. The apostles were in no doubt that God had made these Samaritan believers part of His church. In that total confidence they prayed and laid hands on them. God had shown His approval before the outpouring of the Spirit.

Acts 19

He writes "In keeping with Jesus' promise (1:8), the Spirit descended upon the Jews, the Samaritans, and the Gentiles. After the Spirit was poured out on the members of Cornelius's household (i.e., on Gentiles ['to the ends of the earth,' 1:8]), the promise seems to have been fulfilled. How, then, do we account for the incident in Ephesus?

A possible answer is to consider the extension of the church in Jerusalem, Samaria, and Caesarea as a first phase of mission work among Jews, Samaritans, and Gentiles. A second phase relates to the work of evangelizing persons who have an inadequate knowledge of Christ but are subsequently instructed in the truth of the gospel. If we consider the first phase to be extensive, then the second is intensive."[15]

Answer
There are no solid grounds for suggesting two phases of mission work in Acts. The relatives and friends in Cornelius' house had an inadequate knowledge of Christ (Acts 10:38). They also would fall into the category of the second phase!

Peter Masters, *Only One Baptism of the Holy Spirit*
Acts 19
He says "We can surely see the Lord's purpose here. There were very many Jews scattered around in those parts, and we do not forget the massive Jewish prejudice against gentiles and the new Church order. Even tender-hearted, believing Jews thought, 'Moses can never pass away! God has told us not to swerve in the slightest from the law of Moses! We must protect it and not let anyone add to it or take away from it. But this Christian Church is all so new and so radical. These preachers are saying that our worship must change, and that the ceremonial is of no use. How can this be?'

It was in answer to these misgivings that the signs of Pentecost – designed to rebuke unbelieving Jews and to encourage those who gave up Judaism for Christ – were manifested in this vast, new region of outreach. Thus the Lord gave fresh tokens of Pentecost to liberate the Jewish conscience and to authenticate His messengers."[16]

Answers
From the subsequent events (Acts 19:9–17 shown below) it would not appear that the mini Pentecost, as Peter Masters calls it, would necessarily have been seen by unbelieving Jews or those who later gave up Judaism for Christ. It is feasible that they heard about the happening. But we do read of what happened later, and those events were far more dramatic and were definitely "known to all Jews and Greeks, dwelling in Ephesus." In the light of those later miracles there was no need for a mini Pentecost for the purposes stated by Peter Masters: "But when some were hardened and did not believe, but spoke evil of the Way before the multitude, he departed from them and withdrew the disciples, reasoning daily in the school of Tyrannus. And this continued for two years, so that all who dwelt in Asia heard the word of the Lord

Jesus, both Jews and Greeks. Now God worked unusual miracles by the hands of Paul, so that even handkerchiefs or aprons were brought from his body to the sick, and the diseases left them and the evil spirits went out of them. Then some of the itinerant Jewish exorcists took it upon themselves to call the name of the Lord Jesus over those who had evil spirits, saying, 'We exorcise you by the Jesus whom Paul preaches.' Also there were seven sons of Sceva, a Jewish chief priest, who did so. And the evil spirit answered and said, 'Jesus I know, and Paul I know; but who are you?' Then the man in whom the evil spirit was leaped on them, overpowered them, and prevailed against them, so that they fled out of that house naked and wounded. This became known both to all Jews and Greeks dwelling in Ephesus; and fear fell on them all, and the name of the Lord Jesus was magnified" (Acts 19:9–17).

E.H. Andrews, *The Spirit Has Come*

He writes of Acts 2:1–4, 8:5–17 and 10:1–48, "It seems logical and not inconsistent with any Scripture teaching, that the promise of the Spirit should be fulfilled in separate stages for those who were Jews ('you and your children'), those who were half Jews (the Samaritans) and those who were Gentiles ('all who are far off'). On this view, each of the three effusions of the Spirit was a unique historical event, not to be repeated. If this is so, the two-level experience of the disciples (before and after Pentecost) and of the Samaritans (before and after their visitation from on high) was also historically unique and cannot form a pattern for future generations."[17]

Answer

He mistakes three recorded fulfilments of the promises of the Father through Joel as the gospel advances to new groups, for three stages of a single fulfilment of the promise of the Spirit. He refers to Acts 2:39 "For the promise is to you and to your children, and to all who are afar off, as many as the Lord our God will call," but that verse states explicitly that the promise is to "as many as the Lord our God shall call" throughout the last days. In the sense that the outpourings of the Spirit in those three instances were three fulfilments of the prophecy of Joel they do instruct future generations concerning the ways in which God fulfils His promise of the Spirit to believers.

Acts19:1–6 and 9:1–17

He says, "The Ephesian effusion of Acts 19 is somewhat more obscure in its purpose. It certainly cannot be held to be historically unique, as can the events at Pentecost, in Samaria and in Caesarea. On the other hand it was by no means typical of what happened when the gospel was preached with saving effect."[18] He continues his argument, "It has been suggested that the sequence of events recorded there shows that baptism in the Spirit is a post-conversion experience. . . . The fallacy in this argument lies in its attempt to make regeneration an instantaneous event rather than a Spirit effected process."[19] He then refers to Saul's conversion and asks, "At what point was he born again? Was it in the dust of the Damascus road, when he called Christ 'Lord'? Or was it three days later when he regained his sight and was filled with the Spirit? (Acts 9:1–19). Surely it is idle to speculate on these matters. We recognize that over a period of three days this man was wrought upon by the Spirit of God and brought to new birth. It was not instantaneous, nor should we expect it to be."[20] In a previous chapter concerning Paul he says "the gift of the Holy Spirit was the final act" in the process of conversion. He continues, "Scripture does not tell us at what specific point in the process of conversion a person becomes 'born again'. Indeed, it can be argued that regeneration is itself a process which may occupy a finite span of time, for regeneration is a metaphor based upon physical birth, which is by no means instantaneous. From the onset of labour to the safe delivery of the new-born child, the birth process may occupy many hours, and the Bible says nothing to indicate that the new birth is essentially different in this respect."[21]

Answers

1. His assertion that Acts 19:5–6 was not typical of events when the gospel was preached with saving effect is without even a shred of concrete evidence. Like so many interpreters he decides what is typical from his interpretation of the New Testament, and then assumes and asserts that that is what happened where the scripture record does not tell us what actually occurred. For example there is no record in Acts 2 of the way in which the 3000 converts received the gift of the Holy Spirit. All the following verses record the advance of the gospel: Acts 4:4, 5:14, 6:1, 6:7, 8:35–38, 9:31, 35 and 42, 11:21 and 24, 12:24, 13:12, 13:48, 14:21, 16:5,14–15 and 31–33, 17:4,12 and 34, 18:8, 19:18. Some, but only some, state that water baptism followed faith. From all that the New Testament teaches we may assume that converts were baptized in the cases where there is no mention of their water baptism. Equally from Peter's words in Acts 2:38–39 we may assume that those converts of the last days experienced the promise of the Father (Acts 2:16–18). The Spirit came upon them causing them to prophesy. Indeed all the records that we do

have of the reception of the Spirit are totally consistent with that assumption. Therefore from the apostle's words we have solid ground to assert that Acts 19:5–6 can be taken as typical of what should happen when someone repents and believes in Christ.

2. Concerning the twelve at Ephesus and Saul he treats the experience of the promise of the Father as an integral and final part of the process of conversion. For the twelve there was a point in time when they came to believe in Christ as Saviour. They expressed that faith in water baptism. Paul baptized them *before* laying his hands upon them for the baptism in the Spirit. He treated them as converted. He did not consider them to be partly converted before the Spirit came on them. If what E. H. Andrews says is true then we have an apostle baptizing people partly converted!

James D.G. Dunn, *Baptism in the Holy Spirit, A Re-Examination of the New Testament Teaching on the Gift of the Spirit in relation to Pentecostalism Today*

Acts 2, 8, 9, 10 and 19

He says, "All that the believer receives in conversion – salvation, forgiveness, justification, sonship, etc. – he receives because he receives the Spirit."[22] He affirms, "To become a Christian, in short, is to receive the Spirit of Christ, the Holy Spirit. . . . Man's act in conversion is to repent, to turn and believe; God's act is to give the Spirit to man on believing (Acts 2.38; 11.17; 15.9; 19.2; cf. John 7.39; Gal.3.2). The two together are the essential components of conversion, but in the last analysis it is God's gift which alone counts. Faith would not justify if God did not give His Spirit."[23]

He also says concerning Acts 2:38, "Those who repent and are baptized will receive the gift of the Spirit. It should be noted that no possibility of delay is envisaged here."[24]

Concerning Acts 2 he states with reference to Acts 11:17, "The act of faith which resulted in the gift of the Spirit to the 120 did not take place till Pentecost. . . . so far as Peter was concerned their belief in him and commitment to him as Lord and Christ did not begin until Pentecost."[25]

As regards Acts 8:5–17 he contends that the response and commitment of the Samaritans before Peter and John arrived was defective. They had not met the requirements of Acts 2:38. Therefore the Holy Spirit was not given. The two senior apostles went from Jerusalem to remedy a situation which had gone seriously wrong.[26]

Of Saul's conversion he says, "We conclude then that Paul's conversion was one single experience lasting from the Damascus road to the ministry of Ananias. . . . The experience of being filled with the Spirit was as much an integral part of his conversion as his meeting with Jesus and the three days of solitude and prayer. Paul's conversion was only completed when he called on Jesus as Lord, was filled with the Spirit and had his sins washed away; then, and only then, can he be called a Christian."[27]

He says, "Luke probably regarded the three days of blindness as symbolic, for conversion was frequently thought of as bringing sight to the spiritually blind (John 9.39–41; Acts 26.18; II Cor. 4.4–6; Heb. 6.4; 10.32)."[28]

Concerning Cornelius he says, "The natural implication is that Cornelius at that moment reached out in faith to God for *forgiveness* and received, as God's response, the *Holy Spirit* (cf. 11.17;15.9), not instead of the promised forgiveness but as the bearer of it (cf. Gal 3.2f.). The Spirit was not something additional to God's acceptance and forgiveness but constituted that acceptance and forgiveness."[29]

He writes concerning Acts 19:2 that Paul ". . . is asking twelve 'disciples' who profess belief whether they are Christians."[30]

Of Acts 19:5f he says, "The argument that vv. 5f. relate two quite separate procedures fails to recognize the fact that baptism and the laying on of hands here are the *one* ceremony. . . . It was a single (conversion) experience, . . . Only with the reception of the Spirit did the μαθηταί become Christians." He says that the question of verse three "implies a very close connection between baptism and receiving the Spirit."[31]

Answers

His definition of what is required to become a Christian means that repentance and faith are not sufficient without the gift of the Spirit. This seems to imply that the gift of the Holy Spirit must be an essential part of gospel preaching as well as preaching Christ. He says in his concluding statements, "Has modern evangelism held forth the promise of the Spirit explicitly enough?"[32]

The promise of the Spirit is a part of Peter's gospel message on the day of Pentecost because of the manifestation of the Spirit's outpouring. The explanation of that happening was the content of the start of his message, and he concluded by saying that if they obeyed the gospel they too could experience the promise of the Father. But when we look at the gospel preaching in subsequent days the content of the gospel is repentance and faith in Christ: Acts 3:12–26; 5:42; 8:5,35; 9:20; 10:43; 13:38; 16:31; 17:3, 30–31;18 4–5; 18:28; 20:21; 22:14–15; 26:12–23. Paul defines the gospel in 1 Cor.15:1–4: "Moreover, brethren, I declare to you the gospel which I preached to you, which also you received and in which you stand, by which also you are saved, if you hold fast that word which I preached to you – unless you believed in vain. For I delivered to you first of all that which I also received: that Christ died for our sins according to the Scriptures, and that He was buried, and that He rose again the third day according to the Scriptures." In his letter to the Romans he says, "Paul, a bondservant of Jesus Christ, called *to be* an apostle, separated to the gospel of God which He promised before through His prophets in the Holy Scriptures, concerning His Son Jesus Christ our Lord, who was born of the seed of David according to the flesh, *and* declared *to be* the Son of God with power according to the Spirit of holiness, by the resurrection from the dead" (Rom. 1:1–4); and, "But what does it say? 'The word is near you, in your mouth and in your heart' (that is, the word of faith which we preach): that if you confess with your mouth the Lord Jesus and believe in your heart that God has raised Him from the dead, you will be saved. For with the heart one believes unto righteousness, and with the mouth confession is made unto salvation" (Rom. 10:8–10). In all these scriptures there is no mention of receiving the Holy Spirit. It does not make sense if the baptism in the Spirit is essential for salvation. But it does make sense if the baptism in the Spirit, like water baptism, followed salvation through faith. The attempt to join together faith in Christ for salvation and the reception of the Spirit, and with "no possibility of delay" between the two, does not fit the content of the gospel in the New Testament nor the facts in the book of Acts.

Acts 2: there is nothing to suggest that the outpouring of the Spirit on the day of Pentecost was the result of an act of faith by the 120 which did not take place till Pentecost. Their faith in Christ was rather a constant state during the ten days following His resurrection appearances and Ascension (Acts 1:14). That faith and commitment to Christ was essentially the same on the Day of Pentecost as in the previous days of waiting for the baptism in the Spirit. There was no act of faith and commitment which took place on that day which resulted in the gift of the Holy Spirit. After ten days God's appointed time came, and so He gave the Spirit.

Acts 8: his argument that the Samaritans' faith was defective before Peter and John arrived eliminates an instance where true faith and the reception of the Spirit are separated by a definite time period. If we assume that he is right in saying that the Samaritans' faith was defective we have the incredible fact that the account records nothing about the apostles leading the Samaritans to true faith. We only read of prayer and laying on of hands. There is no record of any correction. This is all the more unbelievable in view of the fact that there is a detailed record of their dealing with Simon's wickedness. According to James D.G. Dunn the Samaritans could well have got a false impression from Philip's preaching about the Kingdom of God, seem to have been caught up in a wave of mass emotion, and gave simply an assent of the mind to Philip's message and an acquiescence to the course of action he advocated rather than true commitment. It these things were true, considerable teaching would have been essential before any prayer and laying on of hands. Yet the record makes no mention of such correction! I submit that the facts which are recorded make his argument utterly absurd.

Acts 9:1–17: when Paul said "Lord what do you want me to do?" he was truly converted before Ananias arrived. His surrender to the Lord Jesus Christ was complete. His lack of knowledge during the first three days after his Damascus road experience concerned ignorance of what he should do, not groping for the truth. He had seen the light when the Lord Jesus spoke to him on the Damascus road. At that point his relationship with Jesus Christ had changed from enmity to reverence and submission. He was no longer in darkness. His spiritual blindness ceased, but he was physically blind for three days. The glory of the light had blinded him (Acts 22:11 and 26:13). His blindness was the result of coming into the light, not a period prior to coming to a knowledge of the truth. We have seen that water baptism is the expression of faith in Christ for the remission of sins. Ananias would not have summoned Paul to be baptized unless he had believed that Paul had come to faith. The words "calling on the name of the Lord" are not to be taken as the point in time when Paul first exercised faith in Christ. He had faith from the moment he saw the light, hence Ananias said, "And now why are you waiting? Arise and be baptized." His water baptism was three days overdue.

Acts 10: the gift of the Spirit to Cornelius, his relatives and close friends was not the gift of forgiveness. Peter expressly says that they received the same gift as he and the other disciples had received on the day of Pentecost recorded in Acts 2 (Acts 11:15–17 and Acts 15:8). On that day the disciples did not receive forgiveness. They were already forgiven. Jesus Himself told them that their names were written in heaven (Luke 10:20). He stated that they were clean because of the word he had spoken to them (John 15:3). He also said that the disciples were not of the world (John 15:19). It is expressly recorded that some of the 120 disciples received the Spirit before Pentecost. From John 20:19 at least ten of them (Thomas may not have been present, John 20:24) received the Spirit when Jesus breathed on them: "When He had said this, He showed them *His* hands and His side. Then the disciples were glad when they saw the Lord. So Jesus said to them again, 'Peace to you! As the Father has sent Me, I also send you.' And when He had said this, He breathed on *them*, and said to them, 'Receive the Holy Spirit' " (John 20:20–22). If Luke 24:33–36 records the same meeting with the risen Christ, then Cleopas and the friend who walked with him to Emmaus were present, and also a number of others with the apostles (Luke 24:33). So at least ten of the apostles and possibly others of the 120 had received the Spirit prior to Pentecost on this occasion. This was a giving of the Spirit to the disciples in relation to His sending them and giving them, as representative of His church, authority to declare sins forgiven or retained. We need to note the following significant facts.

a) The verb breathed is not found anywhere else in the New Testament. It is used in the Septuagint translations of Gen. 2:7 and Ezek. 37:9. These verses record the giving of life. Jesus gives to His followers life in the sense of His authority by the Spirit to act in relation to sins. He instructed them also to wait for the power of the Spirit before commencing to exercise their authority (Luke 24:49, Acts 1:4 and 8).

b) Some would say that Jesus is telling his disciples to receive the Spirit not then, but in the future on the day of Pentecost. The command to receive the Spirit is an aorist imperative. D. Martyn Lloyd-Jones writes, ". . . I defy you to find a single exception – the authorities are all agreed in saying that the Greek aorist imperative never has a future meaning – and I would emphasise the word 'never' . . . when our Lord said to them 'Receive ye the Holy Ghost' they did receive the Holy Ghost. The very word that he used, I repeat, makes it impossible that he was here uttering a prophetic utterance and preparing them for something that was going to happen."[33] Therefore the giving of the Spirit which the 120 received on the day of Pentecost was something distinct from forgiveness, and distinct from the receiving of the Spirit recorded in John 20:22. That something was the promise of the Father. Cornelius, his relatives and close friends received exactly the same gift after having come to faith in Christ for the remission of their sins.

Acts 19: James D.G. Dunn asserts that Paul asked the question in verse 2 to find out whether the twelve were Christians. This creates a profound difficulty. It is stated by Dunn at the very end of his book. He writes, ". . . Accepting that the gift of the Spirit is what makes a man a Christian, how do he and others know if and when he has received the Spirit? In what ways does the Spirit manifest his coming and his presence?"[34]

Paul expected the twelve to know that they had received the Spirit if that event had happened. Therefore for Paul there must have been some clear way that a person knows that he has received the Spirit. The answer is the prophesying in tongues. The events of Acts 19:5–6 are sequential and distinct. Their water baptism was administered and then the laying on of hands for the reception of the Spirit. The two happenings are quite distinct however quickly the second followed the first. The question of verse three does not relate to receiving the Spirit, but was asked because of their ignorance of the Spirit. Moreover the coming upon of the Spirit could not happen until they had become Christians. Jesus said that non-believers could not receive the Spirit: "And I will pray the Father, and He will give you another Helper, that He may abide with you forever – the Spirit of truth, whom the world cannot receive, because it neither sees Him nor knows Him" (John 14:16–17).

Fundamental to James D.G. Dunn's approach to these accounts in Acts is his conviction expressed in the following words, "So far as Paul is concerned, Rom. 8:9 rules out the possibility both of a *non*-Christian possessing the Spirit and of a Christian *not* possessing the Spirit: only the reception and consequent possession of the Spirit makes a man a Christian."[35] He argues that the baptized Samaritans before Peter and John's arrival, Paul before Ananias laid hands on him, Cornelius and his relatives and close friends before the Spirit fell upon them, and the twelve at Ephesus before the Spirit came on them were all unsaved non-Christians. He concludes that until they received the promise of the Father they did not have the indwelling Spirit. He fails to distinguish between receiving the promise of the Father and the indwelling of the Spirit which occurs immediately at regeneration. Rom. 8:9 refers to the latter. Rom. 8:1–9 presents two states of humanity. A person is either "in the flesh" or "in the Spirit." To be "in the flesh" is to be unconverted. It is to live according to fallen human nature. To be "in the Spirit" is to be a believer. It is to be born again by the Spirit of God. It is to have the Son, to have Christ indwelling (Rom. 8:10). As John states, "He who has the Son has life; he who does not have the Son of God does not have life" (1 John 5:12). To have the indwelling of Christ is to have also the indwelling of the Holy Spirit. Notice how Paul speaks in Rom. 8:9–10 of the presence of Christ and the Holy Spirit in the believer: "But you are not in the flesh but in the Spirit, if indeed the Spirit of God dwells in you. Now if anyone does not have the Spirit of Christ, he is not His. And if Christ *is* in you, the body *is* dead because of sin, but the Spirit *is* life because of righteousness."

Thus everyone who truly repents and believes in Christ is regenerate and has the indwelling Spirit of God. Before Paul laid hands on the twelve Ephesian disciples to receive the Holy Spirit they were indwelt by the Spirit having come to faith in Christ. Every true believer is indwelt by the Spirit. As Paul said to the Corinthian Christians, "do you not know that your body is the temple of the Holy Spirit *who is* in you, whom you have from God, and you are not your own?" (1 Cor. 6:19). But not every believer has received the promise of the Father. There is a difference between the indwelling of the Spirit and the pouring out of the Spirit.

The Old Testament saints were regenerate and indwelt by the Spirit. Nicodemus was rebuked for his ignorance of the truth of the new birth (John 3:10). As a teacher in Israel he ought to have known and understood. It is inconceivable that the men and women of faith we read about in the Old Testament lived the way they did without the work of regeneration and the indwelling of the Spirit in their lives. To suggest that the saints recorded in Hebrews 11 behaved, and achieved in the way they did, without the indwelling Spirit is sheer nonsense. Their lives were glorious: "And what more shall I say? For the time would fail me to tell of Gideon and Barak and Samson and Jephthah, also *of* David and Samuel and the prophets: who through faith subdued kingdoms, worked righteousness, obtained promises, stopped the mouths of lions, quenched the violence of fire, escaped the edge of the sword, out of weakness were made strong, became valiant in battle, turned to flight the armies of the aliens. Women received their dead raised to life again. And others were tortured, not accepting deliverance, that they might obtain a better resurrection. Still others had trial of mockings and scourgings, yes, and of chains and imprisonment. They were stoned, they were sawn in two, were tempted, were slain with the sword. They wandered about in sheepskins and goatskins, being destitute, afflicted, tormented – of whom the world was not worthy. They wandered in deserts and mountains, *in* dens and caves of the earth" (Heb. 11:32–38).

There is mention of the indwelling Spirit in the Old Testament. Of Joseph we read, "And Pharaoh said to his servants, 'Can we find *such a one* as this, a man in whom *is* the Spirit of God?' " (Gen. 41:38). Also of Daniel it is recorded by Nebuchadnezzar king of Babylon: "But at last Daniel came before me (his name *is* Belteshazzar, according to the name of my god; in him *is* the Spirit of the Holy God), and I told the dream before him, *saying:* 'Belteshazzar, chief of the magicians, because I know that the Spirit of the Holy God *is* in you, and no secret troubles you, explain to me the visions of my dream that I have seen, and its interpretation' " (Dan. 4:8–9). Bezalel was filled with the Spirit (Exod. 31:3). Of Joshua it is written "a man in whom *is* the Spirit" (Num. 27:18).

Peter refers to the Spirit of God in the prophets of the Old Testament: "searching what, or what manner of time, the Spirit of Christ who was in them was indicating when He testified beforehand the sufferings of Christ and the glories that would follow" (1 Pet. 1:11). Enoch had the testimony that he pleased God (Heb. 11:5). But those who are in the flesh, the unregenerate, cannot please God (Rom. 8:8). There is only one alternative to being in the flesh. It is to be in the Spirit, to have the indwelling of the Spirit of God. These verses reveal important truth concerning God's dealings with mankind. Those who came into fellowship with Him before the coming of Christ experienced great blessings – the regenerating and indwelling of the Holy Spirit, and in some cases the pouring out of the Spirit upon them.

Two verses have been interpreted to argue that the Holy Spirit did not indwell those in fellowship with God before the exaltation of Christ – John 7:39 which reads that the Holy Spirit was not yet given because Jesus was not yet glorified; and John 14:17 the words of Jesus before His death – "the Spirit of truth, whom the world cannot receive, because it neither sees Him nor knows Him; but you know Him, for He dwells with you and will be in you." John 7:39 literally reads "for it was not yet Spirit." The verse does not mean that the Spirit did not indwell or fill men and women before the exaltation of Christ. The Old Testament is clear that He did. But not until the day of Pentecost in Acts 2 was He given according to the terms of the promise of the Father. John 14:17 is translated in the GNB, "He is the Spirit who reveals the truth about God. The world cannot receive him, because it cannot see him or know him. But you know him, because he remains with you and is in you." D.A. Carson says, ". . . . the textual evidence is finely divided between *estin* ('and *is* in you') and *estai* ('and *will be* in you' as in NIV)."[36] He favours the NIV reading. In harmony with all the considerations above there are good grounds to follow the GNB reading. The GNB reading makes more sense. The disciples knew the Spirit because He dwelt with them and also because He was in them. A future indwelling would not cause them to have present knowledge of Him. If this textual reading is correct then the disciples are stated by Jesus to be indwelt by the Spirit at that time.

The New Testament distinguishes between the indwelling of the Spirit and the filling of the Spirit. Paul wrote to the Ephesians, "And do not be drunk with wine, in which is dissipation; but be filled with the Spirit" (Eph. 5:18). The meaning of the verb "be filled" is "go on being filled." It is the present continuous tense of the verb. It follows therefore that a Christian can fail to attain to that state of going on being filled or can lapse from it. The Spirit still indwells them but they are not filled with Him. Eph. 5:18 reveals a distinction between two states of a Christian:

- filled with the Spirit, and
- not filled, but indwelt by Him.

The latter state is that of the believer prior to receiving the baptism in the Spirit.

If every true believer is indwelt by the Spirit then the question arises how can the convert who already has the Spirit have a subsequent experience called receiving the Spirit? The reasons for this are,

a) at conversion the repentant sinner exercises faith in Christ to receive salvation. The sinner's concern is not with the Holy Spirit. But when appropriating the promise of the Father the believer is to be focused on receiving the Spirit. The object of faith in both cases is totally different. Two different blessings are sought.

b) at salvation through repentance and faith there is a conscious experience of new life. The Holy Spirit enters the life as it were silently and mysteriously. The believer is conscious of the change and changes brought about by the Spirit The effects of the Spirit's work are known and felt. The believer is conscious of His blessings. But at the baptism in the Spirit the presence of the Holy Spirit is consciously experienced. He does not come silently. He is consciously received. There is a glorious experience of Him expressed in the terms used – a pouring out of the Spirit, a falling upon of the Spirit, a coming upon of the Spirit, an anointing of the Spirit etc. It is therefore appropriate that the term receiving the Spirit is not used for the indwelling of the Spirit at regeneration, but is used for the baptism in the Spirit.

There is another important argument put forward by James D.G. Dunn. He contends that the disciples entered into the New Covenant at Pentecost. To do this he links Peter's words in Acts 2:38–39 with the covenant of promise made to Abraham. He says, ". . . the words of Acts 2:39 ('the promise is to you and your children') clearly recall the terms of the Abrahamic covenant (Gen 17:7–10) – the covenant of promise – and v.38 identifies the covenant of promise with the gift of the Spirit."[37] Peter is not referring to the Abrahamic covenant in his words of Acts 2:38–39. He is referring back to the promise of the Holy Spirit predicted by Joel (Acts 2:16–18), and received and poured out by the exalted Christ (Acts 2:33). Joel is not prophesying of an action of God to bring people into the New Covenant. He was predicting that those in covenant relationship with God would receive an outpouring of the Spirit specifically for the people of God in the last days. The New Covenant did not begin at Pentecost. It commenced with the death of Christ. Mat. 27:51 and Heb. 10:19–20 tell us that Christ opened up the way into the very Presence of God by his death. This was symbolized by the tearing of the veil in the Temple from top to bottom. It happened precisely at the time of His death (Mat. 27:50). Heb. 9 and 10 are chapters dealing with the replacement of the old Mosaic covenant with the New Covenant. Heb. 9:15 says that Christ is the mediator of the New Covenant by means of His death.

Conclusions

In varied and sometimes in ingenious ways the writers we have considered seek to make Luke fit into their theology of the Spirit and to eliminate a two stage experience. The key to interpreting the Holy Spirit in these events in Acts is found in Peter's words in Acts 2:38–39: "Then Peter said to them, 'Repent, and let every one of you be baptized in the name of Jesus Christ for the remission of sins; and you shall receive the gift of the Holy Spirit. For the promise is to you and to your children, and to all who are afar off, as many as the Lord our God will call.' " The promise he referred to was, "But this is what was spoken by the prophet Joel: 'And it shall come to pass in the last days, says God, That I will pour out of My Spirit on all flesh; Your sons and your daughters shall prophesy, Your young men shall see visions, Your old men shall dream dreams. And on My menservants and on My maidservants I will pour out My Spirit in those days; And they shall prophesy' " (Acts 2:16–18). It is striking that all of these writers, with all their different arguments against a two stage experience, are united in failing to see the true meaning and significance of Peter's words. They miss their true meaning on the day of Pentecost; they do not see them in relation to Acts 8:15–17, 9:17, 10:44–46 and 19:1–6; and they miss their significance for these last days.

They have a further difficulty arising from their stance that the baptism in the Spirit occurs at conversion. They have to explain the experience of Christians who claim to have had the baptism in the Spirit after regeneration. Wayne Grudem does not rule out the possibility of "a genuine work of the Spirit," but suggests an explanation. He thinks that millions of Christians claiming such experience are incorrect to term it a baptism in the Spirit. They define their experience using wrong biblical categories and biblical examples.[38] He says that the term "baptism in the Spirit" leads to a two-category Christianity, dividing Christians into two groups, those baptized in the Spirit and those not baptized.[39] He considers this to be harmful leading to jealousy, pride and divisiveness.[40] Accordingly he considers it appropriate that they should call it *"a large step of growth"* or *"a new empowering for ministry."* His preferred best terminology for " 'second experiences' today (or third or fourth experiences, etc.)", however, is "being filled with the Spirit."[41]

Answers

1. Firstly it is important to clarify one important matter. It is true that the baptism in the Spirit is not repeated in the Christian's life. The various terms used of the experience all indicate this is a single event. For example it is called a sealing. Sealing takes place just once. But after the Christian has experienced the baptism in the Spirit he is commanded to go on being filled with the Spirit. In Acts 4:31 we read of a filling of the Spirit in a particular situation of need. Of those who experienced that filling there be would some (if not all) of the 120 who were previously baptized in the Spirit on the day of Pentecost. It has been well said "one baptism in the Spirit, but many fillings."

2. It is to be noted that Wayne Grudem does not dismiss the experience of Christians baptized in the Spirit as not genuine.

3. He needs to explain their genuine experience by more than simply incorrect labelling. The fact is that they came into their genuine experience because they believed that the baptism in the Spirit was available for them after conversion. They were convinced of the truth from scripture, and sought the experience convinced that it was the promise of God for them. Consequently they had an experience of the Spirit after conversion. Wayne Grudem would have to say that they misunderstood scripture before their experience as well as after it. But the result was genuine experience! The truth is that correct doctrine leads to true experience of the Spirit. Incorrect doctrine results in lack of experience of the Spirit. Where the baptism in the Spirit is taught as an experience subsequent to conversion believers do receive genuine filling of the Spirit. When Christians are taught and accept that they have received the baptism in the Spirit at conversion they usually do not seek a specific experience of the pouring out of the Spirit upon them resulting in prophecy. Why should they? They believe that they have been baptized in the Spirit.

4. The true doctrine of the baptism in the Spirit does mean that there

are Christians who have received the experience and those who have not. In the same way there are believers who have obeyed the Lord's command to be baptized in water by immersion and those who have not. There need be no division because the promise of the Father is for every believer.

There is a further consequence of the belief that the baptism in the Spirit occurs at conversion. The scriptures require believers to be filled with the Spirit (Eph. 5:18). Believers who have not experienced a filling of the Spirit have a deficient understanding of the meaning of the command. Consequently the filling of the Spirit is often diluted to mean a state of total surrender to the will of God. Eph.5:18 is made to be the equivalent of Rom. 12:1–2: "I beseech you therefore, brethren, by the mercies of God, that you present your bodies a living sacrifice, holy, acceptable to God, *which is* your reasonable service. And do not be conformed to this world, but be transformed by the renewing of your mind, that you may prove what *is* that good and acceptable and perfect will of God." Michael Green says, in his book *I Believe in The Holy Spirit*, "To be filled with the Spirit means to allow Jesus to have the fullest control in our lives that we are conscious of. In so far as we do that, we will always be finding new areas of self-centredness to surrender as the Lord who is Spirit possesses us more and more fully. To such submission all Christians are called. And it is no once and for all transaction: 'go on being filled with the Spirit' is the meaning of the original."[42] The conscious experience of the presence and power of the Spirit when He fills a believer is not perceived adequately by this definition. In the verses following Paul's command to be filled with the Spirit in Eph. 5:18 he goes on to state the behaviour that is the expression of being filled with the Spirit. It is expressed in worship, thanksgiving and submitting to one another in the fear of God, "speaking to one another in psalms and hymns and spiritual songs, singing and making melody in your heart to the Lord, giving thanks always for all things to God the Father in the name of our Lord Jesus Christ, submitting to one another in the fear of God" (Eph. 5:19–21). Concerning worship we should note that it is worship in fellowship with other Christians. It is worship that comes from the heart full of song and melody. It is expressed in the psalms of the Old Testament, hymns of New Testament times and spiritual songs, which is singing in tongues (1 Cor. 14:15). Those not baptized in the Spirit are unable to sing in tongues. They are strangers to the prophetic inspiration predicted by Joel, and their worship is without that inspired utterance in song. It also lacks the anointing of the Spirit when singing psalms and hymns. It is unspeakably sublime for believers to sing together in the Spirit, whether a psalm, or a hymn or in tongues. It is to experience a foretaste of heaven. It is "joy inexpressible and full of glory" (1 Peter 1:8). The Spirit-filled life is also one of thanksgiving to God for all His blessings through Jesus Christ. The Spirit-filled life requires the submission of wives, children and employees. Wives are to submit to husbands, children to parents and slaves to their masters. This submission is to be carried out in the fear of God. (Husbands are to love their wives as Christ loved the church and gave Himself for her, fathers are not to provoke their children to wrath but bring them up in the training and admonition of the Lord and masters are to be mindful that they have a Master in heaven and give their slaves what is just and fair.) This worship, thanksgiving and submission is not simply an expression of dedication to the will of God. The believer is empowered by the Spirit of God to rise to these things. This is Paul's definition of the Spirit-filled life.

References

1. R.G. Gromacki, *The Modern Tongues Movement*, The Presbyterian and Reformed Publishing Co. Revised 1972, page 107.
2. *Ibid.*, page 94.
3. *Ibid.*, pages 94–95.
4. *Ibid.*, page 97.
5. *Ibid.*, page 101.
6. *Ibid.*, pages 106–107.
7. A.A. Hoekema, *What About Tongue Speaking?*, Eerdmans and Paternoster Press 1966, pages 70–71.
8. *Ibid.*, page 76.
9. Taken from *Charismatic Chaos* by John F. MacArthur Jr.. Copyright © 1992 by John F. MacArthur Jr. Used by permission of Zondervan, pages 218–219.
10. *Ibid.*, page 226.
11. Donald Bridge and David Phypers, *Spiritual Gifts and the Church*, Christian Focus Publications 1995, page 151.
12. *Ibid.*, page 147.
13. *Ibid.*, page 149.
14. Simon J. Kistemaker, *New Testament Commentary: Acts*, Baker Books 1990, pages 300–301.
15. *Ibid.*, page 681.
16. Peter Masters, *Only One Baptism of the Holy Spirit*, The Wakeman Trust 1994, pages 104–105.
17. E.H. Andrews, *The Spirit Has Come*, Evangelical Press 1991, pages 129–130.

18. *Ibid.*, page 135.
19. *Ibid.*, page 135.
20. *Ibid.*, page 136.
21. *Ibid.*, pages 117–118.
22. James D.G. Dunn, *Baptism in the Holy Spirit*, SCM Press 1970, page 95.
23. *Ibid.*, page 96.
24. *Ibid.*, page 91.
25. *Ibid.*, page 52.
26. *Ibid.*, page 58.
27. *Ibid.*, pages 77–78.
28. *Ibid.*, page 76.
29. *Ibid.*, page 80.
30. *Ibid.*, page 86.
31. *Ibid.*, pages 87–88.
32. *Ibid.*, page 229.
33. D. Martyn Lloyd-Jones, *Joy Unspeakable*, First published 1984, Reprinted 1985 page 253. Used by permission of Kingsway Publications, Lottbridge Drove, Eastbourne.
34. James D.G. Dunn, *Baptism in the Holy Spirit*, SCM Press 1970, page 229
35. *Ibid.*, page 95.
36. D.A. Carson, *The Gospel According To John*, IVP and Eerdmans 1991, pages 509–510.
37. James D.G. Dunn, *Baptism in the Holy Spirit*, SCM Press 1970, page 47.
38. Taken from *Systematic Theology* by Wayne A. Grudem. Copyright © 1994 by Wayne Grudem. Used by permission of IVP and Zondervan, page 775.
39. *Ibid.*, pages 780–781.
40. *Ibid.*, page 775–777.
41. *Ibid.*, page 781.
42. Michael Green, *I Believe in the Holy Spirit*, Revised 2004, pages 198–199. Used by permission of Kingsway Publications, Lottbridge Drove, Eastbourne.

CHAPTER TWENTY NINE

THE BAPTISM IN THE SPIRIT AND THE LAYING ON OF HANDS

The events of Acts 2:4, 8:5–17, 9:1–17, 10:1–48 and 19:1–6 were narrated by Luke to record the spread of the gospel, the enlargement of the church and the fulfilment of the promise of the Father in the last days. Thus we have information concerning the way God chose to fulfil His promise. We find that the laying on of hands was part of God's order for receiving the promise. Indeed in all cases except Acts 2:4 and 10:44 the laying on of hands was always used. The absence of the laying on of hands in Acts 2:4 is simply because it was the first fulfilment of the promise. There was therefore no one to lay hands on the 120. With regard to Acts 10:44 God chose to dispense with the laying on of hands. He could have used Peter to lay hands on the Gentiles just as he did on the Samaritans. From the subsequent accounts of Jewish prejudice in Acts 11 and 15 it is clear that He poured out the Spirit without the laying on of hands to demonstrate emphatically, and in a manner beyond dispute, that He had accepted the Gentiles. The day of Pentecost when the Spirit first was given was obviously unique. The case of Cornelius and those with him was a very special one. But these two occasions do teach that the laying on of hands is an action God may not always require. All the other records of the receiving of the promise of the Father indicate that it is the revealed will of God that hands be laid on the believer who desires the baptism in the Spirit.

It is noteworthy that God sent Ananias to Paul to lay hands on him to be filled with the Spirit (Acts 9:17). God chose to pour out His Spirit on Paul through the ministry of a disciple and the laying on of hands. Ananias was not an apostle. He is described by Luke as a disciple, a devout man according to the law, having a good testimony with all the Jews who dwelt in Damascus (Acts 9:10 and 22:12). There is therefore no ground in scripture for limiting the laying on of hands to apostles.

The Samaritans and the twelve at Ephesus were baptized in the Spirit following the laying on of hands. We may therefore conclude that these records in Acts reveal a pattern. To appropriate the promise of the Father there should be the laying on of hands.

In the letters of the New Testament we find little mention of the laying on of hands for the baptism in the Spirit. Apart from Heb. 6:2 there is only mention of Timothy's baptism in the Spirit with the laying on of Paul's hands: "Therefore I remind you to stir up the gift of God which is in you through the laying on of my hands" (2 Tim. 1:6). The gift of God is the gift of the Holy Spirit. The GNB captures Paul's meaning in the following verse – "For the Spirit that God has given us does not make us timid; instead, his Spirit fills us with power, love, and self control." Paul is recalling Timothy's baptism in the Spirit in verse 6, and in verse 7 he refers to the reception of the Spirit by all believers.

The New Testament pattern was for converts to be baptized in water and to receive the baptism in the Spirit without delay after conversion. When that did not happen at Samaria it was instantly rectified by the apostles. Consequently this lack of mention in the epistles of the laying on of hands for the reception of the Spirit is what we should expect. All the Christians written to had been baptized in the Spirit, just as they had been baptized in water. Frequently the baptism in the Spirit is referred to as a past event (e.g. Rom. 5:5, 8:15–16, 1 Cor. 12:13, 2 Cor. 1:21–22, Gal. 3:2, Eph. 1:13, Tit. 3:4–6, Heb. 6:4,1 John 2:27). In a parallel manner water baptism is stated as a past occurrence (Rom. 6:3; 1 Cor. 1:13; Gal. 3:27 and Col. 2:12). There was no need to mention the laying on of hands when speaking of the experience of being baptized in the Spirit. It would have been unnecessary detail. In the case of Timothy it is mentioned to distinguish the event from another laying on of hands recorded in Paul's first letter to Timothy: "Do not neglect the gift that is in you, which was given to you by prophecy with the laying on of the hands of the eldership" (1 Tim. 4:14). Many writers attempt to make this event the same as 2 Tim. 1:6. There are differences pointing to two events. The gift in 1 Tim. 4:14 was some gift given to minister. It was given through prophecy. It was with the laying on of hands of the elders. The gift in 2 Tim. 1:6 is the Holy Spirit, there is no mention of prophecy, and the laying on of hands is carried out by Paul.

The Meaning of the Laying on of Hands

The scriptures reveal that the laying on of hands was used to impart blessing. This is evident in Jacob's blessing of Ephraim and Manasseh: "And Joseph said to his father, 'They *are* my sons, whom God has given me in this *place.*' And he said, 'Please bring them to me, and I will bless them.' Now the eyes of Israel were dim with age, *so that* he could not see. Then Joseph brought them near him, and he kissed them and embraced them. And Israel said to Joseph, 'I had not thought to see your face; but in fact, God has also shown me your offspring!' So Joseph brought them from beside his knees, and he bowed down with his face to the earth. And Joseph took them both, Ephraim with his right hand toward Israel's left hand, and Manasseh with his left hand toward Israel's right hand, and brought *them* near him. Then Israel stretched out his right hand and laid *it* on Ephraim's head, who *was* the younger, and his left hand on Manasseh's head, guiding his hands knowingly, for Manasseh *was* the firstborn. And he blessed Joseph, and said: 'God, before whom my fathers Abraham and Isaac walked, The God who has fed me all my life long to this day, The Angel who has redeemed me from all evil, Bless the lads; Let my name be named upon them, And the name of my fathers Abraham and Isaac; And let them grow into a multitude in the midst of the earth.' Now when Joseph saw that his father laid his right hand on the head of Ephraim, it displeased him; so he took hold of his father's hand to remove it from Ephraim's head to Manasseh's head. And Joseph said to his father, 'Not so, my father, for this *one is* the firstborn; put your right hand on his head.' But his father refused and said, 'I know, my son, I know. He also shall become a people, and he also shall be great; but truly his younger brother shall be greater than he, and his descendants shall become a multitude of nations.' So he blessed them that day, saying, 'By you Israel will bless, saying, "May God make you as Ephraim and as Manasseh!" ' And thus he set Ephraim before Manasseh" (Gen. 48:9–20).

The impartation of blessing is seen also in Moses' laying his hands upon Joshua. The laying on of Moses' hands not only commissioned Joshua as his successor (Num. 27:15–23), but also imparted an enduement of the Spirit to Joshua: "Now Joshua the son of Nun was filled with the Spirit of wisdom, because Moses had laid his hands on him. So the Israelites listened to him and what the Lord had commanded Moses" (Deut. 34:9; NIV footnote). Before this laying on of hands Joshua was described as 'a man in whom *is* the Spirit' (Num. 27:18). Jesus laid hands on children to bless them (Mark 10:16), and on the sick for healing (e.g. Luke 4:40 and Mat. 9:18). Ananias laid hands on Paul for the recovery of his sight. When Paul and Barnabas ministered on their first missionary journey the Lord bore witness to the word of His grace, granting signs and wonders to be done by their hands (Acts 14:3). God worked unusual miracles by the hands of Paul (Acts 19:11). Paul laid hands on Publius on the island of Malta and healed him (Acts 28:8).

There were other uses of the laying on of hands. Under the Mosaic ritual the laying on of hands was the means of transferring uncleanness and sins to animals for sacrifice. The laying on of hands was also used to commission the seven to serve tables (Acts 6:6), Paul and Barnabas to missionary work (Acts 13:3) and elders into their office (1 Tim. 5:22).

In the light of these scriptures the particular purpose of the laying on of hands in relation to the baptism in the Spirit is for the bestowal of blessing.

Robert P. Menzies says that the laying on of hands commissioned the Samaritans, Paul and the twelve at Ephesus for service. He sees the gift of the Spirit in each of these instances as "a prophetic endowment enabling the recipient(s) to participate effectively in the mission which has been entrusted to the prophetic people of God."[1] This definition of the nature and purpose of the gift of the Spirit does not prove that the purpose of the laying on of hands was to commission in these instances. If the laying on of hands was meant to be a commissioning for all who receive the baptism in the Spirit then we would expect Cornelius and those with him to have hands laid on them after the Spirit fell on them. Also it is clearly stated that Peter and John laid hands on the Samaritans for one reason only – the Holy Spirit had not yet fallen upon them. Paul was commissioned a considerable time after his conversion and meeting with Ananias. His commissioning is recorded approximately thirteen years later in Acts 13:3. Whenever someone was commissioned with the laying on of hands it is stated in the scripture records that this is what the laying on of hands is for. In Acts 8:15–17, 9:17 and 19:6 there is no mention of commissioning. It is an unnatural reading of these texts to interpret them as commissioning.

Conclusions

The laying on of hands is God's appointed way to appropriate the promise of the Father. It is wisdom to submit to His will even though it may not make sense to us or be contrary to our preferred way. Isaiah the prophet said, "'For My thoughts *are* not your thoughts, Nor *are* your ways My ways,' says the LORD. 'For *as* the heavens are higher than the earth, So are My ways higher than your ways, And My thoughts than your thoughts'" (Isa. 55:8–9).

One reason why God has appointed this action may be that it is an aid to the exercise of faith. Faith is necessary when appropriating the promise of the Spirit. Gal. 3:2 tells us that the Spirit is received by the hearing of faith. By a believing response to the message of the promise of the Father the Galatians received the blessing. Maybe the laying on of hands assisted them to believe that *at that time and through that action* God would fulfil His promise and pour out His Spirit upon them. It is necessary to believe to receive. Jesus said, "Therefore

I say to you, whatever things you ask when you pray, believe that you receive *them*, and you will have *them*" (Mark 11:24). The writer to the Hebrews declares "he who comes to God must believe that He is, and *that* He is a rewarder of those who diligently seek Him" (Heb. 11:6). He goes on to say that "through faith" promises were obtained: "And what more shall I say? For the time would fail me to tell of Gideon and Barak and Samson and Jephthah, also *of* David and Samuel and the prophets: who through faith subdued kingdoms, worked righteousness, *obtained promises*, stopped the mouths of lions" (Heb. 11:32–33: italics mine).

Also it may be that God has appointed this action to distinguish the receiving of the Spirit as a separate distinct event not to be confused with the action of baptizing in water. As we have seen in Acts baptism in water and baptism in the Spirit were sometimes very close together in time. The action of laying on of hands marked off the receiving of the Spirit as something separate from water baptism.

Divine wisdom ordained the laying on of hands to show that human ministry has a part in the receiving of the promise of the Father. In the concern to deny a two-stage experience of salvation followed by a baptism in the Spirit, or the concern to refute speaking in tongues as evidence of the baptism in the Spirit little attention has been given to the fact that, except for the outpourings in Acts 2 and 10, the laying on of hands always preceded the receiving of the Spirit. This is highly significant. It reveals that the promise of the Father is a distinct blessing received through human ministry. But many leading expositors and theologians allow no place for the laying on of hands for receiving the promise of the Father. In their view the baptism in the Spirit takes place at conversion without any laying on of hands.

Today there exists the practice of confirmation following infant baptism which employs the laying on of hands as part of the rite for the giving of the Holy Spirit. While such doctrines of confirmation are contrary to the truths of scripture, the laying on of hands for the giving of the Spirit in the ceremony preserves the truth that God appointed the laying on of hands for the receiving of the Spirit. Because the practice of confirmation has been so closely associated with the laying on of hands, based especially on Acts 8:17, 9:17 and 19:6, one suspects that the laying on of hands has sometimes not been given the attention it ought to have received. Laying on of hands has been rejected along with confirmation.

As the church fell away from New Testament truth concerning receiving the promise of the Father it introduced non-scriptural baptismal practices like the anointing with oil (which is only for prayers for the sick, James 5:14). It kept the form of godliness but denied its power. So there arose an empty ceremony where hands were laid upon persons who were told that even though nothing happened they must believe that they had been given the Spirit. This has continued through the centuries from those early days and still persists today. This tragic fact must not cause us to reject the truth that the laying on of hands is God's will for the receiving of the promise of the Father.

Reference

1. Robert P. Menzies *Empowered For Witness: The Spirit in Luke-Acts*, Sheffield: Sheffield Academic Press, 1994, page 225.

CHAPTER THIRTY

THE BAPTISM IN THE SPIRIT AND SPEAKING IN TONGUES

The baptism in the Spirit is the promise of the Father. The promise of the Father is the outpouring of the Spirit with the purpose of inspiring prophetic utterance: "I will pour out My Spirit on all flesh . . . and they shall prophesy" (Acts 2:17–18). The baptism in the Spirit is not the pouring out of the Spirit on a believer. It is the pouring out of the Spirit on a believer causing him to prophesy.

- It is most important that this scriptural definition is kept before our eyes when we consider the relationship between speaking with tongues and the baptism in the Spirit.
- It is equally important that we turn to scripture to define precisely what the promise of the Father means by the words "they shall prophesy."

We shall see that where we have records of what actually occurred when the promise of the Father was fulfilled tongue speaking took place on every occasion. This is stated expressly in Acts 2, 10 and 19. In Acts 8 tongue speaking is not mentioned. The occurrence of tongue speaking fits the facts which are recorded. There are no other accounts of the events accompanying the appropriation of the promise of the Father in the New Testament. The epistles refer back to the baptism in the Spirit as something which took place at the start of the Christian life just as they refer back to water baptism. They do not state what actually happened when believers received the promise of the Father. Paul's actual experience is not recorded (Acts 9:17). Thus all the New Testament accounts of what actually happened when the promise "they shall prophesy" was fulfilled tell us that the prophesying took the form of speaking in tongues. There is nothing indicating that "they shall prophesy" was fulfilled in any other way. This means that speaking in tongues is the fulfilment of the promise of the Father. It also means that it manifests that the pouring out of the Spirit has taken

204

place. It is both an essential part of the baptism in the Spirit, and evidence of the fulfilment of the promise, "I will pour out My Spirit . . . and they shall prophesy." The Spirit is invisible and silent but the tongue speaking is seen and heard (Acts 2:33).

It will be helpful to pause and consider to whom it is acceptable evidence. It is evidence to the one receiving the promise of the Father. It is also evidence that a believer has received the promise of the Father to other believers who have been baptized in the Spirit (Acts 10:46). It is not acceptable evidence to unbelievers because tongues are a sign to them which they reject (1 Cor. 14:21–23). More importantly it is not acceptable evidence to those not baptized in the Spirit. Paul calls them ungifted men in 1 Cor. 14:23: "Therefore if the whole church assembles together and all speak in tongues, and ungifted men or unbelievers enter, will they not say that you are mad?" NASB. When Paul speaks of the unbeliever and the ungifted [Greek: ἰδιῶται] he does not include them in his previous statement that in one Spirit they were all baptized for one body (1 Cor. 12:13 my trans.). These ungifted men, like the unbelievers, are outsiders who come among them. The ungifted are like the twelve at Ephesus before Paul laid hands on them, the Samaritan converts before the arrival of Peter and John, and Saul during the three days before Ananias laid hands on him to be filled with the Spirit. This unacceptability of tongue speaking to the ungifted is a most significant factor which must not be ignored when considering the approach of many who oppose tongue speaking as an essential constituent and evidence of the baptism in the Spirit.

Let us recall the evidence for tongue speaking in Acts and then deal with objections.

The evidence

Acts 2
We saw that the prophesying took the form of speaking in tongues in *every case* on the day of Pentecost. All those filled with the Spirit spoke in tongues.

Acts 10
Cornelius and those with him all spoke in tongues. We also saw that Cornelius and those with him received *exactly the same experience* of the Spirit as the apostles, and elders of the church at Jerusalem (Acts 15:8). We also stated that the words "they heard them speak in tongues and magnify God" recall Acts 2:11. Thus the words "magnify God" are parallel to "speak in tongues."

Acts 19

All of the twelve spoke in tongues. We have parallelism again in Acts 19:6: "they spoke with tongues and prophesied." In Acts 2 the speaking in tongues was described by Peter as prophesying (Acts 2:16–18).

In the book of Acts, in all the instances of the fulfilments of the promise of the Father where the prophesying was described, it took the form of speaking in tongues.

Acts 8

Here the prophesying is not recorded, but there are significant facts in the narrative that must be given due weight. Simon saw that the Holy Spirit was given. Prophesying is visible. Tongue speaking was seen on the day of Pentecost (Acts 2:33). Peter referred to the speaking in tongues on the day of Pentecost as that which his hearers saw (Acts 2:33). Such miraculous utterance explains what Simon saw and was willing to pay for (Acts 8:18). It also explains why the apostles knew with certainty that the Holy Spirit had fallen upon none of the Samaritan believers. Peter and John at Samaria applied some clear criterion by which they judged that not a single one of the converts had experienced the falling upon them of the Holy Spirit. This fact is overlooked, or passed over without due consideration, by many writers. The question therefore arises, "what was that criterion?" Since the promise of the Father was to pour out his Spirit with the result that believers prophesied, and this promise applied to the Samaritans (Acts 2:38–39), it is surely reasonable to argue that the apostles would look for evidence of an experience of the pouring out of the Spirit causing them to prophesy. They found that no one had experienced this. Notice that this deduction is based on Peter's words in Acts 2:38–39 and their reference back to Joel (Acts 2:16–18). It is based on apostolic doctrine.

Objections

Some would argue that inspired utterance in the form of prophesying in one's own language rather than tongue speaking could have occurred when the promise of the Father was appropriated at Samaria

But if the prophesying sometimes took the form of inspired intelligible utterance when receiving the promise of the Father it would not always have been clear that such utterance was inspired by the Spirit. One needs to put oneself in the shoes of the two apostles dealing with the Samaritan converts. Human eloquence can rise to great heights. Doubtless some of those Samaritans, in the joy of having found salvation and the wonderful miracles taking place, would have prayed passionately, witnessed fervently and said beautiful words of thankfulness and praise to God. None of these things were evidence to Peter and John of the Spirit falling upon them. But if tongue speaking always occurred when the promise was appropriated they would have had no difficulty whatsoever in making their judgment. Speaking in tongues manifests Divine inspiration, and would have provided clear cut evidence. As R.W. Menzies says, "Furthermore, how is one to distinguish inspired intelligible speech from that which is uninspired? Although we may all be able to think of instances when intelligible speech was uttered in a manner which indicated the inspiration of the Spirit (spontaneous, edifying, appropriate), the point is that judgments of this kind are rather tenuous or approximate. Tongues-speech, however, because of its unusual and demonstrative character (the very reason it is both often maligned or over-esteemed), is particularly well suited to serve as 'evidence.' In short, if we ask the question concerning 'initial physical evidence' of Luke, tongues-speech uniquely 'fits the bill' because of its intrinsically demonstrative character."[1]

Larry W. Hurtado argues, "Unlike such matters as the Christian doctrine of God, the question of whether there is a separate level of Spirit empowerment subsequent to regeneration, with a required 'evidence' of it, seems not to be reflected at all in the New Testament."[2] His statement is incredible. It flies in the face of Acts 8 where we have proof of a falling upon of the Spirit after regeneration, and where there was some clear evidence of it that the apostles were able to apply. Indeed it shows that the evidence was so clear that it was not an issue slowly worked out and formulated in the process of time. Peter and John knew what the evidence was.

Larry W. Hurtado also argues that the doctrine of tongues as initial evidence of the baptism in the Spirit is built on narratives in Acts, and that Luke had no intention of teaching such doctrine by these accounts
He says "The author's purpose was not to provide a basis for formulating *how* the Spirit is received, but rather it seems to have been to show *that* the Spirit prompted and accompanied the progress of the gospel at every significant juncture and was the power enabling the work of Christian leaders.

This explains why the author sometimes does and sometimes does not (8:14–19; 9:17–19) bother to describe specifically *how* the Spirit was manifested when people are described as 'filled' or otherwise gifted with the Spirit. When the author does emphasise specific phenomena, he does not seem to do so in order to teach a doctrine of the Spirit's reception. At least, there is no hint that this was his purpose"[3] Concerning Acts 10 he says, "The issue is the legitimacy of the proclamation of the gospel to Gentiles and is not a doctrine of 'initial evidence' of a Spirit empowerment distinguishable from regeneration."[4] Of Acts 19:1–7 he writes, "In 19:1–7, the mention of tongues speaking and prophesying in connection with the gift of the Spirit to the disciples of John the Baptist seems to be intended to illustrate the superiority of the gospel of Christ to the message of John, whose disciples, says the author, had 'never even heard that there is a Holy Spirit'(19:2)."[5] He cites Acts 4:31 as a sixth passage narrating a bestowal of the Spirit. He contends that the phenomena accompanying the Spirit varies in the six passages Acts 2:4; 4:31; 8:15–17; 9:17; 10:44–46 and 19:1–6 – tongues, prophecy, boldness, etc.

Acts 4:31 is not an initial reception of the Spirit. It was a subsequent filling for a special need. The doctrine of initial physical evidence of tongue speaking, however, is not based solely on the facts related by Luke of the reception of the Spirit in Acts 2, 8, 9, 10 and 19. It is built on the explanation of those facts by Peter in Acts 2:14–39 with particular reference to verses 16–18 and 38–39. Peter defines precisely and clearly the content and meaning of the promise of the Father (Acts 2:16–18) and precisely to whom the promise is given (Acts 2:38–39). His words are apostolic doctrine on the matter. The events in Acts 8:15–17, 9:17, 10:44–46 and 19:6 are fulfilments of Peter's words in Acts 2:38–39. Luke has thereby provided information concerning the content of the promise of the Father, a definition to whom it applies, and its actual fulfilment by God on several occasions. Doctrine of the promise of the Father must take full account of that revelation. The facts concerning Peter's doctrine *and God's actions* revealed by Luke cannot be dismissed on the ground that they are contained in narratives, nor on the ground of what Luke intended to teach. Those facts, which Luke recorded moved by the Holy Spirit, teach that tongue speaking is an essential part of the baptism in the Spirit and therefore evidence of it.

Many affirm that Paul's question "Do all speak with tongues?"
(1 Cor. 12:30) to which the answer is obviously "No" proves that
speaking in tongues is not the result and evidence of the baptism in
the Spirit
This verse speaks of the gift of tongue speaking for use in the church gathering together with the gift of interpretation of tongues. In 1 Cor. 12:28–30 Paul is stating some of the gifts that God has set in the church universal. Tongues is one of those gifts. Not all believers have this gift of tongues for use when the church meets together. But all believers can

have the tongue speaking inspired by the outpouring of the Spirit when the promise of the Father is received.

The differences between the tongue speaking when receiving the promise of the Father and the gift of tongue speaking in the church are clear when we compare Paul's commandments of the Lord in 1 Cor. 14 with the accounts in Acts. The exercise of the gift of tongues in the church is subject to restrictions stated in 1 Cor. 14:27–28: "If anyone speaks in a tongue, *let there be* two or at the most three, *each* in turn, and let one interpret. But if there is no interpreter, let him keep silent in church, and let him speak to himself and to God." These constraints did not apply to the tongue speaking when receiving the promise of the Father (Acts 2:4, 10:46 and 19:6). Notice that Paul was present at Ephesus (Acts 19:6). Such tongue speaking required no gift of interpretation, and was not limited to three speakers.

Paul also speaks of a private use of tongue speaking, distinct from the gift of tongues for use in the church. This private use of tongue speaking is for all believers (1 Cor. 14:2). It is a further use of the tongues received at the baptism in the Spirit. Paul wants all believers to exercise privately this speaking in tongues (1 Cor. 14:5). He does not want them to stop doing so, because thereby the believer is edified (1 Cor. 14:4). He gives his own experience as guidance for the private use of tongues. He says that in private he practises speaking in tongues to a great degree: "I thank my God I speak with tongues more than you all" (1 Cor. 14:18). The gift of tongues for use in the church gathering with the gift of the interpretation of tongues is not for all who have spoken in tongues at their baptism in the Spirit. Only some will be given that gift (1 Cor. 12:11).

Some argue that the doctrine of tongues as initial physical evidence of the baptism in the Spirit cannot be true because it has only recently been formulated (since 1900), and become part of the doctrinal standards of some Christian denominations and groups
The evidence of church history is conclusive that many true New Testament doctrines were lost for over a thousand years before the Reformation. There were vestiges of some of them from time to time. As we have seen believers' water baptism by immersion is one example. It was only formulated in the sixteenth century.

There is a related objection, if tongue speaking was so important in the early church why has it been absent throughout so much of church history?
Some Pentecostals have said that Joel 2:23 explains the tongue speaking of the early centuries of the Christian church as the former rain, and

the tongue speaking of recent times as the latter rain. The verse reads, "Be glad then, you children of Zion, And rejoice in the LORD your God; For He has given you the former rain faithfully, And He will cause the rain to come down for you – The former rain, And the latter rain in the first *month*." The verse is a promise of restoration after the ravages of the locust. The land will come back to plenteous harvests and fruit-fulness. For this God will give both the former (October–November) and latter (April) rain. Both rains were essential for the production of the crops. Either rain without the other would be useless. This verse therefore does not explain the almost total absence of tongue speaking for over a thousand years.

The speedy departure from true doctrine and practice in the church of Jesus Christ is a fact writ large across church history. As spirituality began to wane, and the form of godliness replaced the power of it (2 Tim. 3:5), one of the first things to be affected would be genuine experience of the promise of the Father. As we have seen, there is evidence that the laying on of hands did continue, but without any real experience of the reception of the Spirit. There was the form of godliness without the power. Even so, why did not those hungry for God not receive the Spirit and speak in tongues? There is evidence in church history that tongue speaking was present in the post-apostolic era. Irenaeus (d.c. 200) related the events of Pentecost of Acts 2 to his own experience: "In like manner we do also hear many brethren in the Church, who possess prophetic gifts, and who do through the Spirit speak all kinds of languages . . ."[6] Tertullian flor. A.D. 197–225 challenged his opponent Marcion to produce from among his followers any "such as have not spoken by human sense, but with the Spirit of God, such as have both predicted things to come, and have made manifest the secrets of the heart." He speaks of utterances inspired "by the Spirit, in an ecstasy, that is in a rapture, whenever an interpretation of tongues has occurred."[7] Novatian, a Presbyter in Rome (d.c. 257) wrote of the Holy Spirit, "This is He who places prophets in the Church, instructs teachers, directs tongues, gives powers and healings, does wonderful works, offers discrimination of spirits, affords powers of government, suggests counsels, and orders and arranges whatever other gifts there are of *charismata*; and thus makes the Lord's Church everywhere, and in all, perfected and completed."[8] Hilary, Bishop of Poitiers in Gaul (d. 367), said of the gifts of either speaking or interpreting divers kinds of tongues that "Clearly these are the Church's agents of ministry and work of whom the body of Christ consists; and God has ordained them."[9]

The advent of infant baptism together with the false belief in baptismal regeneration produced pseudo-Christians devoid of the Holy

Spirit, and therefore without His inspiration to speak in tongues. This situation generally prevailed in Christendom for over a thousand years. Symeon, the New Theologian (949–1022), a monk in the Eastern church, is said to have spoken in tongues. Tongue speaking occurred among some of the Radicals during the reformation; the Quakers and Camisards of the seventeenth century; the Jansenists, the Moravians, the Methodists in the eighteenth century; and the Irvingites of the nineteenth century.[10]

A related objection is that great Christian leaders, mightily used of God, did not speak in tongues. God raised up very great leaders for His purposes before the Pentecost of Acts 2 who did not speak in tongues. Thus the fact that outstanding men have been raised up since then is a continuation of God's will to use men to fulfil His purposes. Their failure to speak in tongues did not negate their gifts to fulfil God's purpose. Apollos (Acts 18:24–29) was a man raised up and greatly gifted for God's service. He was "eloquent", and "mighty in the scriptures." He was also "fervent in spirit." He was "instructed in the way of the Lord," and he "spoke and taught accurately the things of the Lord." He was a great preacher. There was however a limit to his knowledge. He knew "only the baptism of John." He was ignorant of the baptism in water in the name of Jesus, and ignorant of the baptism in the Holy Spirit. Some translate "fervent in spirit" as "boiling over with the Holy Spirit." Both translations are possible, but whichever translation we take we have a great man who was ignorant of the baptism in the Spirit, the promise of the Father. He may have been filled with the Spirit like others in Old Testament times, but he did not speak in tongues, because he did not know of the baptism in the Spirit. This was remedied by Aquila and Priscilla, who explained to him the way of God more fully (Acts 18:26). Down through the centuries great and gifted men like Apollos have accomplished great things in the service of God. But like him, before his meeting with Aquila and Priscilla, they did not speak in tongues. Like the Old Testament men of God doubtless many were filled with the Spirit. For a variety of reasons they did not appropriate the promise of the Father. But their prayers for the power of the Spirit were answered, and at times God sovereignly bestowed His Spirit upon them to fulfil His will even when they did not ask. They were not baptized in the Spirit, but they were filled with Him just like others in Old Testament times. Consequently, though they fell short of the full blessing of the promise of the Father, they were endued with power to fulfil their God given ministry.

Some object because of their interpretation of Joel 2:28–32

John F. MacArthur Jr. says that Pentecost was "only a partial fulfilment, or better, a preview of the prophecy's ultimate consummation," and, "Peter was simply telling those present at Pentecost that they were getting a preliminary glimpse, a projection of the kind of power that the Spirit would release in the millennial kingdom."[11] This view believes in an earthly reign of Jesus Christ at the second coming of the Lord Jesus Christ. Joel's prophecy will not be fulfilled until Christ reigns on earth. Consequently this interpretation does not permit any fulfilment of Joel's prophecy down the centuries from the Pentecost of Acts 2 until the return of Jesus Christ. It contradicts Peter's statement in Acts 2:39. The whole of Joel's prophecy quoted by Peter (Acts 2:16–21) applies throughout the totality of the last days. Verses 19–20 have been fulfilled, and will be fulfilled in God's judgment on Jerusalem: "Jerusalem will be trampled by Gentiles until the times of the Gentiles are fulfilled" (Luke 21:24). The prediction stated in Acts 2:21 "And it shall come to pass *That* whoever calls on the name of the LORD Shall be saved" applies throughout the last days.

There are various arguments that tongues were not meant by God to continue

1.   It is asserted that there was a decline in the occurrence of the miraculous with the passage of time and that this is manifest in the New Testament writings.

There is less mention of miracles in the later chapters of Acts and in the later epistles.

Answer: there is mention of the miraculous in the later chapters of Acts. In Ephesus we see no evidence of decline (Acts 19:11–12). We read of prophesying in Acts 21:9–11. At the end of the book Paul works miracles of healing on the island of Malta (Acts 28:8–9). The lesser mention compared with the earlier chapters in Acts is simply because the subject matter is different. Paul is in captivity from Acts 21:33 to the end of Luke's account. In the same way the later letters continue to mention spiritual gifts (1 Tim. 1:18; 4:14; James 5:15; 1 John 4:1 and Rev. 2:20).

2.   It is similarly argued that miracles are not continuously used by God in His dealings with mankind.

Thus we have a great outbreak of miracles at the time of Moses, an epoch of miracles during the ministries of Elijah and Elisha, and a great number of them at the start of the New Covenant. From these facts it is argued that tongue speaking was not in God's plan after the early days of the Christian church.

Answer: the promise of the Father is for as many as the Lord our God shall call throughout the last days right up to the return of Christ. Those believers who appropriate the promise speak in tongues.

3.   Robert L. Reymond states that Christ and the apostles as those who bore a new body of revelation were authenticated by miracles. After that revelation had been interpreted into permanent scriptural form and authenticated by miraculous power there was no further need for miracles.[12]
Answer: this is too narrow as an interpretation of the purpose of miracles. Again it fails to take any account of Acts 2:39.

4.   The belief that Paul taught in 1 Cor. 13:8 that tongues would cease and that this was fulfilled when the New Testament scriptures were completed.
Answer: the passage reads, "Love never fails. But whether *there are* prophecies, they will fail; whether *there are* tongues, they will cease; whether *there is* knowledge, it will vanish away. For we know in part and we prophesy in part. But when that which is perfect has come, then that which is in part will be done away. When I was a child, I spoke as a child, I understood as a child, I thought as a child; but when I became a man, I put away childish things. For now we see in a mirror, dimly, but then face to face. Now I know in part, but then I shall know just as I also am known" (1 Cor. 13:8–12). "That which is perfect," and "then I shall know just as I also am known" refer to the glorified state of the believer when Christ returns. They do not speak of the completed canon of scripture. As Dr. Martyn Lloyd-Jones says this completed canon view is "nonsense" because "It means that you and I, who have the Scriptures open before us, know much more than the apostle Paul of God's truth."[13]

5.   There is also an interpretation that says "that which is perfect" is a pre-second coming maturity of the Church.
Answer: it is based on the fact that the word translated perfect is used elsewhere in 1 Corinthians to speak of Christian maturity. The meaning of the word has to be determined by the context, and 1 Cor. 13 rules out this meaning. This view imagines a state of knowledge in the future mature church on earth as great as God's knowledge of His people! Again it is nonsense. No local church has ever attained such a state, nor ever will until Christ returns.

6.   Sinclair Ferguson argues that 1 Cor. 13:8 ". . . states no more than the general point that these gifts will cease at some future point; exactly when is not in view."

He continues, "If the New Testament does not make a specific pronouncement, the function of these gifts will determine their longevity. The continuationist – restorationist view does not take sufficient account of the fact that the New Testament itself divides the last days into apostolic and post-apostolic dimensions or periods. There is a foundation-laying period marked by the ministry of the apostles and prophets, and there is a post-foundational, post-apostolic period in view (as Eph. 2:20 implies). It should not surprise us that phenomena occur in the former period which are not designed to continue beyond it, any more than the miracles of Moses, Elijah or Elisha continued to be performed by their gifted successors."[14]

Answers: Paul states exactly when tongues will cease – when that which is perfect is come! Peter states that the promise of the Father applies throughout the last days, apostolic, post-apostolic and down through time right up to the moment of the return of Christ.

7.   *Sinclair Ferguson also argues that". . . outside of 1 Corinthians there is no record of either the occurrence or regulation "of tongue speaking.*[15]

Answer: there is no further mention also in the New Testament epistles of eating the Lord's Supper other than in 1 Corinthians. Does that mean the other churches did not break bread? Of course they did. They carried out the command of the Lord in this matter. Equally the other churches obeyed the commandments of the Lord as regards spiritual gifts: "If anyone thinks himself to be a prophet or spiritual, let him acknowledge that the things which I write to you are the commandments of the Lord" (1 Cor. 14:37). The apostle deals with spiritual gifts throughout chapters 12 – 14 of 1 Corinthians. In chapter twelve he says that spiritual gifts are set in the body of Christ. Here he is not referring to the church at Corinth but to all believers at that time, at Corinth and in every other place, who made up the church on earth, the body of Christ. Thus the commandments he gave to the Corinthians applied to all the other New Testament churches.

8.   *John F. MacArthur Jr. is categoric: "The tongues being spoken today are not biblical."*[16]

He says there are a number of possibilities which could explain the phenomenon. Tongues may be satanic or demonic. Tongues are a learned behaviour, devoid of anything supernatural. Tongues can be psychologically induced.

Answers: one can agree that some tongue speaking is not biblical, and can be explained by the possibilities he suggests. To dismiss all tongue speaking as counterfeit is to deny any value to cast iron assurances that Jesus Himself gave to believers when they seek the Holy Spirit and good gifts from God. He said, "Ask, and it will be given to you; seek, and you will find; knock, and it will be opened to you. For everyone who asks receives, and he who seeks finds, and to him who knocks it will be opened. Or what man is there among you who, if his son asks for bread, will give him a stone? Or if he asks for a fish, will he give him a serpent? If you then, being evil, know how to give good gifts to your children, how much more will your Father who is in heaven give good things to those who ask Him!" (Mat. 7:7–11). Jesus is saying that earthly parents, who are evil, don't give bad gifts to their children. They don't give a stone instead of bread, something utterly useless. They don't give a serpent instead of fish, something dreadfully harmful. They only give good things. Jesus says, "how much more will your Father who is in heaven give good things, not bad things, to those who ask him?" Luke also records similar words of Jesus on another later occasion: "So I say to you, ask, and it will be given to you; seek, and you will find; knock, and it will be opened to you. For everyone who asks receives, and he who seeks finds, and to him who knocks it will be opened. If a son asks for bread from any father among you, will he give him a stone? Or if *he asks* for a fish, will he give him a serpent instead of a fish? Or if he asks for an egg, will he offer him a scorpion? If you then, being evil, know how to give good gifts to your children, how much more will *your* heavenly Father give the Holy Spirit to those who ask Him!" (Luke 11:9–13). This time Jesus adds "if he asks for an egg will he give him a scorpion?" The scorpion stings with its tail. The sting is most painful, and can be deadly. Jesus concludes this time by assuring His disciples that if they ask for the Holy Spirit they will not receive some useless, or harmful alternative gift. John F. MacArthur Jr. is saying that millions of Christians have asked for the Holy Spirit and biblical tongues and have received "stones, serpents and scorpions."

The Historical Perspective

Many Pentecostal denominations declare in their doctrinal tenets that tongues are the initial evidence of the baptism in the Spirit. This particular doctrinal formulation is explained by the course of church history. In 1900 the students of a Bible School in Topeka, Kansas, U.S.A. were instructed to study the Bible individually to see what was the evidence of the baptism in the Holy Spirit. At that time many Christians had come to believe in, and claimed to have experienced, a baptism in the Spirit distinct from and subsequent to the new birth. Their particular doctrines of the baptism in the Spirit were varied. The students of the Bible School concluded that speaking in tongues was the evidence of the baptism in the Spirit. By 1901 the majority of them, and the founder and principal of the Bible School, experienced a Spirit baptism and spoke in tongues. This event was of profound significance. Prior to this there had been instances of speaking in tongues during the preceding decades, but no one linked such speaking with the baptism in the Spirit. That link brought about the formation of the Pentecostal Churches of the twentieth century. It explains the framing of their doctrinal statements. They felt a compelling need to declare what they believed to be the evidence of the baptism in the Spirit. The various denominations and groups which formed adopted differing stances on this contentious matter.

The New Testament did not start at the point of seeking to define the evidence of the baptism in the Spirit. It started with a definition of the baptism in the Spirit. Peter the leading apostle defined very precisely the baptism in the Spirit. He defined it as the promise of the Father "I will pour out My Spirit on all flesh ... and they shall prophesy" (fulfilled in the speaking in tongues). The baptism in the Spirit is receiving a pouring out of the Spirit and thereby being inspired to speak in tongues. It is not merely receiving a pouring out of the Spirit. It is also a promise of inspiration to prophesy. Thus speaking in tongues was an essential part of the baptism in the Spirit. Without it the promise of the Father was not fulfilled. The baptism in the Spirit had not occurred. This definition of the baptism in the Spirit also meant that it was an experience evident to the one receiving the Spirit and to any others who were present. There was the manifestation of speaking in tongues. Therefore there was no need to formulate a doctrine of initial evidence of the baptism in the Spirit. The apostolic definition of the baptism in the Spirit contained it. Speaking in tongues is not merely the initial evidence of the baptism in the Spirit it is an essential part of it.

References

1. Robert P. Menzies *Empowered For Witness, The Spirit in Luke-Acts,* Sheffield: Sheffield Academic Press, 1994, pages 250–251.
2. Larry W. Hurtado *Initial Evidence: Historical and Biblical Perspectives on the Pentecostal Doctrine of Spirit Baptism* Gary B. McGee editor, 1991 by Hendrickson Publishers, Peabody, Massachusetts, page 192. Used by permission. All rights reserved.
3. *Ibid.*, page 194.
4. *Ibid.*, pages 194–195.
5. *Ibid.*, page 195.

6. Irenaeus *Against Heresies* Book V vi.i Ante-Nicene Fathers 1 page 531.
7. Tertullian *Against Marcion* Book V chap.viii. Ante-Nicene Fathers 3 page 447.
8. Novatian *Treatise Concerning The Trinity* xxix. Ante-Nicene Fathers 5 page 641.
9. Hilary *On The Trinity Book* 8.33. Nicene and Post Nicene Fathers Series II Vol ix page 147.
10. Stanley M. Burgess *Initial Evidence: Historical and Biblical Perspectives on the Pentecostal Doctrine of the Spirit* Gary B. McGee editor 1991 by Hendrickson Publishers, Peabody, Massachusetts, pages 14–35. Used by permission. All rights reserved.
11. Taken from *Charismatic Chaos* by John F. MacArthur Jr.. Copyright © 1992 by John F. MacArthur Jr. Used by permission of Zondervan, page 288.
12. Dr. Robert L. Reymond *A New Systematic Theology of the Christian Faith*, Copyright © 1998 Thomas Nelson Inc., page 413.
13. D. Martyn Lloyd-Jones *Prove All Things*, 1985, pages 32–33. Used by permission of Kingsway Publications, Lottbridge Drove, Eastbourne.
14. Sinclair Ferguson *The Holy Spirit* IVP, 1996, pages 228–229.
15. *Ibid.*, page 229.
16. Taken from *Charismatic Chaos* by John F. MacArthur Jr.. Copyright © 1992 by John F. MacArthur Jr. Used by permission of Zondervan, page 297.

CHAPTER THIRTY ONE

THE BAPTISM IN THE SPIRIT IN THE EPISTLES

The baptism in the Spirit closely followed conversion just as water baptism did in New Testament evangelism. The Samaritan converts experienced an abnormal delay between their conversion and baptism in the Spirit. They are unique in this respect in the records of the New Testament. Consequently when the writers of the epistles speak of the baptism in the Spirit they always refer to it as a past event experienced by all the believers to whom they wrote. We shall now examine such verses with the exceptions of Rom. 5:5, 8:15–16, 1 Cor. 12:13, Eph. 1:13–14 and Heb. 6:2 which have already been expounded.

1 Corinthians 2:12

"Now we have received, not the spirit of the world, but the Spirit who is from God, that we might know the things that have been freely given to us by God."

This verse tells us:

a) that Paul and all the Corinthian believers received the Spirit at a point in time in the past. The verb "received" is in the aorist indicative.
b) the Spirit was from God – from the Father (John 14:16, 26; and Acts 2:16–18), and from Christ (John 16:7 and Acts 2:33).
c) one of the purposes of receiving the Spirit is "that we might know the things that have been freely given to us by God" (cf. John 16:13–14).

2 Corinthians 1:21–22

"Now He who establishes us with you in Christ and has anointed us *is* God, who also has sealed us and given us the Spirit in our hearts as a guarantee."

These verses speak of the baptism in the Spirit as an anointing. The anointing in the Old Testament scriptures was linked to the holy anointing oil or simply oil. In both cases the oil symbolised the Holy Spirit. Jacob poured oil on a stone and anointed it (Gen. 28) when God met with him. It marked the presence of God in that place. It also marked a significant meeting with God, when Jacob made a vow to God. God decreed that the Tabernacle and all in it, the altar of burnt offering and the laver and its base were to be anointed with the holy anointing oil. The anointing consecrated these things. It made them holy. In the same way Aaron and his sons the priests were to be anointed, consecrated and set apart so that they may minister to God as priests. After the initial institution of the levitical priesthood only the high priest was anointed to consecrate him to office. Thus anointing was a very special blessing. The holy anointing oil was not to be applied to persons other than those designated by God. There was a severe penalty for breaking this rule – excommunication from Israel. Kings were anointed to consecrate them to their position and to their task. Sometimes prophets were anointed to their office.

In Psa. 105:15 God says, "Do not touch My anointed ones, And do My prophets no harm." The reference in the verse is to Abraham (Gen. 12:17 and Gen. 20:3). It reveals that Abraham was reckoned by God as an anointed one; and that anointed ones together with prophets are to be treated as those who are in a special relationship with God. The anointed must not be harmed, and if anyone does do so, it is regarded by God as great sinfulness. Two examples of this are seen in the life of Abraham. Because of the way he was treated great plagues came upon Pharaoh and his house (Gen. 12:17); and the Lord closed up the wombs of Abimelech's wife and his female servants and would have brought death upon Abimelech and all who were his (Gen. 20:7 and 17–18). David's refusal to kill King Saul, the Lord's anointed, even when Saul sought to kill David, was because of his understanding of God's will concerning the Lord's anointed (1 Sam. 24:6–7 and 26:8–12). David executed the man who killed Saul because he killed the Lord's anointed (2 Sam. 1:6–16).

Anointing was also an enduement: "Then Samuel took the horn of oil and anointed him in the midst of his brothers; and the Spirit of the LORD came upon David from that day forward. So Samuel arose and went to Ramah" (1 Sam. 16:13).

Of particular note is that Cyrus is stated to be the Lord's anointed (Isa. 45:1). He was king of Persia 559–530 B.C. and was appointed by God to give the Jews, who were his subjects, permission to rebuild Jerusalem and its temple even though he was a heathen. In this case the anointing of God indicates simply an appointment to fulfil God's purpose.

Certain offerings had to be anointed with oil under the Mosaic regulations. Unleavened wafers are mentioned in Exod. 29:2, Lev.2:4 and 7:12. Exod. 29:2 was part of the actions to consecrate Aaron and his sons to the priesthood. Lev. 2:4 refers to the cereal offering presented daily each morning and evening. Lev. 7:12 concerns the peace offering expressing thanksgiving to God.

The prophet Zechariah writing of Zerubbabel and Joshua around 500 BC calls them anointed ones (Zech. 4:14). They are respectively governor and high priest. The completion of the building of the Temple by the people of God who had returned from exile could only be achieved by the Spirit of God. The Spirit would work through these two anointed leaders. Here we see the anointing as an enabling to achieve God's purpose which could not be achieved by "might nor by power" (Zech. 4:6). Human resources, both physical and mental, however great, were inadequate. Only those anointed by the Spirit would succeed.

The word Messiah in Dan. 9:25–26, and its New Testament equivalent, Christ, both mean the Anointed One. Both terms come from verbs meaning to anoint with sacred oil. In the Old Testament the anointing oil was poured upon an object or person (Gen. 28:18, 35:14; Exod. 29:7, 30:32; 1 Sam. 10:1; 2 Kings 9:3 and 6; and Psalm 133). The anointing of Jesus by God is recorded in Mat. 3:16–17, Mark 1:9–11 and Luke 3:21–22. "When He had been baptized, Jesus came up immediately from the water; and behold, the heavens were opened to Him, and He saw the Spirit of God descending like a dove and alighting upon Him. And suddenly a voice *came* from heaven, saying, 'This is My beloved Son, in whom I am well pleased'" (Mat. 3:16–17). Luke adds several details – that Jesus was praying, that the Spirit of God descended in a bodily form, and that Jesus began His ministry at that time: "When all the people were baptized, it came to pass that Jesus also was baptized; and while He prayed, the heaven was opened. And the Holy Spirit descended in bodily form like a dove upon Him, and a voice came from heaven which said, 'You are My beloved Son; in You I am well pleased.' Now Jesus Himself began *His ministry at* about thirty years of age" (Luke 3:21–23). This event fulfilled Old Testament prophecies:

Psa. 45:7 predicted the anointing of Jesus, "You love righteousness and hate wickedness; Therefore God, Your God, has anointed You With the oil of gladness more than Your companions" (see Heb. 1:9).

Isa. 11:1–2 was fulfilled, "There shall come forth a Rod from the stem of Jesse, And a Branch shall grow out of his roots. The Spirit of the

LORD shall rest upon Him, The Spirit of wisdom and understanding, The Spirit of counsel and might, The Spirit of knowledge and of the fear of the LORD."

Jesus Himself declared that Isa. 61:1–2 was fulfilled: "And He was handed the book of the prophet Isaiah. And when He had opened the book, He found the place where it was written: 'The Spirit of the LORD *is* upon Me, Because He has anointed Me To preach the gospel to *the* poor; He has sent Me to heal the brokenhearted, To proclaim liberty to *the* captives And recovery of sight to *the* blind, To set at liberty those who are oppressed; To proclaim the acceptable year of the LORD.' Then He closed the book, and gave *it* back to the attendant and sat down. And the eyes of all who were in the synagogue were fixed on Him. And He began to say to them, 'Today this Scripture is fulfilled in your hearing' " (Luke 4:17–21). Jesus was anointed to preach.

Other New Testament scriptures refer to this anointing: "For truly against Your holy Servant Jesus, whom You anointed, both Herod and Pontius Pilate, with the Gentiles and the people of Israel, were gathered together" (Acts 4:27). The significance of mentioning that Jesus was anointed was the utter futility of opposition against Jesus as the Anointed one, as stated prophetically in Psalm 2:1–5, "Why do the nations rage, And the people plot a vain thing? The kings of the earth set themselves, And the rulers take counsel together, Against the LORD and against His Anointed, *saying,* 'Let us break Their bonds in pieces And cast away Their cords from us.' He who sits in the heavens shall laugh; The LORD shall hold them in derision. Then He shall speak to them in His wrath, And distress them in His deep displeasure." The church at Jerusalem used these words in prayer when they were threatened if they continued to preach Jesus. Just like Christ they had been anointed with the Holy Spirit and were opposed by the rulers and authorities. Therefore they confidently asked for God's help to fulfil His will. They received a wonderful answer (Acts 4:29–33). Jesus was anointed to work miracles and to heal. Peter recalls "how God anointed Jesus of Nazareth with the Holy Spirit and with power, who went about doing good and healing all who were oppressed by the devil, for God was with Him" (Acts 10:38). The Father gave the Spirit without measure to Him (John 3:34). This enduement enabled Jesus to work miracles which proved that He was sent by God. Nicodemus recognised that He was "a teacher come from God for no one can do these signs that You do unless God is with him" (John 3:2). The man Jesus healed of blindness said, "If this man were not from God

He could do nothing" (John 9:33). Jesus said, "But I have a greater witness than John's; for the works which the Father has given Me to finish – the very works that I do – bear witness of Me, that the Father has sent Me" (John 5:36). Thus Peter says that Jesus was a man attested by God by miracles, wonders, and signs which God did through Him (Acts 2:22). All those mighty works were wrought by the anointing of the Spirit.

Jesus calls His anointing with the Spirit a sealing by God the Father (John 6:27). The Father said "This is My beloved Son in Whom I am well pleased." He placed His seal of approval on His son at that time. John's gospel tells of that attestation. "John testified saying, 'I have seen the Spirit descending as a dove out of heaven, and He remained upon Him. I did not recognize Him, but He who sent me to baptize in water said to me, "He upon whom you see the Spirit descending and remaining upon Him, this is One who baptizes in the Holy Spirit." I myself have seen, and have testified that this is the Son of God.'" (John 1:32–34 NASB).

His atoning sacrifice for sin was by the Spirit, "how much more shall the blood of Christ, who through the eternal Spirit offered Himself without spot to God, cleanse your conscience from dead works to serve the living God?" (Heb. 9:14).

Christ continued to minister by the Holy Spirit after His resurrection, "The former account I made, O Theophilus, of all that Jesus began both to do and teach, until the day in which He was taken up, after He through the Holy Spirit had given commandments to the apostles whom He had chosen" (Acts 1:1–2). Those commands are stated in Acts 1:4–8.

The truth contained in the scriptures above concerning the anointing of the Spirit reveal the significance of the word "anointed" in Paul's statement, "Now He who establishes us with you in Christ and has anointed us *is* God, who also has sealed us and given us the Spirit in our hearts as a guarantee." "Establishes" is a present tense indicating a continuous experience. "Anointed", "sealed" and "gave" are in the aorist tense pointing to the single event of receiving the promise of the Father. That single experience was at the same time an anointing, a sealing and a giving of the Spirit. The verse puts great emphasis on the fact that it is God who gave this experience. This experience of anointing, sealing and being given the Spirit is a means of grace used by God to establish believers.

The anointing establishes because it is:

1. a vivid experience of the presence of the Holy Spirit. It is a significant meeting with God.

2. a blessing reserved by God only for those to whom He wills to give it.
3. a special relationship with God.
4. God's action of consecrating a believer to His service.
5. God's empowering by the Spirit.

The sealing establishes because it:

1. gives assurance of being His children.
2. gives assurance of security.

The giving of the Spirit establishes because:
The Spirit is the first down-payment assuring the believer of final payment in full. Future glory is certain and already experienced in part now.

Thus the anointing is seen to be a single event of abiding significance for the Christian.

John also writes of the anointing of the Spirit

> "But you have an anointing from the Holy One, and you all know" (1 John 2:20 NASB).

> "But the anointing which you have received from Him abides in you, and you do not need that anyone teach you; but as the same anointing teaches you concerning all things, and is true, and is not a lie, and just as it has taught you, you will abide in Him" (1 John 2:27).

This anointing has come from the Holy One, the Lord Jesus Christ the baptizer in the Holy Spirit. The believers in these verses are being contrasted to those who have left them (verse 19). John is saying in verse 27 that the anointing has taught them so that they know the truth. Also the anointing abides in them and continues to teach them about everything. All of them had been anointed. In stark contrast to the present, all true Christians in New Testament times received the promise of the Father at the start of their Christian lives. Acts 8 reveals that if this did not happen it was remedied without delay. John therefore, just like Paul in 1 Cor. 1:21–22, writes to them in the sure knowledge that they were all anointed. We must not project the current state of Christians, in which some are anointed and some are not, to New Testament times. With the passage of time a profound change has occurred. There has been a grave falling away from New Testament doctrine and experience in this matter.

The anointing, the baptism in the Spirit, is seen in these verses in relation to the attempt of false teachers to deceive the children of God. These deceivers probably claimed superior knowledge, and asserted that the true believers needed the knowledge they could impart. John says that the anointing they have teaches them all things. Their knowledge is sufficient. They are not lacking anything for salvation. They have come into the knowledge of the truth, and in that sense they don't need anyone to teach them. By "anyone" (verse 27) he means these deceivers. He does not mean that they have no need of his letter. Nor does he mean that they have no need of the ministry of apostles, prophets, teachers (Eph. 4:11), and elders (1 Tim. 3:1–7 and 5:17). John says that the anointing remains in them. The baptism in the Spirit is a single event with lasting effect. Consequently the anointing continues to teach them. John exhorts them to hold fast to the teaching already given, and continuing to be given by the Spirit. In this way the anointing will protect them from deceivers.

Galatians 3:1–5

"O foolish Galatians! Who has bewitched you that you should not obey the truth, before whose eyes Jesus Christ was clearly portrayed among you as crucified? This only I want to learn from you: Did you receive the Spirit by the works of the law, or by the hearing of faith? Are you so foolish? Having begun in the Spirit, are you now being made perfect by the flesh? Have you suffered so many things in vain – if indeed *it was* in vain? Therefore He who supplies the Spirit to you and works miracles among you, *does He do it* by the works of the law, or by the hearing of faith?"

Paul is writing to the Galatians to bring them back to the true gospel from which they have been led astray. Instead of believing in Christ for salvation they had turned to the belief that they would be justified by keeping the law and being circumcised. At this point in the letter Paul is treating them as those who are foolish and bewitched. He seeks to bring them back to their senses. Therefore he asks them to reply to *just one* question, "Did you receive the Spirit by the works of the law, or by the hearing of faith?" This question makes sense only if receiving the Spirit was a single definite memorable conscious experience. Moreover, it only has force if all the Galatian believers had received the Spirit. Otherwise only some could answer the question. If, as contended, it was an experience of the Spirit being poured out upon one with the result of speaking in tongues then the Galatian believers would recall the event without difficulty. They would be able to answer Paul's question.

At this point Paul is appealing to this fact of their actual experience. He is absolutely sure that they can only give one answer – the hearing of faith (ἡ ἐξ ἀκοῆς πίστεως). There are several possible translations of this phrase: ἀκοῆς can mean "hearing" or "what is heard", and πίστεως can mean "believing" or "what is believed." Thus the NASB reads "hearing with faith", and the NIV "believing what you heard." Both are in harmony with existing believers appropriating by faith the promise of Joel when they hear it. The phrase "the hearing of faith" is repeated at the end of verse 5, "Therefore He who supplies the Spirit to you and works miracles among you, *does He do it* by the works of the law, or by the hearing of faith?" The supplying of the Spirit and working of miracles is the continuing experience of the Galatians (for a full explanation of the meaning of these words please see 1 Cor. 12–14, 1 Thess. 5:19–22, Rom. 12:6 and 1 Pet. 4:10–11). The phrase "the hearing of faith" has the same meaning in verses 2 and 5. Verse 5 is speaking of faith exercised after believing in Christ for salvation. It is faith in God for the supply of His Spirit and for miracles. It is the same faith which is exercised after salvation to receive the Holy Spirit. It is, however, the same in essence as initial saving faith for justification. It is "the hearing of faith" just as Abraham "believed God, and it was accounted to him for righteousness" (Gal. 3:5–6). As Rom. 1:17 declares, the Christian life is one of faith, "The just shall live by faith."

"Having begun" in verse 3 refers to the fact that receiving the Spirit followed repentance and faith, just as water baptism did. The receiving of the Spirit was one of the first events after they became Christians.

"Have you suffered so many things in vain?" (verse 4) is a possible translation, but the translation "Did you experience so much for nothing?" NRSV is also possible, and suits better the preceding verse 2 and following verse 5.

Galatians 3:13–14, NASB

"Christ redeemed us from the curse of the Law, having become a curse for us – for it is written, 'CURSED IS EVERYONE WHO HANGS ON A TREE' – in order that in Christ Jesus the blessing of Abraham might come to the Gentiles, so that we would receive the promise of the Spirit through faith"

The last part of verse 14, "that we would receive the promise of the Spirit through faith" relates back to verse 2.

The "blessing of Abraham" is justification by faith as stated in verses 6–9.

The "promise of the Spirit" in verse 14 is the promise of the Father through Joel stated in Luke 24:49, Acts 1:4 and 2:16–18.

Christ carried out His redemptive work so that the "blessing of Abraham" might come to Gentiles *in order that* believers might receive the promise of the Spirit. Justification by faith is with the purpose of receiving the Spirit.

Some commentators interpret the blessing of Abraham (justification by faith), and receiving the Spirit as synonymous. They say that both express becoming a Christian in different ways, and that both occur at the same time. To sustain this interpretation the final clause "that we would receive the promise of the Spirit through faith" has to be taken as co-ordinate with the previous clause "that . . . the blessing of Abraham might come to the Gentiles."

Rather the final clause should be taken as subordinate to the first. It will be helpful to highlight the key words as shown:

"Christ redeemed us from the curse of the Law, having become a curse for us – for it is written, 'CURSED IS EVERYONE WHO HANGS ON A TREE' – *in order that* in Christ Jesus the blessing of Abraham might come to the Gentiles, *so that* we would receive the promise of the Spirit through faith" (Gal. 3:13–14 NASB).	Χριστὸς ἡμᾶς ἐξηγόρασεν ἐκ τῆς κατάρας τοῦ νόμου γενόμενος ὑπὲρ ἡμῶν κατάρα, ὅτι γέγραπται, Ἐπικατάρατος πᾶς ὁ κρεμάμενος ἐπὶ ξύλου, **ἵνα** εἰς τὰ ἔθνη ἡ εὐλογία τοῦ Ἀβραὰμ γένηται ἐν Χριστῷ Ἰησοῦ, **ἵνα** τὴν ἐπαγγελίαν τοῦ πνεύματος λάβωμεν διὰ τῆς πίστεως. (Gal. 3:13–14 GNT).

There are other passages in Paul's writings, where in the same way as in Gal.3:14, Paul uses ἵνα (in order that) successively in clauses; and the second ἵνα clause is subordinate to the first ἵνα clause.

> "But when the fullness of the time came, God sent forth His Son, born of a woman, born under the Law, *so that* (ἵνα) He might redeem those who were under the Law, *that* (ἵνα) we might receive the adoption as sons" Gal. 4:4–5 NASB.

The purpose of redemption was adoption. The second ἵνα clause expresses the intended result of the first.

> "I appeal to you, brothers and sisters, by our Lord Jesus Christ and by the love of the Spirit, to join me in earnest prayer to God on my behalf, *that* (ἵνα) I may be rescued from the unbelievers in Judea, and

that my ministry to Jerusalem may be acceptable to the saints; *so that* (ἵνα) by God's will I may come to you with joy and be refreshed in your company" Rom. 15:30–32 NRSV.

Again the second ἵνα clause is subordinate to the first clause.

"Husbands, love your wives, just as Christ also loved the church and gave Himself for her, *that* (ἵνα) He might sanctify and cleanse her with the washing of water by the word, *that* (ἵνα) He might present her to Himself a glorious church, not having spot or wrinkle or any such thing, but *that* (ἵνα) she should be holy and without blemish" Eph. 5:26–27.

The second ἵνα clause expresses the purpose of the first ἵνα clause. The third ἵνα clause is coordinate with the second clause. The sanctification and cleansing of the church is its present state on earth; the presentation of the church is future at the last day in its glorified state.

"meanwhile praying also for us, *that* (ἵνα) God would open to us a door for the word, to speak the mystery of Christ, for which I am also in chains, *that* (ἵνα) I may make it manifest, as I ought to speak." Col. 4:3–4.

Paul wants them to pray for opportunity to preach so that he can reveal the mystery of Christ. Again the second ἵνα clause is subordinate to the first clause.

"And this I pray, *that* (ἵνα) your love may abound still more and more in real knowledge and all discernment, so that you may approve the things that are excellent, *in order* (ἵνα) to be sincere and blameless until the day of Christ." Phil. 1:9–10.NASB.

This is a further example.

Therefore it is contended that the correct interpretation of Gal. 3:14 takes the second ἵνα clause as subordinate to the first ἵνα clause.

2 Timothy 1:6–7 (my trans. of v.7)

"Therefore I remind you to stir up the gift of God which is in you through the laying on of my hands. For God has not given us a Spirit of fear, but of power and of love and of self-control."

Paul is speaking here of Timothy's baptism in the Spirit. It is a separate event from that recorded in 1 Tim. 4:14, NIV "Do not neglect your gift, which was given you through a prophetic message when the body of elders laid their hands on you." In 1 Tim. 4:14 hands are laid on by the presbytery, the elders (see 1 Tim. 3:1–7); in 2 Tim. 1:6–7 only Paul laid hands on Timothy. In 1 Tim. 4:14 a gift was given through prophetic utterance: in 2 Tim. 1:6 Paul makes no mention of prophecy. The gift of God in 2 Tim. 1:6 is the gift of the Holy Spirit.

The meaning of rekindle is to fan into flame his gift. How is Timothy to do this? Timothy spoke in tongues when he received the promise of the Father. A fire of Spirit inspired utterance was lit (cf. Acts 2:3–4). Paul is telling Timothy to go on speaking to God in tongues just as he himself does (1 Cor. 14:18).

In contrast to the rekindling of the gift there is a quenching of the Spirit. Paul commands "Do not quench the Spirit" (1 Thess. 5:19). The word quench means to extinguish a fire. It is the exact opposite of fanning a fire into flame. The command probably referred to behaviour aimed to stop speaking in tongues. Several considerations lead to this conclusion.

a) The words which follow immediately "do not despise prophecies" (1 Thess. 5:20) concern the gift of prophecy, another gift of inspired utterance, which stands alongside tongue speaking in the New Testament (1 Cor. 14).
b) Tongues plus interpretation of tongues was of equal effect and benefit to believers as the gift of prophecy (1 Cor. 14:5).
c) Paul found it necessary to command the Corinthians not to forbid speaking in tongues (1 Cor. 14:39). Some of the believers wanted to quench the Spirit in that way.

This interpretation links with the verse immediately following 2 Tim. 1:6: "For God has not given us a Spirit (πνεῦμα) of fear, but of power and of love and of self-control" (2 Tim. 1:7 my trans.). The Greek πνεῦμα can mean spirit or Spirit. Consequently translators and commentators differ. The arguments for Spirit are:

1. the verb gave – Paul speaks elsewhere of the giving of the Spirit using the same Greek verb (Rom. 5:5, 2 Cor. 1:22, 5:5, and 1 Thess. 4:8).
2. He also writes elsewhere of the Spirit using the idiom "not/but" contrast – not "of fear, but of power and of love and of self-control.":
    "Now we have received, *not* the spirit of the world, *but* the Spirit who is from God, that we might know the things that have been freely given to us by God" (1 Cor. 2:12). "For you did *not* receive

the spirit of bondage again to fear, *but* you received the Spirit of adoption by whom we cry out, 'Abba, Father'" (Rom. 8:15).
3. the aorist tense of the verb "gave" points to a single event in the past. This fits receiving the Holy Spirit.
4. The Spirit is given to "us" namely Christians in general.
5. The fact that the Spirit is accompanied with the genitive "of fear" does not indicate that the Spirit is not meant. The genitive is used in scripture of the Holy Spirit – "of life" (Rom. 8:2), "of adoption" (Rom. 8:15) and "of truth" (John 14:17, 15:26 and 16:13).
6. The Spirit gives power. He gives a consciousness of God's love, producing love towards God and man. He produces self-control, "sound-mindedness in action."[1]

Titus 3:4–7

"But when the kindness and the love of God our Savior toward man appeared, not by works of righteousness which we have done, but according to His mercy He saved us, through the washing of regeneration and renewing of the Holy Spirit, whom He poured out on us abundantly through Jesus Christ our Savior, that having been justified by His grace we should become heirs according to the hope of eternal life."

Christians are saved through the washing of regeneration and the renewing of the Holy Spirit. These words describe the change which takes place when a man is converted. He is spiritually washed. His heart is cleansed (Acts 15:9). He is renewed in his mind by the Holy Spirit. His heart is purified and his thinking transformed. He has come into the knowledge of the truth. This change has been wrought by the Holy Spirit. In addition to, and subsequent to, this change at conversion the Holy Spirit has been "poured out on us abundantly through Jesus Christ our Saviour." This speaks of the promise of the Father, the baptism in the Spirit. He continues, "so that, having been justified by His grace, we might become heirs according to the hope of eternal life." The mention of the pouring out of the Spirit is appropriate because the pouring out is the first instalment of that future inheritance (Eph 1:13–14).

Hebrews 6:4–6

"For *it is* impossible for those who were once enlightened, and have tasted the heavenly gift, and have become partakers of the Holy Spirit, and have tasted the good word of God and the powers of the age to come, if they fall away, to renew them again to repentance, since they crucify again for themselves the Son of God, and put *Him* to an open shame."

The writer to the Hebrews delivers a grave warning against falling away. In it he states the basic elements of Christian experience. They are:

1. receiving the knowledge of the truth at conversion, so that they turned from darkness to light (Acts 26:18; 2 Cor. 4:6; Col. 1:12–13; Eph. 5:8 and Heb. 10:26).
2. tasting the heavenly gift of salvation. Tasting means to experience in the sense of Psa. 34:8 and 1 Pet. 2:3. It means to taste and eat, and experience satisfaction and blessedness.
3. partaking of the Holy Spirit – the word "partakers" indicates a common experience of the Holy Spirit. This probably refers to the baptism in the Spirit.
4. tasting the good word of God – they have experienced its saving power (Rom. 1:16; James 1:21).
5. tasting the powers of the age to come – this links with Eph. 1:13–14, 2 Cor. 1:22 and 2 Cor. 5:5 where the Holy Spirit is the first instalment of future blessedness in the age to come.

Ephesians 4:1–6

"I, therefore, the prisoner of the Lord, beseech you to walk worthy of the calling with which you were called, with all lowliness and gentleness, with longsuffering, bearing with one another in love, endeavoring to keep the unity of the Spirit in the bond of peace. *There is* one body and one Spirit, just as you were called in one hope of your calling; one Lord, one faith, one baptism; one God and Father of all, who *is* above all, and through all, and in you all."

These verses state that all Christians belong to one body, the Church of Jesus Christ. There is only one Spirit Who indwells all of them, the Holy Spirit. They all have been given the same hope, the redemption of the body. They are all called to serve one Lord, Jesus Christ. The same faith has been delivered to all of them. Faith here is objective, the body of truth contained in the New Testament (Acts 6:7, Rom. 1:5 and Jude 3). All believers must embrace and submit to this God given revelation. There is one God and Father of all believers. He is over them, works through them and is in them.

We come to the words which are our particular concern. There is one baptism. Quite clearly Paul is aware that there is water baptism and there is a baptism in the Spirit. Why does he say there is one baptism, and which baptism is he referring to? Paul's concern is to give reasons to endeavour to keep the unity of the Spirit in the bond of peace. Therefore he reminds them of that baptism which was given to each of them with a view to the benefit of the one body of Christ: "For in one Spirit we were all baptized for one body . . . and have all been made to drink of one Spirit" (1 Cor. 12:13, my trans.). The baptism in the one Spirit was given in order to enable the believer to function in the one body of Christ. It was a baptism which related directly to the unity of the Spirit. Water baptism was also the common requirement and experience of all of them, but it related primarily to their individual relationship with Jesus Christ. Therefore it is concluded that Paul was referring to the baptism in the Spirit rather than water baptism.

Conclusions

1. When reading the New Testament epistles it is essential to recognise that there is a vast difference between their doctrine and practice and the doctrine and practice of many Christians even though they affirm the final authority of scripture. For example paedobaptists are unwilling to acknowledge that only believers' baptism was practised: and many who do believe and practise believers' baptism by immersion do not baptize converts as soon as they are saved. It is too easy to impose on the New Testament a preconceived theology backed by the traditions of men, and to force every verse into its framework.

2. Moreover, the fact that the individual experience of the Spirit in New Testament times was supernatural must also be fully acknowledged. The epistles must be read in the light of Acts, not interpreted down to the level of a believer's experience when he has not appropriated the promise of the Father, and when the supernatural gifts of 1 Cor. 12–14 are not part of his experience.

3. Those who deny that the baptism in the Spirit is subsequent to conversion have found it easier to fit Paul's writings into their theology than to account for Luke's scriptures. They have been massively helped to square with Paul by the mistranslation and misinterpretation of 1 Cor. 12:13. Also the fact that all believers to whom the epistles were addressed had received the promise of the Father enables them to argue that there is no teaching in the epistles about a baptism in the Spirit after conversion.

4. The examination of these verses show that there is no conflict between the teaching of Luke and Paul concerning the Spirit in the life of the believer. They are at one. Both were inspired by the one

Holy Spirit as they wrote their God-breathed scriptures. We do not have two differing pneumatologies. Nor is there a superiority in the sense that Paul's pneumatology is more developed than Luke's. Paul's treatment of the Holy Spirit and His work in the believer is far greater in quantity than Luke's. But this is because of the different purposes of each writer. The gospel of Luke focuses on what Jesus did and taught until His ascension (Acts 1:1). The book of Acts records the growth of the church of Jesus Christ. It is primarily about evangelism and missionary work and their results.

Paul's letters to believers delivered doctrine and instruction concerning their faith and walk, (and sometimes correction!), so they naturally contained much about the Holy Spirit. Luke and Paul both taught according to the one body of revelation given by God to believers (Jude 3). Their teachings complement each other. At no point does either contradict, supersede or negate the other.

Reference

1. William Hendriksen, *A Commentary on the Epistles to Timothy and Titus*, Banner of Truth Second British Edition, 1964, page 230.

CHAPTER THIRTY TWO

WHY IS TONGUE SPEAKING PART OF THE PROMISE OF THE FATHER?

There are many reasons given in the word of God for tongue speaking.

It magnifies God

"And how *is it that* we hear, each in our own language in which we were born? Parthians and Medes and Elamites, those dwelling in Mesopotamia, Judea and Cappadocia, Pontus and Asia, Phrygia and Pamphylia, Egypt and the parts of Libya adjoining Cyrene, visitors from Rome, both Jews and proselytes, Cretans and Arabs – we hear them speaking in our own tongues the wonderful works of God" (Acts 2:8–11).

They magnified God as they declared His wonderful works. In the same way it is recorded that Cornelius and those with him spoke in tongues and magnified God (Acts 10:46). On this occasion we do not know if the tongues spoken were understood by any who heard as on the Day of Pentecost. It would appear that none understood the languages being spoken. Even so God heard them speak of His wonderful works. This is in accord with 1 Cor. 14:2 NRSV, "For those who speak in a tongue do not speak to other people but to God; for nobody understands them, since they are speaking mysteries in the Spirit." Mysteries are defined in the New Testament as the wonderful works of God according to His counsel and purpose in history. The Father seeks true worshippers to worship Him in spirit and in truth (John 4:23–24). Speaking in tongues renders glory to God by declaring to Him His marvellous acts. This is praise that is well pleasing to God.

An introduction to the experience of being inspired to prophesy

On the day of Pentecost the literal translation of Acts 2:4 is "they were all filled with the Holy Spirit and began to speak in other tongues as the Spirit gave them to speak forth." Several points are to be noted. The disciples began to speak, not the Spirit in them. They were given the words to speak. Also the Greek word "to speak forth" (ἀποφθέγγεσθαι) means weighty or oracular utterance. They experienced the Holy Spirit moving them and enabling them to speak boldly words given by Him. This experience is an introduction into the whole realm of prophetic inspiration. When He inspires tongue speaking the believer experiences the moving of the Spirit upon him. He gains an understanding of the inspiration of the Spirit. The experience teaches the following important lessons.

1. It is always an act of faith to speak out the words given by the Spirit. The Spirit never forces the believer to speak.
2. The believer is always in control whether to speak or not to speak. This is taught clearly by Paul in 1 Cor. 14:18–19 and 27–28. Ideas of uncontrollable ecstasy or frenzy are utterly foreign to 1 Cor. 14 as the following verses reveal. "I thank my God I speak with tongues more than you all; yet in the church I would rather speak five words with my understanding, that I may teach others also, than ten thousand words in a tongue" (1 Cor. 14:18–19). Paul is setting forth his own example for them to follow. He says that *he chooses* to speak in tongues in private to a degree greater than all of them. But in the church gathering *he chooses* to speak words others can understand rather than tongues which would not be understood by others. He is governed by love to his brothers and sisters in Christ. Therefore he will refrain from the tongue speaking that is to be exercised in private purely for his own personal benefit. He goes on to deal with tongue speaking in the church. In verses 27–28 he says, "If anyone speaks in a tongue, *let there be* two or at the most three, *each* in turn, and let one interpret. But if there is no interpreter, let him keep silent in church, and let him speak to himself and to God." He does see a place for tongue speaking in the church but subject to these rules:

    - there must not be more than three utterances in any gathering,
    - each utterance must be in turn not at the same time as another utterance
    - each time one person only must interpret the utterance.
    - there is to be no speaking in tongues in the church if there is no one in the meeting with the gift of the interpretation of tongues.

Paul's conduct and these rules demonstrate that speaking in tongues is always under the control of the believer.

The Christian who has received the promise of the Father has an experiential understanding of the need for faith to prophesy, and the fact that he is responsible to choose to speak in tongues or not to speak. This understanding also applies to the exercise of the spiritual gifts of interpretation of tongues and prophecy (1 Cor. 12:10;14:5). Faith is necessary to speak forth the interpretation of an utterance in an unknown language; and faith is necessary to deliver a message given by direct inspiration of the Spirit. These gifts must always be exercised with self-control:

"How is it then, brethren? Whenever you come together, each of you has a psalm, has a teaching, has a tongue, has a revelation, has an interpretation. Let all things be done for edification" (1 Cor. 14:26), and,

"Let two or three prophets speak, and let the others judge. But if *anything* is revealed to another who sits by, let the first keep silent. For you can all prophesy one by one, that all may learn and all may be encouraged. And the spirits of the prophets are subject to the prophets" (1 Cor. 14:29–32), and,

"Therefore, brethren, desire earnestly to prophesy, and do not forbid to speak with tongues. Let all things be done decently and in order" (1 Cor. 14:39–40).

At this point it is necessary to define these gifts of the Spirit for use in the church.

The gift of speaking in tongues in the church
As previously explained all believers baptized in the Spirit are able to speak in tongues to God. But not all Christians baptized in the Spirit are inspired to speak forth in tongues in the church gathering for the words to be interpreted. The latter inspiration is a gift of the Spirit to speak words in a language unlearned by the speaker for the benefit of a person or persons present in the meeting of believers, words which will only be understood through the exercise of another gift of the Spirit – the interpretation of tongues.

The gift of interpretation of tongues
This is not an enabling to translate the words given in another language (1 Cor. 14:10). It is the ability by the Spirit to give the meaning of what has been said. The one who interprets is not given knowledge of the

language which was spoken. The Greek word "interprets" in 1 Cor. 14:5 is translated expound in Luke 24:27: "And beginning at Moses and all the Prophets, He expounded to them in all the Scriptures the things concerning Himself." In this verse the Greek word translated "expound" means to make plain what the scriptures said. He stated the meaning of the scriptures to which he directed their attention. In passing, it is appropriate to say that very occasionally there are attested cases of a person recognising the foreign language that is spoken by inspiration of the Spirit. But this is the exception to the norm. The effect is to arrest the attention of the hearer to behold a miracle as on the day of Pentecost (Acts 2:6–11). Speaking in tongues is not used by God to proclaim the gospel. Just as on that day, the gospel must be proclaimed in a language known by both the preacher and the hearers.

The gift of prophecy

It is to speak a message given directly by God. It is to speak with the experience of being moved by the Holy Spirit to speak the message. It is the message of God in the situation. It may be prediction. It is not to be confused with preaching. Paul says expressly in Rom. 12:6–8 that prophesying is different from teaching and exhortation, "Having then gifts differing according to the grace that is given to us, *let us use them:* if prophecy, *let us prophesy* in proportion to our faith; or ministry, *let us use it* in *our* ministering; he who teaches, in teaching; he who exhorts, in exhortation; he who gives, with liberality; he who leads, with diligence; he who shows mercy, with cheerfulness." Paul also says that he does not permit women to teach: "And I do not permit a woman to teach or to have authority over a man, but to be in silence" (1 Tim. 2:12). So when he writes of women prophesying in the church he must be referring to a different gift to teaching: "But every woman who prays or prophesies with *her* head uncovered dishonors her head, for that is one and the same as if her head were shaved" (1 Cor. 11:5). Again in 1 Cor. 14:6 he distinguishes prophesying from teaching: "But now, brethren, if I come to you speaking with tongues, what shall I profit you unless I speak to you either by revelation, by knowledge, by prophesying, or by teaching?"

There are three levels of prophesying in the New Testament church.

- The speaking in tongues practised by all believers.
- The gift of prophecy exercised by some believers in the local church. Those regularly exercising this gift are called prophets in 1 Cor. 14:29 and 32.
- The ministry gift of the prophet (Eph. 4:11). These prophets are mentioned in Acts 11:27–30; 13:1–2, 15:32; and 21:10; 1 Cor. 12:28–29;

Eph. 2:20; 3:3–6; 4:11 and Rev.18:20. They were second only to apostles and above teachers in Paul's ranking. They were gifts of Christ to the church. The prophet spoke God's word declaring what God would say if He were present. The prophet heard from God and delivered His message. Sometimes the prophet gave prediction. They were leaders and leading preachers in the church. An example of their ministry is found in Acts 15:32: "Now Judas and Silas, themselves being prophets also, exhorted and strengthened the brethren with many words." Silas conveyed to Antioch the decree of the Jerusalem council recorded in Acts 15. He also accompanied Paul on his second missionary journey. The ministry gift of prophet must not be confused with the prophet of 1 Cor. 14:29. That verse refers to believers who regularly exercise the spiritual gift of prophecy in the local church. They have a gift of the Holy Spirit, but are not ministry gifts of Christ to the church.

The great value of understanding by experience the moving of the Spirit and the need for faith and self-control in the exercise of these gifts is appreciated fully when it is realised how effective these gifts are.

a) Prophecy edifies, exhorts and comforts believers. Tongues plus the interpretation of tongues has the same blessed effects (1 Cor. 14:5). Edification (οἰκοδομὴν) is the building up of believers. Exhortation (παράκλησιν) means to beseech/urge believers to do something, or to encourage believers, or to comfort them. Comfort (παραμυθίαν) means to draw near to speak kindly to one. It expresses more tenderness than (παράκλησιν) These are truly great blessings which can be ministered to believers. Through prophecy a believer can really give something to brothers and sisters in God's family. "Inasmuch as you did it to one of the least of these My brethren you did it unto Me" said Christ.

b) Prophecy has a wonderfully powerful effect on unbelievers and on Christians not baptized in the Spirit: "But if all prophesy, and an unbeliever or an ungifted man enters, he is convicted by all, he is called to account by all; the secrets of his heart are disclosed; and so he will fall on his face and worship God, declaring that God is certainly among you" (1 Cor. 14:24–25 NASB). This verse does not say that prophecy results in the conversion of unbelievers, but nevertheless it makes a profound impression.

Paul's estimation of prophecy is seen in the following verses in 1 Corinthians: "I thank my God always concerning you for the grace of

God which was given to you by Christ Jesus, that you were enriched in everything by Him in all utterance and all knowledge, even as the testimony of Christ was confirmed in you, so that you come short in no gift, eagerly waiting for the revelation of our Lord Jesus Christ, who will also confirm you to the end, *that you may be* blameless in the day of our Lord Jesus Christ" (1 Cor. 1:4–8). Paul is thankful to God that they do not come short in any gifts of the Spirit. He sees their possession of these gifts as an enrichment given by God. He commands them in 1 Cor. 14:1 to "Pursue love, and desire spiritual *gifts,* but especially that you may prophesy." The word pursue means to pursue with intensity and determination like a hunter pursues the prey. Similarly desire means to desire earnestly. The pursuit of love is to be accompanied with passionate desire for spiritual gifts because through them love can be effective and minister blessings. This is especially true of prophecy so Paul says earnestly desire particularly that gift. Paul enforces these directions: "If anyone thinks himself to be a prophet or spiritual, let him acknowledge that the things which I write to you are the commandments of the Lord. But if anyone is ignorant, let him be ignorant. Therefore, brethren, desire earnestly to prophesy, and do not forbid to speak with tongues" (1 Cor. 14:37–39).

Every Christian is required to obey God's commands in 1 Cor. 14:1 and 39. The fact that the Spirit distributes gifts to each believer as He wills (1 Cor. 12:11) did not permit any of the Corinthians to ignore those commands. Nor does it allow Christians today the liberty to choose not to obey these verses. The truth contained in Deut 29:29 applies in this matter, "The secret *things belong* to the LORD our God, but those *things which are* revealed *belong* to us and to our children forever, that *we* may do all the words of this law." The sovereign will of God in the distribution of gifts is something belonging to the Lord. But the revealed will of God to pursue love and earnestly desire spiritual gifts, especially prophecy, belongs to every Christian. Our conduct must be determined solely by the revealed will of God. If we fail to want these gifts of the Spirit we fall short of God's requirement. Given that obligation, and the effectiveness of prophecy, is it not truly a blessing of very great value to be given an experiential introduction to these things?

A manifestation of the Spirit

The church, which is composed of true believers, is the dwelling place of God in the Spirit (Eph. 2:21–22). It is the temple of the Lord. He does not dwell in temples made with hands (Acts 7:48 and 17:24). He dwells in His people. His presence by the Spirit in the gathering of believers is manifested by spiritual gifts which include speaking in tongues in the church (1 Cor. 12:7). This manifestation of His presence in the meeting of believers is most wonderful and precious. It is to experience the reality of God in the midst. Similarly at the baptism in the Spirit He manifests Himself in the speaking in tongues. He displays His indwelling in the believer. The body of each individual Christian is the temple of the Holy Spirit (1 Cor. 6:19). It is a wonderful manifestation of the Spirit to the believer who is baptized in the Spirit. His prophesying is the open display of the pouring out of the Spirit upon him. This manifestation of His presence through the speaking in tongues also reveals the Spirit in a believer to other believers (Acts 10:45–46).

The means of praying and singing with the spirit

Paul says that praying in tongues is an activity of the human spirit which does not involve the mind in the sense that the Spirit gives the words to utter. The mind is not active in deciding the words to speak. Nor does the mind comprehend the meaning of the words. The same applies to singing with the spirit which is singing in tongues. In contrast, praying and singing with the understanding means that the mind is active in choosing the words to be said or sung, and their meaning is comprehended. We thus have two different sorts of prayer and singing: "For if I pray in a tongue, my spirit prays, but my understanding is unfruitful. What is *the conclusion* then? I will pray with the spirit, and I will also pray with the understanding. I will sing with the spirit, and I will also sing with the understanding" (1 Cor. 14:14–15). This prayer and singing with the spirit was part of Paul's prayer life. He was thankful to God that in private he exercised this speaking in tongues more than all of the Corinthian believers. He valued greatly this means of praying and singing with the spirit. He did not see it as a substitute for praying and singing with the understanding. Rather he concluded that the right action for the believer is to pray and sing with the spirit and also to pray and sing with the understanding. Prayer with the spirit in the church should not be practised because others would not understand the meaning of the words. Paul set forth his own conduct as an example for the Corinthians to follow. It is clear that a full prayer life includes praying in tongues; and a full life of worship and praise includes singing in tongues. It is wonderful indeed to be able to pray and sing in tongues without the mind being active in the sense stated above. It enables communion with God without a continual exercise of the mind. This greatly facilitates prayer and praise. Speaking in tongues is thus a most effective means of grace for every day of the Christian life. A believer without this enabling is missing something of great benefit.

It edifies the believer

Paul said, "He who speaks in a tongue edifies himself" (1 Cor. 14:4). Speaking in a tongue in private builds up the believer spiritually. Consequently Paul went on, "I wish you all spoke with tongues" (1 Cor. 14:5). Many commentators seek to water down the force of Paul's "I wish" (θέλω) to be merely conciliatory or concessive. Paul is not just permitting speaking in a tongue. He really does want them to do so. He also wants them even more to prophesy, because it edifies the church. He wants this more because building up the church is superior to building up oneself.

Some find it impossible to imagine edification taking place without the spoken words being understood. 1 Cor. 14:14–15 reveal that it is a means of communion with God not involving the understanding of what is uttered. Such communion with God edifies.

Self-edification is of great importance not just for the benefit of the believer who speaks in tongues. His edification enables him to minister to others, both Christians and non-Christians. This is one reason why Paul is so grateful for speaking in tongues in private (1 Cor. 14:18). Throughout scripture we have a Divine order. To be a blessing to others one must first be blessed. God said to Abram, "I will bless you and make your name great and you shall be a blessing" (Gen. 12:2). The baptism in the Spirit is the start of an enabling by the Spirit to edify oneself by speaking in a tongue.

It reveals the Deity of the Holy Spirit

When the believer speaks in an unknown language the Holy Spirit gives the words to speak. In that sense the Spirit has absolute control over the speech organ, the tongue, though as we have seen the believer chooses at all times whether to speak forth those words or not to speak. This control over the tongue reveals that the Holy Spirit is God. James says, "For every kind of beast and bird, of reptile and creature of the sea, is tamed and has been tamed by mankind. But no man can tame the tongue. It is an unruly evil, full of deadly poison" (James 3:7–8). Only God can tame the tongue. When the believer speaks in an unknown language by the Spirit the tongue is tamed.

It gives the believer a daily experience of the miraculous

Every day as the believer speaks in a tongue a miracle of utterance takes place. He is not speaking gibberish. He is speaking a language or languages to God (1 Cor. 14:2 and Acts 2:8f.). It may be that he is speaking language used by angels (1 Cor. 13:1). What is certain is that he is given by the Spirit words unlearned and unknown to him but acceptable to God. The words have wonderful meaning. He speaks mysteries in the Spirit. He is in fellowship with a God Who is constantly at work miraculously in his daily life! What an encouragement to his faith.

It declares that believers are living in the last days

The promise of Joel is fulfilled in the last days (Acts 2:16–17). Every time a believer speaks in a tongue they are reminded that the coming of the Lord draws near. The New Testament requires believers to live in the consciousness that they are in the last days. Many scriptures declare this: "The night is far spent, the day is at hand. Therefore let us cast off the works of darkness, and let us put on the armor of light. Let us walk properly, as in the day, not in revelry and drunkenness, not in lewdness and lust, not in strife and envy. But put on the Lord Jesus Christ, and make no provision for the flesh, to *fulfill its* lusts" (Rom. 13:12–14).

"For the grace of God that brings salvation has appeared to all men, teaching us that, denying ungodliness and worldly lusts, we should live soberly, righteously, and godly in the present age, looking for the blessed hope and glorious appearing of our great God and Savior Jesus Christ, who gave Himself for us, that He might redeem us from every lawless deed and purify for Himself *His* own special people, zealous for good works" (Tit. 2:11–14). Christians are to look for the return of Jesus Christ. This means to eagerly wait for His coming as stated in the following verse: "For our citizenship is in heaven, from which we also eagerly wait for the Savior, the Lord Jesus Christ, who will transform our lowly body that it may be conformed to His glorious body, according to the working by which He is able even to subdue all things to Himself" (Phil. 3:20–21).

It is a sign to unbelievers

"In the law it is written: 'With *men of* other tongues and other lips I will speak to this people; And yet, for all that, they will not hear Me,' says the Lord. Therefore tongues are for a sign, not to those who believe but to unbelievers" (1 Cor. 14:21–22). Paul is quoting from Isa. 28:11. There the drunken spiritual leaders mock Isaiah the prophet and speak contemptuously of his messages as "precept upon precept, line upon line, line upon line, here a little, there a little" (Isa. 28:10). Consequently the prophet tells them that God will speak to them by means of a language they do not understand. He will fulfil his threat of punishment for disobedience stated in Deut. 28:49–50, "The LORD will bring a nation against you from afar, from the end of the earth, *as swift* as the eagle flies, a nation whose language you will not understand, a nation of fierce countenance, which does not respect the elderly nor show favor to the young." The nation was Assyria. Their coming against them was a sign to them. Even then they would not listen to God. They ignored the sign of judgment. Paul is saying that in the same way tongues are a sign to unbelievers, and, just as in Isaiah's day, a sign which unbelievers reject. Consequently he says do not speak in tongues when unbelievers are present. They will only reject the sign. This rejection does not mean that the sign is not intrinsically good. It is. The reason for its rejection lies wholly in the sinful refusal of the unbeliever to hear it.

It proclaims the ascension of Jesus Christ

The promise of Joel was fulfilled only because Jesus was exalted to the Father's right hand and received from the Father the promise of the Holy Spirit: "Therefore being exalted to the right hand of God, and having received from the Father the promise of the Holy Spirit, He poured out this which you now see and hear" (Acts 2:33). These are Peter's words on the day of Pentecost concerning the Lord Jesus Christ. Thus the believer is reminded when he speaks in a tongue that Jesus is seated at the Father's right hand in the heavenly places far above all principality and power and might and dominion and every name that is named not only in this age but also in that which is to come, and that the Father has put all things under His feet and has given Him to be head over all things to the church (Eph. 1:20–22).

It enables the believer to fulfil the immediate purpose of the pouring out of the Spirit namely to prophesy

Since speaking in a tongue is addressed to God and not to man it is a form of prophesying that is entirely suitable when the Spirit is poured upon a believer for the first time. In contrast to prophesying in one's own language:

- It is not dependent on the presence of another person or persons.
- It is not limited. Prophesying in one's own language is strictly limited: "Let two or three prophets speak, and let the others judge" (1 Cor. 14:29).
- It does not require the judging of others (1 Cor. 14:29).

Believers are able to prophesy in an unknown language without restriction when the Spirit comes upon them at the baptism in the Spirit. In this way they have a wonderful experience of working out what God is working in them. Moreover as they prophesy the consciousness of communion with God is increased, and can reach wonderful heights of blessedness.

No wonder Paul the great apostle said "I thank my God I speak with tongues more than you all" (1 Cor. 14:18).

CHAPTER THIRTY THREE

RECEIVING THE BAPTISM IN THE SPIRIT

As we have stated converts in New Testament times received the promise of the Father following repentance and faith. The promise of the Father is only for those who are born again. Unbelievers cannot receive the Holy Spirit. Baptism in the Spirit followed faith in Christ without delay in Acts 10, as a next step in Acts 19, three days later in Acts 9:17, and abnormally some days/weeks later in Acts 8. We noted that all these fulfilments of the promise of the Father happened, and were recorded by the Holy Spirit for the instruction of future believers. Taking that instruction and the teaching of the rest of the scriptures the following truths apply concerning receiving the promise of the Father.

Many believers, unlike the New Testament convert, approach this matter having been misled by misinterpretation of the scriptures on the subject. Similarly many believers have received wrong teaching on water baptism. Sometimes their "knowledge" causes them to set themselves against the truth. But others are willing to look again at the matter. The first step for such is to seek God's truth and will from the scriptures. How can a believer come to an assured state of mind about what is the truth? The first thing to say is that it is not always easy.

1. The scriptures must be read and searched.
2. It may require the reading of books expounding the subject.
3. It may require the seeking out of a Christian who can help by their knowledge of the truth.
4. It may require searching for truth as stated in the following scriptures:

> "My son, if you receive my words, And treasure my commands within you, So that you incline your ear to wisdom, *And* apply your heart to understanding; Yes, if you cry out for discernment, *And* lift up your voice for understanding, If you seek her as silver, And search for her as *for* hidden treasures; Then you will understand the fear of the LORD, And find the knowledge of God. For

the LORD gives wisdom; From His mouth *come* knowledge and understanding; He stores up sound wisdom for the upright; *He is* a shield to those who walk uprightly; He guards the paths of justice, And preserves the way of His saints. Then you will understand righteousness and justice, Equity *and* every good path" (Prov. 2:1–9). Such searching must be earnest and determined not to cease until the truth is found. When searching for treasures and silver men go the extra mile. The search is often costly. Truth has to be bought. "Buy the truth" (Prov. 23:23). The price is earnest study of God's word until there is a coming to an understanding of the truth. That involves fervent persevering prayer. There is the cost of surrender of the thoughts to the truth of God's word when it does not say what we would like it to say. It may demolish prejudices. That hurts. The price is surrender of the will to God's revealed will. If we are unwilling to do what God requires it is a barrier to seeing the truth. Willingness to do God's will brings a knowledge and assurance when the truth is found that it is indeed God's truth. Jesus stated this in John 7:17, "If anyone wants to do His will, he shall know concerning the doctrine, whether it is from God or *whether* I speak on My own *authority*." Sometimes buying the truth costs friends, or position or even livelihood. Of course converts who have not received teaching misinterpreting the scriptures on this matter, do not need to pursue this search for the truth. They merely need to be told of the promise of the Father.

Once a believer is convinced from God's word that the promise of the Father is for him then the following principles must be applied.

The believer should have a heart desire for the promise of the Father

Jesus stated this in John 7:37–39, "On the last day, that great *day* of the feast, Jesus stood and cried out, saying, 'If anyone thirsts, let him come to Me and drink. He who believes in Me, as the Scripture has said, out of his heart will flow rivers of living water.' But this He spoke concerning the Spirit, whom those believing in Him would receive; for the Holy Spirit was not yet *given*, because Jesus was not yet glorified." There must be thirst.

The believer should ask for the Spirit

Jesus said, "So I say to you, ask, and it will be given to you; seek, and you will find; knock, and it will be opened to you. For everyone who asks receives, and he who seeks finds, and to him who knocks it will be opened. If a son asks for bread from any father among you, will he give him a stone? Or if *he asks* for a fish, will he give him a serpent instead of a fish? Or if he asks for an egg, will he offer him a scorpion? If you then, being evil, know how to give good gifts to your children, how much more will *your* heavenly Father give the Holy Spirit to those who ask Him!" (Luke 11:9–13).

The believer should ask in faith that he will receive

As Jesus said in Mark 11:24 "Therefore I say to you, whatever things you ask when you pray, believe that you receive *them,* and you will have *them.*"

The Spirit is received by faith. Paul said, "This only I want to learn from you: Did you receive the Spirit by the works of the law, or by the hearing of faith?" (Gal. 3:2). He knew that they would have to answer "by the hearing of faith." They had heard the promise of the Father, they had believed it was for them and they had asked the Lord to fulfil it with an assurance in their hearts that He would do so.

The believer should be willing to allow another believer or believers to pray for the fulfilment of the promise (Acts 8:15 and 9:17)

This includes being willing to receive the laying on of hands.

The believer should be willing to begin to speak in faith the unknown words given by the Spirit (Acts 2:4)

It is an act of faith to begin to prophesy, to begin to speak in tongues. The Spirit Himself does not speak. He does not force the believer to prophesy. He moves the believer to utter the words given by Him. The believer does not know the meaning of the words. It is a new and strange experience to speak words one cannot understand. By faith the believer must begin to speak in response to the moving and enabling of the Holy Spirit.

Because it is always an act of faith to speak in tongues, and because the words are not understood (except on rare occasions), many believers experience after the baptism in the Spirit a spiritual battle against satanic suggestions that they simply made up their tongue speaking. I believe that Jesus gave assurances to believers to deal with this satanic attack. His words are found in Mat. 7:7–11 and Luke 11:9–13. He says in these passages that earthly fathers give good gifts in response to the requests of their children. The fathers are evil but they know how to give good gifts to their children. They don't give something bad instead of the good thing. Jesus concludes "If you then, being evil, know how to give good gifts to your children, how much more will your Father who is in heaven give good things to those who ask Him!" (Mat. 7:11). Similarly He says of the Holy Spirit "If you then, being evil, know how to give good gifts to your children, how much more will *your* heavenly Father give the Holy Spirit to those who ask Him!" (Luke 11:13). It is impossible for the believer who asks for the promise of the Father to receive something spurious.

A convert in the glow of experiencing the new birth will normally have no difficulty with these scriptural conditions if they are presented without delay. Many believers have been stumbled by other Christians employing methods to receive the baptism in the Spirit which have no scriptural warrant or, in some cases, methods which are contrary to the teachings of God's word. Equally many seekers have been disappointed because they have not received the promised blessing, and many of them have given up seeking the baptism in the Spirit. Sadly they have not applied the truths stated above; but happily, if they do, they can receive the promise of the Father.

CHAPTER THIRTY FOUR

THE BAPTISM IN THE SPIRIT AND SPIRITUAL GIFTS

Having been baptized in the Spirit the believer is able to seek and receive the spiritual gifts stated in 1 Cor. 12:8–10

The commands in 1 Cor. 14 to desire earnestly and pray for spiritual gifts were given to believers who had been baptized in one Spirit for one body. These gifts are given to each believer "individually as He wills" (1 Cor. 12:11). But they are given in response to desiring them (1 Cor. 14:1) and prayer for them (1 Cor. 14:13). It is a sinful attitude which refuses to obey 1 Cor. 14:1 and 13 on the grounds that God gives these gifts to whom He will. He gives them to those who desire them and pray for them. Just as Jesus said, "Ask, and it will be given to you; seek, and you will find; knock, and it will be opened to you. For everyone who asks receives, and he who seeks finds, and to him who knocks it will be opened. Or what man is there among you who, if his son asks for bread, will give him a stone? Or if he asks for a fish, will he give him a serpent? If you then, being evil, know how to give good gifts to your children, how much more will your Father who is in heaven give good things to those who ask Him!" (Mat. 7:7–11). By earnestly desiring these gifts the Christian can build on the foundation of the baptism in the Spirit and exercise most wonderful ministries to other believers and unbelievers. The believer can be given by the Spirit any of the following gifts.

A Word of Wisdom

It is not wisdom, but a word of wisdom given by the Spirit in a particular circumstance. The meaning of this term is explained by the following verses: "Now when they bring you to the synagogues and magistrates and authorities, do not worry about how or what you should answer, or what you should say. For the Holy Spirit will teach you in that very hour what you ought to say" (Luke 12:11–12). Jesus is telling his disciples that men will persecute them unto death. He says

248

that they will be brought before ruling bodies, and at that time the Holy Spirit will give them a word of wisdom to speak. We have an example of the fulfilment of this in Acts 4:8f. Peter healed a man who had been lame from birth. He was a beggar and over forty years old. The priests, the captain of the temple, and the Sadducees laid hands on Peter and John and put them in prison. "And it came to pass, on the next day, that their rulers, elders, and scribes, as well as Annas the high priest, Caiaphas, John, and Alexander, and as many as were of the family of the high priest, were gathered together at Jerusalem. And when they had set them in the midst, they asked, 'By what power or by what name have you done this?' " (Acts 4:5–7). At this point Peter, filled with the Spirit, receives a word of wisdom from the Holy Spirit: "Then Peter, filled with the Holy Spirit, said to them, 'Rulers of the people and elders of Israel: if we this day are judged for a good deed *done* to a helpless man, by what means he has been made well, let it be known to you all, and to all the people of Israel, that by the name of Jesus Christ of Nazareth, whom you crucified, whom God raised from the dead, by Him this man stands here before you whole. This is the "stone which was rejected by you builders, which has become the chief cornerstone." Nor is there salvation in any other, for there is no other name under heaven given among men by which we must be saved.' Now when they saw the boldness of Peter and John, and perceived that they were uneducated and untrained men, they marveled" (Acts 4:8–13). The word of wisdom caused them to marvel at the boldness of Peter and John.

A word of wisdom given by the Spirit can also give supernatural guidance. Philip the evangelist was directed first by an angel and then received a word of wisdom given by the Spirit, "Now an angel of the Lord spoke to Philip, saying, 'Arise and go toward the south along the road which goes down from Jerusalem to Gaza.' This is desert. So he arose and went. And behold, a man of Ethiopia, a eunuch of great authority under Candace the queen of the Ethiopians, who had charge of all her treasury, and had come to Jerusalem to worship, was return- ing. And sitting in his chariot, he was reading Isaiah the prophet" (Acts 8:26–28). At this point in time "the Spirit said to Philip, 'Go near and overtake this chariot' " (Acts 8:29). This was not an action Philip would have decided to do if he had not received this word of wisdom from the Spirit. It led to the conversion of the man.

Similarly Peter received a word of wisdom directing him to go the house of Cornelius the Gentile: "And when Peter came up to Jerusalem, those of the circumcision contended with him, saying, 'You went in to uncircumcised men and ate with them!' But Peter explained *it* to them in order from the beginning, saying: 'I was in the city of Joppa praying; and in a trance I saw a vision, an object descending like a great sheet, let down from heaven by four corners; and it came to me. When I observed it intently and considered, I saw four-footed animals of the earth, wild beasts, creeping things, and birds of the air. And I heard a voice saying to me, "Rise, Peter; kill and eat." But I said, "Not so, Lord! For nothing common or unclean has at any time entered my mouth." But the voice answered me again from heaven, "What God has cleansed you must not call common." Now this was done three times, and all were drawn up again into heaven. At that very moment, three men stood before the house where I was, having been sent to me from Caesarea. Then the Spirit told me to go with them, doubting nothing. Moreover these six brethren accompanied me, and we entered the man's house'" (Acts 11:2–12). The actual words are recorded: "While Peter thought about the vision, the Spirit said to him, 'Behold, three men are seeking you. Arise therefore, go down and go with them, doubting nothing; for I have sent them.'" (Acts 10:19–20).

A word of wisdom by the Spirit also gave specific instruction concerning the work to be done by outstanding leaders in the church, "Now in the church that was at Antioch there were certain prophets and teachers: Barnabas, Simeon who was called Niger, Lucius of Cyrene, Manaen who had been brought up with Herod the tetrarch, and Saul. As they ministered to the Lord and fasted, the Holy Spirit said, 'Now separate to Me Barnabas and Saul for the work to which I have called them.' Then, having fasted and prayed, and laid hands on them, they sent *them* away. So, being sent out by the Holy Spirit, they went down to Seleucia, and from there they sailed to Cyprus" (Acts 13:1–4). It may be that this word of wisdom was given by the Spirit through prophetic utterance (cf. 1 Tim. 4:14). Or it may have been declared to those present through one of them as a revelation (1 Cor. 14:6).

A Word of Knowledge

It is not knowledge, but a word of knowledge about the past, or the present or the future given by the Spirit in a particular circumstance. Agabus had words of knowledge of future events: "Then one of them, named Agabus, stood up and showed by the Spirit that there was going to be a great famine throughout all the world, which also happened in the days of Claudius Caesar" (Acts 11:28). This word of knowledge enabled relief to be given, "Then the disciples, each according to his ability, determined to send relief to the brethren dwelling in Judea. This they also did, and sent it to the elders by the hands of Barnabas and

Saul" (Acts 11:29–30). Agabus also had knowledge in advance of Paul's sufferings in Jerusalem, "When he (Agabus) had come to us, he took Paul's belt, bound his *own* hands and feet, and said, 'Thus says the Holy Spirit, So shall the Jews at Jerusalem bind the man who owns this belt, and deliver *him* into the hands of the Gentiles.' " (Acts 21:11).

Peter received a word of knowledge of the deception carried out by Ananias and Sapphira "But a certain man named Ananias, with Sapphira his wife, sold a possession. And he kept back *part* of the proceeds, his wife also being aware *of it,* and brought a certain part and laid *it* at the apostles' feet. But Peter said, 'Ananias, why has Satan filled your heart to lie to the Holy Spirit and keep back *part* of the price of the land for yourself ?' " (Acts 5:1–3). They pretended to give all the proceeds of the sale, but only gave some of the money.

Faith

This is not saving faith, but special faith given by the Spirit for a particular circumstance. In Acts 3:16 there is an example of its operation. The healing of the man over forty years old who had been lame from birth was wrought through this gift of the Spirit: "And His name, through faith in His name, has made this man strong, whom you see and know. Yes, the faith which *comes* through Him has given him this perfect soundness in the presence of you all." The fact that this is special faith by the Spirit is seen when we consider Peter's action: "And a certain man lame from his mother's womb was carried, whom they laid daily at the gate of the temple which is called Beautiful, to ask alms from those who entered the temple; who, seeing Peter and John about to go into the temple, asked for alms. And fixing his eyes on him, with John, Peter said, 'Look at us.' So he gave them his attention, expecting to receive something from them. Then Peter said, 'Silver and gold I do not have, but what I do have I give you: In the name of Jesus Christ of Nazareth, rise up and walk.' And he took him by the right hand and lifted *him* up, and immediately his feet and ankle bones received strength. So he, leaping up, stood and walked and entered the temple with them – walking, leaping, and praising God" (Acts 3:2–8).

Another example is found in Acts 13:6–12, "Now when they had gone through the island to Paphos, they found a certain sorcerer, a false prophet, a Jew whose name *was* Bar-jesus, who was with the proconsul, Sergius Paulus, an intelligent man. This man called for Barnabas and Saul and sought to hear the word of God. But Elymas the sorcerer (for so his name is translated) withstood them, seeking to turn the proconsul away from the faith. Then Saul, who also *is called* Paul, filled with the Holy Spirit, looked intently at him and said, 'O full of all deceit and all fraud, *you* son of the devil, *you* enemy of all righteousness, will you not cease perverting the straight ways of the Lord? And now, indeed, the hand of the Lord *is* upon you, and you shall be blind, not seeing the sun for a time.' And immediately a dark mist fell on him, and he went around seeking someone to lead him by the hand. Then the proconsul believed, when he saw what had been done, being astonished at the teaching of the Lord."

Gifts of healings

Notice the plurals. The one who has these gifts will manifest them at different times for the healing of different persons. Each healing is a gift from God brought about supernaturally by the Spirit through the believer to whom He gives gifts of healings. Ananias had a gift of healing for Saul. Later he recalled that Ananias "came to me; and he stood and said to me, 'Brother Saul, receive your sight.' And at that same hour I looked up at him" (Acts 22:13). Ananias told Saul to receive the gift of healing from blindness.

Workings of miracles

The workings of miracles includes the casting out of demons: "Then Philip went down to the city of Samaria and preached Christ to them. And the multitudes with one accord heeded the things spoken by Philip, hearing and seeing the miracles which he did. For unclean spirits, crying with a loud voice, came out of many who were possessed; and many who were paralyzed and lame were healed" (Acts 8:5–7). These were signs and great works of power (verse 13).

This gift includes raising the dead, "At Joppa there was a certain disciple named Tabitha, which is translated Dorcas. This woman was full of good works and charitable deeds which she did. But it happened in those days that she became sick and died. When they had washed her, they laid *her* in an upper room. And since Lydda was near Joppa, and the disciples had heard that Peter was there, they sent two men to him, imploring *him* not to delay in coming to them. Then Peter arose and went with them. When he had come, they brought *him* to the upper room. And all the widows stood by him weeping, showing the tunics and garments which Dorcas had made while she was with them. But Peter put them all out, and knelt down and prayed. And turning to the body he said, 'Tabitha, arise.' And she opened her eyes, and when she saw Peter she sat up. Then he gave her *his* hand and lifted her up; and when he had called the saints and widows, he presented her alive. And it became known throughout all Joppa, and many believed on the Lord" (Acts 9:36–42).

At Ephesus we read, "Now God worked unusual miracles by the hands of Paul, so that even handkerchiefs or aprons were brought from his body to the sick, and the diseases left them and the evil spirits went out of them" (Acts 19:11–12).

Discernments of spirits

This gift is the ability by the Spirit to distinguish true and false inspiration. It is the power to distinguish between the Holy Spirit, the human spirit and an evil spirit. It is not a mental process but revelation by the Spirit each time the gift is in operation. It is distinct from the doctrinal test of 1 John 4:1–6, the life test of Mat. 7:15–20 and the ability of the Lord's people to flee from strangers (John 10:5). These tests and this ability belong to all of God's people to exercise. The gift of discernments of spirits is given only to some believers.

It is not always necessary for the judging of prophecy. Otherwise Paul would have commanded that there be no prophesying unless someone with the gift of discernments of spirits were present, just as he required the presence of an interpreter when someone spoke in a tongue in the church. All believers were commanded to judge prophecies, "Do not quench the Spirit. Do not despise prophecies. Test all things; hold fast what is good. Abstain from every form of evil." (1 Thess. 5:19–22). The word "test" here means to examine for genuineness as in the testing of metals. When the test is passed then the prophecy, or part(s) of it, is/are to be held fast.

The discernments of spirits is the distinguishing and detection of an evil spirit distinct from the Holy Spirit and the human spirit. We have an example in Acts 16:16–18 "Now it happened, as we went to prayer, that a certain slave girl possessed with a spirit of divination met us, who brought her masters much profit by fortune-telling. This girl followed Paul and us, and cried out, saying, 'These men are the servants of the Most High God, who proclaim to us the way of salvation.' And this she did for many days. But Paul, greatly annoyed, turned and said to the spirit, 'I command you in the name of Jesus Christ to come out of her.' And he came out that very hour." It is striking that the words she said were absolutely true. The apostle discerned an evil spirit.

The gospels reveal that evil spirits causing sickness and ill health are sometimes hidden (Luke 13:11 and 16). The gift therefore perceives the activity of Satan or presence of an evil spirit. The gift sees the real source of "wonderful deeds" done in the name of Christ. Jesus said, "Many will say to Me in that day, 'Lord, Lord, have we not prophesied in Your name, cast out demons in Your name, and done many wonders in Your name?' And then I will declare to them, 'I never knew you;

depart from Me, you who practice lawlessness!' " (Mat. 7:22–23). These acts have all the appearance of being truly done by Christians in the service of Christ. Similarly in 2 Thess. 2:9 the reality of false signs and wonders is stated.

Prophecy

As defined above.

Different kinds of tongues

As defined above.

Interpretation of tongues

As defined above.

Some object that these gifts of the Spirit have been given to believers who deny a baptism in the Spirit distinct from and after regeneration. They conclude that a second stage Spirit baptism is therefore not necessary to receive these gifts. Throughout history before the Spirit was given ten days after the ascension of Christ (John 7:37–39), some men and some women were filled with the Spirit and given supernatural enduement. In their lives are seen all the above gifts of the Spirit, with two exceptions – the gift of speaking in a language they had not learned and the gift of interpretation of a language unknown to them. It should not surprise us therefore that God continues to work supernaturally through some of His children, even if they deny a baptism in the Spirit after the new birth.

Moreover when some seek and ask for the power of the Spirit and a particular spiritual gift without a true understanding of the baptism in the Spirit then sometimes God gives. It does not alter the fact that the baptism in the Spirit is now the foundation appointed by God for believers to move into these gifts of the Spirit.

There are other gifts (χαρίσματα) stated in the New Testament in addition to those in 1 Cor. 12:8–10

In Rom. 12:6–8 we have prophesying, serving, the one who teaches, the one who exhorts, the one contributing to the needs of others, the one taking the lead and the one showing mercy. Paul seems to be deliberately general here in much of his terminology since he is speaking of different gifts within the body of Christ. Paul speaks in this list firstly of the *gifts* of prophecy and service, and then of *persons* with particular abilities by the grace given to each to function in the body.

Also in the context of spiritual gifts in 1 Cor. 12:28 we read "God has appointed these in the church: first apostles, second prophets, third teachers, after that miracles, then gifts of healings, helps, administrations, varieties of tongues." In Eph. 4:11 Paul adds evangelists and instead of teachers writes pastor-teachers, "And He Himself (that is Christ) gave some *to be* apostles, some prophets, some evangelists, and some pastors and teachers." Pastors and teachers should be considered one group. All pastors must teach in order to feed the flock, and all teachers shepherd the sheep by their teaching. These gifts of people – apostles, prophets, pastors and teachers and evangelists are gifts of Christ to the church distinct from the gifts of the Spirit.

In 1 Cor. 12:28 "helps" probably refers to deacons, defined as those who carry out the necessary tasks in the local church but have no ruling authority nor teaching ministry. They are invaluable since they free the elders or church leader/s to devote himself/themselves to prayer and the ministry of the word (Acts 6:4). It may be that the word "helps", however, has a wider meaning, speaking of any believer who performs lowly service. "Administrations" (1 Cor. 12:28) is an inadequate translation. The Greek word (κυβερνήσεις) refers to the ability to steer a ship. It has the meaning of both piloting and leadership. Thus it probably speaks of elders in the local church. Every local church needs both leadership and also piloting through difficult waters.

The New Testament uses the Greek word χάρισμα to refer to marriage and celibacy as gifts to believers from God (1 Cor. 7:7).

Taking all these verses into account we find that there is a list of spiritual gifts (1 Cor. 12:8–10), a list of people who are gifts of Christ (Eph. 4:11) and a list including both spiritual gifts and people who are gifts (1 Cor. 12:28–30). We also find that some gifts are supernatural and some are natural abilities, and these are both included in Rom. 12:6–8. These natural abilities are from God and gifts of grace. Natural gifts are invaluable for ministry in and for the body of Christ. They are essential for ministry to believers and unbelievers. The baptism in the Spirit adds power to the one ministering using a natural gift.

Conclusion

The baptism in the Spirit places the believer in the position to be given the supernatural spiritual gifts of 1 Cor. 12:8–10. It also adds power to the believer when exercising natural gifts.

CHAPTER THIRTY FIVE

THE BAPTISM IN THE SPIRIT PART OF THE ESSENTIAL FOUNDATION

In this chapter we bring together all that has been said about the baptism in the Spirit. First of all it is important to reiterate that Heb.6:2 and the New Testament define the baptism in the Spirit as an experience of the Spirit after the new birth. It does not make a person a Christian: it is given to those who already belong to Christ. It is a first step in the Christian life just as is baptism in water. It is part of the action of laying a foundation for the Christian life. It is a foundation in the following ways:

It is a lesson by vivid experience that the Christian life is a life of faith

Right at the beginning of the Christian life the believer receives the baptism in the Spirit by the hearing of faith. He obtains the promise of the Father, the gift of the Holy Spirit by faith (Gal. 3:2). The essential place of faith in the Christian life is thereby emphasised. It is a lesson of the greatest importance, because he must live and walk by faith for the rest of his days on earth. "The just shall live by faith."

It is a once for all experience, an entrance into the Spirit-filled life

A believer can be baptized in the Spirit once only. That once for all anointing abides (1 John 2:27). The anointing endues the believer with power to serve God and to be His witness. From then onwards he can go on being filled with the Spirit. *The baptism in the Spirit puts a new potential into every part of the believer's life.* By going on being filled with the Spirit his worship has added power (Eph. 5:19). Thanksgiving to God is intensified (Eph. 5:20). Relationships with others in the family and at work are affected by being filled with the Spirit (Eph. 5:18–21). The filling of the Spirit enables submission to one another in the fear of God – wives to husbands, children to parents and employees to employers (Eph. 5:21–6:8). And it enables the husbands, parents and employers to fulfil their responsibilities.

256

Any ministry carried out in the body of Christ by the believer in the will of God can be exercised with the added power of being Spirit-filled.

A fire is lit at the baptism in the Spirit (2 Tim. 1:6). That fire can be maintained. We see this in the events recorded in Acts 4 following the baptism in the Spirit related in Acts 2. The apostles, Peter and John, were threatened and commanded not to preach Christ, and they prayed with the believers, "And when they had prayed, the place where they were assembled together was shaken; and they were all filled with the Holy Spirit, and they spoke the word of God with boldness" (Acts 4:31). They had been filled on the day of Pentecost. This was a further filling. It was not a repeat baptism in the Spirit. It was an enduement to enable them to preach boldly when under serious threat. Before Pentecost they waited for the promise of the Father to receive power. Here they do not ask for a filling of the Spirit. They ask for boldness to speak God's word and for healings, signs and wonders to be done through the name of Jesus (Acts 4:29–30). Their continued faithfulness in doing God's will, despite the threat to them, meant that they maintained the fire. In their particular time of need another filling of the Spirit was given.

The convert after being baptized in the Spirit needs to grow in knowledge and in grace. He needs to develop from being a babe in Christ, to the maturity and strength of youth in Christ, and finally into the wisdom and depth of understanding of God attained by fathers in Christ (1 John 2:12–14). But at each stage of growth he can be Spirit-filled. He has received an anointing that abides. As he works out his salvation he is led into his particular individual service for God. Whatever it is, he is empowered to serve God.

It imparts a knowledge of the truth 1 John 2:20 and 27

The anointing imparts a certain fullness of knowledge. It means that the Christian when confronted with those who would deceive has no need for their false teachings. They assert that his knowledge is deficient but his knowledge is sufficient.

It places the believer in a special relationship with God Psa. 105 :15

The anointed are under the special care of the Almighty.

Through the enabling to prophesy in tongues it gives:

1. an enlarged ability to edify oneself (1 Cor. 14:3)
2. an enlarged prayer life (1 Cor. 14:14).
3. an enlarged ability to praise God (1 Cor. 14:15).
4. a daily experience of the miraculous.

It gives potential to the believer to be given, and to exercise, spiritual gifts in and for the body of Christ 1 Cor. 12:13

The believer having been baptized in the Spirit is commanded to desire earnestly and pray for the spiritual gifts of 1 Cor. 12:8–10. He is endued with power from on high to exercise spiritual gifts given to him.

It gives added assurance of salvation Rom. 8:15–16

This is a source of great strength to the believer.

It gives assurance of final salvation

It is the deposit which guarantees that the full amount will be paid later (Eph. 1:13–14). As such it is an assurance of final glory. This also is a means of giving strength to the believer.

In all these ways the baptism in the Spirit gives strength and potential. It is an essential part of the foundation on which the Christian life is to be built. Without it the building will lack the strength it gives, and certain parts will not be able to be constructed.

It is most important to realise that the experience, wonderful as it is, is only a foundation, indeed only a part of the foundation. The rest of the foundation must be laid for the believer to be able to build successfully a Christian life that grows into maturity. It is only one part of the start of the building of the Christian life to the glory of God.

Once the foundation is completed the believer must walk in obedience and diligently grow in knowledge and in grace. Only that way will the building develop, and the Christian become mature. The baptism in the Spirit does not remove the need to do these things. A believer who is baptized in the Spirit but fails to carry out these duties as he should will only construct a miserable building on his foundation. The New Testament is crystal clear that believers baptized in the Spirit can:

a) be carnal Christians (1 Cor. 3:1).
b) fall into serious error (Gal. 1:6 and 1 Cor. 15:12). Indeed it is likely that Ananias and Sapphira were baptized in the Spirit. But even so they committed a sin unto death (Acts 5:1–10 and 1 John 5:16).

The baptism in the Spirit is an essential part of the foundation on which the Christian life is to be built. It is a necessary support for daily Christian living, and together with the other parts of the foundation makes it possible for the believer to attain his full potential for fruitfulness in the kingdom of God.

*God's Pattern for the
Christian Life*

VOLUME THREE

The Resurrection
of the Dead
and
Eternal Judgment

CONTENTS OF VOLUME THREE

The Doctrine of the Resurrection of the Dead

CHAPTER ONE

DEATH AND THE INTERMEDIATE STATE

We have come to the last two elements of the foundation to be laid for the Christian life – the resurrection of the dead and eternal judgment. They are closely linked, but we shall treat each one in turn. By the term resurrection of the dead we mean the physical resurrection of the bodies of believers and of unbelievers at the return of Christ. Jesus Himself said, "Do not marvel at this; for the hour is coming in which all who are in the graves will hear His voice and come forth – those who have done good, to the resurrection of life, and those who have done evil, to the resurrection of condemnation" (John 5:28–29). Paul stated his belief, which was also the belief of the Jews, "I have hope in God, which they themselves also accept, that there will be a resurrection of *the* dead, both of *the* just and *the* unjust" (Acts 24:15). Consideration of this truth raises a number of questions. What is death? What happens to people who die in the period between physical death and the return of Christ at the last day? When will the bodies of believers and unbelievers be resurrected? What is the nature of the resurrection body of believers, and the resurrection body of unbelievers?

So firstly what is death?

1. It is the death of the body in distinction from the death of the soul. After death the soul and spirit continue to exist. Jesus stated "And do not fear those who kill the body but cannot kill the soul. But rather fear Him who is able to destroy both soul and body in hell" (Mat. 10:28).
2. In Ecc. 12:7 we read concerning the death of the body, "Then the dust will return to the earth as it was, And the spirit will return to God who gave it" (cf. Gen. 3:19 which also says that the death of the body is a returning to dust).
3. James describes the death of the body as the body without the spirit, "the body without the spirit is dead" (Jam. 2:26).

5

4. It is described as a state of sleeping (Dan. 12:2). The body sleeps in the sense that it awaits the awakening of the resurrection at the coming of Christ.
5. This physical death of the body is described as the dismantling of a tent. Paul writes to believers, "For we know that if our earthly house, *this* tent, is destroyed, we have a building from God, a house not made with hands, eternal in the heavens" (2 Cor. 5:1). Accordingly Peter defines his impending physical death as "putting off his tent" (2 Pet. 1:14).
6. Physical death means that man's earthly existence ceases. It is a departing from this life (Phil. 1:23).
7. Luke speaks of it as God requiring the soul (Luke 12:20).
8. It is "the way of no return" (Job 16:22).
9. It strips of all earthly possessions (1 Tim. 6:7).
10. It is appointed by God, "it is appointed for men to die once" (Heb. 9:27). Thus Joshua and David spoke of it as "going the way of all the earth" (Jos. 23:14 and 1 Kings 2:2).
11. It is the consequence of sin (Rom. 5:12).

The body ceases to function, but the spirit and soul continue to exist. This leads us to examine the belief in the immortality of the soul. The scriptures do not teach this doctrine. As regards mankind only believers receive immortality at the return of Jesus Christ. Paul spells out this in Rom. 2:5–11, "But in accordance with your hardness and your impenitent heart you are treasuring up for yourself wrath in the day of wrath and revelation of the righteous judgment of God, who 'will render to each one according to his deeds': eternal life to those who by patient continuance in doing good seek for glory, honor, and immortality; but to those who are self-seeking and do not obey the truth, but obey unrighteousness – indignation and wrath, tribulation and anguish, on every soul of man who does evil, of the Jew first and also of the Greek; but glory, honor, and peace to everyone who works what is good, to the Jew first and also to the Greek. For there is no partiality with God." In 1 Cor. 15:51–54 he says that at the coming of Christ believers will be gloriously changed. Their bodies will be resurrected and put on immortality, "Behold, I tell you a mystery: We shall not all sleep, but we shall all be changed – in a moment, in the twinkling of an eye, at the last trumpet. For the trumpet will sound, and the dead will be raised incorruptible, and we shall be changed. For this corruptible must put on incorruption, and this mortal *must* put on immortality. So when this corruptible has put on incorruption, and this mortal has put on immortality, then shall be brought to pass the saying that is written: 'Death is swallowed up in victory.'"

Unbelievers will not put on immortality when they are resurrected, but the scriptures are clear that the unbeliever will continue to exist spirit, soul and body. Their existence will not be life and immortality but "the second death," a state of eternal conscious punishment and separation from God (Rev. 20:14). The scriptures state that unbelievers are dead in trespasses and sins (Eph. 2:1). Only believers have life (1 John 5:12). The unbeliever does not live in this life nor in the next. Immortality in the scriptures is said to belong only to God. He is the only One Who possesses in Himself deathlessness, freedom from death (1 Tim. 6:16). This is the meaning of immortality in scripture. As W. Hendriksen points out, "This immortality is the opposite of *death,* as is clear from the derivation of the word both in English and in Greek. *Athanasia* is deathlessness."[1] This deathlessness is given only to believers (1 Cor. 15:54). The unbeliever is forever in the state of death. He has an eternal existence, but not immortality.

What happens to believers and unbelievers in the period between physical death and the coming of Christ?

The state of the believer is one of blessedness but awaits the completion of salvation. It is described as Paradise in Luke 23:42–43. In 2 Cor. 5:6–8 it is "to be present with the Lord." It is to see Him in contrast to walking by faith. Paul says that the state of the believer after death and before glorification is very far better. The original uses a triple comparative. This is a thrilling prospect for the Christian. It will be *better* than the fullest enjoyment of God's blessing on earth. More than that it will be *far* better. Even more than that it will be *very* far better. No wonder Paul said, "For to me, to live *is* Christ, and to die *is* gain" (Phil. 1:21). Moreover we shall see that believers also reign with Christ in heaven (Rev. 20:4).

The idea that the soul of the believer sleeps and that the believer is unconscious until the resurrection of the body at the return of Christ cannot stand in the light of these verses. Heb. 12:23 tells of "the spirits of just men made perfect" in heaven. The body awaits resurrection and glorification. The spirit, though perfect, needs the glorified body for salvation to be completed. Thus the state of the Christian after death and before the last day is one of great blessedness, but one awaiting full salvation. That full salvation will not be experienced until the redemption of the body is wrought by God.

The Bible says very little about the state of unbelievers who die before the return of Christ. Jesus told a parable in Luke 19:19–31 which says that they are in a place of suffering and punishment. Peter also states "the Lord knows how to . . . reserve the unjust under punishment for the day of judgment" (2 Pet. 2:9). This verse tells us that God holds the unjust under punishment from the time of their death until the Final Judgment. Until then they are in a continual state of being punished.

The scriptures do not reveal much about man's state from death to the Final Judgment. Concerning the future of mankind the Bible focuses on the resurrection of all the dead, the final judgment of all and the subsequent future eternal state of both believers and unbelievers.

Reference

1. William Hendriksen *A Commentary on the Epistles to Timothy and Titus*, Banner of Truth, Second British Edition, 1964, page 208.

CHAPTER TWO

ONE RESURRECTION OF THE DEAD

When will the bodies of believers and unbelievers be resurrected?

The resurrection of the bodies of believers will take place at the coming of the Lord Jesus Christ. All the following verses declare this truth:

Paul says to believers, "For our citizenship is in heaven, from which we also eagerly wait for the Savior, the Lord Jesus Christ, who will transform our lowly body that it may be conformed to His glorious body, according to the working by which He is able even to subdue all things to Himself" (Phil. 3:20–21).

"But I do not want you to be ignorant, brethren, concerning those who have fallen asleep, lest you sorrow as others who have no hope. For if we believe that Jesus died and rose again, even so God will bring with Him those who sleep in Jesus. For this we say to you by the word of the Lord, that we who are alive *and* remain until the coming of the Lord will by no means precede those who are asleep. For the Lord Himself will descend from heaven with a shout, with the voice of an archangel, and with the trumpet of God. And the dead in Christ will rise first. Then we who are alive *and* remain shall be caught up together with them in the clouds to meet the Lord in the air. And thus we shall always be with the Lord. Therefore comfort one another with these words" (1 Thess. 4:13–18). Some believers will still be alive at the return of Christ. Their bodies will be changed just as the bodies of the Christians who have died ("fallen asleep").

"Behold, I tell you a mystery: We shall not all sleep, but we shall all be changed – in a moment, in the twinkling of an eye, at the last trumpet. For the trumpet will sound, and the dead will be raised incorruptible, and we shall be changed. For this corruptible must put

9

on incorruption, and this mortal *must* put on immortality. So when this corruptible has put on incorruption, and this mortal has put on immortality, then shall be brought to pass the saying that is written: 'Death is swallowed up in victory.'" (1 Cor. 15:51–54). The "last trumpet" will accompany the coming of Christ. "For we know that the whole creation groans and labors with birth pangs together until now. Not only *that*, but we also who have the firstfruits of the Spirit, even we ourselves groan within ourselves, eagerly waiting for the adoption, the redemption of our body. For we were saved in this hope, but hope that is seen is not hope; for why does one still hope for what he sees?" (Rom. 8:22–24).

No one knows the time of the second coming of Christ. Jesus said "But of that day and hour no one knows, not even the angels in heaven, nor the Son, but only the Father. Take heed, watch and pray; for you do not know when the time is" (Mark 13:32–33).

The resurrection of unbelievers will also take place at the coming of Christ, "And many of those who sleep in the dust of the earth shall awake, Some to everlasting life, Some to shame *and* everlasting contempt" (Dan. 12:2). The natural reading of the text is that the godly and ungodly are resurrected at the same time. The word "many" is equivalent to all. H.C. Leupold argues, "There are also other instances in the scriptures where "many" and "all" are used interchangeably, the one emphasising the fact that there are numerically *many*, the other the fact that *all* are involved."[1] He cites Rom. 5:15, "But the free gift *is* not like the offense. For if by the one man's offense many died, much more the grace of God and the gift by the grace of the one Man, Jesus Christ, abounded to many," compared with Rom. 5:12, "Therefore, just as through one man sin entered the world, and death through sin, and thus death spread to all men, because all sinned."

Turning to the New Testament Paul, in his defence before Felix, says, "But this I confess to you, that according to the Way which they call a sect, so I worship the God of my fathers, believing all things which are written in the Law and in the Prophets. I have hope in God, which they themselves" (the Jews) "also accept, that there will be a resurrection of *the* dead, both of *the* just and *the* unjust" (Acts 24:14–15). A.A. Hoekema says, "In the Greek, as well as in the English translation, the word *resurrection* is in the singular (*anastasin*)."[2] The text speaks of a single resurrection.

Some teach that the resurrection of unbelievers takes place 1,000 years after the resurrection of believers. They affirm that an earthly reign of Christ for 1,000 years will take place at His second coming and will be followed by the eternal state. Believers are resurrected at the time of His coming to earth, but unbelievers are not resurrected until the end of the 1,000 years. They also say that there will be a resurrection of those who become believers during the alleged 1,000 year reign. They affirm three resurrections. Some go further. They believe that Christ returns for believers at the start, or in the middle, of a period of seven years of tribulation before His 1,000 year reign on earth. They also believe that unbelievers will not be resurrected until the end of the 1,000 year reign. Thus they have a period of 1,007 or 1,003.5 years between the resurrection of believers and unbelievers. They add two more resurrections to these two resurrections – the resurrection of converts made in the tribulation period, and the resurrection of converts made during the millennium. Consequently they have four resurrections. These prophetic doctrines resulting in more than one single resurrection of all the dead are based on O.T. and N.T. scriptures.

The main passage used is Revelation 20:1–10

"Then I saw an angel coming down from heaven, having the key to the bottomless pit and a great chain in his hand. He laid hold of the dragon, that serpent of old, who is *the* Devil and Satan, and bound him for a thousand years; and he cast him into the bottomless pit, and shut him up, and set a seal on him, so that he should deceive the nations no more till the thousand years were finished. But after these things he must be released for a little while. And I saw thrones, and they sat on them, and judgment was committed to them. Then *I saw* the souls of those who had been beheaded for their witness to Jesus and for the word of God, who had not worshiped the beast or his image, and had not received *his* mark on their foreheads or on their hands. And they lived and reigned with Christ for a thousand years. But the rest of the dead did not live again until the thousand years were finished. This *is* the first resurrection. Blessed and holy *is* he who has part in the first resurrection. Over such the second death has no power, but they shall be priests of God and of Christ, and shall reign with Him a thousand years. Now when the thousand years have expired, Satan will be released from his prison and will go out to deceive the nations which are in the four corners of the earth, Gog and Magog, to gather them together to battle, whose number *is* as the sand of the sea. They went up on the breadth of the earth and surrounded the camp of the saints and the beloved city. And fire came down from God out of heaven and devoured them. The devil, who deceived them, was cast into the lake of fire and brimstone where the beast and the false prophet *are*. And they will be tormented day and night forever and ever."

At first sight these verses may seem to support two resurrections separated by a thousand years. It is vital to understand that the book of Revelation uses symbolism to communicate its message. These symbols are used to denote concrete realities more powerfully than literal language. They are designed to have a greater impact on the mind, heart and will than ordinary words. They present a vivid picture of reality. Thus in Rev. 1:1 the revelation is said to be "signified." As R.H. Mounce says about this word "This should warn the reader not to expect a literal presentation of future history, but a symbolic portrayal of that which must yet come to pass."[3] These symbols are sometimes in stark contrast to heighten the effect. Examples are:

- The Lamb for Christ and the Dragon for the Devil.
- Babylon for the counterfeit Christian Church (having the form of godliness but not the power) and the New Jerusalem, the true church of Jesus Christ.

There are explicit mentions of symbols and their meaning in the following verses:

Rev. 1:20 "The mystery of the seven stars which you saw in My right hand, and the seven golden lampstands: The seven stars are the angels of the seven churches, and the seven lampstands which you saw are the seven churches."

Rev. 4:5 "And from the throne proceeded lightnings, thunderings, and voices. Seven lamps of fire *were* burning before the throne, which are the seven Spirits of God."

Rev. 5:8 "Now when He had taken the scroll, the four living creatures and the twenty-four elders fell down before the Lamb, each having a harp, and golden bowls full of incense, which are the prayers of the saints."

Rev. 7:13–14 "Then one of the elders answered, saying to me, 'Who are these arrayed in white robes, and where did they come from?' And I said to him, 'Sir, you know.' So he said to me, 'These are the ones who come out of the great tribulation, and washed their robes and made them white in the blood of the Lamb'."

Rev. 12:9 "So the great dragon was cast out, that serpent of old, called the Devil and Satan, who deceives the whole world; he was cast to the earth, and his angels were cast out with him."

Rev. 17:9 "Here *is* the mind which has wisdom: The seven heads are seven mountains on which the woman sits."

Rev. 17:12 "The ten horns which you saw are ten kings who have received no kingdom as yet, but they receive authority for one hour as kings with the beast."

Rev. 17:15 "Then he said to me, 'The waters which you saw, where the harlot sits, are peoples, multitudes, nations, and tongues'."

Rev. 17:18 "And the woman whom you saw is that great city which reigns over the kings of the earth."

With these facts in mind we approach Rev. 20:1–10.

Verses 1–3
The meaning of this binding of Satan is explained by the following verses.

"He [the Father] raised Him [Christ] from the dead and seated *Him* at His right hand in the heavenly *places*, far above all principality and power and might and dominion, and every name that is named, not only in this age but also in that which is to come. And He put all *things* under His feet, and gave Him *to be* head over all *things* to the church" (Eph. 1:20–22). The Devil is put under His feet.

John 12:31–32 provides the key to the understanding of Rev. 20:1–3, "Now is the judgment of this world; now the ruler of this world will be cast out. And I, if I am lifted up from the earth, will draw all *peoples* to Myself." Jesus is speaking of His death. It will cast out the ruler of this world, Satan. The devil will not go on deceiving the nations because after His death Christ will draw people from all nations to Himself.

By His death Christ has destroyed the Devil: "Inasmuch then as the children have partaken of flesh and blood, He Himself likewise shared in the same, that through death He might destroy him who had the power of death, that is, the devil, and release those who through fear of death were all their lifetime subject to bondage" (Heb. 2:14–15). He destroyed the Devil in the sense that he rendered him ineffective in wielding the power of death. Satan brought about the fall of man resulting in physical and spiritual death. He was a murderer from the beginning (John 8:44). He works in fallen man, and causes him to walk "according to the prince of the power of the air." Man thus walks in spiritual death (Eph. 2:1–2) and heads for the second death, hell. The Devil has the power of death through his blinding of men's eyes (2 Cor. 4:4). But Christ though His death makes the Devil's power ineffective. Men are delivered from his power. They are turned from the power of Satan to God (Acts 26:18). They are delivered from the power of darkness and transplanted into the kingdom of the Son of His love (Col. 1:13).

God overcomes the blinding of Satan stated in (2 Cor. 4:6): "For it is the God who commanded light to shine out of darkness, who has shone in our hearts to *give* the light of the knowledge of the glory of God in the face of Jesus Christ."

Col. 2:15 tells us of this disarming of principalities and powers, "Having disarmed principalities and powers, He made a public spectacle of them, triumphing over them in it" (Christ with reference to His death). The principalities are Satan and his hosts. They are stripped of their power, and publicly exposed to disgrace.

Rev. 12:9–10 also illuminates the meaning of Rev. 20:1–3, "So the great dragon was cast out, that serpent of old, called the Devil and Satan, who deceives the whole world; he was cast to the earth, and his angels were cast out with him. Then I heard a loud voice saying in heaven, 'Now salvation, and strength, and the kingdom of our God, and the power of His Christ have come, for the accuser of our brethren, who accused them before our God day and night, has been cast down'." The apostle Paul expressed the same glorious truth in Rom 8:33, "Who shall bring a charge against God's elect? *It is* God who justifies." Satan can no longer bring any charge against God's people. He cannot demand the just punishment of death for their sins, because Christ has died for them.

The meaning of numbers in Revelation

The numbers 1, 2, 3, 4, 5, 6, 7, 10, 12 and multiples of some of them have special significance.

- One = unity
- Two = strength (Eccles. 4:9–11, Deut. 17:6 and Luke 10:1).
- Three = a complete and ordered whole, the number of deity.
- Four = symbolic of the world or creation.
- Five = a small quantity, the five loaves and two fish (1 Cor. 14:19).
- Six = the imperfect, the human destined to fail.
- Seven = the complete.
- Ten = fullness (Gen. 31:7, Exod. 26:1,16; 27:12, Num. 14:22, Job 19:3, Dan. 1:12 and Rev. 2:10, 12:3, 13:1 and 17:3).

- Twelve = relates to the people of God.
- Three and a half = hardship.

Years mean a long time distinct from days or months. Therefore the 1000 years is an indefinite ideal long completed period. 1000 = 10×10×10. It is the period between the ascension of Christ and His return. During this period Satan deceives the nations no more. With the death of Christ and the disarming of Satan and his hosts a great change has occurred. Acts 14:16, says that God "in bygone generations allowed all nations to walk in their own ways." Acts 17:30 declares the change: "Truly, these times of ignorance God overlooked, but now commands all men everywhere to repent." God has rendered the Devil ineffective specifically in the matter of continuing to deceive those whom He calls to Himself from all the nations. But the Devil is still active. He still walks about like a roaring lion seeking whom he may devour (1 Pet. 5:8). He still tempts to sin. He still fills men's hearts to commit sin (Acts 5:3). He still works in fallen mankind so that they walk according to his will (Eph. 2:2). He still attacks the people of God (Eph. 6:11–18). He still moves people to worship demons (1 Cor. 10:20). He still has his minis-ters, wolves in sheep's clothing (2 Cor. 11:13–15). Satan still hinders the servants of God in their service for God (1 Thess. 2:18). He still casts servants of God into prison (Rev. 2:10). He still sows tares in God's field (Mat. 13:39). He still takes away the word out of the hearts of some who hear the gospel (Mat. 13:19). He still blinds the eyes of mankind from seeing the truth (2 Cor. 4:4). But as regards the elect, those chosen by God for salvation through the gospel (2 Thess. 2:13–14), he is powerless to prevent them entering the kingdom. As Jesus said, "All authority has been given to Me in heaven and on earth. Go therefore and make disciples of all the nations, baptizing them in the name of the Father and of the Son and of the Holy Spirit, teaching them to observe all things that I have commanded you; and lo, I am with you always, *even* to the end of the age" (Mat. 28:18–20). Rev. 20: 1–3 portrays this particular powerlessness of the Devil.

Notice that after these things he is released for "a little while" (verses 7–8). Gog and Magog are symbolic of the last enemies of the people of God (cf. Ezek. 38–39). 2 Thess. 2:1–12 may explain something about this final period just before the coming of Christ. The passage reads, "Now, brethren, concerning the coming of our Lord Jesus Christ and our gathering together to Him, we ask you, not to be soon shaken in mind or troubled, either by spirit or by word or by letter, as if from us, as though the day of Christ had come. Let no one deceive you by any means; for *that Day will not come* unless the falling away comes first, and the man of sin is revealed, the son of perdition, who opposes and exalts himself above all that is called God or that is worshiped, so that he sits as God in the temple of God, showing himself that he is God. Do you not remember that when I was still with you I told you these things? And now you know what is restraining, that he may be revealed in his own time. For the mystery of lawlessness is already at work; only He who now restrains *will do so* until He is taken out of the way. And then the lawless one will be revealed, whom the Lord will consume with the breath of His mouth and destroy with the brightness of His coming. The coming of the *lawless one* is according to the working of Satan, with all power, signs, and lying wonders, and with all unrighteous deception among those who perish, because they did not receive the love of the truth, that they might be saved. And for this reason God will send them strong delusion, that they should believe the lie, that they all may be condemned who did not believe the truth but had pleasure in unrighteousness."

Verses 4–6

The ones sitting on thrones are Christians who have died and gone to be with Christ. Their thrones are in heaven, where Christ is. They are blessed and holy. They are priests of God and of Christ, and those over whom the second death has no power. They include Christian martyrs, and also those who had not worshipped the beast and had not received his mark on their foreheads or on their hands. John makes specific mention of these two groups, because his whole theme was to encourage fellow believers who were suffering the tribulation of persecution (1:9). Christians even when they are killed for their faith have not suffered defeat. They are alive and reigning! And they will judge those who hated and killed them! They are not yet with glorified bodies, but their spirits are perfected (Heb. 12:23), and they are with Christ (Phil. 1:23) Who is NOW reigning. That present reign is stated in the following verses, "Men *and* brethren, let *me* speak freely to you of the patriarch David, that he is both dead and buried, and his tomb is with us to this day. Therefore, being a prophet, and knowing that God had sworn with an oath to him that of the fruit of his body, according to the flesh, He would raise up the Christ to sit on his throne, he, foreseeing this, spoke concerning the resurrection of the Christ, that His soul was not left in Hades, nor did His flesh see corruption. This Jesus God has raised up, of which we are all witnesses. Therefore being exalted to the right hand of God, and having received from the Father the promise of the Holy Spirit, He poured out this which you now see and hear. For David did not ascend into the heavens, but he says himself: 'The Lord said to my Lord, "Sit at My right hand, Till I make

Your enemies Your footstool."' Therefore let all the house of Israel know assuredly that God has made this Jesus, whom you crucified, both Lord and Christ" (Acts 2:29–36). Peter proclaims that the Risen Ascended Christ has been raised up from death by the Father to sit and reign on David's throne. The reign of Christ began with His ascension, and will continue until His return. As Paul states, "For He must reign till He has put all enemies under His feet" (1 Cor. 15:25).

This present heavenly reign of the departed saints is called the first resurrection.

It will continue until Christ returns to earth. It is called the first resurrection because it occurs after their physical death and before the final general resurrection. Their death was immediately followed by reigning with Christ. In that sense they were resurrected.

The not worshipping the beast or his image, and not receiving his mark on their foreheads or on their hands, are symbolic ways of saying that they did not deny their Lord when persecuted for their faith.

The rest of the dead, that is, all non-Christians, did not live again until the resurrection at the last day. They will rise at the last day (John 5:28–29) when Christ returns. They will be judged and suffer the second death – eternal hell. The first death is physical death.

Some assert that the words in verse 4 "they lived" or "they came to life" (both translations are possible) must have the same meaning as "live again" in verse 5 where it means bodily resurrection:

Rev. 20:4 "And I saw thrones, and they sat on them, and judgment was committed to them. Then *I saw* the souls of those who had been beheaded for their witness to Jesus and for the word of God, who had not worshiped the beast or his image, and had not received *his* mark on their foreheads or on their hands. And *they lived* (ἔζησαν) and reigned with Christ for a thousand years."

Rev. 20:5 "But the rest of the dead did not *live* (ἔζησαν) again until the thousand years were finished. This *is* the first resurrection."

They conclude therefore that this first resurrection must be a bodily resurrection just as the second is. They contend that the two resurrections must be of the same kind.

Against this conclusion are the following considerations:

1. In his gospel John records Jesus speaking of a spiritual resurrection and a literal resurrection in the same context, "Most assuredly, I say

to you, he who hears My word and believes in Him who sent Me has everlasting life, and shall not come into judgment, but has passed from death into life" (spiritual resurrection). "Most assuredly, I say to you, the hour is coming, and now is, when the dead will hear the voice of the Son of God; and those who hear will live. For as the Father has life in Himself, so He has granted the Son to have life in Himself, and has given Him authority to execute judgment also, because He is the Son of Man. Do not marvel at this; for the hour is coming in which all who are in the graves will hear His voice and come forth" (literal resurrection) "– those who have done good, to the resurrection of life, and those who have done evil, to the resurrection of condemnation" (John 5:24–29).

2. There are indications that here in Revelation John is speaking of a spiritual resurrection and a literal resurrection alongside each other.

   a) He uses "live" in different ways. It is used in Rev. 2:8 of the coming to life again of Christ. In 3:1 it describes the spiritual state of a church. In 19:20 it refers to physical existence.

   b) With reference to the words "first resurrection" Meredith G. Kline points out that the word "first" (πρώτη) is sometimes used in scripture to indicate more than sequence. It sometimes means a difference in kind.[4] It is so used in the very next chapter of Revelation. We read in Rev. 21:1 "Now I saw a new heaven and a new earth, for the first (πρῶτος) heaven and the first (πρώτη) earth had passed away. Also there was no more sea." Kim Riddlebarger says, "Then in Rev. 21:1, *prōtos* does not mean the first in a sequence of the same thing. In fact, it refers to a difference in kind, i.e., something which passes away and is replaced, such as the first heaven and earth. The contrast is not between a first earth and a second earth of the same kind, but instead, John contrasted a fallen creation and a redeemed heaven and earth."[5] Kim Riddlebarger points elsewhere in the New Testament where *prōtos* has this same meaning. It designates the Mosaic covenant to distinguish it from the New Covenant (Heb. 8:7). The two covenants are clearly not identical. They stand in contrast. Similarly in 1 Cor. 15:45 we have the "first" man Adam in contrast to Christ. Therefore the word "first" supports the interpretation of two different kinds of resurrection, rather than the interpretation asserting two resurrections of the same kind.

   c) The mention of the "second death" in the immediate context indicates two deaths which are different – physical loss of life, the first death, and everlasting punishment which is the second death. In the same way the first and second resurrections are different.

d) Meredith G. Kline captures John's meaning, "Just as the resurrection of the unjust is paradoxically identified as the 'second death' so the death of the Christian is paradoxically identified as the 'first resurrection.' "[6]

J. Rodman Williams argues against the above interpretation as follows, ". . . there is no other biblical warrant for a present heavenly reign of disembodied souls or spirits. Indeed according to Revelation 6:9–11, souls of martyrs are depicted as 'under the altar' and, crying out for vengeance; they are told to 'rest a little longer.' This is hardly a portrayal of reigning. Also, in Revelation 14:13 the picture is likewise of 'rest' for the 'blessed' dead."[7]

In reply, there is biblical warrant for such a present heavenly reign. It is found in 2 Tim. 2:12 Paul says to Timothy, "If we endure, We shall also reign with *Him*. If we deny *Him*, He also will deny us." The other depictions of departed souls in Rev. 6:9–11 and 14:13 are simply complementary truths concerning their state. It is totally consistent with their reigning, to cry out for righteous judgment to be carried out, and to be at rest from their labours on earth.

Verse 9
The camp expresses the truth that Christians are strangers and pilgrims on the earth. They are also a beloved city Rev. 21:9–10 and Heb. 12:22. Notice the following:

1. The millennial reign is heaven centred.
2. There is no mention of:
   a) the Jews
   b) Palestine
   c) ceremonial ritual
   d) a temple
   e) Jerusalem
   f) a Throne in Jerusalem
   g) Jews having prominence over Gentiles.

Verse 10
The final doom of Satan and his instruments.

Grudem argues for an earthly millennial reign of believers with Christ

Appealing to Luke 19:17,19; 1 Cor. 6:3 and Rev. 2:26–27; 3:21 Wayne Grudem says that the New Testament "frequently" tells us "that believers will reign with Christ and be given authority by him to reign over the earth."[8]

We will examine these verses.

Luke 19:17 and 19

These verses teach that the Lord will reward His servants in accord with their diligence in making use of the opportunity to serve Him. Each servant is given one mina. One servant gains ten minas by trading. He is thus given authority over ten cities. Another servant gains five minas. Accordingly he is given authority over five cities. The "cities" given to them to rule over are not to be taken literally as defining the nature of future rewards for diligent service of Christ. They are simply part of the parable just as the minas the nobleman gave to each of his servants.

1 Cor. 6:3

"Do you not know that we shall judge angels? How much more, things that pertain to this life?" This verse does not say where believers will judge angels.

Rev. 2:26–27

"And he who overcomes, and keeps My works until the end, to him I will give power over the nations – 'He shall rule them with a rod of iron; They shall be dashed to pieces like the potter's vessels' – as I also have received from My Father." These words refer to the Father's promises to the Son recorded in Psalm 2. They are promises in the context of nations acting against the Lord and His anointed. Christ is assured that He will overcome their opposition. The Father says, "Ask of Me, and I will give *You* The nations *for* Your inheritance, And the ends of the earth *for* Your possession. You shall break them with a rod of iron; You shall dash them to pieces like a potter's vessel.'" (Psa. 2:8–9). The Lord Jesus Christ is given absolute assurance that He will gather into His kingdom people from every tribe tongue and kindred throughout the world, and that He will smash with absolute power opposition to this extending of His kingdom.

Thus Christ told his disciples, "All authority has been given to Me in heaven and on earth. Go therefore and make disciples of all the nations, baptizing them in the name of the Father and of the Son and of the Holy Spirit, teaching them to observe all things that I have commanded you; and lo, I am with you always, *even* to the end of the age" (Mat. 28:18–20). The believer who overcomes is promised that gospel power or authority over the nations. It is power to overcome opposition to the extension of the kingdom of Christ throughout the world.

We have an example of the fulfilment of this promise of Rev. 2:26–27 in Acts 4. Peter and John are threatened and commanded by the authorities not to preach the gospel. They go to their fellow believers and pray to God. In their prayer they refer to Psalm 2 and the opposition prophesied against Christ in the opening verses. Then they state that they are now suffering the same opposition. They ask God for victory over those opposing them just as Christ had total victory. God answers in power giving them a marvellous experience of Rev. 2:26–27. Here is the prayer and the answer they received. "So when they heard that, they raised their voice to God with one accord and said: 'Lord, You *are* God, who made heaven and earth and the sea, and all that is in them, who by the mouth of Your servant David have said: "Why did the nations rage, And the people plot vain things? The kings of the earth took their stand, And the rulers were gathered together Against the LORD and against His Christ." For truly against Your holy Servant Jesus, whom You anointed, both Herod and Pontius Pilate, with the Gentiles and the people of Israel, were gathered together to do whatever Your hand and Your purpose determined before to be done. Now, Lord, look on their threats, and grant to Your servants that with all boldness they may speak Your word, by stretching out Your hand to heal, and that signs and wonders may be done through the name of Your holy Servant Jesus.' And when they had prayed, the place where they were assembled together was shaken; and they were all filled with the Holy Spirit, and they spoke the word of God with boldness" (Acts 4:24–31).

Rev. 3:21
"To him who overcomes I will grant to sit with Me on My throne, as I also overcame and sat down with My Father on His throne." When Christ returns "the heavens will pass away with a great noise and the elements will melt with fervent heat; both the earth and the works that are in it will be burned up." There will be a "new heavens and a new earth in which righteousness dwells" (2 Pet. 3:10–13). In that new universe of the age to come, the eternal state, believers will reign with Christ – "And there shall be no more curse, but the throne of God and of the Lamb shall be in it, and His servants shall serve Him. They shall see His face, and His name *shall be* on their foreheads. There shall be no night there: They need no lamp nor light of the sun, for the Lord God gives them light. And they shall reign forever and ever" (Rev. 22:3–5), and possibly, "And they sang a new song, saying: 'You are worthy to take the scroll, And to open its seals; For You were slain, And have redeemed us to God by Your blood Out of every tribe and tongue and

people and nation, And have made us kings and priests to our God; And we shall reign on the earth.'" (Rev. 5:9–10). Textual evidence also supports "And we reign on the earth".

The Christian reigns now in this life, "For if by the one man's offense death reigned through the one, much more those who receive abundance of grace and of the gift of righteousness will reign in life through the One, Jesus Christ" (Rom. 5:17). The believer is seated "in heavenly places in Christ Jesus" (Eph. 2:6). He overcomes the world (1 John 5:4), the flesh (Rom. 6:14) and the Devil (James 4:7). Even death holds no terror, "Who shall separate us from the love of Christ? *Shall* tribulation, or distress, or persecution, or famine, or nakedness, or peril, or sword? As it is written: 'For Your sake we are killed all day long; We are accounted as sheep for the slaughter.' Yet in all these things we are more than conquerors through Him who loved us" (Rom. 8:35–37). More than conquerors! Believers reign in life in all circumstances and at all times through Jesus Christ. They will reign forever with Christ in the eternal state. Thus it is consistent that they also reign in the period from their death to Christ's return.

Looking at all the New Testament we find that there are only two periods in the plan of God. There is the present age, and the age to come. The present age extends from Christ's first coming to His return. It is described as "the last days" (Acts 2:17), "this age" (Luke 20:34), "this present evil age" (Gal. 1:4), and "the last hour" (1 John 2:18). The "age to come" begins with the return of Christ and is eternal. It is described as "that age" in contrast to "this age" – "Jesus answered and said to them, 'The sons of this age marry and are given in marriage. But those who are counted worthy to attain that age, and the resurrection from the dead, neither marry nor are given in marriage'" (Luke 20:34–35). It is contrasted with the present time, "So He said to them, 'Assuredly, I say to you, there is no one who has left house or parents or brothers or wife or children, for the sake of the kingdom of God, who shall not receive many times more in this present time, and in the age to come eternal life'" (Luke 18:29–30). It is defined as "the ages to come" (Eph. 2:7). The age to come will be composed of a number of ages. Indeed Rev. 14:11 defines it as "ages of ages." There will be divisions of time and distinct periods of time within those divisions in the eternal future. The two ages, "this age" and "the age to come" are successive and distinct. "Anyone who speaks a word against the Son of Man, it will be forgiven him; but whoever speaks against the Holy Spirit, it will not be forgiven him, either in this age or in the *age* to come" (Mat. 12:32). See also Luke 18:29–30, and 20:34–35. "He raised Him from the dead and seated *Him* at His right hand in the heavenly *places,* far above all principality and power and might and dominion, and every name that is named, not only in this age but also in that which is to come" (Eph. 1:20–21). These two verses speak of all future time. "This age" ends with the return of Christ. "The age to come" begins with that event. There is no mention of a millennial age between the two in Jesus, or Paul, or Luke, or James, or Peter, or Jude, or the writer of Hebrews. This interpretation of the millennium of Rev. 20:1–6 contradicts the revelation in the rest of the New Testament. It is manifestly an incorrect interpretation.

The alleged earthly millennial reign cannot be fitted into "this age" which ends with the return of Christ, because it only commences when Christ comes to the earth. Nor can it be fitted into "the age to come" as one of the ages of that age to come. The "age to come" is an age of a new heavens and new earth in which righteousness dwells (2 Pet. 3:10). There is unrighteousness present in the alleged earthly millennium. The alleged revolt of Satan and his hordes against Christ and His people and the great presence of evil on the earth flies in the face of the fact that only righteousness dwells on the new earth and throughout the new universe from the start of the "age to come."

Some contend that certain passages in the Old Testament are prophetic of an earthly millennial reign of Christ

Isaiah 65:20 NASB

"No longer will there be in it an infant *who lives but a few* days, Or an old man who does not live out his days; For the youth will die at the age of one hundred And the one who does not reach the age of one hundred Will be *thought* accursed."

This prophecy is of the new heavens and the new earth, the age to come. It will be helpful to show this verse in the context of its surrounding verses:

> " 'For behold, I create new heavens and a new earth; And the former things will not be remembered or come to mind. But be glad and rejoice forever in what I create; For behold, I create Jerusalem *for* rejoicing And her people *for* gladness. I will also rejoice in Jerusalem and be glad in My people; And there will no longer be heard in her The voice of weeping and the sound of crying. No longer will there be in it an infant *who lives but a few* days, Or an old man who does not live out his days; For the youth will die at the age of one hundred And the one who does not reach the age of one hundred Will be *thought* accursed. They will build houses and inhabit *them*; They will also plant vineyards and eat their fruit. They will not build and another inhabit,

They will not plant and another eat; For as the lifetime of a tree, *so will be* the days of My people, And My chosen ones will wear out the work of their hands. They will not labor in vain, Or bear *children* for calamity; For they are the offspring of those blessed by the LORD, And their descendants with them. It will also come to pass that before they call, I will answer; and while they are still speaking, I will hear. The wolf and the lamb will graze together, and the lion will eat straw like the ox; and dust will be the serpent's food. They will do no evil or harm in all My holy mountain,' Says the LORD" (Isa. 65:17–25 NASB).

The prophet is foretelling future blessings in terms familiar to his hearers. He prophesies the future using aspects of their present life and experience of war, defeat and exile. He contrasts the present with the glorious future. Verse 20 is saying that the power of death will be destroyed. He also predicts freedom from sorrow (v. 19), total security (v. 21–23), and total blessedness and peace (v. 24–25). As Alec Motyer says of these verses "Things we have no real capacity to understand can be expressed only through things we know and experience."[9] These future blessings are already being experienced by believers in this age. They have victory over death (John 11:25–26), they have a God given joy (Rom. 14:17), they are secure (Rom. 8:38–39), they experience the Father's love (Mat. 6:8) and a peace that surpasses understanding (Phil. 4:7). In these ways they taste the powers of the age to come (Heb. 6:5). The full experience of these predicted blessings awaits the age to come. Thus Isaiah's prophecy embraces both this age and the age to come. It does not predict an earthly millennial reign of Christ.

Isaiah 11:6–11 NASB

"And the wolf will dwell with the lamb, And the leopard will lie down with the young goat, And the calf and the young lion and the fatling together; And a little boy will lead them. Also the cow and the bear will graze, Their young will lie down together, And the lion will eat straw like the ox. The nursing child will play by the hole of the cobra, And the weaned child will put his hand on the viper's den. They will not hurt or destroy in all My holy mountain, For the earth will be full of the knowledge of the LORD As the waters cover the sea. Then in that day The nations will resort to the root of Jesse, Who will stand as a signal for the peoples; And His resting place shall be glorious. Then it will happen on that day that the LORD Will again recover the second time with His hand The remnant of His people, who will remain, From Assyria, Egypt, Pathros, Cush, Elam, Shinar, Hamath, And from the islands of the sea."

In the previous verse, Isaiah has predicted the coming of the Messiah. He now speaks of the results of His coming. He describes the characteristics of His kingdom. Instead of enmity there will be peace. There will be transformation, holiness and the knowledge of the Lord. Paul writes about the new unity between Jews and Gentiles in Christ: "Therefore remember that you, once Gentiles in the flesh – who are called Uncircumcision by what is called the Circumcision made in the flesh by hands – that at that time you were without Christ, being aliens from the commonwealth of Israel and strangers from the covenants of promise, having no hope and without God in the world. But now in Christ Jesus you who once were far off have been brought near by the blood of Christ. For He Himself is our peace, who has made both one, and has broken down the middle wall of separation, having abolished in His flesh the enmity, *that is*, the law of commandments *contained* in ordinances, so as to create in Himself one new man *from* the two, *thus* making peace, and that He might reconcile them both to God in one body through the cross, thereby putting to death the enmity. And He came and preached peace to you who were afar off and to those who were near. For through Him we both have access by one Spirit to the Father. Now, therefore, you are no longer strangers and foreigners, but fellow citizens with the saints and members of the household of God" (Eph. 2:11–19). This is the wonderful fulfilment of Isaiah's prophecy. The Root of Jesse is Christ the Saviour to Whom Gentiles turn for salvation during this age. They come from all over the world, and Isaiah predicts that by stating that God will gather them from the powers surrounding the Lord's people at that time. As in Isa. 65:20 the prophet is not to be interpreted literally. He is prophesying the blessedness of the kingdom of God in this age using terms of the time in which he lived. Paul quotes Isa. 11:10 as fulfilled in the conversion of the Gentiles in Rom. 15:12.

Psalm 72:8–14 NASB

"May he also rule from sea to sea And from the River to the ends of the earth. Let the nomads of the desert bow before him, And his enemies lick the dust. Let the kings of Tarshish and of the islands bring presents; The kings of Sheba and Seba offer gifts. And let all kings bow down before him, All nations serve him. For he will deliver the needy when he cries for help, The afflicted also, and him who has no helper. He will have compassion on the poor and needy, And the lives of the needy he will save. He will rescue their life from oppression and violence, And their blood will be precious in his sight;"

The reign of the Messiah is predicted in terms applicable to Solomon and his reign. It is fulfilled in the lives of believers now in this age. They belong to a worldwide kingdom. Great ones of the earth are among those believers. The very hairs of the heads of everyone in his kingdom are numbered, so great is His care over them.

Some dismiss such interpretation as "spiritualisation" and insist on a literal interpretation of prophecy. They fail to see that "spiritualisation" declares that certain prophecies have been or will be fulfilled in realities just as concrete as other prophecies which have been fulfilled literally. For example Jesus gave a spiritual interpretation of Mal. 4:5, "Behold, I will send you Elijah the prophet Before the coming of the great and dreadful day of the LORD." He said on two occasions that this prophecy was fulfilled, not literally, but in the coming of John the Baptist, "And if you are willing to receive *it*, he is Elijah who is to come" (Mat. 11:14), and, "And His disciples asked Him, saying, 'Why then do the scribes say that Elijah must come first?' Jesus answered and said to them, 'Indeed, Elijah is coming first and will restore all things. But I say to you that Elijah has come already, and they did not know him but did to him whatever they wished. Likewise the Son of Man is also about to suffer at their hands.' Then the disciples understood that He spoke to them of John the Baptist" (Mat. 17:10–13). Jesus affirms that the scribes are correct in saying that Elijah will come first. But they did not recognize him when he did come in the person of John the Baptist. The insistence on literal interpretation of prophecy can result in failure to see the actual fulfilment.

Zech. 14:5–17 NASB

"You will flee by the valley of My mountains, for the valley of the mountains will reach to Azel; yes, you will flee just as you fled before the earthquake in the days of Uzziah king of Judah. Then the LORD, my God, will come, *and* all the holy ones with Him! In that day there will be no light; the luminaries will dwindle. For it will be a unique day which is known to the LORD, neither day nor night, but it will come about that at evening time there will be light. And in that day living waters will flow out of Jerusalem, half of them toward the eastern sea and the other half toward the western sea; it will be in summer as well as in winter. And the LORD will be king over all the earth; in that day the LORD will be *the only* one, and His name *the only* one. All the land will be changed into a plain from Geba to Rimmon south of Jerusalem; but Jerusalem will rise and remain on its site from Benjamin's Gate as far as the place of the First Gate to the Corner Gate, and from the Tower of Hananel to the king's wine presses. People will live in it, and there will no longer be a curse, for Jerusalem will dwell in security. Now this will be the plague with which the LORD will strike all the peoples who have gone to war against Jerusalem; their flesh will rot while they stand on their feet, and their eyes will rot in their sockets, and their tongue will rot in their mouth. It will come about in that day that a great panic from the LORD will fall on them; and they will seize one another's hand, and the hand of one will be lifted against the hand of another. Judah also will fight at Jerusalem; and the wealth of all the surrounding nations will be gathered, gold and silver and garments in great abundance. So also like this plague will be the plague on the horse, the mule, the camel, the donkey and all the cattle that will be in those camps. Then it will come about that any who are left of all the nations that went against Jerusalem will go up from year to year to worship the King, the LORD of hosts, and to celebrate the Feast of Booths. And it will be that whichever of the families of the earth does not go up to Jerusalem to worship the King, the LORD of hosts, there will be no rain on them."

Verses 1–5 speak of the destruction of Jerusalem, and Jerusalem as representative of the covenant people of God. A remnant, those who receive the Messiah, will escape the terrible judgment (v. 2). The Lord will provide a way of escape (verses 3–5). The state will be overthrown (v. 6) cf. Isa. 13:10, Jer. 4:23–28 and Ezek. 30:3,18. But in that time of judgment the light of the gospel will shine (v. 7). The gospel will go out from Jerusalem to all nations (v. 8–9). Christ's kingdom will spread into all the world (v. 9). The people of God, Jerusalem, will be exalted (v. 10). The Lord's people will be secure (v. 11) cf. Rom. 8:38–39 and John 10:28–29. The people of God shall see their enemies defeated (verses 12–15). There will be those who are converted to Christ (v. 16). Those who do not obey the gospel will not be saved (verses 17–19). The Lord's people will be holy, that is taken out from the world and separated to Him. No one who is of the world will be among them (verses 20–21). Thus we have a description in Old Testament terms of the kingdom of God during this age.

Micah 4:1–5 NASB

"And it will come about in the last days That the mountain of the house of the Lord Will be established as the chief of the mountains. It will be raised above the hills, And the peoples will stream to it. Many nations will come and say, 'Come and let us go up to the mountain of the LORD And to the house of the God of Jacob, That He may teach us about His ways And that we may walk in His paths.' For from Zion will go forth the law, Even the word of the LORD from Jerusalem. And He will judge between many peoples And render decisions for mighty, distant nations. Then they will hammer their swords into plowshares And their spears into pruning hooks; Nation will not lift up sword against nation, And never again will they train for war. Each of them will sit under his vine And under his fig tree, With no one to make *them* afraid, For the mouth of the LORD of hosts has spoken. Though all the peoples walk Each in the name of his god, As for us, we will walk In the name of the LORD our God forever and ever."

These verses also predict the gospel blessings of this age in figurative language. Heb. 12:18–24 records the fulfilment of Micah's prophecy: "For you have not come to the mountain that may be touched and that burned with fire, and to blackness and darkness and tempest, and the sound of a trumpet and the voice of words, so that those who heard *it* begged that the word should not be spoken to them anymore. (For they could not endure what was commanded: 'And if so much as a beast touches the mountain, it shall be stoned or shot with an arrow.' And so terrifying was the sight *that* Moses said, 'I am exceedingly afraid and trembling.') But you have come to Mount Zion and to the city of the living God, the heavenly Jerusalem, to an innumerable company of angels, to the general assembly and church of the first-born *who are* registered in heaven, to God the Judge of all, to the spirits of just men made perfect, to Jesus the Mediator of the new covenant, and to the blood of sprinkling that speaks better things than *that of* Abel."

Some argue that the formation of the nation of Israel in their land in 1948 is related in the purpose of God to a future millennial earthly reign of Christ

Certain New Testament scriptures cast light on this event. Rom. 11:28–29 says: "Concerning the gospel *they are* enemies for your sake, but concerning the election *they are* beloved for the sake of the fathers. For the gifts and the calling of God *are* irrevocable." Paul is stating that, on the one hand, with reference to the gospel, the nation of the Jews are enemies for the sake of the Gentiles. Through their rejection of Christ salvation has come to the Gentiles. Their failure is riches for the Gentiles (verse 12). On the other hand the Jews are also regarded by God as beloved from the standpoint of His election of the nation. They are beloved 'for the fathers' sakes.' The nation came from the fathers – Abraham, Isaac and Jacob. God is faithful to all that He promised to the fathers concerning the nation. So they are beloved. Moreover God has no regrets about His gifts to the nation and His calling of them. This unfailing love for His chosen people may be a reason for their formation as a nation.

During the forty days before His ascension Jesus spoke to the apostles about the things pertaining to the kingdom of God (Acts 1:3). The apostles asked Him, "Lord, will You at this time restore the kingdom to Israel?" (Acts 1:6). They asked about the earthly political kingdom of the Jews. This was distinct from the spiritual kingdom of heaven. Jesus made this distinction in His words in Mat. 8:11–12, "And I say to you that many will come from east and west, and sit down with Abraham, Isaac, and Jacob in the kingdom of heaven. But the sons of the kingdom will be cast out into outer darkness. There will be weeping and gnashing of teeth." The latter kingdom was the national state of Israel distinct from the kingdom of heaven. The sons of the kingdom were Jews belonging to the nation of Israel but who did not receive the Messiah. The apostles were looking for freedom from foreign oppression when they asked this question. They were concerned about the earthly political kingdom. Jesus replied, "It is not for you to know times or seasons which the Father has put in His own authority" (Acts 1:7). The word "times" designates time in its duration, whether a longer or shorter period: the word "seasons" speaks of the characteristics of the period. Jesus is saying most strongly that they should not ask when sovereign power will be restored to the nation of Israel. It must not be their concern. But His reply does not deny that such a restoration will occur in the future. Rather it endorses that expectation. Jesus goes on to say what they must be concerned with, "But you shall receive power when the Holy Spirit has come upon you; and you shall be witnesses to Me in Jerusalem, and in all Judea and Samaria, and to the end of the earth" (Acts 1:8). It is not surprising therefore that we find no mention whatsoever in all the New Testament of a future restoration of the Jews as a nation state. The apostles obeyed their Master's instruction. They directed their attention to the kingdom of God, not to the restoration of the sovereign power of Israel. In the light of these verses the formation of Israel as a sovereign state is indicated by scripture in Acts 1:6. It is an event in the sovereign will of God for a people beloved by Him. Whatever its significance in God's dealings with the Jews and Gentiles, nowhere does the New Testament state that this formation of the nation state of Israel will be a preparation for a millennial earthly reign of Christ.

Attempts are made to insert more than one resurrection into a number of verses in the New Testament

John 5:28–29

"Do not marvel at this; for the hour is coming in which all who are in the graves will hear His voice and come forth – those who have done good, to the resurrection of life, and those who have done evil, to the resurrection of condemnation." It is argued from John 4:21–23 and 5:25 that the word hour means an extended period of time, and therefore can cover resurrections separated by a thousand years or more.

Answer

Throughout the New Testament the word hour (ὥρα) *always* means an unbroken continuous period of time when it does not mean literally sixty minutes. It refers to a situation which prevails unchanged for an undefined period of time. It does not permit a resurrection followed by a long period of no resurrections and then another resurrection.

1 Cor. 15:21–26

"For since by man *came* death, by Man also *came* the resurrection of the dead. For as in Adam all die, even so in Christ all shall be made alive. But each one in his own order: Christ the firstfruits, afterward those *who are* Christ's at His coming. Then *comes* the end, when He delivers the kingdom to God the Father, when He puts an end to all rule and all authority and power. For He must reign till He has put all enemies under His feet. The last enemy *that* will be destroyed *is* death." Some attempt to insert 1000 years or more, between verses 23 and 24.

Answers

Verse 23 says that those who are Christ's are resurrected at His coming. Jesus tells us that they are resurrected at the last day (John 6:39–40 and 54). Therefore they are resurrected at the end, not a 1000 years or more before the end. The *last enemy* to be destroyed is death. The scriptures are clear that death is destroyed at the coming of Christ when believers are glorified, "Behold, I tell you a mystery: We shall not all sleep, but we shall all be changed – in a moment, in the twinkling of an eye, at the last trumpet. For the trumpet will sound, and the dead will be raised incorruptible, and we shall be changed. For this corruptible must put on incorruption, and this mortal *must* put on immortality. So when this corruptible has put on incorruption, and this mortal has put on immortality, then shall be brought to pass the saying that is written: 'Death is swallowed up in victory' " (1 Cor.

15:51–54). Therefore there will no more enemies to be destroyed. But those who teach an earthly millennial reign of Christ after His coming state that during that reign enemies will arise. This conflicts with 1 Cor. 15:26, 51–54.

Mat. 13:30 tells us that the righteous and the wicked remain on earth alongside each other right up to the end of time. Mat. 13:24–30 reads, "Another parable He put forth to them, saying: 'The kingdom of heaven is like a man who sowed good seed in his field; but while men slept, his enemy came and sowed tares among the wheat and went his way. But when the grain had sprouted and produced a crop, then the tares also appeared. So the servants of the owner came and said to him, "Sir, did you not sow good seed in your field? How then does it have tares?" He said to them, "An enemy has done this." The servants said to him, "Do you want us then to go and gather them up?" But he said, "No, lest while you gather up the tares you also uproot the wheat with them. Let both grow together until the harvest, and at the time of harvest I will say to the reapers, 'First gather together the tares and bind them in bundles to burn them, but gather the wheat into my barn.'" There will be a single resurrection and final judgment of all the dead at the return of Christ.

Phil. 3:11

"if, by any means, I may attain to the resurrection from the dead." These words are taken to mean that Paul wanted to be part of a resurrection of believers 1000 years or more before the resurrection of the unbelievers.

Answer

He goes on to say, "Not that I have already attained, or am already perfected; but I press on, that I may lay hold of that for which Christ Jesus has also laid hold of me" (Phil. 3:12).

Clearly Paul's words "Not that I have already attained" rule out a future bodily resurrection. His readers knew he was still alive. Paul meant that he was pressing on to walk in newness of life. He wanted to live to God. Such a life is a resurrection from sin and death (Rom. 6:4–5f.).

1 Thess. 4:16

"The dead in Christ shall rise first" These words are made to mean 1000 years or more before dead unbelievers.

Answer

The words immediately following in verse 17 give the true meaning and sequence of events, "Then we who are alive *and* remain shall be caught up together with them in the clouds to meet the Lord in the air. And thus we shall always be with the Lord." Believers who have died will rise first when the Lord returns. Immediately afterwards believers alive at that time will be raptured and transformed.

Heb. 11:35
"Women received their dead raised to life again. And others were tortured, not accepting deliverance, that they might obtain a better resurrection." The "better resurrection" is interpreted as a resurrection 1000 years or more before the resurrection of the unrighteous.

Answer
The better resurrection is the final resurrection of the righteous in contrast to the bringing back to life as in 1 Kings 17:17–24 and 2 Kings 4:18–37.

Conclusions
1. Rev 20:1–10 does not provide solid ground for a belief in two bodily resurrections separated by a thousand years, or a thousand and seven years, or a thousand and three and a half years or by an indefinite long period indicated by the number 1000.
2. The Old Testament and the New Testament do not support more than one resurrection of all the dead.

References
1. H.C. Leupold *Exposition of Daniel*, Evangelical Press 1969, page 530.
2. A.A. Hoekema *The Bible and the Future*, Paternoster and Eerdmans 1979, page 241.
3. Robert H. Mounce *The Book of Revelation*, Eerdmans 1977, page 65.
4. Meredith G. Kline "The First Resurrection" *Westminster Theological Journal* 37/2 (1975) 366–375.
5. Kim Riddlebarger *A Case for Amillenialism*, IVP and Baker Books 2003, page 219.
6. Meredith G. Kline "The First Resurrection" *Westminster Theological Journal* 37/2 (1975) pages 366–375.
7. Taken from *Renewal Theology* by J. Rodman Williams. Copyright © 1996 by J. Rodman Williams Same author listed with c 1988,1990 and 1992. Used by permission of Zondervan, vol. 3, page 426 footnote.
8. Taken from *Systematic Theology* by Wayne A. Grudem. Copyright © 1994 by Wayne Grudem. Used by permission of IVP and Zondervan, page 1131.
9. Alec Motyer *The Prophecy of Isaiah*, IVP 1994, page 530.

CHAPTER THREE

THE RESURRECTION OF THE BODY

What is the nature of the resurrection body of believers and the nature of the resurrection body of unbelievers?

The scriptures have little to say about the resurrection bodies of unbelievers. Many verses do speak of the sufferings of eternal punishment. Jesus Himself said, "If your right eye causes you to sin, pluck it out and cast it from you; for it is more profitable for you that one of your members perish, than for your whole body to be cast into hell. And if your right hand causes you to sin, cut it off and cast it from you; for it is more profitable for you that one of your members perish, than for your whole body to be cast into hell" (Mat. 5:29–30). He warned, "And do not fear those who kill the body but cannot kill the soul. But rather fear Him who is able to destroy both soul and body in hell" (Mat. 10:28). These verses tell us that the bodies of unbelievers will experience the eternal suffering of Hell. The anguish and torment will not be only felt in the spirit and in the soul. There will be bodily pain.

The Bible, however, does reveal much about the resurrection bodies of believers. The hope of the believer is the redemption of the body (Rom. 8:23). Here on earth salvation is incomplete. The body is one of humiliation (Phil. 3:21). It is humiliated by sin, weakness, sickness and mortality. When Christ comes it will be changed to have a form like the body of the glorified Lord Jesus Christ. Paul tells us about this transformation in 1 Cor. 15:35–54:

"But someone will say, 'How are the dead raised up? And with what body do they come?' Foolish one, what you sow is not made alive unless it dies. And what you sow, you do not sow that body that shall be, but mere grain – perhaps wheat or some other *grain*. But God gives it a body as He pleases, and to each seed its own body. All flesh *is* not the same flesh, but *there is* one *kind of* flesh of men, another flesh of animals, another of fish, *and* another of birds. *There are* also celestial bodies and terrestrial bodies; but the glory of the celestial *is* one, and the *glory* of the terrestrial *is* another. *There is* one glory of the sun, another glory of the moon, and another glory of the stars; for *one* star differs from *another* star in glory. So also *is* the resurrection of the dead. *The body* is sown in corruption, it is raised in incorruption. It is sown in dishonor, it is raised in glory. It is sown in weakness, it is raised in power. It is sown a natural body, it is raised a spiritual body. There is a natural body, and there is a spiritual body. And so it is written, 'The first man Adam became a living being.' The last Adam *became* a life-giving spirit. However, the spiritual is not first, but the natural, and afterward the spiritual. The first man *was* of the earth, *made* of dust; the second Man *is* the Lord from heaven. As *was* the *man* of dust, so also *are* those *who are made* of dust; and as *is* the heavenly *Man*, so also *are* those *who are* heavenly. And as we have borne the image of the *man* of dust, we shall also bear the image of the heavenly *Man*. Now this I say, brethren, that flesh and blood cannot inherit the kingdom of God; nor does corruption inherit incorruption. Behold, I tell you a mystery: We shall not all sleep, but we shall all be changed – in a moment, in the twinkling of an eye, at the last trumpet. For the trumpet will sound, and the dead will be raised incorruptible, and we shall be changed. For this corruptible must put on incorruption, and this mortal *must* put on immortality. So when this corruptible has put on incorruption, and this mortal has put on immortality, then shall be brought to pass the saying that is written: 'Death is swallowed up in victory.'"

Verse 35: Paul states two questions which arise concerning the resurrection of the dead:

How are the dead raised up?
And with what body do they come?

Verses 36–37: Paul rebukes such who ask these questions. He condemns them as fools. He directs them to the natural order of plant life.

What is sown does not come to life unless it dies. "When you sow, you do not plant the body that will be, but just a seed, perhaps of wheat or of something else. But God gives it a body as he has determined, and to each kind of seed he gives its own body" (NIV). Life comes forth out of death, and the body which comes forth is not identical to the body which was sown.

Verse 38: The words "as He pleases" refer to His creation order. Each seed is given its own body designed by God.

Verses 39–41: develops the point that there is a great variety of bodies in creation.

Verses 42–44: Paul now applies what he has said to the resurrection of the body. "So also *is* the resurrection of the dead. *The body* is sown in corruption, it is raised in incorruption. It is sown in dishonor, it is raised in glory. It is sown in weakness, it is raised in power. It is sown a natural body, it is raised a spiritual body. There is a natural body, and there is a spiritual body."

The body will be raised and be subject to decay no longer.

At death the body is in dishonour. Its state of humiliation is manifest.

At resurrection the body will be glorious. Jesus said, "Then the righteous will shine forth as the sun in the kingdom of their Father" (Mat. 13:43).

At death the body is characterised by weakness. It is powerless.

But the resurrected body will be full of power.

The natural body is this present physical body. The spiritual body is suited to the age to come. It will be a body controlled and directed by the Holy Spirit.

Jesus declared one aspect of the difference between the natural body and the spiritual body. He said, "You are mistaken, not knowing the Scriptures nor the power of God. For in the resurrection they neither marry nor are given in marriage, but are like angels of God in heaven" (Mat. 22:29–30).

Paul explains further concerning the natural body and the spiritual body. He contrasts Adam and Christ:

1. Adam "became a living being," but Christ "*became* a life-giving spirit."
2. Adam was of the earth made of dust, but Christ is from heaven.

Christians bear the "the image of the *man* of dust" in their present natural bodies, but will bear "the image of the heavenly *Man*" in their future resurrected spiritual bodies. They will be changed.

Verse 50: Indeed without that change they cannot inherit the kingdom of God, the eternal state of blessedness of the redeemed. The natural body which is perishable cannot inherit that which is imperishable.

Verses 51–54: Therefore all believers both the ones who have died and those alive at the coming of Christ will be changed. Each believer will be transformed in order to enter the heavenly existence. Decay and death will cease for them. Their new bodies will be imperishable and immortal. There will be tremendous change but also continuity. This earthly body will put on incorruption and immortality. This is a mystery, something once hidden but now revealed by God. He calls their attention to it, "Look." It will happen in a split second. It will only take the time it takes to blink an eye. The last trumpet will sound. It will be the last trumpet because it will signal the End.

1 Thess. 4:16–17 adds further detail: "For the Lord Himself will descend from heaven with a shout, with the voice of an archangel, and with the trumpet of God. And the dead in Christ will rise first. Then we who are alive *and* remain shall be caught up together with them in the clouds to meet the Lord in the air. And thus we shall always be with the Lord." This transformation will be wrought by the Lord Jesus Christ Who will exercise the power which enables Him to subject all things to Himself (Phil. 3:21). This fact is the answer to all objections about the feasibility of resurrecting the body, regardless of what happened to the body before, at, and after death.

The resurrection body of believers will be conformed to the glorious body of Jesus Christ (Phil 3:21)

1.   *That body was a body of flesh*
Luke records Jesus coming and appearing to His followers after His resurrection, "Now as they said these things, Jesus Himself stood in the midst of them, and said to them, 'Peace to you.' But they were terrified and frightened, and supposed they had seen a spirit. And He said to them, 'Why are you troubled? And why do doubts arise in your hearts? Behold My hands and My feet, that it is I Myself. Handle Me and see, for a spirit does not have flesh and bones as you see I have.' When He had said this, He showed them His hands and His feet" (Luke 24:36–40). Jesus had a physical body. His flesh and bones could be seen and felt. It was a body capable of taking food – "But while they still did not believe for joy, and marveled, He said to them, 'Have you any food here?' So they gave Him a piece of a broiled fish and some honeycomb. And He took *it* and ate in their presence" (Luke 24:41–43).

2.   *The body of Christ that was raised from the dead was the same body that died*
John also records that same appearing of the resurrected Christ and says Jesus "showed them His hands and his side." Both Luke and John mention the wounds of Jesus to be clearly seen on His resurrected body.

3. *It was a body in which He went to heaven and in which He will return*

It is a body capable of space travel. Our present bodies are truly wonderful, but a body capable of flight through space exceeds what we can imagine. The *same* Jesus Who ascended will come again – "And while they looked steadfastly toward heaven as He went up, behold, two men stood by them in white apparel, who also said, 'Men of Galilee, why do you stand gazing up into heaven? This *same* Jesus, who was taken up from you into heaven, will so come in like manner as you saw Him go into heaven.' " (Acts 1:10–11).

4. *It is a "glorious" body. (Phil. 3:21)*

5. *It was unchanged after His resurrection*

Jesus was not always recognised by His disciples after His resurrection. On one occasion we are told that their eyes were "prevented" from recognising Him (Luke 24:16 NASB). Mary Magdalene did not recognise Jesus. It has been suggested that maybe it was still dark (John 20:1), or that she could not see clearly because she was weeping (John 20:15). She did not recognise His voice until He said "Mary" (John 20:14–16). The disciples initially supposed that they had seen a spirit when He appeared to the eleven in Jerusalem (Luke 24:36–37). The disciples did not recognise Jesus immediately when he came to them at the Sea of Tiberias (John 21:1–12). Matthew tells us that some of the disciples doubted (Mat. 28:17). These facts about the resurrection appearances lead some to conclude that He did not have His glorious body until His ascension into heaven. From the fact that Jesus will come "in the glory of His Father" (Mark 8:38) they argue that His resurrection body underwent a change at the ascension. Rather it would seem that Jesus did not reveal the full glory of His body at those recorded appearances during the forty days before His ascension.

Rom. 8:19–23 The resurrection of believers and creation

"For the earnest expectation of the creation eagerly waits for the revealing of the sons of God. For the creation was subjected to futility, not willingly, but because of Him who subjected *it* in hope; because the creation itself also will be delivered from the bondage of corruption into the glorious liberty of the children of God. For we know that the whole creation groans and labors with birth pangs together until now. Not only *that*, but we also who have the firstfruits of the Spirit, even we ourselves groan within ourselves, eagerly waiting for the adoption, the redemption of our body." Paul says that the whole creation (excluding angels and mankind) is waiting with eager expectation for this resurrection and glorification of believers. He personifies the subpersonal creation. He says that God subjected it to a state in which it is not fulfilling its original intended function. Instead it is in bondage to physical corruption. It is unable to free itself from decay and death. God subjected it to this futility when Adam sinned (Gen. 3:17–19). Since then the sub-human creation has been groaning as if in the pangs of childbirth, continually longing for deliverance but not achieving it. That deliverance will come at the same time as the resurrection and glorification of believers. Then all of irrational creation will fulfil its purpose. Thus the resurrection and glorification of believers will result in the deliverance of the universe.

Paul goes on to say that believers, seeing this glorious prospect of the redemption of the body and the transformed universe, and already experiencing by the Spirit a foretaste of future blessedness, await eagerly the redemption of the body. Indeed, the longing for it is so real that they "groan" in their hearts. Paul refers to this groaning in 2 Cor. 5:1–5: "For we know that if our earthly house, *this* tent, is destroyed, we have a building from God, a house not made with hands, eternal in the heavens. For in this we groan, earnestly desiring to be clothed with our habitation which is from heaven, if indeed, having been clothed, we shall not be found naked. For we who are in *this* tent groan, being burdened, not because we want to be unclothed, but further clothed, that mortality may be swallowed up by life. Now He who has prepared us for this very thing *is* God, who also has given us the Spirit as a guarantee." Paul is saying that believers groan while in this present body ("our earthly house"). They long for the resurrection body ("our heavenly dwelling"). This longing is not a desire to be rid of a body. It is a fervent wish to have the resurrection body. Moreover this glorification is the purpose of God for which He prepares His people. It is salvation brought to completion.

The Doctrine of Eternal Judgment

CHAPTER FOUR

THE FINAL JUDGMENT

The following scriptures declare that there will be a final judgment which will have eternal effect:

Jesus said "Assuredly, I say to you, it will be more tolerable for the land of Sodom and Gomorrah in the day of judgment than for that city!" (Mat. 10:15).

He also said, "But I say to you that for every idle word men may speak, they will give account of it in the day of judgment" (Mat. 12:36).

"He has appointed a day on which He will judge the world in righteousness by the Man whom He has ordained. He has given assurance of this to all by raising Him from the dead" (Acts 17:31).

" . . . in the day when God will judge the secrets of men by Jesus Christ, according to my gospel" (Rom. 2:16).

"For no other foundation can anyone lay than that which is laid, which is Jesus Christ. Now if anyone builds on this foundation *with* gold, silver, precious stones, wood, hay, straw, each one's work will become clear; for the Day will declare it, because it will be revealed by fire; and the fire will test each one's work, of what sort it is" (1 Cor. 3:11–13).

" . . . when the Lord Jesus is revealed from heaven with His mighty angels, in flaming fire taking vengeance on those who do not know God, and on those who do not obey the gospel of our Lord Jesus Christ. These shall be punished with everlasting destruction from the presence of the Lord and from the glory of His power, when He comes, in that Day, to be glorified in His saints and to be admired among all those who believe, because our testimony among you was believed" (2 Thess. 1:7–10).

"I charge *you* therefore before God and the Lord Jesus Christ, who will judge the living and the dead at His appearing and His kingdom" (2 Tim. 4:1).

" . . . the Lord knows how to deliver the godly out of temptations and to reserve the unjust under punishment for the day of judgment" (2 Pet. 2:9).

"But the heavens and the earth *which* are now preserved by the same word, are reserved for fire until the day of judgment and perdition of ungodly men. But, beloved, do not forget this one thing, that with the Lord one day *is* as a thousand years, and a thousand years as one day. The Lord is not slack concerning *His* promise, as some count slackness, but is longsuffering toward us, not willing that any should perish but that all should come to repentance. But the day of the Lord will come as a thief in the night, in which the heavens will pass away with a great noise, and the elements will melt with fervent heat; both the earth and the works that are in it will be burned up. Therefore, since all these things will be dissolved, what manner *of persons* ought you to be in holy conduct and godliness, looking for and hastening the coming of the day of God, because of which the heavens will be dissolved, being on fire, and the elements will melt with fervent heat?" (2 Pet. 3:7–12).

"And the angels who did not keep their proper domain, but left their own abode, He has reserved in everlasting chains under darkness for the judgment of the great day" (Jude 6).

The Time of this Final Judgment

From the above verses it is clear that at the return of Christ the following events occur:

1. the resurrection of all mankind who have died (John 5:28–29).
2. the transporting of believers who are alive at His coming to meet the Lord in the air (1 Thess. 4:17).
3. the glorification of all believers, both those resurrected from death and those who are alive at His coming (1 Cor. 15:51–52).
4. the judgment of all mankind, every human being who has ever lived or will ever live, both believers and unbelievers (Mat. 25:31–46).

5. the judgment of fallen angels (Jude 6).
6. a new heavens and a new earth (2 Pet. 3).

The time of His coming is unknown. Jesus said, "But of that day and hour no one knows, not even the angels in heaven, nor the Son, but only the Father. Take heed, watch and pray; for you do not know when the time is"(Mark 13:32–33).

The Duration of the Day of Judgment

The word day in scripture is used with different meanings. As well as twenty-four hours it means an undefined period of time in some places. 2 Cor. 6:2 is one example: "For He says: 'In an acceptable time I have heard you, And in the day of salvation I have helped you.' Behold, now *is* the accepted time; behold, now *is* the day of salvation." The day of salvation is the time from Christ's ascension to His return. We should think of the Day of Judgment therefore as an undefined period of time, not twenty-four hours.

Who will judge?

Jesus Christ – "For the Father judges no one, but has committed all judgment to the Son, that all should honor the Son just as they honor the Father. He who does not honor the Son does not honor the Father who sent Him" (John 5:22–23). This is stated repeatedly in the New Testament. The Father has placed the eternal destinies of all mankind and all the fallen angels in the hands of His Son. His purpose is that all should honour the Son:

> "When the Son of Man comes in His glory, and all the holy angels with Him, then He will sit on the throne of His glory. All the nations will be gathered before Him, and He will separate them one from another, as a shepherd divides *his* sheep from the goats. And He will set the sheep on His right hand, but the goats on the left. Then the King will say to those on His right hand, 'Come, you blessed of My Father, inherit the kingdom prepared for you from the foundation of the world'. . . . Then He will also say to those on the left hand, 'Depart from Me, you cursed, into the ever-lasting fire prepared for the devil and his angels.' " (Mat. 25:31–34 and 41).

> "He commanded us to preach to the people, and to testify that it is He who was ordained by God *to be* Judge of the living and the dead" (Acts 10:42).

"He has appointed a day on which He will judge the world in righteousness by the Man whom He has ordained. He has given assurance of this to all by raising Him from the dead" (Acts 17:31).

" . . . we must all appear before the judgment seat of Christ, that each one may receive the things *done* in the body, according to what he has done, whether good or bad" (2 Cor. 5:10).

"I charge *you* therefore before God and the Lord Jesus Christ, who will judge the living and the dead at His appearing and His kingdom" (2 Tim. 4:1).

The Lord Jesus Christ will be accompanied with the unfallen angels at His coming and while carrying out judgment (Mat. 25:31). They will carry out the sentence pronounced on the unsaved: "The Son of Man will send out His angels, and they will gather out of His kingdom all things that offend, and those who practice lawlessness, and will cast them into the furnace of fire. There will be wailing and gnashing of teeth" (Mat. 13:41–42).

Some members of mankind will also judge some other members of mankind. Jesus said that at this Final Judgment some would condemn others by their conduct: "The men of Nineveh will rise up in the judgment with this generation and condemn it, because they repented at the preaching of Jonah; and indeed a greater than Jonah *is* here. The queen of the South will rise up in the judgment with this generation and condemn it, for she came from the ends of the earth to hear the wisdom of Solomon; and indeed a greater than Solomon *is* here" (Mat. 12:41–42). These verses may explain the meaning of Paul's statements that believers will judge the world and angels at the Final Judgment: "Do you not know that the saints will judge the world? And if the world will be judged by you, are you unworthy to judge the smallest matters? Do you not know that we shall judge angels? How much more, things that pertain to this life?" (1 Cor. 6:2–3). The conduct of believers while on earth may condemn the world and angels. This interpretation may also explain Jesus's words in Luke 22:29–30: "And I bestow upon you a kingdom, just as My Father bestowed *one* upon Me, that you may eat and drink at My table in My kingdom, and sit on thrones judging the twelve tribes of Israel."

John 5:27 tells us that the Father has given Jesus authority to execute judgment "because He is the Son of Man." This title identifies Jesus with Daniel's vision of One Who receives a universal and everlasting dominion (Dan. 7:13–14). The title speaks of Him as the Messiah and

His glorious future coming and vindication. It also speaks of His humanity. He lived in this world. He lived under the law and was tempted in all points as we are. He understands man by actual experience.

The Father's wisdom is displayed in ordaining Jesus to judge the world. Jesus Himself will be glorified exceedingly by the appointment.

CHAPTER FIVE

THE NATURE OF THE FINAL JUDGMENT (1): A DAY OF WRATH

It will be a day of "wrath and revelation of the righteous judgment of God." The holy wrath of God will be poured out on sinners and fallen angels. In this earthly life sinful men and women enjoy God's goodness. He causes His sun to shine upon them despite their refusal to honour Him. Moreover He exercises forbearance and holds back from fully punishing them for their sins and sinfulness. He is longsuffering in putting up with their attitudes and conduct (Rom. 2:4). His longsuffering provides opportunity for repentance (2 Pet. 3:9). But at the Final Judgment there is no longer any forbearance. There is an end to long-suffering. God's wrath is no longer restrained. It is already manifested in this life in handing the sinner over to his sin (Rom. 1:18–28). This is a real and terrible punishment, but it is not the full and just punishment for sins and sinfulness. On that day the wrath of God against sinners and fallen angels will be expressed and executed without restraint. It will be a fearful thing to fall into the hands of the living God. We find that God's wrath, hot or fierce anger, fury and indignation are writ large in the scriptures from Genesis to Revelation. Generally this attribute of God is not understood and recognised as it is revealed in the scriptures. Therefore it is necessary to state the following verses concerning the wrath of God. Some words are emphasised by me by italic bold type.

Sodom, Gomorrah, Admah and Zeboim. c. 2000 BC

"All its land is brimstone and salt, a burning waste, unsown and unproductive, and no grass grows in it, like the overthrow of Sodom and Gomorrah, Admah and Zeboiim, which the LORD overthrew *in His anger and in His wrath*" (Deut. 29:23 NASB).

Concerning Egypt at the time of the Exodus-c.1440 BC

"When He performed His signs in Egypt And His marvels in the field of Zoan, And turned their rivers to blood, And their streams, they could not drink. He sent among them swarms of flies which devoured them, And frogs which destroyed them. He gave also their crops to the grasshopper And the product of their labor to the locust. He destroyed their vines with hailstones And their sycamore trees with frost. He gave over their cattle also to the hailstones And their herds to bolts of lightning. He sent upon them *His burning anger, Fury and indignation,* and trouble, A band of destroying angels. *He leveled a path for His anger;* He did not spare their soul from death, But gave over their life to the plague, And smote all the firstborn in Egypt, The first *issue* of their virility in the tents of Ham" (Psa. 78:43–51 NASB).

The destruction of Babylon in 539 BC

God used the Medes to conquer Babylon.

"The oracle concerning Babylon which Isaiah the son of Amoz saw. Lift up a standard on the bare hill, Raise your voice to them, Wave the hand that they may enter the doors of the nobles. I have commanded My consecrated ones, *I have even called My mighty warriors, My proudly exulting ones, To execute My anger.* A sound of tumult on the mountains, Like that of many people! A sound of the uproar of kingdoms, Of nations gathered together! The LORD of hosts is mustering the army for battle. They are coming from a far country, From the farthest horizons, *The LORD and His instruments of indignation,* To destroy the whole land. Wail, for the day of the LORD is near! It will come as destruction from the Almighty. Therefore all hands will fall limp, And every man's heart will melt. They will be terrified. Pains and anguish will take hold of *them;* They will writhe like a woman in labor; They will look at one another in astonishment, Their faces aflame. *Behold, the day of the LORD is coming, Cruel, with fury and burning anger,* To make the land a desolation; And He will exterminate its sinners from it. For the stars of heaven and their constellations Will not flash forth their light; The sun will be dark when it rises And the moon will not shed its light. Thus I will punish the world for its evil And the wicked for their iniquity; I will also put an end to the arrogance of the proud And abase the haughtiness of the ruthless. I will make mortal man scarcer than pure gold And mankind than the gold of Ophir. *Therefore I will make the heavens tremble, And the earth will be shaken from its place At the fury of the LORD of hosts In the day of His burning anger.* And it will be that like a hunted gazelle, Or like sheep with none to gather *them,* They will each turn to his own people, And each one flee to his own land. Anyone who is found will be thrust through, And anyone who is captured will fall by the sword. Their little ones also will be dashed to pieces Before their eyes; Their houses will be plundered And their wives ravished. " (Isa. 13:1–16 NASB).

Elam

Jeremiah predicted her downfall which was completed in 539 BC. From 1300 BC for at least 200 years she had been unrivalled in power controlling the plain of Khuzistan, which is now the area north of the Persian Gulf and forming the south west corner of Iran.

"So I will shatter Elam before their enemies And before those who seek their lives; And I will bring calamity upon them, *Even My fierce anger*," declares the LORD; "And I will send out the sword after them Until I have consumed them" (Jer. 49:37 NASB).

Nineveh

The prophet Jonah in the eighth century BC declared "Yet forty days and Nineveh will be overthrown." "Then the people of Nineveh believed in God; and they called a fast and put on sackcloth from the greatest to the least of them. When the word reached the king of Nineveh, he arose from his throne, laid aside his robe from him, covered *himself* with sackcloth and sat on the ashes. He issued a proclamation and it said 'In Nineveh by the decree of the king and his nobles: Do not let man, beast, herd, or flock taste a thing. Do not let them eat or drink water. But both man and beast must be covered with sackcloth; and let men call on God earnestly that each may turn from his wicked way and from the violence which is in his hands. *Who knows, God may turn and relent and withdraw His burning anger so that we will not perish?'* " (Jon. 3:4–9 NASB). This response of the people and the king averted the threatened punishment.

Assyria

Isaiah in the eighth century BC predicts God's judgment on Assyria.

"Behold, the name of *the LORD comes from a remote place; Burning is His anger* and dense is *His* smoke; His lips are filled with *indignation* And His tongue is like a consuming fire; . . . And the LORD will cause His voice of authority to be heard, And the descending of His arm to be seen in *fierce anger*, And *in* the flame of a consuming fire In cloudburst, downpour and hailstones. For at the voice of the LORD Assyria will be terrified, *When* He strikes with the rod" (Isa. 30:27, 30–31 NASB).

Edom

The Edomites descended from Esau, and consequently an Edomite was regarded by the Mosaic law as a brother of the Israelites. Sadly they were constantly hostile to Israel throughout their history. The prophet Malachi some 400 years before Christ, wrote solemn words against them. "Though Edom says, 'We have been beaten down, but we will return and build up the ruins'; thus says the LORD of hosts, 'They may build, but I will tear down; and *men* will call them the wicked territory, and *the people toward whom the LORD is indignant forever.*'" (Mal. 1:4 NASB).

When we turn to God's dealings in wrath with His own chosen nation we find that time after time their sin provokes Him to act in anger against them

In the wilderness

"Now the people became like those who complain of adversity in the hearing of the LORD; and when the LORD heard *it*, **His anger was kindled**, and the fire of the LORD burned among them and consumed *some* of the outskirts of the camp." (Num. 11:1 NASB). "The rabble who were among them had greedy desires; and also the sons of Israel wept again and said, 'Who will give us meat to eat? We remember the fish which we used to eat free in Egypt, the cucumbers and the melons and the leeks and the onions and the garlic, but now our appetite is gone. There is nothing at all to look at except this manna.' . . . Now Moses heard the people weeping throughout their families, each man at the doorway of his tent; and *the anger of the LORD was kindled greatly*, and Moses was displeased. . . . The LORD therefore said to Moses, . . . 'Say to the people, "Consecrate yourselves for tomorrow, and you shall eat meat; for you have wept in the ears of the LORD, saying, 'Oh that someone would give us meat to eat! For we were well-off in Egypt.' Therefore the LORD will give you meat, and you shall eat. You shall eat, not one day, nor two days, nor five days, nor ten days, nor twenty days, but a whole month, until it comes out of your nostrils and becomes loathsome to you; because you have rejected the LORD who is among you and have wept before Him, saying, 'Why did we ever leave Egypt?'" . . . The people spent all day and all night and all the next day, and gathered the quail . . . and they spread *them* out for themselves all around the camp. While the meat was still between their teeth, before it was chewed, *the anger of the LORD was kindled against the people, and the LORD struck the people with a very severe plague*. So the name of that place was called Kibroth-hattaavah, because there they buried the people who had been greedy." (Num. 11:4–6,10,16a, 18–20 and 32–34 NASB).

"While Israel remained at Shittim, the people began to play the harlot with the daughters of Moab. For they invited the people to the sacrifices of their gods, and the people ate and bowed down to their gods. So Israel joined themselves to Baal of Peor, and *the LORD was angry against Israel*. The LORD said to Moses, 'Take all the leaders of the people and execute them in broad daylight before the LORD, so that *the fierce anger of the LORD may turn away from Israel*.' So Moses said to the judges of Israel, 'Each of you slay his men who have joined themselves to Baal of Peor.' Then behold, one of the sons of Israel came and brought to his relatives a Midianite woman, in the sight of Moses and in the sight of all the congregation of the sons of Israel, while they were weeping at the doorway of the tent of meeting. When Phinehas the son of Eleazar, the son of Aaron the priest, saw it, he arose from the midst of the congregation and took a spear in his hand, and he went after the man of Israel into the tent and pierced both of them through, the man of Israel and the woman, through the body. So the plague on the sons of Israel was checked. *Those who died by the plague were 24,000*" (Num. 25:1–9 NASB).

Because of their unbelief after spying out the promised land we read: "Then *the LORD heard the sound of your words, and He was angry* and took an oath, saying, 'Not one of these men, this evil generation, shall see the good land which I swore to give your fathers, except Caleb the son of Jephunneh; he shall see it, and to him and to his sons I will give the land on which he has set foot, because he has followed the LORD fully.' *The LORD was angry with me also on your account*, saying, 'Not even you shall enter there. Joshua the son of Nun, who stands before you, he shall enter there; encourage him, for he will cause Israel to inherit it. Moreover, your little ones who you said would become a prey, and your sons, who this day have no knowledge of good or evil, shall enter there, and I will give it to them and they shall possess it.'" (Deut. 1:34–39 NASB).

When Moses was up the mountain in Horeb receiving the tablets of the covenant they made a golden calf to worship it. Moses said, "I fell down before the LORD, as at the first, forty days and nights; I neither ate bread nor drank water, because of all your sin which you had committed in doing what was evil in the sight of the LORD *to provoke Him to anger. For I was afraid of the anger and hot displeasure with which the LORD was wrathful against you in order to destroy you*, but the LORD listened to me that time also. *The LORD was angry enough with Aaron to destroy him*; so I also prayed for Aaron at the same time" (Deut. 9:18–20 NASB).

The children of Gad and of Reuben wished to remain on the east side of Jordan and not cross over into the promised land. "But Moses said to the sons of Gad and to the sons of Reuben, 'Shall your brothers go to war while you yourselves sit here? Now why are you discouraging the sons of Israel from crossing over into the land which the LORD has given them? ... Now behold, you have risen up in your fathers' place, a brood of sinful men, *to add still more to the burning anger of the LORD against Israel.'* " (Num. 32:6–7,14 NASB).

In the promised land at the time of Joshua

When Achan sinned he brought the wrath of God on all the congregation of Israel. Three thousand men went to attack the city of Ai. The Israelites fled and thirty-six of them were killed. The hearts of the people of God melted. All this because *"the anger of the Lord burned against the sons of Israel"* (Jos. 7:1 NASB).

"Then Joshua and all Israel with him, took Achan the son of Zerah, the silver, the mantle, the bar of gold, his sons, his daughters, his oxen, his donkeys, his sheep, his tent and all that belonged to him; and they brought them up to the valley of Achor. Joshua said, 'Why have you troubled us? The LORD will trouble you this day.' And all Israel stoned them with stones; and they burned them with fire after they had stoned them with stones. They raised over him a great heap of stones that stands to this day, and *the LORD turned from the fierceness of His anger*. Therefore the name of that place has been called the valley of Achor to this day" (Jos. 7:24–26 NASB).

During the days of the Judges 1390–1049 BC

The writer summarises this period of Israel's history in these words: "Then the sons of Israel did evil in the sight of the LORD and served the Baals, and they forsook the LORD, the God of their fathers, who had brought them out of the land of Egypt, and followed other gods from *among* the gods of the peoples who were around them, and bowed themselves down to them; thus *they provoked the LORD to anger*. So they forsook the LORD and served Baal and the Ashtaroth. *The anger of the LORD burned against Israel*, and He gave them into the hands of plunderers who plundered them; and He sold them into the hands of their enemies around *them*, so that they could no longer stand before their enemies. Wherever they went, the hand of the LORD was against them for evil, as the LORD had spoken and as the LORD had sworn to them, so that they were severely distressed. Then the LORD raised up judges who delivered them from the hands of those who plundered them. Yet they did not listen to their judges, for they played the harlot after other gods, and bowed themselves down to them. They turned aside quickly from the way in which their fathers had walked in obeying the commandments of the LORD; they did not do as *their fathers*.

When the LORD raised up judges for them, the LORD was with the judge and delivered them from the hand of their enemies all the days of the judge; for the LORD was moved to pity by their groaning because of those who oppressed and afflicted them. But it came about when the judge died, that they would turn back and act more corruptly than their fathers, in following other gods to serve them and bow down to them; they did not abandon their practices or their stubborn ways. *So the anger of the LORD burned against Israel*, and He said, 'Because this nation has transgressed My covenant which I commanded their fathers and has not listened to My voice, I also will no longer drive out before them any of the nations which Joshua left when he died, in order to test Israel by them, whether they will keep the way of the LORD to walk in it as their fathers did, or not.' " (Judg. 2:11–22 NASB).

At the time of Samuel
God gave them a king *"in My anger"* (Hos. 13:11 NASB).

During the time from Saul to the destruction of Jerusalem in 587 BC
God removed Saul the king *"in My wrath"* (Hos. 13:11 NASB).

In the reign of David *"the anger of the Lord burned against Israel"* (2 Sam. 24:1 NASB). 70,000 men of the people died in a plague sent by the Lord (2 Sam. 24:15). Of Solomon it is written, "Now *the LORD was angry with Solomon* because his heart was turned away from the LORD, the God of Israel, who had appeared to him twice, and had commanded him concerning this thing, that he should not go after other gods; but he did not observe what the LORD had commanded. So the LORD said to Solomon, 'Because you have done this, and you have not kept My covenant and My statutes, which I have commanded you, I will surely tear the kingdom from you, and will give it to your servant.' " (1 Kings 11:9–11 NASB).

When Jehoahaz became king of Israel c. 848 BC, *"So the anger of the LORD was kindled against Israel*, and He gave them continually into the hand of Hazael king of Aram, and into the hand of Ben-hadad the son of Hazael." (2 Kings 13:3 NASB). When the king Josiah c. 640–609 BC found the Book of the Law in the house of the Lord the following account is given: "Then the king commanded Hilkiah the priest, Ahikam the son of Shaphan, Achbor the son of Micaiah, Shaphan the scribe, and Asaiah the king's servant saying, 'Go, inquire of the LORD for me and the people and all Judah concerning the words of this book that has been found, for *great is the wrath of the LORD that burns against us*, because our fathers have not listened to the words of this book, to do according to all that is written concerning us.' So Hilkiah the priest, Ahikam, Achbor, Shaphan, and Asaiah went to Huldah the prophetess, the wife of Shallum the son of Tikvah, the son of Harhas, keeper of the wardrobe (now she lived in Jerusalem in the Second Quarter); and they spoke to her. She said to them, 'Thus says the LORD God of Israel, "Tell the man who sent you to me, thus says the LORD, 'Behold, I bring evil on this place and on its inhabitants, *even* all the words of the book which the king of Judah has read. Because they have forsaken Me and have burned incense to other gods *that they might provoke Me to anger* with all the work of their hands, therefore *My wrath burns against this place, and it shall not be quenched.'* " But to the king of Judah who sent you to inquire of the LORD thus shall you say to him, "Thus says the LORD God of Israel, '*Regarding* the words which you have heard, because your heart was tender and you humbled yourself before the LORD when you heard what I spoke against this place and against its inhabitants that they should become a desolation and a curse, and you have torn your clothes and wept before Me, I truly have heard you' declares the LORD. 'Therefore, behold, I will gather you to your fathers, and you will be gathered to your grave in peace, and your eyes will not see all the evil which I will bring on this place.' " So they brought back word to the king" (2 Kings 22:12–20 NASB).

That wrath was manifested in the destruction of Jerusalem by the Babylonians in 587 BC
Isaiah, Jeremiah, Ezekiel and Daniel all write of this event. Isaiah predicted it in the words, "On this account *the anger of the LORD has burned against His people*, And He has stretched out His hand against and struck them down. And the mountains quaked, and their corpses lay like refuse in the middle of the streets. For all this *His anger is not spent*, But His hand is still stretched out" (Isa. 5:25 NASB).

Jeremiah declared, "Therefore thus says the Lord God, '*Behold, My anger and My wrath will be poured out on this place*, on man and on beast and on the trees of the field and on the fruit of the ground; and *it will burn and not be quenched'* " (Jer. 7:20 NASB). He said to the King Zedekiah, "Thus says the LORD God of Israel, 'Behold, I am about to turn back the weapons of war which are in your hands, with which you are warring against the king of Babylon and the Chaldeans who are besieging you outside the wall; and I will gather them into the center of this city. *I Myself will war against you with an outstretched hand and with a mighty arm, even in anger and wrath and great indignation.* I will also strike down the inhabitants of this city, both man and beast;

they will die of a great pestilence. Then afterwards,' declares the LORD, 'I will give over Zedekiah king of Judah and his servants and the people, even those who survive in this city from the pestilence, the sword and the famine, into the hand of Nebuchadnezzar king of Babylon, and into the hand of their foes and into the hand of those who seek their lives; and he will strike them down with the edge of the sword. He will not spare them nor have pity nor compassion.'" (Jer. 21:4–7 NASB). Jeremiah wrote of the horrors of that invasion and conquest: "Better are those slain with the sword Than those slain with hunger; For they pine away, being stricken For lack of the fruits of the field. The hands of compassionate women Boiled their own children; They became food for them Because of the destruction of the daughter of my people. *The LORD has accomplished His wrath, He has poured out His fierce anger;* And He has kindled a fire in Zion Which has consumed its foundations. The kings of the earth did not believe, Nor *did* any of the inhabitants of the world, That the adversary and the enemy Could enter the gates of Jerusalem." (Lam. 4:9–12 NASB).

Ezekiel uttered words most terrible, "One third of you will die by plague or be consumed by famine among you, one third will fall by the sword around you, and one third I will scatter to every wind, and I will unsheathe a sword behind them. *Thus My anger will be spent and I will satisfy My wrath on them, and I will be appeased*; then they will know that I, the LORD, have spoken in My zeal when *I have spent My wrath upon them*. Moreover, I will make you a desolation and a reproach among the nations which surround you, in the sight of all who pass by. So it will be a reproach, a reviling, a warning and an object of horror to the nations who surround you when *I execute judgments against you in anger, wrath and raging rebukes*. I, the LORD, have spoken" (Ezek. 5:12–15 NASB).

Daniel also speaks of this Babylonian conquest as the wrath of God against Israel: " O Lord, in accordance with all Your righteous acts, *let now Your anger and Your wrath turn away from Your city Jerusalem*, Your holy mountain; for because for our sins and the iniquities of our fathers, Jerusalem and Your people *have become* a reproach to all those around us" (Dan. 9:16 NASB).

The above scriptures are just some which mention the wrath of God. There are more events and verses in the biblical record telling of God's wrath. When these scriptures are meditated upon and accepted as the revelation of God and His ways, we are moved with the prophet Nahum (663–612 BC) to say, "*Who can stand before His indignation? Who can endure the burning of His anger? His wrath is poured out like fire And the rocks are broken up by Him*" (Nah. 1:6 NASB).

The New Testament continues to reveal the wrath of God

Just as the Old Testament tells that "God is a righteous judge, And a God who has indignation every day" (Psa. 7:11 NASB), the New Testament tells us that fallen humanity is handed over to sins and sinfulness because of the wrath of God (Rom. 1:18f.). It tells us that mankind in its natural condition causes God to look upon it with wrath, with a settled indignation against its sinfulness.

1. Jesus prophesied the destruction of Jerusalem which took place in AD 70. He spoke of it thus: "There will be great distress in the land and wrath upon this people" (Luke 21:23)

History tells us something of the horrors of the siege of the city – famine, infant cannibalism and internal strife resulting in terrible bloodshed. The suffering was even greater than that in 587 BC. Paul wrote of this wrath of God upon the Jews which would result in the judgment of AD 70. He said "wrath has come upon them to the uttermost" (1 Thess. 2:16). He refers to the sentence that had been pronounced by Jesus recorded in Mat. 23:34–36: "Therefore, indeed, I send you prophets, wise men, and scribes: *some* of them you will kill and crucify, and *some* of them you will scourge in your synagogues and persecute from city to city, that on you may come all the right-eous blood shed on the earth, from the blood of righteous Abel to the blood of Zechariah, son of Berechiah, whom you murdered between the temple and the altar. Assuredly, I say to you, all these things will come upon this generation." Jesus warned the people: "And a great multitude of the people followed Him, and women who also mourned and lamented Him. But Jesus, turning to them, said, 'Daughters of Jerusalem, do not weep for Me, but weep for yourselves and for your children. For indeed the days are coming in which they will say, "Blessed *are* the barren, wombs that never bore, and breasts which never nursed!" Then they will begin to say to the mountains, "Fall on us!" and to the hills, "Cover us!" ' " (Luke 23:27–30). In AD 70 the wrath of God pronounced on the nation fell upon them.

2. Paul writes of salvation as deliverance from the wrath of the final eternal judgment

"For they themselves declare concerning us what manner of entry we had to you, and how you turned to God from idols to serve the living and true God, and to wait for His Son from heaven, whom He raised from the dead, *even* Jesus who delivers us from the wrath to come" (1 Thess. 1:9–10). He says concerning the believers' future, "For God did not appoint us to wrath, but to obtain salvation through our Lord Jesus Christ" (1 Thess. 5:9).

3.   At the very heart of the gospel, and central in the saving work of Jesus Christ, is His death as a sacrifice for sins to propitiate the Father

> Christ "whom God set forth *as* a propitiation by His blood, through faith, to demonstrate His righteousness, because in His forbearance God had passed over the sins that were previously committed" (Rom. 3:25).

> "Therefore, in all things He had to be made like *His* brethren, that He might be a merciful and faithful High Priest in things *pertaining* to God, to make propitiation for the sins of the people" (Heb. 2:17).

> "And He Himself is the propitiation for our sins, and not for ours only but also for the whole world" (1 John 2:2).

> "In this is love, not that we loved God, but that He loved us and sent His Son *to be* the propitiation for our sins" (1 John 4:10).

To propitiate means to turn away anger by means of a sacrificial offering to the one offended. The propitiation of Christ on the cross turns away God's anger from believers. He bore the punishment of their sins in their place, and thereby delivered them from God's wrath upon them (John. 3:36). To refuse to accept the fact of God's anger against sinners is therefore to overthrow the work of Christ on the cross.

Unbelievers deride the truth of the wrath of God. They are at enmity with the true God. They will not tolerate any suggestion that He is angry with them every day for their sins and sinfulness. They dismiss the fact that He will punish them in wrath and indignation at the day of judgment. They gladly embrace the lies of the Devil that no wrath and no punishment will come upon them. These are the attitudes the scriptures tell us to expect from fallen humanity.

But few believers have a true understanding of the wrath of God. The NIV chooses not to use the word propitiation in Rom. 3:25, Heb. 2:17, 1 John 2:2 and 4:10. "A sacrifice of atonement" (Rom. 3:25), "atonement" (Heb. 2:17), "the atoning sacrifice" (1 John 2:2) and "an atoning sacrifice" (1 John 4:10) are preferred translations. In each verse words meaning propitiation are given as an alternative translation in a footnote. There are no sound reasons for removing the word propitiation from the main text. It is a dilution of the gospel. In this the NIV is a reflection of the general departure from the revelation of God's wrath in the scriptures. The fact that the Day of Judgment will be a day of God's wrath is a truth believers need to know, understand, accept and remember. The Book of the Revelation gives a picture of that day: "And the kings of the earth, the great men, the rich men, the commanders, the mighty men, every slave and every free man, hid themselves in the caves and in the rocks of the mountains, and said to the mountains and rocks, 'Fall on us and hide us from the face of Him who sits on the throne and from the wrath of the Lamb! For the great day of His wrath has come, and who is able to stand?'" (Rev. 6:15–17). At the Final Judgment there will be "indignation and wrath, tribulation and anguish on every soul of man who does evil" (Rom. 2:8–9). The word "indignation" is θυμός which derives from a root conveying the meaning of boiling up. Some translate it "anger." "Indignation and wrath" thus express both the passion and the settled state of God's wrath towards sinners. Tribulation and anguish will result. Leon Morris says the word tribulation "in the literal sense means 'press', 'squash' (as in the treading of grapes), so that θλῖψις denotes not minor discomfort, but acute suffering."[1] It is the feeling of being beaten, battered and bruised to breaking point. It is accompanied by "anguish." This word means literally "narrowness of place."[2] It means great distress, extreme affliction. In the words of Christ there will be "weeping and gnashing of teeth."

References

1. Leon Morris *The Epistle to the Romans*, Eerdmans and IVP 1988, page 119, footnote 59.
2. *Ibid.*, footnote 60.

THE NATURE OF THE FINAL JUDGMENT (2): A DAY OF THE REVELATION OF THE RIGHTEOUS JUDGMENT OF GOD

The Final Judgment will be a day of the revelation of the righteous judgment of God (Rom. 2:5).

On that day everything will be revealed and known

"For God will bring every work into judgment, Including every secret thing, Whether good or evil" (Eccl. 12:14).

"For there is nothing covered that will not be revealed, nor hidden that will not be known. Therefore whatever you have spoken in the dark will be heard in the light, and what you have spoken in the ear in inner rooms will be proclaimed on the housetops" (Luke 12:2–3).

". . . in the day when God will judge the secrets of men by Christ Jesus according to my gospel" (Rom. 2:16).

All actions, words, thoughts and secrets will be revealed and consequently God's judgment will be seen to be absolutely righteous. The Father will be glorified in the manifestation of righteousness through the judgments of Christ. The truth about every individual will be exposed fully. Each one judged will see that God is just and fair in His judgments. Unlike the judgment of human courts there will be no investigation needed to find out the truth. All will be known to God the Father and Jesus Christ before the act of judging. This full knowledge will be an essential part of the revelation that God's judgments will be absolutely righteous.

There will be no partiality in this Judgment (Rom. 2:11)

All sinners who die in their sins will be punished according to their deeds without any partiality. God's judgment will be according to the truth. During this life evil-doers often prosper. Their wrongdoings often go unpunished, or are inadequately punished, sometimes because of partiality of judgment. Indeed they frequently enjoy the pleasures of sin for a season. Justice will at last be done. All those who die in their sins will receive the just punishment for their sins. Not one will escape. Great or small, rich or poor, of whatever nation, all will be judged impartially. Therefore Christians are commanded " 'Beloved, do not avenge yourselves, but *rather* give place to wrath; for it is written, "Vengeance *is* Mine, I will repay," ' says the Lord" (Rom. 12:19). Believers can rest in the confidence that at the Day of Judgment God will repay. Paul stated that assurance to Timothy concerning someone who did him much harm: "Alexander the coppersmith did me much harm. May the Lord repay him according to his works. You also must beware of him, for he has greatly resisted our words" (2 Tim. 4:14–15). God will be seen to be absolutely impartial in judgment.

The Judgment will be according to what is written in the books

"And I saw the dead, small and great, standing before God, and books were opened. And another book was opened, which is *the Book* of Life. And the dead were judged according to their works, by the things which were written in the books" (Rev. 20:12). The books speak of God's complete record of all the acts, words and thoughts, including those done in secret. The book of life contains the names of those who have repented and believed during their life on earth. This book is referred to in Luke 10:20, Phil. 4:3, Heb. 12:23 and Rev. 3:5, 13:8, 17:8, 20:15 and 21:27.

Final Eternal Judgment will depend on deeds done in this life and on one's inclusion or otherwise in the book of life

The scriptures below are clear that all will be judged by their deeds:

"For the Son of Man will come in the glory of His Father with His angels, and then He will reward each according to his works" (Mat. 16:27).

"But I say to you that for every idle word men may speak, they will give account of it in the day of judgment. For by your words you will be justified, and by your words you will be condemned" (Mat. 12:36–37). The words spoken during life will either result in justification (a declaration of being righteous before God) or condemnation (a declaration of being unrighteous before God) at the Final Judgment. Jesus said these words in Mat. 12:36 following His statement: "A good man out of the good treasure of his heart brings forth good things, and an evil man out of the evil treasure brings forth evil things" (Mat. 12:35). Thus words, even careless words, reveal what a man is essentially. They disclose what his treasure is, whether it is good or evil. The treasure a man has determines the heart. As Jesus said, "For where your treasure is, there your heart will be also" (Mat. 6:21).

"the day of wrath when God's righteous judgment will be revealed. For he will render to every man according to his works: to those who by patience in well-doing seek for glory and honor and immortality, he will give eternal life; but for those who are factious and do not obey the truth, but obey wickedness, there will be wrath and fury. There will be tribulation and distress for every human being who does evil, the Jew first and also the Greek, but glory and honor and peace for every one who does good, the Jew first and also the Greek. For God shows no partiality" (Rom. 2:5–11 RSV). Eternal life will be given to those who patiently continue in doing good. Continuance is the mark of true disciples of Christ. He said, "If you abide in My word, you are My disciples indeed" (John 8:31). The word patience speaks of continuance in spite of opposition and difficulty. Believers seek heavenly gifts of glory, honour and immortality. Their hearts are set on these things which they will receive at the return of Christ. Their continuance in doing the will of God and their desire for these heavenly gifts spring from the faith in Christ by which they live.

In contrast the indignation and wrath of God will come upon those who are factious and do not obey the truth but obey unrighteousness. Some commentators translate "factious" as "self-seeking." They argue from the derivation of the Greek word. They say it does not come from ἔρις – strife, but from ἔρῑθος – a hireling. The argument is not conclusive. The derivation of the word is uncertain. The traditional meaning "factious" is in harmony with Paul's statement in his previous words in chapter 1 verses 18–21. There it says that fallen man suppresses the truth in unrighteousness. He has a revelation of His eternal power and Godhead in the creation around him. He refuses to acknowledge these revealed truths. He knows that God is, but he refuses to give Him glory and refuses to give Him thanks. He is God rejecting and rebellious against Him. He is ungodly and unrighteous. He chooses to turn to his own way. Thus in Rom. 2:5–11 we have two different ways of living ending in two different destinies.

Jesus predicted the Final Judgment, "When the Son of Man comes in His glory, and all the holy angels with Him, then He will sit on the throne of His glory. All the nations will be gathered before Him, and He will separate them one from another, as a shepherd divides *his* sheep from the goats. And He will set the sheep on His right hand, but the goats on the left. Then the King will say to those on His right hand, 'Come, you blessed of My Father, inherit the kingdom prepared for you from the foundation of the world: for I was hungry and you gave Me food; I was thirsty and you gave Me drink; I was a stranger and you took Me in; I *was* naked and you clothed Me; I was sick and you visited Me; I was in prison and you came to Me.' Then the righteous will answer Him, saying, 'Lord, when did we see You hungry and feed *You*, or thirsty and give *You* drink? When did we see You a stranger and take *You* in, or naked and clothe *You?* Or when did we see You sick, or in prison, and come to You?' And the King will answer and say to them, 'Assuredly, I say to you, inasmuch as you did *it* to one of the least of these My brethren, you did *it* to Me.' Then He will also say to those on the left hand, 'Depart from Me, you cursed, into the everlasting fire prepared for the devil and his angels: for I was hungry and you gave Me no food; I was thirsty and you gave Me no drink; I was a stranger and you did not take Me in, naked and you did not clothe Me, sick and in prison and you did not visit Me.' Then they also will answer Him, saying, 'Lord, when did we see You hungry or thirsty or a stranger or naked or sick or in prison, and did not minister to You?' Then He will answer them, saying, 'Assuredly, I say to you, inasmuch as you did not do *it* to one of the least of these, you did not do *it* to Me.' And these will go away into everlasting punishment, but the righteous into eternal life" (Mat. 25:31–46). The sheep are those who gave Him food, drink, and clothing when He needed these things. They took Him in when He was a stranger. They visited Him when He was sick and in prison. They did these deeds to those whom Jesus calls His brethren. His brethren are believers. Inasmuch as they did it to them Christ reckons it as done to Him. These sheep go away into eternal life. In contrast the goats gave Him no food, no drink and no clothing when He needed these things. They failed to take Him in when He was a stranger. They did not visit Him when He was sick or in prison. Inasmuch as they did not do it to the least of these His brethren they did not do it to Him. Thus Christ will separate the sheep from the goats by their deeds. It is a gross misinterpretation of these verses to say that good works to one's fellow man are the issue. The works are specifically deeds performed for believers.

In 2 Cor. 5:10 Paul admonishes believers, "For we must all appear before the judgment seat of Christ, that each one may receive the things *done* in the body, according to what he has done, whether good or bad." The word "appear" means to be stripped bare and openly revealed for what we really are. At that judgment believers will receive according to the deeds done.

"For we are God's fellow workers; you are God's field, *you are* God's building. According to the grace of God which was given to me, as a wise master builder I have laid the foundation, and another builds on it. But let each one take heed how he builds on it. For no other foundation can anyone lay than that which is laid, which is Jesus Christ. Now if anyone builds on this foundation *with* gold, silver, precious stones, wood, hay, straw, each one's work will become clear; for the Day will declare it, because it will be revealed by fire; and the fire will test each one's work, of what sort it is. If anyone's work which he has built on *it* endures, he will receive a reward. If anyone's work is burned, he will suffer loss; but he himself will be saved, yet so as through fire" (1 Cor. 3:9–15). Here the apostle is treating one aspect of the Final Judgment, namely rewards to believers for their service in furthering the building of God's temple. God's temple is composed of believers. The foundation of the temple is the saving work of Christ. The church at Corinth had come into being through Paul. He had laid the foundation of the temple by preaching Christ. Now he warns the believers to be careful how they build on it. He says that at the Final Judgment God will test their work. They will not receive a reward unless the test is passed. We shall deal more fully with this subject of rewards later. At this point it is important to see that here is yet another passage in the scriptures telling us again that at the Final Judgment our deeds will be crucial.

Every passage in the New Testament which speaks of the way in which the Final Judgment will be carried out states that it will be according to deeds done. Rev. 20:12–15 is unique in that it says that judgment is according to what is written in the book of life as well as deeds done: "And I saw the dead, small and great, standing before God, and books were opened. And another book was opened, which is *the Book* of Life. And the dead were judged according to their works, by the things which were written in the books. The sea gave up the dead who were in it, and Death and Hades delivered up the dead who were in them. And they were judged, each one according to his works. Then Death and Hades were cast into the lake of fire. This is the second death. And anyone not found written in the Book of Life was cast into the lake of fire." We find this book of life containing the names of all who are the Lord's mentioned also in the following verses:

> "And I urge you also, true companion, help these women who labored with me in the gospel, with Clement also, and the rest of my fellow workers, whose names *are* in the Book of Life" (Phil. 4:3).

"Nevertheless do not rejoice in this, that the spirits are subject to you, but rather rejoice because your names are written in heaven" (Luke 10:20).

"Then those who feared the LORD spoke to one another, And the LORD listened and heard *them*; So a book of remembrance was written before Him For those who fear the LORD And who meditate on His name. 'They shall be Mine,' says the LORD of hosts, 'On the day that I make them My jewels. And I will spare them As a man spares his own son who serves him.' " (Mal. 3:16–17).

"At that time Michael shall stand up, The great prince who stands *watch* over the sons of your people; And there shall be a time of trouble, Such as never was since there was a nation, *Even* to that time. And at that time your people shall be delivered, Every one who is found written in the book" (Dan. 12:1).

"Let them be blotted out of the book of the living, And not be written with the righteous" (Psa. 69:28).

Moses prayed for Israel, "Yet now, if You will forgive their sin – but if not, I pray, blot me out of Your book which You have written" (Exod. 32:32).

The book of life is mentioned several other times in Revelation:

"He who overcomes shall be clothed in white garments, and I will not blot out his name from the Book of Life; but I will confess his name before My Father and before His angels" (Rev. 3:5).

"All who dwell on the earth will worship him, *everyone* whose name has not been written from the foundation of the world in the book of life of the Lamb who has been slain" (Rev. 13:8 NASB).

"The beast that you saw was, and is not, and will ascend out of the bottomless pit and go to perdition. And those who dwell on the earth will marvel, whose names are not written in the Book of Life from the foundation of the world, when they see the beast that was, and is not, and yet is" (Rev. 17:8).

"But there shall by no means enter it anything that defiles, or causes an abomination or a lie, but only those who are written in the Lamb's Book of Life" (Rev. 21:27).

THE NATURE OF THE FINAL JUDGMENT (3): A DAY OF THE REVELATION OF THE RIGHTEOUS JUDGMENT OF GOD continued

The New Testament is emphatic that salvation is not by works but a gift received by faith. So why do the scriptures in the previous chapter tell us that judgment is according to deeds done? There are several reasons.

The deeds done in the case of true believers reveal that they had genuine faith in Christ

True faith always produces works. The Christian is a new creation. His actions, words and thoughts reveal the change that his new birth has wrought within him. They prove that he is living by faith in Christ. They flow from real love for God and His law. The Christian still sins and is conscious of falling short each day (1 John 1:8–9), but his life has been radically changed. He is a partaker of the divine nature (2 Pet. 1:4). He behaves differently from the way he did before conversion, and differently from those who are not believers. From the day of conversion he evidences new conduct. As he grows in grace and knowledge the deeds flowing from his faith increase. Thus in the case of those receiving eternal life Christ's judgment of them will be seen to be a righteous judgment because their faith will be proved by their works. In the will of God this Final Judgment will be a day of revelation of the righteous judgment of God. If Christians were to be judged at that day only on the record that they had faith there would not be manifest proof to others of a righteous and true judgment. On that day non-Christians will see that the deeds of Christians prove that they lived by faith in Christ.

Deeds will also reveal on that day each man's relationship with God

The sheep in Mat. 25:31–46 loved the children of God (Christ's brethren) and evidenced that love by ministering to them. Their love for them was natural because they loved God. Everyone who loves God loves His children. 1 John 5:1 tells us that believers in Christ are born again by God, that they love God and that they love those who are born again by God: "Whoever believes that Jesus is the Christ is born of God, and everyone who loves Him who begot also loves him who is begotten of Him." The love of the sheep for those born of God (the brethren of Christ) therefore was concrete evidence of their love for God. In contrast, the lack of love of the goats for those born again revealed that they had no love for God. Thus Christ's judgment will be seen to be absolutely true and just on that day.

Judgment of deeds will reveal that God is just and righteous in punishing sinners

It will make manifest that His condemnation is righteous. All the truth about each individual will be exposed. Every sin in thought, word and deed and every circumstance in which each sin was committed will be known. God will be seen to be punishing justly even those of mankind who had no knowledge of the scriptures and no knowledge of the gospel. Romans 1 and 2 tells us that they have:

1. the revelation of God given to them in creation Rom. 1:19–21
Man knows that God exists and can see His eternal power and divinity in His handiwork, the creation of the universe. Man refuses to give to God the glory and thanks due to Him. They choose to believe lies instead of this true revelation of God which they have before their eyes. Therefore they are "without excuse." God's wrath in this life is already upon them for sinning against this light. He hands them over to their sinful conduct (Rom. 1:24, 26 and 28).

2. an innate knowledge of the things required by the law of God
Man has a built-in moral sense even when he has never heard of the ten commandments. He does not have them written on his heart, but he has a knowledge of what the law requires. The work of the law is written in his heart (Rom. 2:15). Thus he himself reveals what is right to himself. In that sense he is a law to himself (Rom. 2:14–15). Consequently he does behave according to that moral sense, but he fails to live constantly up to the standard he knows to be right.

3. a conscience
Man has an inward voice which pronounces judgment on his behaviour. The conscience is proof that man has moral standards. The conscience speaks and condemns conduct which breaks those moral standards. This is the universal experience of man. As a consequence of his innate moral consciousness and his conscience, man, even when

he is totally ignorant of the scriptures and the gospel, evidences a moral sense in his reasoning about what is right and wrong (Rom. 2:14:15). Indeed he knows that certain sins deserve death (Rom. 1:32). Despite that knowledge he commits those sins, and he approves others doing such things. At the judgment those who have no knowledge of the scriptures and no knowledge of the gospel will be condemned for sins against all the light given to them. Their condemnation will be revealed as a righteous judgment. Those who have the benefit of knowledge of the scriptures and the gospel, and who die in their sins will judged also for sins committed against that greater revelation of God. This leads us to the next truth.

Judgment of deeds will reveal God's justice in pronouncing different degrees of punishment

Jesus said that some will receive greater condemnation: "Beware of the scribes, who desire to go around in long robes, love greetings in the marketplaces, the best seats in the synagogues, and the best places at feasts, who devour widows' houses, and for a pretense make long prayers. These will receive greater condemnation" (Luke 20:46–47). The greater the sins the greater the punishment. The revelation given by God will be taken into account in His assessment of guilt and punishment. Jesus said, "Woe to you, Chorazin! Woe to you, Bethsaida! For if the mighty works which were done in you had been done in Tyre and Sidon, they would have repented long ago in sackcloth and ashes. But I say to you, it will be more tolerable for Tyre and Sidon in the day of judgment than for you. And you, Capernaum, who are exalted to heaven, will be brought down to Hades; for if the mighty works which were done in you had been done in Sodom, it would have remained until this day. But I say to you that it shall be more tolerable for the land of Sodom in the day of judgment than for you" (Mat. 11:21–24). At the Final Judgment the unrepentant people of Chorazin and Bethsaida who saw His mighty miracles will be reckoned more guilty than the inhabitants of Tyre and Sidon who would have repented had they seen such miracles. Tyre and Sidon were notorious for their wickedness. The prophets Isaiah (23:1–18), Jeremiah (25:22; 27:1–11), Ezekiel (26:1–28:19) and Joel (3:4–8) denounced them. They were unrepentant, and their guilt will be great on that day. But Jesus says the guilt of Chorazin and Bethsaida will be even greater. Jesus then turns to Capernaum. He says in the same way that the guilt of the unrepentant who saw His mighty works there will be even greater than the terrible guilt of Sodom which was a supreme example of wickedness. The greater the amount of revelation given the greater the guilt. Jesus told a parable stating this truth: "And the Lord said, 'Who then is that faithful and wise steward, whom *his* master will make ruler over his household, to give *them their* portion of food in due season? Blessed *is* that servant whom his master will find so doing when he comes. Truly, I say to you that he will make him ruler over all that he has. But if that servant says in his heart, "My master is delaying his coming," and begins to beat the male and female servants, and to eat and drink and be drunk, the master of that servant will come on a day when he is not looking for *him,* and at an hour when he is not aware, and will cut him in two and appoint *him* his portion with the unbelievers. And that servant who knew his master's will, and did not prepare *himself* or do according to his will, shall be beaten with many *stripes.* But he who did not know, yet committed things deserving of stripes, shall be beaten with few. For everyone to whom much is given, from him much will be required; and to whom much has been committed, of him they will ask the more' " (Luke 12:42–48).

Judgment of deeds will mean that the behaviour of some will condemn the conduct of others

In Mat. 12:41–42 Jesus says that the deeds of some of mankind will condemn the behaviour of others of mankind: "The men of Nineveh will rise up in the judgment with this generation and condemn it, because they repented at the preaching of Jonah; and indeed a greater than Jonah *is* here. The queen of the South will rise up in the judgment with this generation and condemn it, for she came from the ends of the earth to hear the wisdom of Solomon; and indeed a greater than Solomon *is* here." Jesus will place the conduct of some alongside the conduct of others. Such comparisons will bear witness to the righteousness of His judgments.

Judgment of deeds will be the means of rewarding believers for their service to Christ while on earth

This will be the subject of the next chapter. The giving of rewards will display the righteousness of God on that day.

CHAPTER EIGHT

THE NATURE OF THE FINAL JUDGMENT (4): REWARDS FOR BELIEVERS

At the Final Judgment believers will inherit the kingdom prepared for them from the foundation of the world (Mat. 25:34). But they will have to give account of their lives and service from the time they became Christians. There are several New Testament passages teaching this truth. 1 Cor. 3:9–15 is our starting point. "For we are God's fellow workers; you are God's field, *you are* God's building. According to the grace of God which was given to me, as a wise master builder I have laid the foundation, and another builds on it. But let each one take heed how he builds on it. For no other foundation can anyone lay than that which is laid, which is Jesus Christ. Now if anyone builds on this foundation *with* gold, silver, precious stones, wood, hay, straw, each one's work will become clear; for the Day will declare it, because it will be revealed by fire; and the fire will test each one's work, of what sort it is. If anyone's work which he has built on *it* endures, he will receive a reward. If anyone's work is burned, he will suffer loss; but he himself will be saved, yet so as through fire." Paul is addressing the believers at Corinth. Through his preaching of Christ the church came into being. He laid the foundation. He says that they can build on the work he has done. He warns them that at the Final Judgment each one's work will be revealed for what it was. The fire will disclose what kind of work each has done. Each man's service will be subjected to this test. Some work will not survive the fire – wood, hay and stubble will be burned up. Before that testing the work may appear to many to be good and acceptable service to Christ. The day will reveal its true nature. The individual whose work is burned up will suffer loss, but he will be saved. The phrase "yet so as through fire" means that he will experience this disclosure of the true nature of his work, and he will suffer the loss of reward for his labour. He will see other believers whose work can withstand the fire of testing, the gold, silver and precious stones, receiving commendation and reward. The rewards will have eternal effect, and the loss of them will be eternal.

The precise nature of these rewards is not revealed to us, but other verses in the scriptures cast light on these things. John tells us that if believers "abide in Him" and truly love other believers they will have confidence and boldness in the day of judgment. If they fail to do these things as they should they will be ashamed before Him on that day (1 John 2:28 and 4:17). John also wrote a warning to "the chosen lady and her children." He may have been writing to a Christian lady and her children who were all believers; or he may have meant those she had led to Christ by the words "her children", that is, her spiritual children. Some think that "the chosen lady and her children" is a metaphorical way of saying "the church and its members." Whatever interpretation we take John is writing to believers. He says that they are in danger of losing what has been worked for, and of losing a "full reward" (2 John 8). The danger came from false teachers, who were deceivers, and who sought to turn them away from the truth and from walking in the truth. So in 1 Cor. 3 we have the possibility of total loss of reward for service, and in 2 John the possibility of losing part of one's reward.

Jesus spoke clearly about rewards for service in the following parables

"For *the kingdom of heaven is* like a man traveling to a far country, *who* called his own servants and delivered his goods to them. And to one he gave five talents, to another two, and to another one, to each according to his own ability; and immediately he went on a journey. Then he who had received the five talents went and traded with them, and made another five talents. And likewise he who *had received* two gained two more also. But he who had received one went and dug in the ground, and hid his lord's money. After a long time the lord of those servants came and settled accounts with them. So he who had received five talents came and brought five other talents, saying, 'Lord, you delivered to me five talents; look, I have gained five more talents besides them.' His lord said to him, 'Well *done,* good and faithful servant; you were faithful over a few things, I will make you ruler over many things. Enter into the joy of your lord.' He also who had received two talents came and said, 'Lord, you delivered to me two talents; look, I have gained two more talents besides them.' His lord said to him, 'Well *done,* good and faithful servant; you have been faithful over a few things, I will make you ruler over many things. Enter into the joy of your lord.' Then he who had received the one talent came and said, 'Lord, I knew you to be a hard man, reaping where you have not sown, and gathering where you have not scattered seed. And I was afraid, and went and hid your talent in the ground. Look, *there* you have *what is* yours.' But his lord answered and said to him, 'You wicked and lazy servant, you knew that I reap where I have not sown, and gather where I have not scattered seed. So you ought to have deposited my money with the bankers, and at my coming I would have received back my own with interest. Therefore take the talent from him, and give *it* to him who has ten talents. For to everyone who has, more will be given, and he will have abundance; but from him who does not have, even what he has will be taken away. And cast the unprofitable servant into the outer darkness. There will be weeping and gnashing of teeth.' " (Mat. 25:14–30). This parable speaks of the return of Christ when each believer will give account of himself to Him. It teaches that Christ will reward equally each one who has made full use of their opportunities and capabilities to serve Him regardless of the differences in those opportunities and capabilities. Thus the servant who gained two talents from the two given to him received an identical reward to the servant who gained five talents from the five given to him. Both rendered faithful service according to their ability. When believers stand before Christ He will assess their works of service in relation to their opportunities and capabilities. The parable also exposes the hypocrite who professes to serve but makes no use of opportunities and abilities to serve his master. At the judgment such will be condemned for what they are.

Jesus told another parable similar to the one in Matthew recorded in Luke 19:11–27: "Now as they heard these things, He spoke another parable, because He was near Jerusalem and because they thought the kingdom of God would appear immediately. Therefore He said: 'A certain nobleman went into a far country to receive for himself a kingdom and to return. So he called ten of his servants, delivered to them ten minas, and said to them, "Do business till I come." But his citizens hated him, and sent a delegation after him, saying, "We will not have this *man* to reign over us." And so it was that when he returned, having received the kingdom, he then commanded these servants, to whom he had given the money, to be called to him, that he might know how much every man had gained by trading. Then came the first, saying, "Master, your mina has earned ten minas." And he said to him, "Well *done*, good servant; because you were faithful in a very little, have authority over ten cities." And the second came, saying, "Master, your mina has earned five minas." Likewise he said to him, "You also be over five cities." Then another came, saying, "Master, here is your mina, which I have kept put away in a handkerchief. For I feared you, because you are an austere man. You collect what you did not deposit, and reap what you did not sow." And he said to him, "Out of your own mouth I will judge you, *you* wicked servant. You knew that I was an austere man, collecting what I did not deposit and reaping what I did not sow. Why then did you not put my money in the bank, that at my coming I might have collected it with interest?" And he said to those who stood by, "Take the mina from him, and give *it* to him who has ten minas." (But they said to him, "Master, he has ten minas.") For I say to you, that to everyone who has will be given; and from him who does not have, even what he has will be taken away from him. But bring here those enemies of mine, who did not want me to reign over them, and slay *them* before me.' "

Verse 11 explains why Jesus told the parable. Jesus tells His disciples that He will be rejected in Jerusalem (v. 14), and that He will go away and return. At His return His servants will have to give account of their stewardship. The disciples need to understand these things. Specifically the parable teaches that there will be different rewards for different uses of equal opportunities to serve Christ. All started with the same opportunity to use the mina. The servant who used it to gain ten minas rendered more service than the servant who gained five minas. Accordingly he received twice as much reward. As in the previous parable the man who put the mina in a handkerchief is a hypocrite, and the opportunity he had for service will be taken away. This is in accord with the fact stated in v. 26: 'For I say to you, that to everyone who has will be given; and from him who does not have, even what he has will be taken away from him.' This is a warning to all those who were rejecting Christ and the truth He spoke to them. If they continued to reject the truth, even the knowledge they had of that truth would be taken away. Their refusal to listen to Him would result in total darkness. Verse 27 predicts the final doom of those who reject Christ.

Jesus taught the necessity to use money in this life to provide benefit in the future life in another parable recorded by Luke: "He also said to His disciples: 'There was a certain rich man who had a steward, and an accusation was brought to him that this man was wasting his goods. So he called him and said to him, "What is this I hear about you? Give an account of your stewardship, for you can no longer be steward" Then the steward said within himself, "What shall I do? For my master is taking the stewardship away from me. I cannot dig; I am ashamed to beg. I have resolved what to do, that when I am put out of the stewardship, they may receive me into their houses." So he called every one of his master's debtors to *him*, and said to the first, "How much do you owe my master?" And he said, "A hundred measures of oil." So he said to him, "Take your bill, and sit down quickly and write fifty." Then he said to another, "And how much do you owe?" So he said, "A hundred measures of wheat." And he said to him, "Take your bill, and write eighty." So the master commended the unjust steward because he had dealt shrewdly. For the sons of this world are more shrewd in their generation than the sons of light. And I say to you, make friends for yourselves by unrighteous mammon, that when you fail, they may receive you into an everlasting home. He who *is* faithful in *what is* least is faithful also in much; and he who is unjust in *what is* least is unjust also in much. Therefore if you have not been faithful in the unrighteous mammon, who will commit to your trust the true *riches*? And if you have not been faithful in what is another man's, who will give you what is your own? No servant can serve two masters; for either he will hate the one and love the other, or else he will be loyal to the one and despise the other. You cannot serve God and mammon.' Now the Pharisees, who were lovers of money, also heard all these things, and they derided Him" (Luke 16:1–14). The dishonest steward's planning for the future is commended, not his dishonesty. He used money wisely to provide for his future after dismissal from his post. Jesus says that in this use of money he was wiser than the "sons of light" Jesus' followers. So He commands His disciples to behave like the steward, and "make friends for yourselves by means of the wealth of unrighteousness; so that when it fails, they will receive you into the eternal dwellings" NASB. The Christian is to use his money so that after he leaves this world it benefits him in the next life. His money is an opportunity for the service of Christ. By using it in that way he will gain rewards at the Final Judgment. Jesus is not telling them to use money in order to get into the kingdom. The kingdom is already theirs. He is telling them to use their money for benefit in the life to come.

1 Tim. 6:17–19 teaches the same truth: "Command those who are rich in this present age not to be haughty, nor to trust in uncertain riches but in the living God, who gives us richly all things to enjoy. *Let them* do good, that they be rich in good works, ready to give, willing to share, storing up for themselves a good foundation for the time to come, that they may lay hold on eternal life." Paul is saying that by the right use of their money the rich believers will store up for themselves a good foundation for the age to come.

A number of commentators interpret these verses differently. They say that they teach that the gifts of money, or things purchased by money, will simply prove true faith at the Final Judgment as in Mat. 25:31–46. It is true that such good works will indeed prove the presence of faith. But the believer will also receive rewards for these works. Paul states that every believer will appear before the judgment seat of

Christ, and will receive the things done in the body, according to what he has done whether good or worthless (2 Cor. 5:10). These words of the apostle affirm again the truths stated by him in 1 Cor. 3. The judgment of the believer will be twofold – a judgment which will separate him as a sheep from the goats, and a judgment of him as a sheep for reward. Paul lived in the consciousness of that judgment for rewards. He spoke of it as something which caused him to have fear, "Therefore, knowing the fear of the Lord, we persuade men" (2 Cor. 5:11 NASB). Paul knew that there would be nothing hidden on that day. Everything would be laid bare before Christ, the Judge. And he would have to give account. Accordingly he devotes himself to his service and apostolic calling. He speaks of reward for his labours in 1 Thess. 2:19: "For what *is* our hope, or joy, or crown of rejoicing? *Is it* not even you in the presence of our Lord Jesus Christ at His coming?" His converts, the believers at Thessalonica, will be his crown at the return of Christ. On another occasion he writes of his determination not to be disapproved when he stands before Christ: "And everyone who competes *for the prize* is temperate in all things. Now they *do it* to obtain a perishable crown, but we *for* an imperishable *crown*. Therefore I run thus: not with uncertainty. Thus I fight: not as *one who* beats the air. But I discipline my body and bring *it* into subjection, lest, when I have preached to others, I myself should become disqualified" (1 Cor. 9:25–27). The word disqualified means not standing the test, in the sense of not being what he ought to be and so not receiving the reward of being a faithful apostle.

Rewards for service are unacceptable to some. They argue that believers serve out of love with no thought of reward, and that to look for reward is unworthy of a Christian. Such views fly in the face of Christ's words: "Blessed are you when they revile and persecute you, and say all kinds of evil against you falsely for My sake. Rejoice and be exceedingly glad, for great *is* your reward in heaven, for so they persecuted the prophets who were before you" (Mat. 5:11–12). Christ encourages His servants with the glorious promise, "And behold, I am coming quickly, and My reward *is* with Me, to give to every one according to his work" (Rev. 22:12). Jesus promised reward at the resurrection of the just for certain conduct: "Then He also said to him who invited Him, 'When you give a dinner or a supper, do not ask your friends, your brothers, your relatives, nor rich neighbors, lest they also invite you back, and you be repaid. But when you give a feast, invite *the* poor, *the* maimed, *the* lame, *the* blind. And you will be blessed, because they cannot repay you; for you shall be repaid at the resurrection of the just.' " (Luke 14:12–14).

Those who depreciate rewards as a motive for service condemn the conduct of Moses which is held before believers as a glorious example of faith in God: "By faith Moses, when he became of age, refused to be called the son of Pharaoh's daughter, choosing rather to suffer affliction with the people of God than to enjoy the passing pleasures of sin, esteeming the reproach of Christ greater riches than the treasures in Egypt; for *he looked to the reward*" (Heb. 11:24–26, my italics).

The apostle Peter held out reward as an incentive. He encouraged his fellow elders to shepherd the flock willingly and be examples to the flock. He promised them a reward for their labour: "The elders who are among you I exhort, I who am a fellow elder and a witness of the sufferings of Christ, and also a partaker of the glory that will be revealed: Shepherd the flock of God which is among you, serving as overseers, not by compulsion but willingly, not for dishonest gain but eagerly; nor as being lords over those entrusted to you, but being examples to the flock; and when the Chief Shepherd appears, you will receive the crown of glory that does not fade away" (1 Pet. 5:1–4). The crown of glory stands in contrast to dishonest gain. Unlike such temporal benefit it is eternal glory. The words "that does not fade away" translate one Greek word ἀμαράντινον which derives its meaning from the amaranth flower which did not fade or wither. Peter says to the elders, "Focus your eyes on that eternal reward."

Paul sought to motivate Christian slaves to serve their earthly masters by reminding them of the reward they would receive at the return of Christ. He said, "Bondservants, obey in all things your masters according to the flesh, not with eyeservice, as men-pleasers, but in sincerity of heart, fearing God. And whatever you do, do it heartily, as to the Lord and not to men, knowing that from the Lord you will receive the reward of the inheritance; for you serve the Lord Christ. But he who does wrong will be repaid for what he has done, and there is no partiality" (Col. 3:22–25). The word "reward" means full recompense. The slave frequently did not get a fair and just return for his labour. Paul assures the believing slave that in serving his earthly master he is serving His heavenly Master Christ, and Christ will reward in full every act of obedience. The reward is the future inheritance of the believer. Paul then adds a warning that doing wrong will also receive due recompense. The slave will suffer loss at the Judgment (1 Cor. 3:15).

Paul himself looked forward in anticipation of reward: "And everyone who competes *for the prize* is temperate in all things. Now they *do it* to obtain a perishable crown, but we *for* an imperishable *crown*."(1 Cor. 9:25). Paul speaks of the athletes competing for a crown or wreath made only of pine fronds or celery. He says that they exercise discipline to gain a perishable reward. How much more should believers make sacrifices for their imperishable crown? He exhorts them to live daily in such a way as to obtain their imperishable crown, which is salvation completed and consummated at the return of Christ. It is not that their efforts or good works will earn them salvation. Salvation is a gift, but it is required of those who receive the gift to endure in following Christ though it costs them self denial, suffering and sometimes even death. As A.W. Pink asserts, "In Scripture 'eternal life' is presented both as a 'gift' and as a 'reward' – the reward of perseverance. . . . That eternal life and glory is set forth in God's Word as the reward and end of perseverance which await all faithful Christians is clear from Heb. 10:35 . . ."[1] Let us look at that verse in its context. "But recall the former days in which, after you were illuminated, you endured a great struggle with sufferings: partly while you were made a spectacle both by reproaches and tribulations, and partly while you became companions of those who were so treated; for you had compassion on me in my chains, and joyfully accepted the plundering of your goods, knowing that you have a better and an enduring possession for yourselves in heaven. Therefore do not cast away your confidence, which has great reward. For you have need of endurance, so that after you have done the will of God, you may receive the promise: 'For yet a little while, *And* He who is coming will come and will not tarry. Now the just shall live by faith; But if *anyone* draws back, My soul has no pleasure in him.' But we are not of those who draw back to perdition, but of those who believe to the saving of the soul" (Heb. 10:32–39). Their confidence is their public confession of faith in Christ for which they are being persecuted. They are in danger of becoming weary and discouraged in their souls because of the hostility of others towards them because of their faith (Heb. 12:3–4). Therefore they need endurance. Christ will fulfil His promise. He will return, and they will receive the reward of eternal life.

James also declares this truth of reward following endurance: "Blessed is a man who perseveres under trial; for once he has been approved, he will receive the crown of life which *the Lord* has promised to those who love Him" (Jam. 1:12 NASB). The believer who perseveres under trial is approved and will receive eternal life at the coming of Christ. Peter writes to believers about this testing of faith: "Blessed *be* the God and Father of our Lord Jesus Christ, who according to His abundant mercy has begotten us again to a living hope through the resurrection of Jesus Christ from the dead, to an inheritance incorruptible and undefiled and that does not fade away, reserved in heaven for you, who are kept by the power of God through faith for salvation ready to be revealed in the last time. In this you greatly rejoice, though now for a little while, if need be, you have been grieved by various trials, that the genuineness of your faith, *being* much more precious than gold that perishes, though it is tested by fire, may be found to praise, honor, and glory at the revelation of Jesus Christ" (1 Pet. 1:3–7).

In Rev. 2:8–10 and 3:7–11 we find this same truth – perseverance rewarded with eternal blessedness: "And to the angel of the church in Smyrna write, 'These things says the First and the Last, who was dead, and came to life: I know your works, tribulation, and poverty (but you are rich); and *I know* the blasphemy of those who say they are Jews and are not, but *are* a synagogue of Satan. Do not fear any of those things which you are about to suffer. Indeed, the devil is about to throw *some* of you into prison, that you may be tested, and you will have tribulation ten days. Be faithful until death, and I will give you the crown of life.' " (Rev. 2:8–10), and "to the angel of the church in Philadelphia write, 'These things says He who is holy, He who is true, He who has the key of David, He who opens and no one shuts, and shuts and no one opens I know your works. See, I have set before you an open door, and no one can shut it; for you have a little strength, have kept My word, and have not denied My name. Indeed I will make *those* of the synagogue of Satan, who say they are Jews and are not, but lie – indeed I will make them come and worship before your feet, and to know that I have loved you. Because you have kept My command to persevere, I also will keep you from the hour of trial which shall come upon the whole world, to test those who dwell on the earth. Behold, I am coming quickly! Hold fast what you have, that no one may take your crown' " (Rev. 3:7–11).

There are two verses in James which speak of the final judgment of believers for rewards. The first is, "So speak and so do as those who will be judged by the law of liberty" (Jam. 2:12). James says that believers will be judged by the law of liberty. This law he has defined earlier in his letter (1:21–25). It is the "implanted" word of God, the word of God received and obeyed at conversion, and continually received and obeyed since that time. It has saved them, is saving them, and will finally result in salvation completed at the return of Christ. The law of liberty therefore is God's word, the scriptures which contain the gospel. This word of God requires absolute obedience: "But be doers of the word, and not hearers only, deceiving yourselves" (1:22). It is the "perfect law of liberty" (1:25). It is perfect because it is God's law. It is a law of liberty because obedience to the gospel brings the power to live according to God's will and gives freedom from slavery to sin. So at the Final Judgment believers will give an account of the deeds done in the body in the light of the word of God. Thus James exhorts them, "So speak and so do as those who will be judged by the law of liberty" (Jam. 2:12). He is instructing them to keep before them each day the fact of the Final Judgment and to behave accordingly. Rewards will be based on God's full knowledge of the believer and all his deeds in the light of the "law of liberty."

A second scripture in James has great significance in the matter of rewards. It reads, "My brethren, let not many of you become teachers, knowing that we shall receive a greater judgment" (Jam. 3:1; my translation). James is saying that Christ will subject teachers of God's people to a greater judgment than believers who are not teachers. By teachers James presumably meant apostles, prophets, possibly evangelists, and elders as well as pastor-teachers (Eph. 4:11 and 1 Tim. 3:1–7). Contrary to much current thinking James did not consider all believers to be teachers. Most versions of the Bible translate μεῖζον κρίμα as "stricter judgment" instead of "greater judgment." But in all judgment Christ will be righteous and just. His judgment will be according to truth. As we have seen, all will be taken into account in every case. There will be no partiality. Therefore the meaning is not that a higher standard will be applied to teachers. Rather James is saying that the judgment of teachers will be greater because they have an additional and very great responsibility. All believers will have to give account for all the deeds done in the body after conversion. For teachers this will also include giving account for the content of their teaching, and for the state of the souls whom they teach. Jesus stated the serious consequences of right and wrong teaching: "Whoever therefore breaks one of the least of these commandments, and teaches men so, shall be called least in the kingdom of heaven; but whoever does and teaches *them*, he shall be called great in the kingdom of heaven" (Mat. 5:19). Moreover teachers, regardless of what designation is used of their office, will have to give an account for each soul in their flock. To look after the sheep for whom Christ died is a great responsibility. The writer to the Hebrews appeals to the believers, "Obey your leaders, and submit *to them*; for they keep watch over your souls as those who will give an account" (Heb. 13:17 NASB). The Final Judgment will assess the lives, deeds and performance of all who held that position of responsibility. It will be a greater judgment for them than for believers who did not have that charge. James says that his readers know this truth.

Conclusion

In the light of all scripture teaching about Christ's judgment of the believer's service the outcome will be either reward or the partial or full loss of reward that could have been obtained. These rewards or loss of rewards will be eternal.

Reference

1. A.W. Pink, *Eternal Security*, Guardian Press, 1974, page 94; later edition by Baker, 1996.

ETERNAL JUDGMENT: SOLEMN WARNINGS

There was an occasion when Jesus gave a warning to His disciples about the Final Judgment: "Then Peter began to say to Him, 'See, we have left all and followed You.' So Jesus answered and said, 'Assuredly, I say to you, there is no one who has left house or brothers or sisters or father or mother or wife or children or lands, for My sake and the gospel's, who shall not receive a hundredfold now in this time – houses and brothers and sisters and mothers and children and lands, with persecutions – and in the age to come, eternal life. But many *who are* first will be last, and the last first.'" (Mark 10:28–31). Jesus was informing His disciples that many who thought that they were first in the kingdom of God would actually be last at the Final Judgment. Also that many who thought that they were last would be judged by Christ to be first. At this time the disciples were concerned about who would be the greatest. He had previously told them, "If anyone desires to be first, he shall be last of all and servant of all" (Mark 9:35). The disciples were not receptive to these words of Jesus. Soon after His words in reply to Peter we find the disciples still occupied with future status. James and John said to Him, "Grant us that we may sit, one on Your right hand and the other on Your left, in Your glory." "But Jesus called them to *Himself* and said to them, 'You know that those who are considered rulers over the Gentiles lord it over them, and their great ones exercise authority over them. Yet it shall not be so among you; but whoever desires to become great among you shall be your servant. And whoever of you desires to be first shall be slave of all'" (Mark 10:37, 42–44). His prediction that "many who are first shall be last, and the last first" relates to this concern about who would be the greatest. God's assessment of the first and the last is very different to the assessment of the disciples.

This reply of Jesus to Peter's assertion – "See we have left all and followed You" – is also recorded by Matthew, "But many *who are* first will be last, and the last first" (Mat. 19:30). In that gospel it is followed immediately by a parable, enforcing the message. The parable reads,

"For the kingdom of heaven is like a landowner who went out early in the morning to hire laborers for his vineyard. Now when he had agreed with the laborers for a denarius a day, he sent them into his vineyard. And he went out about the third hour and saw others standing idle in the marketplace, and said to them, 'You also go into the vineyard, and whatever is right I will give you.' So they went. Again he went out about the sixth and the ninth hour, and did likewise. And about the eleventh hour he went out and found others standing idle, and said to them, 'Why have you been standing here idle all day?' They said to him, 'Because no one hired us.' He said to them, 'You also go into the vineyard, and whatever is right you will receive.' So when evening had come, the owner of the vineyard said to his steward, 'Call the laborers and give them *their* wages, beginning with the last to the first.' And when those came who *were hired* about the eleventh hour, they each received a denarius. But when the first came, they supposed that they would receive more; and they likewise received each a denarius. And when they had received *it*, they complained against the landowner, saying, 'These last *men* have worked *only* one hour, and you made them equal to us who have borne the burden and the heat of the day.' But he answered one of them and said, 'Friend, I am doing you no wrong. Did you not agree with me for a denarius? Take *what is* yours and go your way. I wish to give to this last man *the same* as to you. Is it not lawful for me to do what I wish with my own things? Or is your eye evil because I am good?' So the last will be first, and the first last" (Mat. 20:1–16). Jesus is telling the disciples that rewards from God will not be given according to man's worldly thinking. Contrary to that thinking the owner of the vineyard orders his steward to pay first the ones hired last (at 5 pm), next those hired in the ninth hour (at 3 pm), then the ones hired at the sixth hour (at noon), then those hired at the third hour (at 9 am), and finally last of all those who had laboured all day (from sunrise). Also contrary to man's thoughts he gives the ones who worked for twelve hours no more than he gave those who laboured for only one hour after the heat of the day. Jesus is telling His disciples that in the matter of rewards God will behave contrary to man's thinking. He is also saying in the parable that the owner was totally justified in his actions because:

a) He gave to those who worked twelve hours the wage he had agreed with them. God will be true to His word. He will not break any promise.

b) He had the absolute right to give what belonged to Him. God has the right to give rewards as He will.

c) He was good to those who laboured all day and good to those who worked only one hour. His goodness to the former was in keeping his word. His goodness to the latter was in His generosity to them. God will be good in dispensing rewards.

d) He had a sound reason to be generous to these workers who started at 5 pm. They would have worked all day if they had had the opportunity to do so. God takes all the truth into account.

Thus the owner is seen to be fair and good in all his dealings. In contrast, the ones who worked all day are revealed as greedy, selfish and envious. If His disciples continued in their selfish and envious attitudes of contention to be the greatest they would find to their personal cost that those who think they will be first will end up last.

It is certain that on that Day Christ will shock and surprise. William Hendriksen writes "Not only will many of those who are now regarded as the very pillars of the church be last, but also many who never made the headlines – think of the poor widow who contributed 'two mites' (Mark 12:42), and Mary of Bethany whose act of loving lavishness was roundly criticized by the disciples (Mat. 26:8) – shall be first on the day of judgment (Mark 12:43,44; cf. Mat. 26:10–13)."[1]

There is another passage where Jesus utters a solemn warning and prediction about the Final Judgment: "And He went through the cities and villages, teaching, and journeying toward Jerusalem. Then one said to Him, 'Lord, are there few who are saved?' And He said to them, 'Strive to enter through the narrow gate, for many, I say to you, will seek to enter and will not be able. When once the Master of the house has risen up and shut the door, and you begin to stand outside and knock at the door, saying, "Lord, Lord, open for us," and He will answer and say to you, "I do not know you, where you are from," then you will begin to say, "We ate and drank in Your presence, and You taught in our streets." But He will say, "I tell you I do not know you, where you are from. Depart from Me, all you workers of iniquity." There will be weeping and gnashing of teeth, when you see Abraham and Isaac and Jacob and all the prophets in the kingdom of God, and yourselves thrust out. They will come from the east and the west, from the north and the south, and sit down in the kingdom of God. And indeed there are last who will be first, and there are first who will be last' " (Luke 13:22–30). Jesus is warning the Jews who had not received Him, despite their opportunity to do so, that they will be thrust out of the kingdom of God to which they thought they belonged. The Gentiles who will receive Him will enter it. Thus the Jews, who thought themselves to be first, because of all God's blessings on their nation, will be last. The Jews despised and reckoned the Gentiles to be last, nations who did not have their privileges. But the Gentiles who would receive Christ in the future will be first. This will shock many Jews on that Day. It will result in "weeping and gnashing of teeth."

The passage has a wider application. It is a warning to all who belong to Christian churches but who have not truly received Christ. Such will see others in the kingdom they never thought would be there, and themselves thrust out despite many years of church attendance. Their horror will be beyond description. It will be too late then to receive Christ as saviour. There is no second chance after death.

In His Sermon on the Mount Jesus gave a grave warning: "Not everyone who says to Me, 'Lord, Lord,' shall enter the kingdom of heaven, but he who does the will of My Father in heaven. Many will say to Me in that day, 'Lord, Lord, have we not prophesied in Your name, cast out demons in Your name, and done many wonders in Your name?' And then I will declare to them, 'I never knew you; depart from Me, you who practice lawlessness!'" (Mat. 7:21–23). Here we have those who call Jesus "Lord, Lord." They acknowledge His Divinity. The repetition of Lord indicates devotion and zeal. They will be able to say to the One, before Whom all things will be naked and open to His eyes, that they have prophesied, cast out demons and done many wonders. Notice they can claim many wonders. Moreover they will be able to say that all these works were done in the name of Christ. They were carried out claiming to be acting as servants of Christ and with His power. During their time on earth many reckoned them to be very special servants of God because of these spectacular works. By the power of Satan men not in fellowship with God can work miracles. The magicians of Egypt were able do wonders (Exod. 7:11–12a). Judas Iscariot healed the sick and cast out demons (Mat. 10:1). He was given power by Christ to work those miracles. Way back, God warned his people that false prophets could sometimes give signs and wonders: "If there arises among you a prophet or a dreamer of dreams, and he gives you a sign or a wonder, and the sign or the wonder comes to pass, of which he spoke to you, saying, 'Let us go after other gods' – which you have not known – 'and let us serve them,' you shall not listen to the words of that prophet or that dreamer of dreams, for the LORD your God is testing you to know whether you love the LORD your God with all your heart and with all your soul. You shall walk after the LORD your God and fear Him, and keep His commandments and obey His voice, and you shall serve Him and hold fast to Him. But that prophet or that dreamer of dreams shall be put to death, because he has spoken in order to turn *you* away from the LORD your God, who brought you out of the land of Egypt and redeemed you from the house of bondage, to entice you from the way in which the LORD your God commanded you to walk. So you shall put away the evil from your midst" (Deut. 13:1–5). The New Testament also declares the reality of "lying wonders" – "For the mystery of lawlessness is already at work; only He who now restrains *will do so* until He is taken out of the way. And then the lawless one will be revealed, whom the Lord will consume with the breath of His mouth and destroy with the brightness of His coming. The coming of the *lawless one* is according to the working of Satan, with all power, signs, and lying wonders, and with all unrighteous deception among those who perish, because they did not receive the love of the truth, that they might be saved. And for this reason God will send them strong delusion, that they should believe the lie" (2 Thess. 2:7–11). This mystery of lawlessness was already at work in the time of Paul. Christ predicted in Mat. 7:22 that there will be many who have prophesied, cast out demons and done many wonders in His name who will be condemned at the Judgment Day. Their words reveal their state of self-deception. They thought that eternal blessedness would be their portion. They claimed a relationship with Him. They called Him Lord. They reminded Him of their prophesying and many acts of power in His name. The reply of Christ is devastating, "And then I will declare to them, 'I never knew you; depart from Me, you who practice lawlessness!' " (Mat. 7:23). Christ will say that He had no relationship with them. There was no union of love. He will want nothing to do with them. He will denounce them as those who practice lawlessness. Make no mistake the prediction of Christ will be fulfilled.

Verses 22 and 23 clarify and enforce the meaning of verse 21, "Not everyone who says to Me, 'Lord, Lord,' shall enter the kingdom of heaven, but he who does the will of My Father in heaven." Not even those who can claim prophesying and doing many miracles in His name will enter the kingdom when they fail to do the will of God the Father. If such are rejected, then those who have not done the will of God but plead less spectacular works will also be condemned. Preaching, holding office in the church or a professing Christian organisation, serving people in various ways, writing books and other acts in the name of Christ will be of no avail when life is not lived in submission to the will of God. He who does the will of God the Father is born again, lives by faith in Christ, loves Christ and out of love keeps His commands. His obedience is not perfect, but it is sincere and his life is characterised by doing the will of God from the heart.

The parable of the Marriage Supper is a solemn warning to those who are like the man without a wedding garment: "And Jesus answered and spoke to them again by parables and said: 'The kingdom of heaven is like a certain king who arranged a marriage for his son, and sent out his servants to call those who were invited to the wedding; and they were not willing to come. Again, he sent out other servants, saying, "Tell those who are invited, 'See, I have prepared my dinner; my oxen and fatted cattle *are* killed, and all things *are* ready. Come to the wedding.'" But they made light of it and went their ways, one to his own farm, another to his business. And the rest seized his servants, treated *them* spitefully, and killed *them*. But when the king heard *about it*, he was furious. And he sent out his armies, destroyed those murderers, and burned up their city. Then he said to his servants, "The wedding is ready, but those who were invited were not worthy. Therefore go into the highways, and as many as you find, invite to the wedding." So those servants went out into the highways and gathered together all whom they found, both bad and good. And the wedding *hall* was filled with guests. But when the king came in to see the guests, he saw a man there who did not have on a wedding garment. So he said to him, "Friend, how did you come in here without a wedding garment?" And he was speechless. Then the king said to the servants, "Bind him hand and foot, take him away, and cast *him* into outer darkness; there will be weeping and gnashing of teeth." For many are called, but few *are* chosen.'" (Mat. 22:1–14).

The parable speaks of the union of Christ with His own at His return. The man without a wedding garment portrays the man who thinks that he will be accepted by Christ on that Day. He presumes his acceptance despite his total disregard of the absolutely essential requirement for acceptance. He is an arrogant man who believes he will get to heaven even though he chooses not to submit to the entry requirement. Just as the man in the parable viewed the need to wear the wedding garment with disdain, many treat God's requirement for entry into the kingdom with contempt. Their own thoughts as to how God should act towards them are all that matter. They are opinionated. They have not the slightest fear that they will be rejected and condemned. They put themselves among those who will be acceptable to God. They think they can treat God's word with contempt without any adverse consequence. They are full of their own thoughts, but on that Day they will be speechless. The parable makes the point that they will be given opportunity to explain their lack of the essential requirement. They will offer no arguments, no excuses, no pleas in mitigation. They will be exposed for what they are and damned. The destruction of all their pride and self-delusion will be a fearful experience of exceedingly severe shock and horror.

Conclusion

The Final Judgment will result in judgments very different from what many will expect.

Reference

1. William Hendriksen, *New Testament Commentary The Gospel of Mark*, Banner of Truth, 1976, page 403.

CHAPTER TEN

ETERNAL JUDGMENT: ETERNAL LIFE, ETERNAL REWARDS AND ETERNAL PUNISHMENT

The Final Judgment will declare the eternal destiny of every individual human being and every individual fallen angel. For believers it will be eternal life.

There will also be rewards given to believers for obedience and service. The scriptures do not tell us the precise nature of these rewards. There are indications that they will be of eternal duration. The Christian by service to Christ can lay up treasures in heaven. Jesus said, "Do not lay up for yourselves treasures on earth, where moth and rust destroy and where thieves break in and steal; but lay up for yourselves treasures in heaven, where neither moth nor rust destroys and where thieves do not break in and steal" (Mat. 6:19–20). Treasures laid up on earth in the service of Mammon can perish and can be lost. Treasures laid up in heaven in the service of Christ are lasting. Luke recorded a later occasion when Jesus taught His disciples, "Sell what you have and give alms; provide yourselves money bags which do not grow old, a treasure in the heavens that does not fail, where no thief approaches nor moth destroys" (Luke 12:33). Here again is the indication that the reward in heaven is enduring. In 1 Tim. 6:19 the rich are exhorted to lay up a "good foundation" for the life to come. A foundation speaks of something with lasting effect on the life in the age to come. Rev. 14:13 reads, "Then I heard a voice from heaven saying to me, 'Write: "Blessed *are* the dead who die in the Lord from now on."' 'Yes,' says the Spirit, 'that they may rest from their labors, and their works follow them.'" The works of Christians will be rewarded. The indication is that the reward will be forever. In that sense their works will follow them eternally.

For unbelievers, the devil and fallen angels there will be eternal punishment. The scriptures stating this are crystal clear. Jesus said, "If your hand causes you to sin, cut it off. It is better for you to enter into life maimed, rather than having two hands, to go to hell, into the fire that shall never be quenched – where 'Their worm does not die, And the fire is not quenched.' And if your foot causes you to sin, cut it off. It is better

CHAPTER TEN

ETERNAL JUDGMENT: ETERNAL LIFE, ETERNAL REWARDS AND ETERNAL PUNISHMENT

The Final Judgment will declare the eternal destiny of every individual human being and every individual fallen angel. For believers it will be eternal life.

There will also be rewards given to believers for obedience and service. The scriptures do not tell us the precise nature of these rewards. There are indications that they will be of eternal duration. The Christian by service to Christ can lay up treasures in heaven. Jesus said, "Do not lay up for yourselves treasures on earth, where moth and rust destroy and where thieves break in and steal; but lay up for yourselves treasures in heaven, where neither moth nor rust destroys and where thieves do not break in and steal" (Mat. 6:19–20). Treasures laid up on earth in the service of Mammon can perish and can be lost. Treasures laid up in heaven in the service of Christ are lasting. Luke recorded a later occasion when Jesus taught His disciples, "Sell what you have and give alms; provide yourselves money bags which do not grow old, a treasure in the heavens that does not fail, where no thief approaches nor moth destroys" (Luke 12:33). Here again is the indication that the reward in heaven is enduring. In 1 Tim. 6:19 the rich are exhorted to lay up a "good foundation" for the life to come. A foundation speaks of something with lasting effect on the life in the age to come. Rev. 14:13 reads, "Then I heard a voice from heaven saying to me, 'Write: "Blessed *are* the dead who die in the Lord from now on."' 'Yes,' says the Spirit, 'that they may rest from their labors, and their works follow them.'" The works of Christians will be rewarded. The indication is that the reward will be forever. In that sense their works will follow them eternally.

For unbelievers, the devil and fallen angels there will be eternal punishment. The scriptures stating this are crystal clear. Jesus said, "If your hand causes you to sin, cut it off. It is better for you to enter into life maimed, rather than having two hands, to go to hell, into the fire that shall never be quenched – where 'Their worm does not die, And the fire is not quenched.' And if your foot causes you to sin, cut it off. It is better

84

for you to enter life lame, rather than having two feet, to be cast into hell, into the fire that shall never be quenched – where 'Their worm does not die, And the fire is not quenched.' And if your eye causes you to sin, pluck it out. It is better for you to enter the kingdom of God with one eye, rather than having two eyes, to be cast into hell fire – where 'Their worm does not die, And the fire is not quenched' " (Mark 9:43–48). Whatever the nature of the fire will be, it will be eternal. Whatever is meant by the worm it too will be forever. Jesus is also recorded by Matthew saying on another occasion, "If your hand or foot causes you to sin, cut it off and cast *it* from you. It is better for you to enter into life lame or maimed, rather than having two hands or two feet, to be cast into the everlasting fire" (Mat. 18:8). The words of Jesus in Mat. 25:46 are unambiguous. The goats go to everlasting punishment, and the sheep to eternal life: "These" (the goats) "will go away into eternal punishment, but the righteous" (the sheep) "into eternal life" (Mat. 25:46 NASB). Exactly the same word αἰώνιον translated eternal is used with both punishment and life. It is impossible to say that it means eternal when applying to life, but something less when applying to punishment.

Jude warned of certain ones infiltrating the believers. He stated that their future punishment would be eternal. He called them "raging waves of the sea, foaming up their own shame; wandering stars for whom is reserved the blackness of darkness forever" (verse 13).

In the book of Revelation we have a number of scriptures stating eternal punishment: "Then a third angel followed them, saying with a loud voice, 'If anyone worships the beast and his image, and receives *his* mark on his forehead or on his hand, he himself shall also drink of the wine of the wrath of God, which is poured out full strength into the cup of His indignation. He shall be tormented with fire and brimstone in the presence of the holy angels and in the presence of the Lamb. And the smoke of their torment ascends forever and ever; and they have no rest day or night, who worship the beast and his image, and whoever receives the mark of his name' " (Rev. 14:9–11).

Rev. 19:1–4 reads "After these things I heard a loud voice of a great multitude in heaven, saying, 'Alleluia! Salvation and glory and honor and power *belong* to the Lord our God! For true and righteous *are* His judgments, because He has judged the great harlot who corrupted the earth with her fornication; and He has avenged on her the blood of His servants *shed* by her.' Again they said, 'Alleluia! Her smoke rises up forever and ever!' And the twenty-four elders and the four living creatures fell down and worshiped God who sat on the throne, saying, 'Amen! Alleluia!'." The great harlot is the counterfeit church made up of unregenerate clergy and laity. It is composed of those who profess to be Christians but who have never been born again. They are in churches of many different names all over the world.

"The devil, who deceived them, was cast into the lake of fire and brimstone where the beast and the false prophet *are*. And they will be tormented day and night forever and ever" (Rev. 20:10). Notice that the goats go to the same destiny: "Then He will also say to those on the left hand, 'Depart from Me, you cursed, into the everlasting fire prepared for the devil and his angels'" (Mat. 25:41).

The sufferings in hell will be beyond what we can conceive. The verses above speak of agony and misery which are terrible to contemplate. It will be a punishment designed and prepared by God in His wrath and indignation for the Devil and his angels. The most terrible aspect of hell is the fact that it is unending. There will never be relief from the torment, the anguish and the pain. There will be the blackness of darkness forever. The fire of hell will give no light. To suffer that absolute hopelessness of being sentenced to torment forever will be unspeakably awful. But when one seriously weighs the evil words and actions of the Devil and his angels and the horrendous effects of those words and actions on millions of souls, and also the works of Satan and his angels directed against God, and their evil nature and settled hatred of God one begins to see something of God's justice in ordaining eternal punishment.

Some, who claim to be Christian, and to accept the final authority of the Bible in determining true doctrine, speak against the clear teaching of the scriptures above. They attempt to nullify these scriptures by misinterpreting these texts and other scriptures and by special pleading and human reasoning. They argue for the annihilation of the unsaved. They say that hell is only for a time followed by disintegration into non-existence. They argue that in the following verses destruction means that the unsaved will cease to exist:

"Enter by the narrow gate; for wide *is* the gate and broad *is* the way that leads to destruction, and there are many who go in by it" (Mat. 7:13).

"For many walk, of whom I have told you often, and now tell you even weeping, *that they are* the enemies of the cross of Christ: whose end *is* destruction, whose god *is their* belly, and *whose* glory *is* in their shame – who set their mind on earthly things" (Phil. 3:18–19).

"For when they say, 'Peace and safety!' then sudden destruction comes upon them, as labor pains upon a pregnant woman. And they shall not escape" (1 Thess. 5:3).

"... when the Lord Jesus is revealed from heaven with His mighty angels, in flaming fire taking vengeance on those who do not know God, and on those who do not obey the gospel of our Lord Jesus Christ. These shall be punished with everlasting destruction from the presence of the Lord and from the glory of His power" (2 Thess. 1:7–9).

"By the same word the present heavens and earth are reserved for fire, being kept for the day of judgment and destruction of ungodly men" (2 Pet. 3:7 NIV).

The word destruction in these verses does not mean the cessation of existence. In Mat. 7:13, Phil. 3:19 and 2 Pet. 3:7, the word translated "destruction" is ἀπώλεια from the verb ἀπόλλυμι. When. we examine the use of these words in the New Testament we find the following verses where the meaning is not annihilation:

"And no one puts new wine into old wineskins; or else the new wine bursts the wineskins, the wine is spilled, and the wineskins *are ruined*. But new wine must be put into new wineskins" (Mark 2:22). The wineskins are rendered useless for their intended purpose but they continue to exist.

"But when His disciples saw *it*, they were indignant, saying, 'Why this *waste*?' " (Mat. 26:8). The ointment did not cease to exist. It filled the house with fragrance (John 12:3).

"But on the day that Lot went out of Sodom it rained fire and brimstone from heaven and *destroyed them* all" (Luke 17:29). Jesus said that these people who were destroyed would be at the Final Judgment (Mat. 10:15). Their destruction was not annihilation.

"Yet if your brother is grieved because of *your* food, you are no longer walking in love. Do not *destroy* with your food the one for whom Christ died" (Rom. 14:15). The brother is not annihilated. He is harmed spiritually.

"But go rather to the *lost* sheep of the house of Israel" (Mat. 10:6).

"By these waters also the world of that time was deluged and *destroyed*" (2 Pet. 3:6 NIV). The world continued to exist and to be repopulated.

"People who want to get rich fall into temptation and a trap and into many foolish and harmful desires that plunge men into ruin and *destruction*" (1 Tim. 6:9 NIV). The following verse explains the nature of their destruction: "For the love of money is a root of all *kinds of* evil, for which some have strayed from the faith in their greediness, and pierced themselves through with many sorrows" (1 Tim. 6:10). It is a spiritual destruction of straying from the faith resulting in pain and many sorrows.

In all these examples ἀπώλεια and its related words (shown in italics) do not mean annihilation. The word destruction in Mat. 7:13, Phil. 3:19 and 2 Peter 3:7 means eternal ruin. Moreover in the light of the clear teaching of Christ (Mat. 25:46) it is not possible to give the word destruction in these verses the meaning of annihilation. This would mean that the scriptures contradict themselves! Since they are God-breathed such disharmony is not possible.

Turning to the other word, ὄλεθρος translated "destruction" in 1 Thess. 5:3 and 2 Thess. 1:9, we find verses elsewhere in the New Testament where (shown in italics) it does not mean to annihilate. It is found in 1 Cor. 5:5: "deliver such a one to Satan for the *destruction* of the flesh, that his spirit may be saved in the day of the Lord Jesus." His body, as we have seen, would continue to exist to be transformed at the return of Christ (Phil. 3:21). The word also occurs in 1 Tim. 6:9 NASB: "But those who want to get rich fall into temptation and a snare and many foolish and harmful desires which plunge men into *ruin* and destruction." We have noted above the meaning of that ruin.

Therefore the destruction stated in Mat. 7:13, Phil. 3:19, 1 Thess. 5:3, 2 Thess. 1:9 and 2 Peter 3:7 does not mean that the unrighteous will be annihilated.[1]

An attempt to justify a doctrine of annihilation is also made by interpreting the second death as extinction. The scriptures define the second death:

"And I saw the dead, small and great, standing before God, and books were opened. And another book was opened, which is *the Book of Life*. And the dead were judged according to their works, by the things which were written in the books. The sea gave up the dead who were in it, and Death and Hades delivered up the dead who were in them. And they were judged, each one according to his works. Then Death and Hades were cast into the lake of fire. This is the second death. And anyone not found written in the Book of Life was cast into the lake of fire" (Rev. 20:12–15), and

"But the cowardly, unbelieving, abominable, murderers, sexually immoral, sorcerers, idolaters, and all liars shall have their part in the lake which burns with fire and brimstone, which is the second death" (Rev. 21:8). The lake of fire is where the Devil will go: "The devil, who deceived them, was cast into the lake of fire and brimstone where the beast and the false prophet *are*. And they will be tormented day and night forever and ever" (Rev. 20:10). The second death is the everlasting fire prepared for the Devil and his angels (Mat. 25:41). It is blatant rejection of the clear teaching of scripture to define the second death as annihilation.

Annihilationists refuse to submit to the revelation of God's word. Instead they choose wilfully their own philosophy. They contend:

- that eternal punishment is disproportionate to the sins committed.
- that eternal punishment is inconsistent with God's love for mankind.
- that eternal punishment would mar the new heavens and the new earth.

Eternal punishment disproportionate to the sins committed

The scriptures reveal that men by their sinful natures (Eph. 2:3) and actual sins in thought, word and deed provoke God to wrath and indignation. Man does not see his own sinfulness and sins as God sees them. Man seeks to excuse himself. He does not want to acknowledge the magnitude of his guilt before God. To a greater or lesser extent he is blind to his filthiness and loathsomeness in the sight of God. The deceitfulness of sin is such that it even convinces the doer that he is not sinning! The scriptures tell us plainly that even those who know God sometimes seek to excuse their actions, are deceived by sin and are blind to their sinful state. King David, a man after God's heart, is a striking example. For a time he did not acknowledge his sins of adultery with Bathsheba and the murder of her husband Uriah. The believers at Laodicea did not know that spiritually they were "wretched, miserable, poor, blind and naked." Deceived by sin they thought that their spiritual state was wonderful. They said that they were rich, had become wealthy and had need of nothing. Even believers, who, unlike the Laodiceans are truly rich spiritually, do not see fully the blameworthiness and offensiveness of sin and sinfulness as God sees them. It is through the revelation of God's word that we can know God's estimate of sin. If men rely on their own understanding of the blameworthiness of sin in the sight of God, instead of the revelation of God and His ways in the Bible, then they will conclude that eternal punishment is unreasonable and unjust.

The scriptures tell us the gravity of sin in the sight of God. One sin of disobedience resulted in the fall of mankind. The single transgression of Adam brought condemnation and death upon all mankind (Rom. 5:12), and the whole creation was subjected by God to futility (Rom. 8:20). Ever since that one sin the whole creation continues to groan and labour with birth pangs. Deliverance will only come at the return of Christ. Gen. 3:17–18 give some indication of the meaning of this subjection to futility: "Then to Adam He said, 'Because you have heeded the voice of your wife, and have eaten from the tree of which I commanded you, saying, "You shall not eat of it" Cursed *is* the ground for your sake; In toil you shall eat *of* it All the days of your life. Both thorns and thistles it shall bring forth for you, And you shall eat the herb of the field'." Man, through just one sin, lost paradise, and lives in a world where no longer is everything "very good" (Gen. 1:31). He is subject to terrible suffering and death. Sin is so serious before God that there is no deliverance from the guilt of sin except through the blood of the Son of God. Nothing but the sacrifice of Christ on the cross can propitiate the Father and bring reconciliation between God and man.

The scriptures reveal God's wrath and indignation against those who sin. They also reveal that the Final Judgment and sentence to eternal punishment will not bring about any repentance in those condemned. Their sinful nature will remain. Their enmity towards God will be unchanged. Moreover the scriptures indicate that their sinful deeds will continue. In Rev. 16 we are told repeatedly that fallen man blasphemes the name of God when he experiences His wrath and judgments (Rev. 16:1,9,11 and 21). Man will continue in his sinfulness and active sinning for all eternity, and God will continue in His wrath and indignation for all eternity.

Eternal punishment inconsistent with God's love for mankind

God's love during this life on earth does not free man from His wrath and punishment. The scriptures reveal that God's wrath is upon man until he repents. As we have seen, terrible but just judgments have fallen upon mankind throughout history. Moreover there are many passages revealing God's attitude towards sinful men and women. In ancient times God commanded and warned Israel before their entry into Canaan, "You must not live according to the customs of the nations I am going to drive out before you. Because they did all these things, I abhorred them" (Lev. 20:23 NIV). King David was moved by the Holy

Spirit to write, "For You *are* not a God who takes pleasure in wickedness, Nor shall evil dwell with You. The boastful shall not stand in Your sight; You hate all workers of iniquity. You shall destroy those who speak falsehood; The LORD abhors the bloodthirsty and deceitful man." (Psa. 5:4–6); and "The LORD tests the righteous, But the wicked and the one who loves violence His soul hates." (Psa. 11:5). John tells us that man has the wrath of God abiding upon him until he believes in Christ: "He who believes in the Son has everlasting life; and he who does not believe the Son shall not see life, but the wrath of God abides on him" (John 3:36). As we have seen, that wrath is upon him because of his sinful nature (Eph. 2:3) and because of sins committed (Rom. 1:18–32).

It is not true to say God hates the sin but loves the sinner. Rather scripture says that:

a) God hates sin,
b) that God is angry with sinners, and
c) that God's love for the sinner provides deliverance from God's wrath in this life and the life to come if, and only if, the sinner obeys the gospel.

The love of God to sinners offers salvation to them strictly conditional upon them turning from sin to Christ. God is holy, He is Light and Him is no darkness at all. God is just: "The LORD is slow to anger and great in power, And the LORD will not leave the guilty unpunished. His way is in the whirlwind and the storm, and clouds are the dust of his feet" (Nah. 1:3 NIV). But He is also merciful. As we have noted previously He sends his rain on the righteous and unrighteous (Mat. 5:45), and He is longsuffering and forbearing with sinners (Rom. 2:4). He is moved to reach out to man in his wretched fallen state. He spared not His only Son, and delivered Him up to die to rescue sinners from hell. He is willing to forgive all who will repent of their sins and believe in His Son for salvation. Moreover God is revealed by Ezekiel as the One Who "has no pleasure in the death of the wicked, but that the wicked turn from his way and live" (Ezek. 33:11). Thus God's wrath is upon the sinner, but God's love and mercy is at the same time extended to the sinner in the gospel. There is no contradiction between God's wrath and God's mercy. We have a clear example of God dealing simultaneously in wrath and mercy in the scripture record. God revealed to the prophet Habbakuk (c. 605–589 BC) that He would destroy Judah using the Babylonians. Judah would be punished for her sins. His wrath was upon them. Habbakuk was moved to pray, "In wrath remember mercy." Terrible sufferings came upon Judah when

Babylon conquered the people of God. Jeremiah in the book of Lamentations records the devastation of that time: "How the Lord has covered the daughter of Zion With a cloud in His anger! He cast down from heaven to the earth The beauty of Israel, And did not remember His footstool In the day of His anger. The Lord has swallowed up and has not pitied All the dwelling places of Jacob. He has thrown down in His wrath The strongholds of the daughter of Judah; He has brought *them* down to the ground; He has profaned the kingdom and its princes. He has cut off in fierce anger Every horn of Israel; He has drawn back His right hand From before the enemy. He has blazed against Jacob like a flaming fire Devouring all around. Standing like an enemy, He has bent His bow; With His right hand, like an adversary, He has slain all *who were* pleasing to His eye; On the tent of the daughter of Zion, He has poured out His fury like fire" (Lam. 2:1–4). Notice the repeated statements of God's anger, wrath and fury. The prophet continues his contemplation of the conquest of Judah: "*Through* the Lord's mercies we are not consumed, Because His compassions fail not. *They are* new every morning; Great *is* Your faithfulness" (Lam. 3:22–23). The Lord exercised both wrath and mercy towards sinners at that time.

The sinner is deceived if he is told simply that God loves him. He is under God's wrath. He needs salvation, and God in love offers it on strict conditions of repentance and faith. If he will not meet those conditions he remains under the wrath of God.

God has ordained that the offer of the gospel is confined to life in this age. There is no offer of salvation after death or after the return of Christ. Jesus declared this on several occasions. Concerning the rich man and Lazarus Jesus said that Abraham replied to the rich man, "And besides all this, between us and you there is a great gulf fixed, so that those who want to pass from here to you cannot, nor can those from there pass to us" (Luke 16:26). This tells us that the unsaved cannot pass to the state of the saved after death. Destiny is fixed forever. William Hendriksen in his commentary on Luke points out that the word translated "gulf" is derived from a Greek word meaning to gape, yawn. He says, "What is meant is a ravine, vast in depth, length and breadth; a wadi, gorge."[2] In His parable of the ten virgins Jesus warned that the door was shut after the wise virgins entered and the foolish virgins were unable to gain admittance (Mat. 25:10–12). In response to the question "Lord, are there few who are saved?" Jesus said to them, "Strive to enter through the narrow gate, for many, I say to you, will seek to enter and will not be able. When once the Master of the house has risen up and shut the door, and you begin to stand outside and knock at the door, saying, 'Lord, Lord, open for us,' and He will answer and say to you, 'I do not know you, where you are from,' then you will begin to say, 'We ate and drank in Your presence, and You taught in our streets.' But He will say, 'I tell you I do not know you, where you are from. Depart from Me, all you workers of iniquity.' There will be weeping and gnashing of teeth, when you see Abraham and Isaac and Jacob and all the prophets in the kingdom of God, and yourselves thrust out" (Luke 13:23–28). The saved and lost are separated for eternity at the Final Judgment.

Some say that the following verses teach that an opportunity will be given to those who die in unbelief:

"For Christ also suffered once for sins, the just for the unjust, that He might bring us to God, being put to death in the flesh but made alive by the Spirit, by whom also He went and preached to the spirits in prison, who formerly were disobedient, when once the Divine long-suffering waited in the days of Noah, while *the* ark was being prepared, in which a few, that is, eight souls, were saved through water" (1 Pet. 3:18–20), and

"For this reason the gospel was preached also to those who are dead, that they might be judged according to men in the flesh, but live according to God in the spirit" (1 Pet. 4:6).

1 Pet. 3:18–20 is interpreted to mean that Christ went to preach the gospel to unrighteous dead souls after His death. From this it is reasoned that all the dead who die unsaved will have the gospel preached to them after death. 1 Pet. 4:6 is alleged to support this conclusion. It is contended that it links with Christ preaching to dead souls in 1 Pet. 3:19. It is seen as a further statement that Christ preached the gospel to souls after their death.

In this way these two verses are taken to indicate that after death the gospel will be preached to give the offer of salvation for the first time to those who never heard it during life on earth, and also to give a second chance to those who rejected the gospel before they died. Such interpretation of these verses conflicts with the revelation given in the New Testament.

The following explanations of their meaning are consistent with the New Testament:

One interpretation affirms that 1 Pet. 3:19 states that Christ announced His victory to the fallen angels who are called "spirits in

prison." Gen. 6:1–2, 2 Pet. 2:4 and Jude 6 are quoted in support of this interpretation

"Now it came to pass, when men began to multiply on the face of the earth, and daughters were born to them, that the sons of God saw the daughters of men, that they *were* beautiful; and they took wives for themselves of all whom they chose" (Gen. 6:1–2). The sons of God are taken to be the fallen angels (cf. Job 1:6; 2:1 and 38:7).

"For if God did not spare the angels who sinned, but cast *them* down to hell and delivered *them* into chains of darkness, to be reserved for judgment" (2 Pet. 2:4).

"And the angels who did not keep their proper domain, but left their own abode, He has reserved in everlasting chains under darkness for the judgment of the great day" (Jude 6).

From the above verses it is affirmed that the fallen angels left their appointed domain and married the daughters of men. For this sin they are reserved in chains for judgment to come. This interpretation states that He did not preach the gospel to these fallen angels. He simply declared His triumph to them. The word translated preached in this verse can mean simply proclaim (e.g. Luke 12:3, Rom. 2:21 and Rev. 5:2).

Another interpretation says that 1 Pet. 3:19 refers to the pre-incarnate Christ preaching through Noah to people before the Flood, which people are at the time of Peter's epistle *"spirits in prison."*

Turning to 1 Pet. 4:6, this verse is interpreted as speaking of believers who have died
They had the gospel preached to them while they were alive so that

1. they might be judged according to men in the flesh, and so that
2. they might live according to God in the spirit.

Being judged according to men in the flesh is being defamed by men as evildoers and reviled. It is being maligned and suffering in the flesh for doing good just as Christ suffered (1 Pet. 3:16–18; 4:1–4). This suffering is a major theme in the epistle (2:12; 4:12–19 and 5:10). Such suffering is the calling of the believer: "But when you do good and suffer, if you take it patiently, this *is* commendable before God. For to this you were called, because Christ also suffered for us, leaving us an example, that you should follow His steps" (1 Pet. 2:20–21). Living according to God in the spirit is the glorious experience of the believer both in this life and the next. This interpretation would give great encouragement to the readers of Peter's epistle.

These interpretations of 1 Pet. 3:19 and 4:6 do not reveal an opportunity for salvation after death for those who have died in their sins. After death is the Judgment (Heb. 9:27).

It does not glorify God to suggest that His love rules out eternal punishment. Eternal hell will proclaim the righteous judgment of God. On that Day it will be manifest to all that God's judgments are just and fair. No one will have a just cause to contend that any of His punishments are too severe. Then the magnitude of the guilt of the sin of fallen man and fallen angels will be revealed. When man's guilt is seen in its enormity and God's punishment is revealed to be just, then will be thrown into relief the exceeding greatness of the love and grace of God in salvation. The redeemed will not think that God should ever release those condemned to hell. They will worship Him both for His saving love and for His judgments. His perfection and glory will be seen in both. The revelation of God on that Day will dispel any previous thought that the eternal punishment of sinners is inconsistent with the love of God.

Eternal punishment would mar the new heavens and the new earth

The punishment of evil angels and men will be the triumph of God over sinful opposition manifested to His glory for all eternity. It will not be a failure of the Almighty to bring to fulfilment His purposes. All whom God elects to salvation will be gathered into His kingdom. There will be an innumerable company of angels without sin. The whole sub-human creation will be delivered from the bondage of corruption into the glorious liberty of the children of God. The devil and fallen angels and the unsaved will be banished "from the presence of the Lord" (2 Thess. 1:9). Nothing will mar the peace of the kingdom of God in the age to come. There will be glory, honour and peace for the redeemed (Rom. 2:10). This side of heaven believers can only feel anguish at the thought of their loved ones suffering eternal punishment. In the full revelation given in that future state they will have peace.

In this matter of eternal punishment the choice is to submit to the words of Christ and of scripture or to resort to man's reasoning and philosophy. Man is sinfully blind to his guilt before God, and he sinfully refuses to acknowledge the one true God and His ways. He exchanges Him for a god of his own imagination. It is no surprise that his god does not punish eternally.

References

1. With reference to Mat. 7:13, Phil. 3:19, 2 Peter 3:7, 1 Thess. 5:3 and 2
   Thess. 1:9 I am largely following the arguments of John Blanchard,
   Whatever Happened To Hell?, Evangelical Press, 1993, pages 237–239.
2. William Hendriksen, *New Testament Commentary The Gospel of Luke*,
   Banner of Truth, 1979, page 789.

THE TRUTHS OF THE RESURRECTION OF THE DEAD AND ETERNAL JUDGMENT PART OF THE ESSENTIAL FOUNDATION

The believer is assured of deliverance from eternal punishment at the Final Judgment. Jesus said "Most assuredly, I say to you, he who hears My word and believes in Him who sent Me has everlasting life, and shall not come into judgment" (the Final Judgment resulting in condemnation), "but has passed from death into life" (John 5:24). This assurance fills the believer with gratitude and love for God who is so rich in mercy, love and grace. He knows that he is not appointed to wrath but to obtain salvation through the Lord Jesus Christ (1 Thess. 5:9). That salvation through Christ will be consummated at the believer's resurrection and at the Final Judgment. At that time believers inherit the kingdom prepared for them from the foundation of the world (Mat. 25:34). Then their bodies are transformed and glorified (1 Cor. 15:51–54). Thus the New Testament speaks frequently of salvation as a future event.

It declares this future salvation to be the hope of the believer

Paul wrote to the believers at Rome, "And *do* this, knowing the time, that now *it is* high time to awake out of sleep; for now our salvation *is* nearer than when we *first* believed" (Rom. 13:11).

The writer to the Hebrews speaks of angels ministering for the sake of believers who one day will inherit salvation: "Are they not all ministering spirits sent forth to minister for those who will inherit salvation?" (Heb. 1:14).

The writer also declares, "so Christ was offered once to bear the sins of many. To those who eagerly wait for Him He will appear a second time, apart from sin, for salvation" (Heb. 9:28).

Peter also writes of the believer's salvation as future: "Blessed *be* the God and Father of our Lord Jesus Christ, who according to His abundant mercy has begotten us again to a living hope through the resurrection of Jesus Christ from the dead, to an inheritance incorruptible and undefiled and that does not fade away, reserved in heaven for you, who are kept by the power of God through faith for salvation ready to be revealed in the last time" (1 Pet. 1:3–5).

In the same way adoption and redemption are also spoken of as future: "we also who have the firstfruits of the Spirit, even we ourselves groan within ourselves, eagerly waiting for the adoption, the redemption of our body" (Rom. 8:23). Paul is stating that believers are eagerly waiting for the resurrection at the coming of Christ. Then they will experience the blessing of adoption in its fullness.

Again in his letter to the Ephesian Christians he speaks of redemption as future: "And do not grieve the Holy Spirit of God, by whom you were sealed for the day of redemption" (Eph. 4:30).

It is of course true that the believer at the moment of conversion is saved, adopted and redeemed. Consequently salvation for the believer is also a past event as well as future: "But when the kindness and the love of God our Savior toward man appeared, not by works of righteousness which we have done, but according to His mercy He saved us, through the washing of regeneration and renewing of the Holy Spirit, whom He poured out on us abundantly through Jesus Christ our Savior, that having been justified by His grace we should become heirs according to the hope of eternal life" (Tit. 3:4–7). Believers are already adopted and have the Spirit of adoption (Gal. 4:4–6 and Rom. 8:15). They have been redeemed with the precious blood of Christ. But salvation in all its fulness awaits the resurrection of the dead and Final Judgment. Belief in these events therefore is part of the foundation of the Christian life because they are an essential part of the gospel. Remove either of them and the work of the Triune God to save man is destroyed. It is brought to completion only through these events. Belief in the resurrection of the dead and belief in eternal judgment are absolutely essential for the Christian. The New Testament states hope to be an essential part of the gospel. Paul wrote to the believers at Colossae, "the hope which is laid up for you in heaven, of which you heard before in the word of the truth of the gospel" (Col. 1:5), and "the hope of the gospel which you heard, which was preached to every creature under heaven, of which I, Paul, became a minister" (Col. 1:23). Paul said to some believers who had fallen into the error that there is no resurrection of the dead, "If in this life only we have hope in Christ, we are of all men the most pitiable" (1 Cor. 15:19). He stated that if there is no resurrection of the dead then Christians are so deluded that they are the most pitiable of all people. This is a very strong assertion which bears out the fact that belief in the resurrection of the dead is absolutely essential for the Christian.

Moreover this hope of the believer is essential for living the Christian life

1.   *The believer must live constantly with this hope*
Peter commands believers to "... rest *your* hope fully upon the grace that is to be brought to you at the revelation of Jesus Christ" (1 Pet. 1:13). Believers must not move away from this hope of the gospel (Col. 1:23).

2.   *They are to rejoice in hope at all times (Rom. 12:12)*
The contemplation of the eternal glory that awaits them enables the believer to rejoice always.

3.   *It is a hope which motivates the believer to holiness*
"... everyone who has this hope in Him purifies himself, just as He is pure" (1 John 3:3).

4.   *It is a hope which causes the believer to encourage and build up fellow Christians*
"He died for us so that ... we may live together with him. Therefore encourage one another and build each other up" (1 Thess. 5:10–11 NIV).

5.   *This hope causes them to view this life on earth in a new way*
They live in the knowledge that they are only aliens and strangers in this world (1 Pet. 2:11). Aliens are people who live in a foreign country but who keep their own citizenship. They are strangers. Believers have their citizenship elsewhere. Paul says to believers, "For our citizenship is in heaven, from which we also eagerly wait for the Savior, the Lord Jesus Christ, who will transform our lowly body that it may be conformed to His glorious body, according to the working by which He is able even to subdue all things to Himself" (Phil. 3:20–21). Christians are not of this world. Their home is a future one. Thus Paul says, "brethren, the time *is* short, so that from now on even those who have wives should be as though they had none, those who weep as though they did not weep, those who rejoice as though they did not rejoice, those who buy as though they did not possess, and those who use this world as not misusing *it*. For the form of this world is passing away" (1 Cor. 7:29–31).

6. Hope gives the believer stamina for the work of the Lord

Paul says to believers in the light of their glorious future, "Therefore, my beloved brethren, be steadfast, immovable, always abounding in the work of the Lord, knowing that your labor is not in vain in the Lord" (1 Cor. 15:58).

7. Hope gives comfort to believers when they lose through death someone who was a Christian

"But I do not want you to be ignorant, brethren, concerning those who have fallen asleep, lest you sorrow as others who have no hope. For if we believe that Jesus died and rose again, even so God will bring with Him those who sleep in Jesus. For this we say to you by the word of the Lord, that we who are alive *and* remain until the coming of the Lord will by no means precede those who are asleep. For the Lord Himself will descend from heaven with a shout, with the voice of an archangel, and with the trumpet of God. And the dead in Christ will rise first. Then we who are alive *and* remain shall be caught up together with them in the clouds to meet the Lord in the air. And thus we shall always be with the Lord. Therefore comfort one another with these words" (1 Thess. 4:13–18).

8. Hope enables the believer to endure persecution and tribulation

At the end of holy scriptures we have the words of Christ: "And behold, I am coming quickly, and My reward *is* with Me, to give to every one according to his work" (Rev. 22:12). The book of Revelation was written to persecuted saints. The rewards for suffering for Christ are an incentive to perseverance and faithfulness even unto death. Paul said to believers, "For our light affliction, which is but for a moment, is working for us a far more exceeding *and* eternal weight of glory" (2 Cor. 4:17). This leads us to the next truth.

9. The future judgment for rewards is an incentive to service

There will be a differentiation among believers. All believers will be saved, but their deeds will affect the life to come. Rewards will be given according to the deeds done. This is a glorious prospect, but it will result in different awards. All believers will inherit the kingdom prepared for them from the foundation of the world (Mat. 25:34). But their rewards will, in some way not yet revealed to us, make a difference to the degree of blessedness in the eternal state. At that judgment the believer, and all his deeds, will be made manifest, revealed fully in their true character before Christ. They will be tested by fire. If they fail the test the deeds will be revealed as worthless. They will be seen to merit no reward. Wrong motives will be revealed. Many works will be exposed as done to gain the applause of men (Mat. 6:1–2). On one occasion Paul spoke of those who preached the gospel from envy and strife, from selfish ambition (Phil. 1:15–16). John wrote about one Diotrephes who loved a position of status in the church. Paul evidences true brotherly love, and so many of his letters manifest genuine appreciation of those who laboured in Christ. His words concerning Timothy therefore should make us pause and consider. He said of him to the Philippians, "But I trust in the Lord Jesus to send Timothy to you shortly, that I also may be encouraged when I know your state. For I have no one like-minded, who will sincerely care for your state. For all seek their own, not the things which are of Christ Jesus" (Phil. 2:19–21). There are many who take office in the church of Christ, but there are few who genuinely care for the sheep.

Consequently this day of judgment will be a day of shame for some believers (1 John 2:28). Their service will be seen for what it was – wood, hay and stubble unable to pass the test of fire. The possibility of works not passing the test motivated Paul to fulfil his God given tasks as an apostle of Jesus Christ. He said, "For we must all appear before the judgment seat of Christ, that each one may receive the things *done* in the body, according to what he has done, whether good or bad. Knowing, therefore, the terror of the Lord, we persuade men; but we are well known to God, and I also trust are well known in your consciences" (2 Cor. 5:10–11). His terror or fear of the Lord in view of that day of reckoning moved him to do the will of God. This was alongside the motivation of the love of Christ for him. That love also drove him in his service. He lived constantly in the light of both Calvary and the Final Judgment. The fact of judgment for rewards is a foundation for the Christian life because on that day all one's service will be revealed in its true colours, and the rewards will be great and the loss of them will be a real loss. Belief in the Final Judgment of the believer for rewards will determine the believer's conduct every day. That belief is therefore part of the foundation for a Christian life.

Conclusion

The Christian life begins with faith and hope (Col. 1:4–5,23). It is a life lived by faith and hope. Belief in the resurrection of the dead and eternal judgment is essential each day of the Christian life.

The Sixfold Foundation

CHAPTER TWELVE

SUMMARY AND CONCLUSIONS

We have looked at the parts of the foundation for building the Christian life, each in turn, as we have moved through the six elements of the foundation. Let us recap and summarise the facts concerning each part of the foundation.

Salvation is received through repentance and faith. When these elements of the foundation are laid a person becomes a Christian. They are essential to enter the kingdom of God, and they are also essential as settled states of mind necessary for daily life in that kingdom.

Repentance

- The new view of sin, God and His commands brought about by repentance are essential to walk daily before God.
- The new sense of shame for sins committed before conversion is also essential throughout the Christian life so that sin is renounced continually.
- The new view of self in the sight of God is absolutely necessary. The believer must always see himself as utterly lost without Christ.

Faith

- The Christian is justified by faith and he continues to stand by faith.
- Faith gives access to God the Father.
- Faith governs the life of the Christian.
- Faith enables the believer to overcome the world.
- Continued faith is essential to arrive finally in heaven.

Baptism of believers in water by immersion

- Linked to repentance and faith it is designed by God to be part of the whole experience of conversion to Christ.
- It declares most powerfully, and with great clarity, what has happened through obeying the gospel. The believer is "in Christ."

- The Christian for the rest of his time on earth has the memory of baptism vividly portraying his identification with Christ. That union signified in baptism washed away his sins, and determines the way he lives. He must reckon himself dead to sin and alive to God.
- Water baptism, correctly understood, is a preservative against errors which would destroy the Christian life.

The Baptism in the Spirit

- Because the believer receives the experience of the pouring out of the Spirit by faith, and begins to prophesy by faith, the believer learns in a vivid way that the just shall live by faith.
- The baptism in the Spirit is an entrance into the experience of the Spirit-filled life.
- The enabling to prophesy in tongues gives – an enlarged ability to edify oneself, an enhanced prayer life, an enlarged ability to praise God and a daily experience of the miraculous.
- It gives the potential to exercise spiritual gifts.
- The believer is now anointed, which means consecration for God's service, enduement of power for service, a certain knowledge of the truth and a special relationship with God.
- An added assurance of salvation is given.
- It is the guarantee and foretaste of final salvation.

The Resurrection of the Dead and Eternal Judgment

- These are essential truths of the gospel and the consummation of salvation for the believer.
- They are also essential beliefs for daily Christian life.
- The Final Judgment tells believers that they will have to give account to Christ, and must live at all times in the light of that fact.

THE COMPLETE FOUNDATION

1.   *These six doctrines all concern Christ*

Salvation through repentance and faith is only found in Christ. Water baptism is "into Christ" (Rom. 6:3). He is the Baptizer in the Holy Spirit. He will raise the dead (John 5:28–29). He will judge at the Final Judgment. Therefore knowledge of these doctrines is knowledge of Christ. It is knowledge of His saving work, of His pouring out of the Spirit during these last days and knowledge of the manifestation of His future glory. Such faith in Christ is a foundation of great strength for the new convert.

2.   *The wisdom of God is revealed in designing a foundation which embraces the past, the present and the future*

The believer knows that Christ has saved him. The past is forgiven. As regards the present he is united with Christ, and experiences the reality of the power of the Holy Spirit in his life. His future inheritance is certain and glorious. He has a foretaste and guarantee of it. He awaits it eagerly and he lives in the light of giving account of himself to Christ with the prospect of reward.

3.   *The foundation is a wonderful balance of knowledge of the truth and the experience of God's power*

That balance is essential. Conversion is both a coming into the knowledge of the truth and an experience of the power of God in the new birth. Just like conversion the foundation for the Christian life encompasses both knowledge and experience. The total foundation of these six elements includes both doctrine and the experience of God's power. A Christian life cannot be built on doctrine alone. Nor can it be built on experience alone. The foundation of Heb. 6:1–2 spells out this vital need for both. Sadly many Christians have fallen into imbalance. Some do not give to doctrine the place it ought to have in their lives, and others fail to give due place to the experience of God's power. When a believer lays this foundation at the start of the Christian life he commences his pilgrimage with the right balance. His continued and constant dependence on that foundation is a continual reminder of the need for both doctrine and the experience of God's power.

4.   *There is a collective strength in this sixfold foundation*

God, the Supreme Architect, is the only One Who knows the perfect design for the foundation on which to build the Christian life. He does not give us freedom to modify any part of it. We do not have licence to dispense with any of its elements. The whole of it is divinely appointed and necessary to support the building which each believer is called to build. It is the essential foundation with a wonderful collective strength.

We began by looking at King David's moving of the Ark, and the amazing failure at first to heed God's word concerning the way God required it to be transported. We have looked at God's revealed will in Heb. 6:1–2 in the light of that Old Testament event recorded for the admonition of Christians living in these last days (1 Cor. 10:11).

Conclusions

Every believer is called to lay this foundation
Repentance and faith are the only actions required to become a Christian. But to fulfil God's will the convert must be baptized in water and in the Holy Spirit, and embrace a basic knowledge of the doctrines of the resurrection of the dead and eternal judgment. The foundation should be laid at the start of the Christian life. If a believer did not lay a complete foundation at the beginning then he should complete his foundation.

All involved in evangelism and making disciples must instruct converts to lay this foundation
For many this will mean a great change of practice, and for some personal cost. No price is too great to pay to be true to God's word.

These six elements must be first chronologically. First the foundation and then the superstructure
It is folly to build the superstructure of a building before completing the foundation.

The potential of the Christian for spiritual growth and fruitfulness depends to a significant extent on the soundness and completion of this foundation
This divinely designed foundation can support all the development of the superstructure. The full potential for spiritual growth and fruitfulness is made possible by laying the foundation. Equally there will be loss in some measure if the foundation is incomplete. God's order cannot be ignored without consequences.

A foundation remains essential for the building upon it
It is laid once, but it must remain in place. It must not be removed or weakened. The whole superstructure is threatened with collapse or damage if the foundation is damaged.

Finally as one contemplates the course of church history from New Testament times to now it is wonderful to see the gradual recovery of these doctrines after their loss in the early centuries AD. Today there is a growing understanding of the meaning and significance of Hebrews 6:1–2.